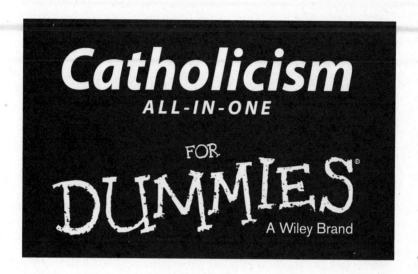

Catholicism
ALL-IN-ONE

FOR DUMMIES®
A Wiley Brand

by Rev. Kenneth Brighenti, PhD,
Rev. Msgr. James Cafone, STD,
Rev. Jonathan Toborowsky, MA, and
Rev. John Trigilio, Jr., PhD, ThD

FOR DUMMIES®
A Wiley Brand

Catholicism All-In-One **For Dummies**®

Published by: **John Wiley & Sons, Inc.,** 111 River Street, Hoboken, NJ 07030-5774, www.wiley.com

Copyright © 2015 by John Wiley & Sons, Inc., Hoboken, New Jersey

Published simultaneously in Canada

The Catholic Edition of the Revised Standard Version of the Bible, © 1965, 1966 by the Division of Christian Education of the National Council of the Churches of Christ in the United States of America. Used by permission. All rights reserved. Excerpts from the English translation of the Catechism of the Catholic Church for use in the United States of America © 1964, United States Catholic Conference, Inc. — Libreria Editrice Vaticana. Used with Permission.

Excerpts from the English translation of The Roman Missal © 2011, International Commission on English in Liturgy Corporation (ICEL); excerpts from the English translation of Rites of Baptism for Children © 1969, ICEL; excerpts from the English translation of Rite of Marriage © 1969, ICEL; excerpts from the English translation of Rite of Confirmation (Second Edition) © 1975, ICEL; excerpts from the English translation of Pastoral Care of the Sick; Rites Anointing and Viaticum © 1982, ICEL; excerpts from the English translation of Order of Christian Funerals © 1985, ICEL. All rights reserved.

For general information on our other products and services, please contact our Customer Care Department within the U.S. at 877-762-2974, outside the U.S. at 317-572-3993, or fax 317-572-4002. For technical support, please visit www.wiley.com/techsupport.

Wiley publishes in a variety of print and electronic formats and by print-on-demand. Some material included with standard print versions of this book may not be included in e-books or in print-on-demand. If this book refers to media such as a CD or DVD that is not included in the version you purchased, you may download this material at http://booksupport.wiley.com. For more information about Wiley products, visit www.wiley.com.

Library of Congress Control Number: 2015941000

ISBN 978-1-119-08468-6 (pbk); ISBN 978-1-119-08470-9 (ePub); ISBN 978-1-119-08469-3 (ePDF)

Manufactured in the United States of America

10 9 8 7 6 5 4 3 2 1

Contents at a Glance

Table of Contents

Introduction

. . . .

*T*hree great religions trace their roots to the prophet Abraham: Judaism, Christianity, and Islam. And one of those religions, Christianity, is expressed in three different traditions: Catholicism, Protestantism, and Eastern Orthodoxy. You may already know that. You may also already know that, currently, more than 1 billion Catholics occupy the earth. That's approximately one-fifth of the world's population.

Whether you're Catholic or not, you may be totally clueless about or just unaware of some aspects of Catholic tradition, history, doctrine, worship, devotion, or culture. No sweat. Regardless of whether you're engaged, married, or related to a Catholic; your neighbor or co-worker is a Catholic; or you're just curious about what Catholics really do believe, this book is for you.

Catholicism All-In-One For Dummies realizes that you're smart and intelligent, but maybe you didn't attend Blessed Sacrament Grade School, St. Thomas Aquinas High School, or Catholic University of America. This book's goal is to give you a taste of Catholicism. It's not a Catechism or religion textbook but a casual, down-to-earth introduction for non-Catholics and a reintroduction for Catholics. It gives common-sense explanations about what Catholics believe and do in plain English, with just enough why and how thrown in to make solid sense.

This book doesn't cover everything about Catholicism, but you do get all the basic stuff so that the next time you're invited to a Catholic wedding, baptism, funeral, confirmation, or First Communion, you won't be totally con- fused. And you may have an edge on other people in your life who are less informed about Catholicism than you.

About This Book

This book covers plenty of material on Catholicism — from doctrine to morality and from worship and liturgy to devotions — but you don't need a degree in theology to comprehend it. Everything is presented in an informal, easy-to-understand way.

This book is also a reference, unlike the schoolbooks you had as a kid. You don't have to read the chapters in order, one after the other, from front cover to back cover. You can just pick the topic that interests you or find the page that addresses the specific question you have. Or you can indiscriminately open the book and pick a place to begin reading.

Icons Used in This Book

This book uses icons to point out various types of information:

This icon draws your attention to information that's worth remembering because it's basic to Catholicism.

This icon alerts you to technical or historical background stuff that's not essential to know. Feel free to divert thine eyes whenever you see this icon.

This icon points out useful tidbits to help you make more sense out of something Catholic.

This icon points out cautionary areas of Catholicism, such as the obligation to attend Mass on Sunday or Saturday evening. (Not doing so without a legitimate excuse, such as illness or severe weather, is a grave sin.)

This icon points out references to the topic in the Good Book.

Beyond the Book

In addition to all the material you find in the book you're reading right now, this product also comes with some access-anywhere goodies on the web. Check out the eCheat Sheet at www.dummies.com/cheatsheet/catholicismaio for helpful insights and shortcuts about the whys and wherefores of the Catholic church. And swing by www.dummies.com/extras/catholicismaio for a handful of bonus articles covering material that didn't quite fit in the book.

Where to Go from Here

Catholicism All-In-One For Dummies is sort of like Sunday dinner at an Italian grandmother's home. Nonna brings everything to the table: bread, antipasto, cheese, olives, prosciutto and melon, tomatoes and mozzarella; then comes the pasta or macaroni in marinara or meat sauce with sausage and peppers, meatballs, and veal; then comes the chicken, the pork, or the beef; followed by salad; and topped off with fruit and cheese, spumoni, gelato, ricotta pie, zabaglione, and an espresso with a splash of sambucca.

Likewise, in this book, you find a little bit of everything on Catholicism: doctrine, morality, history, theology, canon law, spirituality, and liturgy. You can go to any section to discover Catholicism. You can pick and choose what interests you the most, get answers to specific questions on your mind, or just randomly open this book anywhere and begin reading. On the other hand, you may want to start at the beginning and work your way to the end, going through each chapter one by one. You'll get a good taste of what Catholicism is really about.

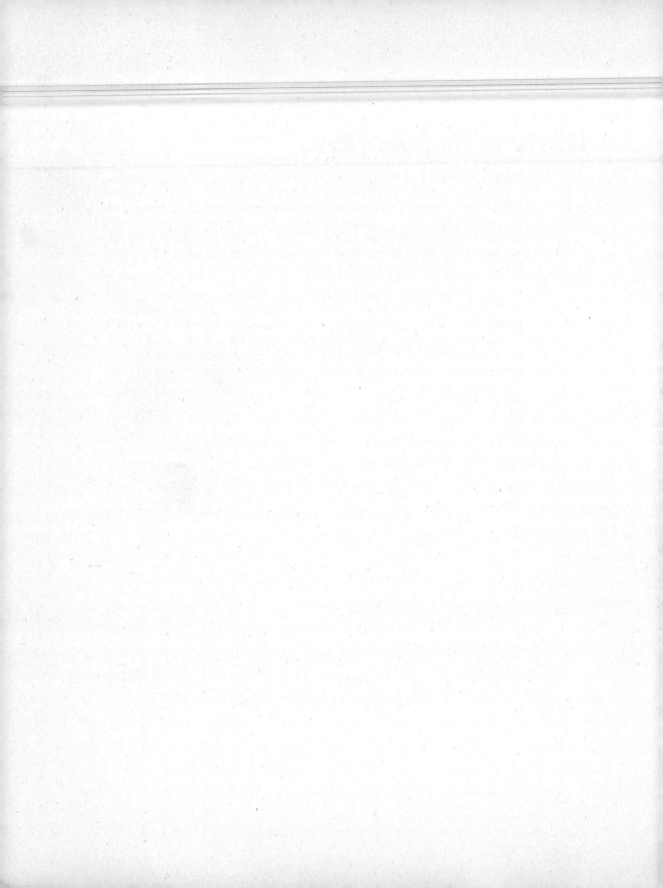

Book I

What Do Catholics Believe?

getting started with

Catholicism

Contents at a Glance

Chapter 1

What It Means to Be Catholic

In This Chapter

▶ Getting a sense of the Catholic perspective

▶ Introducing Church teachings

▶ Participating in Catholic worship

▶ Behaving and praying like a Catholic

*B*eing Catholic means more than attending parochial school or going to religion class once a week, owning some rosary beads, and going to Mass every Saturday night or Sunday morning. It means more than getting ashes smeared on your forehead once a year, eating fish on Fridays, and giving up chocolate for Lent. Being Catholic means living a totally Christian life and having a Catholic perspective.

What is the Catholic perspective? In this chapter, you get a peek at what Catholicism is all about — the common buzzwords and beliefs — a big picture of the whole shebang. (The rest of this book gets into the nitty-gritty details.)

What Exactly Is Catholicism Anyway?

The cut-to-the-chase answer is that *Catholicism* is a Christian religion (just as are Protestantism and Eastern Orthodoxy). *Catholics* are members of the Roman Catholic Church (which means they follow the authority of the bishop of Rome, otherwise known as the pope), and they share various beliefs and ways of worship, as well as a distinct outlook on life. Catholics can be either Latin (Western) or Eastern (Oriental) Catholic; both are equally in union with the bishop of Rome (the pope), but they retain their respective customs and traditions.

Catholics believe that all people are basically good, but sin is a spiritual disease that wounded humankind initially and can kill humankind spiritually if left unchecked. Divine grace is the only remedy for sin, and the best source of divine grace is from the *sacraments,* which are various rites that Catholics believe have been created by Jesus and entrusted by Him to His Church.

From the Catholic perspective, here are some of the bottom-line beliefs:

- ✔ More than an intellectual assent to an idea, Catholicism involves a daily commitment to embrace the will of God — whatever it is and wherever it leads.

- ✔ Catholicism means cooperation with God on the part of the believer. God offers His divine grace (His gift of unconditional love), and the Catholic must accept it and then cooperate with it.

- ✔ Free will is sacred. God never forces you to do anything against your free will. Yet doing evil not only hurts you but also hurts others because a Catholic is never alone. Catholics are always part of a spiritual family called the *Church.*

- ✔ More than a place to go on the weekend to worship, the Church is a mother who feeds spiritually, shares doctrine, heals and comforts, and disciplines when needed. Catholicism considers the Church as important to salvation as the sacraments because both were instituted by Christ.

The Catholic perspective sees everything as being intrinsically created good but with the potential of turning to darkness. It honors the individual intellect and well-formed conscience and encourages members to use their minds to think things through. In other words, instead of just giving a list of do's and don'ts, the Catholic Church educates its members to use their ability to reason and to apply laws of ethics and a natural moral law in many situations.

Catholicism doesn't see science or reason as enemies of faith but as cooperators in seeking the truth. Although Catholicism has an elaborate hierarchy to provide leadership in the Church, Catholicism also teaches individual responsibility and accountability. Education and the secular and sacred sciences are high priorities. Using logical and coherent arguments to explain and defend the Catholic faith is important.

Catholicism isn't a one-day-a-week enterprise. It doesn't segregate religious and moral dimensions of life from political, economic, personal, and familial dimensions. Catholicism tries to integrate faith into everything.

The general Catholic perspective is that because God created everything, *nothing* is outside God's jurisdiction, including your every thought, word, and deed — morning, noon, and night, 24/7.

Knowing What the Catholic Church Teaches

The Catholic religion is built (by Christ) on four pillars of faith: the creed (teachings), the sacraments (liturgical worship), the Ten Commandments (moral code), and the Lord's Prayer or Our Father (prayer and spirituality).

Church doctrine and dogma can be very sophisticated, which may intimidate some people. But the fundamentals are rooted in the Church's creed: the first pillar of faith. Either the Nicene Creed or the Apostles' Creed (which you find out about in Book I, Chapter 2) is said every Sunday and holy day to reaffirm what the Church actually teaches and expects her members to believe and profess. Catholics read the Bible and the *Catechism of the Catholic Church,* the definitive book explaining the official teachings of the Catholic Church on faith and morals.

This section runs through the fundamental tenets of the Church, including what the Church is and who leads it.

Grasping the basic beliefs

Catholics are first and foremost *Christians.* Like Jews and Muslims, Catholics are *monotheistic,* which means that they believe in one God. But Catholics believe that Jesus Christ is the Son of God, which is unique to Christianity. Catholics also believe the following:

- ✔ **The Bible is the inspired, error-free, and revealed word of God.** See Book I, Chapter 2 for an introduction to the Bible.

- ✔ **Baptism, the rite of becoming a Christian, is necessary for salvation.** This is true whether the Baptism occurs by water, blood, or desire (see Book II, Chapter 1).

- ✔ **God's Ten Commandments provide a moral compass — an ethical standard to live by.** You find out about the Ten Commandments in detail in Book II, Chapter 4.

- ✔ **There is one God in three persons: the Holy Trinity.** In other words, Catholics embrace the belief that God, the one Supreme Being, is made up of three persons: God the Father, God the Son, and God the Holy Spirit (see Book I, Chapter 2).

Catholics recognize the unity of body and soul for each human being. So the whole religion centers on the truth that humankind stands between the two worlds of matter and spirit. The physical world is considered part of God's creation and is, therefore, inherently good until an individual misuses it.

The *seven sacraments* — Baptism, Penance, Holy Eucharist, Confirmation, Matrimony, Holy Orders, and the Anointing of the Sick — are outward signs that Christ instituted to give grace. These Catholic rites are based on this same premise of the union of body and soul, matter and spirit, physical and spiritual.

Grace is a totally free, unmerited gift from God necessary for our salvation. Grace is a sharing in the divine; it's God's help — the inspiration that's needed to do His will. Grace inspired martyrs in the early days of Christianity to suffer death rather than deny Christ. Grace bolstered St. Bernadette Soubirous to sustain the derision of the locals who didn't believe she'd seen the Virgin Mary. You can't see, hear, feel, smell, or taste grace because it's invisible. Catholic belief, however, maintains that grace is the life force of the soul. Like a spiritual megavitamin, grace inspires a person to selflessly conform to God's will, and like the battery in the mechanical bunny, grace keeps the soul going, going, going, and going. Because grace is a gift, you can accept or reject it; if you reject it, you won't be saved, and if you accept it, you have to put it into action.

Respecting the role of the Church and its leaders

Catholics firmly believe that Jesus Christ personally founded the Church and He entrusted it to the authority and administration of Saint Peter (the first pope) and his successors. This section explains what Catholics believe the Church really is, as well as how its leadership is structured.

What "the Church" really is

The word *church* has many meanings. Most obviously, it can signify a building where sacred worship takes place. The Catholic Church is not one particular building even though the head of the Church (the pope) lives near Saint Peter's Basilica (the largest church in the world) in Rome.

People who use the church building — the body or assembly of believers — are also known as the *church.* When that body is united under one tradition of worship, it is called a *liturgical church,* such as the Eastern Catholic Church, the Melkite Church, the Ruthenian Church, or the Latin or Roman Rite Church.

Catholic Churches may differ liturgically, but they're still Catholic. The two main lungs of the Church are the Latin (Western) Church and the Eastern Catholic Church. The *Latin (Western) Church* follows the ancient traditions of the Christian community in Rome since the time of St. Peter and St. Paul; most parishes in the United States, Canada, Central America, and South America celebrate this type of Mass, said in either the location's common tongue or Latin. The *Eastern Catholic Church,* which includes the Byzantine Rite, celebrates its Mass like Greek or Russian Eastern Orthodox Churches. Both Masses are cool by the pope, though.

At an even more profound level, the entire *universal* church (meaning the Catholic Church around the world) is theologically considered the Mystical Body of Christ. In other words, the Church sees herself as the living, unifying, sanctifying, governing presence of Jesus Christ on earth today. Not just an organization with members or an institution with departments, the Church is an organic entity; it is alive. Its members, as Saint Paul says in his epistle (1 Corinthians 12:12–31), are like parts in a body. Just as your body has feet, hands, arms, legs, and so on, the Church has many members (parts) but is also one complete and whole *body.*

Unlike a club or association you belong to, the church is more than an informal gathering of like-minded people with similar goals and interests. The church was founded by Christ for a specific purpose: to save us. The church is an extension of Jesus and continues the work begun by Him. He came to teach, sanctify, and govern God's people as the Anointed One (called *Messiah* in Hebrew and *Christ* in Greek).

The Church is necessary for salvation because she is the Mystical Body of Christ, and Christ (being the Savior and Redeemer of the World) is necessary for salvation because He is the One Mediator between God and man. People who do not formally belong to the Church are not *de facto* lost, however, because the church believes in the universal salvific will of God. In other words, God offers salvation to all men and women, yet it is up to them to accept, believe in, and cooperate with that divine grace.

Anyone who has not consciously and deliberately rejected Christ and the Catholic Church can still be saved. In other words, besides the formal members (baptized, registered parishioners), there are many anonymous and unofficial members of the Church who act in good faith and follow their conscience, living virtuous lives. Someone may be innocently ignorant of the necessity of Christ and His Church and still achieve salvation from both.

One body with many members: That is how the Church sees herself. Her mission is to provide everything her members need — spiritually, that is. From the seven sacraments that give us grace to the Magisterium that teaches essential truths to the hierarchy that brings order through laws and governance, the church is there to give the soul what it needs on its journey to heaven. More than a convenient option, the church is a necessary and essential society (community) where members help each other, motivated by the same love.

The Catholic chain of command

Every group of human beings needs a chain of command (authority) and a set of rules (laws), which enable the group to maintain security, provide identity, and promote unity. Families depend on parental authority over the children. Nations have constitutions that delineate and define powers.

The church has authority that she believes comes directly from God. For example, the Lord gave Moses not only the Ten Commandments (see Book II, Chapter 4) but also many other laws and rules to help govern God's people to keep them safe.

Canon law is the set of rules and regulations the Church enacted to protect the rights of persons and the common good of all the members. The word *hierarchy* means "leveled tier." Like the Roman army of old, the Church adopted a chain of command. The highest authority resides in the person of the pope, who is always simultaneously the Bishop of Rome. He is the Successor of Saint Peter, the man to whom Christ entrusted the keys of the kingdom.

The pope is the Church's supreme lawmaker, judge, and visible leader. He is also called the Vicar of Christ on earth. As the Church's ambassador to the world, he possesses full, supreme, and universal power the moment he takes office. He is elected pope by the *college of cardinals,* which exists to elect a pope after the current one dies (or freely resigns) and also to advise, counsel, and assist the reigning pope.

The terms *Vatican* and *Holy See* refer to the various departments, commissions, congregations, and so on that help the pope govern the church, evangelize and teach the faith, and maintain and promote justice.

Jesus not only entrusted the church to Saint Peter and his successors (the popes), but He also had Twelve Apostles whose successors are called *bishops*. A bishop shepherds a local church called a *diocese,* whereas the pope shepherds the universal, global church around the world.

Bishops are helped in each parish church by a pastor who is a priest, and often they are helped by a deacon and/or a parochial vicar (assistant pastor). The bishops of a nation or geographical region form Episcopal conferences, which provide the benefit of pooled resources. For the complete scoop on the church hierarchy, be sure to check out Book I, Chapter 5.

Worshipping As a Catholic: The Holy Mass

The second pillar of faith in the Catholic religion is the seven sacraments — or in more general terms, divine worship of God as celebrated in the sacred liturgy (the topic of Book II). The ceremonies, rituals, and rites performed for the past 2,000+ years were developed by the Church to render worship of the Almighty, to teach the faith to the believers, and to give moral guidance on how to live that faith. The seven sacraments are the most sacred and ancient Catholic rites; they mark the seven major stages of spiritual development:

- ✔ **Baptism:** You are born.
- ✔ **Holy Eucharist:** You are fed.
- ✔ **Confirmation:** You grow.
- ✔ **Penance:** You need healing.
- ✔ **Anointing of the Sick:** You recover.
- ✔ **Matrimony:** You need family.
- ✔ **Holy Orders:** You need leaders.

Because humans have five senses and can't physically see what's happening in the spiritual realm, the seven sacraments involve physical, tangible *symbols* (such as the water used in Baptism, the oil for anointing, and unleavened bread and wine). Symbols help connect us to the invisible spiritual reality, the *divine grace* (God's gift of unconditional love) given in each sacrament. (For more on the seven sacraments, see Book II, Chapter 2.) Catholics belong to their own churches, called *parishes,* which are local places of worship. The *Holy Mass,* the Catholic daily and weekly church service, is a reenactment of *Holy Thursday* (when Jesus celebrated the Last Supper) and *Good Friday* (when He died to purchase the rewards of eternal life in heaven for humankind). In Book III, you find out about the Mass in detail.

Sunday attendance at a parish isn't just expected; it's a moral obligation. Not going to Sunday Mass without a worthy excuse, such as illness or bad weather, is considered a grave sin. (Note that many Christians attend church services on Sunday, but Catholics can also attend Mass on Saturday evening instead to fulfill the Sunday requirement.)

Bringing body and soul into the mix

As Book II, Chapter 1 details, human beings are created as an essential union of body and soul. Material and spiritual worlds are bridged in each and every human person. Because God made us this way, it only makes sense that both body and soul are incorporated in worship.

Attending Mass requires more than just being physically present in Church. That's why Catholics use different postures, such as standing, sitting, kneeling, and bowing, and do plenty of listening, singing, and responding to phrases. For example, if the priest says, "The Lord be with you," Catholics respond, "And with your spirit."

During Mass, the inspired Word of God (see Book I, Chapter 2) is read, proclaimed, and heard through people's eyes, lips, and ears. Holy Communion, food for the soul, is given to believers.

Sacred art adorns the worship space (such as stained glass, statues, icons, paintings, mosaics, tapestries, and frescoes), sacred music is played and sung, bells are rung, incense is burned . . . the senses are stimulated as body and soul are united and nourished in the House of God.

Participating inside and out

Catholics are not spectators while at public worship. Yes, there is a distinction between the *clergy* (ordained ministers who perform the sacred rites and rituals in the name of the Church) and the congregants, but the people in the pews are crucial because they represent the entire human race.

Everyone in the church is asked to get involved in sacred liturgy. Divine worship is the adoration of God by man, and *interior* participation is the most important element. Every person at Mass should be open to God's grace to accept and cooperate with it. Interior participation means going to church not for what you get out of it but for what you can give to God.

Of all the sacraments and all the sacred liturgies, the Mass is par excellence, the source and summit of Christian worship. It is more than a mere reenactment of the Last Supper; it is the unbloody re-presentation of Christ's sacrifice on Calvary (Good Friday).

Mass is first and foremost sacred worship, but it also teaches and supports what Catholics believe in terms of the doctrines and dogmas that form the creed of the religion. Mass communicates religious truths and encourages parishioners to respond morally and spiritually by living holy lives.

Behaving Like a Catholic

The third pillar of the Catholic faith is the Ten Commandments, which represent the moral life of the believer. Behaving as Jesus would want us to is the basic premise. The concept is not puritanical; fun and enjoyment aren't frowned upon. All legitimate pleasures are allowed in moderation — and only if they aren't an end in themselves. The individual's goal is to maintain a happy balance of work and leisure.

As you discover in this section, there are certain activities the church recommends and encourages, and some she requires and demands. In all places and at all times, being docile to the will of God is paramount. For much more detail about how to behave like a Catholic, be sure to check out Book II.

Following the general ground rules

The minimum requirements for being a Catholic are called the *precepts* of the Church:

- Attending Mass every Sunday (or Saturday evening) and holy day of obligation.
- Going to confession annually or more often (or when needed).
- Receiving Holy Communion during Easter. (Receiving weekly or daily Holy Communion is encouraged, though.)
- Observing laws on fasting and abstinence: one full meal on Ash Wednesday and Good Friday; not eating meat on Fridays during Lent.
- Supporting the Church financially and otherwise.

And, in the United States, the American bishops added two more precepts:

- Obeying the marriage laws of the Church.
- Supporting missionary activity of the Church.

You can find out more about the precepts of the Church in Book II, Chapter 3.

Catholics are also required to pray daily, participate in the sacraments, obey the moral law, and accept the teachings of Christ and His Church. If you haven't grown up knowing and accepting the faith, then you need to make sure you know and agree with all that the Catholic Church teaches before you can truly practice the faith.

Practicing the faith is the most difficult part of being Catholic. Obeying the rules isn't just mindless compliance. It involves appreciating the wisdom and value of the various Catholic rules and laws. Believers are asked to put that belief into action, to practice what they believe. Catholics are taught that all men and women are made in the image and likeness of God and that all men and women have been saved by Christ and are adopted children of God. That belief, if truly believed, requires that the person act as if she really means it.

Every organization, society, association, and group has rules. Even individual families and homes have their own rules, which exist for one purpose: the common good of all the members. Just like directions on a bottle of medicine tell you the proper use of something, church laws are signs that warn you of danger and give you the proper directions to your destination. The laws of God — be they the Ten Commandments, the Natural Moral Law, or the moral teachings of the Church — exist to protect us and to ensure our spiritual safety.

Avoiding sin

Sinning is not only breaking the law of God but also much more. Sin is a disease, a germ, an infection of the soul. Just as tumors can be either benign or malignant, sins can be either venial or mortal, either slightly wounding or actually killing the life of grace in the soul.

The best prevention is to avoid sin just as doctors advise us to avoid disease. Good spiritual health requires more than being free of infection, however. Living a virtuous moral life and maintaining a healthy spirituality, when combined with an aggressive program to avoid sin at all cost, is the best plan to live a holy life worthy of a true follower of Christ. Book II, Chapter 5 discusses this subject in detail.

Heeding the Church's stance on tough issues

Certain topics get much more media attention than the substance of Catholic religion (like doctrine, worship, prayer, and spirituality). These topics include the Church's stance on abortion, euthanasia, contraception, homosexuality, and more.

Many of the tough issues that distinguish Catholicism from other faiths are based on the Church's foundational beliefs. Issues such as priestly celibacy are matters of discipline, whereas the ordination of women contradicts a doctrine of the faith. Abortion, euthanasia, contraception, and homosexuality are moral issues that require the application of biblical and doctrinal principals in order to see clearly the spiritual dangers often overlooked by well-meaning people. War and capital punishment are examples where legitimate differences of opinions still exist, yet basic fundamentals must always be respected and upheld. Book II, Chapter 6 covers these tough issues.

Praying as a Catholic: Showing Your Devotion

While public worship (such as the Holy Mass) is governed by the official church, private prayer is more a matter of personal taste and preference. Each person needs to cultivate his own spirituality just as he needs to develop a healthy lifestyle for his body.

When it comes to prayer, what works for one person may not work for another, but certain fundamentals almost always apply. Think of it this way: Your choices with regard to diet and exercise may differ from those of your friends and neighbors, but chances are your choices have a lot in common with those made by people of similar physical health. Likewise, your devotional choices (such as how and when to pray) can be tailored to meet your needs, but many similarities exist among people who share a certain faith.

Praying and using devotions

Devotions are prayers or actions devoted to God, which can be private or public as well. Devotions are minor ways that believers cultivate a love and familiarity with theological truths and revealed mysteries of faith and (most importantly) develop a personal relationship with the Lord. Devotions such as praying the Rosary are some of the more popular and effective ones around.

Realizing the importance of Mary and the saints

The Virgin Mary is the mother of Jesus, and she is also considered one of His most faithful disciples in her own way. While not an Apostle and never holding any authority in the early church, the Mother of Christ nonetheless has always been a model of humility, virtue, and obedience to the will of God.

Mary and the canonized saints of the Church are not objects of worship (which would be idolatry — something condemned by the First Commandment). Instead, they are living examples and models of holiness and sanctity. They are role models and heroes of faith who, in their own way, tried and succeeded in following Jesus as best they could. Book IV introduces you to saints.

Following traditions

The most visible aspects of Catholicism are not usually the most fundamental theological, doctrinal, or moral teachings. In other words, they aren't necessarily the meat-and-potatoes substance of what it means to be Catholic. But some traditions are so public or well known that people associate them with Catholicism much like people associate Judaism with a man wearing a yarmulke or Islam with the use of a prayer rug.

Some such Catholic traditions include meatless Fridays, ashes on the forehead to begin Lent, palms on Palm Sunday, and blessings (of throats, persons, homes, cars, and so on). Such pious practices are not the core of Catholicism, but they do connect and point in that direction.

Defining "The Church" and What Membership Means

The Gospels were originally written in Greek; the Greek word *ekklesia* translates into the English word "church." But *ekklesia* isn't limited to a building where believers worship. The Gospels' notion of church is much more organic and people-related — it's not just a physical structure with a steeple and bell tower.

In the fuller sense of the word, the Church is an assembly of people who share a common faith or belief; it is a building made not of stones but of flesh and blood (called "living stones" in the Bible). In other words, *people* make the Church what it is. In this chapter, we explain how the Church was established, its mission, the benefits of membership, and much more.

Establishing a foundation: Built on rock

Book I

**What Do
Catholics
Believe?**

Jesus said in Matthew 16:18 that Simon, son of John, is to be called Peter (*Petros* in Greek) and that upon this rock (*petra* in Greek), Jesus will build His church (*ekklesia*). Here is the passage from Matthew 16:18–19:

> And I tell you, you are Peter, and on this rock I will build my church, and the powers of death (some versions of the Bible read "gates of hell") shall not prevail against it. I will give you the keys of the kingdom of heaven, and whatever you bind on earth shall be bound in heaven, and whatever you loose on earth shall be loosed in heaven.

This passage makes clear that Christ founded the Church; the Church belongs to Christ. However, Christ gave Peter the authority to care for it. For Catholics, this passage is extremely important because the pope is the successor of St. Peter and the *Vicar* (representative) of Christ on earth. The pope does not replace Christ; he represents Him much like an ambassador represents the president or prime minister who sends him to a foreign nation.

Notice in the Scripture that Jesus gives Peter the keys to the kingdom of heaven. These keys are symbolized in the papal flag, which shows silver and gold keys crossing each other. In the time of Christ, keys were given to prime ministers by the king. The gold key provided access to the treasury where the prime minister kept the king's gold (levied by taxes). The silver key offered access to the royal prison where the enemies of the king were kept.

While Jesus did not give Peter actual, physical keys, He gave him the same authority any king would give his prime minister. That authority is full, supreme, immediate, and universal, as expressed in the phrase "whatever you bind on earth shall be bound in heaven, and whatever you loose on earth shall be loosed in heaven."

Immediately following the death of Peter, the Holy Spirit guided the Church in the election of the next pope, Linus, followed by Cletus, Clement, and so on. Since that time, 266 popes have sat in the Chair of St. Peter — an unbroken line of apostolic succession. Read more about the pope in Book V.

Seeing the Church as the body of Christ and communion of saints

The Church is sometimes called the Mystical Body of Christ, and that analogy comes from the writings of St. Paul. He writes in 1 Corinthians 12:12–13, "Just as the body is one and has many members, and all the members of the body, though many, are one body, so it is with Christ. For by one Spirit we were all baptized into one body." It is in baptism that unity of the Body of Christ is most expressed under the head, Jesus Christ. The Church is one Body, the Church has Christ as her head, and the Church is the Bride of Christ.

Paul refers to Christ as the head of the Church and to the baptized members as the body of the Church. Think of your own body: While you have eyes, ears, hands, and feet, there is only one of you; you're the sum of your parts. Likewise, the Church is the union of all her members, who have unique roles but work together to make a complete whole.

If you're a baptized member of the Church, you have a part to play in the Body of Christ. Here are some examples:

- **The laity** preach the good news of salvation by the way they witness to Christ in the workplace, marketplace, school, and society. Also, through Holy Matrimony (see Book II, Chapter 2) they become supporters of their spouses to become saints and bring forth children to populate heaven.

- **The consecrated religious** give witness to the Kingdom of God by living their religious vows of poverty, chastity, and obedience. These vows are a visible sign for people on earth of the Lord they hope to meet at the end of their lives.

- **The clergy,** by virtue of Holy Orders (see Book II, Chapter 2), share in the task of Christ in dispensing the mysteries of God, the sacraments, to fortify the pilgrim. Through teaching and preaching they instruct the wayfarer toward the correct path to heaven.

The Mystical Body of Christ is also called the *communion of saints* (read more in Book I, Chapter 2). Like Paul's body analogy, the communion of saints model of the Church indicates an organic unity of parts working together — the Church Militant, the Church Suffering, and the Church Triumphant:

- **Militant** refers to the Church's living members on earth who are in a daily battle against the world, flesh, and devil; the war is against evil, not other religions.

- **Suffering** refers to the holy souls in purgatory, who died in the state of grace with no mortal sin on their souls but still had some attachments to their venial sins and to previously forgiven mortal sins. The soul realizes that it is in need of further purification before it can enter into the glories of heaven.

- **Triumphant** refers to the angels and saints in heaven around the banquet table of God. They were victorious in the good fight against sin and evil and are now experiencing the joys of paradise.

Understanding the four marks of the Church

The Nicene Creed (see Book I, Chapter 2) is professed every Sunday and holy day. It speaks of four essential marks, or identifiers, of the Church: "I believe in *one, holy, Catholic* and *apostolic* church." These four elements are the foundation of Catholic Christianity. They are signs to the world that the Church is the work of God and that the Church is of divine origin. Here's what each mark means:

- ✔ **One (unity):** As the preceding section shows you, the Church is one body with many members, each of whom plays a vital role, and all of whom are united. The Church is an organic unity and not artificial, synthetic, or man-made. The pope is the visible head of the global Church, which has more than 1 billion members worldwide. He appoints the local bishops, who in turn assign the local pastors and parish priests and deacons. The Church has one governing authority (hierarchy) and one teaching authority (Magisterium). The Church has one body of truths she teaches (found in the Catechism) and one body of divine worship (the seven sacraments).

- ✔ **Holy (sanctity):** The Church is holy because her founder is Jesus Christ, the Son of God and second person of the Holy Trinity. She is also the Bride of Christ and is considered the Mystical Body of Christ as well. That association and union with divinity itself makes the Church holy. But she also has been given by God Himself all the necessary divine revealed truths and all the necessary divine grace to save souls (help people get to heaven). This does not mean that members have it made and need to do nothing else except belong. It does mean that holiness is possible and promoted by the Church at the will and command of her founder, Jesus Christ. One becomes a saint through, with, and in the Church.

- ✔ **Catholic (universality):** The word *Catholic* derives from the Greek *katholikos,* which means universal. The church's mission is universal. It is to spread the good news about Jesus (also called the *gospel*) to all men and women all over the world. The Church is not confined to any one nation or country. That's why it's not called the Church of Italy, the Church of England, the Church of America, or the Church of Europe. It is the Catholic Church, which belongs to Christ and is found everywhere around the world. Embracing all languages, continents, cultures, and races, the Church is universal and promotes universality. Human beings belong to the same human race even though they live in different parts of the world and speak different tongues.

- ✔ **Apostolic (continuity):** The last mark refers to the fact that the Catholic Church can trace its foundations to Christ Himself and to the 12 apostles. Also, every deacon, priest, and bishop can trace his ordination lineage back to one of the original apostles; this is called *apostolic succession.* A verifiable and direct connection exists between the apostles whom Jesus handpicked and their direct successors, the bishops. Also, there is direct succession of all the popes, from Saint Peter to his 266th successor, Pope Francis.

Fulfilling its mission

The mission of the Church is the continuation of Christ's mission: to proclaim the Gospel to the entire world for all generations. Christ gave the mission to His church when He said, "Go therefore and make disciples of all nations, baptizing them in the name of the Father and of the Son and of the Holy Spirit, teaching them to observe all that I have commanded you" (Matthew 28:19–20). Evangelization is the mission, and all baptized Christians are involved. So if you're a member of the Church, your life's work is intertwined with the salvific duty of the Savior: to reconcile fellow people with God.

Christ won salvation for humanity on the cross, on Good Friday, by shedding His precious blood. He is the great mediator between the Father and mankind. The Church, as the bride of Christ, continues this work through proclaiming the Word of God, teaching revealed truths, dispensing grace through the sacraments, and gathering the multitude into unity.

All members of the Church are commissioned to perform the Corporal Works of Mercy, which are to feed the hungry, give drink to the thirsty, clothe the naked, give shelter to the homeless, visit the sick, ransom the captive, and bury the dead. The baptized also continue the mission of Christ by exercising the Spiritual Works of Mercy, which are to instruct the ignorant, counsel the doubtful, admonish the sinner, bear wrongs patiently, forgive offenses willingly, comfort the afflicted, and pray for the living and the dead.

The mission of the Church is the mission of Christ. Christ Himself was a priest, a prophet, and a king. The *priestly office* of Christ's mission was to sanctify the world. The *prophetic office* of His mission was to teach the truth to the world. His *kingly office* was to be the Good Shepherd and provide governance and leadership. He used all three aspects to achieve the one mission: proclaiming the Good News. The Church, which is an extension of Christ on earth, fulfills that same work via the same three aspects, which we detail next.

Jesus chose 12 apostles and 70 disciples to help continue His mission after He died, rose, and ascended to heaven. Before being able to evangelize, His men needed to be taught the message, sanctified so they could receive the message worthily, and organized to effectively achieve success in the mission. Christ the priest, prophet, and king therefore sanctified, taught, and shepherded His disciples and apostles. The Church continues that process today.

The priestly office: Sanctifying through the sacraments

Jesus Christ the priest instituted the seven sacraments (see Book II, Chapter 2) in order for the faithful to become holy, to receive His divine life, and to become stronger on earth in their journey to heaven. *Sanctifying grace* makes the soul holy and pleasing to God; given at Baptism, this grace is the indwelling of the Triune God (Father, Son, and Holy Spirit) in the soul of the individual person. The priestly (sanctifying) office of Christ and His Church makes the human soul disposed to the gift of divine grace, which makes one holy in the eyes of God.

The sacraments are the visible signs instituted by Christ to confer grace. For the faithful, the sacraments are the necessary vehicles of grace for the sole purpose of salvation. In an analogous way, the Church is what theologians call the *primordial* sacrament, that is, the sacred institution where the seven sacraments are bestowed. The Church and the sacraments both continue the sacred work of Christ's redemption. The effects of the sacraments on the faithful create a bond of unity that is most visible in the Mystical Body of Christ, the Church.

The prophetic office: Teaching through the Magisterium

The official term for the teaching (prophetic) office of the Church is the *Magisterium* (from the Latin *magister*, meaning teacher). The Magisterium is made up of the pope and all the bishops around the world in communion with Him. When the Church teaches on matters of faith and morals, she is *infallible* (free from error). But on matters of science, economics, astronomy, athletics, and so on, she has no *charism* (gift) of infallibility.

The Church's teachings are infallible, but that doesn't mean the Church never updates or refines the explanations of dogmas and doctrines so Catholics can understand them better. Scripture never changes (though the translations do), but teachings can be put in a better context or shown in a different perspective.

There are two levels of infallibility — ordinary and extraordinary — and the same levels apply to the Magisterium. Therefore, you find an Ordinary Magisterium and an Extraordinary Magisterium. Both are infallible in content, but here's how they differ:

- ✔ **Ordinary Magisterium:** These teachings deal with the consistent and perennial common teaching of all the popes and bishops (in union with the pope) throughout history. Examples from this office include papal teachings on birth control or the ordination of women; these are just retellings of guidelines that have always been taught by popes and bishops throughout Catholic history.

✔ **Extraordinary Magisterium:** The name says it all; these teachings are rare. This level proclaims the Church's stance on doctrines formulated by ecumenical councils, after meetings of all Church bishops, or after the pope has made an *ex cathedra* decree. There have been only 21 ecumenical councils and two *ex cathedra* decrees.

The Church has a responsibility to its members to make sense out of the faith, and the Ordinary and Extraordinary Magisteria help Catholics get the word straight from the Vatican's mouth.

The kingly office: Shepherding and governing through the hierarchy

Christ the King provided governance and leadership to his followers. The kingly office of the Church is to make sure that the Church stays organized with the right people in charge, just like Jesus set it up. The Catholic Church is an institution, and as with any organization, it has rules, procedures, and a hierarchy of authority.

The basic structure of the Church was given by the Lord when He formed His Church by calling the 12 apostles, who became the first bishops. Out of the 12, he chose a leader, Peter, the first pope (flip to the section "Establishing a foundation: Built on rock" for more details). That's still the example the Church follows.

Bishops and *presbyters* or priests (successors to the 70 disciples) are ordained to celebrate the sacraments (especially the Mass), to preach, to teach, and to minister in a local church (known as a *parish*). A collection of parishes in a geographical location is known as a *diocese.* The Catholic Church is made up of many different dioceses and archdioceses throughout the world. In addition to priests, there are ordained *deacons* who assist priests and bishops in their local parishes and dioceses.

The pope is the head of the church and the bishop of Rome; as such, his seat of authority *(cathedra)* is the Basilica of St. John Lateran. He is also the head of the Universal Church, and his seat of authority is the Basilica of St. Peter, Vatican City. Cardinals are appointed by the pope and make up the College of Cardinals. As a body, this college advises the pope and, on his death, elects a new pope.

Membership has its benefits

An old axiom states that the whole is greater than the sum of the parts. Belonging to the Church — being a member of the Mystical Body of Christ — has benefits beyond the imagination. Scripture says that eye has not seen and ear has not heard what God has in store for us (1 Corinthians 2:9). While we may not be able to comprehend fully what total union with God fully means, because we are united together, as brothers and sisters, our joy will be more full and intense than if we were all by ourselves.

Although the Church is sometimes called the *societas perfecta* (perfect society), members of the Catholic Church are not in any way perfect or sinless. They are not better than people who do not belong to the Church. Instead, the phrase means that the Church is the source of all necessary divine truth and of all necessary divine grace. It's one-stop spiritual shopping, you could say.

The Church provides for all the spiritual needs of a believer. For spiritual food, there is Holy Communion (also called the Holy Eucharist). For knowledge, there is divine revelation as found in Sacred Scripture and Sacred Tradition, entrusted to the Magisterium (teaching authority of the Church). For spiritual healing, there is the sacrament of Penance and Reconciliation, as well as the sacrament of Anointing the Sick. The Church hierarchy provides necessary leadership, and canon law is the source of justice and discipline. The needs of the individual and the needs of the community are perfectly fulfilled, meaning that members do not need to go anywhere else to fulfill their spiritual requirements.

If all this sounds pretty good to you, and you're not yet a baptized Catholic, we encourage you to check out your local parish's RCIA (Rite of Christian Initiation of Adults) process. It'll give you ample opportunity to learn more about the faith, help find a sponsor for the sacraments of Baptism and Confirmation, and perform all the necessary rites so you can officially join the Church. The process usually takes about nine months, from early fall to spring (Easter), but in some cases can be done privately as well. Baptized Protestants aren't re-baptized, but after instruction are brought into full communion by professing the faith, going to confession, being confirmed, and then receiving their First Communion. Only unbaptized persons can be baptized.

Chapter 2

Having Faith in God's Revealed Word

· ·

In This Chapter

▶ Defining the real, practical meaning of faith

▶ Discovering the ways God reveals truth

▶ Believing in the written and spoken Word of God

▶ Using reason to defend what you believe

· ·

*Y*ou may think that having faith is similar to believing in fantasies or fairy tales, or accepting the existence of UFOs, ghosts, abominable snowmen, the Loch Ness monster, or Bigfoot. But faith is something entirely different. In this chapter, you find out what faith really is and discover all the divine truths that Catholics believe in. You also learn some proofs for God's existence that will make your faith stronger.

How Do You Know If You Have Faith?

St. Thomas Aquinas (theologian of the 13th century) said faith was the assent given by the mind (intellect) to what cannot be seen or proven but is taken on the word and authority of another. The ascertainment of faith is plain and simple: You have *faith* if you trust the word of someone else. When you take what someone says on faith, you believe in what the other person is telling you even though you haven't personally witnessed it, may not understand it, or may find it difficult to believe. In other words, faith means agreeing with, believing in, *trusting* something — without cold, hard evidence — that you can't know or comprehend on your own.

So far, faith doesn't sound all that different from believing in Santa Claus or the Easter Bunny, but having faith is a bit more complicated. Having faith means being able to live with unanswered questions — sometimes, tough ones. For example, why does evil exist in the world? Why do people still go to war? And what about the existence of terrorism, disease, and crime? Faith doesn't answer these questions. (Some people think that the answer "It's God's will" suffices, but it doesn't.) Faith, however, gives you the courage to endure and survive without having the answers. Instead of providing a set of answers to painful and complicated enigmas, faith provides the means to persevere.

The *Catechism of the Catholic Church,* a book defining the official teachings of the Catholic Church, has this to say about faith:

✔ "Faith is first of all a personal adherence of man to God. At the same time, and inseparably, it is a *free assent to the whole truth that God has revealed.*" (150)

✔ "Faith is a personal act — the free response of the human person to the initiative of God who reveals himself. But faith isn't an isolated act. No one can believe alone, just as no one can live alone." (166)

To Catholics, faith is a supernatural virtue given to human beings from God. What you do or don't do with that faith is totally up to you. God offers it freely to anyone and everyone, but it must be freely received as well. No one can be forced to have or accept faith. And when it's presented, each individual responds differently — at different levels, at different times, and in different ways. Some reject it, some ignore it, and some treat it casually. Others cherish their faith deeply. As the adage goes: For those who believe, no explanation is necessary, and for those who do not believe, no explanation is possible.

Having Faith in Revelation

Catholic faith involves more than just believing that God exists. It's about believing *in* God as well as *whatever* God has revealed. Objectively, you can look at faith as the sum total of the truths God reveals, which form the basis for the doctrines of the Church and are often called the *deposit of faith* — the doctrines of the Church. Subjectively, you can consider faith as your personal response *(assent)* to those revealed truths.

So, maybe you wonder: "But what do you mean by revealed truths? And, for that matter, just what *are* God's revealed truths?" *Revealed truths* refer to *revelations,* God's unveiling of supernatural truths necessary for human salvation. (The word *revelation* comes from the Latin *revelare,* meaning to *unveil.*) Some of these are truths that you could never know by science or philosophy; the human mind is incapable of knowing them without divine intervention, so God revealed them to mere mortals. For example, the revealed truth of the Holy Trinity is that there is only one God but three persons (not three gods, mind you). This truth is something that the human intellect could never discover on its own; God had to tell that one himself.

Other revelations, such as the existence of God, can be known by using human reason alone (see the section "Backing Up Your Faith with Reason: Summa Theologica" in this chapter), but God reveals these truths directly anyway because not everyone understands them at the same time and in the same way. The essence of these revelations can be — and is presumed to be — knowable to anyone with the use of reason; so, for example, someone can't claim he didn't know it was wrong to commit murder. But because of original sin, some of the applications and distinctions of these basic truths require more reasoning and thinking. To even out the playing field, God revealed some important truths so that even those people who aren't intelligent or quick-minded won't be caught off guard.

As for what God's revealed truths are, the most concise answer is *His word*. *The Word of God* is the revelation of God to His people. What is the Word of God? Catholics believe that the Word of God comes in two forms:

- ✔ **The written word:** Known also as *Scripture* or the *Bible*
- ✔ **The spoken word:** Also called the *unwritten word* or *Sacred Tradition*

Both the spoken and the written word come from the same source and communicate the same message — the truth. The written word and the spoken word of God are not in competition with one another, nor do Catholics believe one at the expense of the other. Rather, the written word and the spoken word have a mutual partnership. Whenever and wherever the Bible is silent on an issue or its meaning is ambiguous or disputed, the spoken word (Sacred Tradition) steps in to clarify the matter. Catholics believe that God's word reflects what's in His mind, and because God is all truth and all good, His word conveys truth and goodness. Catholics have deep respect for and devotion to the Word of God.

Faith in the written word: The Bible

Catholicism is a biblical religion. Like all Christian religions, it cherishes the Bible as the inspired, infallible, inerrant, and revealed Word of God.

Having faith in the following aspects of the Bible is crucial to being Catholic:

- ✔ The belief in the Bible as one of the two channels of revelation
- ✔ The literal and figurative interpretation of the biblical text
- ✔ The belief in the Catholic Bible as the most authoritative text

Believing in two forms of revelation

Catholic Christianity and Eastern Orthodox Christianity believe in one common source of divine revelation (God himself), but they believe the revelation is transmitted to us through two equal and distinct modes: the written word (the Bible) and the spoken word (the *unwritten word*). Protestant Christianity regards the Bible as the only source of divine revelation. Another way of looking at it is to think of some Christians as seeing only one channel of revelation — *sola scriptura,* which is Latin for *Scripture alone* — and Catholic Christians as seeing two channels of revelation — both the written word and the unwritten word of God. (Just divert thine eyes to the "Faith in the spoken word: Sacred Tradition" section, later in this chapter, for an explanation of what the unwritten word is.)

Interpreting sacred literature both literally and figuratively

Catholics regard the Bible as the inspired and revealed word of God, but it's also seen as a collection of sacred literature. Rather than just looking at the Bible as one big book, Catholicism treats the Bible as a collection of smaller books under one cover: the word of God written by men yet inspired by God. Since the time of the Reformation, opinion on the interpretation of the sacred text has differed significantly. Some Christians hold for a literal interpretation of every word and phrase of Scripture; other Christians hold for a faithful interpretation, which is sometimes literal and sometimes not. (In other words, some text is meant to be interpreted figuratively.) Catholics belong to the second camp.

The Bible tells the history of salvation, but it's much more than a history book. It contains the Psalms of David — songs that the King wrote in honor of God — yet the Bible is much more than a hymnal. It contains poetry, prose, history, theology, imagery, metaphor, analogy, irony, hyperbole, and so on. Because it's not exclusively one form of literature, as you would have in a science textbook, one needs to know and appreciate the various literary forms in the Bible in order to interpret it as the author intended. For example, when Jesus says in the Gospel (Mark 9:43), "And if your hand causes you to sin, cut it off," the Catholic Church has interpreted that to be a *figure of speech* rather than something to be taken *literally*. At the same time, Catholicism interprets literally the passage of John 6:55 — "For my flesh is food indeed and my blood is drink indeed." Because individuals can disagree on what should be interpreted literally and what shouldn't, Catholicism resorts to one final authority to definitively interpret for all Catholics what the biblical text means for the Catholic faith. That ultimate authority is called the *Magisterium* (from the Latin word *magister* meaning *teacher*), which is the authority of the pope and the bishops around the world in union with him to instruct the faithful. (For more on the Magisterium, see Book I, Chapter 5.) Catholics believe that Christ founded the Church ("I will build my Church" [Matthew 16:18]), a necessary institution, to safeguard and protect revelation by authentically interpreting the biblical texts. The Church is not superior to Scripture, but she's the steward and guardian as well as interpreter of the inspired and revealed Word of God. The Church assumes the role of authentic interpreter not on her own but by the authority given her by Christ: "He who hears you, hears me" (Luke 10:16). The Church makes an authentic interpretation and an authoritative decision regarding those issues that aren't explicitly addressed in Sacred Scripture, but only because Christ has entrusted her to do so. To find out how the Church views tough modern-day issues that aren't addressed in the Bible, flip to Book II, Chapter 6.

Book I

What Do Catholics Believe?

Trusting the authority of the Catholic Bible

What follows is a snapshot of how the Bible was created and how different versions evolved — the Catholic versions and the Protestant versions. If you're eager for more information on the Bible, however, check out *The Bible For Dummies* by Jeffrey Geoghegan and Michael Homan (John Wiley & Sons).

To understand the history of the Bible, you really have to go back to around 1800 B.C. when the oral tradition of the Hebrew people started, because Abraham and his tribes were nomadic people and didn't have a written language of their own. Mothers and fathers verbally *(orally)* handed down the stories of the Old Testament about Adam and Eve, Cain and Abel, and so on. (The Latin word *traditio* means to hand down, and it's the root of the English word for *tradition*.) The stories of the Old Testament were all told by word of mouth, which is called *oral tradition*.

Moses appeared sometime around 1250 B.C., when God delivered the Hebrew people from the bondage of slavery in Egypt and they entered the Promised Land. The era of Moses opened the road to some of the written word because Moses was raised in the court of Pharaoh, where he learned how to read and write. But the predominant bulk of revelation was still the oral tradition, handed down from generation to generation, because the rest of the Hebrews were slaves and most were unable to read or write at that time. Substantial writings weren't saved until 950 B.C., during the reign of King Solomon. But after his death, King Solomon's kingdom was divided between the northern and southern kingdoms of Israel and Judah, respectively.

The Assyrians conquered Israel in 721 B.C., and the Babylonians conquered Judah in 587 B.C. During the time of the Babylonian captivity and exile, the Jews of the *Diaspora* (forced exile of Jews) were spread all over the known world. Some retained their Hebrew language, but most lost it and adopted the common language: Greek. (If you could read and write at this time in history, most likely you were reading and writing Greek.)

Consequently, in the year 250 B.C., an effort was underway to translate all Jewish Scripture into the Greek language. The thing is, more Jews lived outside of Palestine than within it. In the third century B.C., nearly two-fifths of the population in Egypt alone, especially in Alexandria, was Jewish and yet unable to read and write in Hebrew. These Greek-speaking Jews were known as *Hellenistic Jews*. Seven books of Scripture were written in Greek by these Hellenistic Jews and were considered as inspired as the 39 Scriptural books written in Hebrew before the Diaspora.

The Greek version of the Old Testament was called the *Septuagint* (symbolized by the Roman numeral LXX for the number 70) because it took 70 scholars allegedly 70 years to complete the task. They met in Alexandria, Egypt, and translated 39 Hebrew Scriptures into Greek and included 7 other books originally written by Jews in the Greek language.

These seven books — the Books of Baruch, Maccabees I and II, Tobit, Judith, Ecclesiasticus (also known as *Sirach*), and Wisdom — were known and used by Jews even in the Holy Land, including Jesus and His disciples. The early Christians likewise accepted the inspired status of these seven books because no one had refuted them during the time of Christ. Because they were later additions to the more ancient Hebrew writings, however, these seven books were called the *Deuterocanonical Books* (meaning *second canon*); the 39 Hebrew books were known as the *Canonical Books*.

Jewish authorities in Jerusalem had no explicit objection to these seven books until the year A.D. 100, well after the Christians had split from formal Judaism and formed their own separate religion. The Temple of Jerusalem was destroyed in A.D. 70, and in the year A.D. 100, Jewish leaders at the Council of Jamnia sought to purify Judaism of all foreign and Gentile influence, which meant removing anything not purely Hebrew. Because the seven Deuterocanonical Books were never written in Hebrew, they got pitched.

By now, though, Christianity was totally separate from Judaism and didn't doubt the authenticity of the seven books, because these books were always considered equal to the other 39. (Much later, Martin Luther would initiate the Protestant Reformation in 1517 and choose to adopt the Hebrew canon [39 books] rather than the Greek canon [46 books], also called the Septuagint.)

So, in the listing of the Old Testament, a discrepancy exists between the Catholic and the Protestant Bibles. Catholic Bibles list 46 books and Protestant Bibles list 39. Recently, many publishers have reintroduced the seven books in Protestant Bibles, such as the King James Version, but they're carefully placed in the back (after the end of the canonical texts) and are identified as being part of the *Apocrypha*, which is from the Greek word *apokryphos* meaning *hidden*.

So what the Catholic Church considers Deuterocanonical, Protestant theologians consider Apocrypha. And what the Catholic Church considers Apocrypha, Protestants call *Pseudepigrapha* (meaning *false writings*), which are the alleged and so-called Lost Books of the Bible. These Lost Books were never considered as being inspired by the Church, so they were never included as part of any Bible, Catholic or Protestant. Such books as the Assumption of Moses, the Apocalypse of Abraham, the Ascension of Isaiah, the Gospel of Thomas, the Gospel of Peter, the Acts of St. John, and others were all considered uninspired and therefore never made it into the Bible.

Interestingly enough, Catholics and Protestants have never seriously disputed the list of the New Testament books, and both the Catholic and the Protestant Bibles have the exact same names and number (27) of books in the New Testament.

Faith in the spoken word: Sacred Tradition

God's word is more than letters on a page or sounds to the ear. His word is *creative.* When God speaks the word, it happens. For example, the book of Genesis in the Bible tells us that God created merely by saying the word: "And God said, 'Let there be light,' and there was light." (Genesis 1:3)

Catholics believe that the Word of God is found not only in the Bible but also in the unwritten or spoken word — *Sacred Tradition.* In this section, you discover Sacred Tradition and the single most important part of that tradition, the Creed.

Filling in the gaps of the written word

Before the word was written, it was first spoken. God first said, "Let there be light," and later on, the sacred author wrote those words on paper. Jesus first spoke the word when He preached His Sermon on the Mount. He didn't dictate to Matthew as He was preaching. Instead, Matthew wrote things down much later, well after Jesus died, rose, and ascended into heaven. None of the Gospels were written during Jesus's life on earth. He died in A.D. 33, and the earliest Gospel manuscript, which is the Aramaic version of Matthew (alluded to by ancient sources), was written between A.D. 40 and 50. The other three Gospels — Mark, Luke, and John — were written between A.D. 53 and 100. Matthew and John, who wrote the first and the last Gospels, were 2 of the original 12 apostles, so they personally heard what Jesus said and saw with their own eyes what He did. Mark and Luke weren't apostles but disciples, and most of their information on what Jesus said and did wasn't a first-hand eyewitness account; rather, their information was handed down to them by others who were witnesses. (Remember that the word *tradition* means *to hand down.*) The unwritten or spoken Gospel was told by word of mouth by the apostles well before the *evangelists,* the Gospel writers, ever wrote one word. Luke received much of his data from Jesus's mother, the Virgin Mary, and Mark received plenty of info from Peter, the apostle Jesus left in charge.

If some time passed between what Jesus actually said and did and when the Gospel writers put His words and actions on paper (actually on parchment), what took place during that period? Before the written word was the unwritten, or spoken, word. In the Old Testament, things happened and were said long before they were written down. So, too, in the New Testament, Jesus preached His sermons and worked His miracles, died on the Cross, rose from the dead, and ascended into heaven long before anyone wrote it down. No one took notes while He preached. No letters were written between Jesus and the apostles. Sacred Tradition predates and precedes Sacred Scripture, but both come from the same source: God.

The New Testament is totally silent on whether Jesus ever married or had children. The Bible says nothing about His marital status, yet Christians believe He had neither a wife nor kids. Sacred Tradition tells that He never married, just as Sacred Tradition says that the Gospels number only four. Without a written list, who decides (and how) if the Old Testament contains 39 books in Protestant Bibles or 46 books in Catholic Bibles and the New Testament has 27? If Catholics were to believe only in the written word, then no answer would exist. But another avenue exists — the unwritten word.

Existing separately from human tradition

Catholicism carefully distinguishes between mere human tradition and divinely inspired Sacred Tradition:

✔ **Human traditions** are man-made laws that can be changed. An example of a human tradition is Catholics not eating meat on Fridays during Lent. Celibacy for priests of the Western (Latin) Church is another human tradition, which any pope can dispense, modify, or continue.

✔ **Sacred Tradition** is considered part of the unwritten Word of God because it has been believed for centuries, since the time of the Apostolic Church, which refers to that period of time in Church history from the first (while the Apostles were still alive) to the second century A.D. (before the second-generation Christians died). It's called *Apostolic* because the apostles lived at that time.

An example of a Sacred Tradition is the dogma of the Assumption of Mary. A *dogma* is a revealed truth that's solemnly defined by the Church — a formal doctrine that the faithful are obligated to believe. Although it's not explicit in Sacred Scripture, the Assumption of Mary means that Mary was *assumed* (physically taken up), body and soul, into heaven by her divine Son. Even though it wasn't solemnly defined until 1950 by Pope Pius XII, this doctrine has been believed (and never doubted) by Catholic Christians since the time of the apostles. Other examples of Sacred Tradition can be found in the doctrines defined by the 21 General or Ecumenical Councils of the Church, from Nicea (A.D. 325) to Vatican II (1962–1965).

The Creed

The most crucial and influential part of Sacred Tradition is the Creed. The word comes from the Latin *credo,* meaning "I believe." A Creed is a statement or profession of what members of a particular church or religion believe as being essential and necessary. The two most ancient and most important creeds are the *Apostles' Creed* and the *Nicene Creed;* the latter is recited or sung every Sunday and on holy days of obligation at Catholic Masses all over the world. (Like Sundays, *holy days of obligation* are specific days in the calendar year on which Catholics are required to go to Mass. See Book I, Chapter 6 for more on holy days.) The *Nicene Creed* was the fruit of the Council of Nicea, which convened in A.D. 325 to condemn the heresy of Arianism and to affirm the doctrine of the divinity of Christ. The oldest creed, however, is the Apostles' Creed. Although it's doubtful that the 12 apostles themselves wrote it, the origin of this creed comes from the first century A.D.

A sophisticated development of the *Apostles' Creed,* which is a Christian statement of belief attributed to the 12 apostles, the Nicene Creed reflects one's loyalty and allegiance to the truths contained in it. The *Catechism of the Catholic Church* explains that the Creed is one of the four pillars of faith, along with the Ten Commandments, the seven sacraments, and the Our Father. The text of the Apostles' Creed and the Nicene Creed, which follows, succinctly summarizes all that Catholicism regards as divinely revealed truth:

> **The Apostles' Creed:** I believe in God, the Father almighty, Creator of heaven and earth, and in Jesus Christ, his only Son, our Lord, born of the Virgin Mary, suffered under Pontius Pilate, was crucified, died and was buried; he descended into hell; on the third day he rose again from the dead; he ascended into heaven, and is seated at the right hand of God the Father almighty; from there he will come to judge the living and the dead. I believe in the Holy Spirit, the holy catholic Church, the communion of saints, the forgiveness of sins, the resurrection of the body, and life everlasting. Amen.

The following list explains the Apostles' Creed in detail, so you can get a better understanding of this Sacred Tradition and the Catholic belief system. (It's divided into 12 articles for easier digestion.)

- **Article 1: I believe in God, the Father Almighty, the Creator of heaven and earth.** This affirms that God exists, that He's one God in three persons, known as the Holy Trinity, and that He created the known universe.

  Creation is understood as making something from nothing. The created world includes all inanimate matter, as well as plant, animal, human, and angelic life.

- **Article 2: And in Jesus Christ, His only Son, our Lord.** This attests that Jesus is the Son of God and that He's most certainly divine. The word *Lord* implies divinity, because the Greek word *Kyrios* and the Hebrew

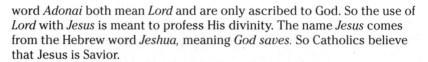

word *Adonai* both mean *Lord* and are only ascribed to God. So the use of *Lord* with *Jesus* is meant to profess His divinity. The name *Jesus* comes from the Hebrew word *Jeshua*, meaning *God saves.* So Catholics believe that Jesus is Savior.

✔ **Article 3: Who was conceived by the Holy Spirit [and] born of the Virgin Mary.** This affirms the human nature of Christ, meaning that He had a real, true human mother, and it also affirms His divine nature, meaning that He had no human father, but by the power of the Holy Spirit He was conceived in the womb of the Virgin Mary. Therefore, He's considered both God and man by Christians — fully divine and fully human.

The union of the two natures in the one divine person of Christ is called the *Incarnation* from the Latin word *caro* meaning *flesh.* The Latin word *Incarnatio* or *Incarnation* in English translates to *becoming flesh.*

✔ **Article 4: [He] suffered under Pontius Pilate, was crucified, died, and was buried.** The human nature of Christ could feel pain and actually die, and He did on Good Friday. The mention of Pontius Pilate by name wasn't meant so much to vilify him forever in history but to place the Crucifixion within human history. So reference is made to an actual historical person, the Roman governor of Judea appointed by Caesar, to put the life and death of Jesus within a chronological and historical context. It also reminds the faithful that one can't blame all Jews for the death of Jesus, as some have erroneously done over the ages. Certain Jewish leaders conspired against Jesus, but a Roman gave the actual death sentence, and Roman soldiers carried it out. So both Jew and Gentile alike shared in the spilling of innocent blood. Anti-Semitism based on the Crucifixion of Jesus is inaccurate, unjust, and erroneous.

✔ **Article 5: He descended into hell. The third day He arose again from the dead.** The *hell* Jesus descended into wasn't the hell of the damned, where Christians believe that the devil and his demons reside. *Hell* was also a word that Jews and ancient Christians used to describe the place of the dead, both the good and the bad. Before salvation and redemption, the souls of Adam and Eve, Abraham, Isaac, Jacob, David, Solomon, Esther, Ruth, and so on, all had to wait in the abode of the dead, until the Redeemer could open the gates of heaven once more. They weren't paroled from hell for good behavior.

This passage affirms that on the third day He *rose,* meaning Jesus came back from the dead of His own divine power. He wasn't just clinically dead for a few minutes, He was *dead* dead; then He rose from the dead. More than a resuscitated corpse, Jesus possessed a glorified and risen *body.*

✔ **Article 6: He ascended into heaven and is seated at the right hand of God the Father Almighty.** The Ascension reminds the faithful that after the human and divine natures of Christ were united in the Incarnation, they could never be separated. In other words, after the saving death and Resurrection, Jesus didn't dump His human body as if He didn't need it anymore. Catholicism teaches that His human body will exist forever. Where Jesus went, body and soul, into heaven, the faithful hope one day to follow.

✔ **Article 7: From there He will come to judge the living and the dead.** This article affirms the Second Coming of Christ at the end of the world to be its judge. Judgment Day, Day of Reckoning, Doomsday — they're all metaphors for the end of time when what's known as the General Judgment will occur. Catholics believe that after the death of any human person, immediate private judgment occurs, and the person goes directly to heaven, hell, or *purgatory* — an intermediate place in preparation for heaven. At the end of time, when General Judgment happens, all the private judgments will be revealed, so everyone knows who's in heaven or hell and why. Private judgment is the one that Catholics are concerned about most, because immediately after death, people are judged by their faith or lack of it and how they practiced that faith — how they acted and behaved as believers. General Judgment is merely God's disclosure of everyone's private judgment. It's *not* an appeal of prior judgment, nor is it a second chance.

✔ **Article 8: I believe in the Holy Spirit.** This part reminds the believer that God exists in three persons: the Holy Trinity — God the Father, God the Son, and God the Holy Spirit. What's referred to as *the Force* in the movie *Star Wars* isn't the same as the Holy Spirit, who is a distinct person equal to the other two — God the Father and God the Son.

✔ **Article 9: [I believe in] the holy Catholic Church, the communion of saints.** Catholics believe that the Church is more than a mere institution and certainly not a necessary evil. It's an essential dimension and aspect of spiritual life. Christ explicitly uses the word *church* (*ekklesia* in Greek) in Matthew 16 when He says, "I will build My Church."

The role of the Church is seen as a continuation of the three-fold mission Christ had while He walked the earth — to *teach, sanctify,* and *govern* — just as He was simultaneously *prophet, priest,* and *king.* The Catholic Church continues His *prophetic* mission of *teaching* through the *Magisterium,* the teaching authority of the Church. She continues His *priestly* mission of *sanctification* through the celebration of the seven sacraments. And the Church continues His *kingly* mission of being shepherd and pastor through the *hierarchy.* The phrase *communion of saints* means that the Church includes not just all the living baptized persons on earth but also the saints in heaven and the souls in purgatory as well. (See Book II, Chapter 2 for an overview of the seven sacraments; see Book I, Chapter 5 for more on Church hierarchy.)

✔ **Article 10: [I believe in] the forgiveness of sins.** Christ came to save the world from sin. Belief in the forgiveness of sins is essential to Christianity. Catholicism believes sins are forgiven in Baptism and in the Sacrament of Penance, which is also known as the Sacrament of Reconciliation or Confession. Mother Teresa of Calcutta said, "It is not that God is calling us to be successful, rather He is calling us to be faithful." In other words, Catholicism acknowledges that all are sinners and all men and women are in need of God's mercy and forgiveness. Religion and the Church are not for perfect people who never sin (perfect people don't exist anyway), but they're for sinners who need the help that religion and the Church provide.

✔ **Article 11: [I believe in] the resurrection of the body.** From the Catholic perspective, a human being is a union of body and soul, so death is just the momentary separation of body and soul until the world ends and all the dead are resurrected. The just will go, body and soul, into heaven, and the damned will go, body and soul, into hell.

Belief in the Resurrection leaves no room for reincarnation or past-life experiences. Catholics believe that you're unique, body and soul, and neither part of you can or will be duplicated even if human cloning is perfected someday. This tenet is why Christians believe that death isn't the last chapter in anyone's life. For the believer, death is a doorway for the soul. The body and soul will eventually get back together again because the body participated in the good that the soul performed or the evil it committed. So the body as well as the soul must be rewarded or punished for all eternity.

✔ **Article 12: [I believe in] life everlasting.** As Christ died, so, too, must mere mortals. As He rose, so shall all human beings.

Death is the only way to cross from this life into the next. At the very moment of death, private judgment occurs; Christ judges the soul. If a person was particularly holy and virtuous on earth, the soul goes directly to heaven. If an individual was evil and wicked and dies in the state of mortal sin, that soul is damned for eternity in hell.

But what if a person lived a life not bad enough to warrant hell but not holy enough to go right to heaven? Catholics believe that *purgatory* is a middle ground between heaven and earth. It's a place of *purgation,* hence the name *purgatory.* Everyone in purgatory eventually gets into heaven.

Backing Up Your Faith with Reason: Summa Theologica

So are having faith and hoping to be saved the same as believing in the Tooth Fairy and hoping for a dollar bill under your pillow? Of course not. The First Vatican Council (1869–1879; also known as *Vatican I*) taught that you need the intervention of supernatural revelation to be saved, but certain truths, like the existence of God, are attainable on your own power by using human reason.

In the 13th century, St. Thomas Aquinas, a philosopher, explained how the human mind seeks different kinds of truth. He said that

- ✔ **Scientific truth** (also known as *empirical truth*) is known by observation and experimentation. So, for example, you know that fire is hot by burning your finger with a lit match.

- ✔ **Philosophical truth** is known by using human reason. You know that two plus two equals four, for example. So if two chairs are in a room and someone says, "I'll get two more," you know by using reason that the total will be four chairs. You don't need to count the chairs after they arrive.

- ✔ **Theological truth,** known only by faith, is the final and highest level of truth. It can't be observed, and it can't be reasoned; it must be believed by faith — taken on God's word, because He revealed it.

St. Thomas Aquinas also delineated five philosophical proofs for the existence of God in a monumental work called the *Summa Theologica.* Because Vatican I taught that the human mind can know some things of religion on its own without having to depend on divine revelation, it's good to see the example given by St. Thomas. Aquinas reasoned that humans can prove the existence of God through motion, causality, necessity, gradation, and governance. Granted, you may not be able to persuade an atheist to become a missionary priest this way, but these proofs are still pretty compelling.

Through motion

Before you were conceived in your mother's womb, you were merely a *potential* being. You didn't become real, or actual, until the occurrence of the act that created a new human life.

Likewise, at one time, everything now in existence was merely potential, because everything has a beginning. In other words, to get to the actual here and now, you first must have an actual beginning — a start. So at some point, all human beings — and all things — never were.

Some force had to start the motion from potential existence to actual existence. And that force could never have been potential itself; it always was, is, and shall be. Otherwise, that force would've had to be started by some other force, which would've had to be started by some other force, and so on. This chain of forces means that an actual beginning would never have been. And, again, the here and now must have an actual beginning.

Before the Big Bang, when the universe was only potential, what force started the motion for it to become actual and real? St. Thomas said that the force is God, the Prime Mover — moving the potential universe into becoming the actual one.

Through causality

Our parents caused us to be born, just as yours did. Our grandparents caused our parents to be born. And so on. So every cause was first an effect of a previous cause. So if you go all the way back to the beginning of everything, something or someone had to be the cause of all causes. Just as the force that started the motion from potential existence to actual existence could never have been potential itself, the cause of all causes could never have been the effect of a previous cause. In other words, the cause of all causes was never an effect but always a cause — or, as philosophers put it, an uncaused cause. St. Thomas said that uncaused cause is God. He caused everything to be by starting creation in the first place.

Through necessity

The universe would not blow up or crash to a screeching halt if you had never been born. This fact is a real ego-popper.

No one individual is necessary. Everything in the universe is basically contingent on — dependent on — something else to exist. Think of it this way: If you turn off a light switch, the flow of electricity to the light bulb is cut off. Without the electricity, you don't have light. If God removed His Being from sustaining you, you'd be like a turned-off light bulb.

One being must be necessary in order to keep the contingent (unnecessary) beings in existence. Otherwise, nothing would exist at all. St. Thomas said the necessary being is God.

Through gradation

Existence and being have different levels. Following is a gradation, or hierarchy, from the lowest level of existence to the highest level of being:

- **Inanimate matter:** Look at inanimate matter, such as rocks. They represent a basic level of existence. They're just there.
- **Plant life:** The next level is plant or vegetative life — simple but able to reproduce.
- **Animal life:** Farther up is animal life. Not only can it reproduce and grow like plant life, but it also has *sense* knowledge. Animals can detect information from their eyes, ears, nose, mouth, and so on.
- **Human life:** Next is human life, which can do all the stuff animal life can, as well as reason. Plus, human life has free will.

✔ **Angelic life or pure beings:** Angelic life consists of pure spirits without bodies. Angels are superior to men and women in that their minds have all the knowledge they will ever have all at one time. Their minds are much more powerful than the minds of mere mortals, too, because they're not distracted by having a body. Without bodies, they never get sick, feel pain, or need food or sleep or shelter. They're immortal and, as pure spirits, have power over the material world.

✔ **The Supreme Pure Being:** The final and ultimate level of existence is a Supreme Pure Being who has no beginning and no end. St. Thomas said that this Supreme Being is God. Like angels, God has no mortal body but is pure spirit. Unlike angels, He has no beginning, whereas He created the angels. Unlike angels, who have limited knowledge and power, God has infinite power, which means that He's *omnipotent;* He has infinite knowledge, which means that He's *omniscient;* and He's everywhere — He's *omnipresent.*

Through governance

Ever wonder why the earth is just the right distance from the sun and has just the right balance of gases to maintain an atmosphere that supports life? The balance is delicate, much like the ecosystem in which plants produce oxygen and animals produce carbon dioxide to keep one another alive.

The planets rotate and orbit at fixed rates instead of crashing into one another. The fundamental laws of physics, chemistry, and biology must be followed; otherwise, life wouldn't exist. These facts point to a higher intelligence — a being that made these physical laws, because they didn't just happen on their own.

Nature tends to go from order to chaos. Who put things in order to begin with? A higher intelligence is indicated when you study how human DNA is so intricate, orderly, and consistent. Rather than being mere chance, life on earth is no mistake, and it follows a plan. St. Thomas said that the Great Governor is God.

These five proofs alone can't convince atheists or agnostics, but they may get their minds clicking. The bottom line is that the existence of God is reasonable and that faith doesn't contradict or oppose reason. Rather, faith complements reason.

Chapter 3

In the Beginning: Catholic Teachings on Creation and Original Sin

....

In This Chapter

▶ Acknowledging that creation has a Creator

▶ Seeing where the devil and hell came from

▶ Experiencing the fallout of Adam and Eve's sin

▶ Expecting the world to end

....

Since the dawn of civilization, humankind has sought to discover the origins of the world and of the universe itself. Where did we come from? How did we get here? These questions inevitably lead to others, such as who are we? And where are we going?

Catholics believe that God is the Creator of heaven and earth because that's what Divine Revelation (as found in Sacred Scripture and Sacred Tradition — see Book I, Chapter 2) tells us. This belief is supported by human logic and science, which tell us that time and space had a beginning, whether you call that moment *creation* or the *Big Bang*. Catholics also believe that because of Adam and Eve's Original Sin, all of us have a wounded sinful nature. We all face judgment at the end of the world, and Catholicism has certain beliefs about what the end of the world will look like.

In this chapter, you explore what Catholicism teaches about the moment when the material world came into existence, the moment when the devil and sin were introduced, and what we know about the end of creation.

Making Something out of Nothing

Technically speaking, *creation* is the act of making something out of nothing, or *creatio ex nihilo* in Latin. (Changing something into something else is called *transmutation* and is a different subject entirely.) Catholics believe that God created the earth and the heavens, meaning that He made them out of nothing.

To grasp how profound this concept is, consider what scientists do in a laboratory. They mix elements to come up with new compounds, and they combine compounds to make all sorts of materials. And when they produce something that has widespread applications, such as plastic, their efforts revolutionize how people live. Their efforts can seem truly miraculous at times.

But who made the elements themselves? Who created the stuff out of which all other stuff is made? To literally make something out of thin air is something no scientist can do (not even the Professor on *Gilligan's Island*). Moving a potential thing into actuality is what a creator does, and Catholics believe that the Creator of heaven and earth is God.

The first chapter of Genesis, the first book of the Bible, tells us that in the beginning nothing existed but God. His first act of creation was to make light: "and God said, 'Let there be light' and there was light." (Genesis 1:3) If plastic has revolutionized the way we live, how much more revolutionary was the creation of light?! (Keep in mind that scientists tell us the beginning of the physical universe took place after what they call the Big Bang. That super-stellar explosion just happened to cause an enormous amount of — you guessed it — *light*.)

Breathing Life into the World: Creationism or Evolution?

A great battle has waged for centuries between those who call themselves pure creationists and those who call themselves pure evolutionists. The Catholic Church has solemnly defined that God is the Creator of the universe. At the same time, the Church has never condemned any modified version of evolution that allows for a Creator and for the spiritual creation of the immortal soul.

Intelligent design is one way Catholics approach creation from a standpoint that accommodates both faith and reason (religion and science). Are not the laws of physics and chemistry part of the divine plan of God? Because God made the universe, didn't He also make the laws that govern the planets and all the beings that exist on them?

A purely atheistic theory of evolution is incompatible with Christianity. Life did not create itself, nor is pure chance or randomness the master of the universe. All of creation works according to a design and plan — so much so that scientists can discern and ascertain that design. The planets rotate around the sun and follow orbits in such a way that enables people to determine every day when sunrise and sunset will occur, when the seasons will take place, and when a whole calendar year will elapse. The planetary movement is orderly; it is not chaotic or spontaneous. Otherwise, the planet would have crashed into Mars or Venus or the sun long ago.

Order does not happen by itself. If you throw marbles in the air, they do not land spelling words. Chaos is what happens when order is removed, and without a guiding design and plan, all of creation would be in chaos. Intelligent design and order are obvious everywhere you look. Consider these examples:

- ✔ Every human being has human DNA, which is distinct from animal DNA and can be used to determine paternity or who committed a crime.

- ✔ Seasons are predictable enough that farmers know when to plant and when to harvest.

- ✔ Chemists know what elements combine with other ones to form stable and safe compounds.

Studying the order of our universe got a man to the moon and offers medical science the ability to treat deadly diseases, but Catholics trace it all back to the Creator. Evolution is still a theory and not a proven law of science. But as long as room is made in that theory for the intelligent design of a Creator, nothing is intrinsically wrong with evolution. Only when evolution kicks God out of the equation is it an offense to religion (as well as illogical).

Angels and Devils: Following God or Lucifer

The Catholic Church teaches that before the first human beings (Adam and Eve) were created in the Garden of Eden, God created beings known as *angels:* beings with no bodies. Angels are pure spirit. An angelic nature consists of an angelic intellect (mind) and an angelic will (heart). In this section, you discover Catholic beliefs about God's creation of angels — and how some of them decided to become devils.

Infused knowledge, eternal decisions

You are a union of body and soul. Our souls are where our rational intellect and free will reside, but our souls depend on our bodies to retrieve all necessary data. Like the memory in a brand-new computer, a soul begins life on earth totally clean and needs input from your keyboard (your body). As the body transmits that data to the soul, humans gain what is called *acquired* knowledge.

Angels have no bodies, so they cannot acquire knowledge; they need *infused* knowledge. Whereas you and I learn each day and extrapolate more from that knowledge, angels know everything at the moment of their creation. Their knowledge is gained all at once, and their will makes one choice that lasts for all eternity. In other words, angels cannot change their minds after they have made a decision. Unfortunately, some of the angels in heaven made the decision to turn away from God.

The angels' test and the devil's choice

After the angels were created but before they were in heaven, God put them to a test. To explain the point of this test, you first need to know what Catholics believe about heaven.

The Catholic Church teaches that once you are in heaven, you can never leave. (That's a good thing!) You can never be tempted, either — whether you're a saint (a human soul) or an angel. Heaven is being in the immediate, direct presence of God (called the *Beatific Vision*). Your intellect, which seeks truth, and your will, which seeks the good, are both perfectly fulfilled and satisfied in heaven. The same is true for angels. So, no one in heaven can sin or be tempted to sin.

Outside of heaven is a different story. Man and angel alike can be tested and tempted. Angels were created first, so their test was different than ours. Theologians over the ages have speculated on the exact nature of the angels' test. Here are two such speculations:

- The angels were given a glimpse of the creation of human beings, and then God disclosed to them that out of pure love, He was going to invite the human race into heaven.

- God disclosed that men and women would sin, but God would forgive them and actually redeem them by becoming one of us.

No matter what the exact nature of the test, the end result is that one-third of the angels were unhappy with what God disclosed to them. Perhaps their pride resented that humans would be invited to heaven, or they were disdainful of the possibility that God would lower Himself to become a man and then raise human nature above angelic nature. Humans can look at Jesus as both King and as brother, but the angels in heaven see Christ only as Lord and King, surely another source of irritation to the rebellious angels.

Lucifer was the most intelligent of all the angels. He and one-third of the angels rebelled against God and refused to submit to His dominion. Saint Michael and the other two-thirds decided to remain loyal to God and fought against the angels who rebelled. Hell was created by God as a place of eternal punishment for Lucifer (who was thereafter known as the *devil*) and all the fallen angels who accompanied him.

It is not accurate to say that God created the devil. God created the angel Lucifer, who was intrinsically good and who freely chose to become bad. His evil decision cast him into hell.

Witnessing the Original Sin

The Book of Genesis begins with the story of creation in general and then focuses on Adam and Eve and their fall from God's grace. In this section, you find out about the choice they made, God's punishment for it, and the everlasting effect of that choice on human nature.

Tempting our first parents

Just as God tested the angels (see the preceding section), He also tested the first human beings: Adam and Eve. He told them not to eat of the forbidden fruit, which was found on only one tree in the entire, bountiful Garden of Eden: the Tree of Knowledge of Good and Evil. All they had to do was overlook one tree! A serpent, who was the devil in disguise, told Eve that she and Adam wouldn't die if they ate the fruit of the tree forbidden by God. Eve ate from the tree and got her husband to do likewise. Adam and Eve chose to defy God and disobey His command. God punished them both — and one of the penalties was death. They didn't die on the spot, but had they not disobeyed the Lord, mankind would have remained immortal.

Of course, the serpent does get some of the blame. But he never coerced the free will of Eve or Adam. Another name for the devil is the Author of All Lies, which is evident in his distortion and perversion of the truth.

Temptation comes from the world, the flesh, or the devil. It is a proposition in our mind to choose an inferior good over a superior one. No rational person chooses evil for the sake of evil; such a person is a sociopath. Nonetheless, rational people do sometimes choose evil: They choose lower goods, ignore higher goods, and often employ immoral means to fulfill (supposedly) morally good ends.

The devil takes a lesser good — like pleasure, convenience, or comfort — and tempts us to raise it above higher goods like life, honor, duty, commitment, family, friendship, and faith. Adam and Eve succumbed to the temptation, and there were consequences.

Losing gifts

When Adam and Eve sinned by disobeying God, they felt ashamed and hid from God. But immediate consequences occurred. After all, sin is not just breaking the law of God; it's also engaging in activity that's dangerous (sometimes lethal) to the soul. Sin causes separation from the Lord.

Here is how Genesis 3:16–19 describes God's punishment:

> To the woman He said, "I will greatly multiply your pain in childbearing; in pain you shall bring forth children, yet your desire will be for your husband, and he shall rule over you."

> And to Adam He said, "Because you have listened to the voice of your wife and have eaten of the tree of which I commanded you, 'You shall not eat of it,' cursed is the ground because of you; in toil you shall eat of it all the days of your life; thorns and thistles it shall bring forth to you, and you shall eat the plants of the field. In the sweat of your face you shall eat bread until you return to the ground, for out of it you were taken; you are dust and to dust you shall return."

The main gifts Adam and Eve lost were *sanctifying grace* (that which makes a person holy and allows him to be in the presence of God), *immortality* (freedom from death), and *impassibility* (freedom from all pain). Without sanctifying grace, heaven was not possible, ever. Adam and Eve were subjected to disease, illness, pain, misery, suffering, toil, labor, and death itself.

As if all this weren't enough, Original Sin had another effect, which the next section explains.

Wounding our nature

Concupiscence is the inclination of the human soul toward evil. It's a consequence of the wounds created by the sin of Adam and Eve, which every human being inherits, and is called *Original Sin*. The wound in human nature that took place immediately was the darkening of the intellect, the weakening of the will, and the disordering of the lower passions and emotions:

- ✔ **Darkening of the intellect:** This wound is the reason many times people can't see clearly the right path to take even though it's right under our nose, so to speak. Sometimes, our wounded human nature clouds our intellect's ability to see with precision the proper course to take. Often, you need good advice, counsel, and perhaps even fraternal correction to compensate when your mind is unable to digest the situation or you find it difficult to figure out the proper solution to your problem.

- ✔ **Weakening of the will:** Even if your mind knows what to do, you might lack the patience or courage to see it through. An addict needs to quit and knows the drugs he takes are killing him, but his will is so weak that he can't just say no. Ask anyone who's on a diet or trying to quit smoking how hard it is. The intellect *knows* the body can do better, but the will is too weak to hang in there and do what needs to be done.

- ✔ **The disordering of the senses:** This phenomenon occurs when your emotions override or overcome your reason. Anger, lust, envy, and so on can become so strong and powerful that your mind is blinded to the evil within it. How many sins and crimes have been committed in the heat of anger or lust? Man was not made of stone with no emotions. Jesus had emotions in His human nature. But Original Sin wounded our human nature so that sometimes our emotions are no longer under the immediate control of our intellect.

Being redeemed by God's grace

If the wound resulting from Original Sin was the end of the human story, it would be bleak and pathetic, for sure. But God's mercy and love are without limit. God's justice condemned and punished humankind for disobeying, and God's mercy promised that a Messiah would redeem and save the human race. Salvation would then be possible for everyone, past, present and future. The Book of Genesis tells of punishment but also of promise.

Speaking to the serpent, God said:

> Upon your belly you shall go and dust you shall eat all the days of your life. I will put enmity between you and the woman, and between your seed and her seed; he shall bruise your head, and you shall bruise his heel (Genesis 3:14-15).

The Catholic Church sees a prophecy in this verse, which is fulfilled in the person of the Virgin Mary. She is considered the woman whose offspring (Jesus) will crush the head of the serpent (the devil). By His grace, God devised a plan to save and redeem man by sending the Son. When Jesus died on the cross (on Good Friday) and rose from the dead (on Easter), He opened the gates of Paradise and made heaven possible once again (see Book I, Chapter 4).

Facing the four last things

The Catholic Church teaches that when a person experiences *death,* she also experiences *particular judgment, heaven,* or *hell.* These are called the *four last things.* Why do they fall into a chapter about creation? Because without the Original Sin of Adam and Eve, humankind wouldn't experience the four last things. So at the beginning of the human experience, the seeds were sown for what occurs at the end of each human life.

When a person dies, there is immediate judgment on his soul, or *particular judgment.* If a person has lived an evil, immoral, sinful life and is unrepentant at the moment of death, he condemns himself to eternal damnation in hell. On the other hand, a holy person who has lived a virtuous and saintly life and dies in the state of grace is rewarded with eternal happiness in heaven. Most people are not bad enough to go to hell yet not good enough to go directly to heaven. These are people who die with some attachments to their former sins. In this case, the person is cleansed (purged) of his attachments in a state of being called *purgatory.* Purgatory is not hell with parole. Purgatory is the state of purification from sins. Sin leaves a scar on the soul, and if the scar is deep, more treatment is needed to heal it and restore the former beauty.

Hell is pure punishment for evil — divine retribution. Purgatory is medicinal and therapeutic. Like gold that is purified in fire, purgatory cleanses our attachments to sin so when someone does go through the pearly gates, that person is wearing the proper wedding garment.

Anticipating What's to Come: Moving toward the End of Creation

For Catholics (and most other Christians), inherent in the story of creation is the belief that God will create a new heaven and a new earth at the end of time. No one knows when the end of this present creation will occur, but the faithful believe in the Second Coming of Christ, the resurrection of the dead, the general judgment, and the end of the world: the four last things of the entire universe (for the four last things that each individual person encounters, check out the preceding section).

The Second Coming

Catholics believe that Jesus died on Good Friday, rose from the dead on Easter Sunday, and 40 days later ascended into heaven. They also believe there will be a Second Coming of Christ to mark the end times. He will not be born as a baby again. Instead, He will return to earth as a full-grown man, the same as He was when He ascended into heaven. The first time around, He entered the world in abject poverty and humility. He will return as the victorious conqueror of sin, death, and the devil.

Before the Second Coming of Christ, which will usher in the end times, these things will happen:

- ✔ All Gentiles will be united in the Church.
- ✔ All Jews will be one in the Messiah's salvation.
- ✔ The Church will be assailed one last time by the Antichrist, who will try to sway many people by deception.
- ✔ Christ will be victorious over this final unleashing of evil through a cosmic battle (Armageddon).

Notice that this list does not mention the *rapture* (a belief that certain "chosen" people will be taken up to heaven before the Second Coming of Christ) nor a reign of a thousand years of the Evil One (the Antichrist). That's because the Catholic Church does not ascribe to these beliefs, which tend to be held more frequently by evangelical Christians.

The tribulation of the church by the Antichrist may last a short or long period of time; the jury is out on that one. There will be a test of faith and a battle for souls. The end will happen when the Second Coming of Christ takes place and the Antichrist and the *Whore of Babylon* (the Antichrist's accomplice, who is mentioned in the Book of Revelation, or the Apocalypse) are defeated and vanquished.

Resurrection of the dead

Catholics believe that after Jesus returns, the dead will be raised. Bodies and souls will be reunited, but not like in any horror movie or thriller video you've seen. The dead bodies of the souls in heaven will be resurrected and then be *glorified* (meaning they will be like Jesus's resurrected body, which was immortal, was impervious to pain and injury, never aged, and never got sick) and taken into heaven. The damned will get their bodies back, but they'll not be glorified. The souls in purgatory will be released and get glorified bodies, which will enter heaven.

General judgment

Immediately after the resurrection of the dead, the general judgment will take place. The general judgment is not an appeal or second chance; it's merely the public disclosure of all the private judgments that took place earlier. The general judgment will manifest both divine justice (in rewarding good and punishing evil) and divine mercy (in the forgiveness of sinners). This way, nobody in heaven is going to ask, "How did *he* get in here?"

The end of the world

The Catholic Church teaches that after general judgment, the risen bodies go back to heaven or hell, and the world ends. The material universe ceases to exist, and reality consists only of heaven and hell — nothing else. Theologians and scientists are in agreement that the universe will end someday. *When* the world ends is irrelevant because your eternal destiny of heaven or hell is already decided well before that happens. Better to be worried and prepared for your *particular* judgment (see the earlier section "Facing the four last things") because you don't know the day or hour for that one, either. The Catechism also talks about the creation of a new heaven and new earth for the glorified, resurrected bodies, since the old earth will be destroyed at the end of the world. But no one knows what that'll be like except God alone.

You don't have to be worried about hell or the end of the world if you live a moral life by obeying the Ten Commandments (see Book II, Chapter 4), seeking God's forgiveness for your sins, and trying to live a saintly life. Thanks to Jesus, Original Sin doesn't prevent people from getting to heaven.

Chapter 4

Believing in Jesus

In This Chapter

▶ Understanding the human nature and the divine nature of Jesus

▶ Examining the Gospels from the Catholic perspective

▶ Looking at some nasty rumors about Jesus that ran wild

*L*ike all Christians, Catholics share the core belief that Jesus of Nazareth is Lord and Savior. The term *Lord* is used because Christians believe Jesus is *divine* — the Son of God. The term *Savior* is used because Christians believe that Jesus saved all humankind by dying for our sins.

Some people may think that Catholicism considers Jesus a hybrid — half human and half divine. That's not the case at all. Catholicism doesn't see Jesus as having a split personality or as a spiritual Frankenstein, partly human and partly divine. He's regarded as fully human and fully divine — true man and true God. He's considered one divine person with two equal natures, human and divine. This premise is the cornerstone of all Christian mysteries. It can't be explained completely but must be believed on faith. (See Book I, Chapter 2 for the scoop on what faith really means.)

The Nicene Creed, a highly theological profession of faith, says volumes about what Christianity in general (and the Catholic Church in particular) believes about the person called Jesus. This chapter doesn't say volumes, but it does tell you the need-to-know points for understanding Catholicism's perspective on Jesus.

Understanding Jesus, the God-Man

Jesus, the God-Man, having a fully divine nature and a fully human nature in one divine person, is the core and center of Christian belief.

"True God" and "became man" are key phrases in the Nicene Creed, which highlights the fundamental doctrine of Jesus as the God-Man:

✔ As God, Jesus possessed a fully divine nature, so He was able to perform miracles, such as changing water into wine; curing sickness, disease, and disability; and raising the dead. His greatest act of divinity was to rise from the dead Himself.

✔ As man, Jesus had a human mother, Mary, who gave birth to Him and nursed Him. He lived and grew up like any other man. He taught, preached, suffered, and died. So Jesus had a fully human nature as well.

The Old Testament usually uses the word *Lord* (*Adonai* in Hebrew) in connection with the word *God* (*Elohim* in Hebrew). An example is the phrase "Hear, O Israel, the Lord our God is one Lord" in Deuteronomy 6:4. But the New Testament asserts through the Epistle of St. Paul to the Philippians (2:11) "that Jesus Christ is Lord."

The human nature of Jesus

Jesus had a physical body with all the usual parts: two eyes, two ears, two legs, a heart, a brain, a stomach, and so on. He also possessed a human intellect (mind) and will (heart) and experienced human emotions, such as joy and sorrow. The Gospel According to John, for example, says that Jesus cried at the death of his friend Lazarus. Jesus wasn't born with the ability to speak. He had to learn how to walk and talk — how to be, act, and think as a human. These things are called *acquired* knowledge. Other things were directly revealed to His human mind by the divine intellect; these are called *infused* knowledge.

Jesus did *not* share sin with human beings. As a Divine Person, He could not sin because it would mean negating Himself (sin is going against the will of God). Being human doesn't mean being capable of sinning, nor does it mean that you've sinned somewhere along the line. Being human means having a free will and rational intellect joined to a physical body. Humans can choose to do good or choose to do evil.

Catholics believe that human beings don't determine what's good or evil because that's intrinsic to the thing itself. Whether something is good or evil is independent of personal opinion. Murder is evil in and of itself. Someone may personally think an action is okay, but if it's intrinsically evil, that person is only fooling himself and will eventually regret it. Jesus in His humanity always chose to do good, but that didn't make Him any less human. Even though He never got drunk, swore, or told a dirty joke, He was still human.

It's important to keep in mind that Catholicism doesn't depend *exclusively* on the Bible for what's known about Jesus. *Sacred Tradition* (see Book I, Chapter 2) fills in some of the gaps when the Bible is silent or ambiguous on certain points, such as whether Jesus ever married or had any siblings.

Did Jesus have a wife and kids?

The last verse of the Gospel According to John (21:25) says, "There are also many other things which Jesus did; were every one of them to be written, I suppose that the world itself could not contain the books that would be written." The Bible is silent in some areas. Was Jesus ever married? Did He have a wife and children? The Bible doesn't say either way. You could presume He was unmarried, because a wife is never mentioned. (The Bible does mention Peter's *mother-in-law* being cured, but the Bible never classifies the other disciples and apostles as married or single.)

No Christian denomination or religion has ever believed that Jesus was married, even though the Bible never categorically states that He remained unmarried. The reason? Tradition. Christianity has maintained the tradition that Jesus was celibate and never married, even though the Bible at best implies it by never mentioning a wife or children.

Despite what you may read in some modern novels, Jesus and Mary Magdalene were never a couple, legally or romantically. Counterfeit Gospels were written a few hundred years after the legitimate ones that alleged such a relationship with the intent to undermine the Church. No one ever took them seriously, and no accredited scholar today gives them any credibility.

Medieval literature is filled with stories on the *Holy Grail,* which was the alleged chalice Jesus used at the Last Supper. Folklore and legend imply that the Knights Templar may have found it while on Crusade, but there has never been any evidence whatsoever to establish or even suggest that the Grail symbolizes a bloodline running through European monarchies going back to the supposed offspring of Christ and Mary Magdalene. These stories are all fiction; there is no historical or biblical evidence to suggest otherwise.

Whenever the Bible is silent or ambiguous, Sacred Tradition fills in the gaps. So to Catholics, a written record in the Bible is that He was a man, His name was Jesus, and His mother was Mary, and a revealed truth of Sacred Tradition is that He never married.

Did Jesus have any brothers or sisters?

Some Christians believe Mary had other children after she had Jesus, but the Catholic Church officially teaches that Mary always remained a virgin — before, during, and after the birth of Jesus. She had one son, and that son was Jesus.

Another belief among some Christians is that Joseph had children from a prior marriage, and after he became a widower and married the mother of Jesus, those children became stepbrothers and stepsisters of Jesus. Those who believe that Jesus had siblings invoke Mark 6:3: "Is not this the carpenter, the son of Mary and brother of James and Joses and Judas and Simon and are not his sisters here with us?" And Matthew 12:46 says, "His mother and his brothers stood outside."

So who were these brothers and sisters mentioned in the Gospel, if they weren't actual siblings of Jesus? The Catholic Church reminds its members that the original four Gospels were written in the Greek language, not English. The Greek word used in all three occasions is *adelphoi* (plural of *adelphos*), which can be translated as *brothers*. But that same Greek word can also mean *cousins* or *relatives,* as in an uncle or a nephew.

An example is shown in the Old Testament. Genesis 11:27 says that Abram and Haran were brothers, sons of Terah. Lot was the son of Haran and thus the nephew of Abram, who was later called Abraham by God. Ironically, Genesis 14:14 and 14:16 in the King James Version of the Bible refer to Lot as the *brother* of Abraham. The Greek word used in the Septuagint version of the Old Testament, the version used at the time of Jesus, is again *adelphos.* Obviously, a word that denoted a nephew-uncle relationship was unavailable in ancient Hebrew or Greek. So an alternative use of *brother* (*adelphos* in Greek) is used in those passages, because Lot was actually Abraham's nephew.

The Catholic Church reasons that if the Bible uses *brother* to refer to a nephew in one instance, then why not another? Why can't the *adelphoi* (brothers) of Jesus be his relatives — cousins or other family members? Why must that word be used in a restrictive way in the Gospel when it's used broadly in the Old Testament?

The Church uses other reasoning as well. If these *brothers* were siblings, where were they during the Crucifixion and death of their brother? Mary and a few other women were there, but the only man mentioned in the Gospel at the event was the Apostle John, and he was in no way related to Jesus, by blood or marriage. And before Jesus died on the cross, He told John, "Behold your mother" (John 19:27). Why entrust His mother to John if other adult children could've taken care of her? Only if Mary were alone would Jesus worry about her enough to say what He did to John.

And the Church asks this: If Jesus had blood brothers, or even half-brothers or stepbrothers, why didn't they assume roles of leadership after His death? Why allow Peter and the other apostles to run the Church and make decisions if immediate family members were around? Yet if the only living relatives were distant cousins, nieces, nephews, and such, it all makes sense.

The debate will continue for centuries to come. The bottom line is the authoritative decision of the Church. Catholicism doesn't place the Church above Scripture but sees her as the one and only authentic guardian and interpreter of the written word and the unwritten or spoken word, or Sacred Tradition.

The divine nature of Jesus

Catholics believe that Jesus performed miracles, such as walking on water; expelling demons; rising from the dead himself and raising the dead, such as Lazarus in Chapter 11 of the Gospel According to St. John; and saving all humankind, becoming the Redeemer, Savior, and Messiah. He founded the Catholic Church and instituted, explicitly or implicitly, all seven sacraments. (The *seven sacraments* are Catholic rituals marking seven stages of spiritual development. See Book II, Chapter 2 for more on the seven sacraments.)

Jesus is the second person of the Holy Trinity — God the Son. And God the Son (Jesus) is as much God as God the Father and God the Holy Spirit.

Although Christians, Jews, and Muslims all believe in one God, Christians believe in a *Triune God,* one God in three persons — God the Father, God the Son, and God the Holy Spirit — also known as the *Holy Trinity.* The mystery of the Holy Trinity is how you can have three divine persons but not three gods. Catholics don't perceive the Holy Trinity as three gods but as three distinct — but not separate — persons in one God.

The divine mind of Jesus was infinite, because He had the mind of God; the human mind of Jesus was, like the human mind, limited. The human mind could only know so much and only what God the Father wanted it to know. When asked about the time and date of the end of the world, Jesus's apparent ignorance in Mark 13:32 "of that day or that hour, no one knows, not even the angels in heaven, nor the Son, but only the Father," is proof that the human intellect of Christ was not privy to all that the divine intellect of Christ knew.

To the Catholic Church, overemphasizing Jesus's humanity to the exclusion of His divinity is as bad as ignoring or downplaying His humanity to exalt His divinity. To understand the Catholic Church's stance on Jesus's divinity even better, check out the doctrine of the Hypostatic Union in the section "Monophystism."

The Savior of our sins; the Redeemer of the world

The study of Christ evokes two key questions. The first is "Who is Jesus Christ?" So far in this chapter, we've been addressing this question like this: Jesus is the son of God, and He is both God and man, divine and human. The second question is "Why did Jesus become man?" This question is answered by the Cross.

Catholics firmly believe that Jesus is the Savior of the world and the Redeemer of the human race. Jesus died for our sins and ransomed us from sin and death. As you find in Book I, Chapter 3, the first (original) sin of Adam and Eve incurred guilt and punishment on all human beings. Their act of disobedience resulted in a serious wound to human nature. Because of original sin, humans lost God's sanctifying grace; were expelled from paradise; and faced lives full of sickness and death, toil and labor. No one could enter heaven until a Savior was born.

Messiah is the Hebrew word for Savior, and in Greek the word is *Christos.* Both words also mean "Anointed One." The Old Testament prophesied that a Savior would be sent to save the human race from sin and death, and Christians believe that God sent His son, Jesus, to be that Savior.

As the Son of God, Jesus offered his life on the Cross as a supreme sacrifice to atone for sin. His blood redeemed us and freed us from the grip death had on us. Before Christ, no one could go to heaven after death. But because Jesus opened the gates by dying for our sins, everyone has the chance to enter Paradise forever. Appropriately, the word *redeemer* means someone who rescues others from danger.

The Catholic Church graphically reminds her members of the human nature of Jesus by conspicuously placing a crucifix in every church. A *crucifix* is a cross with the crucified figure of Jesus attached to it. It's a reminder to Catholics that Jesus didn't pretend to be human. The nails in His hands and feet, the crown of thorns on His head, and the wound in His side where a soldier thrust a lance into His heart all poignantly remind the faithful that Jesus's suffering, which is known as his *Passion,* was real. He felt real pain, and He really died. He was really human. If He had been only a god pretending to be human, His pain and death would have been faked.

If you look closely at a crucifix, you may see the letters INRI on it. Those letters are an abbreviation for the Latin words *Iesus Nazarenus Rex Iudaeorum,* which mean "Jesus of Nazareth, King of the Jews." These words were written on the cross above Jesus's head by order of Pontius Pilate, the Roman governor who condemned Jesus to death.

In addition to reminding believers of Jesus's human nature and His painful sacrifice, the crucifix reminds them that Jesus commanded us to take up our cross daily and follow Him. (For this reason, many Catholics have a crucifix at home.) The concept of *dying to self* is something spiritual writers speak of often. The process of dying to self involves enduring unavoidable suffering with dignity and faith. Seeing Jesus depicted on His cross is meant to encourage the devout to do likewise and offer up their sufferings as did Jesus.

The obedient Son of God

Catholicism regards Jesus as the eternal Son of the Father and teaches that the relationship between Father and Son is one of profound love. To understand this dynamic even better, see the nearby sidebar "Deep thoughts about Father and Son."

The belief that the relationship between Father and Son is so close, intense, and perfect led St. Thomas Aquinas to say that the third person of the Holy Trinity — the Holy Spirit — is the living, personified fruit of that mutual love.

Obedience is a sign of love and respect, and Catholics believe that Jesus obeyed the will of the Father. To Catholics, "Thy will be done" is more than just a phrase of the Our Father. It's the motto of Jesus Christ, Son of God.

And Catholic belief maintains that God the Father's will was for Jesus to

✔ Reveal God as a community of three persons (Father, Son, and Holy Spirit) united in divine love

✔ Show God's love for all humankind

✔ Be humankind's Redeemer and Savior

The Gospel Truth: Examining Four Written Records of Jesus

The New Testament contains four *Gospels,* books of the Bible that tell the life and words of Jesus. The four evangelists, Matthew, Mark, Luke, and John, each wrote one of the four Gospels, considered by Christians to be the most important of all biblical text, because these four books contain the words and deeds of Jesus when He walked this earth.

Even though a different man wrote each of the four Gospels, the same Holy Spirit inspired each man. *Inspiration* is a special gift of the Holy Spirit given to the *sacred authors* (those who wrote the Bible) so that only the words that God wanted written down *were* written down.

Catholic beliefs about the Gospel

The Catholic Church emphasizes that it's imperative to consider the four Gospels as actually forming one whole unit. The four Gospels aren't four *separate* Gospels but four *versions* of one Gospel. That's why each one is called *The Gospel According to Matthew* or *The Gospel According to Mark,* for example, and not *Matthew's Gospel* or *Mark's Gospel.* No one single account gives the entire picture, but like facets on a diamond, all sides form to make one beautiful reality. The faithful need all four versions to appreciate the full depth and impact of Jesus.

Catholicism cherishes each different perspective but stresses that all four together, in conjunction with the other inspired writings of the New and Old Testaments, give a better portrait of Jesus.

Both the Holy Spirit and the author, inspired by the Holy Spirit, intended to use or not use the same words and to present or not present the same ideas and images based on the particular author's distinct audience. For more on how the Gospels are both inspired and audience-savvy, see the section "Comparing Gospels."

Figure 4-1 shows how Matthew, Mark, Luke, and John are often depicted in art from Revelation (Apocalypse) 4:7. According to St. Ambrose (339–397), a Father of the Church (learned scholar), a man with wings symbolizes Matthew because he begins his Gospel account with the human origins and birth of Christ. Mark starts his account with the regal power of Christ, the reign of God, and is therefore symbolized by a lion with wings, which was held in high esteem by the Romans. Luke begins his account with the father of John the Baptist, Zachary, the priest, and is symbolized by an ox with wings because the priests of the temple often sacrificed oxen on the altar. John is shown as an eagle because he soars to heaven in his introduction to the Gospel with the preexistence of Christ as the Word (*logos* in Greek).

How the Gospels came to be

Were Matthew, Mark, Luke, and John standing on the sidelines taking notes as Jesus preached or performed miracles? No. In fact, only two of the four, Matthew and John, were actual apostles and eyewitnesses, so you can't think of Matthew, Mark, Luke, and John as, say, reporters covering a story for the media.

Matthew, The Man   Mark, The Lion

Luke, The Ox   John, The Eagle

© John Wiley & Sons, Inc.

Figure 4-1: The writers of the four Gospels are often depicted like this from Revelation (Apocalypse) 4:7.

Before the Gospels were written, the words and deeds of Jesus were told by word of mouth. In other words, the Gospels were preached before they were written. The spoken word preceded the written word. And after it was written, because the papyrus on which the scrolls were written was so fragile, expensive, and rare, most people didn't read the Word but heard it as it was spoken in church during Mass. The Church calls it the three-level development of the Gospel: first, the actual sayings and teachings of Christ; second, the oral tradition where the apostles preached to the people what they saw and heard; and third, the writing by the sacred authors to ensure that the message wouldn't be altered.

The New Testament was written between A.D. 35 and 100. St. Irenaeus (c. 130-200) in A.D. 188 was the first person to mention the four Gospels. But it wasn't until the Council of Carthage in A.D. 397 that the final and official judgment of the Church came out and explicitly listed the 27 books in the New Testament, including the four Gospels. St. Jerome (c. 341-420) was the first one to combine both the Old and New Testaments into one volume and to translate all the books from Hebrew, Aramaic, and Greek into Latin, which was the common tongue of his time. This Latin version of the Bible is the *Vulgate.* It took him from A.D. 382 to 405 to finish this monumental task, but he was the first person to coordinate the complete and whole Christian Bible.

Comparing Gospels

The Catholic Church regards the entire Bible as the inspired and inerrant (error-free) Word of God, so the Gospels in particular are crucial because they accurately relate what Jesus said and did while on earth. As you discover in Book I, Chapter 2, the Catholic Church believes that the Bible is sacred literature, but as literature, some parts of it should be interpreted literally, and other parts are intended to be read figuratively. The Gospels are among the books that are primarily interpreted literally insofar as what Jesus said and did.

Matthew and Luke

Matthew opens his Gospel with a long genealogy of Jesus, beginning with Abraham and tracing it all the way down to Joseph, the husband of Mary, "of whom Jesus was born, who is called the Messiah."

Matthew was addressing potential converts from Judaism. A Jewish audience was probably interested in hearing this family tree because the Hebrew people are often called the Children of Abraham. That's why Matthew began with Abraham and connected him to Jesus to open his Gospel.

Luke offers a similar genealogy to Matthew's, but he works backward from Jesus to Adam, 20 generations before Abraham. Luke was a Gentile physician, and his audience was Gentile, not Jewish. Neither Matthew nor Luke used editorial fiction, but each carefully selected what to say to his respective audience through the inspiration of the Holy Spirit. A Gentile audience wasn't as concerned with a connection to Abraham as a Jewish audience. Gentiles were interested in a connection between Jesus and the first man, Adam, because Gentiles were big into Greek philosophy. Plato, Socrates, and Aristotle — just to mention a few famous Greek thinkers who lived before Christ — philosophized about the origins of humanity and, thus, making a link between Jesus and the first man would have greatly appealed to them. In the Sermon on the Mount, Matthew mentions that prior to giving the sermon, Jesus "went up on the mountain" (Matthew 5:1), but Luke describes Jesus giving a Sermon on the Plain, "a level place" (Luke 6:17). Both men quote the teachings from these sermons, called the *Beatitudes*. See the following version from Matthew 5:

> Seeing the crowds, he went up on the mountain, and when he sat down his disciples came to him. And he opened his mouth and taught them, saying:
>
> "Blessed are the poor in spirit, for theirs is the kingdom of heaven.
>
> "Blessed are those who mourn, for they shall be comforted.
>
> "Blessed are the meek, for they shall inherit the earth.
>
> "Blessed are those who hunger and thirst for righteousness, for they shall be satisfied.
>
> "Blessed are the merciful, for they shall obtain mercy.
>
> "Blessed are the pure in heart, for they shall see God.
>
> "Blessed are the peacemakers, for they shall be called sons of God.

"Blessed are those who are persecuted for righteousness' sake, for theirs is the kingdom of heaven.

"Blessed are you when men revile you and persecute you and utter all kinds of evil against you falsely on my account. Rejoice and be glad, for your reward is great in heaven, for so men persecuted the prophets who were before you."

Now contrast the Sermon on the Mount in the Gospel of Matthew with Luke 6:17–26, which follows:

And he came down with them and stood on a level place, with a great crowd of his disciples and a great multitude of people from all Judea and Jerusalem and the seacoast of Tyre and Sidon, who came to hear him and to be healed of their diseases; and those who were troubled with unclean spirits were cured. And all the crowd sought to touch him, for power came forth from him and healed them all. And he lifted up his eyes on his disciples, and said:

"Blessed are you poor, for yours is the kingdom of God.

"Blessed are you that hunger now, for you shall be satisfied.

"Blessed are you that weep now, for you shall laugh.

"Blessed are you when men hate you, and when they exclude you and revile you, and cast out your name as evil, on account of the Son of man! Rejoice in that day, and leap for joy, for behold, your reward is great in heaven; for so their fathers did to the prophets.

"But woe to you that are rich, for you have received your consolation.

"Woe to you that are well fed now, for you shall hunger.

"Woe to you that laugh now, for you shall mourn and weep.

"Woe to you when all men speak well of you, for so their fathers did to the false prophets."

So why the difference in location for these sermons — mount and plain?

Any good preacher knows that when you have a good sermon, you can use it more than once, especially if you're preaching in another place to a different crowd. It's not unreasonable to presume that Jesus preached His Beatitudes more than once, because He moved around quite a bit and, aside from the apostles, no one in the crowd would have heard the message before.

Matthew mentions the occasion of the Sermon on the Mount because his Jewish audience would have been keen on such a detail. The reason? Moses was given the Law, the Ten Commandments, on Mount Sinai. So Jesus was giving the law of blessedness, also known as the Beatitudes, also from a mount. Matthew also makes sure to quote Jesus, saying that He had "come not to abolish them [the law and the prophets], but to fulfill them," (Matthew 5:17) also appealing to a Jewish listener. Moses gave the Ten Commandments that came from God to the Hebrew people, and now Jesus was going to fulfill that Law.

Luke, on the other hand, mentions the time that the sermon was given on a plain. Why mention the obscure detail of a level ground? Luke was writing for a Gentile audience. Unlike the Jewish audience of Matthew, which was used to the Law being given from God to Moses on Mount Sinai, the Gentiles were accustomed to giving and listening to philosophical debates in the Greek tradition. Philosophers such as Plato, Socrates, and Aristotle debated one another on level ground, standing shoulder-to-shoulder, eye-to-eye, instead of lecturing from an elevated podium, in order to give a sense of fairness and equality to the discussion. Because a Gentile audience would have been more interested in a speech given by Jesus in similar fashion, Luke retold such an occurrence.

A slight difference can be detected in some of the wording of Luke's account versus that of Matthew, as well as an addition of "woe to you" given by Jesus to correspond with each "blessed are you," which isn't found in Matthew. Again, a preacher often adapts an older sermon by adding to, subtracting from, or modifying his original work, depending on his second audience. The Catholic Church maintains that the discrepancy comes from a change Jesus made because neither sacred author would feel free to alter anything Jesus said or did on his own human authority.

Mark

Mark is the shortest of the four Gospels, due to the fact that his audience was mainly Roman. When you belong to an imperial police state, you're not as concerned about making intricate connections to a Hebrew past, and you're not interested in lengthy philosophical dialogues. You want action. That's why the Gospel According to Mark has fewer sermons and more movement. It's fast-paced, nonstop, continuous narrative, like an excited person telling the events "a mile a minute." Romans would have been far more attentive to the Gospel According to Mark than to the Gospels of Matthew, Luke, or John.

Mark explicitly describes the Roman Centurion, a military commander of a hundred soldiers, at the Crucifixion as making the proclamation, "Truly, this man was the Son of God" (Mark 15:39). His Roman audience would've certainly perked up when that was said because it was an act of faith from one of their own kind.

Like Luke, Mark wasn't one of the original 12 apostles. Matthew and John were apostles, but Luke and Mark were 2 of the 72 disciples. The *apostles* were there in person to witness all that Jesus said and did. The *disciples* often had to resort to secondhand information, told to them by other sources. Luke most likely received much of his information from Mary, the mother of Jesus, and Mark undoubtedly used his friend Peter, the chief apostle, as his source.

John

John was the last one to write a Gospel, and his is the most theological of the four. The other three are so similar in content, style, and sequence that they're often called the *Synoptic Gospels,* from the Greek word *sunoptikos,* meaning *summary* or *general view.*

John, who wrote his Gospel much later than the others, was writing for a Christian audience. He presumed that people had already heard the basic facts, and he provided advanced information to complement the Jesus 101 material covered in Matthew, Mark, and Luke. In other words, The Gospel According to John is like college calculus, whereas the Synoptic Gospels are like advanced high-school algebra.

John sets the tone by opening his Gospel with a philosophical concept of preexistence: Before Jesus became man by being conceived and born of the Virgin Mary, He existed from all eternity in His divinity because He's the second person of the Holy Trinity. Take a look at the first line from the Gospel According to John: "In the beginning was the Word, and the Word was with God and the Word was God."

This is a very philosophical and theological concept. John wanted his audience to see Jesus as being the living Word of God: As he says, "The Word became flesh and dwelt among us" (John 1:14). He was saying that Jesus was the incarnate Word — the Word taking on flesh. The first book of the Bible, Genesis, starts with the same phrase John uses in the opening of his Gospel: "In the beginning." According to Genesis 1:3, God said, "Let there be light; and there was light." In other words, by merely speaking the word, God *created.* John built on that in his Gospel, saying that Jesus *was* the Word. The Word of God wasn't a thing but a person. The Word was creative and powerful. Just as God said the word and light were created, Jesus spoke the word and the blind received their sight, the lame walked, and the dead came back to life.

Dealing with Heresy and Some Other $10 Words

Christians were violently and lethally persecuted for the first 300 years after the death of Jesus — from the time of Emperor Nero and the burning of Rome, which he blamed on the Christians. So for the first 300 years, Christianity remained underground. Through word of mouth, Christians learned about Jesus of Nazareth and his preaching, suffering, death, Resurrection, and Ascension.

It wasn't until A.D. 313, when Roman Emperor Constantine legalized Christianity in his Edict of Milan, that Christians were even allowed to publicly admit their religious affiliation. But once Christianity became legal, it soon became predominant and even became the state religion.

Leaving the *catacombs* (underground cemeteries sometimes used by Christians to hide from the Romans and as places of worship during times of persecution) and entering the public arena, Christians began devoting themselves to theological questions that the Bible didn't specifically address. For example, Scripture teaches that Jesus was God and man, human and divine. Yet *how* was He both? How were the human and divine natures of Jesus connected? So the second 300 years after Jesus's death, the fourth to seventh centuries, became a Pandora's box of theological debate.

To the Catholic Church, *heresy* is the denial of a revealed truth or the distortion of one so that others are deceived into believing a theological error. After Christianity was legalized, the *Christological heresies* that referred to the nature of Christ became rampant. Debates often degenerated into violent arguments, and the civil authorities, such as the Roman Emperor, often intervened, urging or even demanding that the religious leaders, such as the pope, patriarchs, and bishops, cease the unrest by settling the issues once and for all. This section explains some of the heresies, or false rumors, that plagued the Church during early Christianity.

Gnosticism and Docetism

Gnosticism comes from the Greek work *gnosis,* for *knowledge.* From the first century B.C. to the fifth century A.D., Gnostics believed in secret knowledge, whereas the Judeo-Christians were free and public about disclosing the truth divinely revealed by God. Gnostics believed that the material world was evil and the only way to salvation was through discovering the "secrets" of the universe. This belief flew in the face of Judaism and Christianity, both of which believed that God created the world (Genesis) and that it was good, not evil. Keeping revelation secret wasn't meant to be; rather, it should be shared openly with others.

Docetism, a spin-off from Gnosticism, comes from the Greek word *dokesis,* meaning *appearance.* In the first and second centuries A.D., Docetists asserted that Jesus Christ only appeared to be human. They considered the material world, including the human body, so evil and corrupt that God, who is all good, couldn't have assumed a real human body and human nature. He must have pretended.

The Gnostic antagonism between the spiritual and the material worlds led Docetists to deny that Jesus was true man. They had no problem with His divinity, only with believing in His real humanity. So if that part was an illusion, then the horrible and immense suffering and death of Jesus on the cross meant nothing. If His human nature was a parlor trick, then His Passion also was an illusion.

The core of Christianity, and of Catholic Christianity, is that Jesus died for the sins of all humankind. Only a real human nature can feel pain and actually die. Docetism and Gnosticism were considered hostile to *authentic Christianity,* or, more accurately, *orthodox Christianity.* (The word *orthodox* with a small letter *o* means correct or right believer. However, if you see the capital letter *O,* then *Orthodox* refers to the eastern Orthodox Churches, such as the Greek, Russian, and Serbian Orthodox Churches.)

Even today, remnants of neo-Gnosticism are in some modern ideologies and theories of religion. New Age spirituality and Dianetics, which is the Church of Scientology, propose to reveal secrets and unlock secret powers of human nature. Docetism seems to have pretty much died out, however.

Arianism

Arianism was the most dangerous and prolific of the heresies in the early Church. (By the way, this Arianism isn't about modern-day skinheads with swastikas and anti-Semitic prejudices.) *Arianism* comes from a cleric named Arius in the fourth century (A.D. 250–336), who denied the divinity of Jesus. Whereas Docetism denied his humanity, Arianism denied that Jesus had a truly divine nature equal to God the Father.

Arius proposed that Jesus was created and wasn't of the same substance as God — He was considered higher than any man or angel because He possessed a similar substance, or essence, but He was never equal to God. His Son-ship was one of adoption. In Arianism, Jesus *became* the Son, whereas in orthodox Christianity, He was, is, and will always be the Son, with no beginning and no end. Arianism caught on like wildfire because it appealed to people's knowledge that only one God existed. The argument was that if Jesus was also God, two gods existed instead of only one.

Emperor Constantine, living in the Eastern Empire, was afraid that the religious discord would endanger the security of the realm. He saw how animate and aggressive the argument became and ordered that a council of all the bishops, the patriarchs, and the pope's representatives convene to settle the issue once and for all. The imperial city of Nicea was chosen to guarantee safety. In Nicea, the world's bishops decided to compose a creed that every believer was to learn and profess as being the substance of Christian faith. That same creed is now recited every Sunday and Holy Day at Catholic Masses all over the world. It's known as the Nicene Creed, because it came from the Ecumenical Council of Nicea in A.D. 325.

The punch line that ended the Arianism controversy was the phrase "one in being with the Father" in the Nicene Creed (the phrase that has recently been replaced by "consubstantial with the Father"). The more accurate English translation of the Greek and Latin, however, is *consubstantial* or *of the same substance as the Father.* This line boldly defied the Arian proposition that Jesus was only similar but not equal in substance to the Father in terms of His divinity.

Nestorianism

Another heresy was Nestorianism, named after its founder, Nestorius (c. 386–451). This doctrine maintained that Christ had two *hypostases* (persons) — one divine and one human. Nestorius condemned the use of the word *Theotokos,* which was Greek for *bearer* or *mother of God.* If Jesus had two persons, the most that could be said of Mary was that she gave birth to the human person of Jesus and not to the divine. Nestorius preferred the use of the word *Christotokos* or Christ-bearer to *Theotokos.*

Another Ecumenical Council was convened, this time in the town of Ephesus in A.D. 431, where the participants ironed out the doctrine that Jesus had one person, not two, but that two natures were present — one human and one divine. Because Christ was only one person, Mary could rightly be called the Mother of God because she gave birth to only one person.

In other words, Jesus didn't come in parts on Christmas Day for Mary and Joseph to put together. He was born whole and intact, one person, two natures. The Church says that because Mary gave birth to Jesus, the Church could use the title Mother of God *(Theotokos),* realizing that she didn't give Jesus His divinity. (This concept is similar to the belief that your mother gave you a human body, but only God created your immortal soul. Still, you call her *mother.*)

Monophysitism

The last significant heresy about Jesus was known as *Monophysitism.* This idea centered on a notion that the human nature of Jesus was absorbed into the divine nature. Say, for example, that a drop of oil represents the humanity of Jesus and the ocean represents the divinity of Jesus. If you put the drop of oil into the vast waters of the ocean, the drop of oil, representing His humanity, would literally be overwhelmed and absorbed by the enormous waters of the ocean — His divinity.

The Ecumenical Council of Chalcedon in A.D. 451 condemned Monophyistism. A simple teaching was formulated that one divine person with two distinct, full, and true natures, one human and one divine, existed in Jesus. These two natures were *hypostatically* (from the Greek *hypostasis,* for *person*) united into one divine person. Thus the *Hypostatic Union,* the name of the doctrine, explained these things about Jesus:

- ✔ **In His human nature,** Jesus had a human mind just like you. It had to learn like yours. Therefore, the baby Jesus in the stable at Bethlehem didn't speak to the shepherds on Christmas Eve. He had to be taught how to speak, walk, and so on. Likewise, His human will, like yours, was free, so He had to freely choose to embrace the will of God.

  In other words, in His humanity, Jesus knew what He learned. And He had to freely choose to conform His human will to the divine will. (*Sin* is when your will is opposed to the will of God.) Any human knowledge not gained by regular learning was infused into His human intellect by His divine intellect. Jesus knew that fire is hot just as you've learned this fact. He also knew what only God could know, because He was a divine person with a human and a divine nature. The human mind of Christ is limited, but the divine is infinite. His divinity revealed some divine truths to His human intellect, so He would know who He is, who His Father is, and why He came to earth.

- ✔ **The divine nature** of Jesus had the same (not similar) divine intellect and will as that of God the Father and God the Holy Spirit. As God, He knew and willed the same things that the other two persons of the Trinity knew and willed. Thus, in His divinity, Jesus knew everything, and what He willed, happened.

- ✔ **As both God and man,** Jesus could bridge the gap between humanity and divinity. He could actually save humankind by becoming one of us, and yet, because He never lost His divinity, His death had eternal and infinite merit and value. If He were only a man, His death would have no supernatural effect. His death, because it was united to His divine personhood, actually atoned for sin and caused redemption to take place.

It's a mouthful to be sure, but the bottom line in Catholic theology is that the faithful fully and solemnly believe that Jesus was one divine person with a fully human nature and a fully divine nature. Each nature had its own intellect and will. So the divine nature of Jesus had a divine intellect and will, and the human nature of Jesus had a human intellect and will.

Some modern scholars have proposed that Jesus didn't know that He was divine, as if His human nature were ignorant of His divinity. But the Catholic Church points to Luke 2:42–50, which says that when Jesus's parents found the 12-year-old Jesus preaching in the Temple, the young Jesus responded that He was in His Father's house and that He was about to do the work of the Father. So even the young Jesus knew that He was divine. To the Church, "I and the Father are one" (John 10:30) and "before Abraham was, I am" (John 8:58) dispel any identity crisis in Jesus.

Chapter 5

Who's Who in Catholic Practice

*E*very structured environment has a chain of command — from governments to corporations to schools to sports programs. The Catholic Church is no exception. This chapter explains who's who in the Catholic Church and gives you a glimpse into the authority and duties of its various members. Check out Table 5-1 for a quick look at who's in charge, from highest to lowest (top to bottom) in terms of rank.

Table 5-1	The Catholic Church Chain of Command
Clergy Members' Titles	*What They Do*
The pope	He's the bishop of Rome and the head of the whole Church.
Cardinals	They elect the pope and work in different departments as his right-hand men.
Bishops and archbishops	They take charge of the churches in their respective geographical areas, called dioceses.
Vicars general	They are priests who help the bishop govern the local churches.
Parish priests, or pastors	They take care of all the big day-to-day duties in their churches, from leading Mass to hearing confessions.
Monks and nuns	They choose to live together, work together, and spend many hours devoted in prayer.

Getting to Know the Pope

Best known throughout the world and among more than 1 billion Catholics as *the pope,* the bishop of Rome is the supreme and visible head of the Catholic Church. The word *pope* is actually an English translation of the Italian *il Papa,* meaning *father,* which leads you to another title for the pope — *Holy Father.* Just as a Catholic priest is called "Father" in a spiritual sense, the pope is called "Holy Father" by Catholics all over the world.

He has a slew of other titles, too: Successor of St. Peter, Vicar of Christ, Primate of Italy, Supreme Pontiff, Roman Pontiff, Sovereign of the Vatican City State, and Head of the College of Bishops. The most common and best-known titles, however, are pope, Holy Father, and Roman Pontiff.

Think you're under pressure at work? The pope has *two* big jobs: He's the bishop of Rome (see the section "Bishops and archbishops" for more about bishops) *and* the head of the entire Catholic Church.

How the pope gets his job

The *College of Cardinals* elects the pope. Nope, that's not a university where priests and bishops learn how to become cardinals. Unlike Notre Dame and The Catholic University of America, the *College of Cardinals* merely refers to all the cardinals around the world, just as the *College of Bishops* is a way of describing all the world's Catholic bishops.

The pope handpicks bishops to become *cardinals,* and their primary function in life is to elect a new pope when the old pope dies or resigns. Because most modern popes live at least ten years in office (except Pope John Paul I, who lived only one month), cardinals do have other work to do instead of just waiting around for the boss to pass on. (For details about cardinals and their jobs, see the section "Cardinals," later in this chapter.) Cardinals under the age of 80 are eligible to vote for the next pope.

The limit of electors is set at 120, but at one point Pope John Paul II (who was pope from 1978 to 2005) had appointed so many that the number of eligible voters reached 137. With retirements and deaths, only 117 eligible voting cardinals remained when Pope John Paul II died in 2005. His successor, Pope Benedict XVI, created 90 new cardinals in 5 consistories. At the time of this writing, Pope Francis has created 39 cardinals in 2 consistories, yet with retirements and deaths there are currently 122 electors; 32 have been created by Pope John Paul II; 59 by Pope Benedict XVI; and 31 by Pope Francis. (You'll find out about the consistories in the upcoming "Cardinals" section.)

The electors can vote for any other cardinal or any Catholic bishop, priest, deacon, or layman, anywhere in the world and of any liturgical rite, such as Latin, Byzantine, and so on. Normally, the cardinals select another cardinal, both because they know each other better and because the number of cardinals to choose from is small compared to the 5,000 bishops around the world and more than 410,000 priests. Although extremely rare, if a layman is elected pope (as in the case of Benedict IX), he first has to be ordained a deacon, then a priest, and then a bishop before he can function as pope, because the authority resides in his office as bishop of Rome. If a priest is chosen, he needs to be ordained a bishop prior to being installed as pope.

Are there pope primaries?

The government of the Catholic Church, called the *hierarchy,* is more like a monarchy than a democracy. Catholicism is hierarchical in that one person, the pope, is supreme head over the universal Church. Yet bishops govern the local churches in a geographical district called the *diocese,* and pastors (or priests) represent the bishop in each local parish. Individual Catholics don't vote for the next pope or for their bishop or pastor. The Catholic hierarchy operates like a military chain of command as opposed to an elected, representative government. So nope — no local primaries, no election campaigns, no debates, no political ads, and no popular vote.

Other religions and Christian churches allow for lay participation in positions of authority from a little to a lot, but Catholicism has been predominantly monarchical since the appointment of St. Peter. (See Book IV, Chapter 2 for more on St. Peter, the first pope.) Laypersons are encouraged to participate in other ways. While they aren't allowed to have jurisdictional power, laity serve as consulters and advisors to pastors and bishops. Parish councils and finance committees are composed of lay parishioners who advise the pastor before he makes important decisions. Laity also even serve in the Vatican to advise, counsel, and represent the Holy See to organizations like the United Nations.

You may have heard the saying: He who enters the conclave a pope leaves a cardinal. The meaning? When a pope becomes sick or elderly or dies, rumors run rampant as to who will take the Chair of St. Peter. Often, the press names certain cardinals as the most likely candidates; they're called *papabile* (meaning *pope-able*) in Italian. But the *papabile* are usually the ones that the other cardinals *never* elect. So if a man enters the *conclave* — the private meeting of all the cardinals for the specific purpose of electing the pope — as a favorite (or worse yet, if he comes off as wanting the job), chances are he will leave a cardinal because his fellow cardinals will choose someone more humble.

Dimpled, pimpled, or hanging chads?

No sooner than 15 days and no later than 20 days after the death or resignation of the pope, all the cardinals are summoned to Rome for the secret conclave. *Conclave* comes from the Latin *cum clave,* meaning *with key,* because the cardinals are literally locked into the Sistine Chapel, the pope's private chapel at the Vatican, until they elect a new pope.

After the cardinals from around the world assemble inside the conclave, they begin discussions and deliberations. Almost like a sequestered jury, the cardinals are permitted no contact with the outside world during the conclave. Under pain of excommunication, no cardinal is ever allowed to discuss what transpires at these elections — to keep the element of politics and outside influence to a bare minimum.

Historically, the election of a new pope could take place in one of three different forms:

- ✔ **Acclamation:** A name is presented, and everyone unanimously consents without the need of a secret ballot.

- ✔ **Compromise:** Each cardinal casts a secret ballot. If no one achieves a two-thirds majority after several rounds of voting, then the entire College of Cardinals may choose one or several electors to select a candidate, and the entire body is bound to accept that choice. A unanimous vote to employ compromise is necessary for it to be valid.

- ✔ **Scrutiny:** Each cardinal proposes a candidate and gives reasons for his qualifications before the individual cardinals cast their secret ballot. A two-thirds majority decision is needed to elect a new pope.

    This is the only valid method currently permitted in papal conclaves.

Want a peek at what's going on behind those closed doors? When voting for a new pope, each cardinal writes a name on a piece of paper, which is placed on a gold *paten* (plate). The paten is then turned upside down, so the ballot can fall into a *chalice* (cup) underneath. This symbolism is deep, because the paten and chalice are primarily used at the Catholic Mass to hold the wafer of bread and cup of wine that, when consecrated, become the body and blood of Christ during the Eucharistic Prayer.

If no one receives two-thirds of the votes or if the nominee declines the nomination, then wet straw is mixed with the paper ballots and burned in the chimney. The wet straw makes black smoke, which alerts the crowds gathered outside that a two-thirds majority decision hasn't yet been made. One vote occurs in the morning and one in the evening. The election continues twice a day, every day. In 1996, Pope John Paul II introduced a variation in which if no one was elected by a two-thirds majority after 21 votes, then on the 22nd ballot, the man who received a simple majority (50 percent plus one) was elected pope. Pope Benedict XVI subsequently rescinded that change in 2007 and returned the requirement of two-thirds no matter how long the conclave takes. If someone receives two-thirds of the votes and he accepts, the ballots are burned without the straw, which blows white smoke to alert the crowds.

After a cardinal has received a two-thirds majority vote, he's asked whether he accepts the nomination. If he accepts, he's then asked, "By what name are you to be addressed?"

Pope John II (A.D. 533) was the first to change his name when he was elected pope because he was born with the name Mercury after the pagan god. So he chose the Christian name John instead. But it was not until Sergius IV (1009) that all subsequent popes continued the tradition of changing their name at the time of election. So, for example, Pope Pius XII (1939) was originally Eugenio Pacelli, John XXIII (1958) was Angelo Roncalli, Paul VI (1963) was Giovanni Montini, John Paul I (1978) was Albino Luciani, John Paul II (1978) was Karol Wojtyla, Benedict XVI (2005) was Josef Ratzinger, and Francis (2013) was Jorge Mario Bergoglio.

Is he really infallible?

Catholicism maintains that the pope is *infallible,* incapable of error, when he teaches a doctrine on faith or morals to the universal Church in his unique office as supreme head. When the pope asserts his official authority in matters of faith and morals to the whole church, the Holy Spirit guards him from error. Papal infallibility doesn't mean that the pope can't make *any* mistakes. He's not infallible in scientific, historical, political, philosophical, geographic, or any other matters — just faith and morals.

It boils down to trust. Catholics trust that the Holy Spirit protects *them* from being taught or forced to believe erroneous doctrines by preventing a pope from issuing them. Whether the Holy Spirit's intervention is as subtle as getting the pope to change his mind or as drastic as striking him dead, in any event, Catholics firmly believe that God loves them and loves the truth so much that he would intervene and prevent a pope from imposing a false teaching upon the whole Church. This belief doesn't mean that personally and individually the pope is free from all error. He could privately be wrong as long as he doesn't attempt to impose or teach that error to the universal Church, because at that point the Holy Spirit would somehow stop him from doing so.

So what does infallibility mean?

Infallibility is widely misunderstood. It's *not* the same as the Catholic beliefs of *inspiration* or *impeccability:*

- ✔ **Inspiration** is a special gift of the Holy Spirit, which He gave to the *sacred authors,* those who wrote the Sacred Scripture (the Bible), so that only the things God wanted written down *were* written down — no more, no less. So the pope isn't inspired, but Matthew, Mark, Luke, and John were when they wrote their Gospels.

- ✔ **Impeccability** is the absence and inability to commit sin. Only Jesus Christ, being the Son of God, and His Blessed Mother had impeccability — via a special grace from God. Popes aren't impeccable, so they're capable of sin — which, by the way, was visible in the case of the first pope, St. Peter, when he denied Christ three times just before the Crucifixion (Matthew 26:69–75).

Everything the sacred authors wrote in the Bible is inspired, but not everything every pope says or writes is infallible. *Infallibility* means that if the pope attempts to teach a false doctrine on faith or morals, the Holy Spirit prevents him (even by death) from imposing such an error on the faithful. So, for example, no pope can declare, "As of today, the number of commandments is nine instead of ten." Nor can he declare, "Jesus was not a man" or "Jesus was not the Son of God."

Infallibility also doesn't mean perfection. Infallible statements aren't perfect statements, so they can be improved so that subsequent popes can use better or more accurate language. Yet infallible statements can never be contradicted, rejected, or refuted.

So according to Catholicism, an immoral pope (you'll find several in Church history) can sin like any man and will answer to God for his evil deeds. However, as supreme head of the Church, the pope retains his infallibility on matters of faith and morals as long as he remains pope.

No pope in 2,000 years has formally and officially taught an error of faith or morals to the universal Church. Individually, some may have been poor or inadequate theologians or philosophers, and some may have had erroneous ideas about science. That has nothing to do with papal infallibility, however, because the main objective is to preserve the integrity of Catholic faith for all the members at all times and in all places.

The pope can exercise his papal infallibility in two ways. One is called the *Extraordinary Magisterium,* and the other is called *Ordinary Magisterium.* The word *magisterium* is from the Latin word *magister* meaning *teacher,* so the *Magisterium* is the teaching authority of the Church, which is manifested by the pope alone and or the pope along with the bishops all over the world.

The Extraordinary Magisterium

Extraordinary means just that, out of the ordinary. When an Ecumenical (General) Council is convened, presided over, and approved by the pope, and he issues definitive decrees, they're considered infallible because they come from the Extraordinary Magisterium. The Church has held an all-time total of only 21 councils. These are gatherings of the world's bishops and cardinals. Sometimes priests, deacons, and laity are invited to observe, but only bishops and the pope can discuss and vote. The culmination of these councils is a written letter that explains the faith, interprets Scripture, or settles disputed topics of faith and morals. They never contradict the Bible but apply biblical truths to contemporary concerns and problems, as well as giving more understanding to essential core beliefs. The names and years of the councils throughout Church history are as follows:

1. Nicea (325)
2. First Constantinople (381)
3. Ephesus (431)
4. Chalcedon (451)
5. Second Constantinople (553)
6. Third Constantinople (680–81)
7. Second Nicea (787)
8. Fourth Constantinople (869–70)
9. First Lateran (1123)
10. Second Lateran (1139)
11. Third Lateran (1179)
12. Fourth Lateran (1215)
13. First Lyons (1245)
14. Second Lyons (1274)
15. Vienne (1311–12)
16. Constance (1414–18)
17. Basel-Ferrara-Florence (1431–45)
18. Fifth Lateran (1512–17)
19. Trent (1545–63)
20. First Vatican (1869–70)
21. Second Vatican (1962–65)

The Ecumenical Councils have defined doctrines such as the divinity of Christ (Nicea); the title of Mary as the Mother of God (Ephesus); the two natures of Christ, human and divine, being united in the one divine person (Chalcedon); *transubstantiation* (see Book III, Chapter 1) to describe how the bread and wine are changed at Mass into the Body and Blood of Christ (Lateran IV); the seven sacraments, Sacred Scripture and Sacred Tradition (see Book I, Chapter 2), and other responses to the Reformation (Trent); and papal infallibility (Vatican I). These conciliar decrees and *ex cathedra* papal pronouncements form the Extraordinary Magisterium.

Ex cathedra (Latin for *from the chair*) pronouncements from the pope are considered infallible teachings. The only two *ex cathedra* pronouncements in 2,000 years have been the dogmas of the Immaculate Conception (1854) and the Assumption (1950). When the pope teaches *ex cathedra,* he's exercising his universal authority as Supreme Teacher of a doctrine on faith or morals, and he's incapable of error. Catholics consider the Assumption of Mary and the Immaculate Conception infallible teachings because they involve the solemn, full, and universal papal authority.

The word *cathedral* comes from the Latin *cathedra* because it's the church where the bishop's chair *(cathedra)* resides. The chair is symbolic of authority going back to Roman days when Caesar or his governors sat on a chair and made public decisions, pronouncements, or judgments. When the pope teaches *ex cathedra,* he's not physically sitting on a particular chair but exercising his universal authority as Supreme Teacher.

Unlike governments that separate their executive, legislative, and judicial branches, in the Catholic Church, the pope is all three rolled into one. He's the chief judge, the chief lawmaker, and the commander in chief all at the same time. That's why the triple crown (also known as a *tiara* or *triregnum*) was used in papal coronations — to symbolize his three-fold authority and that he's higher in dignity and authority than a king (one crown) or even an emperor (double crown). (Pope Paul VI was the last pope to wear the tiara. It's a matter of personal choice and preference now.)

The Ordinary Magisterium

The second way that an infallible teaching is taught to Catholics is through the *Ordinary Magisterium,* which is the more common and typical manner, hence the reason why it's called *ordinary.* This teaching of the popes is consistent, constant, and universal through their various documents, letters, papal encyclicals, decrees, and so on. It's never a new doctrine but rather one that has been taught *ubique, semper et ab omnibus* (Latin for *everywhere, always and by all*). In other words, when the pope reinforces, reiterates, or restates the consistent teaching of his predecessors and of the bishops united with him around the world, that's considered the Ordinary Magisterium and should be treated as infallible doctrine.

When popes write papal documents (anything authored by a pope), the title they use to refer to themselves the most is *Servant of the Servants of God* (*Servus Servorum Dei* in Latin). St. Gregory the Great (590–604) was the first pope to use this title. Check out the different types of papal documents from the most solemn on down:

- ✔ Papal Bulls
- ✔ Papal Encyclicals
- ✔ Papal Briefs
- ✔ Apostolic Exhortations

✔ Apostolic Constitutions

✔ Apostolic Letters

✔ Motu Proprios

Prior to the Second Vatican Council (1962–65), more commonly known as Vatican II, the type of papal document the pope chose determined how much authority he intended to exercise. (See Book V, Chapter 1 for more on Vatican II.) The preceding list indicates the order of authority that various papal documents traditionally had. For example, the lowest level was the *Motu Proprio,* which is a Latin phrase meaning *of his own initiative.* Somewhat like an international memo, it's a short papal letter granting a dispensation or making a modification applying to the whole world but on a disciplinary matter only, such as an issue that has nothing to do with doctrine. An example of Motu Proprio was when John Paul II granted permission to celebrate the Tridentine Mass (the order and structure of the Mass as it was celebrated between the Council of Trent and Vatican II). On the other hand, *Papal Bulls* were considered the highest authority.

Since Vatican II, however, the *content* and *context* of the document determine the degree of authority and not just the type of papal document. If the pope intends to definitively teach the universal Church on a matter of faith or morals, then he is expressing his supreme authority as head of the Church. When John Paul II issued his Apostolic Letter *Ordinatio Sacerdotalis* in 1994, he officially declared that the Catholic Church has no power to ordain women. *Ordinatio Sacerdotalis* was *not* an ex cathedra papal statement, but it's part of the Ordinary Magisterium, and thus, according to the Prefect for the Sacred Congregation for the Doctrine of the Faith, the teaching is infallible. The Cardinal Prefect is the pope's watchdog to investigate all suspected cases of *heresy* (false teaching) and to explain official church dogma.

Papal encyclicals are letters addressed to the world on contemporary issues and concerns. *Encyclical* comes from the Latin word for *circular,* because these documents are meant to circulate around the world. The name of each letter consists of the first two words of the letter in Latin, because every official document coming from the Vatican is still written in Latin. Encyclicals aren't *ex cathedra* pronouncements. Some examples of popes who put encyclicals to good use include:

✔ **Leo XIII** wrote *Rerum Novarum* in 1891, which discusses capital and labor. It defends private property and business, as well as the right of workers to form trade unions and guilds.

✔ **Paul VI** presented the Church's teaching on abortion and artificial contraception in *Humanae Vitae* in 1968. It's not an *ex cathedra* statement, but *Humanae Vitae* is a part of the constant, consistent, and universal teachings of the popes and bishops over the ages. (For more about the church's stand on artificial contraception, as well as other sticky issues, turn to Book II, Chapter 6.)

- ✔ **John Paul II** wrote *Laborem Exercens* in 1981 on human work; *Veritatis Splendor* in 1993 on the natural moral law; *Evangelium Vitae* in 1995 on the dignity, sanctity, and inviolability of human life and the things that threaten it, such as abortion, euthanasia, and the death penalty; and *Fides et Ratio* in 1998 on the compatibility of faith and reason.

- ✔ **Benedict XVI**'s first encyclical was *Deus Caritas Est* (2005) on the biblical passage that "God is Love." It explains that divine love and human love are based on the same premise: All love must be both "give and take," sacrificial and possessive.

Encyclicals are the routine, day-to-day, consistent teaching of the Ordinary Magisterium, which is equally infallible when it concerns faith and morals and reiterates the constant, consistent, and universal teaching of the popes and bishops. Their content requires religious submission of mind and will of faithful Catholics around the world. So-called dissent from papal teaching in encyclicals isn't part of Catholic belief. The Catholic faithful willfully conform to papal teaching and don't dispute it.

Now that's job security

Popes are elected for life unless they voluntarily — without pressure or coercion — resign from office. (Pope Pontian was the first one to abdicate from the office in A.D. 235. Pope St. Peter Celestine V was the most famous one to resign, going back to monastic life in 1294. Pope Gregory XII quit in 1415. Pope Benedict was the last one to voluntarily resign in 2013. No one can depose a pope even if he becomes insane, sick, or corrupt.) No ecumenical council has the authority to remove him from office. So when a bad pope gets in (and from time to time, a bad pope has been elected), the only course of action is to pray to St. Joseph for a happy death of the pope in question. (St. Joseph is the patron of a happy death, because he probably died of natural causes in the arms of Mary and Jesus.)

Although even one bad pope is one too many, Jesus himself picked 12 imperfect sinners to be his apostles. The first pope, St. Peter, weakened and denied Christ three times, and Judas, one of the first bishops, betrayed him for 30 pieces of silver. One repented; the other hanged himself instead of seeking mercy.

This is our two cents' worth: Of the 266 popes in history, only a dozen were real scoundrels and caused great scandal. Eighty popes are recognized as holy saints (see Book IV), leaving 174 pretty good, all-right guys. Better stats than for presidents, prime ministers, or monarchs around the world.

Where the pope hangs his hat

The pope's home is *Vatican City,* an independent nation since the Lateran Agreement of 1929, when Italy recognized its sovereignty. Vatican City covers only 0.2 square miles (108.7 acres), has fewer than a thousand inhabitants, and rests in the middle of Rome.

After 300 years of Roman persecution, the Emperor Constantine legalized Christianity in A.D. 313 with the Edict of Milan and thus formally ended the state-sponsored persecutions of the Christians. In A.D. 321, he donated the imperial property of the Lateran Palace to the bishop of Rome, which began a trend of donating property in recompense for all the land and possessions that the Romans took from the early Christians during the pagan era.

The donation of large estates stopped around A.D. 600, but 154 years later, King Pepin (the Short) of the Franks (who was also the father of Charlemagne) issued the Donation of A.D. 754: The pope would govern the territory of central Italy (16,000 square miles). From 754 to 1870, Vatican City was part of the Papal States, also known as *Patrimonium Sancti Petri* (the Patrimony of St. Peter). During the unification of Italy, Giuseppe Garibaldi and Count Camillo Benso di Cavour, the two men most responsible for creating the Kingdom and modern nation of Italy in 1870, seized the Papal States and, for all practical purposes, ended the secular rule of the popes. Today, Vatican City is the smallest independent nation in the world. Ironically, it also has the largest number of embassies and ambassadors around the globe. Guglielmo Marconi, the inventor of radio, built a radio for Pope Pius XI; thus Vatican Radio began in 1931. Now, in addition to a radio and short-wave antennae, the Vatican also has television and Internet programming.

The only real citizens of Vatican City, aside from the pope, are the cardinals who live in Rome, directors of other Vatican offices, and full-time diplomats who work for the *Holy See* (the pope and the various offices of Church government in the Vatican). These diplomats, clergy and laity alike, come from countries all over the world. They still retain their own nationality and citizenship but are given a Vatican passport while employed to represent the Vatican. Originally sent to Rome in 1506, about 107 Swiss guards protect the pope, decorating the *Piazza* (outdoor square where people gather) with their colorful costumes. In addition, plain-clothes Swiss guards, with electronic surveillance and sophisticated weapons, also keep a close eye on the Holy Father, especially since the attempted assassination of John Paul II in 1981.

Who's Next in the Ecclesiastical Scheme of Things

Because the Catholic Church has a billion-plus members, the pope depends on many helpers to govern the vast institution. The ranking system goes like this: The pope's at the helm, followed by cardinals, archbishops/bishops, vicars general, monsignors, and priests. The rest of the Church is made up of deacons, monks, nuns, brothers, sisters, and laypersons. (The latter — lay men and lay women — make up 99.9 percent of the Church.)

Cardinals

Although the primary responsibility of the College of Cardinals is to elect a pope (see the section "How the pope gets his job", earlier in this chapter), cardinals have many other responsibilities as well. The *Roman Curia* is the whole group of administrators (Cardinal Prefects) who head up their departments (congregations, tribunals, and so on), working together as the right hand of the pope. The pope governs through the Roman Curia, something like cabinet members who assist the president or department ministers who assist the prime minister. For example, a Cardinal Secretary of State represents the Holy See to foreign governments, because Vatican City is the world's smallest independent country. And you can find a different cardinal heading up each congregation, such as the Congregation for

- Doctrine of the Faith
- Bishops
- Catholic Education
- Causes of the Saints
- Clergy
- Divine Worship and Discipline of the Sacraments
- Evangelization of Peoples
- Institutes of Consecrated Life and Societies of Apostolic Life
- Oriental Churches

A different cardinal also heads up each of several commissions and councils, as well as three high courts of the Catholic Church: the Apostolic Penitentiary, the Apostolic Signatura, and the Roman Rota, all of which deal with canon law and its application and interpretation.

Cardinals who don't work in the Curia run an (arch)diocese, mostly functioning as an (arch)bishop would — ordaining, confirming, and doing the day-to-day business of being chief shepherd of the archdiocese. These cardinals are also often the *metropolitans,* which means that they supervise the province of two to several dioceses, usually all in the same state or region. (The next section defines archdiocese and diocese.) A metropolitan doesn't have immediate authority over neighboring bishops or their dioceses even though they're within the cardinal archbishop's province as metropolitan.

A metropolitan does report to Rome, however, if one of the bishops in his province is derelict in his duties, commits scandal or crime, and so on. Often, the *apostolic nuncio,* the papal ambassador to that country, consults with the cardinal when vacancies appear in his province, as in the case of a bishop dying or retiring. For example, the Cardinal Archbishop of Philadelphia is the Metropolitan for Pennsylvania, which incorporates the eight dioceses of Philadelphia, Pittsburgh, Erie, Harrisburg, Scranton, Allentown, Greensburg, and Altoona-Johnstown.

The pope personally selects the men who become cardinals. The ceremony where new cardinals are created is called a *consistory,* and it usually occurs every few years to replace those who have retired (or will soon retire), as well as those who have died since the last consistory. This way, the goal of 120 cardinal electors is more likely achieved should the pope die, in which case a conclave is called to elect a new pope. Since the pontificate of John Paul II, a concerted effort has been made to have a diverse spectrum of cardinals from all continents and from both Latin and Eastern Catholic Rites.

Bishops and archbishops

Besides being the head of the Catholic Church, the pope is also the bishop of Rome. The pope isn't more a bishop than any other bishop, but his authority covers more territory. The pope has supreme, full, immediate, and universal jurisdiction all over the world, whereas a local bishop, who may also be an archbishop or a cardinal, possesses jurisdiction only in his *diocese,* which is the typical geographical designation in Catholic governance — an administrative territory.

Dioceses and archdioceses: The areas that bishops govern

Each individual bishop retains his own authority, which comes from episcopal ordination and consecration. *Episcopal* refers to anything that has to do with a bishop or bishops, and episcopal ordination and consecration is the sacrament by which a priest becomes a bishop. It's the third and fullest level of the Sacrament of Holy Orders. (The first level is the ordination of a deacon, and the second is the ordination of a priest. Deacons, priests, and bishops are all considered *clergy.*)

The local bishop runs the diocese. He's not an ambassador of the pope but governs the local diocese as an authentic successor of the apostles, just as the pope governs the universal Church as the successor of St. Peter.

The pope appoints the bishops, and they must make a visit to the Holy Father every five years and give a report on their particular diocese. The rest of the time, the bishop goes around the diocese confirming adults and teenagers, ordaining men to the *diaconate* (the office of deacon), and ordaining men to the priesthood once a year. Only bishops have the authority to administer the Sacrament of Holy Orders whereby men are ordained deacons, priests, or bishops. Bishops make pastoral visits to the parishes and chair numerous meetings with their staff. (See Chapter Book II, Chapter 2 for more on the sacraments.) A bishop is like a pastor of an extra-large parish. (See the section "The parish priest" for details about pastors.)

The local diocese is a collection of local parishes, just like a state is a collection of counties and cities. Many dioceses are comprised of several state counties, and in a few places, the entire state makes up one diocese.

In general, you can think of a local parish as being like a town or city, and the local pastor as being like the mayor. The diocese is like a state or province, and the bishop is like the governor. (The pope is like the prime minister, governing the entire nation, except that he governs the universal Church all over the world.)

An archbishop runs a really large diocese, known as an *archdiocese*. For example, an archbishop is given authority in each of the following archdioceses: Newark, San Francisco, Denver, Hartford, Miami, St. Louis, and Omaha. Sometimes, though, the archbishop is also a cardinal, which is often the case in Philadelphia, New York City, Boston, Chicago, Baltimore, Los Angeles, Detroit, and Washington, D.C.

The bishops within an entire country or nation get together at least once a year in a gathering known as an *episcopal conference.* The American bishops belong to the United States Conference of Catholic Bishops (USCCB); the Canadian Bishops belong to the Canadian Conference of Catholic Bishops (CCCB); in Australia, it's the Australian Catholic Bishops Conference (ACBC); and in Great Britain, it's the Catholic Bishops' Conference of England and Wales (CBCEW).

Cathedrals: The place where bishops hang out

The cathedral is to the local diocese what the Vatican is to the universal Church. The cathedral is the official church of the diocese where the bishop's chair resides, and his chair (*cathedra* in Latin) is a symbol of his authority as a successor to the apostles.

Ironically, St. Peter's Basilica in the Vatican, where the pope celebrates most of his Masses, isn't technically the pope's cathedral church. The cathedral for the diocese of Rome is actually St. John Lateran, where the popes originally lived before moving to the Vatican in the 14th century.

Bishops celebrate most Masses at the cathedral church. In addition, it's often the place where the Chrism Mass (also known as the *Mass of the Oils*) takes place — unless the bishop decides to have it elsewhere in the diocese. (Curious? See the sidebar "Nope, the Mass of the Oils has nothing to do with your car's engine" for details about this special Mass.)

Cathedrals also have daily and weekly Mass like other parishes, as well as weddings, funerals, baptisms, and such. But the pride of the cathedral is in the ordinations to the episcopacy, priesthood, or diaconate, as well as the Chrism Mass.

Note: Only the bishop may sit in his *cathedra,* so any other priest celebrating Mass must use another chair.

The vicar general

Vicars general aren't military leaders like Generals Montgomery, De Gaulle, and MacArthur. They're priests who are second in command in the diocese and appointed by the bishop to help him govern the local Church. Sometimes, episcopal vicars are also appointed to assist the bishop in certain areas, such as vocations, the marriage tribunal, clergy personnel, Hispanic or minority ministries, and so on. In large dioceses, such as New York or London, vicars general are often *auxiliary bishops,* ordained bishops who assist the bishop of the diocese in the same way any other vicar general does except that they can help the bishop ordain deacons and priests and celebrate the Sacrament of Confirmation.

Some priests are given the honorary title of *monsignor* at the request of the local bishop. This title has no extra authority, dignity, or salary. You can recognize a monsignor by the color of his *cassock* — a long, close-fitting garment worn by clerics. Until recently, this honorary title could be bestowed in three different forms:

- **Papal Chamberlain:** Also known as *Chaplain of His Holiness,* this is the lowest ranking of the title of monsignor. These monsignors wear black cassocks with purple buttons and trim.

- **Domestic Prelate:** These monsignors are also known as *Prelates of Honor,* and they wear purple or black cassocks with red buttons and trim.

- **Protonotary Apostolic:** This is the highest ranking of the title. It's designated by a purple *ferraiolone,* a silk cape worn over the cassock.

Pope Francis issued a revision for the honorary title of monsignor at the end of 2013. He has limited this title to diocesan priests at least 65 years old, and now all will only receive the title *Chaplain of His Holiness*. The change is not retroactive and does not affect Vatican officials or members of religious orders.

The parish priest

The *parish priest* (also known as a *pastor*) is the next clergy in the hierarchy after the vicar general. Pastors are appointed by the bishop and represent the bishop to the local *parish,* which is a collection of neighborhoods in one small region of the county within a given state.

Some pastors are helped by a priest called a *parochial vicar* (formerly known as a *curate* or an *assistant pastor*) and/or sometimes by a permanent deacon, religious sister, or a lay parishioner as a *pastoral associate.* The parish council and finance committees, which are made up of lay parishioners for the most part, advise and counsel the pastor but don't have administrative or executive authority.

Tough training

The typical Catholic priest isn't what you see in movies or on TV. Priests are expected to obtain a graduate, post-graduate, or doctoral degree, and they often spend anywhere from 4 to 12 years in the *seminary,* which is the equivalent of Protestant divinity school. Most have at least a master's degree in divinity or theology, if not a higher academic degree on par with medical doctors and attorneys.

Besides scholastic training, seminarians also receive practical experience from *apostolates,* which are weekly or summertime assignments in parishes, hospitals, nursing homes, prisons, classrooms, and such, to unite pastoral education with theological and philosophical education.

A busy job

A parish priest celebrates daily Mass, hears confessions every week, gives marriage counseling, provides prenuptial counseling, gives spiritual direction, anoints and visits shut-ins and the sick in hospitals and nursing homes, teaches *Catechism* (a book that contains the doctrines of Catholicism) to children and adults, baptizes, witnesses marriages, performs funerals and burials, attends numerous parish and diocesan meetings, prays privately every day, does spiritual and theological reading, and finds time to relax now and then with family and friends. And once a year, he's expected to make a five-day retreat in addition to doing his regular spiritual direction and daily prayer. Yeah, it's a busy job.

With 1.23 billion Catholics worldwide and only about 414,313 priests to minister to their spiritual needs, that leaves an average of about one priest per 2,968 Catholics. Some areas have as many as 6,000 or more people per priest.

The hub in the wheel: The parish church

The parish church is where the priest does his job and where most Catholics hang out on Saturday evening or Sunday morning to attend Mass.

The local Catholic parish is often named after a title of the Lord Jesus Christ, such as *Blessed Sacrament* or *Sacred Heart;* after a title of the Blessed Virgin Mary, such as *Our Lady of Good Counsel* or *Our Lady of Seven Sorrows;* or after one of the saints, such as *St. Ann, St. Bernadette,* or *St. Joseph.* The parish is the heart of the diocese because it's where most Catholics get baptized, go to confession, attend Mass, receive Holy Communion, are confirmed, get married, and are buried from.

Some American parishes have a parochial school connected to them, but few of them have a convent of nuns who staff the school, although you can still find them here and there. Catholic grade schools were once the bread and butter of vocations and often fed into Catholic high schools and colleges. In other words, these parish schools encouraged boys and girls to consider becoming priests and nuns, and most students continued their Catholic education all the way through college even if they didn't have a religious vocation. But economics, demographics, and declining numbers of religious sisters and brothers have resulted in the consolidation and closing of many parish schools. Public schools in many places are well staffed, well funded, and more accessible.

An even rarer occurrence is the parish cemetery. Nowadays, the diocese has centralized schools and cemeteries, but a few old country parishes still have a graveyard in the back of the property.

Father, are you a diocesan or religious priest?

Catholic priests are *diocesan* (secular) or *religious* (regular). Diocesan priests belong to the diocese that they're located in, but religious order priests, such as Franciscan or Dominican, belong to that order.

Diocesan (secular) priests

The typical parish priest is usually a diocesan priest, meaning he belongs to the geographical area of the diocese, which often comprises several counties in one state. He makes a promise of obedience to the local bishop and a promise of celibacy. Diocesan priests are also called *secular* priests to distinguish them from the priests who belong to communities and orders.

A diocesan priest gets a modest monthly salary from the parish. In addition, the parish or diocese normally provides room and board (meals and lodging) and health insurance, but only a few dioceses also provide car insurance. Diocesan priests live in parishes alone or with another priest, but basically have their own living quarters inside the *rectory* — the house where the parish priests live. They do their own work and relax on their own, usually just sharing one meal together.

Diocesan priests are responsible for buying and maintaining their own automobiles as well as personal property — clothing, books, computers, televisions, and so on. The individual diocesan priest pays his federal, state, and local taxes, including Social Security taxes. After making monthly car payments, paying for insurance, and possibly paying off bank loans from college, not much is left of the monthly salary, but the parish or diocese provides his necessities. Honoraria and gifts from baptisms, weddings, and funerals differ from parish to parish and from diocese to diocese, but it's *very important* to note that a priest never charges any fees for his services. Free will offerings are often made to him or to the parish, but it's sinful, sacrilegious, and rude for any cleric to ask for money while performing his sacred ministry.

Canon law guarantees every priest one day off per seven-day week and one month (30 days) of vacation per year, not including the one-week annual retreat. If you think 30 days of vacation every year seems like a lot, keep in mind that most people get two days off per week. Priests work an extra 52 days each year to earn their 30 days of vacation!

Religious (regular) priests

Religious priests are referred to as *regular* because they follow the *regula*, which is Latin for *rule,* the structured life of a religious community. The Rule refers to how a religious order trains, lives, governs itself, and practices. Religious priests are more commonly known as *order priests* after the religious *order* that they belong to, such as the Franciscans, Dominicans, Jesuits, Benedictines, and Augustinians. They wear particular *habits* (religious garb) and take solemn vows of poverty, chastity, and obedience. They don't own their own cars or personal possessions. Many use community automobiles that everyone in the order shares. They have the clothes on their back and little else. They don't get salaries like diocesan priests but are given an extremely modest monthly allowance to buy toiletries and snacks, as well as to go out for dinner or a movie once in a while. If they need to buy something expensive or want to take time off for vacation, they must ask permission of the superior who authorizes the money to be given them or for the bill to be paid.

They normally live together with three or more (sometimes more than 20) members of the community in the same house, sharing everything: one television, one computer, and so on. This arrangement encourages them to recreate together, because they must also live together, pray together, and work together. Unlike diocesan (secular) clergy who get small salaries and pay taxes, religious clergy own nothing. If they inherit anything whatsoever, it goes to the community or to the order, whereas a diocesan priest could inherit the family home but would also have to pay all the taxes and upkeep.

Deacons

Deacons are the clergy next in the hierarchy, right after priests. *Permanent deacons* are men ordained to an office in the Church who normally have no intention or desire of becoming priests. They can be single or married.

If the latter, they must be married *before* being ordained a deacon. If their wife dies before them, they may be ordained a priest if the bishop permits and approves. Married deacons cannot remarry if their wife dies unless they petition the Pope for a dispensation (for example, when there are small children to be raised).

Transitional deacons are *seminarians,* students in training for the priesthood, at the last phase of their formation. After being a deacon for a year, they're ordained a priest by the bishop.

Deacons can baptize, witness marriages, perform funeral and burial services outside of Mass, distribute Holy Communion, preach the *homily* (the sermon given after the Gospel at Mass), and are obligated to pray the Divine Office (150 psalms and Scriptural readings for clergy) each day.

Permanent deacons, especially those who are married, have secular jobs to support their families. They help the local pastor by visiting the sick, teaching the faith, counseling couples and individuals, working on parish committees and councils, and giving advice to the pastor.

Monks and nuns, brothers and sisters

Technically speaking, monks and nuns live in *monasteries* (from the Greek *monazein,* meaning *to live alone*), buildings that have restricted access to the outside world, allowing them to spend as much time as possible in work and in prayer. Monasteries are places where only women as nuns reside or where only men as monks live. Few monasteries have guest accommodations, and the monks or nuns live a monastic type of spirituality, such that they all gather in the chapel to pray together, they all eat together, and they all work somewhere in the monastery — cooking, cleaning, and so on.

Religious sisters, on the other hand, live in *convents,* a word that comes from the Latin *conventus* meaning *assembly.* Convents offer more open access inside and out to the secular world. Residents typically live and pray in the convent but work outside in schools, hospitals, and so on. *Friaries* (from the Latin word *frater* meaning *brother*) are the male version of convents, a place where religious men called *brothers* live and pray together. Their work is done outside the friary.

St. Dominic and St. Francis of Assisi both founded the first group of friars in the Church. Friars bridged the gap between the urban parish and the monastery, and they aren't as cloistered or semi-cloistered as their monk and nun counterparts. How cloistered the group is depends on the religious order or community and the founder who started it.

You can find hundreds of different religious orders, communities, and congregations in the world today. Each community and order bases its spirituality on the founder of its congregation; for example, St. Francis founded the Franciscans, St. Clare founded the Poor Clares, St. Lucy Filippini founded the Religious Sisters Filippini, and Mother Teresa founded the Missionaries of Charity. Some communities specialize in teaching and others in hospital work. Some engage in several active apostolates, and a few devote themselves to a cloistered life of contemplative prayer.

For example, the Sisters of St. Joseph, the Sisters of Mercy, Religious Sisters Filippini, Dominican Sisters, Daughters of Charity, and Sisters of Saints Cyril and Methodius often work in schools, hospitals, and nursing homes. But Carmelite, Dominican, Poor Clare, and other nuns stay in the monastery and pray, fast, and work for the sanctification of souls. You may have seen Mother Angelica and the other Poor Clare nuns on television from time to time and noticed that even while they're in the chapel, they're separated *(cloistered)* from the general public. Cloistered nuns live and stay in the monastery whereas religious sisters work outside the convent.

In contrast, the sisters in parochial schools aren't nuns but religious sisters; they don't live in a cloistered monastery but in a convent, and they teach in the parish school.

You can tell the order of the monk, nun, sister, or friar by their *habit* (religious garb). Franciscans typically wear brown, the Dominicans wear white, the Benedictines wear black, and the Missionaries of Charity wear white with blue stripes. Some communities of women no longer wear a veil on their head but wear a pin that identifies them with their order instead. The style, size, and color of the women's veils also designate their community.

Religious brothers and sisters aren't members of the clergy, but they aren't members of the lay faithful, either. They're called *consecrated religious,* which means that they've taken sacred vows of poverty, chastity, and obedience. They share all meals together and try to work together, pray together, and recreate together. Because they take a vow of poverty, they don't own their own cars (no insurance, loan payments, or gasoline to buy either), and they have no personal savings or checking accounts. The religious order provides all these things, and they must ask their superiors when they need or want something. This is where that vow of obedience kicks in.

The Non-Ordained Ministers

Clergy (ordained ministers) may be assisted in Sacred Worship by *non-ordained ministers,* certain lay parishioners and consecrated religious (monks, nuns, sisters, brothers, and so on). Some ministries, or roles, are part of the formation and process of becoming a deacon or priest. Other ministries are called *extraordinary* in that they function whenever ordinary ministers are not available to do the job. Men studying in the seminary or formation program leading toward Holy Orders (diaconate or priesthood) are admitted to ministries such as lector and acolyte (formerly known as minor orders) as part of their preliminary education.

Acolyte

The word *acolyte* comes from Greek and means *attendant* or *helper.* The acolyte's duty, as described in the General Instruction of the Roman Missal, is "to serve at the altar and assist the priest and deacon." At Mass, acolytes light altar candles, carry candles in procession, assist deacons and priests at the Mass, bring the wine and water to the altar at the offertory, ring bells during the consecration, help in distribution of Holy Communion by placing a paten under recipients' chin or hands, and wash the celebrant's fingers in purifying vessels after Holy Communion. A *formally instituted* acolyte (meaning a seminarian authorized by his bishop to help distribute Holy Communion) can also distribute Holy Communion as an extraordinary minister of Holy Communion.

Because Holy Orders (the roles of bishop, priest, and deacon) are reserved for baptized males, the *installed ministries* or *minor orders* of acolyte and lector are also only for men. In the present Code of Canon Law, the ministry of acolyte is open to all laymen (nonclergy male members of the congregation). In the reform of the liturgy after the Second Vatican Council, the pope intended to extend the role of acolyte beyond seminarians who are preparing for priesthood.

Although the office of acolyte is reserved for men, the function is not. In the Ordinary form of the Roman Rite, women with the consent of the local bishop and parish pastor may function as *readers* (similar to lectors) and as *altar servers* (similar to acolytes).

The proper vesture for an acolyte is cassock and surplice or an alb-like robe.

The Extraordinary form and the Eastern Catholic Church still retain the minor order of subdeacon, which ranks above acolyte, but in the Ordinary form of the Latin Rite, that office was taken over by the installed acolyte. Subdeacons in the Eastern Orthodox and Extraordinary form of the Latin Rite assist the deacon as the deacon in turn assists the celebrant. Subdeacons prepare by pouring the wine into the chalice, carrying the chalice with wine to the altar, and reading the Epistles before the people.

Extraordinary ministers of Holy Communion

Extraordinary ministers of Holy Communion are not instituted by the bishop; rather they have been given temporary permission from the bishop to distribute Holy Communion. At Mass they help the bishop, priest, and deacon (the ordinary ministers of Holy Communion) to distribute the Blessed Sacrament. The extraordinary ministers of Holy Communion also customarily transport the Eucharist to sick and shut-in members of the congregation, especially on Sundays.

The term *extraordinary* has a literal definition here; it refers to exceptional occasions when an ordinary minister of Holy Communion is unavailable. All members of the ordained clergy — bishops, priests and deacons — are considered ordinary ministers of Holy Communion and normally perform all the tasks of the extraordinary ministers. Religious men and women and laity can be authorized by the local bishop to be extraordinary ministers of Holy Communion.

To be eligible to become an extraordinary minister of Holy Communion, a layperson must have received all the Sacraments of Initiation (Baptism, Confirmation, and Holy Eucharist). Extraordinary ministers are trained and authorized by the bishop.

Vesting for an extraordinary Eucharistic minister is Sunday dress clothes. Some dioceses permit extraordinary Eucharistic ministers to wear albs. However, normally albs are reserved for the ordinary ministers.

Lector

The General Instruction of Roman Missal defines the lector as a congregant who is instituted to proclaim the readings from Sacred Scripture, with the exception of the Gospel. The lector may also announce the intentions for the Prayer of the Faithful and, in the absence of a psalmist, proclaim the psalm between the readings. The proper place for a lector to do Scripture readings at Mass is the ambo or pulpit, and he normally reads the General Intercessions at the lectern. When a deacon isn't present, the lector may carry the Book of the Gospels in procession.

Like acolytes, lectors are also formally installed ministers, and therefore the positions can be filled only by men from the lay congregation. Being a lector is also one of the steps toward entering the Holy Orders.

Reader

Laymen and laywomen may function as *readers* if an instituted lector is not present. Their duties are the same as lectors', and they are trained to read Scripture clearly and audibly. Like extraordinary Eucharistic ministers, commissioned readers must have received all the Sacraments of Initiation and, if married, have a valid marriage. Bishops authorize lay readers to function in the diocese for a period of one to three years. From time to time, priests may appoint a reader to read at a certain Mass without a formal commissioning.

Psalmist/cantor

The General Instruction for Roman Missal outlines the position of *psalmist,* or *cantor,* a layperson who sings the psalm in between the Old and New Testament readings. The cantor aids the congregation in singing. The cantor often works in conjunction with the choir. Psalmists can wear choir robes or Sunday dress.

Organist/music director

The *organist* can be the parish music director or someone else. The organist and/or music director must not only be well versed in music, but also have a working knowledge of Catholic liturgy and the liturgical calendar. In addition, the organist/music director is integral with the choir and works very closely with the clergy to plan the music to be sung at the liturgy. The organist can wear a cassock and a special sleeveless surplice to play the organ and conduct the choir, or may wear Sunday dress clothes.

Choir

The *choir* augments the singing of the congregation during Mass. The choir should never serve as a substitute for the congregation's singing, although at times the choir may sing pieces separate from the congregation. Members of the choir often wear choir robes or Sunday dress clothes.

Commentator

Not to be confused with the cantor, psalmist, or lector, the *commentator* provides the congregation with brief explanations and commentaries. Normally, the commentator speaks from the lectern where the cantor leads music. Commentators are not mandatory but are used at important celebrations for the sole purpose of introducing the particular celebration. They are appropriately employed at Solemn Pontifical Masses, dedications of churches, anniversaries of parishes, celebrations of priestly or religious vocations, and state functions in which Mass is being celebrated, as in the case in papal visits.

Altar servers

Most Catholics are generally familiar with the people who serve at Mass, the *altar servers*. They assist the celebrant at Mass and serve in place of instituted acolytes. They can have the following roles:

- **Thurifer:** A thurifer carries the censer to be used at Mass and also leads processions while gently swinging it so that billows of incense ascend to God. In addition, the thurifer can incense at the consecration of the Mass.

- **Crucifer:** The crucifer, the cross-bearer, carries the processional cross situated atop a long staff. He is employed anytime a procession takes place. When a thurifer is not present, he leads the procession.

- **Book bearer:** The book bearer holds the missal at Mass for the celebrant.

- **Episcopal attendants:** At celebrations when the bishop is present, two altar servers are employed to hold the miter and crosier during the ceremony. The server wears a special garment, the vimp, over his cassock and surplice in order not to soil the sacred vestures.

- **Servers:** Servers aid the celebrant at the altar.

None of these types of server is an instituted ministry, and as with extraordinary Eucharistic ministers and readers, laymen and laywomen can function as altar servers. Normally, altar servers wear a cassock and surplice. However, in some parishes, white albs are used.

Ushers

The General Instruction for the Roman Missal mentions ushers' role of preserving orderliness at Holy Mass:

> Ushers take up the collection in the church. Those who, in some places, meet the faithful at the church entrance, lead them to appropriate places and direct processions.

In addition to collecting the offertory giving of the faithful, ushers can distribute the bulletins after Mass, aid congregants who have physical disabilities, help direct the ordinary or extraordinary minister of the Eucharist to distribute Holy Communion, especially to disabled people, and serve as a reference for people attending the Mass.

Ushers often are the first people you meet when arriving at Mass. They can be very useful in disseminating valuable information. In special processions, ushers control the crowd and promote orderliness in the sacred march. In many parishes, ushers wear a uniform jacket with the parish coat-of-arms on the breast pocket so that the congregants can easily identify them.

Master of ceremonies

At Solemn Masses, a *master of ceremonies* is often used. He acts as a director of the flow of the liturgy.

Ordinary Catholics often come into contact with a master of ceremonies when the bishop comes to their parish for a specific celebration, such as conferring the Sacrament of Confirmation. The master of ceremonies can also be employed for solemn celebrations in which the bishop isn't present, such as the Easter Triduum.

Whether a priest, deacon, or layman, the master of ceremonies is well versed in the norms of the liturgy. He works closely with all the key players of the liturgy — the main celebrant, the musicians, and the servers. In complicated ceremonies in which many variables arise, especially when a bishop is the main celebrant, the master of ceremonies has to have a fine sense of judgment, well-organized thoughts, and, most of all, good coordination in order for the liturgy to proceed smoothly.

The master of ceremonies typically leads the rehearsals of servers and musicians. During the liturgy, he must be able to look ahead at the pending action in order to be prepared and on time with the elements and servers. The proper dress for master of ceremonies is usually a cassock and surplice. If the master of ceremonies is a priest or deacon, he wears a stole during Holy Communion.

Sacristan

The *sacristan* is very important to the liturgy. The General Instruction for the Roman Missal describes the sacristan as one "who carefully arranges the liturgical books, the vestments, and other things necessary in the celebration of Mass." He provides an invaluable service to the priest by setting up the Missal, placing on the credence table the chalice, ciboria, and cruets, making sure the church is opened and either the heat or air conditioning is turned on, and handling anything else that must be taken care of prior to the start of Mass.

A sacristan also takes charge of the care of the vestments and vessels of the church. This person makes sure the sacred linens, altar cloths, albs, and vestments are cleaned and plentiful; he makes sure that chalices, ciboria, and candlesticks are polished; and that flowers and other devotional items are in good condition and in their correct places.

Chapter 6

The Liturgical Year

*T*he idea of marking significant events during the year isn't exclusive to Christianity. From pagan times, people observed a calendar that was usually centered on the agricultural cycle: Spring meant planting and new birth among the animals, summer symbolized growth, fall represented the harvest, and winter stood for dormancy, not just for the animal kingdom but the plant kingdom as well.

Christianity also has its own seasonal *liturgical* calendar. Just as the pagan calendar observed holidays according to nature's cycle of life, the Christian calendar celebrates holy days according to historical biblical events.

Judaism plays a significant role in the Christian liturgical calendar. The Christian observance of Easter originally took place during the Jewish feast of Passover; Christians believe Holy Thursday is when Christ instituted the Sacraments of Holy Eucharist and Holy Orders, one day before his Passion and Crucifixion. Three days later was his Resurrection.

The Church liturgical year has two cycles, the Temporal and the Sanctoral. The Temporal (from Latin *tempus,* meaning *time* or *season*) cycle focuses on the life of Christ, from Birth to Death, Resurrection to Ascension. The entire paschal mystery (Passion, Death, and Resurrection) is ceremonially celebrated in the divine worship given each Sunday and holy day of the year during the Temporal cycle. The Sanctoral (from Latin *sanctus,* meaning *saint*) cycle focuses on the various holy men and women of faith who the Church endorses as saints. These heroes of the Catholic religion are normally celebrated on the day of their death, which is considered their heavenly birthday. While the Sanctoral cycle follows the days of the Gregorian calendar (the normal January to December calendar), the Temporal cycle follows the seasons of the year, beginning in winter with Advent and Christmas, going through spring with Lent and Easter, continuing through summer (Ordinary Time), and ending in fall with the Feast of Christ the King.

Worshipping through the Temporal Cycle

The liturgical year is a year of grace. Christians view it as an opportunity to enter into the Sacred Mysteries of redemption and receive God's life. This prospect unfolds itself throughout the year through the different aspects of salvation from the beginning of Christ's life — the Advent and Christmas season — to the earthly end — the Lent and Easter season. The months in between mark Ordinary Time and the celebration of the saints.

The liturgy not only recalls the sacred events of our salvation from history, but also makes them alive in the annual celebration of the Temporal cycle. After the Roman Empire fell and Europe was overrun by the barbarian invaders, the Dark Ages ensued, and many common folk were unable to read and write. They were taught, however, not by books, but by the Sacred Liturgy. The Temporal cycle of the liturgical year taught the faithful about the Birth, Death, Resurrection, and Ascension of Jesus, year after year. Just as the same four seasons occur year after year, the Birth of Christ happens every winter and the Resurrection of Christ every spring. Although Christmas is a fixed date, Easter changes every year based on the equinox and full moon in the lunar cycle.

Preparing for Christ Our Light: Advent and Christmas

The season of Christmas and the four weeks of preparation, known as Advent, begin the new liturgical year of grace and the Temporal cycle. This new year is marked by the changing lectionary cycle, or cycle of readings. Sundays are divided into three lectionary volumes, and weekdays are divided into two volumes. The First Sunday of Advent means a change of volumes for both Sundays and weekdays.

Christmas developed as a liturgical celebration of the birthday of the Savior. The word itself means *Christ's Mass,* the Mass in honor of the Birth of Jesus Christ. Christians wanted to celebrate and commemorate the Birth of Christ, but no one knew the exact date. Emperors and kings and other powerful people had their birthdays remembered because of public celebrations. Ordinary folks, like a son of a carpenter in Nazareth, would not have had his birthday marked down on any calendar. Only after his Death, Resurrection, and Ascension did the followers of Jesus want to honor his Birth (since they already were celebrating the day he died).

Many theories concern the date of the Savior's Birth in Bethlehem. Some scholars believe it occurred in the spring because the shepherds and their animals were outside at night, and even in the Mediterranean the nights are chilly during spring and summer and quite cold in December.

Although the pagan Romans celebrated the feast of the sun at the winter solstice, St. Augustine (who lived in the fourth century AD) wrote that Christians also used that time of year to honor the birthday of their beloved founder. The reason was based on the symbolism of daylight. The shortest day of the year occurs in December, and by December 25 (Christmas), the amount of daylight begins to increase in the Northern hemisphere. Conversely, the longest day of the year occurs in June, so that by June 24 the amount of daylight begins to slowly decrease day by day until the shortest day arrives and the opposite takes place.

According to St. Augustine, two passages in the Bible relate to the shortest and the longest days of the year.

> ✔ In John 3:30, "I must decrease while he must increase" was spoken by St. John the Baptist in reference to his cousin, Jesus Christ the Lord.
> ✔ Jesus said "I am the Light of the world" in John 9:5.

So the Church celebrates the birthday of John the Baptist on June 24 (when sunlight is beginning to decrease) and the birthday of Jesus on December 25 (when sunlight is beginning to increase).

Advent

The four-week season of Advent helps prepare Christians for the Solemnity of Christmas. *Advent* comes from the Latin and means *arrival,* a fitting word because the season is in preparation for the arrival of Christ. The season is broken up into the various weeks of preparation: the Sundays are First, Second, Third (Gaudete Sunday), and Fourth, beginning on the Feast of the Apostle Andrew on November 30 and ending on December 24, the Vigil of Christmas. Each season in the liturgical calendar is symbolized by a specific color, and for Advent, the liturgical color is purple.

Advent focuses on the historical arrival of Jesus over two millennia ago and also symbolizes the Second Coming of Christ that will take place at the end of world. Advent is a season characterized by preparation, reflection, hope, and anticipation. Spiritual reflections are taken from key people noted in Scripture: Isaiah the prophet; John the Baptist; Elizabeth and Zechariah, the parents of John; and Joseph.

The Solemnity of the Immaculate Conception of Mary is during the Advent season, on December 8. The feast is a celebration of the Divine Plan, which provides that Mary was preserved from Original Sin while in the womb of Ann, her mother. Nine months later, the birthday of Mary is celebrated on September 8.

Following are other Advent season feasts, which each have their own unique customs and traditions that add to the festivity of the season:

- December 6: St. Nicholas Day (the origin of Santa Claus)
- December 12: Our Lady of Guadalupe, patroness of the Americas
- December 13: St. Lucy, virgin and martyr, and patron saint of eye maladies

Changes to the Mass and additional prayers

The Gloria praise hymn, originally a Christmas hymn, is not sung during Advent's preparation season. Unlike during Lent, which is more penitential, the Alleluia still can be sung during the liturgy in Advent in the Ordinary Rite, but is omitted in the Extraordinary form of the Roman Rite. Flowers may adorn the altar during this season, and often greenery is brought into the church.

A special novena known as the Christmas Novena is prayed during this season as a tool of preparation. The novena asks God to grant a request in the honor of the Birth of his Son at Christmas. It is a pious custom that revolves around the family, as many of the customs of Advent and Christmas do.

Christmas Novena

Hail, and blessed be the hour and moment
At which the Son of God was born
Of a more pure Virgin
At a stable at midnight in Bethlehem
In the piercing cold
At that hour vouchsafe, I beseech thee,
To hear my prayers and grant my desires [mention request]
Through Jesus Christ and his most Blessed Mother. Amen.

The Advent wreath

The Advent wreath has become a very popular sacramental in the Universal Church. Three of the candles are purple, symbolizing the preparation and anticipation of the season. The fourth candle is rose and is lit on Gaudete Sunday. Before electricity, candles were the source of light in the church, so lighting these candles during the darkest time of year gave a great expression of Christ, the light of the world.

The following prayer is used on the First Sunday of Advent. The subsequent candles are lit in silence on the following Sundays until Christmas Eve.

> **Prayer of Blessing of the Advent Wreath**
>
> O God, by whose word all things are sanctified
> Pour forth thy blessing upon this wreath
> Grant that who use it may prepare our hearts
> For the coming of Christ and
> May receive from thee abundant graces.
> Through Christ our Lord. Amen.

Christmas

The season of Christmas begins at the evening liturgy of Christmas Eve and lasts until the Feast of the Epiphany. In Europe, Epiphany falls on January 6, which coincides with the traditional count of the 12th day of Christmas. By special permission in many dioceses, including those in the United States, this solemnity has been transferred to the Sunday nearest January 6. However, the Christmas season actually extends to the Feast of the Baptism of the Lord, which is observed the Sunday after Epiphany.

Christmas is the celebration of the Birth of the Light of the World, Jesus Christ, when the long promised Messiah of the Old Testament materialized. For Catholics in the Northern Hemisphere, it is the darkest and coldest time of the year. Though the actual date of the Lord's Birth is not known, December 25 became the set date; for Orthodox Christians who observe the Julian calendar, however, Christ's Birth is celebrated on January 6.

Four special Masses are assigned for Christmas, each with its own prayers, and readings: the Vigil Mass, Mass during the Night, Mass at Dawn, and Mass during the Day. Any one of these Masses fulfills the Catholic obligation to attend Mass on the holy day.

Traditionally, the Mass at Midnight is the most special, with much pomp and ceremony exhibited. Usually a long procession takes place with a figurine of the Baby Jesus placed in a crèche (nativity set) in the crib, which is blessed with the Prayer of Blessing:

Prayer of Blessing

God of every nation and people, from the very beginning of creation
You have made manifest your love:
When our need for a Savior was great
You sent your Son to be born of the Virgin Mary.
To our lives he brings joy and peace, justice, mercy, and love.
Lord bless all who look upon this manger;
May it remind us of the humble Birth of Jesus,
And raise up our thoughts to him, who is God-with-us and Savior of all,
And who lives and reigns for ever and ever. Amen.

The formal Proclamation of the Birth of Christ is also recited at the Midnight Mass. The text, which comes from the Roman Martyrology, situates the Birth of Christ within the context of salvation history. It begins with the creation of the world and culminates with the Birth of the Savior during the Roman Empire. Note the connection with human history (Caesar Augustus, Greek Olympiad) and biblical events to help situate the Birth of Christ.

The Proclamation

Today, the twenty–fifth day of December,
unknown ages from the time when God created the heavens and the earth
and then formed man and woman in his own image.
Several thousand years after the flood,
when God made the rainbow shine forth
as a sign of the covenant.
Twenty–one centuries from the time of Abraham and Sarah;
thirteen centuries after Moses led the people of Israel
out of Egypt.
Eleven hundred years from the time of Ruth and the Judges;
one thousand years from the anointing of David as king;
in the sixty–fifth week according to the prophecy of Daniel.
In the one hundred and ninety–fourth Olympiad;
the seven hundred and fifty–second year from the foundation
of the city of Rome.
The forty–second year of the reign of Octavian Augustus;
the whole world being at peace,
Jesus Christ, eternal God and Son of the eternal Father,
desiring to sanctify the world by his most merciful coming,
being conceived by the Holy Spirit,
and nine months having passed since his conception,
was born in Bethlehem of Judea of the Virgin Mary.
Today is the nativity of our Lord Jesus Christ according to the flesh.

Christmas symbols

Many Christmas symbols that seem to have a secular appearance have religious significance, as well. The Christmas tree, which originated in Germany, developed from medieval religious plays. One such play was about the mystery of Paradise and the expulsion of the first parents, and the Garden of Eden was presented as an evergreen tree. The plays always ended on a hopeful note promising the Messiah, and this was portrayed by Christmas candles on the tree that reflect the deep mystery of Christ the Light of the world.

Other symbols of Christmas are holly, Christmas roses, and poinsettia. Holly berries symbolize Christ's blood and the holly represents the crown of thorns, which prefigures the Passion of Christ. The Christmas rose is a symbol of Jesus, who is the Rose of Sharon, and his Mother, the Mystical Rose. Poinsettia flowers are indigenous to Mexico, and the Mexicans have always seen the red leaves of this plant in relationship to the deep love for Jesus.

After Christmas: The celebration continues

Christmas Day doesn't end the Christmas season. The following feasts are celebrated after December 25:

- The **Octave of Christmas** starts December 26 with the Feast of St. Stephen, which commemorates the first martyr for Christ.

- December 27 is the **Feast of St. John the Beloved Disciple** and one of the four Gospel writers, known as Evangelists.

- December 28 is the **Commemoration of the Holy Innocents**, the babies that Herod had destroyed in Bethlehem in pursuit of killing the Christ child. Today they are patron saints of the aborted child and the pro-life movement.

- **Holy Family Sunday** is observed on the Sunday following Christmas. The liturgy remembers Jesus, Mary, and Joseph as the patrons of Christian families.

- January 1, in the secular sphere, marks the passing of the year. In the liturgical calendar it is the **Celebration of Mary as the Mother of God.**

- The **Feast of the Epiphany** in Rome and many European countries is observed on January 6, the 12th day of Christmas. In countries where Catholicism is not the state religion, the Epiphany is transferred to the Sunday after the Feast of Mary the Mother of God, January 1. Therefore, instead of being an immovable feast it changes from year to year.

  Epiphany means *manifestations*. It is the day that celebrates the arrival of the Three Wise Men or Three Kings, known as the Magi, who are called Caspar, Melchior, and Balthazar. The manifestation of the Savior to the

Magi is significant, because it's when God makes his appearance known to the world. The Magi brought gifts of gold, frankincense, and myrrh, which represent the threefold role of the Messiah: King, Prophet, and Priest. The magnificent cathedral in Cologne, Germany, is believed to hold the relics of the Magi.

✔ The **Solemnity of the Baptism of the Lord**, celebrated after the Epiphany, is the last major feast of the Christmas season. It commemorates the Baptism of Jesus in the Jordan River by John the Baptist and signals the next season of the Church. On this day, the Holy Father celebrates the Sacrament of Baptism in which he baptizes a select few in the Sistine Chapel.

Celebrating Christ Our Life: Lent, Holy Week, and Easter

Easter, the celebration of the Passion, Death, and Resurrection of the Lord, is the high point of the liturgical year. Lent, the 40-day period before Easter, is a time of preparation that includes increased prayer, penitence, almsgiving, and self-denial.

Churches themselves seem to undergo a sort of decorative fast as well. The absence of flowers and ornate decorations and the use of purple offer a certain austerity for the season of penance. The Gloria and Alleluia usually sung at Mass and the Liturgy of the Hours are omitted for Lent, and ostentatious displays of music are also skipped.

Closer to Holy Week — the week before Easter, beginning with Palm Sunday — the statuary and crucifixes may be covered as a reminder that parishioners are readying themselves for something much more important, the world to come, and that things of this world are transient. This season has also been known as the "Great Retreat," which commemorates the 40-day fast and retreat the Lord made before his passion.

Lent is a time to receive many graces by God. The faithful grow closer to the Lord through self denial (prayer, fasting, and almsgiving) and other Lenten disciplines. Examples include the Stations or Way of the Cross (usually celebrated in parish churches on Friday nights during Lent); praying the rosary, especially as a family in the home; having a poor man's meal of soup and bread one day a week; and giving up a favorite food, alcoholic beverages, movie theaters, dances, and so on.

In the Extraordinary form of the Roman Rite, the three weeks prior to Ash Wednesday contain a series of specially named Sundays in preparation for

Lent: Septuagesima (seventh), Sexagesima (sixth), and Quinquagesima (fifth). It was considered a time of preparation for the season of Lent that culminated on Carnival, the day before Lent actually commenced. In the Ordinary form of the Roman Rite this time of preparation has been dropped and replaced simply by the season of Ordinary Time.

Book I

**What Do
Catholics
Believe?**

Lent

In the Western Church (Latin Rite), Lent begins with the imposition (marking on the forehead) of ashes on Ash Wednesday, which takes place 46 days before Lent. Sundays aren't technically included in the 40 days of Lent as they are considered "Little Easters."

For Byzantine Catholics, Lent does not begin on Ash Wednesday but on Clean Monday, two days prior to Ash Wednesday. On the two preceding Sundays, Byzantines observed Cheesefare Sunday and Meatfare Sunday; the customary practice was to abstain from dairy products during Lent from Cheesefare Sunday to Easter, and from meat products from Meatfare Sunday to Easter. In addition to fasting, abstinence, prayer, confession, and almsgiving are common in the Byzantine Church.

Lent concludes with Easter, which occurs on a different Sunday from year to year.

The date of Easter is determined according to a lunar calendar; it is the first Sunday after the full moon after the spring equinox, believed to be the actual date of the Jewish feast of Passover. The Last Supper (Holy Thursday) happened during Passover.

The Fourth Sunday of Lent is known as *Laetare* Sunday. This is considered the halfway point of Lent. It gets its name from the opening lines of the antiphon of the Mass, "Laetare Jerusalem," meaning "Rejoice, O Jerusalem." Like Gaudete Sunday, the color of the vestments, antependium, chalice veil and burse, and tabernacle veil is rose. Rose symbolizes joy and hope in the midst of penance. Flowers are permitted on this Sunday, and exuberant music pieces are performed.

Some of the Sundays during Lent have been reconfigured. In the Extraordinary form of the Roman Rite, the Sunday before Palm Sunday is known as Passion Sunday, and it is on this day that the Passion is read and the statues in the church are veiled. In the Ordinary form of the Roman Rite, which most parishes follow, the reading of the Passion has been transferred to Palm Sunday (and no Passion Sunday is celebrated).

The following three major feasts may fall during Lent:

- ✔ February 22: The Chair of St. Peter
- ✔ March 19: Solemnity of St. Joseph
- ✔ March 25: The Annunciation of the Blessed Virgin Mary

Each of these feasts can be celebrated with solemnity unless they fall during Holy Week, which takes precedence over any other celebration. St. Joseph and Annunciation can be observed before or after Holy Week depending upon their proximity to it.

Ash Wednesday

On Ash Wednesday, ashes are placed on the foreheads of the faithful during the liturgy and are put in the sign of the cross, the symbol of salvation. The traditional prayer of imposition, from Genesis 3:19, is recited:

> Remember, O man, that you are dust, and unto dust you shall return.

Ashes are traditionally made from old palms from Palm Sunday of the previous year. Burnt, sifted, and blessed ashes become a sacramental and synonymous with the day. They're a symbol of penance and serve to remind the faithful that they have embarked on a 40-day religious journey of prayer, fasting, and almsgiving. All these things are done not only to improve the religious character of the person, but to prepare the soul for heaven in general.

Fasting and abstinence during Lent

Fasting has many meanings. When the doctor tells the patient to fast the night before a procedure, that means to eat and drink *nothing*. Some people have interpreted religious fasting as eating nothing at all or as only having bread and water once or twice during the day. But typically the modern Church defines fasting as the eating of two small meals along with one regular, full meal. The small meals if combined would not to equal the one normal meal.

Today the Catholic Church only demands that the faithful between ages of 18 and 59 fast a minimum of two days — Ash Wednesday and Good Friday. In previous eras, the entire season of Lent was a time of fasting (except on Sundays to honor the day of Resurrection). Some Eastern Catholics and Eastern Orthodox maintain the older tradition of fasting most if not all of Lent.

Along with fasting, another discipline of Lent is abstinence. Catholics are required to abstain from eating meat on Ash Wednesday and all Fridays of Lent. Meat is defined as the flesh of warm-blooded animals. This rule binds Catholics aged 14 and older.

Catholics should abstain from meat on *all* Fridays throughout the year. However, in his Apostolic Constitution *Paenitemini* of 1966, Pope Paul VI allowed the faithful to substitute another form of penance in place of abstaining from meat on Fridays outside of Lent.

The Stations of the Cross

The Stations (or Way) of the Cross are prayed publicly in church during Lent, usually on Wednesdays and Fridays. The celebrant is usually vested in a cassock, surplice, stole, and possibly a cope. The colors for the Stations are usually purple, red, or black.

Two acolytes typically accompany the celebrant, holding lit candles and a crucifer, as the celebrant walks through the church and the stations. The traditional hymn, "Stabat Mater" ("Sorrowful Mother"), is sung between each Station.

Holy Week

The Sixth Sunday of Lent is traditionally known as Palm Sunday of the Lord's Passion, or Palm Sunday, and it marks the beginning of Holy Week. The liturgy takes a dramatic turn and focuses more on the Passion of Christ and the immediate preparation for the Holy Triduum and Easter. Statues and crosses are still veiled on this day, although it is an optional custom. Once they're veiled, the statuary remains this way until the Vigil of Easter. The only statuary never veiled during the Lenten season are the Stations of the Cross.

In the Ordinary form of the Roman Rite, the Passion is read in a dialogue fashion, and a procession takes place at the beginning of Mass with newly blessed palm fronds. Palms are a commemoration of the triumphant entry of Jesus into Jerusalem directly before his Passion. The Byzantine Church substitutes pussy willow branches for the palms because they were more accessible in their native countries than palms.

Holy Week ends with the Easter Triduum, consisting of Holy Thursday, on which the Mass of the Lord's Supper is celebrated, Good Friday, on which the Passion of Our Lord is remembered, and Holy Saturday, on which the vigil of the Lord's resurrection held. This is the heart of the liturgical year and technically the end of the 40 days of Lent.

The Chrism Mass

The Chrism Mass, in which the sacred oils used in some of the Sacraments are blessed, occurs during Holy Week. Priests renew their commitment and surround the bishop during this Mass, as well. Traditionally, this Mass took place on the morning of Holy Thursday, but it's now most commonly observed on Holy Monday due to the distance many pastors must drive to the cathedral and their busy parish schedules during Holy Week.

Following are the three oils to be blessed:

- ✔ Oil of catechumen, used in the Sacrament of Baptism
- ✔ Oil of the infirmed, used in the Anointing of the Sick
- ✔ Chrism oil, used in the Sacraments of Baptism, Confirmation, and Holy Orders and to consecrate a church or altar

Enough oil must be blessed for every parish or religious institution in the diocese. It is a symbol of unity that the bishop blesses the oil and then disperses it amongst his parishes in the diocese.

In preparation of this Mass, parish oil stocks are usually collected and the remaining oil is burned. After being cleaned out, the parishes are ready to receive fresh stock of blessed oil. Each parish brings the new oils back to their churches, and usually they are solemnly presented at the evening Mass of the Lord's Supper on Holy Thursday. They are stored in an *ambry,* a special box, which is usually visible to the congregation.

Holy Wednesday

Holy Wednesday, sometimes called Spy Wednesday for Judas's paid betrayal of the Lord, is marked by the reading of Tenebrae. *Tenebrae,* the Latin word for *shadows,* is a set of readings from Psalms and the Book of Lamentations. The Tenebrae candle, a 15-candle candelabra, is lit. After each major section of the readings, two candles are extinguished, until the middle candle, the Christ candle, is all that remains. The Christ candle is then taken away from the sanctuary by a server, and a large crashing sound is made. The crashing sound is in remembrance of the earthquake that took place upon the Death of the Savior on Good Friday. Then the still-lit candle is brought back into church as a sign of hope in the Resurrection.

Holy Thursday

On Holy Thursday, the central part of the Mass of the Lord's Supper is the remembrance of the two Sacraments Christ instituted at the Last Supper — Eucharist and the Mass, and the Priesthood, the way Mass is perpetuated throughout the centuries. The sanctuary, although it can have some decorations and flowers, still remains simple. The color of vestments can be white or gold. The three oils blessed at the Chrism Mass are announced and brought into the church and placed in the ambry. The Gloria is sung and bells are rung, and from this point until the Easter Vigil the organ and bells remain silent. Liturgy of the Word begins and the Gospel is proclaimed. The homily focuses on the Institution of the Blessed Sacrament and the Holy Sacrifice of the Mass that was instituted at the Last Supper.

The traditional washing of the feet takes place after the homily, commemorating Jesus' washing his Apostles' feet at the Last Supper. It is a symbol of humility and service, both qualities to emulate in the priesthood.

The Mass continues in the usual fashion until the last prayer. In a section of the church or even a chapel, a temporary altar with a tabernacle is created. Suitable decoration of flowers and candles is arranged. The Blessed Sacrament that was prepared at this Mass and enough for the following day's service is carried throughout the church by a priest in vestments and with humeral veil. A traditional hymn called the "Pange Lingua," composed by St. Thomas Aquinas, is sung. Then the Blessed Sacrament is placed in the repository (a temporary tabernacle to hold the Holy Eucharist, consecrated hosts), and after proper incensation (ritual burning of incense in a brass container held by chains), there is time for private adoration.

Normally, the sanctuary is stripped bare of any of its refinements before the final prayer. The main tabernacle doors are left open. The sanctuary lamp is extinguished. Holy water fonts are emptied. These gestures symbolize the great Passion of the Lord and his Sacred Death. After midnight, if the repository is in the main church, it's usually dismantled and the Blessed Sacrament is placed in a secure area with a sole candle lit to note the Real Presence.

Good Friday

Good Friday commemorates the Passion of our Lord on the cross, and the vestments are red. This service usually takes place at 3 p.m., the hour at which Christ died, but for pastoral reasons the ceremony can take place in the evening. In addition, the Stations of the Cross can be prayed publicly before or after the service. Between noon and 3 p.m., the Church traditionally preaches and meditates on the Seven Last Words uttered by Christ on the Cross. Not literally only seven words, the Seven Last Words, or Sayings, of Jesus are:

1. Father forgive them, for they know not what they do.

2. Today you will be with me in paradise.

3. Behold your son; behold your mother.

4. My God, my God, why have you forsaken me?

5. I thirst.

6. It is finished.

7. Father, into your hands I commit my Spirit.

The Passion of the Lord, the Good Friday Service, is not a Mass. In fact, Good Friday is the only day of the year in which Mass cannot be celebrated. The service is divided into three parts:

1. The Liturgy of the Word is given, including the dialogue of the Passion, followed by a homily and chanting of the General Intercessions.

2. Veneration of the cross is done solemnly. The celebrant, flanked by candles, brings a veiled crucifix into the church and stops three times, each time chanting, "Behold the wood of the cross, on which hung the Savior of the World," and revealing a bit of the cross. When he reaches the sanctuary he venerates the whole crucifix.

3. The final part of the liturgy is Holy Communion. The altar is dressed with a simple cloth, upon which the candles from the procession of the crucifix are placed. A corporal, purificator, ablution cup, and sacramentary are all placed on the altar and the Blessed Sacrament is brought into the sanctuary. Our Father is prayed and Communion is distributed, and after the closing prayer all depart in silence. The simplicity of the liturgy expresses the deep-hearted sorrow every Christian has in reflecting that it is their sins that have crucified the Lord.

Easter Vigil

The Easter Vigil is by far the oldest and most respected of all the Church's liturgies. The church is decorated for Easter with candles, flowers, a white tabernacle veil, white antependium (full frontal altar cloth), and white vestments, but the church usually has all its lights off, and the congregation waits in anticipation in darkness. They are all given candles that will be lit during the liturgy.

The Easter Vigil has many components. First is the Service of Light. In the entrance of the church or in another suitable place where the faithful can gather, a fire is prepared, lit, and blessed. The Easter or paschal candle, usually 6 to 9 feet tall, is prepared for its blessing. It is a symbol of the Risen Jesus.

The candle is lit and the procession into the dark church commences. When inside the church, the candle is lowered three times and the people light their little vigil candles from the Easter candle.

The second part of the liturgy is the Easter Proclamation. The deacon or priest makes the proclamation in darkness except for the paschal candle and vigil candles that are lit. The chanted Easter Proclamation is a review of the history of our salvation culminating in Christ.

The third section of the liturgy is the Liturgy of the Word. Seven readings and psalms from the Old Testament, ranging from the Book of Genesis to the Book of the Prophet Ezekiel, can be done. At a minimum, readings 1, 3,

5, and 7 must be used, but the priest may choose to add readings 2, 4, and 6. After the last psalm, the choir and congregation sing the Gloria again, the church bells are rung, the lights are turned on, the candles used at Mass are lit from the Easter candle, and if the church has a statue of the Risen Christ, it is unveiled. Afterward is a reading from the New Testament, followed by the solemn chanting of the Alleluia, which was omitted during Lent, and a homily.

The fourth part is the celebration of the Sacraments of Baptism and Confirmation of people who are joining the Catholic Church. To prepare for these Sacraments, the Litany of Saints is sung, the priest blesses water as holy water, the candidates pledge their renunciation of sin and profession of faith, and then the actual Baptism takes place. Following the Sacrament of Baptism, the congregation gives a general renewal of the renunciation of sin and profession of faith. The priest then blesses all the people with the Easter water.

If any candidates have already been baptized in non-Catholic churches, before the celebration of the Sacrament of Confirmation they make their formal reception into Full Communion with the Church. The Confirmation concludes the celebration of Baptism and Confirmation. Mass continues as usual, but at the conclusion of Mass a double Alleluia is sung by the celebrant and congregation.

After the Easter Vigil, the Easter season has begun. For the entire Easter season the paschal candle remains in a prominent place, usually near the pulpit, and is lit for every liturgy. White is the color used for the season.

Easter

Easter is the primary solemnity of the Church. It is first celebrated in a special Octave; that is, a liturgical period of eight days. Each day of the Octave ranks the same as Easter Sunday — the highest level. Any saints' feast days that fall in the Octave are not commemorated at that time. Whitsunday, which is also known as Divine Mercy Sunday, ends the Octave, and the Easter season continues until Ascension Thursday. This feast falls 40 days after Easter and commemorates the Ascension of the Lord into heaven. In some dioceses this feast is celebrated on the Seventh Sunday of Easter. After the Octave, the paschal candle is moved to the area of the baptismal font and used only for the Sacraments of Baptism and Confirmation and Mass of Christian Burial.

Pentecost, 50 days after Easter, finishes this season, and it commemorates the descent of the Holy Spirit upon the Apostles and the Blessed Virgin Mary in the Upper Room. Pentecost is considered the birthday of the Church. The vestment color of red represents the fire of faith that the Holy Spirit imparts.

Pentecost is an appropriate day for adult celebration of the Sacrament of Confirmation, because the first Confirmations took place at Pentecost. The diocesan bishop typically visits the local parish during the calendar year to confirm boys and girls (anywhere from 2nd to 8th grades to high-school age), and he also likes to have all the adults of the diocese who need to be confirmed do so with him at the cathedral.

The Pentecost liturgy ends with the double Alleluia at the dismissal, and the Easter season ends. This service also usually ends *mystagogy,* the period of postinstruction for adults who received the Sacraments of Initiation at the Easter Vigil.

Filling in the Gaps with Ordinary Time

Ordinary Time is the period when the Church celebrates the mystery of Christ in all its aspects. Also called *ferial days* and *time throughout the year,* it is the part of the liturgical calendar between the major seasons. It follows Christmas and ends at Ash Wednesday, and then resumes after the Solemnity of Pentecost and concludes at the First Sunday of Advent. In the calendar of the Extraordinary form of the Roman Rite, Ordinary Time is called *the season after Epiphany* and *the season after Pentecost.* It is the longest liturgical season of the Church and can last up to 34 weeks of the year. The normal color for this season is green, the color of hope.

Following are some special feasts observed on Sundays in Ordinary Time.

- ✔ **Solemnity of the Blessed Trinity** is the Sunday directly after Pentecost. This feast focuses on the theological fact of the One God in Three Divine Persons. In the liturgy of the Blessed Trinity the special preface, prayers, and Scripture readings try to unfold this deep and most important element of doctrine in what it means to be a Christian.

- ✔ **Corpus Christi (Body of Christ) Sunday** follows the Solemnity of the Blessed Trinity. It was established in the 13th century to mark a Eucharistic miracle that took place in Bolsena, Italy. Today it is technically known as the Solemnity of the Most Holy Body and Blood of Christ, but most people still remember and refer to the older Latin designation of Corpus Christi.

- ✔ **Solemnity of Christ the King** is celebrated on the last Sunday of the liturgical year, which falls the week before the First Sunday of Advent. It was established by Pope Pius XI in 1925 to counteract the effects of nationalism and secularism. The feast highlights the culmination of all the Church's doctrines and beliefs in the Second Person of the Blessed Trinity, Jesus Christ. It also makes Catholics aware that they are made for the Kingdom of Heaven and not for this earth.

Coming not long after the Christmas season, the **Feast of the Presentation of the Lord** on February 2 is formally known as the **Purification of the Blessed Virgin Mary**. It commemorates the Jewish tradition of the presentation of firstborn male children in the Temple in Jerusalem 40 days after their birth by their mothers, who in turn received a blessing. Before the Second Vatican Council, this day marked the end of Christmas instead of the Baptism of the Lord, but now it falls in Ordinary Time. This day is also called *Candlemas Day* because it was also the day the candles to be used in Divine worship in the church were blessed.

On February 3, some of the candles that were used on the preceding day are used for the commemoration of St. Blaise. On **St. Blaise Day**, after Mass the priest holds two candles in a crisscross fashion under the chin of the faithful and makes a special blessing for deliverance of any maladies of the throat or other illnesses:

> **St. Blaise Prayer**
>
> Through the intercession of St. Blaise, bishop and martyr
> May God deliver you free from every ailment of the throat
> And from every other illness.
> In the name of the Father and of the Son And of the Holy Spirit, amen.

The following solemnities or feasts are celebrated instead of the regular liturgy when they fall on a Sunday in Ordinary Time:

- February 2: Solemnity of Presentation of the Lord

- June 24: Solemnity of the Birth of St. John the Baptist

- June 29: Solemnity of SS. Peter and Paul

- August 6: Feast of the Transfiguration of Christ

- August 15: Solemnity of the Assumption of the Blessed Virgin Mary into Heaven

- September 14: Exaltation of the Holy Cross

- November 1: Solemnity of All Saints

- November 2: Commemoration of All Souls

- November 9: Dedication of the Basilica of St. John Lateran (in honor of both St. John the Baptist and St. John the Evangelist)

In addition, the Feast of the Sacred Heart of Jesus falls 19 days after Pentecost on a Friday. This feast day is a culmination of devotion to the Sacred Humanity of the Lord that began in the 12th century. St. Margaret Mary Alacoque, a cloister Visitation Nun in France, received private revelations of the Sacred Heart of Jesus, raising interest in holding a Feast of the

Lord under this specific title, and in the 19th century Pope Pius IX instituted this feast day. In the 20th century Pope Pius XII elevated it liturgically to the highest rank of importance, without attaching an obligation to attend Mass.

Honoring Saints in the Sanctoral Cycle

The *Sanctoral cycle,* or Proper of the Saints, is the listing of the feast days of the saints commemorated in the Church, according to the Roman Missal. The feast days are given in sequence, from January through December.

Catholics worship God alone and only *venerate,* or honor, the saints. The theological distinction is as follows:

- ✔ *Latria* is worshipping God exclusively.
- ✔ *Dulia* is honoring the saints.
- ✔ *Hyperdulia* is highest honor given to the Virgin Mary.

In no way does the Catholics' love and respect for the saints supersede or even rival their love and adoration of God.

Feasts of the Virgin Mary

Mary is the premier saint because of her attributes, all of which are related to the fact that she is *Theotokos:* the Mother of God. She is mother in the sense that she gave the Jesus, the Second Person of the Blessed Trinity, his Sacred Humanity. Mary is celebrated for her part in the Incarnation, making flesh from the word of God.

The angel Gabriel announced to Mary that she was pregnant with Jesus, the Son of God (celebrated March 25 with the Feast of the Annunciation). Jesus is the Divine Person, but he has two natures, Divine and Human. In the sense that you cannot split the Divine Person, Mary is the Mother of God (celebrated January 1). As the Mother of God, she could not have been under the contagion of sin, even Original Sin, because God prepared a perfect receptacle to give humanity to the Redeemer (the fact of which is celebrated as the Immaculate Conception, December 1). If she did not have Original Sin, she therefore did not have to suffer the consequences (celebrated as Dormition or Assumption of Mary, August 15). And as Christ is our King, then Mary is Queen Mother (and is honored on the day of the Queenship of Mary, August 22).

Following are other feasts of Mary:

- ✔ January 8: Our Lady of Prompt Succor
- ✔ February 11: Our Lady of Lourdes
- ✔ May 13: Our Lady of Fatima
- ✔ May 24: Our Lady Help of Christians
- ✔ May 31: Visitation of Our Lady
- ✔ June 27: Our Lady of Perpetual Help
- ✔ July 16: Our Lady of Mount Carmel
- ✔ September 8: The Nativity of Mary
- ✔ September 12: The Most Holy Name of Mary
- ✔ September 15: Our Lady of Sorrows
- ✔ October 7: Our Lady of the Most Holy Rosary
- ✔ October 8: Our Lady of Good Remedy
- ✔ November 21: Presentation of Our Lady
- ✔ December 12: Our Lady of Guadalupe

Feasts of the saints

The saints are celebrated according their distinction in life. The Litany of Saints distinguishes angels, patriarchs, prophets, apostles, evangelists, martyrs, bishops, confessors, priests, monks, hermits, virgins, and widows. Pope John Paul II highlighted another class of saints, holy men and women who are secular but attained holiness according to their state in life.

Devotion to the saints was developed in early Christian times during the severe persecution by the Roman Empire and the many martyrs. Early Christians would visit martyrs' tombs and often celebrate Mass there, bringing the faithful closer to the saint. Many people would pray to God that they receive the same strength exhibited by these martyrs.

The names of the saints were collected into a list called the *Roman Martyrology*. In the 16th century, Pope Gregory XIII published the first edition of this list with his reform of the calendar, the Gregorian calendar. The current edition, published in 2001, contains over 7,000 officially canonized saints, beatified and blessed, and the current liturgical calendar of saints takes its form from this list.

Not every country celebrates every saint. Local saints of a certain geographical area may only appear on the local Episcopal Conference Calendar. However, some saints have universal appeal.

The saints are seen as bringing us closer to God by what they said and did and their prayers for the faithful. Christian men and women have distinguished themselves in their dedication and service to Christ and his Church in their lives, some to the point of shedding their blood (martyrs). When Catholics venerate a saint, they are acknowledging and proclaiming the victorious grace of Christ at work in the holy person's life.

Book II

Walking the Catholic Walk

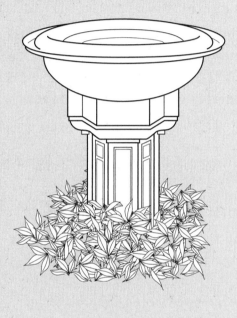

Contents at a Glance

Chapter 1

Worshipping Catholic Style

*O*ne of the most familiar and yet mysterious aspects of Catholicism is its way of worship, which is chock-full of ancient rites and rituals. Catholic worship is based on the principle that humankind stands between the worlds of matter and spirit. In other words, human beings belong to both the material world, which the body interacts with through the five senses, and the spiritual world, which the soul interacts with by divine grace.

So Catholic worship — from kneeling to burning incense to using symbols — centers on the dynamic relationship between the material and spiritual worlds. This chapter shows you what worshipping Catholic style is all about.

Three of the seven sacraments — Baptism, Holy Eucharist, and Confirmation — are classified as *Sacraments of Initiation.* Through Baptism, people enter (are *initiated* into) the Catholic Church. Through Holy Eucharist, which is also called *Holy Communion,* they express their unity with the Church — all her doctrines, laws, and practices. Through Confirmation, they're considered personally responsible for their faith.

The Eastern Catholic Church administers all three Sacraments of Initiation at the same time — at infancy. The Latin (Western) Catholic Church separates the three sacraments into completely different celebrations at different ages. Normally, *infants* are baptized, *children* receive Holy Eucharist at the age of reason (around 7 years of age), and *adolescents* or *young adults* are confirmed at ages ranging from 7 to 18 years old, but many Catholics are confirmed at around 14 years old. This chapter explains the Sacraments of Initiation and offers insight into the ceremonies of Baptism, First Communion, and Confirmation. (Book II, Chapter 2 explains the rest of the seven sacraments.)

Getting Your Body and Soul into the Act

Christians believe that a human being is made up of a body and a soul, both of which are created by God and are, therefore, good. In addition, because Jesus, the Son of God, had a human body and a human soul united in His divine nature, connecting the body and soul in worship is essential to the Catholic faith.

To capitalize on the dynamic relationship between body and soul — between the material world and the spiritual world — Catholic worship engages the entire human person in its rites and rituals.

✔ **Rites:** *Rites* are the necessary words and actions of a particular religious ceremony. For example, the Rite of Baptism requires that water be poured over the head (or that the person be immersed in water) while a priest says, "I baptize you in the name of the Father and of the Son and of the Holy Spirit." Each of the seven sacraments has its own proper rite.

On a broader scale, *rite* also refers to the four main Liturgical traditions (Roman, Antiochian, Alexandrian, and Byzantine or Constantinopolitan, which originated in the four patriachates) in which the Holy Eucharist is celebrated.

✔ **Rituals:** *Rituals* are the official books that contain the essential words and actions of particular religious ceremonies. For example, the Roman Ritual is the book that priests and deacons use when they celebrate rites. It tells them what materials to use, what sequence of events to follow, and what words and actions to say when celebrating rites. The Roman Ritual used to be one volume, but it's now printed in individual volumes for each sacrament — one volume for performing weddings, one for funerals, one for Baptisms, and so on.

During a Catholic Mass, the priest and the congregation engage their bodies by speaking aloud and by sitting, standing, or kneeling. They also perceive tangible symbols that exist outside the body — the water used for baptizing, for example, or the oil used for anointing — through one or more of the five senses. These outward symbols and ritual actions remind the faithful of the internal action of invisible divine grace entering the human soul.

Understanding Some Symbols and Gestures

Kneeling and making the sign of the cross, hanging crosses depicting a crucified Jesus, and sprinkling holy water on this and that are telltale Catholic practices. In this section, you find the meanings behind these symbols and gestures as they relate to the body and soul.

The sign of the cross

The most common Catholic gesture is the sign of the cross. Latin (Western) Catholics make the sign of the cross by using their right hand to touch the forehead, then the middle of the breast, then the left shoulder, and finally the right shoulder. As they make this gesture, they say, "In the name of the Father and of the Son and of the Holy Spirit, Amen." This one complete gesture makes a cross. Eastern Catholics say the same thing as they make a similar sign of the cross; the only difference is that they go to the right shoulder first and then to the left.

No matter which shoulder Catholics touch first, the sign of the cross has the same meaning. It symbolically reaffirms two essential Christian doctrines: The Holy Trinity — Father, Son, and Holy Spirit — and humankind's salvation through the cross of Christ.

The genuflection

Another telltale sign of Catholic worship is *genuflection,* which is the act of touching the right knee to the floor while bending the left knee, and making the sign of the cross at the same time.

Catholics genuflect only in front of the Holy Eucharist. Why? Because the Holy Eucharist *is* the real body and blood of Jesus and Catholics want to show the ultimate form of respect by genuflecting or kneeling before Him. Catholic churches keep the Holy Eucharist in a large metal container or vault called a *tabernacle,* or sometimes they display the Eucharist behind glass in a gold container called a *monstrance.*

The crucifix

The *crucifix,* a cross bearing an image of Jesus being crucified, is a typical Catholic symbol. Protestant Christians usually have crosses with no *corpus* (that's Latin for *body*) of Jesus attached. The graphic symbol of the crucifix became predominant in the Western Church to remind Catholics that Jesus was true man as well as true God and that His suffering and death were very real and painful. The crucifix calls attention to the high price paid for human-kind's sins and inspires believers to repent of their sins and be grateful for the salvation that Jesus offered through His death on the cross. The *rubrics* (liturgical laws for celebrating Mass) require a crucifix to be visible to the people during divine worship. The faithful are encouraged to have a crucifix in their homes, and many wear a small one around their neck to remind them of the supreme love Christ showed in dying for our sins.

Holy water

Holy water, which is water blessed by a priest, bishop, or deacon, is a *sacramental,* or a religious object or action that the Catholic Church — not Jesus — created. Helpful and beneficial but totally optional, sacramentals are subordinate to the seven sacraments, which are necessary for believers to live a life made holy by the gift of grace from God. In other words, sacra-ments give grace no matter what the spiritual state of the recipient. For example, a groom who is in the state of mortal sin when he gets married (the Sacrament of Matrimony) is still validly married. On the other hand, a groom who has a mortal sin on his soul gets no grace from the blessing (a sacra-mental) the priest gives to the newly married couple after they pronounce their vows.

Think of the sacraments as food for the soul and sacramentals as supplemen-tal vitamins.

Holy water is the most widely used sacramental. Non-Catholics may think of holy water as the stuff that burned the face of the possessed 12-year-old in the movie *The Exorcist.* Although the Church does use holy water to drive out demons on rare occasions, it more regularly uses holy water to *sanctify* (bless) objects, to protect people from supernatural evil, and to serve as a symbolic reminder of Baptism.

When entering or leaving a church, Catholics dip their right hand, usually with two fingers, into a *font,* a cup of holy water that's on a wall near the doors of the church. Then they make the sign of the cross, wetting their forehead, breast, and shoulders. In doing so, they visibly remind themselves that they're entering the House of God. Plus, blessing with holy water is good preparation for worship.

Catholics also take small quantities of holy water home with them to fill fonts on their walls. They then bless themselves whenever leaving home, because the home is the *domestic Church* for Catholics. Home is where the family lives, and it's from the family that the Church grows and lives. After all, priests, deacons, and bishops must come from families, and churches can't grow without the families who attend church and support them.

At some Masses, the priest sprinkles holy water on the congregation in place of the Penitential Rite. (See Book III, Chapter 2 for what's what at the Mass.) And anytime a priest or deacon blesses a religious article, such as rosary beads, a statue, or a medal of one of the saints, he sprinkles holy water on the object after saying the prayers of blessing. The holy water reminds the owner that the object is now reserved for sacred use — to enhance prayer life, for example — and shouldn't be used for profane (nonreligious) use. This is why the blessed cup, called a *chalice,* that the priest uses at Mass to hold the wine that he consecrates can't be used for any other purpose, like to drink wine or juice at the dinner table.

In case you're wondering, a priest, bishop, or deacon blesses holy water when they celebrate in the church, particularly at the Easter Vigil (or Holy Saturday night), which takes place the evening before Easter Sunday. They can also bless holy water anytime during the year when the quantity runs out or evaporates.

Book II

Walking the Catholic Walk

Sensing God

Catholic worship incorporates all five senses — sight, touch, smell, hearing, and taste. Catholics believe that they can't see, feel, smell, hear, or taste the internal action of divine grace entering the human soul. But because the senses can perceive external symbols, Catholics can use many external symbols for the human body to perceive while the soul receives the divine grace.

Through sight

If you've been blessed with a good set of eyes, you gather more information by the sense of sight than any other. From the words you read to the pictures and images you look at, the ability to see impacts your perception of the world significantly.

Depicting God

Catholicism teaches that God the Father has no human body. He's pure spirit and totally invisible. But because of the importance of sight, people have felt the need to represent God visually somehow — to create a visible symbol of the invisible God. One problem with representing visible symbols of God is that the First Commandment forbids *graven images,* which are objects of worship, or idols.

The pagans, such as the ancient Babylonians, Egyptians, Persians, Greeks, and Romans, had many gods and goddesses, which they represented in stone or metal and worshipped. The Hebrew people, on the other hand, were one of the few ancient cultures to have a *monotheistic* religion (*mono* meaning *one* and *theos* meaning *god*). Although their pagan counterparts had plenty of idols to worship, the Hebrews were forbidden from making an image or idol of God.

From Abraham until Moses, no one even knew the name *God*. He was the *nameless* or *ineffable One*. This invisible, imageless deity was different from pagan gods because he had no name. According to the ancient way of thinking, after a person knew the name of the god — or of the evil spirit or demon, for that matter — he could control it somehow. So invoking the name and having an image of the god gave the believer some influence over that being. But the one true God had no name and couldn't be depicted by any image.

After paganism died out in Western culture and the Roman Empire embraced Christianity, the danger of distorting the nature of the one true God evaporated. After God the Son took on a human nature in the person of Jesus, who had a real and true human body, fear about symbolically representing God the Father or God the Holy Spirit in Christian art disappeared.

Today, you can see God the Father, Jesus, and the Holy Spirit portrayed in paintings on walls and canvases, as well as in stained glass. God is most often represented in visible form as follows:

- ✔ *God the Father* is usually depicted as an old man with a long flowing beard, an image that came from the early Europeans. In modern and contemporary Christian art, however, artists also represent God the Father with Asian or African features, for example. The modern reasoning is that if God is a spirit, why portray Him just as a Caucasian man?

- ✔ *Jesus (God the Son)* had a face and a body, but with no pictures of Him to draw from, artists have used their own creativity to depict the Savior — often as a young man with a full beard. Many works of art have been modeled on the image of the Shroud of Turin, which is considered by many to be the actual burial cloth of Jesus and has a miraculous image of His face and body on it.

- ✔ *God the Holy Spirit* is almost always portrayed as a dove because the Bible speaks of a dove descending on Jesus at His baptism by John the Baptist.

Conveying meaning through colors and symbols

The Catholic Church uses symbols to show us the connection of the material and spiritual worlds because human beings are both body and soul. One of the most well-known symbols used in the Catholic Church is the stained-glass window. Some of the most popular churches, like St. Patrick's Cathedral in

New York City and the Cathedral of Notre Dame in Paris (not the football shrine), contain hundreds of magnificent stained-glass windows full of color, light, and symbolism.

Originally, churches used stained-glass windows to teach the Catholic faith to illiterate peasants. Unable to read, these peasants could look at the pictures and symbols depicted in the stained glass and learn all about salvation history from biblical stories to Church history to the seven sacraments.

You see another important symbol in the priest's garb. Depending on the occasion, priests and deacons wear different-colored liturgical *vestments* (garments for worship services) for Mass — green, white, red, purple, black, rose, or gold. Vestments often have symbols on them, such as a cross; the first and last letters of the Greek alphabet (the *alpha* and *omega*), which represent Jesus, who is the beginning and the end; and the letter *M* for Mary, the Mother of Jesus.

Marble altars and floors often include engraved symbols, such as

- **Two keys:** This image symbols St. Peter and comes from the Gospel of Matthew, which describes Jesus entrusting the keys of the kingdom to Peter.
- **An eagle:** This symbol represents St. John the Evangelist.
- **A pelican pecking her own heart to feed her young with her blood:** This image symbolizes Christ, who feeds Catholics with His blood in Holy Communion.

In addition, Catholic architecture and art use visual symbols to enhance the faith. For example, the gothic cathedrals spiral up toward heaven to remind the faithful to remember their destiny in the next world — and not to get too comfortable in this earthly one. To literally see the beauty of Catholic worship, you can visit the Shrine of the Most Blessed Sacrament in Hanceville, Alabama. The marble, the gold, the stained glass, the light, the altar, the tabernacle, and especially the 7-foot-tall monstrance surrounded by gold and jewels all attract the human eye and inspire the human soul to aspire to heaven. These symbols, which are attractive to the five senses, also help the soul transcend the material world into the spiritual realm.

Through touch

Just as no one has seen God because He's invisible, no one has touched Him either. Yet everyone knows how vital the sense of touch is to human beings from the moment they're born. Being held by a parent and feeling tender, loving hands offers a sense of security.

Like the sense of sight, the sense of touch is also an important part of Catholic worship. For instance, each of the following sacraments incorporates the sense of touch in some way:

- ✔ **Baptism:** You literally feel the water that the priest pours over your head.

- ✔ **Anointing of the Sick:** You feel the oil that the priest applies to your forehead and the palms of your hands.

- ✔ **Matrimony:** The bride and groom join right hands before pronouncing their vows.

- ✔ **Confirmation:** You feel the chrism oil being put on your forehead.

- ✔ **Holy Orders:** Men being ordained feel the two hands of the bishop touching the top of their heads.

Another way that Catholics embrace the sense of touch in prayer is by saying the Rosary. They can feel the beads as they pray the Hail Marys and meditate on the mysteries of Jesus and Mary. Catholics also encounter the sense of touch on Ash Wednesday when they feel the ashes of burnt palms (from last year's Palm Sunday) being spread on their foreheads in the sign of the cross. On the Feast of St. Blaise, which is February 3, Catholics feel two crossed candles on their throats when the priest blesses them. Plus, holy water fonts are at every entrance and exit of Catholic churches, so believers can touch the holy water with their right hands and bless themselves.

Through smell

The sense of smell is as much a part of human beings as the other four senses, so Catholic worship also appeals to this function of the body.

Burning incense

The most obvious appeal to the nose in Catholic worship involves burning *incense,* which is the powder or crystalline form you get when you dry the aromatic resins of certain trees. When you place incense on burning charcoal, it produces a visible smoke and a recognizable aroma that fills the church. The smoke represents prayers going up to heaven, and the sweet aroma reminds people of the sweetness of God's divine mercy.

Incense has been a part of worship since biblical times. In the Old Testament, Psalm 141 speaks of prayers rising up to heaven "as incense." God commanded Moses to burn incense on the altar before the Ark of the Covenant, which held the Ten Commandments.

On a more practical level, churches burned incense in the Middle Ages when they didn't have decent air circulation and parishioners didn't wear deodorant. On a hot summer Sunday, the smell in the church became quite potent unless the clergy burnt plenty of incense and thoroughly swung it around the entire congregation. Yep, in pre-air-freshener days, incense was the best thing going. Keep in mind, though, that this practical application of incense didn't take away from its symbolic significance.

Incense remains an integral part of Catholic worship today. Eastern Orthodox Catholics use incense every day and every week during liturgical worship. Latin (Western) Catholics may use it on special holy days (like Easter and Christmas), maybe once a week at Sunday Mass, and almost always at Catholic funerals.

Note: At funerals, Catholics burn incense at the coffin as well as the altar because the body was a temple of the Holy Spirit when the soul lived inside. Jesus will reunite the body with its soul at the resurrection of the dead.

Book II

Walking the Catholic Walk

Anointing with oil

Another familiar smell to Catholics is *chrism oil,* sometimes called *oil of chrism.* Chrism is olive oil that the local diocesan bishop has blessed. Catholic worship uses this oil to consecrate bishops, anoint the hands of priests, confirm Catholics, baptize Catholics, bless bells, and consecrate altars and churches. The strong but pleasant odor comes from *balsam,* an aromatic perfume that's added to the oil.

The local bishop blesses three oils during Holy Week (the week before Easter) at a special Mass called the *Chrism Mass,* or *Mass of the Oils.* At this special Mass, the bishop blesses Chrism Oil, the Oil of the Sick, and the Oil of Catechumens. The bishop blesses all three olive oils in multigallon containers. Then he distributes the oil to the priests and deacons of the diocese. Chrism oil is the only one that has balsam added to it.

Through sound

Catholics use their sense of hearing in worship by listening to the Word of God read aloud. Catholics hear the words of the Bible read aloud at every Catholic Mass, whether it's Sunday or daily Mass. Readings come only from the Bible because Catholics believe that no other poetry or prose can replace the inspired Word of God. The readings come from both the Old and New Testaments. After the Old Testament reading and before the New Testament Epistle reading, the congregation normally sings or recites a Psalm. Then, after the Epistle reading, the priest or deacon reads a passage from one of the four Gospels. In addition, many of the hymns Catholics sing throughout the Mass are based on scriptural citations.

Although the words of Scripture are the primary way that Catholic worship incorporates the sense of hearing, the prayers of the priest and congregation are also important, so the congregation pays attention to these prayers and responds at the appropriate times. The *homily,* or sermon, that the priest, deacon, or bishop gives immediately after the Gospel is another important sense-of-sound part of the Catholic Mass because it offers the congregation an application of the Gospel.

The Catholic Church also uses plenty of music, especially organ music, choirs, and *Gregorian chant* (Latin chant named after Pope St. Gregory the Great, who was pope from A.D. 590–604). The beautiful sounds of the pipe organ and the delicate tones of the human voice are also reminders of God that the congregation can physically hear.

Through taste

Catholicism even employs the sense of taste in its worship at Communion time. The Holy Eucharist is the most important, sacred, and pivotal aspect of Catholic worship because it is when the bread and wine become the real, true, and substantial body and blood, soul and divinity of Christ. The appearance of the bread and wine appeals to and is perceived by the sense of taste.

When it's time for Communion, believers receive the Holy Eucharist, which still tastes like unleavened bread and grape wine. (The Latin Church uses unleavened bread, but the Eastern Church uses leavened bread.) The believers' sense of taste doesn't perceive the change of substance, hence the term *transubstantiation* (see Book II, Chapter 3), from bread and wine into the body and blood of Christ — which is definitely a good thing because if the Holy Eucharist tasted like flesh and blood, no one would take it.

The appearances of the bread and wine during Communion are sometimes called the *accidents,* but they have nothing to do with mishaps or car crashes. Catholic theology uses the philosophical term *accident* to distinguish outward appearances from the invisible but underlying essence.

Come On In — The Water's Fine

Baptism is the first of the seven sacraments. It's the one sacrament that all Christian denominations share in common, even though each faith community baptizes at different ages and some only in one way, such as immersion. A few Christian denominations only baptize by completely immersing or dunking the person head to toe in the water, but most allow immersion or infusion such as the pouring of water over the head of the new Christian. Like the Sacrament of Confirmation and the Sacrament of Holy Orders (see book II, Chapter 2), you're baptized only once. These three sacraments confer an indelible mark on the soul, which can never be repeated and is never removed. So, no one can ever be unbaptized or re-baptized.

In the eyes of the Catholic Church, any Baptism that uses water and the invocation of the Holy Trinity, as well as the intention to *do* what the Church *does* — that is, "I baptize you in the name of the Father and of the Son and of the Holy Spirit" — is a valid sacrament. So Catholicism regards Episcopalian, Anglican, Lutheran, Methodist, Presbyterian, Baptist, United Church of Christ, Assembly of God, Church of the Nazarene, Church of the Brethren, Amish, Church of God, Disciples of Christ, Adventist, and Evangelical Baptisms to be valid. And if a follower of one of these Christian churches wants to become Catholic, he doesn't have to be re-baptized.

That said, Catholicism doubts the Baptisms in the following faith communities to be a valid sacrament: Christian Scientists, Quakers, Salvation Army, Jehovah's Witnesses, Unitarians/Universalists, Christadelphians, and Mormons (Church of Jesus Christ of Latter Day Saints). The reason has nothing to do with the religions themselves or their members, because all espouse a true love of God and neighbor. The reason merely has to do with what Catholicism considers to be a valid sacrament.

Book II

Walking the Catholic Walk

Becoming Christ's kith and kin

Your first birth from your mother's womb made you a member of the family established by your parents and their respective families. You have an immediate family of parents and siblings and an extended family of grandparents, aunts, uncles, cousins, in-laws, and such.

Just as natural birth ushers people into blood and marriage relationships, Baptism — as a supernatural birth — establishes ties to spiritual families. By being baptized, *born again* of water and the Spirit, new Christians become children of God by adoption. In other words, they're adopted into the family of God; they can't be born into that family because they're human and God is divine. Jesus Christ, God and man, divine and yet human, becomes their brother. Mary, the Mother of Jesus, becomes their spiritual mother because siblings share a relationship with the parents. If Jesus is their brother by adoption, then His mother, Mary, becomes their mother by adoption.

Baptism also connects the new Catholic to the Church. The title *Father* is given to the priest because he typically does the baptizing. The Holy *Mother* Church, the Catholic Church, gives birth to the new Christian from the spiritual womb of the baptismal font. The water of the baptismal font has been likened to the waters that surround the baby in the womb — thus the reason it's called the *spiritual womb*. A person is reborn through the waters of Baptism with the assistance of the priest doing the baptizing. It's only an analogy, but it has endured for 2,000 years.

At the moment of Baptism, a new Catholic joins the local parish and diocese as well. The *parish* is the faith community of a neighborhood, composed of Catholic families in that area; the *diocese* is the faith family of many parish communities in one geographic region of the state. So, if you were baptized at Notre-Dame de Paris in France, for example, you'd be a member of the Roman Catholic Church at large, a member of the Archdiocese of Paris, and a member of the Notre-Dame Cathedral Parish, all at the same time.

Washing away original sin

More than making connections and relationships, Baptism also washes away *original sin,* the sin of the original parents of the whole human race: Adam and Eve. The Book of Genesis (1:26–27) says that God created man in his own image and likeness, male and female. The first man was called Adam, and the first woman, the wife of Adam, was called Eve. They were the prototype man and woman, and their sin affected all men and women after them. And the Bible says that their sin was disobedience.

Biology has shown that you inherit many physical characteristics from your natural parents — eye and hair color, facial features, body shape, and so on. Good and bad traits and some diseases are handed down from generation to generation. In the same way, original sin is transmitted from generation to generation by birth.

Original sin doesn't mean that a baby in the womb somehow commits a sin before being born. If Junior kicks too much inside, he's not being a bad boy, for example. Mom just may have had too much spicy Italian sausage. To the Catholic Church, original sin isn't a personal sin of the unborn but a sin transmitted from generation to generation by birth. All men and women are born with original sin, and only Baptism can wash it away.

Catholicism sees original sin differently from *actual sin,* which is what a rational person does when she consciously, deliberately, and willingly disobeys God. Original sin is the natural inclination to sin.

Think of it this way: Nobody is born with polio, measles, or chicken pox, but folks aren't born with any immunity to these diseases, either. A baby needs to be vaccinated so the human body can produce its own antibodies and fight these diseases when it's exposed to them. Likewise, on the spiritual level, human beings are born with a weakened resistance to temptation and sin, and this condition is part of original sin.

Baptism is to original sin what the polio vaccination is to the polio virus. Baptism restores what should have been — a spiritual resistance to sin and temptation. The first sin of the first parents, Adam and Eve, wounded human nature, and everyone inherited that wounded nature from them. Baptism washes it away.

In addition to getting rid of original sin, Baptism also imparts or infuses *sanctifying grace,* a special free gift from God. Sanctifying grace makes the new Christian a child of God and applies the merits of Jesus Christ, His suffering and death for sins, to the new Christian personally because the person being baptized is mentioned by name. Catholicism believes that sanctifying grace allows human beings to enter heaven. It justifies them in the eyes of God by uniting them with the Savior and Redeemer, Jesus Christ. Without sanctifying grace, one can't stand before the utter holiness of God who is sanctity personified. Normally, you receive this special grace only through the sacraments, but God does provide some means to make sure all men and women have the potential and possibility of salvation (that is, baptism by blood or baptism of desire).

Book II

Walking the Catholic Walk

Baptizing with water

The most common form of Baptism is by water (you discover what blood and desire have to do with Baptism later in this section). The Gospels say that one must be born again of water and the Holy Spirit (John 3:5). The early Christians and their successors have been baptizing with water for almost two millennia but with some slight differences:

- ✔ **Immersion:** Some Christian denominations fully immerse a person in water up to three times while saying the invocation of the Holy Trinity, also known as the *Trinitarian formula,* "I baptize you in the name of the Father and of the Son and of the Holy Spirit."

- ✔ **Aspersion:** Other Christians sprinkle water on the forehead of the one being baptized and then invoke the Trinitarian formula.

- ✔ **Infusion:** Catholics (mostly Latin) baptize by pouring water over the head of the one being baptized while the Trinitarian formula is pronounced.

All three methods use water and the invocation of the Holy Trinity. Water (good old H_2O) is the only liquid that can be used for this form of Baptism.

(The priest or bishop can't use oil, milk, or any other liquid.) Immersion or infusion is preferred to aspersion.

Many people ask why Catholics baptize infants whereas other Christians wait until the individual is old enough to decide for himself whether he wants to be baptized. Fair question. Think of it this way:

- ✔ At your birth, you were given a name by your parents. You had no choice in the matter. Once you're 18 and a legal adult, you can change your name, but from the day you are born, you need an identity. Imagine if your mom and dad waited until you were old enough to choose your own name. Not practical, is it? Similarly, Baptism defines you as a child of God. Your identity as a Christian is established at baptism.

- ✔ Where you're born and/or the nationality of your parents determines your citizenship; it isn't deferred until you can decide for yourself. Citizens have rights and obligations. Likewise, Baptism makes you a member of the family of faith called the Church. As a member, you benefit from your rights from day one.

In the past, infant mortality was so high that many babies didn't survive birth or early childhood, so Baptism as an infant insured that their souls wouldn't be denied heaven. In ancient times, there was no firm teaching on baptism of desire. Medieval theologians developed a theory of Limbo being a place where unbaptized infants went. Later came a fuller and expanded understanding of the baptism of desire and the universal salvific will of God (that all men and women be given the possibility of salvation). Today, with modern medicine and progress, it's not the fear of death but rather the hope for great potential and wonderful possibilities that encourages Catholic parents to baptize their children. It gives them an identity and a spiritual beginning. Anyway, the New Testament affirms that *entire households* were baptized, which meant the parents and children as well. So infant Baptisms have occurred from the very beginning.

Recognizing the role of sponsors or godparents

Every child or adult about to be baptized must have a sponsor unless he or she is in danger of death. The sponsors in Baptism have traditionally been called *godparents*. The minimum requirement is one sponsor, but usually when infants are baptized, they get two, one of each gender.

Canon law permits only one godparent of each gender — a godmother and godfather. For an adult or a child being baptized, these sponsors

- ✔ Can't be the parents of the one being baptized
- ✔ Must be at least 16 years old

  ✔ Must be practicing Catholics who go to Mass every week, are not invalidly married, and live a good Christian life

  ✔ Must be already confirmed

If someone can't find two practicing Catholics to be the godfather and godmother, then one sponsor can be Catholic and the other a Christian witness if that person is a baptized Protestant Christian in good standing.

Being a godparent carries with it no legal right or ecclesiastical authority to the custody of the children. Prior to the medical advances of the 20th century, when people died at an earlier age because of illness, godparents were the practical choice to raise a child if both parents died before the son or daughter grew up. Babies had two godparents in case one would not be able to fulfill the job of raising the child. Nowadays, however, custody is a strictly legal matter that parents must decide with their attorney. Being a godparent means more than giving Christmas and birthday gifts every year. It means actively being a good Christian witness and example, a role model, and a supporter by regularly and faithfully practicing the religion.

Book II

Walking the Catholic Walk

What goes on at a Baptism?

Baptisms in the Catholic Church usually take place on Sundays, during the parish Mass or in the early afternoon after all the Masses are over. It all depends on the parish, the pastor, and the parents. Adults who were never baptized are an exception to this rule; they're highly encouraged to be baptized with other adults on Holy Saturday evening, during a service known as the Easter Vigil, because it's held on the night before Easter Sunday. Children, however, are baptized once a month or every Sunday, depending on the diocese and parish.

The person being baptized is asked to dress in white. Some parishes put a small white garment on the child, especially if she isn't already dressed in white. When adults are baptized, they typically put on a full-length white gown known as an *alb,* from the Latin word for *white.*

The white garment symbolizes the white garments that Jesus wore when he was placed in the tomb after his death on Good Friday. When the women and disciples returned on Easter day, they found the tomb empty except for the white robes. So it represents the promise of the Resurrection, made at Baptism. The promise is that the baptized body will one day die, like Christ's did, but it'll be raised from the dead someday by Christ. White also symbolizes purity of faith and cleansing.

The priest or deacon is usually the minister of Baptism, but anyone can baptize in an emergency, such as in a hospital or whenever someone's life is in danger. Here are the steps that occur during both infant and adult Baptism:

1. **During the Baptism of an infant, the priest or deacon asks the parents, "What name do you give your child?"**

   He doesn't ask this question because he's too senile to remember or too blind to read the child's name on the card in front of him, but because that person becomes a child of God by name and Jesus becomes her brother by name as soon as the person is baptized. The parents respond aloud, ideally with a Christian name, such as one of the saints or heroes of the Bible.

   In adult baptism, skip this step.

2. **The priest or deacon asks, "What do you ask of God's church for your child?"**

   The parents respond, "Baptism." If an adult is being baptized, she answers the same.

3. **In infant baptism, the priest or deacon asks the parents and the godparents whether they're willing and able to fulfill their duties to bring up this child in the Christian faith.**

4. **As a symbolic gesture, the priest or deacon makes the sign of the cross with his thumb gently on the forehead of the child or adult.**

   This sign is made to show that the cross of Christ has saved her.

   The parents and godparents do the same.

5. **A particular passage from the Bible is read, usually from the New Testament, where Baptism is mentioned or alluded to.**

6. **After some other prayers, the first anointing takes place.**

   The infant's white garb is pulled slightly beneath the neck so the priest or deacon can smear a little *Oil of Catechumens* (blessed olive oil) on the infant's neck with his thumb. The same anointing takes place for an adult.

   The oil symbolizes that the person, born into the world, is now being set apart from the world by the anointing. She is soon to be baptized and therefore belongs not to the world but to God and heaven.

7. **The priest or deacon blesses the water of Baptism.**

   The prayer recalls how water has played an important role in salvation history as recorded throughout the Bible: It represents a sign of new life, the washing of sin, deliverance from slavery, and a new beginning.

8. The first part of the baptismal promises are made: renunciation of evil.

Because an infant can't speak for herself, mom, dad, and the godparents answer for her. The priest or deacon asks, "Do you renounce Satan? And all his works? And all his empty promises?" If things go well, everyone says "I do." If not, you have to check for devil worshippers among the crowd. Later, probably when she's 14 years old, the child answers those same questions on her own before the bishop. Adults who are being baptized answer for themselves.

9. The second part of baptismal promises follows, with the *Apostles' Creed* put in question form: "Do you believe in God, the Father Almighty, Creator of heaven and earth?"

Again, the hoped-for response is "I do." Then the other two persons of the Trinity are mentioned: "Do you believe in Jesus Christ. . . ?" and "Do you believe in the Holy Spirit. . . ?" And, once again, parents and godparents answer for infants; adults answer for themselves.

10. The actual Baptism takes place.

In infant Baptism, the immediate family gathers around the baptismal font (see Figure 1-1), and the child is held over the basin while the priest or deacon pours water three times over the child's head and says his first and middle name, and then, "I baptize you in the name of the Father and of the Son and of the Holy Spirit. Amen." Usually, the baby cries, because the water tends to be a little cool. (In the Eastern Catholic Church, the formula is: "The servant of God, [name], is baptized in the name of the Father, and of the Son, and of the Holy Spirit." Confirmation (Chrismation) and Holy Communion are also given at the ceremony when one is baptized in the Eastern Church.)

In adult baptism, the catechumen holds her head over the basin, and the priest pours water over her head; or, if baptized by immersion, she enters the pool, and the priest dips her head into the water three times.

11. The priest or deacon anoints the top of the new Christian's head with chrism oil.

The anointing symbolizes that the newly baptized Christian is now exactly that — a *Christ*ian. The word *Christ* means *anointed,* and a *Christian* is someone who's anointed in Jesus Christ. This anointing also means the person is now to share in the three-fold mission of Christ — to sanctify, proclaim, and give Christian leadership and example to the world. Now, a white garment is usually presented to the newly baptized.

12. A Baptismal candle is lit from the burning Easter Candle, which is present throughout the ceremony.

It symbolizes that the new Christian is a light to the world.

13. The Our Father is said and a blessing is given for mom, dad, and the family, and everyone celebrates.

Book II

Walking the Catholic Walk

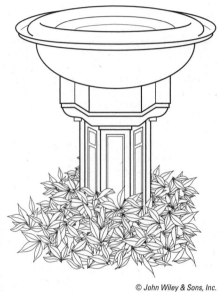

Figure 1-1:
A baptismal
font.

If you're invited to a Baptism

- ✔ You don't need to be Catholic or even a Christian to attend. Your presence is a sign of love, support, and friendship for the parents and for the baptized.
- ✔ If you're a Christian, you may want to join in the renewal of baptismal promises when they're asked.

Receiving the sacrament of Baptism in other ways

Every person must be baptized to receive salvation. Baptism by water is probably what you think of when you imagine Baptism, but people can still receive the sacrament of Baptism sans the water, white garment, and priest. Baptism by blood and by desire are two valid forms of Baptism under certain circumstances.

Shedding blood for Christ

From A.D. 60 to the end of the third century, the Romans violently persecuted the early Christian Church. Christianity wasn't even legal until after Emperor Constantine's Edict of Milan in A.D. 313. During those first 300 years of Roman persecution, many who believed in Christ as the Son of God weren't yet baptized with water. These unbaptized believers were called *catechumens,* which meant that they were preparing for Baptism by study and prayer but were not yet baptized. After all, people coming from a decadent pagan lifestyle needed time to clean up their act before being baptized, and some took several weeks, months, or even a year or two to prepare for their Baptism. After Baptism, they renounced their pagan ways and did no more dabbling in the idolatry and immorality of their secular contemporaries.

These catechumens and students of Christianity, otherwise known as the pre-baptized, were treated just as if they were full-fledged baptized Christians. The Roman gladiators and animals in the arena didn't distinguish between baptized Christians and those preparing for Baptism. Both were violently persecuted.

The notion of being baptized by shedding your own blood for Christ and/ or His Church grew up during the Roman persecutions. And the Catholic Church has always revered these unbaptized *martyrs* — people who are killed because of their faith — maintaining that the divine mercy of God wouldn't penalize them or ignore their sacrifice merely because they died before their Baptism by water.

In addition, Herod killed many infants (Matthew 2:16) in a failed effort to kill the newborn Christ. Those infants, known as the *Holy Innocents,* are martyrs, too, because they shed their blood so Christ could live. So Baptism by blood is as valid as Baptism by water. The following quote from the *Catechism of the Catholic Church* shows what the Church has to say about Baptism by blood:

> The Church has always held the firm conviction that those who suffer death for the sake of the faith without having received Baptism are baptized by their death for and with Christ. This *Baptism of blood,* like the *desire for Baptism,* brings about the fruits of Baptism without being a sacrament. (1258)

Having the will but not the way

Part of Catholic theology is the *Universal Salvific Will of God,* which is just a fancy way of saying that God basically would like for everyone, all men and women, to join Him in heaven. Men and women have free will, though, so He *offers* the gift of grace, but men and women must freely accept and then cooperate with it.

St. Augustine (A.D. 354–430) taught that God offers everyone *sufficient* grace to be saved, but it only becomes *efficacious* (successful) for those who freely accept and cooperate with that grace. In other words, God gives every human being the chance and possibility of going to heaven. Whether they get beyond the pearly gates, however, depends on the individual person.

The official church doctrine of God's desire that everyone have the possibility of going to heaven is clearly stated in a document from a declaration by the Congregation for the Doctrine of the Faith (the Vatican office in charge of defending and explaining the faith) in 2000, which says:

> "The universal salvific will of God is closely connected to the sole mediation of Christ: 'God desires all men to be saved and to come to the knowledge of the truth.' (1 Tim 2:4)" (Dominus Iesus, #13).

So, on the one hand, you have the doctrine of the necessity of baptism, and on the other hand, you have the doctrine of the universal salvific will of God. How can God impose a requirement if, at the same time, he wants everyone to have the same chance?

As long as a person doesn't explicitly reject Christ and his Church and deliberately refuse Baptism, he can be saved. Nonbelievers can have an implicit desire to know and accept Christ. People who lack any knowledge of Christ and His teachings are sometimes called *anonymous Christians*.

Therefore, the Church believes in Baptism by desire, which allows salvation for non-Christians who, through no fault of their own, do not know or have never heard about Jesus Christ. God, being all-knowing, also knows with certitude if any person would have accepted or rejected Christ had they been given the chance and opportunity.

The Catechism of the Catholic Church has this to say about Baptism by desire:

> Since Christ died for all . . . we must hold that the Holy Spirit offers to all the possibility. . . . Every man who is ignorant of the Gospel of Christ and of his Church, but seeks the truth and does the will of God . . . can be saved. It may be supposed that such persons would have *desired Baptism explicitly* if they had known its necessity. (1260)

So while the Church consistently teaches the absolute necessity of Baptism for salvation, she also understands that it can accomplished by water, blood, or desire.

The Holy Eucharist

The Holy Eucharist refers to the consecrated bread and wine consumed by Catholics during Communion. Like Baptism, the Holy Eucharist is also considered a Sacrament of Initiation because new members are encouraged to participate regularly and often in Holy Communion.

Of all seven sacraments, the Holy Eucharist is the most central and important to Catholicism because of the staunch belief that the consecrated bread and wine are actually, really, truly, and substantially the body and blood, soul and divinity of Christ. For Catholics, the presence of Christ in the Holy Eucharist is not just symbolic, allegorical, metaphorical, or merely spiritual. It's real. That's why it's also called the *Real Presence* — because Christ *really is present.*

Understanding the consecrated host

Catholicism maintains that Christ's body and blood are present in the *consecrated host* (the wafer of bread upon which the priest says the words of Jesus from the Last Supper: "This is my body") and in the consecrated wine (over which the priest says the words of Jesus: "This is the chalice of my blood"). *Holy Eucharist* refers to the three aspects of Christ's body and blood — as *sacrifice* during the Consecration of the Mass, as Holy *Communion,* and as *Blessed Sacrament.* These three aspects form the core of Catholic belief on the Holy Eucharist.

The word *Eucharist* comes from the Greek *eucharistein,* meaning "thanksgiving." Catholics are grateful and give thanks to God for providing the Holy Eucharist to feed and nourish the soul.

Only wheat bread and grape wine can be used. The moment the priest or bishop says the words of consecration — the words of Christ at the Last Supper, "This is My body" and "This is My blood," (Matthew 26:26–29) — Catholics believe that the bread and wine become the body and blood, soul and divinity of Christ.

On the natural level, whatever you eat becomes part of you. On the supernatural plane, when Catholics eat the body and blood of Christ, they're supposed to become more like Christ in his obedience to the Father, humility, and love for neighbors.

To Catholics, the physical act of eating the consecrated host or drinking the consecrated wine from the *chalice,* a blessed cup (see Figure 1-2), is secondary to the underlying invisible reality that the human soul is being fed by the very body and blood, soul and divinity of Christ. The body merely consumes the *appearances* of bread and wine while the soul receives Christ personally and totally.

Book II

Walking
the
Catholic
Walk

Figure 1-2:
A chalice
from which
Catholics
drink
consecrated
wine.

The Holy Eucharist is food for the soul, so it's given and eaten during Holy Communion at the Mass. However, the form and manner of distribution bear slight differences, depending on whether you attend a Latin (Western) Rite Mass or an Eastern Rite Mass:

- ✔ **Latin (Western) Rite:** Holy Communion is in the form of consecrated unleavened hosts made from wheat flour and water, just like the unleavened bread used by Jesus at the Last Supper. The host is flat and the size of a quarter or half-dollar. Latin Catholics may receive the host on their tongue or in their hand if the local bishop and the national conference of bishops permit.

- ✔ **Eastern Rite:** Catholics receive consecrated leavened bread (the yeast or leaven symbolizes the Resurrection), which is placed inside the chalice (cup) of consecrated wine. The priest takes a spoon and gingerly places a cut cube of consecrated bread soaked in the consecrated wine inside the mouths of the communicants without ever touching their lips or tongue.

Discovering who can receive Holy Communion

The word *Communion* comes from Latin: *Co* means "with" and *unio* means "union." *Communio* means "union with." Catholics believe that Communion allows the believer to be united with Christ by sharing His body and blood. The priest and deacon, sometimes with the assistance of *extraordinary ministers* (nonclerics who have been given the authority to assist the priest), distribute Holy Communion to the faithful (see Chapter 10 for more on what happens during Mass). Because this is really and truly the body and blood, soul and divinity of Christ, receiving Holy Communion, God's intimate visit with His faithful souls, is most sacred.

When believers receive Holy Communion, they're intimately united with their Lord and Savior, Jesus Christ. However, Communion isn't limited to the *communicant* (the one receiving Holy Communion) and Jesus Christ. By taking Holy Communion, the Catholic is also expressing her union with all Catholics around the world and at all times who believe the same doctrines, obey the same laws, and follow the same leaders. This is why Catholics (and Eastern Orthodox Christians) have a strict law that only people who are *in communion* with the Church can receive Holy Communion. In other words, only those who are united in the same beliefs — the seven sacraments, the authority of the pope, and the teachings in the Catechism of the Catholic Church — are allowed to receive Holy Communion.

In the Protestant tradition, Communion is often seen as a means of building unity among various denominations, and many have open Communion, meaning that any baptized Christian can take Communion in their services. Catholics and Eastern Orthodox Christians, on the other hand, see Communion not as the means but as the final fruit of unity. So only those in communion can receive Holy Communion. It has nothing to do with who's worthy.

Think of it this way: If a Canadian citizen moves to the United States, lives in Erie, Pennsylvania, works in Erie, and has a family in Erie, he can do so indefinitely. However, he can't run for public office or vote in an American election unless and until he becomes a U.S. citizen. Does being or not being a citizen make you a good or bad person? Of course not. But if citizens from other countries want to vote, they must give up their own citizenship and become U.S. citizens.

Being a non-Catholic in the Church is like being a non-citizen in a foreign country. Non-Catholics can come to as many Catholic Masses as they want; they can marry Catholics and raise their children in the Catholic faith, but they can't receive Holy Communion in the Catholic Church until they become Catholic. Becoming Catholic is how a person gets united with and experiences union with the whole Catholic Church. Those in union can then receive Holy Communion.

Similarly, Catholics who don't follow the Church's laws on divorce and remarriage, or who obstinately reject Church teaching, such as the inherent evil of abortion, shouldn't come forward to receive Communion because they're no longer in communion. This prohibition isn't a judgment on their moral or spiritual state because only God can know that. But receiving Holy Communion is a public act, and therefore, it's an ecclesiastical action requiring those who do it to be united with all that the Church teaches and commands and with all the ways that the Church prays.

Book II

Walking the Catholic Walk

Partaking of First Holy Communion

When boys and girls (usually in second grade) make their First Holy Communion, it's a big occasion for Catholic families. Like their Baptism, the day of First Communion is one filled with family, friends, and feasting after the sacred event has taken place in church.

Girls typically wear white gowns and veils and often look like little brides, and boys wear their Sunday best or new suits and ties bought just for the occasion. Some parishes have the entire class make their First Communion together at a Sunday or Saturday Mass, but other parishes allow each child to go on a different weekend.

The children are generally too young to appreciate all the theological refinements of *transubstantiation,* the act of changing the substances of bread and wine into the substances of the body and blood of Christ, but as long as they know and believe that it's not bread or wine they're receiving but the real body and blood of Jesus Christ, they are old enough to take Holy Communion.

Like Penance and the Anointing of the Sick, Holy Eucharist can be received more than once. (However, Baptism, Confirmation, and Holy Orders can't be repeated.)

First Penance (see Book II, Chapter 2), which is going to confession for the first time, *must come before* First Communion.

Adult converts normally make their First Communion at the Easter Vigil, the same night they are baptized and confirmed.

Coming of Age: Confirmation

The final Sacrament of Initiation is Confirmation. Soon after babies are born and get fed, they start to grow. Growth is as vital to human life as nourishment. The body and mind must grow to stay alive. Catholics believe that the soul also needs to grow in the life of grace. Just as the human body must grow through childhood, adolescence, and then adulthood, the human soul needs to grow into maturity.

Catholics believe that Confirmation is the supernatural equivalent of the growth process on the natural level. It builds on what was begun in Baptism and what was nourished in Holy Eucharist. It completes the process of initiation into the Christian community, and it matures the soul for the work ahead. The Eastern Catholic Church confirms *(chrismates)* at Baptism and gives Holy Eucharist as well, thus initiating the new Christian all at the same time.

Too often, Confirmation is the bribe to get Catholic kids who go to public school to attend CCD (Confraternity of Christian Doctrine), also known as religious education classes. As long as they attend eight years of CCD, they're eligible for Confirmation.

But Confirmation is more than a carrot on a stick to keep kids in CCD classes. This Sacrament of Initiation means that they become young adults in the Catholic faith. During an infant's Baptism, parents and godparents make promises to renounce Satan and believe in God and the Church on behalf of the child. At Confirmation, before the bishop, the young adult renews those same promises, this time in her own words.

So what occurs during Confirmation? The Holy Spirit is first introduced to a Catholic the day that she's baptized, because the entire Holy Trinity — Father, Son, and Holy Spirit — are invoked at the ceremony. During Confirmation, God the Holy Spirit comes upon the person, accompanied by God the Father and God the Son, just as he did at *Pentecost.* The Feast of Pentecost commemorates the descent of the Holy Spirit from heaven to earth upon the 12 apostles and the Virgin Mary, occurring 50 days after Easter and 10 days after Jesus's Ascension (Acts 2:1–4).

This sacrament is called *Confirmation* because the faith given in Baptism is now confirmed and made strong. Sometimes, those who benefit from Confirmation are referred to as *soldiers of Christ.* This isn't a military desig-nation but a spiritual duty to fight the war between good and evil, light and darkness — a war between the human race and all the powers of hell.

Traditionally, the 12 fruits of the Holy Spirit are charity, joy, peace, patience, kindness, goodness, generosity, gentleness, faithfulness, modesty, self-control, and chastity. These are human qualities that can be activated by the Holy Spirit. The seven gifts of the Holy Spirit are wisdom, understanding, counsel, fortitude, knowledge, piety, and fear of the Lord. These gifts are supernatural graces given to the soul. With these fruits and gifts, confirmed Catholics are now equipped to live out their baptismal call to holiness as adult members of the faith.

A bishop is the ordinary minister of the Sacrament of Confirmation. However, priests can be delegated by the bishop to confirm young people of the parish or adult converts being brought into full communion.

Book II

Walking the Catholic Walk

The following occurs during the Sacrament of Confirmation:

- ✔ The ceremony may take place at Mass or outside of Mass, and the bishop usually wears red vestments to symbolize the red tongues of fire seen hovering over the heads of the apostles at Pentecost.

- ✔ Each individual to be confirmed comes forward with his sponsor. The same canonical requirements for being a godparent in Baptism apply for sponsors at Confirmation. At Baptism, Junior's mom and dad picked his godfather and godmother; for Confirmation, he picks his own sponsor. The sponsor can be the godmother or godfather if they're still practicing Catholics, or he may choose someone else (other than his parents) who's over the age of 16, already confirmed, and in good standing with the Church. One sponsor is chosen for Confirmation.

- ✔ Each Catholic selects his own Confirmation name. At Baptism, the name was chosen without the child's consent because the child was too little to make the selection alone. Now, in Confirmation, another name — in addition to the first and middle names — can be added, or the original baptismal name may be used. It must be a Christian name, though, such as one of the canonized saints of the Church or a hero from the Bible. You wouldn't want to pick a name like Cain, Judas, or Herod, for example, and no secular names would be appropriate.

- ✔ The Catholic being confirmed stands or kneels before the bishop, and the sponsor lays one hand on the shoulder of the one being confirmed. The Confirmation name is spoken, and the bishop puts chrism oil on the person's forehead, says his name aloud, and then says, "Be sealed with the gift of the Holy Spirit." The person responds, "Amen." The bishop then says, "Peace be with you." And the person responds, "And with your spirit."

Latin (Western) Rite Catholics are usually baptized as infants, receive First Communion as children, and are confirmed as adolescents. Adult converts who've never been baptized are baptized when they become Catholic; they're confirmed and receive their First Communion at the same time. Or, if adult converts were baptized in a Protestant Church, they make a Profession of Faith, are confirmed, and receive Holy Eucharist — typically at the Easter Vigil Mass on Holy Saturday. Eastern Rite Catholics are confirmed at the same time they are baptized.

Confirmation means accepting responsibility for your faith and destiny. Childhood is a time when you're told what to do, and you react positively to reward and negatively to punishment. Adulthood, even young adulthood, means that you must do what's right on your own, not for the recognition or reward but merely because it's the right thing to do. Doing what's right can be satisfying, too. The focus is on the Holy Spirit, who confirmed the apostles on Pentecost (Acts 2:1–4) and gave them courage to practice their faith. Catholics believe that the same Holy Spirit confirms Catholics during the Sacrament of Confirmation and gives them the same gifts and fruits.

Chapter 2

The Sacraments of Service and Healing

In This Chapter

▶ Making marriage vows stick

▶ Caring for the Church community through Holy Orders

▶ Spilling your guts in the confessional

▶ Strengthening the spirit through the Anointing of the Sick

The seven sacraments are the most sacred and ancient Catholic rites of worship. They mark seven sequential stages of spiritual development, so if you missed the first three — Baptism, Confirmation, and Holy Eucharist — head over to Book II, Chapter 1 before hearing all about Catholicism's final four (sacraments, that is).

In this chapter, you find out about the two Sacraments of Community and Service: Matrimony and Holy Orders. They're all about uniting and ministering. Then you discover the last two sacraments — Penance and the Anointing of the Sick — which are Sacraments of Mercy and Healing.

The Sacraments of Service and Community

Following the three sacraments for the sake of initiation (see Book II, Chapter 1) are the two sacraments for the sake of social development. The Sacrament of Matrimony takes care of the family, and the Sacrament of Holy Orders takes care of the society of the Church. Both are of service to others.

Marriage — Catholic style

The Catholic Church distinguishes between a legal, state-recognized marriage and the Sacrament of Matrimony. Marriage is regulated by the civil government, which has certain rules that must be followed to make a marriage legal. But being legally married doesn't necessarily mean that two people have participated in the Sacrament of Matrimony. The Sacrament of Matrimony means becoming husband and wife through a sacred covenant with God and each other. In this section, you discover what must occur for the marriage to be a valid sacrament in the eyes of the Church.

Responding to the vocation

A Christian (Protestant, Catholic, Orthodox) marriage is between one baptized man and one baptized woman. A Catholic marriage is a Christian union where one or both parties are of the Catholic faith. The sacrament of Matrimony is a vocation, a calling from God, from the Latin *vocare,* to call. Just as priests, deacons, religious sisters and brothers, nuns and monks have a calling from God, so do married people, as well as single persons.

Being a good husband or wife — then a good father or mother — is as much a sacred calling from God as the call to become a monk or nun. Married people are to be sanctified as much as clergy and religious brothers and sisters.

Because marriage is a vocation *and* a sacrament, marriage imparts a special grace that gives the recipients the strength and ability to assume and fulfill all the duties and responsibilities of Christian marriage. Three elements are required for a marital union to be a valid sacrament: The participants must enter the Sacrament of Matrimony with the intention that their union will be

- ✔ **Permanent:** Unto death
- ✔ **Faithful:** Without adultery
- ✔ **Fruitful:** Open to the possibility of children if God wills it

The term *fruitful* means only that both bride and groom have to be open to the *possibility* of children. They do not have to give birth to as many children as biologically possible, but they cannot purposefully avoid having any kids whatsoever.

The Sacrament of Matrimony gives the bride and groom the necessary graces to bring those vows to fruition. However, getting married in the Catholic Church isn't as complicated as some may think. At least one person must be Catholic, but the other person can be any other religion. If the non-Catholic was baptized in a non-Catholic church, the non-Catholic needs documentation verifying Baptism. If the non-Catholic is unbaptized, unchurched, or of a non-Christian religion, a special dispensation from the local bishop is needed. The priest or deacon doing the ceremony can obtain it.

If two baptized but non-Catholic Christians get married in a civil ceremony or in any religious denomination, the Catholic Church does recognize that as being valid as long as it's the first marriage for both of them.

Committing to a lifetime and avoiding annulments

Like the Sacraments of Baptism, Confirmation, and Holy Orders, the Sacrament of Matrimony can take place only once in someone's life, unless his or her spouse dies. Due to the lifelong commitment that's required for the Sacrament of Matrimony, Catholics can only marry someone who's widowed or wasn't married before. If a person was previously married and the spouse is alive, it must be demonstrated that the marriage was invalid so the previous union can be declared null and void through an annulment.

In most dioceses, Catholics who want to marry are asked to meet with a priest or deacon at least 9 to 12 months before the wedding. This period is called *Pre-Cana* after the name of the town, Cana, where Jesus and his mother, Mary, went to a wedding feast, and Jesus changed water into wine. During the Pre-Cana period, the priest or deacon offers practical financial and emotional advice to the couple, as well as instructions on the spiritual nature of marriage and Natural Family Planning (NFP), which, by the way, is not the old, forsaken Rhythm Method. (Because the Catholic Church forbids artificial contraception, regulating birth must be based on morally allowable means.)

Why so much time spent in preparation? Why can't weddings be spontaneous? Because the Sacrament of Matrimony is a vocation for life. The Catholic Church wants to prevent impulsive, shotgun weddings, or anything done in haste, rashness, or imprudence.

An *annulment* is not a Catholic version of divorce. Divorce is a civil decree from the state that a legal marriage is no longer in force. An annulment, on the other hand, is an ecclesiastical decree that a marriage, even if entered in good faith, was determined to be an invalid sacrament from the first moment (when vows were exchanged at the wedding ceremony).

How could this sacrament be invalid? When a baptized man and a baptized woman marry for the first time, the Church presumes the marriage to be valid unless proven otherwise in a Church court. That same assumption applies for all baptized persons: Catholic, Protestant, or Eastern Orthodox. If, however, one or both of the participants did not intend on their wedding day to enter a *permanent, faithful,* and *fruitful* union, then no sacrament took place, and the Church can declare the marriage null and void. If that happens, both parties are free to marry someone else — the Church hopes *validly* this time.

Likewise, if one or both parties had a lack of due competence or a grave lack of due discretion, the marriage is invalid. The latter concerns the requisite

Book II

Walking the Catholic Walk

knowledge and comprehension of the essential rights and obligations of marriage, whereas the former concerns the emotional and psychological ability to fulfill them.

Keep in mind that because Church annulments are *not* a form of divorce, they have no effect whatsoever on the legitimacy of children because that's a purely legal matter. Annulments *don't* make the children born of that union illegitimate.

Making it valid

A valid Sacrament of Matrimony requires the presence of a priest or deacon, a bride and groom (no same-sex marriages), and two witnesses of any religion. All the other stuff is icing on the wedding cake — the ushers, bridesmaids, groomsmen, parents, grandparents, photographer, videographer, caterer, ring bearer, flower girl, organist, and soloist. (See the sidebar "Food, flowers, and faith" for our opinion on prioritizing wedding preparations.)

The bride and groom are the real ministers of the sacrament because their "I do" makes them husband and wife. The priest or deacon is just an official witness for the Church — necessary, yes, but just a witness.

Only Scripture readings from the Bible can be read and only approved vows recited during the ceremony. Secular or other writings from other faiths can be read at the wedding reception before grace is prayed and the toast given, but they don't belong in church.

Three types of Catholic wedding ceremonies are available. The first is a wedding at Mass; the second is a wedding without a Mass; and the third is a *convalidation* ceremony, in which a couple who was previously married invalidly in the eyes of the Church (perhaps by a Justice of the Peace or Protestant minister) now seeks to have that marriage recognized by the Church or, as the canon lawyers call it, *convalidated.*

Getting the full treatment with a Nuptial Mass

A *Nuptial Mass,* the Sacrament of Matrimony with a Mass, normally occurs on Saturdays (and sometimes Friday evenings and Sundays, with special permission from the bishop). The Nuptial Mass is highly recommended and encouraged when *both* the bride and groom are Catholic because two sacraments are received at this ceremony: the Sacrament of Matrimony and the Sacrament of the Holy Eucharist. Participating in two sacraments is a great way to start the marriage.

Just like a Sunday parish Mass, the wedding Mass has four Scripture readings: one from the Old Testament read by a friend or relative, a Psalm that's sung, one from the New Testament Epistles read by a friend or relative, and one from the Gospels read by the priest or deacon. Then the priest or deacon gives the sermon and proceeds to witness the vows.

Just before the formal vows, the priest or deacon asks the couple three important questions:

1. **Have you come here freely and without reservation to give yourselves to each other in marriage?**
2. **Will you love and honor each other as husband and wife for the rest of your lives?**
3. **Will you accept children lovingly from God and bring them up according to the law of Christ and his Church?**

Book II

Walking the Catholic Walk

Assuming that both say "Yes!" to all three questions, the priest or deacon can proceed to the marriage vows.

The vows may be stated by the priest or deacon and repeated by the bride and groom, or the vows may be addressed as a question, to which the bride and groom merely respond, "I do." Following are examples of the two accepted versions:

> I, Concetta, take you, Salvatore, to be my husband. I promise to be true to you in good times and in bad, in sickness and in health. I will love you and honor you all the days of my life.

Or:

> Do you, Salvatore, take Concetta for your lawful wife, to have and to hold, from this day forward, for better, for worse, for richer, for poorer, in sickness and in health, until death do you part?

After the vows, the rings are blessed. Then the groom places one ring on the bride's finger and says, "Take this ring as a sign of my love and my fidelity, in the name of the Father and of the Son and of the Holy Spirit. Amen." The bride takes the other ring and places it on the groom's finger and says the same words.

The couple become husband and wife at the moment they exchange consent, not rings. Rings are merely a symbol.

After the exchange of rings, the prayers of the faithful are said (just like at Sunday Mass), followed by an offertory hymn and the preparation of the gifts on the altar. A relative or friend may bring up the bread and wine, and Mass proceeds as normal. (See Book III for a detailed look at the Mass.) After the Our Father, the priest gives a special nuptial blessing to the couple. Then they stand, give a sign of peace (hug or kiss) to their respective parents, and return to the sanctuary. Communion proceeds as usual.

Often, after Communion and the final prayer, the bride and groom walk to a statue of Mary. They place some flowers before the statue, while a soloist sings *Ave Maria,* the *Hail Mary* sung in Latin, or another song in honor of Mary. This custom arose from a pious practice of newlyweds asking for Mary's prayers because Mary's intercession at the wedding feast of Cana prompted her son, Jesus, to change water into wine. The new husband and wife ask Mary, the Mother of Jesus, to pray to Jesus for them as well.

Finally comes the big announcement: The priest or deacon introduces "Mr. and Mrs. Nicastro." Then they smooch and exit down the main aisle.

Opting for a wedding without a Mass

The Catholic wedding ceremony without a Mass is often celebrated when the bride or groom isn't of the Catholic faith. Without a Mass, Communion doesn't take place. If Communion took place, the non-Catholic wouldn't be able to receive it, because you must be Catholic to receive Communion. (See Book II, Chapter 1 for more on Communion.) So to spare any embarrassment, misunderstandings, or hurt feelings, the Church usually suggests a wedding ceremony without Mass for a Catholic and non-Catholic.

The ceremony (formally called *Rite of Marriage Outside of Mass*) is the same as the Nuptial Mass in that selections from the Old Testament and New Testament are read, along with a Psalm and a Gospel. The priest or deacon preaches a sermon after proclaiming the Gospel, and then the wedding vows are pronounced, followed by the exchange of rings. Some prayers are offered on behalf of the new husband and wife, followed by the Our Father, after which the priest or deacon gives the nuptial blessing to the couple. Then comes the sign of peace (a hug and/or kiss), a final prayer, and the big announcement. The difference between the two ceremonies is that in the Nuptial Mass, right after the vows are pronounced and rings exchanged, the Mass continues.

Making it Catholic: Convalidation

A *convalidation ceremony* is needed when a Catholic couple gets married in a civil or non-Catholic ceremony, which makes it an invalid marriage in the eyes of the Church. Even if only one of them is Catholic, it's an invalid sacrament because Catholics must always follow Church law, which says they must be married in a Catholic church.

After the mandatory waiting period of six months or more, if the couple decides to have their civil marriage recognized (sometimes erroneously called having it *blessed*) by the Catholic Church, then a *convalidation* is in order. This is a simple and private ceremony involving the couple, two witnesses, and the priest or deacon. The vows are pronounced, and the rings may be exchanged. If the rings can't be taken off, then they're simply blessed.

It's not a renewal of vows but a making of the vows for the first time in the eyes of the Church. The convalidation makes a merely civil marriage a Sacrament of Matrimony.

Convalidations are a way to remedy a hasty decision to marry too soon. If a couple marries in haste but later realizes that, yes, they will remain together, the couple can have the union recognized by God and the Church through convalidation. It's not considered an option but a remedy to an unfortunate situation, because the Church prefers couples to marry validly the first time.

Sadly, some couples run off and get married in a modest non-Catholic ceremony just to avoid an expensive Catholic wedding. The Church *never* demands or even suggests big weddings with huge bridal parties, stretch limousines, and country club receptions. Brides and grooms are allowed that, but if a couple wants a simple, dignified, and reverent ceremony with a few family and friends and without all the high-priced, big-ticket items, they can still opt for that in the Catholic Church. The Nuptial Mass or the Rite of Marriage Outside of Mass is appropriate in either situation: expensive or economical. The choice is that of the bride and groom.

If a Catholic gets married by a Justice of the Peace, a captain on a ship, a mayor, or a Protestant minister, and hasn't obtained a dispensation from the local Catholic bishop, then that marriage is invalid, and the Catholic isn't allowed to receive Holy Communion until that union is sanctioned by the Church in a convalidation. This situation often happens when a nonpracticing Catholic doesn't realize that a non-Catholic minister can still marry the couple in a non-Catholic ceremony with the Catholic Church's blessing as long as the couple meets with a priest or deacon and still fulfills all the same Pre-Cana preparations as everyone else. A dispensation from the local bishop is possible and can allow a Catholic bride or groom to be validly married in the eyes of the Church, by a non-Catholic minister, and in a non-Catholic church of the non-Catholic spouse, but the Catholic priest or deacon must fill out the necessary forms, and the couple still has to make the same preparations as other Catholic couples.

Occasionally, a Catholic goes against the advice and laws of the Church and marries a divorced person who hasn't obtained an annulment. This marriage takes place in a civil ceremony or by a non-Catholic minister, but it's not considered valid in the eyes of the Catholic Church. If an annulment is granted later on, and the couple wants to have their union recognized and sanctioned as a valid sacrament, then a convalidation is the appropriate and only remedy.

Because annulments aren't guaranteed, Catholics shouldn't *presume* that they'll get a convalidation after marrying in an invalid civil ceremony.

The Sacrament of Matrimony entails a lot more than just getting hitched. Society often places more emphasis on the wedding and less importance on the entire marriage. What the Church cares about is the sacrament's spiritual dimension, and the fact that marriage is a lifelong vocation.

Holy Orders

Along with Matrimony, the other sacrament of community and service is *Holy Orders*. In the Catholic Church, *sacred ministers,* those who serve the spiritual needs of others, are ordained by a bishop by means of Holy Orders, which creates the hierarchy of deacon, priest, and bishop. Book I, Chapter 5 provides detailed information about the rank and file of the Catholic Church and the specific duties of deacons, priests, and bishops.

This sacrament can be received only once, just like Baptism and Confirmation, but a man may also be ordained to a higher order up to the third degree. A man must first be ordained a deacon before being ordained a priest, and he must be ordained a deacon and then a priest before being ordained a bishop. So every priest and every bishop has experienced the Sacrament of Holy Orders more than once, yet he can never be re-ordained a deacon, priest, or bishop, because it's for life.

Only baptized men can receive the Sacrament of Holy Orders.

Celebrating the sacrament

Jesus Christ instituted the Sacrament of Holy Orders at the Last Supper simultaneously with His institution of the Sacrament of Holy Eucharist. To change bread and wine into the body and blood, soul, and divinity of Christ, you need priests who've been given this power by virtue of their ordination. (See Book I, Chapter 1 for a discussion of the Holy Eucharist.)

Bishops receive the highest level of Holy Orders, and it's often said in the Church that bishops have the "fullness of the priesthood" because they alone have the authority to offer all seven sacraments: Baptism, Penance, Holy Eucharist, Matrimony, Anointing of the Sick, Holy Orders, and Confirmation. Priests have the power and authority (also known as *faculties*) to celebrate only five: Baptism, Penance, Holy Eucharist (Mass), Matrimony, and Anointing of the Sick. Deacons can celebrate only two: Baptism and Matrimony (provided that the wedding is without a Nuptial Mass).

Preparing for the responsibility

Deacons, priests, and bishops receive plenty of pastoral and theological training. Catholic clergy candidates attend *seminary,* the Catholic equivalent to Protestant divinity school. A college degree, however, is a prerequisite for seminary, and then most *seminarians,* students who attend a seminary, start work on a master's degree — Master of Divinity (MDiv) or Master of Arts (MA) — in Theology. Post-college studies can range from four to eight years, depending on the candidate and the diocese he's studying for. Now and then, a few students go farther and earn a Doctorate in philosophy (PhD), theology (STD or ThD), or canon law (JCD).

Having a similar academic background as physicians, lawyers, and Protestant ministers gives the Catholic clergy a good foundation, but the academic background must also be complemented with solid prayer life. Seminarians must also receive *pastoral formation,* which is learning how to listen to people, counsel them, work with others (especially the sick and the needy), and so on, so they can function as good pastors, as well as adequate theologians.

The Sacrament of Holy Orders doesn't make a man a Church aristocrat, but it does confer the dignity of the sacrament, which entails the obligation to obey the pope and be of service to the people of God. In previous ages, though, some opportunistic and ambitious men rose through the clerical ranks and used their office of deacon, priest, or bishop to abuse ecclesiastical authority and satisfy personal needs. Nevertheless, the original purpose of Holy Orders was not to create an upper class but to provide spiritual leadership. Pastors are to see their role as shepherds who love and know their sheep instead of seeing their people as servants and peasants.

Removing the clergy from service, but not the sacrament from the clergy

Holy Orders impart an indelible mark on the soul (much like Baptism and Confirmation), which means this sacrament cannot be removed or undone. Hence, deacons, priests, and bishops cannot have their ordination removed or dissolved. What can happen, though, is that their sacred ministry can be constrained in such a way that they're not allowed to dress or function like clergy.

What is commonly called being "defrocked" is technically known as an *involuntary laicization* or formal dismissal from the clerical state. This step is taken as a punishment for crime and to remove from public ministry a cleric who either promotes heretical teaching and/or engages in immoral and abhorrent behavior. While still having the power to validly celebrate the sacraments, a laicized cleric is not legally permitted to do so. The only exception is if the defrocked priest is the only one available to anoint a dying person or hear a confession before death. Otherwise, laicized clergy are forbidden to function as clergy.

In addition, an ordained man may, of his own accord, request being dispensed from his vows of celibacy in order to marry validly in the Church — a step called *voluntary laicization*. This request is not automatically granted. The priest in question must demonstrate that being ordained either was a mistake in the very beginning or that he is now involved in a serious relationship with serious obligations (in other words, he has a pregnant girlfriend or she recently gave birth to his child). It is not enough for him to say that he's bored with being a priest or tired of living as a single man and now wants to try married family life.

Laicized priests can't wear the Roman collar, be called "Father," or publicly celebrate the sacraments. All requests for laicization must go to Rome, and only the Vatican can approve them. A voluntarily or involuntarily laicized cleric isn't given a salary, housing, or insurance. He can validly and licitly get married in church, but he can never celebrate any of the sacraments publicly.

The Sacraments of Mercy and Healing

The two Sacraments of Healing are Penance and the Anointing of the Sick. The following sections provide the details of these sacraments.

Penance

Catholics believe that the Holy Mother Church gives birth in the Sacrament of Baptism, nourishes in Holy Eucharist, helps Catholics grow in Confirmation, and heals in the *Sacrament of Penance*.

Healing the spirit

Medicine and therapy can heal a wounded body, but Catholics believe that only God's grace can heal a wounded soul. That's why Jesus left the Sacrament of Penance to heal spiritual wounds, or *sin*. Often, people think of sin only as breaking God's laws. Sure, stealing, lying, and murdering break some of the Ten Commandments and are considered sinful. But Catholics believe that God said, "You shall not" because he knew these sinful actions would wound spiritually.

Sin is like a bacteria or virus to the soul. When a person lies, cheats, steals, or murders, it's like being infected with millions of deadly germs. The longer the infection is left untreated, the more it spreads and worsens. It wounds and can even kill the life of grace that enables entry into heaven.

Just as tumors are benign or malignant, Catholics believe that sins are venial or mortal. In other words, some sins aren't considered as serious as others and merely inflict a slight wound to the soul, but others are so intrinsically evil that they're considered deadly. The latter are called *mortal sins* because they can kill grace. (For more on mortal sin, see Book II, Chapter 5.)

The Sacrament of Penance (also known as the *Sacrament of Reconciliation* or *Confession*) is for spiritual healing. According to the Gospels, after the Resurrection, Jesus appeared to the apostles, breathed on them, and said, "Receive the Holy Spirit. If you forgive the sins of any, they are forgiven; if you retain the sins of any, they are retained" (John 20:22–23).

Because Jesus gave the apostles the power to forgive sins, he must have wanted them to use it. So the Sacrament of Penance has been the very will of Christ from day one.

Understanding penance in the past

The actual confession of sins (verbally admitting the wrongs you have done) is — and always has been — done privately to a priest or bishop. Private or secret confession of sins ensures the absolute confidentiality (also called the *Seal of Confession*) of the *penitent:* the sinner. However, the *penance* (acts of sorrow) performed as part of the Sacrament used to be done in public for *public sins* (those done openly and known by the community). For example, in the early Church, penance for *apostasy* — denying the faith — was done publicly before the entire Church community. (People who denied their Christian faith [called *lapsi* in Latin] in court to be spared from death in the arena during the Roman persecution period might perform public acts of penance.) A public penance may have involved making a pilgrimage to the Holy Land and visiting the places where Jesus lived, visiting a local shrine, or wearing sackcloth and ashes. The idea was that to repair the scandal caused by public sin, public penance was done to encourage others to repent and be reconciled with God and the Church.

On the other hand, for *private sins* (sins nobody else knew about), the penance was performed privately. Private penance would entail saying some prayers quietly in church, doing a good deed anonymously, reading passages from the Bible, giving alms to the poor, and so on.

In reality, because Christians were clustered into small groups at first, everyone knew what everyone else did anyway. But as Christianity's status changed from persecuted religion to the state religion, more and more members filled the ranks, and admitting faults before a large crowd became more embarrassing and delicate.

Also, more sins became private and less public, so the need for private and discreet penances arose. In the ancient church, believers lived in close-knit communities, and everyone knew what you said and did, whether it was

Book II

Walking the Catholic Walk

cheating on your spouse or getting drunk. Later, as Christianity was no longer illegal in the Roman Empire, behavior became more private. Discreet penances meant that no one could figure out your sins by merely observing your performed penance.

Absolving sins

Whether a sin was public or private, only a priest (or bishop) had the power and authority to absolve sin in the name of Jesus Christ. Additionally, the penance had to be completed before the absolution took place. So a sinner would first confess his sins to the priest, who would impose a penance. Then the penitent would go and do the prescribed acts of sorrow. Once finished, he would then return to the same priest and receive sacramental absolution.

The Irish monks of the sixth and seventh centuries refined the practice of private confessions, which became the norm for the rest of the Church. The monks gave absolution immediately after confession but before the penance was performed. This practice took place because the monks were *itinerant,* meaning they traveled from place to place and would not be in the same area later on.

You gotta confess

Just like the Sacrament of the Holy Eucharist, the Sacrament of Penance may be received many times throughout a person's life. However, the first time that a young Catholic confesses his sins is before his First Communion, which in the Western Church is around the age of reason: 7 years old.

Catholics must confess all known mortal sins to a priest.

To receive the Holy Eucharist without having gone to confession and without receiving absolution for mortal sins makes matters worse. Receiving the Eucharist with mortal sin on your soul is a *sacrilege,* the use of something sacred for an unworthy purpose. A sacrilege expresses disrespect for the sacrament and is another mortal sin.

If you're in danger of death and no priest is available, you can make a *perfect act of contrition.* A perfect act of contrition (which can be as easy as saying "Jesus, have mercy on me, a sinner" to the more elaborate act of contrition said by penitents in the confessional) means that the sinner is sorry for his sins out of love for God and remorse for offending Him rather than just a fear of punishment in the afterlife. Hence, the reason for the sorrow determines whether it's a perfect act of contrition. The sinner must have the absolute intention of going to confession to a priest or bishop as soon as possible if she survives. In situations where no threat to a person's life exists, however, the Church believes that mortal sins can only be forgiven in the Sacrament of Penance. Otherwise, the soul damns itself to hell without absolution from a priest.

Assuming that your death is not imminent and you *can* make it to confession, the perfect act of contrition doesn't apply. Instead, you go to see a priest, confess your sins, and express your remorse and desire to avoid sinfulness in the future. One way to do so is to say aloud the Act of Contrition prayer.

Trusting in absolute secrecy

Telling sins to a priest isn't as scary as people think. Most people tell sensitive, delicate, and confidential information to their physicians and attorneys, so why not to their pastor? The priest is bound by the most absolute secrecy and confidentiality known to humankind. Not even the pope can get a priest to tell who went to him for confession or what was confessed. The priest must be willing to endure prison, torture, and death before violating the *Seal of Confession,* the secrecy of the sacrament.

Over 2,000 years, many bad, immoral, unethical, and unscrupulous priests have existed, and many of them left or were thrown out of the priesthood. But none have ever revealed the secrets they knew from hearing confessions. The fact that even the bad or mediocre ones throughout all history haven't done so — even after they've left the active ministry or the Catholic religion — is, to Catholics, a great sign of the power of the Holy Spirit protecting the dignity and sanctity of the Sacrament of Penance. C'mon, you may say — priests *never* blab about what they hear in confession? Nope. Never.

The confidentiality of the sacrament is so strict and sacred that even enemies of the Church are often in awe of its endurance. The absolute secrecy ensures that anything can be confessed without fear of any retaliation, reaction, or response. Knowing that the priest can never tell anyone anything he hears gives penitents the strength and courage to confess everything.

If a priest does violate the seal of secrecy of the Sacrament of Penance, he's automatically excommunicated, and only the pope can give him absolution for such a crime.

Confessing in three ways

Confession may take place in one of three different ways:

- ✔ **Private confession** is the most common form of confession. The *penitent* (person telling his sins) goes into a Catholic church and enters a *confessional,* also known as a *reconciliation room* or *penance room.*

  Although some older confessionals don't allow the penitent the option of seeing the priest and confessing face-to-face, the newer penance rooms give the penitent the choice of kneeling behind a screen (just like in the older confessionals) and maintaining anonymity, or confessing face-to-face, thus revealing the penitent's identity (if only by face) to the priest.

Book II

Walking
the
Catholic
Walk

The penitent confesses all known and remembered mortal sins since the last confession. See the section "Are you really, truly sorry?" for more on what to confess.

This form of confession happens almost every Saturday afternoon or evening in every parish around the world. A priest sits in a confessional every week, waiting for parishioners to confess. St. John Vianney (1786–1859), the patron saint of parish priests, heard confessions for nearly 20 straight hours, but most priests hear confessions for about 30 to 90 minutes straight every weekend.

But Catholics don't have to wait for Saturday to go to confession. They can ask the priest to hear their confession anytime it's convenient. It's just easier and more practical for people to take advantage of the "man in the box" whenever possible.

✔ **Parish Penance services** are the second form of confession. Usually during Advent (before Christmas) and Lent (before Easter), parishes get several priests to visit as *confessors* — priests hearing the confessions. The whole congregation sings a hymn, listens to a Scripture reading, hears a brief sermon, and then everyone prays the *Act of Contrition* together as a group. Next, people individually go to a priest of their choosing, verbally confess *at least* all mortal sins in confidence, get a penance, and receive absolution.

This form of confession is helpful, because often before Christmas and Easter — times of year when faith is foremost on people's minds — the lines for confessions on Saturdays are longer than the check-out lines in the stores.

✔ **General confession and absolution** is the third and rarest form. In a time of war, natural disaster, or when lives are in danger, if a large number of sinners can't logistically get to confession because only one priest is available to hear the confessions of hundreds of penitents and time is of the essence, the priest can ask the bishop for permission to give general absolution without individual confession.

Simply having a large crowd and one priest isn't a serious enough reason to give general absolution. It's not like a spiritual car wash. General absolution without individual confession is valid only if the local bishop gives permission *and* for a grave and serious reason, such as when the Three Mile Island nuclear power plant incident occurred in 1979. And the proviso is stated that all persons taking advantage of general absolution make a private confession as soon as possible — first chance they get if they survive — and confess at least all their mortal sins, including those that they had on their souls when they participated in the general confession.

Soldiers and sailors going off to battle are often given general absolution by the Catholic chaplain. If they survive, they must make a private confession as soon as possible.

Are you really, truly sorry?

Confessing all known and unconfessed *mortal* sins (any acts or thoughts that turn away from God and turn toward a created thing instead) is absolutely necessary. Any and all *venial* sins (lesser violations than mortal sins) committed since the last confession may be and are encouraged to be confessed as well. If a person has no mortal sins or simply wants to include her venial sins with the mortal sins she needs to confess, then telling the priest all her sins is a helpful thing (like telling the doctor about your minor aches and pains as well as the serious injuries). The best part is that any forgotten sins are also forgiven. Only the ones intentionally withheld make the sacrament invalid.

Being truly sorry for your sins should go without saying, but saying it anyway is important: The *contrition* (sorrow) for sins must be genuine. The priest gives everyone the benefit of the doubt, but no one can fool God. If a man confesses the sin of adultery but isn't sorry — just sorry that his wife caught him — then none of his sins are absolved (forgiven), venial or mortal, because he made a bad confession. Verbal confession must coincide with interior contrition for the sin.

Perfect contrition is being sorry for your sins merely because God is good and sin offends him. *Imperfect contrition* is being sorry because you fear the pains of hell. The church believes that either will do, but perfect is obviously better. Still, when you're in a weak moment, those images of fire and brimstone can help keep you on the straight and narrow.

After you list your sins, the priest asks you to say an Act of Contrition, but you have to really mean what you're saying. Just as the responsibility for receiving the Holy Eucharist without being in the state of mortal sin rests with the conscience of the individual, the validity of the penitent's confession rests with the penitent and his own conscience. The priest doesn't know whether you're in the state of mortal sin, whether you're telling all your sins, whether you're really sorry, or whether you really don't intend to avoid committing sin again, but *you* know. Only you and God know the exact state of your soul.

Doing penance

After you confess your sins, the priest gives you a penance to perform. A penance may be to do something nice for your enemy every day for a week or every week for a month. It may be to visit a nursing home or hospital one day a week for a month. It may be to donate time to a soup kitchen or clothing bank. It may involve any one of the corporal or spiritual works of mercy. On the other hand, quite often, the penance is a set of prayers, such as saying the Our Father or the Hail Mary five to ten times.

Book II

Walking the Catholic Walk

Whatever the penance, it's merely a token, because Catholics believe that the sacrifice of Christ on the cross is what made atonement for our sins. Your penance is for your benefit — to remind yourself that God comes first and you come last.

Absolving the sinner

After you're told what the penance is and you agree to do it (if you really can't perform the penance the priest assigns, tell him and he'll give you a different one), the priest gives his sacramental absolution:

> God the Father of mercies through the death and resurrection of His Son has reconciled the world to Himself and sent the Holy Spirit among us for the forgiveness of sins. Through the ministry of the Church may God give you pardon and peace, and I absolve you from your sins, in the name of the Father, and of the Son, and of the Holy Spirit. Amen.

If the person shows no sorrow or no firm purpose of amendment, then the priest can't give absolution. For example, if a man confesses to being in an adulterous relationship but refuses to end it and go back to his wife, the priest can't give absolution because the man not only fails to feel sorrow but also intends to continue committing this sin — he has no firm purpose of amending his life. Also, if the person fakes out the priest by only pretending to be sorry, the absolution is invalid because you can't fool God.

Only a priest or bishop (which includes cardinals and popes) can give absolution. Deacons don't have the power to celebrate this sacrament.

Anointing of the Sick

Paired with penance, the second sacrament of mercy and healing is *Anointing of the Sick.*

Receiving strength, not a death sentence

In the past, Anointing of the Sick was called *Extreme Unction,* or last anointing, because it was the last anointing a person received in this life (Baptism and Confirmation are the first two times a person is anointed). This sacrament was also commonly called *Last Rites* because before antibiotics and penicillin, more people died than recovered from disease and injury.

Modern medicine has given folks tremendous hope for recovery and remission from diseases, and many surgeries are now quite successful, unlike in the days before blood transfusions, sterile instruments, and anesthesia. Back when sickness and injury usually resulted in death, Catholics called for the priest to anoint based on St. James's Epistle: "Is any among you sick? Let him call for the elders of the church, and let the them pray over him, anointing him with oil" (James 5:14).

When the sick and injured weren't expected to survive, Extreme Unction was the sign that no more could be done, so the sick and injured were spiritually preparing for death. That's why even today, many of the elderly get a bit nervous when the Catholic hospital chaplain brings his purple stole and oils. They may presume the worse and only see the sacrament as the beginning of the end.

In reality, the Anointing of the Sick is to offer prayers for possible recovery, but the more important intention is to give strength to the soul of the sick person. Often, when people are sick, they get discouraged, depressed, angry, annoyed, and afraid. The Church believes that the sacrament offers a special grace to calm the spirit. If physical recovery is God's will, so be it. If not, then the person needs the grace, strength, and encouragement to bear the illness with dignity. The Sacrament of Anointing of the Sick also remits (absolves) all sins the person is sorry for but did not previously confess in the Sacrament of Penance. On occasion, there isn't time for the person to make a confession, or the person is unconscious or not lucid enough to make a confession, so the anointing compensates by forgiving sins, which the person would have confessed were he able to do so. Because of this aspect of absolving sins, deacons can't anoint, but priests and bishops can.

Book II

Walking the Catholic Walk

The Catholic notion of redemptive suffering — that is, uniting your own suffering with the crucified Jesus — gives a person's unavoidable suffering meaning and purpose. This notion is explicitly and implicitly expressed in the Sacrament of the Anointing of the Sick. Most of the time, the innocent are the ones who suffer, and guilty sinners seem to escape pain and misery. So instead of seeing suffering as a punishment, Catholics are asked to see suffering as (in the words of Mother Teresa of Calcutta) being personally kissed and embraced by the Crucified Lord. He holds us so close and so tight; we can feel the nails and thorns in our own body (analogously, of course).

Administering the sacrament

The Anointing of the Sick involves using Oil of the Sick *(oleum infirmorum)* — olive oil blessed by the bishop during Holy Week. Anointing with oil is not a magical or good-luck gesture but a sincere sign of supernatural assistance to coincide with the physical medicine and treatment already being given. Those suffering are reminded of St. Paul's words: "Now I rejoice in my sufferings for your sake, and in my flesh I complete what is lacking in Christ's afflictions for the sake of his body, that is the church," (Colossians 1:24), and "For we share abundantly in Christ's sufferings, so through Christ we share abundantly in comfort too" (2 Corinthians 1:5). Catholic Christians firmly believe in *redemptive suffering*, whereby a person willingly offers up his personal aches and pains, trials and tribulations with Christ on the Cross.

Because many sick and injured people recover nowadays, or at least go into remission, Catholics are able to receive the Sacrament of Anointing of the Sick more than once — as many times as needed. The elderly, people with many ailments, and those with a deadly or serious disease, chronic pain and suffering, or recurring illness can and should be anointed often.

Some Catholics see Anointing of the Sick as a spiritual oil change and feel that every three months (or 3,000 miles) is a good time to anoint the bedridden, people in nursing homes, and others with chronic and pathological conditions. Coauthor Father Trigilio relates, "When my brother Michael was alive and suffering from muscular dystrophy, and when my dad was alive and endured his leukemia, I often anointed them whenever I came home to visit, which was often every three months or so."

Some parishes have a Mass of Anointing once or twice a year for the sick of the parish. (That's not people who are sick of the parish. It's parishioners who are sick.) The only caveat is that often, people with minor illnesses, aches, and pains and those suffering from nonphysical conditions that aren't life threatening want to be anointed, but the sacrament is for those in danger of death or in critical condition medically speaking. In minor cases, a prayer for healing is appropriate. The sacrament shouldn't be overused or trivialized for every upset stomach and toe ache.

Many older Catholics have a "sick call set" crucifix hanging on the wall. This special crucifix opens up in preparation for the priest to make a *sick call,* a visit to the sick to anoint them, and inside are two white beeswax candles, a bottle of holy water, and a white cloth. The cloth is placed on a table near the sick person before the priest arrives to anoint him. The crucifix is laid on top of the cloth, and the two candles are put in their holders and lit, unless the patient is on oxygen, in which case, *no candles.* A family member greets the priest and escorts him to the sick person's room, which is *quiet.* In other words, the television isn't blaring *Wheel of Fortune.* The priest anoints the sick person, and if the person is dying, the priest also administers *viaticum.* Viaticum is Latin for *something for the journey.* Viaticum offers a dying person that last opportunity on earth to have intimate union with Christ by receiving his body and blood in Holy Communion. This conveys the teaching that death is but a journey from this life to the next, where the union with Jesus is forever. If a person is unconscious or is unable to eat and swallow the sacred host, then the priest doesn't administer viaticum. Whether or not Holy Communion has been administered, the Anointing of the Sick closes with the priest sprinkling holy water on the person and room.

The Catholic Church suggests that a dying person have a crucifix nearby to meditate on, a rosary, a Bible, holy water, and candles, if safe to use. These items make the setting sacred because the suffering person is going through his own form of Calvary and literally walking with the Lord as he approaches the place where Jesus was crucified.

The priest sticks his finger in the oil stock, which often has cotton squished inside to absorb the oil and keep it from spilling and going bad. He dabs some on his thumb and then anoints the head, saying, "Through this holy anointing may the Lord in his love and mercy help you with the grace of the Holy Spirit." Then, if possible, he anoints the palms of the person, saying, "May the Lord who frees you from sin save you and raise you up." If it's an emergency, such as a patient in the trauma center, the priest can anoint any part of the body that's available if the doctors and nurses are working on the head and hands of the injured person.

Priests and bishops aren't anointed on the palms when given the Sacrament of the Anointing of the Sick because their hands were already anointed at their ordination. Priests and bishops are anointed on the back of the hands instead.

Chapter 3

Obeying the Rules: Catholic Law

*L*aws aren't just arbitrary rules made by those in authority. Governments, clubs, organizations, families, and religions have laws for the common good of their members. Whether for professional baseball or a friendly game of basketball in someone's driveway, an Elks meeting or a session of Congress, all groups have rules of behavior to protect their members from possible abuse or neglect, as well as to preserve the unity and integrity of the whole group.

The Church is considered the family of God, and rules exist to protect that family as a whole, as well as the individual members. Specifically, Catholics are obligated to follow all the divine laws of God, the natural moral law, Church law (also known as *canon law*), and all the legitimate and ethical civil laws of their city, state, and nation as long as they don't contradict the laws of God or the Church. In short, a Catholic is expected to be a law-abiding citizen. This viewpoint is reinforced by what Christ said: "Render to Caesar the things that are Caesar's and to God the things that are God's" (Mark 12:17).

Every morally binding law must make sense, be known, and be of benefit to people. This chapter covers such laws, as they're understood by the Church.

Following the Eternal Law of God

In the 13th century, philosopher and theologian St. Thomas Aquinas defined *law* as "a command of reason promulgated by a competent authority for the common good." He divided it into the three categories that follow under the main title *the Eternal Law of God:*

- ✔ Divine positive law
- ✔ Natural moral law
- ✔ Human positive law
  - Civil (also known as *secular*) law
  - Ecclesiastical (also known as *canon*) law

Note that human positive law also comprises civil and ecclesiastical law. But first, you need to understand what *eternal law* means. From all eternity, God has willed that all things act according to their nature. Created things must obey the laws of nature (physics, mathematics, chemistry, gravity, and so on), animals must obey their instincts, and humans must act according to their nature, which is rational. Being rational creatures, humans must also obey authentic laws that conform to reason, are made known, and exist for the common good. So the eternal law is nothing more than the combination of all laws that conform to reason and exist for the common good of everyone.

Only rational beings can know philosophical, theological, and moral laws — so only rational beings are obligated to obey them. Catholics regard these laws as chemists regard formulas, cooks regard recipes, and pharmacists regard prescriptions: If you follow the rules, the results are guaranteed. If you fudge the figures or disregard the directions, the end product is in danger. The soul needs God's laws to find eternal happiness, and obeying them is as crucial for Catholics as following the correct formula is for scientists.

The divine positive law

According to Exodus in the Old Testament, God issued his own set of laws, known as the *Ten Commandments,* which were given to Moses on Mount Sinai. God didn't give Moses ten suggestions or ten proposals but Ten Commandments. These laws aren't negotiable, and they apply to every human being who's at least 7 years old (the age of reason).

The first three commandments deal with your personal relationship with God: Love but one God, honor His name, and honor His day. The last seven deal with interpersonal relationships: Honor your parents and honor other people's lives, property, spouses, and their right to know the truth. Chapter 12 spells out all the details concerning the Ten Commandments.

Because God himself revealed the Ten Commandments, they're considered *divine* law. And because they were spelled out specifically with no room for ambiguity, they're also *positive* law. Hence the term *divine positive law.* For many people, the Ten Commandments — whether or not they're classified under the term *divine positive law* — are still treated as rules and regulations.

But the divine positive law isn't abstract or arbitrary. It's simple and explicit: Thou shall not kill; Thou shall not commit adultery; Thou shall not steal; and so on. The Ten Commandments are all simple and clear. Although the last seven of the ten can be known by reason alone via the natural moral law (see "The natural moral law" section, coming up next), God chose to reinforce and equalize the playing field by divinely revealing them, too, instead of just leaving them for people to figure out on their own.

Think of it like the sticker on a hair dryer that says, "Do not immerse in water while plugged in to outlet." Even though most people know via common sense not to do so, some people don't know that it's dangerous and lethal to let a plugged-in hair dryer fall into water. That's the reason for the stickers. Common sense should also tell folks to honor their parents, not to take an innocent life, not to cheat on their spouses, not to lie, not to steal, and so on. But for some people, common sense doesn't do it. So in His divine mercy, God revealed His divine positive law to remove all doubt and ambiguity.

Book II

Walking the Catholic Walk

The natural moral law

The Bible tells the story of Cain murdering his brother Abel centuries before Moses ever received the Ten Commandments, which included the injunction "Thou shall not kill." So if he'd had a good lawyer, such as *Rumpole of the Bailey* or the Dream Team — F. Lee Bailey, Johnny Cochran, and Barry Scheck — could Cain have had his day in court and been acquitted, because the law hadn't been promulgated until *after* the alleged crime took place?

> But your Divinity, my client is innocent of murder because he didn't have access to a Bible, and there's no way he could've known about the Fifth Commandment because it wasn't written down by You and given to Moses until centuries after my client allegedly committed the deed.

Case closed? Not.

The Bible explains that because Cain *knew* he did something wrong, immoral, and sinful, he hid from the Lord. And Moses broke the same commandment (Exodus 2:12) before he got the Ten Commandments. After killing an Egyptian, Moses fled into the desert because he *knew* he did wrong — even though he didn't get the Fifth Commandment for another 18 chapters.

So how did both Cain and Moses know it was wrong to murder an innocent person? And why did other civilizations, such as the Egyptians, Persians, Assyrians, Babylonians, Greeks, and Romans, all have laws forbidding murder, stealing, adultery, perjury, and so on, if they didn't have the revealed Word of God like the Hebrews did? How could Nazi soldiers and officers be condemned at the Nuremburg War Trials for crimes of genocide if they and their government had no religion and no belief in God, let alone any respect for His chosen people? Can all men and women be aware of an unwritten law merely by the use of reason? Does this naturally knowable law apply to all human beings at every time and in every place?

A century before Christ, the Roman stoic philosopher Cicero wrote:

> There is truly a law, which is right reason, fitted to our nature, proclaimed to all men, constant, everlasting. It calls to duty by commanding and deters from wrong by forbidding, neither commanding nor forbidding the good man in vain when it fails to move the wicked. It can neither be evaded nor amended nor wholly abolished. No decree of Senate or people can free us from it. No explainer or interpreter of it need be sought but itself. There will not be found one law at Rome and another at Athens, one now and another later, but one law, everlasting and unchangeable, extending to all nations and all times. (*De Republica*, III, xxii, 33)

And St. Paul the Apostle said:

> When Gentiles who have not the law do by nature what the law requires, they are a law to themselves, even though they do not have the law. They show that what the law requires is written on their hearts (Romans 2:14–15a).

Natural moral law is unwritten but is known by all men and women who have the use of reason. It uses basic common sense, prudence, and justice. Because it's known by reason, not written in stone or on paper, like the Commandments or the Bible, the moral law is *natural.* It's *moral* because it applies only to moral acts — actions of human beings that involve a free act of the will. (It doesn't apply to animals because they don't have the use of reason.)

Because of the natural moral law, Cain and Moses knew it was wrong to commit murder before the Fifth Commandment ever came along. And because of the natural moral law, trials for war crimes can be conducted against anyone who commits genocide or mass murder regardless of the person's religion or lack thereof. A Nazi couldn't have used the defense that he didn't recognize the authority of the Bible because even the most evil of Nazis still had the use of reason, and reason is what discovers the natural moral law for each and every man and woman.

Just obeying orders or following the civil law won't cut it either. An immoral act violates the natural moral law even if it conforms to the local civil law. Slavery was immoral and contrary to natural moral law even though the U.S. Supreme Court (1857) upheld it until it was overturned by the 14th Amendment (1868) after the Civil War. The Nuremburg Laws of Nazi Germany (1935) also violated the natural moral law because they deprived Jews of their citizenship; paved the way for confiscation of personal property, deportation, and incarceration; and doomed many to the concentration camps. Apartheid is another example: The legalized racial segregation in South Africa from 1948 to 1991 defied the natural moral law. In all these cases, the civil law endorsed, tolerated, or promoted horrible injustices precisely because the natural moral law was being violated. A government, a constitution, a law, or an amendment doesn't grant personhood. It comes from human nature made in the image and likeness of God. Jew and Christian, born and unborn: The natural moral law exists despite what political parties and civil authorities legislate to the contrary.

Book II

Walking the Catholic Walk

The human positive law

People — not God or nature — create *human laws.* The Church maintains that natural and divine laws are immutable and eternal because they come from God. However, human laws — whether they come from the Church or the government — are conditioned by contemporary circumstances, such as time, place, and culture. They're *positive* in that they're clearly written and promulgated.

Speed limits of 15 miles per hour in a school zone, income tax laws, and the Patriot Act are all human laws. They're not perfect and can always be improved, changed, interpreted, dissolved, or re-created.

Human laws apply to humans, obviously, so when an animal does damage to property or people, the owners are often responsible. Also, human laws aren't meant to restrict activity and behavior but to protect and defend the inalienable rights of life and liberty of all people. So even though one of the Commandments is "Thou shall not steal," and the natural moral law tells people with reason that taking something that doesn't belong to them is unethical and wrong, civil laws also make theft a crime — a punishable one.

Human positive law comprises both civil law and canon (Church) law.

Civil law

Civil laws are all the laws written and enforced by cities, states, nations, and international communities, such as the United Nations (UN) and the North Atlantic Treaty Organization (NATO). Calgary, Alberta, has laws that apply only to residents of the municipality, but Alberta has laws that apply to all the cities and towns in the province. The Canadian Parliament makes laws that are binding in all its provinces because the Canadian government oversees the whole country.

Some civil laws apply only to residents of the area, and other laws apply to anyone who works at or visits that place, too. For example, speed-limit laws are for everyone, regardless of where you live, vote, or have citizenship, but laws for where and when you vote depend on exactly where you live. Because civil laws (being human laws) aren't perfect, they can and must be interpreted and applied by a recognized authority.

Canon (Church) law

Canon law is the supreme law of the Church, and it specifies the universal norms and regulations for the entire Church. The Catholic Church is a religion and an institution. With more than 1 billion members worldwide and thousands of cardinals, bishops, priests, and deacons to govern the Church, having laws that pertain to activities and people in the Church is both a necessity and a matter of justice.

Getting a taste of canon law

The word *canon* comes from the Greek *kanon,* which means *rule* and refers to decrees that are binding on all persons. *Canon law* refers to the laws that apply to all members of the Catholic faith. The Roman Church has 1,752 canons, and 1,546 canons are in the Eastern Catholic Church. That's quite a few more than the Ten Commandments, eh? It could be worse — the number of Roman Catholic canons actually decreased in 1983; 2,414 canons filled the Code from 1917 to 1982! The *Code of Canon Law* is the book containing the laws of the Catholic Church. The edition for the Western (Latin) Church is separate from the Eastern (Byzantine) Church edition.

The Code of Canon Law is patterned according to the Vatican II document *Lumen Gentium* (Dogmatic Constitution on the Church), which describes the Catholic Church as the living and continuing presence of Christ on earth — his mystical body and spotless bride. The Church that Christ himself founded continues his three-fold mission as priest, prophet, and king — to sanctify, teach, and govern. Laws allow the Church to govern.

Some laws protect rights and privileges; others define obligations and duties. Following are some examples:

- ✔ Canon 226 reminds parents that they're the primary teachers of their children and, therefore, they are responsible to God for their sons' and daughters' religious education and practice.

- Canon 208 emphasizes the genuine equality of dignity and action among all of Christ's faithful. This means that clergy aren't better than laity, and both have equal importance, although they have different functions.

- Canon 212 guarantees that everyone has a right to make known their spiritual needs to their pastors.

- Canon 221 states that all the faithful (laity and clergy) have a right to due process in church tribunals and ecclesiastical courts.

- Canon 281 guarantees clergy fair wages, and Canon 283 assures them reasonable time off — one weekly day off and 30 days of annual vacation (533).

- Canon 276 highly encourages priests, deacons, and bishops to participate in daily Mass and obliges them to daily pray the Liturgy of the Hours, make an annual retreat, go to confession often, and honor and venerate the Virgin Mary.

Facing punishment for violations

Law exists to protect the common good, and sometimes that requires disciplining those who violate the rules and thereby endanger the community as well as themselves. Sanctions are medicinal punishments meant to encourage a person to stop doing something harmful. Normally, the penalty is removed soon after the offender repents and ceases to break the law.

Some of the punishments handed down by the ecclesiastical court system include interdict, suspension, and excommunication.

- **Interdict:** This is a temporary penalty that can be applied to one or more persons, either of the clergy or laity. Under this punishment, the persons named can't receive the sacraments, but they aren't excommunicated, so they still can receive income, hold office, and so on. The sanction is lifted when the person repents and seeks reconciliation.

- **Suspension:** Applying to clergy only, the Church forbids priest, deacon, or bishop to exercise his ordained ministry and to wear clerical garb. However, suspension doesn't deprive the cleric of receiving the sacraments.

- **Excommunication:** The most severe form of penalty, *excommunication*, which means being outside of the Church, is used only as a last resort, with the hope that the excommunicated person, whether cleric or layperson, will repent and seek reconciliation. Excommunicated people are deprived of the sacraments, such as receiving the Holy Eucharist at Mass. The excommunicated are also forbidden from employment or holding any position of authority in a diocese or parish and are deprived of a Catholic burial. However, penalties are suspended in danger of death. If the excommunicated person shows a sign of repentance before he dies, then he's allowed Catholic funeral rites.

Some excommunications are automatic and occur as soon as the offense is committed, without formal declaration by the Church. Others are imposed by the local bishop by formal decree.

Of the three, excommunication is the most serious and most severe. Often people ask, "Why, then, are not murder, rape, or sexual abuse of children listed as crimes worthy of excommunication?" The main reason is that these horrible sins are also violations of civil law and already incur serious penalties that only the state can impose, such as imprisonment.

Sins that violate divine, natural, and/or Church law are not always in violation of civil law. Abortion is legal in many places but is still considered a grave evil because it's the direct and actual killing of an innocent human life. The sin of abortion incurs an automatic excommunication (Canon 1398) for all direct participants and necessary accomplices as long as each one knows there is a serious penalty for that crime.

Canon 1323, however, stipulates that no one can be excommunicated who

- Has not turned 17
- Was, without fault, ignorant of violating the law
- Acted under physical force or under a chance occurrence that could not be foreseen or avoided
- Acted under compulsion of grave fear
- Lacked the use of reason

Some penalties (for example, those for heresy, pretended celebration of the Holy Eucharist, or procuring an abortion) can be lifted by any priest when the offender goes to confession in the Sacrament of Penance. Other penalties are so serious that only the local bishop or, in some grave offenses, only the pope can remove them. For example, only the pope can remove the offenses of desecration of sacred species (Holy Communion) or physical attack on the pope himself. To find out more about punishment for different offenses, check out the Code of Canon Law.

Playing by the Church's Rules

While the 1983 Code of Canon Law has 1,752 laws, the Church has only five *precepts,* which are the Catholic Church's house rules — the basic recipe for spiritual health for each and every Catholic. Just as schoolchildren must at least attend school daily in order to remain in school and employees must show up for work each day to keep their paychecks coming, so, too, Catholics must do the minimum by following these five precepts. These simple precepts are, of course, in addition to the Ten Commandments, which apply to every Christian (Protestant, Catholic, and Orthodox) and Jew alike. But the precepts of the Church are binding only on Catholics. To be a good, practicing Catholic means believing what the Church teaches and obeying these rules:

✔ Attend Mass on all Sundays and holy days of obligation.

✔ Receive the Holy Eucharist during Easter season.

✔ Confess your sins at least once a year.

✔ Fast and abstain on appointed days.

✔ Contribute to the support of the Church.

In the United States, the American bishops added two more precepts:

✔ Observe the marriage laws of the Church.

✔ Support missionary work of the Church.

Except for the Ten Commandments and the natural moral law, most Catholics aren't well versed in the 1983 *Code of Canon Law* because so many laws exist. But Catholics are aware of the precepts of the Church, which are personal applications of the numerous canons from the Code.

Nowadays, the minimum requirements for the precepts are manageable — they're not nearly as burdensome as they were in the old, old days (back when monks were monks and nuns were nuns). Of course, personal piety may motivate some people to go beyond the minimum by, for example, praying the Rosary daily, going to confession once a week, or attending Mass once or twice during the week in addition to Sunday.

Attending Mass on all Sundays and holy days of obligation

Catholics must regularly and faithfully attend and participate in a Catholic Mass each and every Sunday and holy day of obligation. Missing Mass on one of these days is a mortal sin. Only inclement weather and bad health that would prevent you from leaving home at all excuse you from the obligation of going to Mass that day.

Even on vacation, Catholics are obliged to attend Mass. Non-Catholic religious services are fine as long as Catholics don't attempt to substitute a non-Catholic worship service for the Mass. So, for example, if you attend a Lutheran Sunday service, you still have to go to Sunday Mass in addition if you're a Catholic.

Book II

Walking the Catholic Walk

Receiving the Holy Eucharist during Easter season

Catholics must receive the Holy Eucharist at least once during the Easter season, which for U.S. Catholics is from Ash Wednesday to Trinity Sunday. In the Middle Ages, many Catholics, feeling personally unworthy, received the Eucharist only rarely even though the Church never endorsed that they go only occasionally. Pope St. Pius X (he was pope from 1903–1914), however, felt that Catholics should receive Christ every time that they went to Mass as long as they were without the blemish of mortal sin. So Catholics were encouraged and prepared for more frequent reception, which is why this precept was created. The Church requires that Catholics fast for an hour before receiving the Eucharist. This means that Catholics can't eat or drink anything besides water or necessary medication for at least an hour before receiving the Holy Eucharist.

Receiving Holy Eucharist once a year during the Easter season is the minimum requirement for Catholics, and receiving it twice a day — if you attend two Masses — is the maximum allowed.

Confessing your sins at least once a year

Confessing your sins once a year applies only if you're guilty and conscious of a mortal sin. Full consent of the will, full knowledge, and grave matter are all required elements for mortal sin. Missing Sunday Mass without a valid excuse (such as really bad weather or serious illness), a sin of the flesh, and blasphemy by using God's name in vain are all mortal sins. These sins and all other mortal sins must be confessed before a Catholic can worthily receive the Holy Eucharist. The bare-minimum requirement is that those in a state of mortal sin must go to confession before receiving the Holy Eucharist. Otherwise, they've committed another mortal sin — the *sacrilege* of receiving Communion when in the state of mortal sin, a sort of spiritual double jeopardy. Before Vatican II, most Catholics went to confession every week before going to Communion.

Fasting and abstaining on appointed days

Today, *abstaining* applies to all Catholics age 14 and older and means that they must not eat meat on Ash Wednesday, Good Friday, and all Fridays in Lent. (Meat is any beef, pork, chicken, or fowl.) *Fasting* applies to all Catholics ages 18 to 59 and means they must eat only one full meal on Ash Wednesday and

Good Friday, which means no snacks between meals. However, two smaller meals, such as breakfast and lunch, can be eaten in addition to the one full meal (supper) as long as they don't equal the one full meal if combined.

Some Eastern Catholics and many Orthodox Christians observe the *Great Fast,* meaning they don't eat any meat, egg, or dairy products during all 40 days of Lent, and they often fast every Friday — if not every day — of Lent (from midnight to noon) except on Sundays (to honor the Resurrection).

Before Vatican II, *every* Friday of the year — Lent or not — was a day of abstinence from meat. Today, in most countries, only Fridays in Lent are obligatory, but the Church highly recommends abstinence on Fridays during the rest of the year to show respect for the day Christ died and sacrificed his flesh on the cross. The Church also recommends that if Catholics don't abstain on Fridays outside of Lent, they should do some small form of penance or work of mercy, nevertheless.

Contributing to the support of the Church

Although *tithing,* giving 10 percent of your income to the parish, is mentioned in the Bible (Leviticus 27:30–34), it isn't mandatory in the Catholic Church. Most Catholics are encouraged to donate at least 5 percent of their income to the parish and 5 percent to their favorite charities. Statistically, though, Catholics are notoriously the lowest givers of all Christians, dedicating 1 percent of their incomes to the Church. Mainline Protestants give 2 percent, and Evangelical and Fundamentalist Christians give 5 to 10 percent.

But those who can't give much financial support can and often do donate an abundance of volunteer time to the parish by holding fundraisers and supporting other parish events and projects. Volunteers sometimes teach religious education programs for children, sometimes known as the Confraternity of Christian Doctrine (CCD) classes and the Rite of Christian Initiation of Adults (RCIA) classes (convert classes for adults). Catholic children who can't attend a Catholic school learn about the Catholic faith through CCD classes, and non-Catholics who are interested in the Catholic faith attend RCIA classes, usually at a local parish. Those volunteers who are too old or infirm for other types of service support the parish with their prayers. Giving of one's time and talent, as well as giving of your treasure (financial contributions), are ways that Catholic Christians support their church, from the parish to the diocese.

In the eyes of the Church, nobody goes to heaven merely by earning their way through obedience, because salvation is a free gift from God. But following the laws of God (divine and natural laws) and the laws of His Church help a person be a better person, a better Christian, and a better Catholic. These rules and regulations help promote holiness just as following your doctor's advice and prescriptions helps promote good health.

Observing Church marriage laws

Although this precept isn't given in the Catechism as one of the five, Catholics in America are asked to abide by it. Catholics must be married with two witnesses before a priest, bishop, or deacon in a Catholic Church at a Catholic wedding ceremony, unless a special *dispensation* (a special allowance in light of circumstances that warrant it) has been granted from the local bishop for the couple to be married by a non-Catholic minister in a non-Catholic ceremony at a non-Catholic church.

In addition, Catholics ought to take 9 to 12 months to prepare for their marriage. During this prep time, called the *Pre-Cana period,* the couple receives practical advice and instructions from the priest or deacon. Catholics can only marry someone who has never been married before, or the intended spouse must have an official annulment from a previous marriage. And both the bride and groom must intend to enter a permanent, faithful, and (God willing) fruitful union for it to be a valid sacrament. (See Book II, Chapter 2 for much more information about the Sacrament of Matrimony.)

Supporting missionary work of the Church

American bishops ask that the faithful pray regularly for the success of the Church's missions abroad, provide financial support when possible, and encourage priests, brothers, and sisters to enter *vocations,* or callings, to be missionaries around the world. Spiritual and material support for those who are helping others is a challenge to all the faithful, since Catholics belong to a universal and not just a local church community.

Chapter 4

Loving and Honoring: The Ten Commandments

In This Chapter

▶ Honoring God, His name, and His day

▶ Loving the folks next door and all down the block

▶ Going neck and neck on the Ten Commandments

The Catholic Church sees the Ten Commandments as one of the four *pillars of faith,* along with the Creed (the Apostles' Creed and the Nicene Creed), the seven sacraments, and the Our Father. They're called the *pillars of faith* because they're the foundations upon which the Catholic Church is built, just as an altar would have four solid pillars to support itself. Each pillar represents a major component of Catholicism, and all four together establish the core of Catholic belief and practice. The Church treats the Ten Commandments as divine laws from God that the Church and pope can never change, add to, or subtract from.

The Church doesn't see the Ten Commandments as arbitrary rules and regulations from the man upstairs but as commandments for protection. Obey them, and eternal happiness is yours. Disobey them and suffer the consequences.

The Ten Commandments have also been called the *Decalogue* (Greek) and the *Debarim* (Hebrew), both of which mean *the Ten Words.*

Many a preacher has said, "These are the Ten Commandments, not the Ten Suggestions." True enough. Just as a prescription tells you how many pills to take and how often, the Commandments tell us what to do and what not to do in the moral life. Disregard the formula in the laboratory, and the chemicals you mix may explode. Ignore grandma's favorite recipe and carelessly fail to measure the ingredients, and the end result won't taste good. Likewise, disobey the Commandments now, and expect eternal misery in the afterlife.

Demonstrating Love for God

The first three commandments focus on the individual's relationship with God. The main objectives are to honor God, His name, and His day.

I: Honor God

The First Commandment is "I am the Lord your God, you shall not have strange gods before Me." This commandment forbids *idolatry*, the worship of false gods and goddesses, and it forbids *polytheism*, the belief in many gods, insisting instead on *monotheism*, the belief in one God. So the obvious and blatant ways to break this commandment are to

- ✔ Worship a false god, be it Hercules, Zena, or Satan
- ✔ Consciously and willingly deny the existence of God, as in the case of atheism or having no religion whatsoever

The Catholic Church looks at the commandment — the letter of the law and the spirit of the law — and tries to apply it to daily life. Granted, in the 21st century, the Church doesn't see many people worshipping idols like they used to do in pagan Greece and Rome. But refraining from building golden calves or statues of Caesar in your house aren't the only ways you can obey the First Commandment.

Rejecting false belief systems

You can break the First Commandment by willingly and consciously being ignorant of what God has revealed in Sacred Scripture (the Bible) and Sacred Tradition (see Book I, Chapter 2), as well as by believing in and/or seriously using *astrology* (horoscopes), numerology, and *dianetics*, which refers to the Church of Scientology.

Another way to break this commandment is to become involved with *New Age spirituality*, which is an informal religion of no creed, no liturgy, no doctrine, and no church structure, leadership, or institution. This type of religion blends ancient paganism with the occult, superstition, Gnosticism, and so on. It's extremely different from the three monotheistic religions of Judaism, Christianity, and Islam.

Dabbling in witchcraft, sorcery, devil worship, white or black magic, voodoo, *spiritism* (communicating with the dead), *fortune telling* (which is also known as psychic reading), tarot cards, Ouija boards, lucky charms, and such are all violations of this commandment, too.

Sacrilege, the desecration of holy objects, and *simony,* trying to buy or sell spiritual favors or graces, are also ways in which you can break the First Commandment. The Church believes that all these things are forbidden by the first commandment because they don't put the one, true God before all else — and many of them put credence in superstition.

Tuning out the distractions and putting God first

Today, the most common way that the First Commandment is broken seems to be when you put someone or something before God. In other words, God isn't your highest priority. According to Catholicism, when career, fame, fortune, comfort, pleasure, family, or a friend, for example, is your most important object, value, or priority, you're violating the First Commandment.

Even though you're not denying the existence of God or showing contempt for God or things symbolizing the divine, the Church believes that you're showing disrespect by not making God your highest priority and most cherished relationship. When you're too busy to go to church every week or going to church becomes too inconvenient, yet you have time to attend every soccer game for Susie, music recital for Johnny, and football game at your favorite college, then God's no longer *numero uno* in your life.

The Bible, Jesus Christ, and the Catholic Church say that you're to love God "with all your heart, and with all your soul, and with all your strength, and with all your mind" (Luke 10:27). So no one and no thing can be number one in your heart except God.

Spending QT with God

To the Church, the First Commandment implies that if God is the most important person in your life, you'll want to honor Him, spend quality time with Him, and communicate with Him daily through prayer. Prayer enables you to speak to God with your heart and mind — vocally or mentally — and neglecting to pray, or intentionally not praying, violates the First Commandment.

Honoring, not idolizing, Mary and the saints

According to the First Commandment, only God the Father, God the Son, and God the Holy Spirit are entitled to and deserve worship and adoration. Worshipping or adoring anyone or anything else is idolatry and forbidden. Yet Catholics are sometimes accused of idolatry for the prayer and honor they give to the saints — especially the highest honor and respect they give to Mary, the Mother of Jesus. While worship of anyone or anything other than God is idolatry, adoration is only one form of prayer. Intercessory prayer addressed to the Virgin Mary and the Saints isn't worship, but spiritual communication.

Book II

Walking the Catholic Walk

In Catholicism, the devotion to and veneration of Mary and the saints aren't considered idolatry because devotion, honor, and veneration aren't considered the same as worship and adoration. The Fourth Commandment, "Honor your father and mother," shows the faithful that honoring a human being, like mom or dad, is permissible — even commanded — because honor isn't adoration or worship. And in the Gospel, even Jesus showed honor to dead people, such as Abraham and Moses, speaking of them with great respect.

Catholics believe that if humans can and must honor their parents, then it's only logical to honor the faithful servants of God who lived holy lives on earth and are now in heaven before the throne of God.

II: Honor God's name

The Second Commandment, "You shall not take the name of the Lord your God in vain," tells the faithful to honor the name of God, which goes hand in hand with the First Commandment saying to honor the person of God by not worshipping anyone else. It makes sense that if you're to love God with all your heart, soul, mind, and strength, then you're naturally to respect the name of God with equal passion and vigor.

Avoiding blasphemy

Imagine a man using his fiancée's name whenever he wants to curse. How can he say that he loves his girlfriend if he shows contempt for her very name? A person's name is part of who that person is, and respect for the name is respect for the person. Disrespect and contempt for the name equal disrespect for the person.

So Catholics believe that using God's name — especially the name *Jesus Christ* — to swear and curse when, say, a car cuts you off in traffic, a bird leaves a little surprise on your new suit, or a stranger waves with his middle finger is disrespectful to God. It's using the sacred name of the Lord and Savior to show anger and hostility. It's ironic that many who claim to be followers of Christ show their anger and animosity by using His name. Think about it. When was the last time you heard someone say *Jesus Christ?* Was it in prayer or shouted from an open window?

Using God's name in a disrespectful manner is *blasphemy,* and it's the essence of the Second Commandment.

Respecting holy things and holy oaths

Any act of disrespect to anything holy — be it a holy image, place, or person — is considered a *sacrilege,* and it's forbidden by the Second Commandment. The Church believes that you're being irreligious when you show contempt for God, such as by desecrating a holy object or place. When a house of worship — a church, temple, synagogue, or mosque — is vandalized, the Church maintains that the sin of sacrilege has been committed; a house of God was desecrated, and contempt was shown not solely for those who attend the house's services but also and preeminently for the person the place was built for.

You're also violating the Second Commandment if you make jokes, watch movies, or read books that are disrespectful to God or anything considered holy. So for a Catholic, if you ridicule or laugh at a Jewish man for wearing a *yarmulke* (skull cap), a Muslim woman for wearing a *khimar* (head covering), a nun for wearing her religious habit, or a priest for wearing a *cassock* (a long, close-fitting garment, usually black), you're being sacrilegious. Human beings wear certain things out of religious tradition, or they perform certain rituals as an external way of showing their love for God. When others make fun of religious garb or religious practices, it's an insult to the one being honored by them, in other words, God Himself.

The Second Commandment also forbids false oaths and perjury. So to place your hand on the Holy Bible and swear to tell the whole truth and nothing but the truth, "so help me God," and then tell a lie is considered perjury and a serious violation of this commandment. Also, when a couple plans to get married, they meet with a priest or deacon and fill out papers that ask questions, such as "Were you ever married before?" and "Do you intend to enter a permanent, faithful, and, God willing, fruitful union?" They're asked to sign this document, and by doing so, they're placing themselves under oath and saying that they've answered all the questions truthfully. Lying about any of the questions is considered a false oath — a mortal sin.

III: Honor God's day

The Third Commandment is "Remember to keep holy the Lord's day." The Jewish celebration of Sabbath *(Shabbat)* begins at sundown on Friday evening and lasts until sundown on Saturday. So, basically, Saturday is the Sabbath Day. It's the last day of the week, the seventh day, the day (according to the Book of Genesis) on which God rested after six days of creation. Even modern calendars have Saturday as the last day of the week and Sunday as the first day of the new week.

So why, then, do Catholic, Protestant, and Orthodox Christians go to church on Sunday, treating it as the Lord's Day instead of Saturday? In general, Catholicism and Christianity moved the celebration of the Lord's Day from Saturday to Sunday because Jesus Christ rose from the dead on Easter Sunday. In other words, Sunday has become the Christian Sabbath, the day of rest, to honor the day Christ rose from the dead. Jesus said in the Gospel that the Sabbath was made for man, not man for the Sabbath. So, Christians who wanted to honor their Risen Lord on the day of the week that He rose from the dead made Sunday their day of worship instead of the former day of Saturday, which the Hebrews had honored from the time of Moses.

Catholics are also bound to attend a Catholic Mass on each and every Sunday or the Vigil Mass on Saturday of every weekend in the calendar year. To miss Mass on Sunday is considered a mortal sin unless the person has a legitimate excuse, such as serious illness.

Ever wonder why some Catholics go to Mass on Saturday evening instead of Sunday morning? Using the Hebrew method of time reckoning, after sundown on Saturday evening is actually the beginning of Sunday, so the Church allows parishes to offer a Saturday evening *Vigil Mass* to satisfy the Sunday obligation.

But just going to a Christian Sunday worship service isn't good enough. In order for Catholics to satisfy and fulfill the Third Commandment, they must attend a valid Catholic Mass. Going to another denomination for a Sunday worship service is nice, but Catholics must also attend Mass the evening before or sometime during the day on Sunday. The reason is that the Church maintains that only the Mass has the real, true, and substantial presence of Christ in the Holy Eucharist. Even if a Catholic doesn't receive Holy Communion, she still satisfies the Sunday obligation by attending and participating at Mass.

The Third Commandment also forbids doing any servile work — unnecessary hard labor — on the Lord's Day, because it's a day of rest. And Pope John Paul II wrote a document about Sunday, *Dies Domini* (Latin for *Day of the Lord*), in which he reminded Catholics of the serious obligation to attend Mass each and every weekend and to refrain from doing unnecessary manual work.

To meet this obligation, all Catholics would optimally have Sunday off, so they'd have the opportunity to go to church and spend time with family. But in reality, some people must work frequently on Sundays — doctors, nurses, pharmacists, police officers, firefighters, and so on. Pastors can transfer the obligation to another day, but only on an individual basis and only for serious reasons.

Loving Your Neighbor

The last seven of the Ten Commandments focus on the individual's relationship with others. The main objectives are to honor your parents, human life, human sexuality, the property of others, and the truth.

IV: Honor your parents

The Fourth Commandment, "Honor your father and mother," obliges the faithful to show respect for their parents — as children *and* adults. Children must obey their parents, and adults must respect and see to the care of their parents when they become old and infirm.

Therefore, the Catholic Church believes that adult children who abandon, abuse, or neglect their elderly parents are violating the Fourth Commandment as much as teenage children who refuse to show respect or obedience to their parents. Likewise, being ashamed or embarrassed of your parents is considered as much a sin as disobeying them when you're a child or harboring feelings of hatred or revenge for them even if they weren't the parents they should have been.

This commandment is meant to protect the dignity and integrity of the family, which consists of a father, a mother, and their children. Obviously, some families are headed by a single parent because of the death or illness of the absent parent or because the absent parent was abusive or delinquent; in such sad circumstances, some people manage to do a terrific job at parenting solo. However, many single-parent households exist simply because the parents never married in the first place. Catholicism teaches that this commandment frowns on the option of freely and willingly choosing to establish a single-parent family. Voluntary single parenthood is considered an abuse because, all things being equal, a child deserves both a loving mother and a loving father.

Whether it's adopting a child or having your own, parenthood should be sought and tried within the context of the family, which means a husband and a wife to be the mother and the father, rather than just being a parent by yourself. Just as the Church discourages parenthood outside of marriage, she also condemns artificial insemination — especially from donors not married to the potential mother.

According to the Church, children deserve (if possible) to have both parents. The Church also believes that even if the children are adopted, parenthood means both genders. So two men or two women can't replace the divine plan that everyone deserves — a father and a mother.

The Catholic Church believes this commandment means more than just keeping order in the home and preventing the kids from establishing anarchy. It also entails and implies a respect and honor for everyone in legitimate positions of authority — be they civilian, military, or *ecclesiastical* (church-related). Teachers, employers, police officers, and so on have some degree of authority over others, and the Fourth Commandment requires that respect be shown to those given the responsibility of taking care of others. Whether you like or dislike the person who was elected president or prime minister, for example, the office demands some respect and dignity if, say, the prime minister enters the room. To show contempt or disrespect is considered sinful.

In the same line of thinking, this commandment also involves respect and love for your country. Patriotism isn't the same as nationalism. The former is a healthy love and respect for your country, but the latter is blind, total, and unrestricted support for any and all legislation, policies, or activities of a nation. Nationalism is the extreme, whereas patriotism is the goal, because good patriots know when to challenge their political leaders, laws, and policies when they become unjust or immoral.

For Catholics, this commandment recognizes the natural right of the family and of the state to form society. The family is the primary and fundamental building block from which comes the civil union of many families into a local and national government. And the family is the basis for the faith community of the Church, which is the family of God and the union of all the natural families around the world.

V: Honor human life

In English, the Fifth Commandment is read as "You shall not kill," but the Hebrew word *ratsach* (murder) was used rather than *nakah* (kill), so the better translation would be "Thou shalt not murder." And St. Jerome used the Latin word *occidere* (to murder) instead of *interficere* (to kill) when he translated the Hebrew into the *Latin Vulgate,* which was the first complete Christian Bible combining the Old and New Testaments in one volume and translated.

It's a subtle distinction but an important one to the Church. Killing an innocent person is considered murder. Killing an unjust aggressor to preserve your own life is still killing, but it isn't considered murder or immoral by any means. The use of deadly force is morally permitted *only* if it's the last resort and if the person isn't innocent — he or she must be guilty of a most serious offense or threatening to commit such horrible evil.

Forbidding unjust killings

The Catholic Church believes that murder is the sin prohibited in the Fifth Commandment. Killing in self-defense has always been considered justifiable and morally permissible. This distinction is the reason that when God ordered the Israelites to kill sometimes in the Old Testament, it wasn't a violation of the Fifth Commandment. Only unjust killing (taking innocent life) or murder is forbidden. Likewise, police officers and soldiers may have to use deadly force in certain well-defined and restricted circumstances. Again, this is morally permitted. Yet the legitimate taking of life isn't casual, unlicensed, unrestricted, or uncontrolled. The Church sees it as only a last resort — rare rather than common.

In broader terms, the Church believes that the intentional taking of innocent life includes murder (homicide or manslaughter), abortion, euthanasia, suicide, in most cases the death penalty, and even the old custom of dueling. The Church also condemns terrorism, violence, and any unjust war or physical abuse.

Taking issue with capital punishment

Capital punishment, whereby the death penalty is inflicted on someone guilty of a grisly murder, is obviously not the same as the murder of an innocent person. The pope and the Catechism acknowledge the theoretical right of the state (civil government) to resort to this extreme measure, but its actual implementation must be morally done across the board.

Because capital punishment is not currently performed universally, uniformly, and equitably, the Church claims that very few if any circumstances or situations today fulfill the moral criteria to allow the death penalty to be carried out. Because some countries outlaw it and others do not; some states and provinces allow it and others do not; location has plenty to do with capital punishment. How just is it to put criminals to death based on where the crime took place? Is life more or less sacred in one location than another? Also, several means of capital punishment are more humane than others. Does making it *painless* make it more acceptable?

Finally, it's often the poor who get executed because the rich and famous can hire expensive lawyers to appeal their cases. The poor people are given public defenders and don't have the money to make appeals. Based on the inequities of place, diversity of means, and unfairness of economics as to who has access to aggressive attorneys and long appeal processes, the reality of the death penalty overrules the theory that some criminals can be morally executed as a last resort. Although not totally condemning capital punishment, the Catechism does strongly discourage it. Whenever an innocent life is unjustly taken, it is always condemned as murder.

Recognizing other violations

More subtle violations of this commandment, according to the Church, include growing angry in your heart with your neighbor, harboring feelings of hatred or revenge, being criminally negligent (such as refusing to save someone's life when you're able to do so), and committing personal abuse (which is intentionally neglecting to take care of your own health and safety).

Abusing drugs and alcohol is considered breaking the Fifth Commandment because it recklessly endangers the user's life and potentially endangers others if someone under the influence becomes violent and irrational. Drunk driving is considered a violation because drunk drivers are jeopardizing their own lives and the lives of others by using an auto under the influence.

Mutilation and torture of human or animal life is also considered breaking the Fifth Commandment. Using animals for medical and scientific research is permitted as long as no suffering or unnecessary death is involved. To boot, psychological or emotional abuse is considered forbidden because such abuse attacks the victim with unjust consequences.

Because the natural moral law (see Book II, Chapter 3) tells anyone with the use of reason that the intentional, direct taking of innocent life is immoral and wrong, the Fifth Commandment is no secret nor is it a change from general human experience. In the Bible, Cain knew it was wrong to murder his brother Abel, even though it was centuries before Moses ever received all Ten Commandments. And the Nazis who were convicted of war crimes, such as genocide, were found guilty not by reason of the Fifth Commandment but because of the natural moral law, which also outlaws such atrocities.

VI and IX: Honor human sexuality

The Sixth Commandment is "You shall not commit adultery," and the ninth is "You shall not covet your neighbor's wife." Both deal with honoring human sexuality.

The Sixth Commandment forbids the actual, physical act of having immoral sexual activity, specifically adultery, which is sex with someone else's spouse or a spouse cheating on his or her partner. But this commandment also includes *fornication,* which is sex between unmarried people, prostitution, pornography, homosexual activity, masturbation, group sex, rape, incest, pedophilia, bestiality, and necrophilia.

The Ninth Commandment forbids the intentional desire and longing for immoral sexuality. To sin in the heart, Jesus says, is to lust after a woman or a man with the desire and will to have immoral sex with that person. Committing the act of sex outside of marriage is sinful, and wanting to do it is immoral as well, just as hating your neighbor is like killing him in your heart (Matthew 5:21-22). Just as human life is a gift from God and needs to be respected, defended, and protected, so, too, is human sexuality. Catholicism regards human sexuality as a divine gift, so it's considered sacred in the proper context — marriage.

Taking the cake: Marriage

The Church believes that sexual intercourse was ordained by God and designed exclusively for a husband and wife. Marriage is the best, most sacred, and most efficient union of man and woman because God created marriage. It's a sign of the permanent, faithful, and hopefully fruitful covenant that's made on the day that the man and woman make their vows and exchange consent. Human sexual activity is designed to promote love (unity) and life (procreation). And whenever that formula is altered or divided, the Church believes that sin enters the equation.

Only sex between a husband and wife is considered moral, and even then, the couple must be mutually respectful of each other. If the sole objective is personal pleasure and nothing more, then even a husband or wife sins by reducing his or her partner to a sex object or just a means to self-gratification. For example, using pornography or any kind of sex toy is strictly forbidden in the eyes of the Church.

So married sex is considered holy and sacred when it focuses on the unity of the couple as husband and wife — two human people who deserve dignity, respect, communication, honesty, fidelity, and compassion. To the Church, human sexuality isn't an end but a means to an end — the greater unity between husband and wife and the possibility of new life.

Book II

Walking the Catholic Walk

Planning a family the natural way

Catholicism doesn't teach that married couples *must* have as many children as biologically possible. It allows for Natural Family Planning (NFP), which is *not* the old, archaic, and unreliable rhythm method. So responsible parents can morally decide how large or small a family they can reasonably afford, raise, and maintain, as long as moral means are employed to do so.

Contraceptive sex, the Church says, divides the bond of love and life, unity and procreation — isolating the dimension of human sexuality that unites two people from the possible procreative level. Likewise, any form of human reproduction that results from anything other than sexual intercourse, such as surrogate mothers, sperm banks, in vitro fertilization, human cloning, and all methods of artificial conception are equally sinful because they isolate and separate the God-intended bond of the unitive and procreative. Sex outside of marriage and conception outside of sex are considered violations of the unity within human sexuality. For more info about the Church's stand on these and other sticky issues, turn to Book II, Chapter 6.

Cheating and philandering don't cut it

The Church teaches that sex outside of and/or before marriage is considered sinful and immoral, but strictly speaking, *adultery* is having sex with someone else's spouse or cheating on your own spouse by having sex with someone else. Catholicism says that adultery is primarily a sin against justice because all married couples make a solemn oath, a sacred covenant, to be faithful to each other until death. So marital infidelity is an injustice as well as a selfish and irresponsible sin of the flesh. Don Juans and desperate housewives needn't apply.

Playing footsie with fire

Even though the average Joe may think nothing of experimenting with sex before marriage, the Church says that true love means wanting what's best for the other person — body and soul. Having sex before or outside of marriage, whether it's a one-night stand or a long-term shack-up, isn't sanctioned or blessed by God and lacks respect for the people involved. True love and respect mean you'd never want to lure the one you love into a sinful situation any more than you'd intentionally lead that person into a scenario that would endanger his or her life or health. So having sex supposedly just to show your love is considered a lie.

Engaging in sexual intercourse without a lifelong commitment blessed by God is also dishonest. Having sex before or outside of marriage is considered dishonest because the people involved deserve only the best, and the best is the total gift of self — lifelong commitment, fidelity, and openness to the possibility that God may use this couple to bring a new human life into the world.

VII and X: Honor the property of others

The Seventh Commandment, "You shall not steal," and the tenth commandment, "You shall not covet your neighbor's goods," focus on respecting and honoring the possessions of others.

The Seventh Commandment forbids the act of taking someone else's property, and the Tenth Commandment forbids wanting to do so.

Explicitly, these two commandments condemn theft and the feelings of envy, greed, and jealousy in reaction to what other people have. The Catholic Church believes that, implicitly, these commandments also denounce cheating people of their money or property, depriving workers of their just wage, or not giving employers a full day's work for a full day's pay. Embezzlement, fraud, tax evasion, and vandalism are all considered extensions of violations of the Seventh Commandment. Showing disrespect for the private ownership of someone else's property — be it money or possessions — occurs when these sinful acts take place.

In addition, the Church believes that governments have no right to usurp private property and nationalize businesses, and they do have an obligation to protect private property and to help individuals and other nations in great need.

The Church maintains that personal property is a fundamental right, but it's not considered an absolute right. If a person owns more food than he needs, and someone comes along who is starving, the person with more food than he needs is obligated to share with the one who's starving. In the same way, governments and corporations have no right to deny the individual his inalienable right to private property. But although private property is a right, it's subservient to higher values, such as human life and national security.

VIII: Honor the truth

The Eighth Commandment, "You shall not bear false witness against your neighbor," condemns lying. Because God is regarded as the author of all truth, the Church believes that humans are obligated in the Eighth Commandment to honor the truth. The most obvious way to fulfill this commandment is not to *lie,* to intentionally deceive another by speaking a falsehood.

Figures of speech, metaphors, hyperboles, fairy tales, and such aren't considered lies because the listener isn't expecting accurate facts or exclusive truth, and the speaker isn't intending to deceive but to make a point.

Keep reading, because you haven't heard it all yet. *Mental reservation* is considered a means by which you can withhold some aspects of the truth without telling a lie, usually by not telling all the details. The Church believes it can be used in very limited circumstances:

✔ When someone isn't entitled to know all the facts and seeks to know them for evil purposes

✔ To protect the safety of self or others

✔ To protect confidentiality of penitent and confessor, doctor and patient, or attorney and client

This line of thinking is why the Church considers it moral to keep certain secrets confidential. For example:

✔ Catholicism regards the secrecy of the confessional as absolute, and no priest can ever reveal who went to confession or what was confessed. This is what's known as the *Seal of the Confessional.* Yet a priest can't lie to protect the penitent because the ends can never justify the means. He can and must simply remain silent rather than tell a falsehood.

✔ Doctor-patient and lawyer-client confidentiality is considered close to, but not synonymous with, the Seal of Confession and priest-penitent secrecy.

Book II

Walking the Catholic Walk

   ✔ The government can have secrets to protect the national security of the country and all its citizens, but just like the individual, the government isn't allowed to tell a lie even to save lives. Governments can use mental reservation to keep strategic information from enemies.

Concealing the truth (or some details of it) is different from distorting it, which would be a lie. Telling bedtime stories, writing fiction, using figures of speech, and using mental reservation are all permissible acts when done in the proper context. But intentionally lying is always considered sinful, even if the reasons may be noble. According to the Church, God created the human intellect to know the truth, just as He made the human will to seek the good.

Coming Out Even Steven

Certain differences exist between the Catholic and Lutheran version and the Protestant version of the Ten Commandments. The content is just the same, but the numbers differ. See Table 4-1 for a side-by-side comparison.

Table 4-1   **Comparing the Catholic/Lutheran and Protestant Ten Commandments**

Catholic/Lutheran	Protestant
1. I am the Lord your God, you shall not have strange gods before Me.	1. I am the Lord your God who brought you out of the land of Egypt. You shall have no other gods before Me.
2. You shall not take the name of the Lord your God in vain.	2. You shall not make unto you any graven images.
3. Remember to keep holy the Lord's day.	3. You shall not take the name of the Lord your God in vain.
4. Honor your father and mother.	4. You shall remember the Sabbath and keep it holy.
5. You shall not kill.	5. Honor your father and mother.
6. You shall not commit adultery.	6. You shall not murder.
7. You shall not steal.	7. You shall not commit adultery.
8. You shall not bear false witness against thy neighbor.	8. You shall not steal.
9. You shall not covet your neighbor's wife.	9. You shall not bear false witness against your neighbor.
10. You shall not covet your neighbor's goods.	10. You shall not covet your neighbor's house, nor his wife, nor anything that belongs to him.

The Bible doesn't number the Ten Commandments; it merely states them in Exodus 20:1–17 and Deuteronomy 5:6–21. Both Roman Catholics and Lutherans use a numbering sequence devised by St. Augustine in the fifth century, because Martin Luther (1483–1546), a German theologian, had been an Augustinian priest before he left the priesthood in favor of his new Lutheran religion. The Augustinians were followers of St. Augustine. Protestant denominations other than the Lutheran Church, however, use the sequence of commandments devised by English and Swiss reformers in the 16th century.

The Catholic/Lutheran version has the First Commandment prohibiting idolatry (no strange gods = no graven images). The Protestant version separates false worship and graven images into the First and Second Commandments. Additionally, in the Catholic/Lutheran version, one commandment forbids you to covet your neighbor's wife and another commandment forbids you to covet your neighbor's goods. Contrarily, the Protestant version combines all forms of coveting into one commandment.

Book II

Walking the Catholic Walk

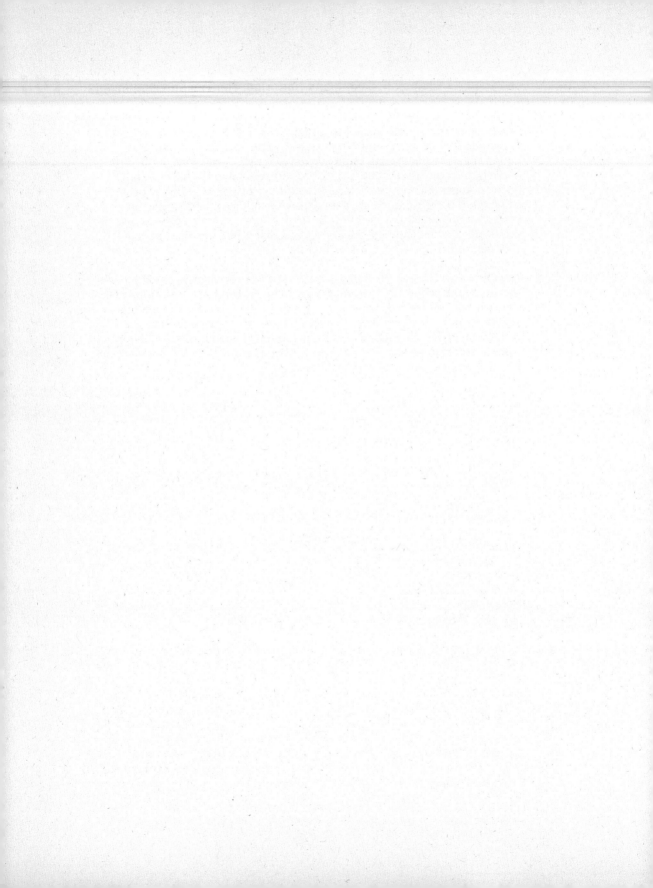

Chapter 5

Being Good When Sinning Is So Easy

Catholic morality is more than just avoiding what's sinful. Just as peace is more than the mere absence of war and good health is more than the mere absence of disease, holiness is more than the mere absence of sin and evil. Being able to say, "I've committed no sin today" isn't enough. A cat could say the same.

If a doctor gives you a prescription to cure a disease or infection, you must choose to follow the directions — such as "Take twice daily with plenty of water" — to make it work. If you don't, you can't blame the doctor if you don't get better. Similarly, God gave humans the Ten Commandments — a prescription for protection from spiritual disease (sin). But consciously choosing to follow the directions is up to the individual.

A good doctor does more than just give a prescription to cure the infection. She also gives overall directions for good and sustained physical health, such as "Drink plenty of fluids and get plenty of sleep and exercise," and "Stay away from high-fat and high-cholesterol foods." Likewise, Catholics believe that God did more than give the Ten Commandments for protection from sin. He also gave overall directions for good and sustained spiritual health — specifically, how to cultivate good habits, eliminate bad habits, and recognize the difference between the two. In this chapter, you find out all about the four cardinal virtues Catholics cling to and the seven biggest sins they steer away from to keep their souls pure and disease-free.

Cultivating Good Habits

A *virtue* is a habit that perfects the powers of the soul and disposes you to do good. Catholics believe that divine grace is offered to the soul because, without God's help, humans can't do good on their own due to *original sin:* the sin of Adam and Eve, the first human beings and the parents of the human race. Their disobedience wounded human nature, and all people inherit that sinful nature from them. Grace, which is God's intervention, bolsters a person's soul, providing the necessary oomph to do the right thing — that is, *if* the recipient recognizes grace's value. Catholics believe that virtues prepare and dispose people so that when grace is offered, people readily recognize, accept, and cooperate with it. In other words, God's grace is necessary, and virtues make it easier to work with.

Traditionally, the Catholic Church recognizes four cardinal virtues, but you don't have to be a cardinal in the Catholic Church to possess them. The root meaning of *cardinal* is *cardo,* which is Latin for *hinge.* These four virtues are the hinges on which the rest of the moral life swings:

- ✔ Prudence
- ✔ Justice
- ✔ Temperance
- ✔ Fortitude

The four cardinal virtues are also called *moral virtues* to distinguish them from the *theological virtues* of faith, hope, and love (charity), which are given to the soul at Baptism.

Taking virtuous actions doesn't make you a virtuous person. A virtuous person is able to do what's virtuous because he's committed to doing the right thing for the right reason. Doing good merely because it's the right thing to do — instead of for profit, fame, or esteem — is the motivation for a virtuous person to do virtuous acts.

Prudence: Knowing what, when, and how

Too many people today carelessly blurt out statements that, although true, aren't spoken in charity and compassion but with cold, deliberate, and calculated harshness. That's where prudence can help.

Prudence is basically practical common sense. It's saying or doing the proper thing at the proper time and in the appropriate manner. It's also the ability to know and judge whether to say something or nothing at all.

You don't need a high IQ to be prudent. Prudence, like wisdom, isn't measured by intelligence but by the willingness of a person to think, discern, and then act. For example, asking a friend for the $500 he owes you while you're both at a funeral parlor for the viewing of his deceased brother isn't prudent. Knowing what to say, how to say it, and when to say it is prudence.

As another example, prudence can help you find the right time to appropriately confront a family member or friend who has an eating disorder. With prudence, you're not negligent, saying nothing at all, but neither are you abrupt or rude, saying something like "Hey, you look anorexic!" or "You really need to eat a cheeseburger!"

An alcoholic practices prudence when declining an invitation to lunch at a bar, even though the person doing the inviting assures the alcoholic that they won't sit at the bar but merely eat at a table. Prudence tells the alcoholic that entering a room where the aroma of booze permeates the air, where old drinking buddies hang out, and where she has memories of getting plastered is too dangerous for her. Prudence tells the alcoholic to decline or offer an alternative — a restaurant with no bar or, better yet, one where no alcohol is served.

Book II

Walking the Catholic Walk

Prudence takes time and practice. In the olden days, when good manners were more important, noblemen and peasants alike strove to show respect for their fellow man through the practice of prudent speech. Today, manners often come in two extremes: Some people are politically correct, live in fear of offending anyone, and, as a result, say nothing controversial — even when someone is in danger; other people adopt the shock-jock approach, which is to bludgeon you over the head with the raw, unadulterated truth, hoping to hurt your feelings and get a violent reaction from you rather than help you. Prudence lies in the middle of these two extremes. Prudent people speak the truth when it's needed and appropriate, in an inoffensive way, but they never lose their force and conviction.

Acting prudently requires mature deliberation, wise choice, and the right execution:

- **Mature deliberation:** When you exercise mature deliberation, you think carefully before acting or not acting. Mature deliberation involves contemplating past experience, examining the current situation and circumstances, and considering the possible results or outcome of your decision. Mature deliberation means that you're not content with just personal knowledge, either. You seek the good advice of others — the opinions of well-respected, good, and morally upright people whom you respect and admire. You consult with peers and colleagues, and research authoritative sources and documents. For Catholic Christians, these sources include both the Bible and the Catechism of the Catholic

Church. In any event, mature deliberation means not just depending on your own personal experience and opinion but also testing your knowledge and beliefs and getting good advice.

✔ **Wise choice:** Making a wise choice involves determining which of the available options is most feasible and appropriate. Getting input is the first step, and deciding which course to take after examining all the possibilities is the second. This route may not be the quickest or easiest one, but prudence enables you to judge the most beneficial path to take.

✔ **The right execution:** The right execution is one in which you don't delay after you make a wise choice, but swiftly and thoroughly follow through on what you've decided to do. Procrastination and haste are the two foes to look out for. The right execution means that you've planned and prepared and now know what to do. You don't hesitate; you follow through.

Justice: Treating others fairly

Justice is the virtue that seeks to promote fair play. It's the desire and resolve to give each person his due. It demands that you reward goodness and punish evil. Justice can be one of three different types: commutative, distributive, and social.

Quid pro quo: Commutative justice

Commutative justice concerns the relationship between individuals — between two people, such as a customer and a merchant. Commutative justice demands, for example, that the customer be asked to pay a fair price for a product and that the merchant be honest about the condition and history of the item, so the buyer can know whether the price is indeed fair. So if a merchant tries to sell a coin that allegedly belonged to Abraham Lincoln, the consumer needs some proof to verify the claim. It's unfair to charge an enormous amount of money for something that can't be authenticated or, worse yet, isn't really as old as or in as good condition as advertised.

Commutative justice is based on the principle *quid pro quo,* which is Latin for *this for that.* I'm willing to pay you the price that you ask for this item, and you're willing to sell it to me at that price. But the item must actually be what it's advertised to be. If the advertised price isn't correct or facts about the item are wrong, then commutative justice is violated.

Cheating the consumer *and* cheating the merchant are both ways of violating commutative justice.

Another situation in which commutative justice comes into play is when you're robbed. Commutative justice demands that the thief make restitution by giving back the stolen money or property or, if that's impossible, recompensing you in another way, such as giving you something equal in value or providing services. So when you were a kid and smashed your next-door-neighbor's window, your mom or dad rightfully enforced commutative justice. And after apologizing to Mr. Wilson, you had to save your allowance until you could pay for the replacement window.

All for one and one for all: Distributive justice

Distributive justice involves the relationship between one and many — between an individual and a group. This kind of justice is most obvious in the relationship between a citizen and her government. The city, state, and federal governments are required by distributive justice to levy fair taxes to pay for services provided. Charging excess taxes is a violation of distributive justice, as is not charging enough taxes to pay for services, resulting in cuts to essential services. A flip-side violation is when a citizen refuses to pay her fair share of taxes and yet often benefits from the government's services.

Distributive justice means that taxpayers have a right to know where their money goes, who spends it, and on what. The government has a right to ask citizens to financially support police, ambulance, firefighter, national defense, and other social services.

Here's another example of how distributive justice comes into play. Suppose that Fred and Barney belong to the Loyal Order of Water Buffaloes, a private club. They pay their annual dues, and in return they get a monthly newsletter, an annual membership card made of bedrock, and an invitation to the annual convention. Distributive justice demands that members pay their dues and that the board of directors be responsible for the monies collected, giving an accounting each year so that everyone knows where the loot went. If Mr. Slate skims some money off the top for personal use or if favoritism or nepotism creep in, this type of justice has been violated. All members should be treated fairly and equally.

Fair play from Dan to Beersheba: Social justice

Social justice concerns the relationship of both individuals and groups between one another and everyone. The bottom line is the common good — the public welfare of all. Social justice is concerned with the environment, the economy, private property, civil rights, and church-state relations.

Although businesses have the right to make a profit by manufacturing and selling goods and services, increasing profit share at the harmful expense of others is unacceptable. For example, polluting the local water system just to make a greater profit is a violation of social justice. At the same time, environmental extremists violate social justice when they take the law into their own hands and perpetrate property damage or seek to close a business, which results in many lost jobs that families depend on for survival. Cooperating

Book II

Walking the Catholic Walk

and communicating in order to balance the needs of the community and the needs of the business are better for both sides.

Note that neither the right to profit nor the right to property is absolute. So if a community is suffering from a severe drought, for example, a company that has access to drinkable water is obliged to share with those who are dying of thirst.

Social justice demands that everyone be treated fairly and equally under the law. It also recognizes the inalienable right and duty of every human being to work and receive a fair and just wage for that work. This type of justice defends the right of workers to form unions, guilds, and societies. And it defends the right of managers to expect reasonable and fair requests that won't put them out of business or make them lose money rather than make it.

Treating all citizens — regardless of gender, color, ethnicity, or religion — with the same dignity and human rights is a mandate of social justice to all governments. For their part, citizens are expected to support their governments and nations in return for the protection and services they provide.

Temperance: *Moderating pleasure*

Feast or famine. Many people live at extremes — too much or too little. Some party hearty, and some are party poopers. From Puritans to Hedonists, the practices of self-deprivation and self-indulgence run the gamut, but the choice doesn't have to be an either/or proposition. Having some fun, enjoying your leisure time, taking pleasure, and relaxing aren't sinful, immoral, illicit, or juvenile. Really!

Christians can and ought to have fun without it degenerating into depravity and debauchery. That's where temperance comes in.

 Temperance is the virtue by which a person uses balance. It's the good habit that allows a person to relax and have fun without crossing the line and committing sin.

 The Catholic Church believes that human beings are permitted to participate in legitimate pleasures but that, often, society and culture lure people into excesses in the direction of either extreme. For example, enjoying a good meal is a good thing, but if you continually eat more than you need and become obese, that's gluttony. On the other hand, if you deprive yourself of food until your health suffers, all for the sake of looking good, well, that's vanity.

Temperance is nothing more than moderation and balance in using lawful pleasures. Temperance is having an alcoholic beverage without abusing it.

Drinking to get drunk and drinking and driving are violations of the virtue of temperance. So are eating, sleeping, or recreating to excess.

Temperance is the habit of using prudence and restraint and doesn't require total abstinence unless someone has a problem. For example, an alcoholic can never have one or two social drinks. An alcoholic must forever abstain from booze, but she can still have a good time at parties with soft drinks instead.

Practicing temperance isn't about Carrie Nation and the Women's Christian Temperance Union and a bunch of old ladies banging a drum and decrying the evils of gin and rum. Rather, practicing temperance means knowing when to say when. It's knowing your limits and sticking to them. For example, a kiss and a hug don't have to end in passionate sex, and an argument doesn't have to deteriorate into a fistfight. Temperance is establishing, respecting, and enforcing boundaries. Self-control is the key. Having a good time without it becoming an occasion of sin or a sinful act is what temperance is all about.

Fortitude: Doing what's right come hell or high water

Fortitude isn't about physical strength or mental intelligence, nor is it about being macho or bullying people around. Instead, this cardinal virtue centers on strength of character.

Fortitude is the ability to persevere in times of trial and tribulation — the strength to hang in there when the going gets tough. It's having the courage to do the right thing no matter what the cost.

It's not enough to be fair, use self-control, and be prudent. The virtue of fortitude gives you the strength to fulfill your commitments to God, family, and friends. This virtue enables

- ✔ You to keep your promise and your word even when the world and everyone else is telling you to forget it
- ✔ Teenagers to combat peer pressure, avoiding drugs and sex
- ✔ Adults to remain chaste, abstaining from sexual relations until marriage despite the social pressures to have premarital relations
- ✔ People of conscience to speak up and out when injustice occurs at work or in society

When practiced faithfully and consistently, fortitude empowers people to remain courageous and overcome even the fear of death in order to help others and/or do the right thing for the right reason.

Book II

Walking the Catholic Walk

The Seven Deadly Sins

As you may have guessed, along with cultivating good habits, you need to avoid some bad habits. The Church maintains that seven vices in particular lead to breaking one or more of the Ten Commandments. These particular bad habits are called the seven deadly sins because, according to Catholicism, they're *mortal sins* — sins that kill the life of sanctifying grace. The Church believes that if you commit a mortal sin, you forfeit heaven and opt for hell by your own free will and actions. (See Book II, Chapter 2 for more on mortal sin.) Remember, too, that the Catholic Church teaches that God can and will forgive any sin if the person is truly repentant (through the Sacrament of Penance, Baptism, and Anointing of the Sick, or a perfect act of contrition in extreme necessity). Don't commit the vices described in this section. But you can always seek God's grace and mercy (read more in Book II, Chapter 2).

A mortal sin is any act or thought of a human being that turns away from God (*aversio a Deo* in Latin) and turns toward a created thing instead (*conversio ad creaturam* in Latin). In other words, mortal sin is completely turning away from God and embracing something else in His place. It's deadly to the life of grace because it insults the honor of God and injures the soul of the sinner himself. Mortal sin is like a malignant tumor or a critical injury that's lethal to the spiritual life. Three conditions are necessary for mortal sin to exist:

- **Grave matter:** The act itself is intrinsically evil and immoral. For example, murder, rape, incest, perjury, adultery, and so on are grave matters. These actions are in and of themselves deadly to the life of grace.

- **Full knowledge:** The person must *know* that what he's doing or planning to do is evil and immoral. For example, say someone steals a postage stamp, thinking that it's worth only 50 cents. She knows that it's sinful, but if she's unaware that the stamp is rare and actually worth $1,000, she's not guilty of mortal sin but of venial sin (more on that is coming up in this section).

- **Deliberate consent:** The person must *freely choose* to commit the act or plan to do it. Someone who's forced against his will doesn't commit a mortal sin. For example, a man who is drugged and brainwashed to assassinate a leader hasn't done so of his own free will; therefore, he's not guilty of mortal sin.

Venial sins are any sins that meet only one or two of the conditions needed for a mortal sin but do not fulfill all three at the same time, or are minor violations of the moral law, such as giving an obscene gesture to another driver while in traffic. Venial sin is less serious than mortal sin. Like a benign tumor or a minor infection, venial sin only weakens the soul with sickness; it doesn't kill the grace within. Venial sins aren't deadly to the life of grace, but like minor infections in the body, if casually ignored and left untended, they may deteriorate into a more serious condition. For example, someone who tells so-called "white lies" commits venial sin, but if he does it long enough, he'll be much more easily tempted to tell a big lie later on that would, in fact, be a mortal sin, such as cheating on a test or on his income tax return.

In the sixth century, Pope Gregory the Great made up the list of the seven deadly sins, which are pride, envy, lust, anger, gluttony, greed, and sloth. Later, in the 14th century, Geoffrey Chaucer popularized these sins in his *Canterbury Tales*.

This section covers the seven deadly sins. As a bonus, it gives you the remedies. Yep, *remedies*. Some specific virtues, lesser known than the four cardinal virtues, have traditionally been linked with a particular deadly sin. These virtues (listed in Table 5-1) help to defeat their counterparts.

Table 5-1	The Seven Deadly Sins and the Virtues That Defeat Them
Deadly Sin	*Conquering Virtue*
Pride	Humility
Envy	Kindness or meekness
Lust	Chastity
Anger	Patience
Gluttony	Periodic fasting and abstinence
Greed (avarice)	Generosity
Sloth (acedia)	Diligence

Pride goeth before the fall

Parents and teachers say to be proud of yourself, so why is pride considered a deadly sin? In the context they're talking about, it's not a sin. Parents and teachers are talking about healthy pride, such as taking joy from belonging to a family, a church, or a nation. Being proud to be an American, a Canadian, a good student, a hard worker, and so on isn't sinful.

The sin of *pride* is an inordinate love of self — a super-confidence and high esteem in your own abilities. It's also known as vanity. It exaggerates your abilities, gifts, and talents, and ignores your weaknesses, frailties, and imperfections.

In Catholicism, sinful pride is the deviation or distortion of the legitimate need of self-affirmation. Liking yourself isn't sinful; in fact, it's healthy and necessary. But when the self-perception no longer conforms to reality, and you begin to think that you're more important than you actually are, the sin of pride is rearing its ugly head.

The sin of pride gives you a fat head. You think you're better and more important than anyone else. It leads to resenting others whom you consider inferior, and you become impatient with others because you think they're not perfect like you.

Pride is the key to all other sins because after you believe that you're more important than you actually are, you compensate for it when others don't agree with your judgment. You rationalize your behavior and make excuses for lying, cheating, stealing, insulting, ignoring, and such, because no one understands you like *you* do. In your mind, you're underestimated by the world.

That's the extreme expression of pride. A subtler example is when you refuse to accept the authority of someone else over you, be it a parent, teacher, employer, pastor, bishop, or pope. The refusal to obey others is a by-product of pride. Showing disrespect for those in authority is pride as well. The ego can't stomach someone else having more power, intelligence, influence, or authority, so it rebels against the lawful superiors.

Pride also prevents you from seeking, listening to, or applying advice from others. Do you ever wonder why it is that most men refuse to ask for directions when they're lost? Pride prevents them from admitting that they can't read a map or follow directions properly. They can't let their wives, girlfriends, or mothers know the truth, so they drive on and on, hoping that something familiar appears before it gets too dark or too late.

The Catholic Church teaches that *humility* is the best remedy for pride. It's not a false self-deprecation, where you beat yourself up verbally only so others can say otherwise. It's not denying the truth. If you have a good singing voice, for example, responding to a compliment with "Oh, no, I can't carry a tune" isn't humility. Catholicism regards humility as recognizing that the talent is really a gift from God and responding with, "Thank you — I've been blessed by the good Lord." Pride would say, "You're darn right I have a good voice. It's about time you realized it."

In other words, although acknowledging your talents is good, humility reminds you that your talents come from God. Pride fools you into thinking that you're the source of your own greatness.

Envying what others have or enjoy

Envy, another deadly sin, is the resentment of another person's good fortune or joy. Catholicism distinguishes between two kinds of envy:

- ✔ **Material envy** is when you resent others who have more money, talent, strength, beauty, friends, and so on, than you do.

- ✔ **Spiritual envy** is resenting others who progress in holiness, preferring that they stay at or below your level instead of being joyful and happy that they're doing what they're supposed to be doing. Spiritual envy is far worse and more evil than material envy.

Book II

Walking the Catholic Walk

Note that spiritual writers and moralists make a distinction between envy and jealousy. Envy is the resentment of what others have, such as possessions, talent, fame, and so on, whereas jealousy is the fear of losing what you already have. So a jealous husband fears that he may or will lose his wife to another man. If he happens to think Julia Roberts is the most beautiful woman in the world, then that same husband may also be envious of Julia Roberts's husband. Jealousy is considered to be as much a sin as envy because it closely resembles that deadly sin.

Jealousy among professional people is common, because they often fear losing their own status, position, notoriety, or esteem to rival colleagues. Jealous people are insecure, apprehensive, and fearful of peers taking what they have, surpassing them, or leaving them behind with less than they started out with. The same fears exist among students. A student ranked with the best grades in his class is jealous when he fears losing that ranking to another student who's getting better grades day by day and is moving up the list faster and faster. On the other hand, a B student is envious when he resents a straight-A student.

The Church maintains that *meekness* or *kindness* can counter envy. For example, Genesis 37–47 tells the story of Joseph's brothers, who were envious of Joseph because he was the favorite son of their father, Jacob. They sold Joseph into slavery, but Joseph rose through the ranks from slave to personal advisor to pharaoh. Later, when he met his brothers again, instead of seeking revenge, Joseph showed them kindness and brought them and their father into Egypt.

Lusting after fruit that's forbidden

The Catholic Church believes that being attracted to and appreciating the opposite sex is normal and healthy. That's not lust, and it's not considered a sin.

Lust is looking at, imagining, and even treating others as mere sex objects to serve your own physical pleasures, rather than as individuals made in the image and likeness of God. Lust is having someone become something merely to please you, in fantasy or reality.

The Church says that lust depersonalizes the other person and the one having the lustful thoughts. It makes both parties nothing more than instruments of enjoyment instead of enabling them to focus on the unique gift of person-hood. And it seeks to separate, divide, and isolate what God intended to be united — love and life, the unitive and procreative dimensions of marriage.

The pleasure that lustful thoughts provide is only a sign of the human condition and its wounded nature from original sin, which is *concupiscence,* the proclivity to sin, especially the tendency toward sins of the flesh. The fact that you're entertained by impure thoughts isn't sinful; rather, sin comes into play when you entertain them — you engage in the conscious and deliberate act of having lustful thoughts. The sin occurs when you initiate, consent to, and/or continue fantasizing about sexual activity with another person, because all sin involves a free act of the will. Spontaneous thoughts — especially during puberty and adolescence — are primarily involuntary and aren't considered sinful. Such thoughts become sinful when the person recognizes them and has the ability to dismiss and reject them as soon as possible, yet doesn't do so.

Chastity, the virtue that moderates sexual desire, is the best remedy for lust. Chastity falls under temperance and can help to keep physical pleasure in moderation.

Without chastity, men and women become like animals that copulate when in heat. Animals have sex driven by instinct, but men and women have the gift of reason and can choose when and with whom to be intimate. Desirous of chastity, men and women can freely abstain from sexual activity until the wedding night. If they allow lust to drive their actions, however, they sin and commit *fornication* (sex between two unmarried people) or they commit *adultery* (having sex with someone else's spouse or cheating on your own spouse). Cultivating and clinging to chastity separate them from the animals.

Anger to the point of seeking revenge

You have no control over what angers you, but you do have control over what you do after you become angry. The deadly sin of *anger* is the sudden outburst of emotion — namely hostility — and sustaining thoughts about the desire for revenge. The key here is that the wrath persists for more than a moment. You want harm to come to someone else. In the worst case, anger can lead to willfully inflicting suffering on others.

If someone sticks you with a needle or pin, for example, or slaps you in the face, your initial reaction is probably one of anger. You resent what was done to you. The sin of anger occurs when you react by swearing, cursing, shouting, ranting, or raving. (Don't confuse these last three reactions with the shouting, ranting, and raving that occur at a typical Italian meal. Everyone screams and yells at those.) In the same vein, if you brood over injuries and insults others have heaped on you and begin to yearn for revenge, the Church asserts that you're committing the sin of anger. Inordinate, violent, and hateful anger is always a mortal sin. Bloodthirsty revenge also comes from anger.

But what if, say, someone robs you? In that case, wouldn't those feelings be merited? No. Being upset that someone robbed you is normal and is properly called *righteous indignation,* but seeking revenge and desiring to see the culprit suffer isn't. Instead, with the virtue of justice, you can desire for the police to catch the thief and for a court to sentence her to a fair punishment.

Patience, the virtue that allows you to adapt and endure evil without harboring any destructive feelings, is the best countermeasure for anger. When you give yourself the time and opportunity to cool off, anger dissipates and more practical concerns come to the front line.

Book II

Walking the Catholic Walk

Gluttony: Too much food or firewater

Gluttony is immoderate, excessive eating, and/or drinking too much alcohol. Enjoying a delightful dinner isn't sinful, but intentionally overeating to the point where you literally get sick to your stomach is. So, too, having an alcoholic beverage now and then (provided that you don't suffer from alcoholism) is *not* sinful in the eyes of the Church. Responsible consumption of alcohol is allowed. Making a champagne toast to a bride and groom or having a mixed drink with friends at a dinner party is all fine and well — that is, as long as you aren't a recovering alcoholic. But drinking to the point of drunkenness *is* a sin. Abusing alcohol is sinful, and it doesn't necessarily mean only getting drunk. People who use alcohol to lessen their own (or others') inhibitions are committing sin. Driving under the influence or while intoxicated or impaired is a grave matter and can be a mortal sin (if you meet all three conditions for a mortal sin covered in the section "The Seven Deadly Sins"), because you endanger your own life and the lives of others. Underage drinking is also considered a serious sin.

Legitimate eating disorders, such as anorexia and bulimia, aren't gluttony; they're medical conditions that require treatment and care. The sin of gluttony is freely choosing to overconsume.

Like lust, gluttony focuses on *pleasure*. Gluttony finds it in food and drink, whereas lust finds it in sexual activity. Both enslave the soul to the body, even though the soul — being superior to the body — should be in charge. Gluttons don't eat out of necessity or for social reasons, but merely to consume and experience the pleasure of taste.

Gorging yourself on appetizers, several courses, desserts, and so on — with no concern for the possibility of getting sick or the reality that millions of people are starving around the world — is the ugliness and evil of gluttony. In addition, gluttony endangers your life by jeopardizing the health of your body.

Periodic *fasting*, restricting the amount of food you eat, and *abstinence*, avoiding meat or some favorite food, are the best defenses against gluttony. Unlike dieting where the goal is to lose weight, fasting and abstinence purify the soul by controlling the desires of the body. Occasionally giving up favorite foods and beverages promotes self-control and temperance. In addition, deciding ahead of time what and how much to eat and drink is considered prudent and helpful.

Greed: The desire for more and more

Greed is the inordinate love of and desire for earthly possessions. Greed entails cherishing things above people and relationships. Amassing a fortune and foolishly trying to accumulate the most stuff is greed, which is sometimes called *avarice*. "It's never enough. I have to have more." That's the battle cry of greed.

Greed is also a sign of mistrust. "I doubt that God will take care of me, so I try to gather as much as possible now in case no more is left later." The Gospel relates the parable about such a greedy man. He had so much grain that he tore down his bin to hold more — only to die that very night (Luke 12:16–21). But you can't take it with you. That saying was true then, and it's true now. Some time ago, a rich woman stipulated in her will that she be buried in her Rolls Royce. Where's she going to drive that thing?

Greed, the apex of selfishness, has ruined marriages, families, and friendships. *Generosity*, however, is the best weapon against greed. Freely giving some of your possessions away, especially to those less fortunate, is considered the perfect antithesis to greed and avarice. Generosity promotes detachment from material things that come and go. Things can be broken, stolen, destroyed, or lost. They can be replaced, but people can't.

Sloth: Lazy as a lotus-eater

Sloth (sometimes called *acedia*) is laziness — particularly when it concerns prayer and spiritual life. It centers on doing nothing or doing just trivial things. A slothful person always wants to rest and relax, with no desire or intention of making a sacrifice or doing something for others. It's an aversion to work — physical, mental, and spiritual. Sloth inevitably leads to lukewarmness and tepidity and then deteriorates into disinterest, discouragement, and finally despair. Sloth breeds indifference, which prevents joy from ever being experienced.

The Church says that the evil habit of being inattentive at religious worship services — being physically present but not consciously participating — or being careless in fulfilling your religious duties is a sin of sloth. Other examples include never getting to Church on time, before Mass starts; just sitting in church but not singing, praying, kneeling, or standing; never reading the Bible or the Catechism of the Catholic Church; and not praying before eating a meal or going to bed.

Proverbs has something to say about sloth:

- **Proverbs 10:26:** Like vinegar to the teeth, and smoke to the eyes, so is the slothful to those who send him.

- **Proverbs 18:9:** He who is slothful in his work is a brother to him who destroys.

- **Proverbs 19:15:** Slothfulness casts into a deep sleep, and an idle person will suffer hunger.

- **Proverbs 19:24:** A slothful man hides his hand in the dish, and will not even bring it back to his mouth.

Spiritual laziness can only be overcome by practicing the virtue of *diligence,* which is the habit of keeping focused and paying attention to the work at hand — be it the work of employment or the work of God. Diligent prayer and diligent worship can make you more reverent. Diligence in all things ensures that you don't become idle and then start daydreaming, leaving reality for Fantasy Island.

Catholics, like all other human beings, are asked to practice virtue and avoid vice. Going even farther, religion and faith ask God's children to seek holiness and avoid all sin and evil at the same time. The motivation for believers is simple: the choice of heaven or hell — eternal happiness, joy, and peace, or eternal pain, misery, and damnation.

Book II

Walking the Catholic Walk

Chapter 6

Standing Firm: The Church's Stance on Some Sticky Issues

*C*atholicism may appear at times to go against the grain, risk unpopularity, or even chance rejection and persecution of some of its beliefs and practices. Like most religions, Catholicism seeks to conform to the Almighty rather than go along with the hoi polloi. Moods change, tastes differ, and crowds can be fickle, ugly, or just plain apathetic. Whether something is popular doesn't determine whether it's true or good. When most of the people thought the world was flat, their belief didn't make it so. Moral and spiritual leaders have an obligation to conform to a higher authority than their own. Even though they serve and minister to the common folk, they owe their obedience not to the *vox populi* (voice of the people) but to the *vox Dei* (voice of God).

Most religions have some controversial teachings, doctrines, disciplines, and policies that the outside world rejects or misunderstands. A few members may even dislike or oppose some doctrine or another. Yet these positions remain part and parcel of the official religion because at the very core is an obligation to speak the truth "in season and out of season" because there will always be those who'd rather have their ears tickled than hear what's true (2 Timothy 4:2–3). For this reason, the Catholic Church stands by her convictions and teachings on artificial birth control, abortion, euthanasia, capital punishment, and the like. In this chapter, you discover the Church's position on a number of controversial issues that people face today.

Celibacy and the Male Priesthood

Even before the advent of clergy sex scandals, the issue of celibacy intrigued non-Catholics. Some claim it contradicts nature and goes against biblical teachings on marriage and the ministry, such as "Be fruitful and multiply" (Genesis 1:28) and "Do we not have the right to be accompanied by a wife?" (1 Corinthians 9:5). Although the number of Catholics in the world continues to increase (there are more than 1 billion Catholics worldwide), the number of priests to minister to all of them has decreased. Because of this vocations crisis (not enough shepherds to take care of the sheep), many people are questioning celibacy and the restriction of ordination to males only. Married clergy and women priests, some contend, would alleviate the shortage of personnel and bring a fresh perspective to the vocation. Protestant Christians have had both for decades now and wonder when Catholics will catch up. Legitimate questions and valid points to be sure, but Catholicism has some good answers and replies, as we point out in this section.

Celibacy and the male priesthood are two separate and distinct issues and entities, even though they overlap in practice. Celibacy is a discipline of the Church that isn't absolute; exceptions and modifications have been made through the centuries. But the male priesthood is a part of doctrine and divine law that can never be changed or altered by any pope or council.

Flying solo for life

Celibacy is the formal and solemn oath never to enter the married state. Celibate men and women willingly relinquish their natural right to marry in order to devote themselves completely and totally to God and His Church.

The Catholic Church doesn't teach (and never has taught) that *all* clergy must be celibate. From day one, clergy of the Eastern Catholic Churches, such as the Byzantine, have consistently and perennially had the option of marrying. Only in the United States was celibacy imposed on the Byzantine Catholic clergy. This ban was lifted in November 2014.

Celibacy isn't necessary for valid Orders in the Roman Catholic Church. It's a *discipline* of the church, not a doctrine. The East never made it mandatory. The Western (Latin) Church made it normative in A.D. 306 at the Council of Elvira and mandatory in 1074 by Pope Gregory VII. The Second Lateran Council reaffirmed it in 1139. Although the Eastern Catholic and Orthodox Churches have always had an optional celibacy for clergy, both have a celibate episcopacy, meaning that only celibate priests can become bishops. So although they have a married clergy, the upper hierarchy remains celibate and, to a degree, quasi-monastic. (They live and pray more like monks than like parish priests.)

A rolling stone gathers no moss

Celibacy is legitimate for both the East and the West, even though it's optional for the former and mandatory for the latter. But why the difference between the two? Well, politics and culture. Even before East split from West in 1054 and formed the Orthodox Church, the Eastern part of the Holy Roman Empire operated differently from the Western part.

In the East, a close association existed between the secular and religious spheres, which was dramatically different from the situation in the West. After Rome fell in A.D. 476, no single, powerful, and influential secular ruler arose until Charlemagne was crowned Holy Roman Emperor in A.D. 800.

Book II

Walking the Catholic Walk

So from the fifth to the eighth centuries, the most powerful and influential person in the West was the bishop of Rome. As pope and head of the world-wide Catholic Church, he became the icon of stability and power as Western Europe survived the fall of the ancient Roman Empire, the barbarian invasions, and the so-called Dark Ages.

Instability in the secular realm meant that the clergy, especially the bishops, took on more than just spiritual leadership, just as the pope wielded more than pastoral power in Rome and around the world. And the West found that celibacy among the clergy was beneficial and helpful because that meant no divided loyalties.

Kings, princes, barons, earls, dukes, counts, and other nobility married first to make political alliances and second to establish families. Mandatory celibacy prevented the clergy from getting involved in the intrigue of who marries whom. Mandatory celibacy ensured that the priests were preoccupied with Church work and had no ties or interests in local politics among the fighting factions, which were trying to establish the infant nation states.

Priests with families would have been vulnerable to the local nobility, because their extended families would have been under secular dominion. A celibate clergy made for a more independent clergy, free from earthly concerns and corruption, enabling them to serve the people and the hierarchy with full attention and loyalty.

Biblical background for celibacy

As noted earlier in this section, some people think that celibacy goes against biblical teachings on marriage and the ministry. But the Catholic Church actually uses the Bible as part of its reasoning for priestly celibacy.

Jesus Christ never married and was celibate, and the New Testament affirms the value of celibacy:

> ✔ **1 Corinthians 7:8:** To the unmarried and the widows I say that it is well for them to remain single as I do.

> ✔ **1 Corinthians 7:27–34, 38:** Are you bound to a wife? Do not seek to be free. But if you marry, you do not sin, and if a girl marries she does not sin. Yet those who marry will have worldly troubles, and I would spare you that. I mean, brethren, the appointed time has grown very short; from now on, let those who have wives live as though they had none, and those who mourn as though they were not mourning, and those who rejoice as though they were not rejoicing, and those who buy as though they had no goods, and those who deal with the world as though they had no dealings with it. For the form of this world is passing away. I want you to be free from anxieties. The unmarried man is anxious about the affairs of the Lord, how to please the Lord; but the married man is anxious about worldly affairs, how to please his wife, and his interests are divided. . . . So that he who marries his betrothed does well; and he who refrains from marriage will do better.

According to Catholicism, to claim that celibacy is nonbiblical is erroneous. Many significant people in the Bible were unmarried, and the preceding passages show that the New Testament and the Early Church didn't frown on or merely tolerate celibacy. They saw it as a gift — as much a gift as the gift of faith and the gift of a vocation to serve the Church.

Mandatory celibacy for the priesthood is a discipline of the Church, not a doctrine or a dogma. Theoretically, any pope can modify or dissolve mandatory celibacy at any time, but it's highly improbable because it has been part of the Western Church's priesthood since the fourth century. Additionally, the Church teaches and affirms that celibacy isn't just a sacrifice; it's also a gift.

Is celibacy to blame for the priest shortage?

Because of the declining number of newly ordained Catholic priests, some people think that allowing married clergy would alleviate the shortage of personnel. But statistics show that even Protestant ministers and clergy — who *can* be married and, in many cases, can be women or men — are decreasing in numbers, too. The Church believes that relaxing or eliminating celibacy isn't the panacea that would answer the priest shortage in the West.

Socially and culturally, first-world nations, such as the United States, Canada, and most of Western Europe, are having smaller and smaller families. The birth rate has dropped to an all-time low because many couples in these affluent countries are having only one or two children. Big families aren't the only, or primary, source of priests and nuns, but they do bring possible vocations into the world.

But if a pope were to decide to change, modify, or end mandatory celibacy for the Western church, the Church would still maintain and follow the same tradition observed by the Eastern Catholic Church concerning married clergy. Among the married clergy in the Eastern Church, marriage must come before ordination; if a cleric is ordained unmarried, he must remain unmarried. Therefore, ending mandatory celibacy would affect only those yet to be ordained. In addition:

- ✔ Seminarians would have to decide before ordination whether they wanted to be married. They'd have to find a wife prior to their ordination or remain celibate.

- ✔ Anyone having aspirations to be ordained a bishop would have to remain celibate.

- ✔ Catholic priests who were ordained celibate and then later left the active ministry to get married would *not* be allowed back into the active ministry as a married priest.

The pros and cons

Celibacy can be difficult for those who don't come from a large, extended family. An only son may feel anxiety and tension when his elderly parents become sick and need attention, and no other adult children are available to care for them. And a priest who comes from a small family may feel lonely more often during the holidays. He sees married families in his parish sharing the joy of the season with one another, and yet he doesn't have many aunts and uncles, brothers and sisters, and nieces and nephews to visit.

Another sacrifice is not having a lifelong companion to support, encourage, advise, and, of course, correct you at times. Not having a baby to rock to sleep, a son to watch in his first little league baseball game, and a daughter to walk down the aisle on her wedding day are all sacrifices required by celibacy.

But at the same time, celibacy gives a priest the time and opportunity to love hundreds of people and to give 100 percent of his attention, effort, zeal, and talent, whereas a married man must balance family and work. A celibate priest doesn't have to make the painful decision of whether to respond to an emergency phone call at 3 a.m. or stay home with a seriously ill wife or child.

Celibacy can be distorted into being only a sacrifice ("I gave up a wife and children"), or it can be seen as the Church intended — as both a sacrifice and a gift. ("I freely gave up a wife and children so that I can love and serve my parishioners as if they're my children.")

Catholic priests use the title *Father* because they're spiritually considered the father of many children through the sacraments. Catholic Christians are spiritually born in Baptism, fed in the Holy Eucharist, made mature in

Confirmation, and healed during Penance and the Anointing of the Sick. The responsibilities of parents parallel those of the priest: Parents give birth to their children, feed them, heal them, and help them grow and mature. So the Church is considered the spiritual mother. Catholics call the Church the *Holy Mother Church,* and the priest is their spiritual father.

Pope John Paul II's letter *Pastores Dabo Vobis* (I Will Give You Shepherds) reminded Catholic priests that although they have no wife and children of their own, they're not alone. They do have a spouse — the Church. A priest is to treat the people of his parish (and every member of the Church, for that matter) as his beloved bride. The parishioners aren't to be treated as stockholders, employers, employees, servants, customers, or clients. They're to be treated as a beloved spouse. The priest marries the Church because the Church is considered the Bride of Christ, and the priest is considered "another Christ" by virtue of the Sacrament of Holy Orders. So the priest must love the Church as Christ loves the Church. It's a spousal relationship and covenant of love.

When put in this context, celibacy is merely the means to making the reality more possible and more dynamic. Married clergy can do a superb and phenomenal job, no matter what their denomination or gender. But celibacy for the Catholic priesthood in the Latin tradition makes sense, and although it's not always easy, neither is married life.

The sexual abuse issue

Celibate clergy aren't more likely or prone to sexual misconduct (homosexual or heterosexual) than any other group, despite the rhetoric that ensued soon after the blitz of pedophilia cases came to light in the United States a while back. Catholic priests were the focus of much media attention — mostly because of the unconscionable actions of a very small minority of deviant clergy and a few bishops who merely transferred clergy known to be sex offenders from one assignment to another.

Sadly, 80 percent of physical abuse of children is perpetrated by parents, and other family members account for another 7 percent. Teachers, coaches, neighbors, daycare providers, scoutmasters, youth ministers, and clergy are among the remaining 12 percent who know the children. (Complete strangers account for only 1 percent of this abuse.)

The 2004 John Jay Report, a study based on 10,667 allegations of Catholic clergy engaging in sexual abuse of minors between 1950 and 2002, showed that 4,392 priests had been credibly accused. That number amounted to 4 percent of the 109,694 priests in active ministry during that same time period. Estimates indicate that between 2 and 5 percent of Protestant ministers, Eastern Orthodox priests, Jewish rabbis, and Islamic imams use their position of authority to sexually abuse minors as well.

Even one case is one too many, of course, because abusing children is one of the most heinous evils any adult can commit. But this horrible behavior isn't limited to — or even primarily found in — the celibate male clergy. It's an evil that afflicts a few pastors of all denominations, as well as people from all other walks of life.

In no way do the statistics take away from the horror, shame, and diabolical evil of a few celibate priests committing the heinous crime and sin of child sex abuse. But it's important to also look at the whole picture — to see that the overwhelming majority of child abuse cases are committed by married laymen who are related to the kids and that the overwhelming majority of celibate priests aren't pedophiles and have never abused any boy, girl, man, or woman.

The evil of child abuse makes no distinction between Catholic or Protestant, Christian or Jewish, celibate or married, black or white, young or old. All ethnic, religious, and racial groups have a few deviants and perverts in their ranks. Indiscriminately associating the Catholic priesthood and its discipline of celibacy with pedophilia doesn't make sense. Yes, sadly, some priests and bishops did abuse children, and more disturbing is that some bishops merely moved these weirdoes from place to place instead of stopping them once and for all. Nonetheless, no credible or logical argument or data supports the notion that celibacy encouraged or promoted sexual misconduct among the clergy. And from now on, those found ought to be — and will be — removed from active ministry, suspended of their ordained faculties, and reported to the civil authorities.

No-woman's-land

With an apparent priest shortage and so many Protestant denominations embracing women ministers, some people wonder why the Catholic Church doesn't allow female priests. First of all, it's *not* because women aren't qualified or that they're somehow not worthy of this calling.

Having a male clergy is a *constitutive element* of the Sacrament of Holy Orders — no pope, council, or bishop can change it. The same is true about the use of water for Baptism and wheat bread and grape wine for Holy Eucharist. The elements of every Sacrament can't be changed because Christ established them. This belief is shared by the Eastern Orthodox, who don't ordain women for the very same reason. It has nothing to do with who's more worthy or suitable for Holy Orders, in the same way that the ban on non-Catholics receiving Holy Communion has nothing to do with any moral or spiritual judgment on the persons involved. It has to do with Sacred Tradition, which is considered as divinely inspired as Sacred Scripture.

The reason the Roman Catholic and Eastern Orthodox Churches are unable to ordain women — be it to the diaconate, priesthood, or episcopacy — is actually threefold:

- ✔ The Church can't change what constitutes valid matter for any of the seven sacraments.
- ✔ Sacred Tradition, nearly 2,000 years old, has never had an instance of women priests.
- ✔ Jesus didn't ordain any women or call any of them to be apostles — not even his own mother!

The Sacrament of Holy Orders

No pope, bishop, or council can change the constitutive elements of any of the seven sacraments, and a valid Sacrament of Holy Orders requires a baptized male to be ordained by a validly ordained bishop. Maleness is as essential to the Sacrament of Holy Orders as wheat bread and grape wine are to the Sacrament of the Holy Eucharist. So just as the pope can't change the requirements of valid matter for the Holy Eucharist, he can't change the requirements of valid matter for Holy Orders.

Sacred Tradition

Both the Catholic and Orthodox Churches believe that the revealed Word of God is both written (Sacred Scripture) and unwritten (Sacred Tradition). When the Bible is silent or ambiguous, Sacred Tradition authentically fills in the gaps. Sacred Tradition shows that women were never ordained, and Pope John Paul II's apostolic letter *Ordinatio Sacerdotalis* (1994) clearly stated that women can't be ordained.

Ordaining only males is not considered a matter of injustice because not all men are allowed to be ordained. Just having a personal vocation isn't enough. The local bishop must call the man, giving an official recognition from the Church that a man may indeed have a priestly vocation. No man can demand or expect ordination because it's a gift, not a right. Think of it like this: Just as it's not unjust for men not to be able to give birth, it's not unjust for women not to be ordained.

Jesus and his apostles

The Church points to the fact that Jesus was both God and man. From all eternity, He was divine with a divine nature, intellect, and will. But He was also born of a human mother and took on a human nature as well. In His divinity, Jesus was God and pure spirit, but in His humanity, He was a man. His gender was more than accidental because the Church is His bride. And because the priest acts *in persona Christi* (in the person of Christ) as an *alter-Christus* (another Christ), the priest reflects Christ to the entire Church whenever he celebrates any of the sacraments. The maleness of Christ was part of who He was, and therefore, Jesus only called men to be His apostles (even though His mother would have been a far better choice). If a woman were to be ordained, she couldn't be espoused to the Church because the Church is considered *mother*. A mother needs a father to complement the equation.

Catholicism regards Jesus as the groom and the Church as his bride. The priest is another Christ who acts in the person of Christ. The male priest represents the male Christ, and the priest is in a spousal relationship with the Holy Mother Church. Women priests don't fit into that typology.

The changing roles of women

Women have come a long way since the early and medieval Church. Although they can't be ordained priests, women have equal rights to be sponsors at Baptism and Confirmation. In Matrimony, they're treated and regarded as 100-percent full, equal partners with their husbands. Women can serve on the parish council and finance committees. They can be readers at Mass, *extraordinary ministers* (laypersons who assist the priest at Mass to give out Holy Communion) if needed, and ushers. They can work in the parish office, teach religious education courses, and so on, just like their male counterparts. And many parishes have women *pastoral associates* — usually nuns, religious sisters, or laywomen who help the pastor with many spiritual and pastoral duties. In addition, women can even hold positions of influence and power in the diocesan chancery. The Church has women who are canon lawyers, judges, and chancellors across the country. The Church has allowed local bishops and pastors the option to permit female altar servers at Mass. Now many parishes have both altar girls and altar boys.

Matters of Life and Death

The Catholic Church's stand on various life and death issues — abortion, euthanasia, the death penalty, and war — doesn't always go with the flow. To find out exactly what each stand is and the reasoning behind it, keep reading.

Abortion

The Catholic Church opposes and condemns any and all direct abortions. Even pregnancies that result from rape or incest or that present a danger to the life of the mother aren't reasons for abortion. Although the Catholic position on abortion may seem extreme to some, it coincides consistently and completely with Catholic morality, which is based on the natural moral law, the Bible, and the official teachings of the Magisterium. (For more on natural moral law, see Book II, Chapter 3; for more on the Magisterium, see Book I, Chapter 2.)

The ends can never justify the means. Catholics believe that willingly, knowingly, and deliberately committing evil is never justifiable — no matter how good the intention and no matter how noble the cause. This belief is a moral absolute for Catholics, and it can't be diluted or altered one iota. The Church believes that if, in even one circumstance, someone is allowed to knowingly and willingly commit evil so that good may come from it, then Pandora's box is opened for anyone to claim he was merely doing a so-called necessary evil for the greater good in the long run. So the Church teaches that one innocent life can't be taken even if it would save hundreds, thousands, or millions.

The Catholic Church sees abortion as the termination of an innocent, though unborn, life. Therefore, it's always wrong, sinful, and immoral. The circumstances by which that life was conceived are considered irrelevant to the question, "Is this an innocent person?"

The Church teaches that human life is created and begins at the moment of conception. A whole unborn child is growing and living in the womb — not a half-human or pre-human. At the moment of conception, when the father's sperm fertilizes the mother's egg, God infuses an immortal soul into this brand new member of the human race. The embryo may not survive the nine months of pregnancy, but nature — not man — should decide when life should be terminated. The baby's DNA is human and distinct from the DNA of mom and dad, too. That means that only a human being exists in the womb, nothing less.

Often, people say that the Catholic Church opts for the child over the mother. Not the case at all. The real teaching is that each and every innocent life must be protected, and intentionally ending the life of the mother or the unborn child is immoral.

So if a pregnant woman has a heart attack and needs emergency surgery, it's considered morally permissible to put her under anesthesia and operate, even though it's likely that she'll spontaneously abort the unborn fetus on her own as a consequence. The distinction is that her body is doing the act of ejecting the fetus as an effect of the primary action of the doctors who are trying to save both lives — the mother and the baby. If the baby dies naturally, the Church believes that no sin has been committed. But if the doctor or nurse directly kills the baby, that's considered murder, the taking of an innocent life.

Likewise, say a pregnant woman has a cancerous uterus, and it must be removed immediately or she and the baby will die. It's considered morally permissible for the uterus to be removed as long as the unborn child isn't directly killed. If the womb is diseased and threatening the life of the mother, the Church permits removing both the uterus and the child while the child is still alive. In this case, the unborn are often too young to survive outside the womb even with the best of prenatal care, and the baby dies a natural death. The sin of abortion occurs if the doctor or nurse intentionally causes the death of the unborn while still in the womb or on the way out. The Church sees a drastic difference between causing death and allowing the process of certain death to continue.

The same applies to ectopic pregnancies. This pathologic condition can warrant the immediate removal of the fallopian tube even though an embryo is attached or embedded to it. As long as the unborn is never directly killed, the Church doesn't consider the procedure an abortion.

Killing an embryo while in the womb or removing an unviable fetus from the womb with the intent and purpose to end its life is considered an abortion. Treating a life-threatening, pathological condition that indirectly results in the unborn child dying naturally is considered a tragedy but not an abortion. So it's not a question of who lives or who dies. It's not a battle of mother versus child.

Even the horror and tragedy of rape or incest isn't considered cause to kill an innocent unborn life. If possible, the woman — who is also considered an innocent victim — can get treatment as soon as possible to try to *prevent* conception from occurring immediately after the rape or incest. Moral theologians and doctors say that it takes several hours to a day for the sperm to reach the egg, so the Church permits a female rape victim to be given a contraceptive *(anovulent) only* if ovulation or conception haven't yet taken place *and* the drug given isn't an *abortifacient* — a so-called contraceptive that doesn't prevent fertilization and conception but rather removes, destroys, or prevents implantation of the embryo. If she waits too long, usually more than 24 hours, conception may take place, and any procedure or treatment to eject the unviable human embryo is an abortion. The Church's stand is that even though she's an innocent victim of a horrible evil, the unborn child is also an innocent victim. No matter what the circumstances that led to the conception, once conceived, that child has an immortal soul and has as much right to live as the mother. In the United States, 98 percent of abortions have nothing to do with rape or incest, and throughout much of the world, the greater percentage of abortions also have nothing to do with rape.

Book II

Walking the Catholic Walk

Euthanasia

The same principles used to condemn abortion are also used to condemn euthanasia. Catholicism regards life as sacred, and taking any innocent life is immoral and sinful, whether it's doctors, nurses, family members, or friends who are taking the life.

The Church believes that no one ought to suffer a long, painful death and that the sick must be treated and the dying must be comforted. The dying and those suffering enormous pain from disease or injury can and should have as much painkilling medication as they can tolerate, as long as the medication isn't the cause of death. Modern medicine has created a plethora of chemicals to diminish or even remove pain, even if it means the patient loses consciousness. So giving someone morphine is permitted and encouraged, for example, but the dosage can't be large enough to be the direct cause of death.

The Church distinguishes between two types of euthanasia. In active euthanasia, you're causing death by doing something to hasten death. In passive euthanasia you intend and cause death by not doing what's necessary to preserve or sustain life, as follows:

- **Active:** Any procedure or treatment that directly causes the death of a patient. Giving someone a lethal injection or drinking poison are examples. This type is always considered immoral and sinful because it's the direct taking of an innocent life. The reasoning is that because the ends can't justify the means, causing the death of someone — even someone you love and hate to see in pain and suffering — is still immoral. Better to make them comfortable and give them pain medication, water, air, and nutrition.

- **Passive:** Intentionally withholding life-sustaining treatment. If the treatment is sustaining life and stopping or removing it ends life, then doing so is considered passive euthanasia. Omitting medicine that's needed to preserve life — such as not giving a diabetic insulin — or starving someone to death by not feeding her are examples. Like active euthanasia, passive euthanasia is considered immoral and sinful because its primary purpose is the death of an innocent person. The means are different, however.

The Church also distinguishes between direct and indirect passive euthanasia:

- **Direct passive:** Intentionally causing death by withholding medicine or a procedure or stopping one that has begun. This type is always immoral.

- **Indirect passive:** Withholding treatment or medicine knowing that doing so may cause death, but death isn't the intent or direct cause of withholding it. This type isn't considered immoral. For example, someone dying of cancer who's also on dialysis can refuse (or his family can refuse) that particular treatment as long as he has already started the dying process and will die of cancer or complications of it well before he'd die of kidney failure. As long as the medicine or treatment being withheld isn't the direct cause of death, it can be refused. Likewise, say that a 98-year-old person in a nursing home is in bad health and bedridden, has cancer, and has begun the dying process (the organs are starting to shut down one by one). It's considered morally permissible to have a Do Not Resuscitate (DNR) order on the chart in case the patient has a heart attack because doing cardio-pulmonary resuscitation (CPR) would be fruitless or would only prolong death by cancer. The Catechism of the Catholic Church clarifies when medical treatment can be refused or stopped: "Discontinuing medical procedures that are burdensome, dangerous, extraordinary, or disproportionate to the expected outcome can be legitimate; it is the refusal of 'overzealous' treatment. Here one does not will to cause death; one's inability to impede it is merely accepted" (2278).

Book II

Walking the Catholic Walk

When Pope John Paul II was in his last months of life suffering from Parkinson's disease, he issued a statement that the terminally ill must always be given at least *hydration* (water), *nutrition* (food), and *normal care* (clean clothes, bathing, shelter, and so on). All ordinary means to sustain life and treat disease or injury are to be done, while extraordinary means can be withheld. The only exception is a person whose digestive system has shut down. Then the use of a feeding tube would be redundant because the stomach is no longer working and is therefore unable to absorb any food or drink. Otherwise, ordinary procedures, like performing an emergency tracheotomy or inserting a feeding tube into the stomach, ought to be done to any and all sick persons, whether terminally ill or not. If these are not done and the person starves to death or dies of asphyxiation, it is considered euthanasia. Those directly involved may be guilty of the sin of murder or negligent homicide, even if the state never presses charges against them.

The death penalty

The Catechism of the Catholic Church says, "The traditional teaching of the Church does not exclude recourse to the death penalty, *if this is the only possible way* of effectively defending human lives against the *unjust aggressor*" (2267). This teaching assumes that the truly guilty party's identity and culpability have been firmly established. But the death penalty is not an absolute right of the state as would be the case in defending the right to life of the innocent. Remember: It's always immoral to intentionally take the life of an innocent person, such as in the case of abortion or euthanasia.

If the innocent can never be intentionally killed, then what about the guilty? The Catechism and the pope, quoting St. Thomas Aquinas, affirm that legitimate defense is not only a *right* but may even be a *duty* for someone responsible for another's life. Sadly, sometimes the only way to render an unjust aggressor incapable of causing harm may involve the use of deadly force, such as a policeman in the line of duty may use or a soldier in time of war would do. But the very significant restriction, according to the Catechism, is "if, however nonlethal means are sufficient to defend and protect people's safety from the aggressor, authority will limit itself to such means" (2267).

What does this all mean? It's consistent Church teaching that the state *possesses* the right to impose the death penalty, but there is no unlimited or unrestricted *use* of that right. According to the Catechism, because the state can effectively prevent crime by stopping the perpetrator without the use of deadly force, "the cases in which the execution of the offender is an absolute necessity 'are very rare, if not practically non-existent'" (2267). This severe restriction on the application of the death penalty is rooted in the fact that punishment isn't meant to be revenge but the restoration of justice, deterrence, and possible rehabilitation. Conversion of the criminal is an aspect not often brought into the public debate on the death penalty.

What about terrorists? There is significant evidence, argumentation, and sound reasoning that says you can invoke the rules of a Just War. (The Just War Doctrine is discussed in the next section.) This would mean that you could try terrorists in a military tribunal as enemy combatants. The thinking is that a terrorist is at war with the civilian (and in most cases) non-combatant population. So those who planned and executed the attacks of September 11, 2001, aren't just criminals; they're war criminals.

The Just War Doctrine

Catholicism has a tradition of discerning a Just War Theory, which says that all things being equal, the state has a right to wage war — just like it has a right to use capital punishment. However, just like capital punishment, the right to wage war isn't an absolute right.

St. Thomas Aquinas (1226–74) developed a theory of St. Augustine (354–430) into the now-known Just War Theory. Its basis is the natural moral law, and it incorporates a moral evaluation before going to war (the reasons for it) and during war (the means used). Everything leading up to war and every act during it must fulfill the criteria listed due to the seriousness of the actions. Otherwise, the war is judged to be immoral. So the Church's stand is that in theory war is justified at times, and a just war can be waged. And the Church believes that throughout history, some wars were morally right, but many wars could've and should've been avoided.

It's actually more accurate to call the Just War Theory the *Just War Doctrine* because theories are ideas not yet proven. The doctrine uses the natural moral law as a litmus test, so its premises and conclusions are sound and morally binding.

The Just War Doctrine can be broken down into two components: *Ius ad bellum* (Latin for *right to war* or moral reasons that justify a country's going to war) and *Ius in bello* (Latin for *right in war* or moral conduct during war). The upcoming sections discuss each component in turn.

Book II

Walking the Catholic Walk

Justifying a country going to war

Before war, these issues must be considered:

- ✔ Just cause
- ✔ Competent authority
- ✔ Comparative justice
- ✔ Right intention
- ✔ Last resort
- ✔ Probability of success
- ✔ Proportionality

The upcoming sections explain each consideration.

Just cause

For a war to be morally permissible, the reasons for going to war must be morally correct. One example of a just cause is to repel invading enemy forces, which are considered unjust aggressors. Imperial Japan's attack on Pearl Harbor in 1941 was sufficient reason to go to war because the enemy was in the process of making attacks on the United States.

Another moral and just cause for going to war is to rescue or assist an ally who was attacked by an unjust aggressor, as Great Britain did in World War II when Poland was invaded by Nazi Germany. Removing or repelling an invading aggressor is sufficient reason to go to war. Gaining new territory or financial or political superiority, however, aren't good reasons.

If citizens are captured, property is seized, land is occupied, or allies are being attacked or invaded, the Church believes that going to war is justified. Defending or protecting lives and territory is considered a just cause. But aggression, revenge, or economic, political, or territorial gain is considered an immoral, or unjust, cause.

Competent authority

Morally speaking, only legitimate, authentic, and authorized leaders can declare and involve the nation in war. Private citizens, corporations, special interest groups, associations, political parties, and so on have no moral authority to declare war. Only presidents and congresses, prime ministers and parliaments, kings and queens — those who wield executive power — have the capacity to engage the entire nation in a war. The press and media may cover the war, but they don't declare it. And they don't sue for peace or have the authority to sign treaties. Individual soldiers, sailors, admirals, or generals have no authority to declare war either.

Comparative justice

Are the values at stake worth the loss of life, the wounding of others, the risk of innocent victims, and damage to property? There must be greater goods at risk, like freedom and liberty, which are in jeopardy if one does not go to war.

Right intention

Morally acceptable reasons for going to war are a just cause, such as the stopping of an unjust aggressor, or having the goal of restoring peace rather than seeking revenge, retaliation, or total destruction of the enemy (without any possibility of surrender).

Last resort

Morally speaking, all viable alternatives must be exhausted before resorting to war. These alternatives include but aren't limited to diplomatic dialogue and debate, quarantine, blockade, sanctions, economics, negotiation, mediation, arbitration, political and public pressure, and sufficient warning. Going to war shouldn't be the first step but the last one. All peaceful attempts must be tried. However, a country can't allow the unjust aggressor who has invaded time to regroup and strike again.

Probability of success

A just war demands that the hope of winning the war is reasonable. Fighting just to make or prove a point or merely defending honor when enemy forces are vastly superior in number, ammunition, or resources is foolish. Sacrificing troops and endangering citizens unnecessarily are irresponsible. The Mutual Assured Destruction (MAD) policy of the former Union of Soviet Socialist Republics and the United States during the Cold War had no probability of success because the goal and objective were to totally destroy the enemy, knowing that the enemy had the same capability; there could be no winners and no survivors.

Proportionality

The evils and suffering that result from the war must be proportionately less than the evils or suffering that would have ensued had there been no conflict. If more misery will result by going to war than deciding not to go, the moral choice is to wait, defer, or use other means. Part of proportionality includes the aftermath and cost of the war — in lives, injuries, property damage, and economic consequences.

Displaying right conduct during war

During war, these two issues are in play:

- ✔ Proportionality
- ✔ Discrimination of noncombatants

Proportionality

A just war uses moral means during the execution of the war. Biological weapons are considered immoral because they disproportionately harm more people and in more severity than is necessary for victory. Furthermore, germ and biological weapons of mass destruction are intrinsically evil because there is little control over the chance of harming innocent noncombatants. Tactical nuclear weapons are permissible only if employed as a last resort and there are no other means to deter the aggressor; in addition, there must be significant accuracy and control to target only valid sites. Conventional weapons, troops, and tactics should first be tried.

Discrimination of noncombatants

The last criterion for a just war is that collateral damage must be kept to an absolute bare minimum. Military and strategic targets are the only morally permissible sites for attack. Major population centers and any place where noncombatants reside shouldn't be directly targeted. Terror bombing of civilians, for example, is immoral.

The old distinction between *military* and *civilian* no longer applies because not all combatants wear uniforms. Guerilla warfare that uses both military and civilian forces is common, so now the distinction is made between *combatants* (those who carry and use firearms or weapons) and *noncombatants* (those who don't).

Wars are declared, whereas military operations may not require such formality. Rescuing hostages; protecting innocent noncombatants; and making humanitarian deliveries of food, clothing, and medicine are not considered acts of war but still must be done prudently. Certain actions may instigate or be the catalyst for all-out war; hence, nations and their leaders are urged to resort to diplomacy and economic pressure when possible.

The sticky part comes when enemy action is imminent and probable. No one argues that a person or country should not defend itself when attacked. But what happens when there is only the threat and nothing more? What if the enemy is working on a secret weapon or is in the process of planning, preparing, and implementing an attack? Here is where credible intelligence may not be enough. There may not be enough information to determine precisely what the enemy is about to do and when it intends to do it. Preemptive wars normally do not fall into the category of being permissible. Strategic military operations may be necessary, however, if an attack is considered imminent, probable, and potentially devastating to many innocent victims.

Planning Your Family Naturally

Catholicism does *not* teach that wives are to have as many children as biologically possible. Women aren't baby factories. So why, then, is the Church against artificial contraception? Keep reading to get a glimpse of the Church's reasoning and to find out about what the Church considers a morally permissible alternative — Natural Family Planning (NFP).

The moral argument against artificial contraception

Pope Paul VI issued his encyclical *Humanae Vitae* (1968), which articulates and reiterates the Church's moral opposition to the use of artificial contraception. The Catholic Church has always said that artificial contraception is immoral. In fact, until 1930, every Christian denomination in the world — Protestant, Catholic, and Orthodox — believed that artificial contraception was sinful. The Anglican Lambeth Conference in 1930, however, permitted contraception in limited cases. Soon afterward, most Protestant churches followed suit. Today, Catholicism and a few Evangelical and Fundamentalist churches still maintain that the use of artificial contraception isn't part of God's plan.

For the Church, the worst aspect of birth control pills is that many of them aren't true contraceptives; they don't prevent the sperm and egg from conceiving. Instead, they work as an *abortifacient,* causing the uterus to eject a fertilized egg, which, according to Catholicism, is now an embryo and a human person. Many women think that their birth control pills are really contraceptives, when they're actually abortifacients.

The Church also says that artificial contraception is morally wrong because it synthetically divides and separates what God intended to always be together. Morally, each and every sex act can occur only between husband and wife *and* must be directed toward two ends: love and life, that is, the intimate unity between the man and woman (love) and the possible procreation of another human being (life). Married conjugal love — the intimacy between husband and wife — is the most profound union on earth at the natural level. The physical union of bodies in married sex represents the spiritual reality of two becoming one flesh, but that unity is also present to be open to the possibility of new life. Conception and pregnancy don't have to occur each time, but no manmade barriers should prevent what God may intend to happen. For example, if a middle-age woman, having gone through menopause and lost the natural ability to become pregnant, marries, then her marriage is just as valid in the eyes of the Church as those who are young enough to conceive.

When love and life — unity and procreation — are separated, then sex becomes an end in itself rather than a means to an end. Birth control makes sex recreational, and removing what may be perceived as the "danger" of pregnancy means that couples no longer need to communicate about when and when not to have sex and whether they want or can afford another child. The communication and consideration that's necessitated by the possibility of having a child actually strengthens the marriage. Without the necessity for consideration, communication, and cooperation, their ties to one another may weaken or fail to live up to their full potential.

Whether it's the pill, a condom, an intrauterine device (IUD), or a sponge, any artificial method of contraception is deemed immoral because the Church believes that it divides what God intended and may frustrate a divine plan to bring a new life into the world.

The natural alternative to contraception

The Catholic Church permits and encourages married couples to space births and plan how big or small their families will be. But if artificial contraception is out, what's in? Definitely not the archaic and undependable rhythm method. That's not what the Church means by Natural Family Planning (NFP).

Because no two women are exactly alike, no two menstrual cycles are exactly alike, either. But science does show that women are infertile more times during the month than they're fertile. Each woman has a unique cycle in which she goes from producing eggs to being infertile and vice versa. By using natural science — taking body temperature, checking body fluids, and using some computations — a woman can determine with 95 percent accuracy when to have sex without getting pregnant.

Unlike artificial methods, NFP doesn't require foreign objects to be inserted into the woman's body. This method is completely natural, organic, and 100-percent safe, with no chemical side effects, no recalls, and no toxic

Book II

Walking the Catholic Walk

complications. And it's a *team* effort. When using the pill or a condom, one person takes responsibility for spacing the births and regulating conception. But *both* the husband *and* the wife practice NFP. This makes sense in the eyes of the Church because *both* get married on the wedding day and *both* are involved if a baby comes along.

When practiced properly, NFP is as effective as any artificial birth control method. And it's not difficult to learn. Mother Theresa taught illiterate women how to effectively use NFP. In addition, no prescription and no expensive devices are involved, so it's easy on the budget. Birth control pills, on the other hand, are commodities bought and sold for profit. Pharmaceutical companies have a vested interest as well.

A woman is fertile during approximately seven to ten days per cycle and is infertile the rest of the time. During periods of fertility, a couple seeking to space out their family can abstain from sex.

The Catholic Church believes that these times challenge the couple to remain romantic without becoming sexual. All too often, our culture and society have exclusively united the two so that people can't imagine how someone can be romantic without ending up in bed. Yet men still court women before marrying them. Courtship means being affectionate, romantic, and loving without any sex, because it's saved for the wedding night. The Church says that the brief period of abstinence that's observed by those practicing NFP enables husbands and wives to see each other as more than objects of desire and still encourages them to be close, romantic, and loving toward one another in other, nonsexual ways. It demonstrates that one can be romantic without being sexual.

For more information on this topic, check out The Couple-to-Couple League at www.ccli.org. This international, interfaith, nonprofit organization teaches Natural Family Planning (NFP).

What if you can't conceive naturally?

What about the other side of the coin? What if a man and woman are using Natural Family Planning (NFP) to have a baby but find that they can't conceive? Infertility is one of the most painful and agonizing crosses some married couples have to carry. Just as contraceptive sex is immoral because it divides love and life (unity and procreation), conception outside of normal sexual intercourse is considered immoral, too. The Church teaches that the ends can't justify the means, so immoral means can never be used, even to promote the birth of another human being to two loving parents who desperately want a child. Children are a gift from God and not an absolute right that people can demand. Moral means must be employed when married couples have sex and when they want to have children.

One alternative to using biological procedures to conceive children is the ancient tradition of adoption. Saint Joseph is often invoked as the patron saint of adoptive parents as he wasn't the natural father of Jesus, but as the husband of Mary, the mother of Jesus, he loved her son as if He were his own flesh and blood. Adoption can save many unborn children from a horrible death by abortion and can also bring love and joy to infertile married couples.

That said, fertility drugs aren't per se forbidden, but the warning is that they often lead to multiple births, which then prompts some physicians to play God and say to the mother, "It's unlikely that all will survive, so let's terminate the least likely to survive to increase the chances of the rest." So a selective abortion is done. Kill one to save two, three, or more. To the Church, the end doesn't justify the means. Evil can never be knowingly, willingly, and intentionally done, no matter how great and good the final effect.

Book II

Walking the Catholic Walk

When conception occurs artificially, the Church claims that it isn't in God's plan, which is found naturally (in nature as opposed to manmade). Therefore, the following methods of artificially creating new life are considered immoral:

- ✔ **Artificial insemination (AIH):** The husband's sperm are inserted into the wife with a device. And often, because the man's sperm count is low, some of the husband's sperm are mixed with donor sperm. The mixture is used, but it takes only one sperm to fertilize the egg, so it's possible that someone else is going to be the genetic father of the child.

- ✔ **In vitro fertilization (IVF) and embryo transfer (ET):** With in vitro fertilization, several eggs are fertilized with plenty of sperm in a test tube or petri dish. Every fertilized egg becomes an embryo — a human person with an immortal soul. The clinic picks the best-looking embryo(s), transfers one or more into the womb of the mother, and discards the rest, which Catholicism regards as an abortion. The Church believes that at the moment of conception, a human being is created and that freezing or throwing away a person — no matter how small and developing — is gravely immoral.

- ✔ **Donor sperm and donor eggs:** These methods are forbidden because, again, artificial means are used to achieve conception. Even more importantly, one of the spouses is completely absent from the act of procreation because another person's egg or sperm is being used; a third party becomes involved in the birth. The donor isn't married to the husband and wife, and yet he or she is going to genetically create a new human person with one of them. For the same reason, sperm banks and surrogate mothers are considered immoral because they literally exclude the husband or the wife in the very act of procreating. Also, clinics often overfertilize and then select good embryos from not-so-good ones. The ones that are tossed out are human beings nevertheless.

✓ **Human cloning:** This method attempts to replicate rather than procreate. Using genetic material from mom and/or dad, a healthy egg is wiped clean of DNA, only to have someone else's put inside. Human cloning is an attempt to play God — as if a mere mortal can create life — and Catholicism teaches that it's dangerous and wrong.

Despite the sadness of infertility, the Catholic Church maintains that modern science doesn't offer moral solutions — only immoral alternatives. Natural sex between husband and wife is the only morally accepted means to conceive and have children.

Defending Traditional Family Life

The Catholic Church firmly believes in the sanctity of human life and in the sanctity of the human family. Both the Bible and the Catechism teach that God intended human beings to be born, be raised, and live within the nurturing protection of the family. More than just a social agreement among individuals to live together, family is a covenant relationship blessed by God.

The family is often called the *domestic church* because it is the place where persons first learn about God and His love for His children from the love shown by mom and dad to their kids. It is the building block of society, both church (religious) and state (secular). As such, family has defined parameters, obligations, duties, privileges, and rights.

Family is intimately connected to marriage, which itself reflects the covenant between the Lord and His people. Marriage is the permanent, faithful, and fruitful union of one man and one woman. This institution was created by divine design and cannot be changed or undone by any person, state, or religion. Likewise, family is built on marriage. Parents are supposed to be married to each other so they can best raise their children.

Biologically, most adults can have offspring, whether they are married or single. Being a mother or father is more than just procreating; it's a vocation that is simultaneously connected to and built on the foundation of marriage. Unmarried parents can certainly love and care for their children as much as married couples; however, the children are deprived of the blessings of full family life when mom and dad are not husband and wife.

The Church does not condone any denial or violation of human rights. All human beings are made in the image and likeness of God and deserve equal treatment and protection. At the same time, there is no inalienable right to redefine or remake marriage and the family.

Marriage is between one man and one woman by divine, natural, and ecclesiastical law regardless of whether the local civil law says otherwise. Hence, homosexual (same-sex) unions cannot become or be considered true marriages. This issue is not a matter of discrimination because not just one group of people is affected. Whether you're talking about an unmarried heterosexual couple or a civilly united homosexual couple, neither of these unions constitute the divinely instituted estate of marriage. And without marriage, there cannot be full family life. Polygamous and incestuous unions are also not considered true marriages.

There may be commitment and even love between adults, and they may have all the financial resources necessary, but being open to an exclusive, permanent, and fruitful union is the foundation of marriage. A same-sex union is no different than a polygamous union or an unmarried couple in the eyes of the Church. None fully coincide with the mandate of God as does the traditional family. Christ Himself is described as the bridegroom and the Church as His bride by Saint Paul in his epistles.

Pope John Paul II said in his letter *Familiaris Consortio* (1981) that individuals are born into a family so they may more easily see their membership in the family of faith, known as the Church. Baptism makes one a child of God and a member of God's family, being able to call Him Father and seeing Jesus as our brother. Familial relationships are not artificial but organic, like the unity in a body among all its parts.

That is why the family has a natural right to exist as it was intended to be. Unfortunately, human sin and weakness have entered the equation, and all too often innocent victims, namely the children, suffer when families are divided due to broken marriages. Sometimes even the economy and the culture — if not governments themselves — work against family life by making it easier for parents to live together without the grace and stability of marriage. Tragedies like death, illness, abuse, and abandonment also inflict harm on families and family members. All the more reason, Pope John Paul II said, that people need the spiritual family of the Church to sustain them when even their own natural family falls short.

Book II

Walking the Catholic Walk

Book III

Catholic Mass

Contents at a Glance

Chapter 1

Understanding Mass and Its Foundations

*W*hat Catholic Christians believe and how they worship are integrally connected. Those beliefs are efficiently expressed in the worship service known as the Holy Mass, also sometimes called Divine Liturgy and Sacred Worship. This chapter looks at how the keystone of Catholic doctrine is celebrated in Mass around the world, including the roots of the traditions and the roles of those who participate.

Introducing the Catholic Mass

Catholicism is a Christian religion. It professes the belief that Jesus Christ is the Son of God and the Second Person of the Holy Trinity, and therefore its followers are to worship him with the same adoration given to God.

With its roots in Judaism, Catholicism shares many steadfast beliefs and traditions with that religion; most prominently, the belief in one God (monotheism) and the use of sacred texts divinely inspired by God. Both faiths perform certain rituals, such as praying, giving blessings, reading the texts from God, and offering some sort of sacrificial offering. In ancient times an animal was sacrificed as a symbolic rite for the purification of sins.

Christian worship, and Catholic Mass in particular, is rooted in both word and ritual. Its followers consider Mass to be the ritual reenactment of the Last Supper and the unbloody reenactment of the Sacrifice of Calvary when Jesus died on the cross.

The Mass is the heart and soul of Catholic worship and belief. It is rooted in the Bible, and this sacred text is read aloud during Mass. The Church has foundations in both parts of the Bible, the Old Testament (the Hebrew Scriptures) and the New Testament. Both testaments show the enormous value of ritual sacrifice as signs of *covenant*. The Old Testament is the covenant between God and his Chosen People, the Jews; the New Testament is the covenant between God and the whole human race, which is at the core of Catholicism.

The Hebrew word for covenant is *berit,* in Greek it is *diatheke,* and in Latin it is *testamentum*. All three biblical and ancient translations refer to a sacred oath and agreement, much more permanent, personal, and profound than a mere legal contract. Covenants are not temporary and cannot be dissolved. Covenants can be broken insofar as one party may neglect to fulfill its obligations, but even that neglect doesn't destroy the relationship it created. Catholicism believes in and celebrates in Mass the covenant between God and his faithful followers.

Honoring God every week on a special day is very important to Catholics. Jews have observed the Sabbath day, Saturday, since the time of Moses and the giving of the Ten Commandments, but Christians worship on Sundays. The Church didn't change the Sabbath from Saturday to Sunday, as some people claim; rather, it considers itself bound by the New Law of the New Testament, not the Old Law of the Old Testament, so the day of worship became the day of Resurrection, which was Sunday.

Christian Churches, including the Catholic Church, remember the Last Supper on Holy Thursday when Jesus celebrated the Passover (the annual Jewish sacred feast) with his Apostles. Bread and wine are used during the Mass, and the words Christ spoke at that event are repeated by the ordained priest: "this is my body" (over the bread) and "this is my blood" (over the wine).

What Mass Means to Catholics

Latin, or Western, Catholics are familiar with the word *Mass,* from the Latin word *missa,* which is said by the priest or deacon at the end of the liturgy. *Ite missa est* has been inaccurately translated over the years as "Go, the Mass is ended." Literally, however, it should read "Go, [the congregation] is sent." In other words, the command is to go, because the people are now sent *(missa est)* into the world.

These last words of the Mass, *missa est,* were used to describe the entire sacred liturgy that is the heart and soul of Catholic divine worship. Why the last and not the first words? Well, every Catholic prayer and sacrament begins with the same words: *in the name of the Father, and of the Son and of the Holy Spirit.* Each sacrament and prayer have different endings. Latin is also a language where the verb and/or the most important word of the sentence appears at the end and not the beginning.

A Communion service is not the same as a Mass. Only a priest or bishop can celebrate Mass, but any deacon or designated layperson (called an *extraordinary minister of Holy Commun*ion) may preside at the distribution of Holy Communion outside Mass. A Communion service has Scripture readings, meditation, prayers, the Our Father (Lord's Prayer), and concludes with Holy Communion. These services are common in places where no priest is available for weekly Mass but the faithful are in need of the sacraments.

Holy Mass, on the other hand, is more than the giving of Holy Communion. It is foremost a sacrifice (of Jesus to his heavenly Father) and then a sacrament (a source of divine grace) and sacred banquet (spiritual food for the soul). The Sacred Liturgy is the worship of God, so the focus is on the Lord and not on mankind.

In Catholicism, Holy Communion (also called the Holy Eucharist) is not only believed to be the Body, Blood, Soul, and Divinity of Christ, but also the intimate union of God and believer. Simultaneously, it is also the union of all the members who partake of the same Body and Blood of Christ. The analogy used by St. Paul is that the Church is like a human body with many parts but is one whole, unified being. Each part is distinct but connected to the whole.

Book III

Catholic Mass

People often refer to the Mass using other terms. Here are a few examples:

- **Breaking of Bread:** The *breaking of bread* is the first reference to the unique form of Christian worship rooted in the Last Supper, commemorating the moment Jesus took the loaf of bread, broke it into pieces, and handed it to the apostles.

- **Liturgy:** *Celebrating the liturgy,* a phrase common in Apostolic times, is what Latin or Western Catholics call the Holy Mass. Liturgy is a public service or ministry, and the *Divine Liturgy* was the public worship of God. Catholicism used the term *liturgy* to refer to the Mass and the other sacraments as well as the Divine Office or Breviary (also known as the Liturgy of the Hours).

- **Lord's Supper:** The *Lord's Supper* was a term coined by St. Paul in his first epistle to the Corinthians (11:20) to describe the sacred event. He chastises the Corinthians, however, for misbehaving at these gatherings, admonishing them that the sacred liturgy is not the place to get drunk, have arguments, or spread false teachings. (Imagine going a Mass where that happened!)

- ✔ **Sacrifice, Offering,** or **Oblation:** *Sacrifice, offering,* or *oblation* were other common terms during the time of the Apostles and Fathers of the Church to describe the main offering of Jesus the Son of God the Father to save mankind from sin. Christian priests, particularly Catholic and Orthodox, offer the sacrifice of the Son to the Father because they act in the name and in the person of Jesus Christ by virtue of their ordination.

- ✔ **Gathering** or **Synaxis:** Sometimes the words *gathering* or *assembly* are used to describe the congregating of people, but the many secular and nonreligious uses of the words make them not unique to worship. The Greek usage, however, is predominantly religious and sacred, hence *synaxis* is used to refer to the Divine Liturgy and also to Vespers, Matins, Lauds, and for commemorating several saints in one service.

- ✔ **Eucharist:** The word *Eucharist,* meaning *thanksgiving,* can be traced to the ancient church. It was used by Justin Martyr in the second century as a means of describing the attitude of thankfulness the faithful must present when participating in the divine worship of God. Christians then adopted the word, and the Sacrament of Holy Eucharist refers not only to the Holy Communion but to the worship service in which it occurs.

Different Catholics, Different Masses

The substance of the Mass is the same everywhere in the world. Sacred Scripture is read, prayers are offered, and the Last Supper is commemorated. Wheat bread and grape wine are used, and only ordained priests or bishops perform the celebration of Mass, the holiest ceremony and service in the Catholic religion.

The word *catholic,* however, comes from the Greek word *katholikos,* meaning *universal.* "Unity among diversity" is the definition St. Thomas Aquinas (a 13th-century Catholic theologian) gave for beauty, and it is the description he gives to the Church. While Catholicism professes unity of doctrine (teachings), discipline (law), and divine worship (sacraments), the Church still has a lot of diversity. The language of worship ranges from ancient Greek and Latin to modern-day English, Spanish, Italian, Polish, Vietnamese, Korean, and so on.

The Church's liturgical division between East and West predates the division of the Roman Empire in the fourth century. Christianity began in Jerusalem then spread to Antioch (Syria) and Alexandria (Egypt) and finally found its way to Rome. This is how Constantine's mother, St. Helena, embraced the Christian religion. While no specific date is evident, over time the Christian communities in the East (at Antioch, Alexandria, and Constantinople) had profound influence over liturgical practice.

The Church's liturgical division led to the development of different rites. A *rite* is a tradition of how the seven sacraments are celebrated. In other words, rites are ways in which sacred liturgy is said and done. According to Canon 28 of the Code of Canon Law for the Eastern and Oriental Churches, a rite is "the liturgical, theological, spiritual and disciplinary patrimony, culture and circumstances of history of a distinct people."

The Catholic Church has four major liturgical rites: Western (also called Latin) and three Eastern branches: Antiochian, Alexandrian, and Byzantine. Within the four rites, numerous ritual churches are associated within Catholic Christianity. A ritual church is a group of Christian faithful united by a hierarchy and, especially among the Eastern (sometimes called Oriental) Catholics, with its own patriarch or metropolitan.

Western Rite

Some small liturgical traditions exist in the Western, or Latin, Church, from religious orders like the Dominicans to new converts from the Protestant Anglican Church. But the most predominant form by far is the Roman Rite, which originated in Rome, the diocese of the pope. The Roman Rite takes two forms: Ordinary and Extraordinary.

Book III

Catholic Mass

Celebrating Mass regularly in the Ordinary form

Mass in the Ordinary form is celebrated according to the *Missale Romanum* of 1970, promulgated by Pope Paul VI, currently in its third edition (2002). The vernacular editions of this Missal, as well as the rites of the other sacraments, are translated from the Latin typical editions revised after the Second Vatican Council. As its name suggests, the Ordinary form is the typical and most common form of the Mass celebrated in the Western Catholic Church.

Preserving the traditional Mass as the Extraordinary form

The Extraordinary form of the Mass is celebrated according to the *Missale Romanum* of 1962, promulgated by Blessed Pope John XXIII. It is sometimes inaccurately referred to as the Tridentine Mass (after the Council of Trent from the 16th century) or the TLM (Traditional Latin Mass), but technically it is different. Pope Benedict XVI clarified that the Extraordinary form was never abolished and has remained valid and allowable at all times since the Second Vatican Council established the Ordinary Mass. Any priest is allowed to celebrate the Extraordinary form of the Mass without special permission from his bishop.

The Extraordinary form is exhibited in different ways:

- ✔ **Anglican Use:** Since the 1980s, the Holy See (the pope) has granted some former Anglican and Episcopal clergy converting with their parishes the right to celebrate the sacramental rites according to the Book of Common Prayer.

- ✔ **Mozarabic:** The rite of the Iberian Peninsula (Spain and Portugal) dates from the sixth century. Beginning in the 11th century it was generally replaced by the Roman Rite, although it has remained the Rite of the Cathedral of the Archdiocese of Toledo, Spain, and six parishes that sought permission to adhere to it. Its celebration today is generally semiprivate.

- ✔ **Ambrosian:** The Rite of the Archdiocese of Milan, Italy, consolidated by St. Ambrose, continues to be celebrated in Milan, though not by all parishes.

- ✔ **Bragan:** The Rite of the Archdiocese of Braga, the Primatial See of Portugal, dates from the 12th century or earlier. It is occasionally used in the United States and Brazil but is very rare.

- ✔ **Carmelite:** The Rite of the Order of Carmel was founded by St. Berthold around 1154.

- ✔ **Carthusian:** The Rite of the Carthusian Order was founded by St. Bruno in 1084.

- ✔ **Dominican:** The Rite of the Order of Friars Preacher (OP) was founded by St. Dominic in 1215.

Eastern Rite

The Eastern Rite is made up of the Churches that developed in Constantinople, Alexandria, and Antioch and all the Rites that stem from those patriarchates. The East-West Schism of 1040 separated many of the Eastern Churches, subsequently called *Orthodox,* from the Western Church and Rome. The Eastern Catholic Church of today is comprised of the formerly Orthodox Churches that later reunited with Rome and the other Churches in the Eastern part of the world that didn't separate in the schism.

The largest number of Eastern Catholics practice the Byzantine Rite. This rite developed in Constantinople, which was established by Emperor Constantine as the second capital city of the Roman Empire in the fourth century AD. (The name *Byzantine* comes from the city's original name, which was also given to the whole region.) But many other Eastern Catholics use rites that stem from the Churches of Antioch and Alexandria. In this section we explore some of the smaller rites within the Eastern Church as well as the Byzantine.

Antiochian family of liturgical rites

The Church of Antioch in Syria was founded by St. Peter, and its liturgy is attributed to St. James and the Church of Jerusalem. This branch of liturgical churches is primarily divided by Eastern or Western Syriac language (dialect of Aramaic) usage, and then each of those branches is further subdivided by language and tradition.

Following are the rites categorized as West Syriac:

- ✔ **Maronite:** Under the jurisdiction of the Maronite Patriarch of Antioch, this Church never separated from Rome. Three million Maronites in Lebanon (the place of origin), Cyprus, Egypt, Syria, Israel, Canada, the United States, Mexico, Brazil, Argentina, and Australia are members of the Maronite Church. The liturgical language is Aramaic.

- ✔ **Syriac:** Under the jurisdiction of the Syriac Patriarch of Antioch, the Syriac Orthodox Church reunited with Rome in 1781 from the Monophysite heresy. About 110,000 Syriac Catholics live in Syria, Lebanon, Iraq, Egypt, Canada, and the United States. They use the Liturgy of St. James.

- ✔ **Malankarese:** Under the jurisdiction of the Major Archbishop of the Syro-Malankara Catholic Church, this Church was started in the south of India by St. Thomas, using the West Syriac liturgy. The Church reunited with Rome in 1930. Liturgical languages are West Syriac and Malayalam. India and North America are home to 350,000 Malankarese Catholics.

The following rites fall under the umbrella of East Syriac:

- ✔ **Chaldean:** Under the jurisdiction of the Katholicos Patriarch of Babylon in Baghdad, Babylonian (Chaldeon) Catholics returned to Rome in 1692 from the Nestorian heresy. Liturgical languages are Syriac and Arabic. There are 310,000 Chaldean Catholics in Iraq, Iran, Syria, Lebanon, Egypt, Turkey, and the United States.

- ✔ **Syro-Malabarese:** Under the jurisdiction of the Major Archbishop of Kerala for the Syro-Malabar Catholic Church, this church was started in southern India using the East Syriac liturgy. It never severed ties to Rome and has 3.5 million members worldwide, mostly in India.

Alexandrian family of liturgical rites

The Church of Alexandria in Egypt was one of the original centers of Christianity; like Rome and Antioch, it had a large Jewish population that was very open and amenable to early Christian evangelization. Its liturgy is attributed to St. Mark the Evangelist and shows the later influence of the Byzantine Liturgy in addition to its unique elements.

Book III

Catholic Mass

- ✔ **Coptic:** This Church was started by Egyptian Catholics who were separated from the pope but returned to communion with Rome in 1741. The Patriarch of Alexandria leads the 200,000 faithful of this rite, who are spread throughout Egypt and the Near East. The liturgical languages are Coptic (Egyptian) and Arabic.

- ✔ **Ethiopian/Abyssinian:** Comprised of Ethiopian Coptic Christians who returned to Rome in 1846. The liturgical language is Ge'ez. The 200,000 faithful are found in Ethiopia, Eritrea, Somalia, and Jerusalem.

Armenian liturgical rite

The Armenian Apostolic Church formally broke from Rome in the fifth century, and despite the early efforts of some Armenian bishops to reestablish unity with Rome, unity wasn't established until the Crusades in the 15th century. That reunion was short-lived, though, and only in 1742 was full communion achieved when Pope Benedict XIV formally established the Armenian Catholic Church.

Considered either its own rite or an older version of the Byzantine (see the following section), the exact form of the Armenian Rite is not used by any other Byzantine Rite. It is composed of Catholics from the first people to convert as a nation, the Armenians (northeast of Turkey), and who returned to Rome at the time of the Crusades. Under the jurisdiction of the Patriarch of Cilicia of the Armenians in Lebanon, the 350,000 Armenian Catholics are found in Armenia, Syria, Iran, Iraq, Lebanon, Turkey, Egypt, Greece, Ukraine, France, Romania, the U.S., and Argentina. The liturgical language is classical Armenian. Most Armenians are Orthodox, not in union with Rome.

Byzantine family of liturgical rites

Although all Byzantine Catholics are Eastern Catholic, not all Eastern Catholics are Byzantine. Many Roman or Latin Rite Catholics erroneously identify all Eastern Catholic Churches as "Byzantine," when in reality the term is specifically used to identify mainly those formerly Eastern Orthodox communities that independently reestablished union with Rome in the 17th and 18th centuries. Orthodox (non-Catholic) Churches use some of the doctrine of the Catholic Church:

- ✔ *Oriental* Orthodox Churches refer to those traditions that only accept the first three Ecumenical Councils (Nicea in 325, I Constantinople in 381, and Ephesus in 431).

- ✔ *Eastern* Orthodox Churches refer to those traditions that embrace those three councils and the four that followed (Chalcedon 451, II Constantinople 553, III Constantinople 681, II Nicea 787), thus making the first seven councils their source of doctrinal authority.

Both the Oriental Orthodox and the Eastern Orthodox Churches are separated from Rome and exist as independent religions. However, Eastern Catholic Churches, including the Byzantine Rite, are in full communion with the Bishop of Rome (also known as the pope) while retaining their own autonomy in terms of local jurisdiction.

Changes to the Mass Over the Years

The Eastern Liturgical Rites have not had significant changes over the past few centuries. The Roman Rite, however, has gone through a few modifications of significance.

No matter what changes take place, the substance of the Mass has remained the same from the time of the Last Supper. What Jesus used (wheat bread and grape wine) and what he said over them ("this is my body . . . this is my blood") have been repeated in the Mass by an ordained minister for two millennia.

The early days

The first changes took place when the language of the Sacred Liturgy went from Aramaic (the dialect of Hebrew spoken by Christ and his Apostles) to Greek (the proper and eloquent tongue of the educated) and finally to Latin (the common and official language of the Roman Empire). After Christianity spread throughout the Empire, those parts that spoke Greek (the Eastern Empire) used Greek for the Sacred Liturgy, and those parts that spoke Latin (the Western Empire) used Latin for public worship.

At that time, the Romance languages, like French, Spanish, Portuguese, and Italian, and the Germanic tongues, like German and English, were just starting to be formulated with rules of grammar and syntax. Latin and Greek, however, were ancient languages that had vast vocabularies and had been around long enough to have set rules and defined meanings. In that time, if you were literate, you could read and write in Latin and/or Greek. The other European languages weren't developed enough to use at any scholarly or liturgical level.

After 300 years of illegality and persecution by the Roman Empire, Christianity was legalized in AD 313 by the Edict of Milan, issued by Emperor Constantine. Five centuries later, when Charles the Great was crowned Holy Roman Emperor by the pope on Christmas Day in AD 800, he sought to solidify Christendom in the West under one faith and one sword. The Roman Rite became the predominant liturgical way of worshipping God just as the Byzantine did for much of the Eastern Empire.

Book III

Catholic
Mass

The Middle Ages and Renaissance

When Martin Luther and the Protestant Reformation appeared in the 16th century, the vernacular was more sophisticated and formalized. Some people were concerned, however, that because of all the new languages then spoken, mistranslations of Sacred Scripture and liturgical texts used for Divine Worship could easily happen. For the sake of uniformity and accuracy, liturgical and biblical language remained the fixed and structured Latin in the West and Greek in the East.

The use of Latin, therefore, was not intended to make the Bible's contents difficult for people to understand, but rather to keep the structure and form in a uniform language. Latin ensured accuracy, formality, and, most of all, universality in a religion that used the very word (*catholic* means *universal*) as one of its names.

When the Protestant Church openly embraced vernacular language, the Catholic response was to even more vigilantly maintain the use of Latin in the Western Church. This difference helped Catholicism maintain a unique identity distinct from Protestant Christianity and from Eastern Orthodoxy (which separated from Rome in 1054).

Adapting in the 20th century

The modern world of the 1960s saw another change in the celebration of the Mass as a result of the Second Vatican Council (1962–1965), also called Vatican II. After two world wars, depression, and globalization, the Catholic bishops of the world were called by Pope John XXIII to see how the Church could adapt its methods while retaining its content.

Pope Pius XII had done tremendous work during the post–World War II era to develop more external participation by the faithful at the Mass. Vatican II suggested some use of the vernacular and offered the option of the priest facing the people while he celebrated Mass. Until then, the priest and the people both faced the same direction — either geographical east or liturgical east (facing the tabernacle). The orientation toward the east was ancient, historical, biblical, theological, and liturgical. Christ rose at the break of day. The sun rises in the east every morning. And eastward orientation was seen as an orientation toward the Lord. But during the aftermath of the Second Vatican Council, a push was made by some liturgists to have the celebrant face the people. The Missal never mandated the change in position, but because of the spreading use of free-standing altars that accommodate facing the people, the practice merely disappeared on its own.

Three generations of Catholics have known only the *Novus Ordo* of Pope Paul VI (1970), which is now called the Ordinary form of the Roman Rite. The old traditional Latin Mass (TLM, also sometimes called Tridentine Mass and now classified as the Extraordinary form) was given more opportunity for use by Pope John Paul II in 1988. Finally, Pope Benedict XVI issued his own *motu proprio, Summorum Pontificum,* granting universal authorization for any priest of the Latin Rite to celebrate the Extraordinary form and urging him to do so whenever requested by his parishioners. Previously, priests had to secure permission from their own bishops.

Roots of Judaism within the Mass

Knowing the past, how and why things came to be, leads to a deeper understanding of the present, which can ultimately point to where things are going. Exploring the roots of Catholicism in the Jewish texts give the faithful a foundation on which to base their beliefs and thoughts about what happened long ago, what is happening now, and what will happen in the years to come.

Genesis and the creation story

If you want to gain a better understanding of the Catholic Mass, you're best off starting at the beginning. Biblically speaking, that's the Book of Genesis, or the book of *beginnings,* which is the first book in the Bible. Scholars believe that the people of Israel told this story of beginnings to their children and to each other for many years before it was ever recorded in writing.

Genesis tells the story of God creating the universe and everything in it. It describes the making of the sun, moon, stars, and earth, with its dry land, oceans, and streams. It teaches about the creation of animals, and says that God made humans in his own image (Genesis 1:26).

By giving humans this certain resemblance to himself, God enabled humans to be his friends. And although human beings were made in much the same way as all of God's creation — from the earth — God gave them one thing that made them special and godlike: free will.

God provided that unique friendship to the first humans he created, Adam and Eve. He made a special garden, Eden, in which they could live in peace and have an abundance of food and shelter. And though they had free will, the one caveat to their peaceful living was that they stay away from the tree in the middle of the garden.

Book III

Catholic Mass

An evil voice came to Adam and Eve in the body of a serpent and convinced them to pick the fruit from the tree and eat it. By giving in to the temptation, the two demonstrated their lack of gratitude to God for all he had given them. They were cast out of the garden and forced to live their lives, as were all of their descendants, with Original Sin — thoughts of greed and lust and other impurities would always be present.

In a story of redemption, the Old Testament tells of God's anger at the humans he created. He was prepared to drown them all in a great flood, but relented a bit and told his friend Noah to build a great ark and fill it with good people and pairings of animals (Genesis 8:20). Those survivors then repopulated the earth.

Beyond the story of creation, the Old Testament tells the stories of the relationship between God and his people and of his love for them despite their unfaithfulness to him. The Old Testament highlights God's refusal to abandon the humans he created. And it doesn't highlight just the ways God's people disappointed him; there are many stories of God's followers offering sacrifice to their Lord in a showing of true love and faith.

Pope Benedict XVI wrote that love is both possessive and oblative (sacrificial). In other words, true love involves both need to be with and the willingness to sacrifice for the one you love. As described in numerous Old Testament stories, God expected his children to make sacrifices to him in appreciation and gratitude for his love and friendship. While the people were the recipients of God's generosity, mercy and forgiveness, they also were to give back worship and adoration, but of him alone. God did not tolerate any idolatry or false worship of other deities.

Sacrifice of Abel

According to the Book of Genesis, Adam and Eve had two sons, Cain and Abel. Both sons offered sacrifice to God, but Abel's gift of the best of his livestock was pure and spotless, and Cain's gift of inferior, inedible produce was cheap and irreverent. When the offerings were burned, the smoke from Abel's sacrifice rose right up to heaven and the smoke of Cain's inferior offerings blew back into his own face. Cain was so infuriated by the rebuke that he killed Abel out of pure envy. Abel's sacrifice, however, is a model of the proper kind of sacrifice a child of God should always perform.

Sacrifice of Abraham

Later in Genesis you meet Abraham and his wife Sarah, who were old and childless. Their faithfulness to the Lord was rewarded with a son, Isaac, who was to be with them the rest of their days.

God called Abraham to enter a covenant, or sacred agreement, that they would love each other. As part of this covenant, God asked Abraham to prove his love by sacrificing his only son, Isaac. Abraham loved his son dearly, but his love for God was stronger, and Abraham showed that he was willing to obey God and sacrifice his only son. God spared Isaac and entered into another sacred covenant with Abraham promising that he would make Abraham's descendants "as numerous as the stars in the heavens and the sands on the shore of the sea" (Genesis 22:17). In fact, as noted earlier in this chapter, all three monotheistic religions (Judaism, Christianity and Islam) consider themselves spiritual children of Abraham.

Sacrifice of Melchizedek

Abraham met the mysterious priest Melchizedek as he was returning from a victorious battle. Melchizedek, king of Salem, is described in both the Old and New Testaments as a "priest of God Most High" (Genesis 14:18, Hebrews 7:1–28). At this meeting Melchizedek offered a sacrifice (priestly act) of bread and wine as an expression of praise and gratitude to God. Melchizedek was not a Hebrew priest and not a member of a priestly family (dynastic according to the tribe of Levi and the lineage of Aaron), but he gave Abraham a priestly blessing. Melchizedek's priesthood was recognized by the Scriptures and became part of the priestly inheritance of the Old Testament, foreshadowing the eternal priesthood of Jesus Christ. Both have a priesthood which is not hereditary but unique to their person. Both offered bread and wine. Both were kings (Melchizedek, King of Salem; Jesus, King of Kings).

Book III

Catholic Mass

The memory of the Old Testament's long procession of priestly sacrifices ultimately were fulfilled and pointed to the sacrifice that would be offered by Jesus on the cross and by the long line of Christian priests who would come after him.

Passover (Seder) meal

The Passover, or Seder, meal is a symbolic ritual that pays homage to the freeing of the Hebrew people by Moses under the Lord's direction.

Joseph, one of the two youngest of Jacob's 12 sons, was sold into slavery by his older brothers and sent to Egypt. He was used by God as a trusted counselor and advisor to the pharaoh and eventually became Governor of Egypt and moved his family out of the desert.

The dynasty of the pharaohs who ruled Egypt at that time was overthrown, and a new line of kings took the throne. The new rulers enslaved the Hebrews, including the Twelve Tribes of Israel.

Hundreds of years later, Moses was appointed by God to deliver his Chosen People into freedom and deliver them to the Promised Land. Moses knew all too well that danger accompanied the pharaoh's anxiety: The pharaoh had ordered the execution of the infant Moses and all firstborn Hebrew males to slow the procreation of the Hebrew people. Moses's mother saved him by putting him in a bassinet and floating him down the Nile River, where he was found by the pharaoh's daughter and raised as her own.

He grew into adulthood in the court of the pharaoh, only to be exiled when his Hebrew roots were discovered.

The Lord came to Moses in the form of a burning bush and instructed him to return to Egypt and "let my people go" (Exodus 5:1). Ten plagues were cast upon the people in Egypt, the last of which was to be death of the firstborns in each home. The night before this final plague, however, Moses told the Hebrew people to sacrifice a lamb and sprinkle its blood on the doorpost, identifying the home as one the Angel of Death must "pass over."

Faithful Jews still celebrate the Passover with a Seder meal, in which unleavened bread (to symbolize the Hebrews' hasty departure from Egypt) and grape wine are used just as in the time of Moses. That same meal was celebrated by Jesus and his Apostles the night before his Crucifixion and Death.

Sacrifice by Levite priests in the Temple

Levi was a son of Jacob and great-grandfather to Moses, Aaron, and Miriam. His descendants became the tribe of Levi, or Levites.

The Tribe of Levi was the Priestly tribe, which meant that all Levite males were expected to learn ritual worship as prescribed by God and recorded in the *Torah* (the Hebrew word for *law* and the first five books of the Bible).

Sacrifice is an integral part of the Levite's history. In the early years, Levite priests offered up animal sacrifices in the wilderness to honor God. The deaths of these animals would be considered a symbolic act later when the Messiah offered himself as a sacrifice to atone for the sins of the world.

Centuries later, when the Israelites became a civil entity and kingdom, the son of King David built a temple to house the Ark of the Covenant (the special receptacle or tabernacle that housed the stone tablets on which God wrote the Ten Commandments). This Temple of Solomon was also the place where the high priest would celebrate the sacrifice of the lamb for Passover and where the services for Yom Kippur (Day of Atonement) took place.

The Levitical Priesthood performed ritual worship on the Sabbath and all Jewish holy days as mandated by Mosaic Law. They continued the tradition of blood sacrifice in the Temple of Jerusalem, accepting offerings of sheep, oxen, and doves as an expression of gratitude and praise to God. The priests would slaughter the sacrificial animal and allow its blood to run down the altar as a sign of atonement for sin. The smoke then rose heavenward as the animal was cooked over the fire, and then the people would eat the animal as a sign of their covenanted relationship with the Lord.

The physical Temple of Jerusalem would one day be destroyed by the Romans in AD 70. Jesus, however, spoke of the temple of his body: "Destroy this temple and in three days I shall raise it up" (John 2:19). Later, after his Death and Resurrection, the Christian Church sees herself as the living temple on earth. The baptized (men and women of faith) are the living stones which make up the temple of God.

> *Coming to him as to a living stone, rejected indeed by men, but chosen by God and precious, you also, as living stones, are being built up a spiritual house, a holy priesthood, to offer up spiritual sacrifices acceptable to God through Jesus Christ. (1 Peter 2:4–5)*

Biblical covenants

The Bible is filled with covenants made between God and his people. God made a covenant with Noah after the flood, promising that the waters of the sea would never again drown the whole earth. Later, God made a covenant with Abraham, promising him that his descendants would be as numerous as the stars in the heavens and the sand on the shore of the sea. After that, through Moses, God made what is called the Old Covenant, or Mosaic Covenant. This was God's definitive covenant with his chosen people, but what exactly did this mean?

The Old Covenant was a sacred promise and permanent contract that God made with the Jewish people through Moses on Mount Sinai. It was a mutual pact or treaty: I will be your God if you will be my people.

But in the Old Testament writings of the prophet Jeremiah, God promises a *New Covenant,* which would not be written on stone, but rather on the people's hearts (Jeremiah 31:31–34). Jesus offers this New Covenant to his Apostles at the Last Supper. This new covenant is discussed in the New Testament, the second part of the Bible, which teaches about the fulfillment of the Old Covenant in the person of Jesus and of a new covenant between God and all his people, Jew and Gentile alike (that is, the whole human race).

New Testament: Origin of Christianity

Long before the coming of Christ, which is told of in the New Testament, God made promises of a glorious future for the Chosen People. The Book of Jeremiah in the Old Testament offers prophetic glimpses of an eternal kingdom that God would create with the coming of the Messiah. Many examples of these hope-filled expectations can be found in the messianic prophecies scattered throughout the Old Testament, especially in the prophetic books.

By the time Jesus was born into the world, however, many of these messianic prophecies had been given false interpretations by some of the religious leaders of his day. Their country was occupied by Roman armies, and many viewed the Messiah (the Anointed One) as a political and military leader whose mission would be to save the people of Israel from foreign oppression at the hands of the Roman forces.

As is clear in the New Testament, Jesus is a very different kind of Messiah. This part of the Bible contains many of the stories and teachings that Catholicism is based on. The foundation of the relationship between God and people changes from the Old to New Testament in ways that significantly affect the Church's beliefs.

Making a new covenant at the Last Supper

The Last Supper was a significant event in Jesus' time, and its remembrance remains a sacred part of the Catholic Mass today. The events of the Last Supper explain how Jesus represents the New Covenant, the definitive relationship between God and people.

Jesus sat at the table with his Apostles and celebrated the Jewish Passover meal just before being arrested and taken away by soldiers. The words spoken by Jesus at this Last Supper are found in the Gospels of Matthew, Mark, and Luke and serve as the basic foundation for the Christian Eucharistic Liturgy. Jesus gave his Apostles bread and wine, telling them: "This is my body which is given for you. . . . This cup which is poured out for you is the new covenant in my blood."

Jesus describes the giving of his Body and Blood as the new and eternal covenant because it symbolizes the start of a new relationship between God and his people. The suffering that Christ would endure on the cross is God's way of expressing that his love for humanity has no limit; in the Passion and Death of Jesus, God has gone as far as he can go. After the Crucifixion of Christ, there is nothing else God can do to convince people that he loves them; that he longs to forgive all their sins; that he has an unconditional and infinite desire to share his divine life with them.

Jesus makes a New Covenant because he wants people to know that he is no longer bound to the Old Testament way of doing things. His New Covenant with all the people of the earth will no longer depend upon the people's faithfulness to God. God's faithfulness to his people is what will bind them to him — God will faithfully love them, whether or not they are faithful to him (Romans).

Nevertheless, in the New Covenant, an element of reciprocity remains. In fact, this aspect of reciprocity is a very important part of the messianic message and Jesus articulates it clearly and carefully in many passages of the New Testament. The parable of the Good Samaritan is a powerful expression of the reciprocity that Jesus teaches: "Go and do likewise," he says. "Love one another as I have loved you. . . . My heavenly Father will treat you in exactly the same way that you treat your neighbor. The measure you measure out to others will be measured back to you." The heart and soul of Christ's moral and ethical teaching can be summed up in his words to the disciples: "Whatsoever you do to the least person, you did to me."

Seeing how the New Covenant changes things

The New Covenant offered by Jesus differs from the Old Covenant in two specific ways.

Under the Old Covenant, to stay in God's good graces, God's people were expected to perform rituals and sacrifices and obey the Ten Commandments as given to Moses. With the New Covenant, however, God's people are no longer under penalty of law. Instead, they're given the chance to receive salvation as a free gift as part of the Lord's true sacrifice, that of his Son dying on the cross.

Another important difference between the Old and New Covenants is that the New Covenant is not offered for only one group of people, but for all humanity. God's Son, the Second Person of the Trinity, took on a human nature and was born of a woman (Virgin Mary). He died for all men and women, Jew and gentile (non-Jew) alike.

The Old Covenant between God and the Hebrews was rooted in the promise "I will be your God and you will be my people." The New Covenant did not dissolve or cancel out the first one; instead, it is considered by Christians to

Book III

Catholic Mass

be the fulfillment of the Old Covenant — "For God so loved the world that he gave his only Son" (John 3:16).

The Old Covenant was remembered and celebrated with the slaughter of an innocent lamb whose blood was poured out, which saved the Chosen People from death. Likewise, the New Covenant is sealed in the blood of the Lamb of God (the name John the Baptist calls Jesus while baptizing him in the River Jordan), which was shed on the wood of the cross on Good Friday.

Remembering the covenant and the Last Supper

In the telling of the Last Supper in the Gospel of Luke (22:19), Jesus adds the sentence that instructs his followers to: "Do this in remembrance of me." In other words, celebrate the Lord's Supper as a sacred ritual, again and again. The ancient Christians did this every Sunday, and when the state finally legalized the religion, every day (when possible, of course).

Bread and wine are used during Mass, just as they were at the Last Supper. The words of Jesus — "this is my body" and "this is my blood" — have been meticulously preserved and repeated over bread and wine all over the world for more than 2,000 years. The Mass always includes these *exact words* spoken at the Last Supper (usually translated into whatever language the Mass is spoken in). The words are included regardless of whether Mass is celebrated in a basilica, cathedral, or local parish church; or whether by a pope, bishop, or priest.

Discovering the Real Presence

The first words of John's Gospel are a conscious attempt to parallel the opening of the Book of Genesis: "In the beginning. . . ." Genesis tells the story of the physical creation of man and earth, whereas John's Gospel speaks of God's spiritual creation that occurs with the coming of Jesus the Messiah. John the Baptist (a different John) points at Jesus and tells the people, "Behold the Lamb of God who takes away the sins of the world." John (the writer of the Gospel) makes a special effort to compare Jesus to the paschal lamb by making it clear that not a bone of his was broken: the same requirement for the lambs offered by the Israelites in their Passover meals (John 19:36).

Although John's narration of Jesus's words to his Apostles at the Last Supper is much longer than that of any other Gospel and doesn't specifically contain the words of Consecration ("this is my body; this is my blood"), Scripture scholars tell us that the entire sixth chapter of the Gospel of John is Eucharistic in nature and intent.

The sixth chapter of John's Gospel provides the strong foundation for the Catholic belief in the *Real* Presence of Christ in the Eucharist. When Jesus tells the people that he will give them his Body and Blood as food and drink, many listeners find this hard to believe: "How can this man give us his flesh to eat?" (John 6:52). But Jesus does not back down from his words, telling them: "Truly, truly, I say to you, unless you eat the flesh of the Son of man and drink his blood, you have no life in you" (John 6:53). Catholics believe that Jesus meant exactly what he said, so when they receive Holy Communion, they have faith that they are truly receiving the Body and Blood of Jesus.

According to Scripture scholars, the sixth chapter of the Gospel of John provides even more preparation for the gift of the Eucharist that Jesus will give to his followers. After multiplying the loaves and fishes to feed the people, he assures them that he is the bread of life, sent by God the Father. "I am the living bread which came down from heaven; if anyone eats of this bread, he will live forever; and the bread that I will give for the life of the world is my flesh" (John 6:51). When his followers argue among themselves, asking how Jesus can give them his flesh to eat, he responds in a passage that beautifully describes the gift of the Eucharist: ". . . he who eats my flesh and drinks my blood has eternal life, and I will raise him up at the last day. For my flesh is food indeed and my blood is drink indeed" (John 6:53–55). He goes on to say, "This is the bread which came down from heaven, not such as the fathers who ate and died; he who eats this bread will live forever" (John 6:58).

Book III

Catholic Mass

Other New Testament foundations

The Epistle to the Hebrews compares the bloody sacrifice of Jesus on the cross to the blood sacrifices in the Temple of Jerusalem and refers very directly to the Blood of Christ cleansing and sanctifying those defiled by sin (Hebrews 9:13–14). Paul's First Letter to the Corinthians contains the words of consecration (the words Jesus spoke at the Last Supper over the bread and wine: *this is my body . . . this is my blood*) as well as many other references to the Eucharist (I Corinthians 10:16, 10:17, 11:20, 11:27, 11:28, and more).

In the Book of Revelations, the Bible's last book, the name given to Jesus by John the Baptist is brought to its fulfillment. Jesus is again referred to as *the lamb* (at Passover, a lamb had to be slain in sacrifice. Then the night before he died on the cross, Jesus became the lamb who would be sacrificed on the wood of the cross), indicating that the sacrifice of his Body and Blood on the cross becomes the fulfillment of the Old Covenant Passover meal. The marvelous description of heaven's eternal liturgy of praise and gratitude to God is referred to as *the supper of the lamb* and the *marriage supper of the lamb* (Revelations 19:7–9). The image of Jesus as the *lamb of god* not only appears in the mouth of John the Baptist.

Getting the Most Out of Mass

Catholics are obligated by church law to attend Mass each and every Sunday (or Saturday evening) and holy day of obligation. And not only are they required to be physically present, but they are also expected to participate fully, actively, and consciously. When someone says "I don't get anything out of the Mass," the priest or deacon responds that "it is not what you or I *get out of* Mass that counts, rather, it is what we ourselves *give to* the Mass." Being there in the church is one component, and the other is offering up yourself to God. Spending time each weekend in the House of God is a sign of love for God.

The job of the priest and his crew

When a priest celebrates Mass without a congregation, he is united with all the believers around the world (called the Pilgrim Church or the Church Militant) as well as with all the saints in heaven (called the Church Triumphant) and all the faithful departed, deceased souls in purgatory (called the Church Suffering). The priest-celebrant prays for and with the Universal as well as local Church.

Acolytes and/or lectors are men installed in these offices by the local bishop who are in the process of formation to later be ordained deacons or priests. The lector reads the Scripture readings of the Mass (except the Gospel), and the acolyte assists the deacon during Mass and can help distribute Holy Communion (only in the Ordinary form of the Roman Rite, however).

Laymen and laywomen — that is, the non-ordained and non-religious (meaning not monks or nuns) common folk — can also help in the Ordinary form as readers and as extraordinary ministers of Holy Communion in those dioceses where the local bishop authorizes them to do so. Most parishioners who attend Mass, however, do not have any liturgical office. Nevertheless, their participation is still real and valid.

The role of the congregation

The clergy in the sanctuary have specific things to do and say, but so does the congregation in the pews. The Ordinary form requires the whole congregation to sit, stand, and kneel at specified times. They are required to make the proper responses to the priest or deacon, sing hymns, and say aloud prayers and creeds.

Participation doesn't mean everybody does or says the same thing. In parts of the Mass, the congregation and the celebrant jointly pray together (for the Gloria, Creed, Sanctus, Our Father, and Agnus Dei), and other parts are reserved for one or the other. For example, the priest says, "the Lord be with you," and the people respond, "and with your spirit."

Body gestures and positions are the same for the entire congregation. Everyone kneels during the Consecration while the priest stands at the altar and says the Eucharistic Prayer (which is reserved for the priest alone). The harmony of combining the separate actions and words of the people and the celebrant is like the different sections of a symphony orchestra coming together to make a song.

The highest form of external participation by the faithful is the physical reception of Holy Communion at Mass. Holy Communion is available only to people in full communion (meaning that they accept all Catholic doctrine-teachings, discipline-laws and worship-sacraments and in fact are members of the Catholic Church). They must also be properly disposed, which means they are validly married or single, have fasted for one hour, and are in the state of grace (free from mortal sin).

Internally, people participate by listening and meditating on what is happening. Making a deliberate and conscious intention to give glory and praise to God is internal participation at the Sacred Liturgy. Spiritually uniting with the Sacrifice on the Altar is internal participation. Asking Jesus to come into your heart and soul, especially when you are unable to receive physical Holy Communion, is called making a Spiritual Communion.

Book III

Catholic Mass

Running Through the Roles of Liturgical Ministers

Just as the Mass can be broken down into its various elements, those ministers offering the Mass, too, play different roles within the hierarchy of the Church. Of course you have the celebrant, who presides at the Mass.

But other folks take part as well, including acolytes and non-ordained lay ministers. This chapter covers the functions of these different roles.

According to the Second Vatican Council, all the baptized faithful are required to participate in the Sacred and Divine Liturgy fully, actively, and consciously. The level and type of participation, however, is distinctly different for the ordained ministerial priesthood and for the common priesthood of the baptized. The *clergy* (ordained ministers: bishops, priests, and deacons) participate through the sacrament of Holy Orders at the altar, and the *lay faithful* (parishioners; common folk) participate through the sacrament of Baptism in the pews of the congregation. Non-ordained lay ministers also play a distinct role.

Identifying the celebrants

The ordained celebrant participates in Mass in a very public, obvious, and official capacity. The *celebrant* is the clergyman (usually a priest but could also be a bishop) who offers the Mass. He represents the institutional and hierarchical Church founded by the Savior and entrusted to St. Peter and the Apostles. The celebrant's participation in the Mass is very prescribed, and his location in the sanctuary, visible vestments, words, actions, gestures, and posture are all part of his mode of participation.

Bishop

The principal celebrant at Mass is the bishop of the diocese, who is the chief teacher of the faith, shepherd of the faithful, and dispenser of the Sacraments. The General Instruction of the Roman Missal, known as GIRM, states in paragraphs 91 and 92,

> *The celebration of the Eucharist is the action of Christ and of the Church, namely, of the holy people united and ordered under the Bishop . . . every legitimate celebration of the Eucharist is directed by the Bishop, either in person or through Priests who are his helpers.*

The episcopacy ("bishophood") contains the fullness of the priesthood — bishop, priest, and deacon. In the celebration of the Mass, the unity of the diocese is best expressed when the bishop gathers around the altar with his priests and deacon. As main celebrant, he emphasizes his role as the chief pastor of the diocese.

Priest

The General Instruction on the Roman Missal delineates the duties of the Priest. Number 93 states,

A Priest, also, who possesses within the Church the sacred power of Orders to offer sacrifice in the person of Christ, presides by this fact over the faithful people. . .presides over their prayer, proclaims to them the message of salvation, associates the people with himself in the offering of sacrifice through Christ in the Holy Spirit to God the Father.

Through his priestly ordination, the priest has the power to offer the Sacrifice of the Mass, preach, bless, baptize, and anoint the sick. Although the priest, through the Sacrament of Holy Orders, has the power to forgive sins in the Sacrament of Penance, witness marriages, and confer the Sacrament of Penance, the bishop of the diocese must delegate or give the faculties to exercise these powers to the priest.

In the absence of the bishop, the priest dispenses the Sacraments. The priest celebrates Solemn or Simple Mass; Solemn Mass often takes place on solemnities, the patronal feast of the parish, and Sundays during the liturgical year. The principal Mass on Sunday is typically a Solemn Mass. Simple Masses often occur during the week and at the nonprincipal Masses on Sundays. Simple masses may include music but often exclude incense. They also often exclude processions, though at Sunday Masses processional and recessional processions are customary. Priests may wear a black cassock but must wear an alb, cincture, stole, and chasuble for all Holy Masses.

Deacon

Deacons function as ordained ministers and typically assist the priest at Mass. The name *deacon* comes from the Greek *diakonos,* meaning *minister* or *servant.* Paragraph 94 of the General Instruction of the Roman says,

> *At Mass the Deacon has his own part in proclaiming the Gospel, from time to time in preaching God's Word, in announcing the intentions of the Universal Prayer, in ministering to the Priest, in preparing the altar and in serving the celebration of the Sacrifice, in distributing the Eucharist to the faithful, especially under the species of wine, and from time to time in giving instructions regarding the people's gestures and posture.*

During the Mass, the celebrant is flanked by the deacons; the Deacon of the Word stands and sits to the left of the celebrant and the Deacon of the Eucharist stands and sits to the right. When only one deacon is present, he stands and sits to the celebrant's right. In addition to functioning at Mass, deacons can also baptize, witness marriages, bury the dead, and celebrate Evening Prayer.

Deacons may wear a cassock but must wear an alb and cincture and then place a stole over the top. Typically on Sundays and solemn feast days, deacons also wear a dalmatic over the alb and stole just as the priest and bishop wear the chasuble over their alb and stole.

Book III

Catholic Mass

The non-ordained ministers

Clergy (ordained ministers) may be assisted in Sacred Worship by *non-ordained ministers,* certain lay parishioners and consecrated religious (monks, nuns, sisters, brothers, and so on). Some ministries, or roles, are part of the formation and process of becoming a deacon or priest. Other ministries are called *extraordinary* in that they function whenever ordinary ministers are not available to do the job. Men studying in the seminary or formation program leading toward Holy Orders (diaconate or priesthood) are admitted to ministries such as lector and acolyte (formerly known as minor orders) as part of their preliminary education.

Acolyte

The word *acolyte* comes from Greek and means *attendant* or *helper.* The acolyte's duty, as described in the General Instruction of the Roman Missal, is "to serve at the altar and assist the priest and deacon." At Mass, acolytes light altar candles, carry candles in procession, assist deacons and priests at the Mass, bring the wine and water to the altar at the offertory, ring bells during the consecration, help in distribution of Holy Communion by placing a paten under recipients' chin or hands, and wash the celebrant's fingers in purifying vessels after Holy Communion. A *formally instituted* acolyte (meaning a seminarian authorized by his bishop to help distribute Holy Communion) can also distribute Holy Communion as an extraordinary minister of Holy Communion.

Because Holy Orders (the roles of bishop, priest, and deacon) are reserved for baptized males, the *installed ministries* or *minor orders* of acolyte and lector are also only for men. In the present Code of Canon Law, the ministry of acolyte is open to all laymen (nonclergy male members of the congregation). In the reform of the liturgy after the Second Vatican Council, the pope intended to extend the role of acolyte beyond seminarians who are preparing for priesthood.

Although the office of acolyte is reserved for men, the function is not. In the Ordinary form of the Roman Rite, women with the consent of the local bishop and parish pastor may function as *readers* (similar to lectors) and as *altar servers* (similar to acolytes).

The proper vesture for an acolyte is cassock and surplice or an alb-like robe.

The Extraordinary form and the Eastern Catholic Church still retain the minor order of subdeacon, which ranks above acolyte, but in the Ordinary form of the Latin Rite, that office was taken over by the installed acolyte. Subdeacons in the Eastern Orthodox and Extraordinary form of the Latin Rite assist the deacon as the deacon in turn assists the celebrant. Subdeacons prepare by pouring the wine into the chalice, carrying the chalice with wine to the altar, and reading the Epistles before the people.

Extraordinary ministers of Holy Communion

Extraordinary ministers of Holy Communion are not instituted by the bishop; rather they have been given temporary permission from the bishop to distribute Holy Communion. At Mass they help the bishop, priest, and deacon (the ordinary ministers of Holy Communion) to distribute the Blessed Sacrament. The extraordinary ministers of Holy Communion also customarily transport the Eucharist to sick and shut-in members of the congregation, especially on Sundays.

The term *extraordinary* has a literal definition here; it refers to exceptional occasions when an ordinary minister of Holy Communion is unavailable. All members of the ordained clergy — bishops, priests and deacons — are considered ordinary ministers of Holy Communion and normally perform all the tasks of the extraordinary ministers. Religious men and women and laity can be authorized by the local bishop to be extraordinary ministers of Holy Communion.

To be eligible to become an extraordinary minister of Holy Communion, a layperson must have received all the Sacraments of Initiation (Baptism, Confirmation, and Holy Eucharist). Extraordinary ministers are trained and authorized by the bishop.

Vesting for an extraordinary Eucharistic minister is Sunday dress clothes. Some dioceses permit extraordinary Eucharistic ministers to wear albs. However, normally albs are reserved for the ordinary ministers.

Lector

The General Instruction of Roman Missal defines the lector as a congregant who is instituted to proclaim the readings from Sacred Scripture, with the exception of the Gospel. The lector may also announce the intentions for the Prayer of the Faithful and, in the absence of a psalmist, proclaim the psalm between the readings. The proper place for a lector to do Scripture readings at Mass is the ambo or pulpit, and he normally reads the General Intercessions at the lectern. When a deacon isn't present, the lector may carry the Book of the Gospels in procession.

Like acolytes, lectors are also formally installed ministers, and therefore the positions can be filled only by men from the lay congregation. Being a lector is also one of the steps toward entering the Holy Orders.

Reader

Laymen and laywomen may function as *readers* if an instituted lector is not present. Their duties are the same as lectors', and they are trained to read Scripture clearly and audibly. Like extraordinary Eucharistic ministers, commissioned readers must have received all the Sacraments of Initiation and, if married, have a valid marriage. Bishops authorize lay readers to function in the diocese for a period of one to three years. From time to time, priests may appoint a reader to read at a certain Mass without a formal commissioning.

Psalmist/cantor

The General Instruction for Roman Missal outlines the position of *psalmist,* or *cantor,* a layperson who sings the psalm in between the Old and New Testament readings. The cantor aids the congregation in singing. The cantor often works in conjunction with the choir. Psalmists can wear choir robes or Sunday dress.

Organist/music director

The *organist* can be the parish music director or someone else. The organist and/or music director must not only be well versed in music, but also have a working knowledge of Catholic liturgy and the liturgical calendar. In addition, the organist/music director is integral with the choir and works very closely with the clergy to plan the music to be sung at the liturgy. The organist can wear a cassock and a special sleeveless surplice to play the organ and conduct the choir, or may wear Sunday dress clothes.

Choir

The *choir* augments the singing of the congregation during Mass. The choir should never serve as a substitute for the congregation's singing, although at times the choir may sing pieces separate from the congregation. Members of the choir often wear choir robes or Sunday dress clothes.

Commentator

Not to be confused with the cantor, psalmist, or lector, the *commentator* provides the congregation with brief explanations and commentaries. Normally, the commentator speaks from the lectern where the cantor leads music. Commentators are not mandatory but are used at important celebrations for the sole purpose of introducing the particular celebration. They are appropriately employed at Solemn Pontifical Masses, dedications of churches, anniversaries of parishes, celebrations of priestly or religious vocations, and state functions in which Mass is being celebrated, as in the case in papal visits.

Altar servers

Most Catholics are generally familiar with the people who serve at Mass, the *altar servers.* They assist the celebrant at Mass and serve in place of instituted acolytes. They can have the following roles:

✔ **Thurifer:** A thurifer carries the censer to be used at Mass and also leads processions while gently swinging it so that billows of incense ascend to God. In addition, the thurifer can incense at the consecration of the Mass.

✔ **Crucifer:** The crucifer, the cross-bearer, carries the processional cross situated atop a long staff. He is employed anytime a procession takes place. When a thurifer is not present, he leads the procession.

✔ **Book bearer:** The book bearer holds the missal at Mass for the celebrant.

✔ **Episcopal attendants:** At celebrations when the bishop is present, two altar servers are employed to hold the miter and crosier during the ceremony. The server wears a special garment, the vimp, over his cassock and surplice in order not to soil the sacred vestures.

✔ **Servers:** Servers aid the celebrant at the altar.

None of these types of server is an instituted ministry, and as with extraordinary Eucharistic ministers and readers, laymen and laywomen can function as altar servers. Normally, altar servers wear a cassock and surplice. However, in some parishes, white albs are used.

Ushers

The General Instruction for the Roman Missal mentions ushers' role of preserving orderliness at Holy Mass:

> Ushers take up the collections in the church. Those who, in some regions, welcome the faithful at the church doors, seat them appropriately, and marshal them in processions.

In addition to collecting the offertory giving of the faithful, ushers can distribute the bulletins after Mass, aid congregants who have physical disabilities, help direct the ordinary or extraordinary minister of the Eucharist to distribute Holy Communion, especially to disabled people, and serve as a reference for people attending the Mass.

Ushers often are the first people you meet when arriving at Mass. They can be very useful in disseminating valuable information. In special processions, ushers control the crowd and promote orderliness in the sacred march. In many parishes, ushers wear a uniform jacket with the parish coat-of-arms on the breast pocket so that the congregants can easily identify them.

Master of ceremonies

At Solemn Masses, a *master of ceremonies* is often used. He acts as a director of the flow of the liturgy.

Book III

Catholic Mass

Ordinary Catholics often come into contact with a master of ceremonies when the bishop comes to their parish for a specific celebration, such as conferring the Sacrament of Confirmation. The master of ceremonies can also be employed for solemn celebrations in which the bishop isn't present, such as the Easter Triduum.

Whether a priest, deacon, or layman, the master of ceremonies is well versed in the norms of the liturgy. He works closely with all the key players of the liturgy — the main celebrant, the musicians, and the servers. In complicated ceremonies in which many variables arise, especially when a bishop is the main celebrant, the master of ceremonies has to have a fine sense of judgment, well-organized thoughts, and, most of all, good coordination in order for the liturgy to proceed smoothly.

The master of ceremonies typically leads the rehearsals of servers and musicians. During the liturgy, he must be able to look ahead at the pending action in order to be prepared and on time with the elements and servers. The proper dress for master of ceremonies is usually a cassock and surplice. If the master of ceremonies is a priest or deacon, he wears a stole during Holy Communion.

Sacristan

The *sacristan* is very important to the liturgy. The General Instruction for the Roman Missal describes the sacristan as one "who carefully arranges the liturgical books, the vestments, and other things necessary in the celebration of Mass." He provides an invaluable service to the priest by setting up the Missal, placing on the credence table the chalice, ciboria, and cruets, making sure the church is opened and either the heat or air conditioning is turned on, and handling anything else that must be taken care of prior to the start of Mass.

A sacristan also takes charge of the care of the vestments and vessels of the church. This person makes sure the sacred linens, altar cloths, albs, and vestments are cleaned and plentiful; he makes sure that chalices, ciboria, and candlesticks are polished; and that flowers and other devotional items are in good condition and in their correct places.

Ministers in the extraordinary form of the Roman mass

As you may expect, the functions of some of the ministers in the Extraordinary form of the Roman Mass are slightly different from those in the Ordinary form of the Mass. In addition, another type of minister, called a subdeacon, plays a role in the Mass.

Acolytes

In the Extraordinary form of the Roman Mass, acolytes function as they do in the Roman Rite. They are exclusively male and wear a cassock and surplice.

In the Eastern Catholic Church, acolytes serve in a similar fashion with some differences. They can carry liturgical fans, which are decorated with icons, prepare the hot water to be added to the chalice, and arrange the *antidoron* — unconsecrated bread that is distributed to the faithful after the Divine Liturgies and feast days.

Lectors

In the Extraordinary form of the Roman Rite and Eastern Churches, lectors are among the four minor orders in which a cleric is ordained. The lectors in these cases function like lectors of the Ordinary Rite. Because they belong to the minor orders, only males are to be admitted to this step. As in the case of the Ordinary Rite, lectors read the liturgical passages of Sacred Scripture.

Subdeacon

The role of *subdeacon* is one that has been omitted from the Ordinary Latin form (and the duties have been taken over by the acolyte), but it remains in use in the Extraordinary form of the Roman Rite and Byzantine Rite.

In Solemn High Masses, subdeacons sing the Epistle, hold the Book of the Gospels while the deacon proclaims it, and then carry the Book back when the deacon is finished. The subdeacon assists the priest and deacon in setting the altar. A subdeacon wears a cassock, amice, cincture, maniple, alb, and tunic, but no stole. He also wears a humeral veil while holding the paten from the Offertory to the recitation of the Our Father.

In the Byzantine Rite, the subdeacon's role is primarily that of servant to the bishop. During liturgies without the bishop present, he serves as the highest ranking minor clergy serving the liturgy. Normally he coordinates and leads the serving team. Subdeacons wear a sticharion, which functions like an alb in the Roman Rite, and the color corresponds to the liturgical season. In addition, the orarion is tied around his waist. This vestment distinguishes the priest, deacon, and subdeacon.

Deacon

In the Extraordinary form of the Roman Rite, deacons wear a cassock, amice, alb, cincture, maniple, stole, and dalmatic. The function of the deacon is

Book III

Catholic Mass

similar to that in the Ordinary form of the Roman Rite, but it has some minor additions. In the Eastern Church, the deacon reads the Gospel, assists in distributing Holy Communion, incenses the icons and people, leads the litanies, calls people to prayer, and has a role in the dialogue of the Eucharistic Prayer. Like the subdeacon, he wears a sticharion and orarion. However, he also wears epimanikia, or cuffs.

Chapter 2

Ordinary Form of the Mass

*T*he Ordinary form of the Mass is just as its name implies — it's the normal or standard form of Mass with which most Catholics are generally familiar. It differs from the Extraordinary form and Tridentine Mass (sometimes called the Traditional Latin Mass), which developed during the time of Charlemagne in the 9th century and was made normative in the 16th century by the Council of Trent.

This chapter walks you through the Ordinary form of the Mass from the opening procession to the closing hymn.

The most recent changes to the English translation of the Mass appear in **boldface** type.

Introductory Rites

The first part of the Ordinary Mass is the introductory rites. Mass typically starts with a procession from the back of the church, near the front door, down the middle aisle and into the sanctuary. During weekday Masses, particularly those with just a few congregants in attendance, the priest, deacon, and any servers may just enter the sanctuary from the sacristy.

An entrance hymn is sung during Sunday and Saturday evening Mass. When the procession and hymn are omitted, the Introit or Entrance Antiphon may be recited.

The Extraordinary form of the Roman Rite has the celebrant begin Mass by praying at the foot of the altar. The *Novus Ordo* Mass of Paul VI, now called the Ordinary form, eliminated those prayers and starts Mass with the priest making the sign of the cross and introducing the Mass from the altar or chair.

Greeting

The Mass formally begins when the priest blesses himself. He says, "In the name of the Father, and of the Son, and of the Holy Spirit" while tracing a cross over his torso: He places his right hand first on his forehead and then moves it down to his breast; then he moves his hand across to his far left and then to his far right. The people make the same gesture and respond, "Amen."

Next, the celebrant can say simply "the Lord be with you" (taken from Ruth 2:4) or he may use a more elaborate address taken from St. Paul: "the grace of our Lord Jesus Christ, and the love of God, and the **communion** of the Holy Spirit be with you all." The one change here in the new version of the Mass is the replacement of the word *fellowship* with the more accurate word, *communion* (*communicatio* in Latin). Although similar in meaning, the word *communion* has much more theological impact. *Fellowship* expresses a fraternal relationship, whereas *communion* goes further to express an organic and necessary connection that transcends body and soul.

The big change to this greeting occurs in the people's response to the priest's invitation, "**the Lord be** with you." Previously, the congregation said "and also with you." Now the people give the literal translation of the Latin text *et cum spiritu tuo*, **"and with your spirit."** This phrase is biblical; we see it in Galatians 6:18 and 2 Timothy 4:22 when St. Paul addresses a community of believers.

"And also with you" became too colloquial and pedestrian. It was like someone saying "yeah, you, too," which isn't appropriate, because the spirit of the priest or bishop who celebrates the Holy Mass is changed when he is ordained. He is made an *alter Christus* (another Christ) so he can celebrate the sacraments *in persona Christi* (in the person of Christ). (That is why the first-person singular pronoun is used at the consecration of the bread and wine: "this is *my* body . . . this is *my* blood" as the ordained minister speaks in the name and in the person of Christ himself by virtue of Holy Orders.) Now, by saying "and with your spirit," the congregation affirms the doctrine that the priest and bishop are ordained to represent Christ whenever the Sacred Worship is given to God.

When the bishop is the main celebrant at Mass, he begins with "Peace be with you," as found in John 20:26. However, a priest is only allowed to say "the Lord be with you." This is a subtle way the Sacred Liturgy identifies the distinction between the bishop and the priest (who represents the local bishop at every parish celebration of the Holy Mass).

Rite of Sprinkling or Penitential Rite

Either the Rite of Sprinkling or the Penitential Rite takes place after the greeting. During Easter time and particularly at Pentecost, the Rite of Blessing and Sprinkling holy water is an appropriate part of the Mass. The holy water reminds the congregation of the waters of Baptism and the invocation of the Holy Spirit.

Water is blessed by the priest, and he may add exorcised salt, because holy water is believed to be a potent weapon against the Devil. The priest then takes a bucket of holy water and sprinkles with a reed of hyssop or a metal aspergillum (special device to hold a few ounces of holy water with holes at the end to allow drops to flow out into congregation).

The Penitential Rite is used on most Sundays and weekdays. If a deacon is present, he may introduce three petitions to which the congregation responds: "Lord, have mercy; Christ, have mercy; Lord, have mercy."

Although in no way a replacement or substitute for individual celebration of the sacrament of Penance and Reconciliation (confession), the Penitential Rite still allows a communal admission of personal sin and the need for divine mercy and forgiveness.

Book III

Catholic Mass

Confiteor

The priest may choose to invoke the *Confiteor* (Latin for "I confess"). This ancient prayer for forgiveness may be used in the confessional during the sacrament of Penance and Reconciliation, but when said at Mass, it does not mean that the sins of the congregants have been absolved. It is not a private or individual confession; rather, it is a communal admission that as human beings, we are all sinners, we all make mistakes, and we all can and ought to do and be better.

> I confess to Almighty Godand to you, my brothers and sisters, that I have greatly sinned, in my thoughts and in my words, in what I have done and in what I have failed to do, **through my fault, through my fault, through my most grievous fault;** therefore I ask blessed Mary ever-virgin, all the angels and saints, and you, my brothers and sisters, to pray for me to the Lord our God.

The big change here is the inclusion of the triple *mea culpa* (Latin for "my fault"), whereas in the former English translation it was only said once.

Kyrie

The Church has used for millennia the ancient petition: "Lord, have mercy; Christ, have mercy; Lord, have mercy." It's called the *Kyrie*.

Kyrios is Greek for *Lord*. *Christos* is Greek for *Anointed One* (*Messiah* in Hebrew). The original Greek text retained in the Latin Mass is *Kyrie, eleison; Christe, eleison; Kyrie, eleison.*

Gloria

On Sundays (except during Advent and Lent) and holy days, the Gloria is said, chanted, or sung by the celebrant and congregation. It begins with the angelic salutation given to the shepherds at the first Christmas when Jesus was born in Bethlehem, "Glory to God in the highest" (*Gloria in excelsis Deo* in Latin), as found in Luke 2:14.

Just as the Penitential Rite is intended to make congregants contrite and soberly repentant, the Gloria is used to uplift the congregation as a reminder of the hope, salvation, and redemption brought by God's grace. The Gloria is suspended during the penitential seasons of Advent and Lent because these seasons are meant to accentuate sadness for sin and the desire for true repentence, but it returns with Christmas and Easter.

"Peace to his people on earth" has been changed to **"on earth peace to people of good will."** This phrase conforms more accurately to the Latin text (*in terra pax hominibus bonae voluntatis*). The phrase "Lord God, Heavenly King, Almighty God and Father, we worship you, we give you thanks, we praise you for your glory" now reads **"We praise you, we bless you, we adore you, we glorify you, we give you thanks for your great glory, Lord God, heavenly King, O God, Almighty Father."** The meaning is the same, it just has a more accurate sentence structure.

Opening Prayer (Collect)

The Opening Prayer (also called the *Collect*) sets the tone for the liturgical act of divine worship. It reminds the assembly that adoration of God is directed to the Father through the Son and in the Holy Spirit. In other words, it is always Trinitarian because the one God is in Three Persons.

Liturgy of the Word

The next section of the Mass is called the Liturgy of the Word because the emphasis is on the written and spoken Word of God. It includes multiple readings, a sermon, the Creed, and a prayer.

Rather than having Bibles in the pews for the people to follow along, many Catholic parishes have what is known as a *missalette,* an abbreviated form of the lectionary. The lectionary, a liturgical book, is the official ceremonial book containing Sacred Scripture. It is the same as the Bible in that it contains only biblical passages; the only difference is the order in which the passages are listed. Instead of being arranged somewhat chronologically, the lectionary's passages are arranged by their assignment in the liturgical year. The Church assigns specific passages from the Old and New Testaments for every weekday, Sunday, and holy day, and the weekly missalette includes the relevant passages from the lectionary for each Mass.

First reading

While everyone is seated, a reader or lector walks up to the ambo or pulpit and reads aloud the assigned passage from Sacred Scripture. Normally, the first reading comes from one of the 46 books of the Old Testament in the Catholic Bible. The passage is prefaced by the phrase "a reading from . . ." and then the name of the book of the Bible is mentioned.

The precise chapter and verse of the reading are not mentioned. The Bible itself was originally written without any chapter or verse identification. In fact, the Bible had no chapters until 1248 when Archbishop Stephen Langton assigned divisions, and no verse numbers until Robert Stephanus worked out versification in 1555.

When the reader or lector comes to the end of the passage, he or she says "The word of the Lord" and the people respond "Thanks be to God." The book (lectionary) is not to be lifted up as the person says "the word of the Lord," because the spoken and proclaimed word is being affirmed more than the written text.

Protestant Bibles have the same 39 canonical books as Catholic Bibles but do not have the other seven deuterocanonical books (Baruch, Maccabees 1 and 2, Tobit, Judith, Ecclesiasticus, and Wisdom). These books originated in the Greek version of the Hebrew Bible (called the Septuagint), which goes back to between 250 and 150 BC. Christian Bibles had all 46 books until Martin Luther and the other reformers removed the deuterocanonical books (called *Apocrypha* by Protestants) in the 16th century.

Psalm

The Bible includes 150 psalms, and many of them are incorporated into the Sacred Liturgy of the Ordinary form. A psalm is always included in weekday and Sunday Masses.

The only psalms not used in divine worship are the curse or deprecatory psalms, which are requests for harsh retribution against one's enemies. Although they're considered equally inspired revealed Scripture, they don't make for elegant worship of the Almighty.

Either a cantor sings or chants the psalm or a lay reader or lector reads (recites) the verses of the psalm. The congregation repeats the response.

Second reading

The second Scripture reading from the Bible comes from the New Testament. Usually it's an Epistle, or sometimes a passage from the Acts of the Apostles or from the Book of Revelation (Apocalypse). Weekday Masses don't include this second reading, but Sundays and holy days always do.

Like the first reading, the second is introduced merely by the name of the Book and not by chapter and verse. At the end of the passage, the reader says "The word of the Lord" and the people respond "Thanks be to God."

Gospel

Before the Gospel is proclaimed, the Alleluia is sung or chanted. (It may be omitted during weekday Masses.) The entire congregation stands and stays standing during the proclamation of the Gospel.

If a deacon is present, he takes the Book of Gospels to the ambo, or pulpit. When no deacon is present, the priest proclaims the sacred text. Although both male and female laity and religious can do the first and second readings, only an ordained minister (deacon, priest, or bishop) can read the Gospel at Mass.

If a deacon reads the Gospel, he first goes to the bishop or priest and receives the following blessing:

> May the Lord be in your heart and on your lips that you may proclaim his Gospel worthily and well, in the name of the Father and of the Son and of the Holy Spirit, amen.

The Gospel is introduced:

> *Deacon/Priest:* The Lord be with you.
>
> *People:* **And with your spirit.**
>
> *Deacon/Priest:* A reading from the holy Gospel according to [Name of the book of the Bible].
>
> *People:* Glory to you, O Lord.

Then after the Gospel is proclaimed:

> *Deacon/Priest:* The Gospel of the Lord.
>
> *People:* Praise to you, Lord Jesus Christ.
>
> *Deacon/Priest:* Through the words of the Gospel may our sins be wiped away.

The deacon (or priest) reverences the book with a kiss before the last line is said quietly. Like the lectionary, the Book of Gospels is not lifted up, because the proclaimed spoken word is what's being affirmed at this moment, not the written text.

On Sundays and solemn feasts, the Book of Gospels can be incensed prior to reading it aloud.

Book III

Catholic Mass

Homily

A *homily* is a sermon preached by an ordained cleric at Mass or any Sacred Liturgy. While canon law allows laity and religious to preach (outside of Mass) in some very rare occasions, only a deacon, priest, or bishop can preach the homily during Mass. Mass includes a homily on all Sundays and holy days of obligation. Parishes are encouraged to include a homily in weekday Masses during Advent, Lent, Easter Season, and on feast days and festive occasions when more people than usual come to Mass.

Usually the celebrant preaches the homily, but he can entrust it to a concelebrant or to the deacon. Special circumstances may also allow a priest or bishop who is present but who is not concelebrating to preach the homily.

The homily may explain the Scripture passages just read or give moral or doctrinal instruction, especially on particular feasts. It also may bring to light certain spiritual aspects for later meditation and consideration.

Profession of Faith (Creed)

On all Sundays and holy days, the Creed must be recited or sung by the celebrant and congregation. A *creed* is a summary of doctrines written in a format meant to be easy to memorize. Long ago when many people were unable to read and write, most learning was done by sheer memory. People memorized passages, chapters, and even whole books of the Bible centuries before they were written down.

Think of the Creed like a blueprint, recipe, or formula for the beliefs of the Catholic Church. The Creed says what is important to Catholic Christianity in terms of basic tenets, which is why it's so important for believers to know and understand the Creed. Every official doctrine of Catholicism is somehow connected to or derived from it.

Some background on the Creed

The current Creed (also called the Profession of Faith) goes back to the year AD 325. At that time, the heresy of Arianism was rampaging Christendom. Arius was a cleric who maintained that Jesus was indeed human but not quite divine. He insisted that Christ had a similar but not the same divine substance as God the Father. In other words, he portrayed God the Son as a hybrid of divinity and humanity. Arianism is the false doctrine that Jesus Christ is not equal to God. He is the highest creature God made, higher than angels or men, but not equal to the Lord God.

Christianity, however, tenaciously clings to the belief that Jesus is not like Mr. Spock, who is half human and half alien. Christians believe that Jesus is true God and true man. Rather than being 50/50, he is 100 percent human and 100 percent divine. That is the mystery of the Incarnation.

The Creed, developed at the Council of Nicea by the bishops of the world in union with the pope in Rome, clearly defined that Christ is God the Son and has the same substance (*homoousios* in Greek, or *consubstantialem* in Latin) as the God the Father. Arius's notion that Christ only had a *similar* substance (*homoiousios* in Greek) was condemned as heresy.

Recent updates to the English translation

When the Mass was translated into English in 1970, the word *consubstantialem* in Latin was rendered as "one in being." The revised translation now retains the more accurate word **consubstantial,** meaning "of the same substance," to convey that God the Son is equal to God the Father (and God the Holy Spirit) because a single divine nature is shared by all three divine Persons of the Trinity.

Another tweak in the text is the phrase **"I believe"** to replace "We believe." The official Latin uses the word *credo,* which is first person singular (I). Were it first person plural (we), it would use the word *credimus.* The emphasis is merely that each believer must affirm for himself that he personally accepts and embraces the faith. While the Church is always a community of believers, each member retains his identity as an individual. Catholic Christians are taught to cultivate personal relationships with God as well as communal relationships with their neighbors.

"Born of the Virgin Mary" has been changed to **"was incarnate of the Virgin Mary."** This new phrase is a more accurate translation of the Latin text *incarnatus est,* and it conveys the doctrine that Jesus's human nature began not at his birth but from the very first moment of his conception within the womb of his mother, Mary.

Catholics show reverence for the Incarnation by bowing at the phrase "and became man." On Christmas (December 25) and the Feast of the Annunciation (March 25) the custom is to genuflect rather than bow.

Two other translations have been altered in the Creed for greater accuracy. "He suffered, died and was buried" now reads **"he suffered death and was buried."** The phrase "on the third day he rose again in fulfillment of the Scriptures" has been changed to **"and rose again on the third day in accordance** (*secundum* in Latin) **with the Scriptures."**

Prayer of the Faithful (General Intercessions)

After the Creed on Sundays or after the homily on weekdays, the Prayer of the Faithful follows. The General Instruction on the Roman Missal (#69) says,

> *In the Universal Prayer or Prayer of the Faithful, the people respond in some sense to the Word of God which they have received in faith and, exercising the office of their baptismal Priesthood, offer prayers to God for the salvation of all.*

If a deacon is present, he prays aloud the intercessions; otherwise, in his absence, it is done by a lay reader or the priest celebrant. The petitions presented for prayer should always try to incorporate these concepts:

- ✔ The needs of the Church, especially the pope and local bishop
- ✔ Public authorities and the salvation of the whole world
- ✔ Those burdened by any kind of difficulty, especially the poor and the sick

✔ The local community, especially the members of the parish and those preparing for sacraments

✔ The faithful departed and the souls in Purgatory

Liturgy of the Eucharist

After the Liturgy of the Word is the part of Mass called the Liturgy of the Eucharist. It is the heart and soul of the Mass, with the zenith being the consecration of the bread and wine into the Precious Body and Blood of Christ.

Preparation of Gifts (Offertory)

On Sundays and holy days, someone from the congregation usually brings the gifts (bread and wine that will become the Holy Eucharist) down the main aisle to the deacon or priest at the altar. On weekdays when the number of people attending is very small, the priest may just leave them on a side table before Mass. The Latin (Roman) tradition is to use only unleavened bread, whereas the Byzantine and other Eastern Catholic Churches use bread cooked with yeast.

The deacon prepares the altar; if he's not present, it's done by the priest. Taking bread and holding it over the altar, the priest celebrant says:

> Blessed are you, Lord God of all creation, for through your goodness we have received the bread we offer you: fruit of the earth and work of human hands; it will become for us the bread of life.

The people respond:

> Blessed be God forever.

Then the deacon or priest pours wine into the chalice(s), saying:

> By the mystery of this water and wine may we come to share in the divinity of Christ who humbled himself to share in our humanity.

Then taking the chalice and holding it over the altar, the priest says:

> Blessed are you, Lord God of all creation, for through your goodness we have received the wine we offer you: fruit of the vine and work of human hands; it will become our spiritual drink.

The people respond:

> Blessed be God forever.

The priest bows and quietly prays:

> With humble spirit and contrite heart may we be accepted by you,
> O Lord, and may our sacrifice in your sight this day be pleasing to you,
> Lord God.

Then he washes his fingers, saying:

> Wash me, O Lord, from my iniquity and cleanse me from my sin.

Lastly, the priest says:

> Pray, brethren (brothers and sisters), that **my sacrifice and yours** may
> be acceptable to God, the Almighty Father.

The change here is the distinction between the sacrifice of the priest (my) and that of the people (yours), whereas in the older translation it merely said *our sacrifice.*

Then the people respond:

> May the Lord accept the sacrifice at your hands for the praise and glory
> of his name, for our good and the good of all his **holy** Church.

The only change here is the addition of the adjective *holy* (*sanctae* in Latin).

Book III

Catholic Mass

Offertory Prayer

Each Sunday and holy day is assigned a specific prayer to be said over the gifts. On weekdays the celebrant may choose from options. The priest says this prayer, and the people respond with the usual "amen."

Preface and Sanctus

This part of the Mass precedes the Eucharistic prayer and begins as follows:

> *Priest:* The Lord be with you.
>
> *People:* **And with your spirit.**

Priest: Lift up your hearts.

People: We lift them up to the Lord.

Priest: Let us give thanks to the Lord our God.

People: **It is right and just.**

The phrase "the Lord be with you" previously had the response "and also with you," but now the response is **"and with your spirit."** The other change is the last response. Previously, it had been "It is right to give him thanks and praise." Now it reads **"It is right and just"** to conform to the official Latin text.

Next, the following lines are either sung or spoken:

Holy, Holy, Holy Lord God of **hosts.** Heaven and earth are full of your glory. Hosanna in the highest. Blessed is he who comes in the name of the Lord. Hosanna in the highest.

The only change here is the replacement of **hosts** for the previous phrase "power and might." Again, this simply conforms the text to the official Latin.

Eucharistic Prayer

At this point, the most important part of the Mass begins: the Eucharistic Prayer. The Eucharistic Prayer has several components to it.

- **Thanksgiving:** The word *Eucharist* comes from the Greek word for thanksgiving. The priest first gives thanks to God on behalf of the people for all the blessings and gifts the Lord has given. This gratitude is expressed primarily in the Preface prayer of the Mass (the introduction to the Eucharistic Prayer in which the priest begins with "the Lord be with you" and also says "let us give thanks to the Lord our God").

- **Acclamation:** The congregation affirms their gratitude by singing the thrice-holy angelic hymn, the *Sanctus* (Holy).

- **Epiclesis:** The priest acting in *Persona Christi* invokes the Holy Spirit to come down from heaven and bless the gifts of bread and wine. This invocation is expressed physically by the stretching out of the celebrant's arms and hands over the gifts.

- **Institution narrative and Consecration:** The holiest part of the Mass is when the priest acting in *Persona Christi* uses the exact same words used by Jesus at the Last Supper and speaks them over the bread and wine, thereby consecrating them. The prayer includes the narrative of the Last Supper where Jesus took bread and wine and said "This is my body . . . this is my blood."

- ✔ **Anamnesis:** The anamnesis recalls and reaffirms Christ's command to "do this in memory of me" and the recollection of the mystery of Jesus's Passion, Death, and Resurrection.

- ✔ **Offering:** The priest offers the Son *to* the Father *with* the Holy Spirit on behalf of the entire human race and the whole world. Jesus offers himself to God the Father on behalf of the human race. The priest represents both mankind and Christ, so he is able to mystically offer the Son to the Father for us.

- ✔ **Intercessions:** The priest requests that the fruits of the sacrifice be applied to both the living and the dead.

- ✔ **Final doxology:** The glory of God, Father, Son, and Holy Spirit is manifested in this solemn prayer, which is affirmed by the people in their response of "amen."

The Eucharistic Prayer is the chief of the priestly prayers of the Mass. Only the ordained priest or bishop can say them, because only he has the ordained power and authority to consecrate bread and wine into the Body and Blood of Christ.

The previous prayer was missing some of the elegant and beautiful vocabulary the Church used to describe holy and sacred things and persons, like Jesus himself. Hence the revised translation inserts words like *holy, venerable,* and *sacred* where the previous version omitted them.

One significant change among several incidental ones in the Eucharistic Prayer occurs at the Consecration itself.

Over the bread the priest says the first half of *the most important words of the entire missal:*

Take this, all of you, and eat of it, for this is my body, which will be given up for you.

Over the wine the priest completes the most important part of the Missal:

> Take this, all of you, and drink from it, for this is the chalice of my blood, the blood of the new and eternal covenant, which will be poured out for you and for many for the forgiveness of sins. Do this in memory of me.

Previously, the phrase had been "for you and for *all,*" but now it's more conforming to the Latin, which says "for you and for **many**" *(pro vobis et pro **multis**).*

Book III

Catholic Mass

Memorial Acclamation

After the consecration of the bread and wine into the Body and Blood of Christ, the priest continues the Eucharistic Prayer, saying:

> The Mystery of Faith.

The people respond based on which option the choir or celebrant chooses:

> We proclaim your Death, O Lord, and profess your Resurrection until you come again.

Or

> When we eat this bread and drink this cup, we proclaim your Death, O Lord, until you come again.

Or

> Save us, Savior of the world, for by your cross and Resurrection, you have set us free.

After the acclamation, the priest continues the Eucharistic Prayer with intercessions to the Virgin Mary and the saints on behalf of the Church and all her members. Particular mention can be made for the deceased person for whom the Mass is being offered.

Doxology and Great Amen

A doxology is a short hymn of praise to God. Following the Eucharistic Prayer is a doxology to the Triune God (Father, Son, and Holy Spirit) as a sign of public thanks for the consecration of the bread and wine into the Body and Blood of Christ. It is also appreciation for the Holy Sacrifice of the Mass where the Son was offered to Father with the Holy Spirit for the salvation of souls.

The priests concludes the Eucharistic Prayer:

> Through him, and with him, and in him, O God, Almighty Father, in the unity of the Holy Spirit, all glory and honor is yours, forever and ever.

The people respond, "Amen."

Pater Noster (Our Father or Lord's Prayer)

When asked by his disciples how to pray, Jesus gave them the Lord's Prayer (also called the *Our Father*). This prayer is said before the reception of Holy Communion, which is truly our daily bread:

> Our Father, who art in heaven, hallowed be thy name; thy kingdom come, thy will be done on earth as it is in heaven. Give us this day our daily bread, and forgive us our trespasses, as we forgive those who trespass against us; and lead us not into temptation, but deliver us from evil.

"For thine is the kingdom, the power, and the glory, forever and ever" is not said at the end of the prayer, because it was never part of the original passage in Matthew 6:13. It is not in the original Greek or in the Latin of St. Jerome (who in AD 400 translated and edited the first one-volume Christian Bible from Hebrew and Greek into Latin). This closing phrase is found in the King James Version of the Bible, however, and is common to Protestant Christians around the world.

However, Catholic Christians are used to saying it at Mass after the priest says (after the Lord's Prayer):

> Deliver us, Lord, we pray, from every evil, graciously grant peace in our days, that, by the help of your mercy, we may be always free from sin and safe from all distress, as we await the blessed hope and the coming of our Savior, Jesus Christ.

Then the people respond:

> For the kingdom, the power, and the glory are yours now and forever.

Book III

Catholic Mass

Sign of Peace

After the *Pater Noster* the priest says, "The peace of the Lord be with you always" and the congregation replies, "And with your spirit." The priest or deacon may then invite everyone to share a sign of peace.

Originally called the Kiss of Peace, this gesture of fraternity or brotherly love flows from the truth that all men and women are made in the image and likeness of God and by Baptism we become brothers and sisters in Christ. It can be done as a solemn and reverent gesture as done in the Extraordinary form or as a simple hand-shake or small bow while placing both hands on shoulder of the other person. Waving and bear-hugs are not appropriate forms.

Fraction Rite — Agnus Dei (Lamb of God)

Agnus Dei is Latin for *Lamb of God,* and while this prayer is said or sung aloud by the congregation, the priest breaks (fractions) the host he just consecrated into two equal parts. Then he places a small fragment into the chalice containing the consecrated wine (Precious Blood). This mingling of the two symbolizes the unity of the Body and Blood of Christ in every drop and every fragment.

The priest holds the consecrated host over the chalice of consecrated wine and says:

> Behold the Lamb of God; behold him who takes away the sins of the world. **Blessed** are those called to the supper **of the Lamb.**

"Of the Lamb" is newly included, but **blessed** is a replacement for *happy.*

The people respond:

> Lord, I am not worthy **that you should enter under my roof,** but only say the word and **my soul** shall be healed.

Here, the change is the addition of words. Previously, the response was "I am not worthy to receive you, but only say the word and I shall be healed." Now it references Matthew 8:8 where a Roman centurion tells Jesus, "I am not worthy to have you enter under my roof."

The other new element is the addition of the word **soul** instead of just saying *I.* Spiritual healing of the soul is the preeminent objective here.

Communion Rite

The priest consumes the host first and then drinks some of the Precious Blood from the chalice. He then gives a host to the deacon, and after he eats it, the priest gives him the chalice to drink. Then the two of them begin to administer Holy Communion to the altar servers and, if needed, to the extraordinary ministers of Holy Communion. Finally, the congregation comes forward and, either standing in a line or kneeling at the altar rail or *prie dieux* (kneeler for one person), receives first the consecrated host and may also be offered the chalice of Precious Blood (consecrated wine).

The minister says, "The Body [or the Blood] of Christ" and the communicant responds, "Amen."

Prayer after Communion

Just as the Opening Prayer begins Mass and the Prayer over the Gifts is in the middle, a Prayer after Communion completes the rite. Each Sunday and holy day has an assigned prayer. It usually ties together the themes mentioned beforehand and asks for divine assistance to live out the Christian life.

At the end of the prayer, the people say, "Amen."

Concluding Rite

The priest gives the final blessing at the end of the Mass:

> May Almighty God bless you, the Father, the Son, and the Holy Spirit.

Then comes the dismissal:

> *Deacon/Priest:* Go in Peace [or go forth], the Mass is ended.
>
> *People:* Thanks be to God.

On Sundays and holy days, a recessional hymn is usually sung as the priest, deacon, and other ministers process from the sanctuary to the back of the church.

Book III

Catholic Mass

Discovering Variations in the Ordinary Form

The Holy Mass is the center of all Catholic worship of Jesus Christ, and in addition to the weekly, obligatory Sunday church services, special liturgies are offered on certain occasions in the lives of the congregants and days of celebration in the Church. These variations on the Mass are spiritual bookmarks in the lives of the faithful.

Many of the Masses covered in this chapter are *Ritual Masses,* which are Sacred Liturgies celebrated on any day of the week. *Ritual* means a set of actions, gestures, or words performed on certain occasions and having symbolic meaning to reaffirm Church teaching. These Masses focus on one of the seven sacraments or the final sacrament possible, a Catholic burial.

Nuptial (wedding) Mass

Weddings in the Catholic Church may take place with or without a Mass. If both the bride and groom are Catholic, they typically have a Nuptial or wedding Mass, but if one is not Catholic and a majority of the invited guests aren't either, then they usually have a wedding service alone without a Mass, because only Catholics who are *in full communion* with Church teachings and laws are permitted to receive Holy Communion. Which way to go is determined by the pastor after discussion with the bride and groom and based on the policies of the local diocese.

Exchanging vows is the essential part of a Catholic wedding. Mutual consent of the bride and groom is what makes them husband and wife, and therefore the actual ministers of the Sacrament of Matrimony are the couple themselves. The priest or deacon is not the minister; rather, he is the official witness for the Church of this union.

Requiem (funeral) Mass

The death of a loved one is always painful and difficult, and more than any other occasion needs the spiritual support and strength of the Church through the Holy Mass. The funeral rites of the Catholic Church are first and foremost for the assistance of the departed person and secondarily for the surviving family and friends.

The funeral Mass is offered for the soul of the deceased. Even if this person lived a virtuous and holy life and went straight to heaven when he or she died, the Mass is not in vain. The spiritual benefits are still given to the family and friends who attend.

Funeral wakes usually take place the night before the burial services. Typically, Catholics either have a Rosary prayed at the funeral parlor the night before the burial or have a formal vigil service, also called a wake. The custom in some countries is to hold the wake in the deceased person's home and then have the body transferred to the church for the Mass the next day.

The Sacred Liturgy for the Deceased is much like a Sunday parish Mass in that there are two readings from Scripture before the Gospel, the psalm is usually sung, and a cantor or choir (or both) is usually present to help sing the hymns and acclamations.

Mass with Baptism

Baptism is the first sacrament a Catholic receives and is called the gateway to the other sacraments, because only a baptized person can receive them. It is the first of three Sacraments of Initiation into the Church and makes you an adopted Child of God.

Catholicism considers Baptism the spiritual process of being "born again of water and the Spirit." The sacrament removes the Original Sin of Adam and Eve and infuses Sanctifying Grace which allows the soul the possibility of heaven, but it is not a get-out-of-hell-for-free card. More than a cultural or symbolic act, Baptism makes an indelible mark on the soul. That is why no one can be *un*-baptized or *re*-baptized. Once is forever.

Most babies in Catholic families are baptized within two to five weeks of their birth, as soon as mommy and daddy are confident enough to take their bundle of joy out of the house and into the public. Parents and godparents sit with the child to be baptized and are accompanied by friends and family as well.

When done within Mass, the Rite of Baptism is divided into parts: the reception of the child, anointing, blessing of the baptismal water, renunciation of sin and Profession of Faith, Baptism, second anointing, clothing with the white garment, and lighting the candle.

Book III

Catholic Mass

Confirmation Mass

Confirmation is the second Sacrament of Initiation and confirms what was done in Baptism. The Creed is repeated and the questions formerly answered by the parents and godparents are now answered by the young man or young woman about to be confirmed. While the Holy Trinity (Father, Son, and Holy Spirit) fill the soul of the newly baptized, the Holy Spirit is one who fills the soul of the newly confirmed.

The Sacrament of Confirmation is done at different times in the Eastern and Latin (Western) Catholic Church. In the Eastern Church, the three Sacraments of Baptism, Confirmation (also called Chrismation), and Holy Eucharist are done at the same time, usually in infancy. In the Latin Church, the three events are separated by several years. Usually the bishop visits each parish annually to confirm its teenagers.

Mass for Anointing of the Sick

Not everyone who's sick is in a hospital or nursing home — some are home-bound. For these faithful, the Church offers an optional Mass of Anointing that takes place in the home. St. James said in his epistle in the New Testament,

> If there are any sick among you, then let them call for the priests of the church and the priest will pray over them and anoint the sick person with oil and the prayer of faith will save the sick person. (James 5:14)

The Mass begins with the usual introductory rites, and then the priest may welcome all the sick together by saying:

> Christ taught his disciples to be a community of love. In praying together, in sharing all things, and in caring for the sick, they recalled his words: "Insofar as you did this to one of these, you did it to me." We gather today to witness to this teaching and to pray in the name of Jesus the healer that the sick may be restored to health. Through this Eucharist and anointing we invoke his healing power.

The Mass then continues with the Confiteor or other Penitential rite options as listed in the Missal.

Weekday Mass

Weekday Mass is just like Sunday Mass except that only one Scripture reading is done before the Gospel instead of two. The congregation attending the weekday Mass is typically much smaller than on Sundays, so hymns may be omitted. No offering is collected during the week in parishes.

Holy day Mass (Solemnities)

Holy day Masses are treated like Sundays. Two readings from Scripture are done before the Gospel reading, and chanting and incense are typically part of the Mass, as well. The celebrant may also wear more formal albs at these special Masses.

Easter and Christmas are two most important solemnities and holy days of the Church year, followed by the feasts of the Lord (Corpus Christi, Ascension Thursday, Epiphany), feasts of the Virgin Mary (Immaculate Conception, Assumption, Nativity), and feasts of some of the more significant saints (St. Joseph, SS. Peter and Paul, Holy Apostles, All Saints, patron saint of the parish, patron saint of the diocese). You can find out more about special celebrations of the liturgical year in Book I, Chapter 6.

Some holy days have proper sequences (poetic verses) recited before the Gospel listed in the lectionary (the Catholic book of Bible readings for Mass). The *Stabat Mater* is read on the feast of Our Lady of Sorrows (September 15); *Veni Sancte Spiritus* on Pentecost (50 days after Easter); *Victimae paschali laudes* on Easter; *Lauda Sion Salvatorem* on Corpus Christi. The Extraordinary form of the Roman Rite also includes the *Dies Irae* on All Souls Day.

Book III

Catholic Mass

Chapter 3

Extraordinary Form: Traditional Latin Mass

In This Chapter

▶ Checking out the history of this ancient form of Mass

▶ Examining the types of the Extraordinary form

▶ Running through the complete Extraordinary Mass

*N*o matter what it's called — Traditional Latin Mass (TLM), Tridentine Mass, Old Mass, Extraordinary form of the Roman Rite — this form of Catholic Mass has been around almost as long as the Church itself.

Introducing the Extraordinary Form of the Mass

The Latin Mass goes back to the time of the Roman caesars. Thanks to the missionary efforts of SS. Peter and Paul, many Jews and pagans in Rome converted to Christianity. What is today called the Extraordinary form of the Roman Rite is the offspring of that early period of Church history when there was one church and one state.

Discovering the origins of the Extraordinary form

The Roman Mass took on more prestige during the time of Charlemagne, who was crowned Holy Roman Emperor by Pope Leo III on Christmas day, AD 800. As the secular ruler of a united Christendom, Charlemagne wanted stability and uniformity throughout the realm. One way of doing that was to have a standard Sacred Worship so Mass would be the same any-where and every-where within the empire.

Nevertheless, over time nation states emerged and monarchs wanted to be more and more independent. When Martin Luther in Germany and John Calvin in Switzerland began the Protestant Reformation in the 16th century, vernacular (the common, local languages) entered Sacred Worship.

The Council of Trent (1545–1563) was convened to address the issues and concerns raised by the Reformers. One response was to make sure the Holy Mass was meticulously preserved and protected from any attempts to dilute or distort Catholic doctrine especially on the priesthood, the Real Presence in the Holy Eucharist. The Mass of Pope St. Pius (otherwise known as the Tridentine Mass or Traditonal Latin Mass) became the normal and staple form of Catholic worship for Europe and the New World.

Replacing and restoring the Extraordinary form

For more than four hundred years the Tridentine Mass was the typical form of Catholic worship (except in Eastern Europe and the Middle East where Eastern Catholic liturgy was the common form). When Pope John XXIII convened the Second Vatican Council (1962–1965), one of the goals was to present the timeless truths of faith to the modern world in a new voice. Same message but new medium.

The Mass that came out of Vatican II, first called the Mass of Paul VI (who was the pope who closed the Council), was later called the *Novus Ordo* (New Order) to distinguish it from the previous version, then called the Tridentine or the Traditional Latin Mass. The biggest innovation was the introduction of the vernacular (common tongue) into the Mass.

The Ordinary form (the New Mass) became normative around the world in 1970. However, some Catholics, clergy and laity alike, felt that the vernacular language and the changing of the posture of the priest (from facing east, called *ad orientem,* to facing the people, *versus populum*) were not conducive to their spiritual needs. So in 1988 Pope John Paul II issued *Ecclesia Dei,* which permitted priests to celebrate the old Mass in the old tongue and in the old way. Pope Benedict XVI went further and issued *Summorum Pontificum* in 2007, which allowed any and all priests the ability to celebrate the TLM.

Celebrating the Extraordinary Mass today

Not all parishes offer the Extraordinary form, but most dioceses have at least one parish where all the Masses are in Latin and according to the 1962 Missal. (The rest and majority of parishes are using the vernacular Ordinary form according to the 2002 Missal.) The Extraordinary Mass can take the following forms:

- ✔ **Low Mass (Missa Privata):** Mass in which the priest does not chant the proper parts but quietly reads (recites) them instead

- ✔ **High Mass (Solemn High Mass):** Sung Mass assisted by sacred ministers (a deacon and subdeacon)

- ✔ **Missa Cantata:** Sung Mass without any assisting sacred ministers (no deacon or subdeacon)

- ✔ **Pontifical Mass:** Mass celebrated by a bishop (or an archbishop or cardinal)

- ✔ **Pontifical High Mass (Solemn Pontifical Mass):** Mass celebrated by a bishop and assisted by a deacon and subdeacon

- ✔ **Apostolic (Papal) Pontifical High Mass:** Mass celebrated by the pope and assisted by a deacon, subdeacon, and cleric of the Eastern Catholic Church, who chants the Epistle and Gospel in Greek (after they're chanted in Latin by Western Catholic clerics)

Book III

Catholic Mass

Most parishes in the United States and Canada that have the Extraordinary form do either the Low Mass or the Missa Cantata. The Pontifical Mass is rare.

A Rundown of the Entire Mass

In the sections that follow, we describe from start to finish the parts of the Extraordinary form.

The Mass is divided into two main parts, Mass of Catechumens and Mass of Faithful. This division is similar to the Ordinary form designation of the Liturgy of the Word and Liturgy of the Eucharist.

The *Ordinary of the Mass (Ordo Missae)* is the set of liturgical texts that remain constant and invariable. The passages from Sacred Scripture and the prayers specific for the day or season do change and are listed in the Roman Missal for the celebrant's convenience.

The following abbreviations are used to help distinguish the various participants in the Holy Sacrifice of the Mass according to the Extraordinary form of the Roman Rite:

P. Priest

D. Deacon

L. Lector/subdeacon

S. Server/congregation

C. Choir

V. Versicle

R. Response

Asperges (Sprinkling of holy water)

The priest sprinkles holy water over the congregation while this hymn (*asperges me*) is sung/chanted. This act symbolizes the purifying waters of Baptism that wash away Original Sin and venial sins.

P. Asperges me,	P. Thou shalt sprinkle me,
C. Domine, hyssopo, et mundabor: lavabis me, et super nivem dealbabor. Miserere mei, Deus, secundum magnam misericordiam tuam.	C. Lord, with hyssop, and I shall be cleansed; thou shalt wash me, and I shall be made whiter than snow. Have mercy on me, O God, according to thy great mercy.
V. Gloria Patri, et Filio, et Spiritui Sancto.	V. Glory be to the Father, and to the Son, and to the Holy Spirit.
R. Sicut erat in principio, et nunc, et semper, et in saecula saeculorum. Amen.	R. As it was in the beginning, is now, and ever shall be, world without end. Amen.
(Antiphon:) Asperges me, Domine, hyssopo, et mundabor: lavabis me, et super nivem dealbabor.	(Antiphon:) Thou shalt sprinkle me, Lord, with hyssop, and I shall be cleansed; thou shalt wash me, and I shall be made whiter than snow.

Mass of the Catechumens

Before entering the sanctuary, the priest and altar server(s) say preparatory prayers to show great awe of and reverence to the sanctuary where the Holy Sacrifice will take place. They need to adequately prepare for the worship rather than rushing into it too hastily, clumsily, or casually.

Prayers at the foot of the altar

The priest begins by making the sign of the cross and reciting the prayers of Psalm 42:

P. In nomine Patris, et Filii, et Spiritus Sancti.	P. In the Name of the Father, and of the Son, and of the Holy Spirit.
S. Amen.	S. Amen
P. Introibo ad altare Dei	P. I will go to the altar of God.
S Ad Deum qui laetificat juventutem meam.	S. To God, the joy of my youth.
P. Judica me, Deus, et discerne causam meam de gente non sancta: ab homine iniquo et doloso erue me.	P. Do me justice, O God, and fight my fight against an unholy people: Rescue me from the wicked and deceitful man.
S. Quia tu es, Deus, fortitudo mea: quare me repulisti, et quare tristis incedo, dum affligit me inimicus?	S. For thou, O God, art my strength: Why hast thou forsaken me? And why do I go about in sadness, while the enemy harasses me?
P. Emitte lucem tuam et veritatem tuam: ipsa me deduxerunt et adduxerunt in montem sanctum tuum, et in tabernacula tua.	P. Send forth thy light and thy truth: for they have led me and brought me to thy holy hill and thy dwelling place.
S. Et introibo ad altare Dei: ad Deum qui laetificat juventutem meam.	S. And I will go to the altar of God: to God, the joy of my youth.
P. Confitebor tibi in cithara, Deus, Deus meus quare tristis es anima mea, et quare conturbas me?	P. I shall yet praise thee upon the harp, O God, my God. Why art thou sad, my soul, and why art thou downcast?
S. Spera in Deo, quoniam adhuc confitebor illi: salutare vultus mei, et Deus meus.	S. Trust in God, for I shall yet praise him, my Savior, and my God.
P. Gloria Patri, et Filio, et Spiritui Sancto.	P. Glory be to the Father, and to the Son, and to the Holy Spirit.
S. Sicut erat in principio, et nunc, et semper: et in saecula saeculorum. Amen.	S. As it was in the beginning, is now, and ever shall be: world without end. Amen.
P. Introibo ad altare Dei.	P. I will go to the altar of God.
S. Ad Deum qui laetificat juventutem meam.	S. To God, the joy of my youth.
P. Adjutorium nostrum in nomine Domini.	P. Our help is in the name of the Lord.
S. Qui fecit coelum et terram.	S. Who made heaven and earth.

Book III

Catholic Mass

The priest, by virtue of ordination, represents both God and man during Sacred Worship. As a fellow human being, the priest is as much in need of mercy and forgiveness as the rest of sinful humanity. Hence, he confesses his weakness. As an ordained minister, he represents the loving forgiveness that God bestows on his children.

Confiteor

The priest bows profoundly low and begins the Confiteor (I confess).

P. Confiteor Deo omnipotenti, beatae Mariae semper Virgini, beato Michaeli Archangelo, beato Joanni Baptistae, sanctis Apostolis Petro et Paulo, omnibus Sanctis, et vobis fratres: quia peccavi nimis cogitatione verbo, et opere: mea culpa, mea culpa, mea maxima culpa. Ideo precor beatam Mariam semper Virginem, beatum Michaelem Archangelum, beatum Joannem Baptistam, sanctos Apostolos Petrum et Paulum, omnes Sanctos, et vos fratres, orare pro me ad Dominum Deum Nostrum.	P. I confess to Almighty God, to Blessed Mary ever-virgin, to Blessed Michael the Archangel, to Blessed John the Baptist, to the Holy Apostles Peter and Paul, to all the angels and saints, and to you my brothers and sisters, that I have sinned exceedingly in thought, word, deed, [he strikes his breast three times, saying:] through my fault, through my fault, through my most grievous fault, and I ask Blessed Mary ever-virgin, Blessed Michael the Archangel, Blessed John the Baptist, the Holy Apostles Peter and Paul, all the angels and saints, and you my brothers and sisters, to pray for me to the Lord our God.
S. Misereatur tui omnipotens Deus, et dimissis peccatis tuis, perducat te ad vitam aeternam.	S. May Almighty God have mercy on you, forgive you all your sins, and bring you to everlasting life.
P. Amen.	P. Amen.

The Confiteor continues with the People's Confession. The servers bow profoundly low.

S. Confiteor Deo omnipotenti, beatae Mariae semper Virgini, beato Michaeli Archangelo, beato Joanni Baptistae, sanctis Apostolis Petro et Paulo, omnibus Sanctis, et tibi Pater: quia peccavi nimis cogitatione verbo, et opere: mea culpa, mea culpa, mea maxima culpa. Ideo precor beatam Mariam semper Virginem, beatum Michaelem Archangelum, beatum	S. I confess to Almighty God, to Blessed Mary ever-virgin, to Blessed Michael the Archangel, to Blessed John the Baptist, to the Holy Apostles Peter and Paul, to all the angels and saints, and to you my brothers and sisters, that I have sinned exceedingly in thought, word, deed, [strike your breast three times, saying:] through my fault,

Joannem Baptistam, sanctos Apostolos Petrum et Paulum, omnes Sanctos, et te Pater, orare pro me ad Dominum Deum Nostrum.	through my fault, through my most grievous fault, and I ask Blessed Mary ever-virgin, Blessed Michael the Archangel, Blessed John the Baptist, the Holy Apostles Peter and Paul, all the angels and saints, and you Father, to pray for me to the Lord our God.
P. Misereatur vestri omnipotens Deus, et dimissis peccatis vestris, perducat vos ad vitam aeternam.	P. May Almighty God have mercy on you, forgive you your sins, and bring you to everlasting life.
S. Amen.	S. Amen.
P. Indulgentiam absolutionem, et remissionem peccatorum nostrorum, tribuat nobis omnipotens et misericors Dominus.	P. May the Almighty and Merciful Lord grant us pardon, absolution, and remission of our sins.
S. Amen.	S. Amen.
P. Deus, tu conversus vivificabis nos.	P. Turn to us, O God, and bring us life.
S. Et plebs tua laetabitur in te.	S. And your people will rejoice in you.
P. Ostende nobis Domine, misericordiam tuam.	P. Show us, Lord, your mercy.
S. Et salutare tuum da nobis.	S. And grant us your salvation.
P. Domine, exaudi orationem meam.	P. O Lord, hear my prayer.
S. Et clamor meus ad te veniat.	S. And let my cry come to you.
P. Dominus vobiscum.	P. May the Lord be with you.
S. Et cum spiritu tuo.	S. And with your spirit.
P. Oremus.	P. Let us pray.

The priest prays the following words inaudibly while ascending to the altar.

P. Aufer a nobis, quaesumus, Domine, iniquitates nostras ut ad Sancta sanctorum puris mereamur mentibus introire. Per Christum Dominum nostrum. Amen.	P. Take away from us, O Lord, our iniquities, we beseech you, that we may enter with pure minds into the Holy of Holies. Through Christ our Lord. Amen.

Book III

Catholic Mass

The priest kisses the altar where the relics are, praying the following.

P. Oramus te. Domine, per merita Sanctorum tuorum, quorum reliquiae hic sunt, et omnium Sanctorum: ut indulgere digneris omnia peccata mea. Amen.	P. We beseech you, O Lord, by the merits of your saints, whose relics lie here, and of all the saints, deign in your mercy to pardon me all my sins. Amen.

At High Mass, the priest then incenses the altar, saying:

P. Ab illo benedicaris, in cuius honore cremaberis. Amen.	P. May this incense be blessed by him in whose honor it is to be burned. Amen.

Introit

Introit means *to introduce*. The Introit is a psalm that introduces the Mass.

The priest reads the specific Introit from the Roman Missal for the specific Mass from the Epistle (right) side of the altar. When finished, he concludes with:

P. Gloria Patri, et Filio, et Spiritui Sancto. Sicut erat in principio, et nunc, et semper, et in saecula saeculorum. Amen.	P. Glory be to the Father, and to the Son, and to the Holy Spirit, as it was in the beginning, is now and ever shall be. Amen.

The priest then proceeds to the middle of the altar.

Kyrie

Kyrie eleison is Greek for Lord have mercy, and *Christie eleison* means Christ have mercy.

The priest stands in the middle of the altar and says, alternating with the server(s):

P. Kyrie eleison.	P. Lord, have mercy.
S. Kyrie eleison.	S. Lord, have mercy.
P. Kyrie eleison.	P. Lord, have mercy.
S. Christe eleison.	S. Christ, have mercy.
P. Christe eleison.	P. Christ, have mercy.
S. Christe eleison.	S. Christ, have mercy.
P. Kyrie eleison.	P. Lord, have mercy.
S. Kyrie eleison.	S. Lord, have mercy.
P. Kyrie eleison.	P. Lord, have mercy.

Gloria

Following the somber admission of unworthiness and need for mercy and forgiveness, the tone turns more joyful, and the choir sings the angelic hymn proclaimed to the shepherds at the time of Christ's birth, the Gloria.

The Gloria is omitted for penitential seasons, Masses for the dead, and certain other Masses.

Standing at the middle of the altar, the priest extends and joins his hands, makes a slight bow, says:

P. Gloria in exceslis Deo.	P. Glory to God in the highest.

The priest sits while the choir sings the Gloria:

C. Et in terra pax hominibus bonae vol- untatis. Laudamus te. Benedicimus te. Adoramus te. Glorificamus te. Gratias agimus tibi propter magnam gloriam tuam. Domine Deus, Rex coelestis, Deus Pater omnipotens. Domine Fili unigenite, Jesu Christe. Domine Deus, Agnus Dei, Filius Patris, Qui tollis pec- cata mundi, miserere nobis. Qui tollis peccata mundi, suscipe deprecationem nostram. Qui sedes ad dexteram Patris, miserere nobis. Quoniam tu solus Sanctus. Tu solus Dominus. To solus Altissimus, Jesu Christe. Cum Sancto Spiritu in gloria Dei Patris. Amen.	C. And on earth peace to people of good will. We praise you. We bless you. We worship you. We glorify you. Lord God, Heavenly King, God the Father Almighty. Lord Jesus Christ, the Only Begotten Son. Lord God, Lamb of God, Son of the Father. You who take away the sins of the world, have mercy on us. You who take away the sins of the world, receive our prayer. You who sit at the right hand of the Father, have mercy on us. For you alone are holy. You alone are Lord. You alone are the Most High, Jesus Christ, with the Holy Spirit, in the Glory of God the Father. Amen.

Turning toward the people, the priest says:

P. Dominus Vobiscum.	P. May the Lord be with you.
S. Et cum spiritu tuo.	S. And with your spirit.
P. Oremus.	P. Let us pray.

Collect

In ancient times, Christians would form processions to various churches where the local people would gather. This gathering was known as the _ecclesia collect_ (church assembly). At these places, Mass was celebrated with a community prayer for specific intentions.

The Collect is a brief prayer assigned for that day, season, or occasion. It is equivalent to the Opening Prayer in the Ordinary form.

Epistle

The congregation sits for the reading of the Epistle, one of the letters of the New Testament found in the Bible after the Gospel.

The priest stands at the Epistle (right) side of the altar and reads the Epistle from the Mass he is celebrating, after which the server says:

S. Deo gratias.	S. Thanks be to God.

Gradual, Tract, and Sequence

The server begins preparing for the Gospel, moving the Missal from the Epistle (right) side of the alter to the Gospel (left) side of the alter. Meanwhile, the Gradual (similar to a sequence, it is a liturgical hymn or poem) is sung by the choir. The Alleluia is sung along with the proper Sequence: *Paschale victimae* in the Easter Vigil; *Veni, sancte Spiritus* on Pentecost; *Lauda Sion* on Corpus Christi; *Stabat Mater* on Our Lady of Sorrows; *Dies Irae* on All Souls and in Requiem Masses. In Lent and at Masses for the dead, the Alleluia is omitted, and a tract is sung instead.

Before reading the Gospel, the deacon (if a Solemn or High Mass) returns to the center, bows down, joins his hands, and says:

D. Munda cor meum ac labia mea, omnipotens Deus, qui labia Isaiae Prophetae calculo mundasti ignito: ita me tua grata miseratione dignare mundare, ut sanctum Evangelium tuum digne valeam nuntiare. Per Christum Dominum nostrum. Amen. Jube, Domine benedicere.	D. Cleanse my heart and my lips, O Almighty God, who cleansed the lips of the Prophet Isaiah with a burning coal. In your gracious mercy deign so to purify me that I may worthily proclaim your Holy Gospel. Through Christ our Lord. Amen. Lord, grant me your blessing.
P. Dominus sit in corde meo et in labiis meis. ut digne et competenter annuntiem evangelium suum.	P. The Lord be in your heart and on your lips that you may worthily and fittingly proclaim his Holy Gospel. In the name of the Father, and of the Son, and of the Holy Spirit.
D. Amen.	D. Amen.

If the Mass is a Missa Cantata or Low Mass, no deacon is used, and the priest says the lines above.

Gospel

The Gospel is one of the four accounts of the life, sayings, and deeds of Jesus Christ written by the Evangelists, Matthew, Mark, Luke, and John.

Everyone in the church stands for the Holy Gospel.

P./D. Dominus vobiscum.	P./D. May the Lord be with you.
S. Et cum spiritu tuo.	S. And with your spirit.
P./D. Sequentia (or Initium) sancti Evangelii secundum [N].	P./D. A continuation of the Holy Gospel according to St. [name].

The Gospel Book is then incensed.

S. Gloria tibi, Domine.	S. Glory to you, O Lord.

The Holy Gospel is sung or read aloud. At the end, the deacon or server says:

D./S. Laus tibi, Christe.	D./S. Praise to you, O Christ.

At High Mass, the deacon takes the Missal to the celebrant, who kisses it and says:

P. Per evangelica dicta deleantur nostra delicta.	P. May the words of the Gospel wipe away our sins.

If laity are present, the priest may go to the pulpit and read the Epistle and the Gospel aloud in the vernacular language. All stand again for the reading of the Gospel.

Homily

After the Epistle and Gospel, the priest goes to the pulpit to deliver a theological or spiritual reflection to inspire the congregation to aspire to heavenly goals and objectives. The people sit for this sermon, the homily.

Credo

The Profession of Faith, or Creed, that was ironed out and codified at the Ecumenical Council of Nicea in AD 325 is a summary of Christian religion. It is sung, chanted, or spoken at this part of the Mass.

After the homily, the priest goes to the middle of the altar and begins the Creed. As with the Gloria, he intones the first words of the Creed and then sits while the choir sings (the people also sit):

Book III

Catholic Mass

C. Credo in unum Deum, Patrem omnipotentem, factorem coeli et terrae, visibilium omnium et invisibilium. Et in unum Dominum Jesum Christum, Filium Dei unigenitum. Et ex Patre natum ante omnia saecula. Deum de Deo, lumen de lumine, Deum verum de Deo vero. Genitum, not factum, consubstantialem Patri: per quem omnia facta sunt. Qui propter nos homines, et propter nostram salutem descendit de coelis. Et incarnatus est de Spiritu Sancto ex Maria Virgine: *et homo factus est.* Crucifixus etiam pro nobis; sub Pontio Pilato passus, et sepultus est. Et resurrexit tertia die, secundum Scripturas. Et ascendit in coelum: sedet ad dexteram Patris. Et iterum venturus est cum gloria judicare vivos et mortuos. cujus regni non erit finis. Et in Spiritum Sanctum, Dominum et vivificantem: qui ex Patre Filioque procedit. Qui cum Patre, et Filio simul adoratur et conglorificatur: qui locutus est per Prophetas. Et unam, sanctam, catholicam et apostolicam Ecclesiam. Confiteor unum baptisma in remissionem peccatorum. Et exspecto resurrectionem mortuorum. Et vitam venturi saeculi. Amen.	C. I believe in one God, the Father Almighty, Maker of heaven and earth, and of all things visible and invisible. And in one Lord, Jesus Christ, the Only Begotten Son of God. Born of the Father before all ages. God of God, Light of Light, true God of true God. Begotten, not made, of one substance with the Father. By whom all things were made. Who for us men and for our salvation came down from heaven. [Here all present kneel.] And became incarnate by the Holy Spirit of the Virgin Mary: *and was made man.* [Here all arise.] He was also crucified for us, suffered under Pontius Pilate, and was buried. And on the third day he rose again according to the Scriptures. He ascended into heaven and sits at the right hand of the Father. He will come again in glory to judge the living and the dead, and his kingdom will have no end. And in the Holy Spirit, the Lord and Giver of life, who proceeds from the Father and the Son. Who together with the Father and the Son is adored and glorified, and who spoke through the prophets. And one holy, Catholic, and Apostolic Church. I confess one Baptism for the forgiveness of sins and I await the resurrection of the dead and the life of the world to come. Amen.

All stand, and the priest continues:

P. Dominus vobiscum.	P. May the Lord be with you.
S. Et cum spiritu tuo.	S. And with your spirit.
P. Oremus.	P. Let us pray.

The people sit.

At this point, the Mass of the Catechumens ends and the Mass of the Faithful begins. In the ancient Church, the Catechumens (unbaptized persons preparing for conversion) were dismissed here because they could not receive Holy Communion, which happens in the second half of the Mass.

Mass of the Faithful

Historically, when upbaptized people left the church after the Mass of the Catechumens, the people who did remain in church were baptized members of the Church, the faithful. Therefore, the second part of the Mass is called Mass of the Faithful.

This part of the Mass is more than just the second half, though; it is the heart and soul of the Mass. The Mass of the Faithful contains the offertory where the oblation (sacrifice) is made, where the bread and wine are consecrated into the Body and Blood of Christ, and where the faithful are spiritually fed with Holy Communion.

Unbaptized, unchurched, or uncatechized persons are no longer asked to leave or escorted out of church prior to the Mass of the Faithful. Anyone and everyone is welcome to attend the entire Mass. Only those baptized Christians who are in full communion (members of the Catholic Church) can receive Holy Communion, but all are free to be present during the Mass from beginning to end.

Offertory

The priest says the Offertory Prayer, which offers unleavened wheat bread and grape wine. These gifts of the earth also represent the whole human race who unite themselves to the supreme sacrifice made by Jesus, that of his life for the salvation of the world.

Book III

Catholic Mass

The priest says the offertory prayers in a low voice while the choir sings the Offertory Verse, also called the Offertory Antiphon.

All sit during the Offertory.

P. Suscipe, sancte Pater, omnipotens aeterne Deus, hanc immaculatam hostiam, quam ego indignus famulus tuus offero tibi, Deo meo vivo et vero, pro innumerabilibus peccatis, et offensionibus, et negligentiis meis, et pro omnibus circumstantibus, sed et pro omnibus fidelibus Christianis vivis atque defunctis. Ut mihi, et illis proficiat ad salutem in vitam aeternam.	P. Accept, O Holy Father, Almighty and Eternal God, this spotless host, which I, your unworthy servant, offer to you, my living and true God, to atone for my numberless sins, offenses, and negligences; on behalf of all here present and likewise for all faithful Christians living and dead, that it may profit me and them as a means of salvation to life everlasting.
S. Amen.	S. Amen.

P. Deus, qui humanae substantiae dignitatem mirabiliter condidisti, et mirabilius reformasti: da nobis per hujus aquae et vini mysterium, ejus divinitatis esse consortes, qui humanitatis nostrae fieri dignatus est particeps, Jesus Christus Filius tuus Dominus noster: Qui tecum vivit et regnat in unitate Spiritus Sancti Deus. Per omnia saecula saeculorum. Amen.	P. O God, who established the nature of man in wondrous dignity, and still more admirably restored it, grant that by the mystery of this water and wine, may we come to share in his Divinity, who humbled himself to share in our humanity, Jesus Christ, your Son, our Lord. Who lives and reigns with you in the unity of the Holy Spirit, one God, forever and ever. Amen.
Offerimus tibi, Domine, calicem salutaris tuam deprecantes clementiam: ut in conspectu divinae majestatis tuae, pro nostra et totius mundi salute cum odore suavitatis ascendat. Amen.	We offer you, O Lord, the chalice of salvation, humbly begging of your mercy that it may arise before your Divine Majesty, with a pleasing fragrance, for our salvation and for that of the whole world. Amen.
In spiritu humilitatis, et in animo contrito suscipiamur a te, Domine, et sic fiat sacrificium nostrum in conspectu tuo hodie, ut placeat tibi, Domine Deus.	In a humble spirit and with a contrite heart, may we be accepted by you, O Lord, and may our sacrifice so be offered in your sight this day as to please you, O Lord God.
Veni, Sanctificator omnipotens aeterne Deus. Et benedic hoc sacrificum tuo sancto nomini praeparatum.	Come, O Sanctifier, Almighty and Eternal God, and bless this sacrifice prepared for the glory of your holy name.

When Mass is sung, the priest blesses the incense, saying:

P. Per intercessionem beati Michaelis Archangeli, stantis a dextris altaris incensi, et omnium electorum suorum, incensum istud dignetur Dominus benedicere, et in odorem suavitatis accipere. Per Christum Dominum nostrum. Amen.	P. Through the intercession of Blessed Michael the Archangel, standing at the right hand of the altar of incense, and of all his elect may the Lord vouchsafe to bless this incense and to receive it in the odor of sweetness. Through Christ our Lord. Amen.

The priest incenses the offerings and the cross, saying:

P. Incensum istud a te benedictum, ascendat ad te, Domine, et descendat super nos misericordia tua.	P. May this incense blessed by you arise before you, O Lord, and may your mercy come down upon us.

The priest incenses the altar and says:

P. Dirigatur, Domine, oratio mea sicut incensum in conspectu tuo: elevatio manuum mearum sacrificium vesperti-num. Pone, Domine, custodiam ori meo, et ostium circumstantiae labiis meis : ut non declinet cor meum in verba malitiae, ad excusandas excusationes in peccatis.	P. Let my prayer, O Lord, come like incense before you; the lifting up of my hands, like the evening sacrifice. O Lord, set a watch before my mouth, a guard at the door of my lips. Let not my heart incline to the evil of engaging in deeds of wickedness.

He then hands back the thurible to the deacon or server, saying:

P. Accendat in nobis Dominus ignem sui amoris, et flammam aeterne caritatis. Amen.	P. May the Lord enkindle in us the fire of his love and the flame of everlasting charity. Amen.

The celebrant, the ministers, the servers, and the people are incensed, in that order.

Lavabo

Lava is Latin for *wash*. The priest washes his hands in a ritual purification symbolizing his own personal unworthiness to offer the Mass. Only by God's grace of the sacrament of Holy Orders is he able to continue and complete the offering and the sacrifice.

Book III

Catholic Mass

Going to the Epistle (right) side of the altar, the priest washes his fingers and says:

P. Lavabo inter innocentes manus meas. et circumdabo altare tuum, Domine. Ut audiam vocem laudis. et enarrem universa mirabila tua. Domine, dilexi decorem domus tuae: et locum habitationis gloriae tuae. Ne perdas cum impiis, Deus animam meam: et cum viris sanguinum vitam meam: in quorum manibus iniquitates sunt: dextera eorum repleta est muner-ibus. Ego autem in innocentia mea ingressus sum: redime me, et miser-ere mei. Pes meus stetit in directo: in ecclesiis benedicam te, Domine.	P. I wash my hands in innocence, and I go around your altar, O Lord, giving voice to my thanks, and recounting all your wondrous deeds. O Lord, I love the house in which you dwell, the tent-ing place of your glory. Gather not my soul with those of sinners, nor with men of blood my life. On their hands are crimes, and their right hands are full of bribes. But I walk in integrity; redeem me, and have pity on me. My foot stands on level ground; in the assem-blies I will bless you, O Lord.
Gloria Patri, et Filio, et Spiritui Sancto. Sicut erat in principio, et nunc, et semper: et in saecula saeculorum. Amen.	Glory be to the Father, and to the Son, and to the Holy Spirit. As it was in the beginning, is now, and ever shall be: world without end. Amen.

Facing the middle of the altar, the priest continues.

P. Suscipe sancta Trinitas, hanc oblationem, quam tibi offerimus ob memoriam passionis, resurrectionis, et ascensionis Jesu Christi Domini nostri: et in honorem beatae Mariae semper Virginis, et beati Joannis Baptistae, et sanctorum Apostolorum Petri et Pauli, et istorum, et omnium Sanctorum: ut illis proficiat ad hon-orem, nobis autem ad salutem: et illi pro nobis intercedere dignentur in coelis, quorum memoriam agimus in terris. Per eumdem Christum Dominum nostrum. S. Amen.	P. Accept, most Holy Trinity, this offering which we are making to you in remembrance of the Passion, Resurrection, and Ascension of Jesus Christ, our Lord; and in honor of Blessed Mary, ever-virgin, Blessed John the Baptist, the Holy Apostles Peter and Paul, and of [name of the saints whose relics are in the altar] and of all the saints; that it may add to their honor and aid our salvation; and may they deign to intercede in heaven for us who honor their memory here on earth. Through the same Christ our Lord.
S. Amen.	S. Amen.

The priest kisses the altar, turns to the people, and says:

P. Orate fratres, ut meum ac vestrum sacrificium acceptabile fiat apud Deum Patrem omnipotentem.	P. Pray brethren, that my sacrifice and yours may be acceptable to God the Father Almighty.
S. Suscipiat Dominus sacrificium de manibus tuis ad laudem et gloriam nominis sui, ad utilitatem quoque nostram, totiusque Ecclesiae suae sanctae.	S. May the Lord receive the sacrifice from your hands to the praise and glory of his name, for our good, and that of all his holy Church.

Secret prayers

With his hands extended, the priest says the secret prayers. They are called *secret* not because the priest is a agent of the CIA or MI6, but because he says them quietly. In the Ordinary form of the Roman Rite, this prayer is called the *Oblation* or *Prayer Over the Gifts.*

The preface to the prayer, which begins "Per ominia saecula saeculorum" (forever and ever), is where we give thanks and praise to God. It concludes with the Sanctus, a prayer of union with the heavenly hosts and of adoration of the most "Holy, Holy, Holy" triune God.

Most often the preface is the Preface of the Most Holy Trinity (below) unless substituted with another, such as the Preface of the Nativity or the Preface of the Epiphany. When using the Preface of the Most Holy Trinity, the priest says (in a louder voice):

P. Per omnia saecula saeculorum.	P. World without end.
S. Amen.	S. Amen.
P. Dominus vobiscum.	P. The Lord be with you.
S. Et cum spiritu tuo.	S. And with thy spirit.
P. Sursum corda.	P. Lift up your hearts.
S. Habemus ad Dominum.	S. We have them lifted up unto the Lord.
P. Gratias agamus Domino Deo nostro.	P. Let us give thanks to the Lord our God.
S. Dignum et justum est.	S. It is meet and just.
P. Vere dignum et justum est, aequum et salutare, nos tibi semper, et ubique gratias agere: Domine sancte, Pater omnipotens, aeterne Deus. Qui cum unigenito Filio tuo, et Spiritu Sancto, unus es Deus, unus es Dominus: non in unius singularitate personae, sed in unius Trinitate substantiae. Quod enim de tua gloria, revelante te, credimus, hoc de Filio tuo, hoc de Spritu sancto, sine differentia discretionis sentimus. Ut in confessione verae, sempiternae-que Deitatis, et in personis proprietas, et in essentia unitas, et in majestate adoretur aequalitas. Quam laudant Angeli, atque Archangeli, Cherubim quoque ac Seraphim: qui non cessant clamare quotidie, una voce dicentes:	P. It is truly meet and just, right and profitable, for us, at all times, and in all places, to give thanks to thee, O Lord, the Holy One, the Father Almighty, the everlasting God: Who, together with thine Only Begotten Son and the Holy Ghost, art one God, one Lord, not in the singleness of one Person, but in the Trinity of one substance. For that which, according to thy revelation, we believe of thy glory, the same we believe of thy Son, the same of the Holy Ghost, without difference or distinc- tion; so that in the confession of one true and eternal Godhead we adore distinctness in persons, oneness in essence, and equality in majesty: Which the angels praise, and the archangels, the cherubim also and the seraphim, who cease not, day by day crying out with one voice to repeat:

Here the bell is rung three times.

Sanctus

The thrice-holy hymn comes from the Old Testament of the Bible, in Isaiah 6:3: "Holy, holy, holy, is the Lord of hosts: the whole earth is full of his glory." It signifies that this is the beginning of the most holy part of the

Mass as even the angels in heaven now stand at attention as the priest is about to begin the Eucharistic Prayer.

P. Sanctus, Sanctus, Sanctus, Dominus Deus Sabaoth. Pleni sunt coeli et terra gloria tua. Hosanna in excelsis. Benedictus qui venit in nomine Domini. Hosanna in excelsis.	P. Holy, holy, holy, Lord God of hosts. The heavens and the earth are full of thy glory. Hosanna in the highest. Blessed is he who cometh in the name of the Lord. Hosanna in the highest.

The people kneel at this point of the Mass.

Canon of the Mass

Canon comes from the Greek word for *measuring rod.* The Canon of Scripture is the list of sacred books the Church officially endorses as authentically inspired. The Canon of the Mass is the set of official prayers said by the priest which authentically effect the Holy Sacrifice, and it's the holiest part of the Mass. The celebrant remembers Salvation History and retells the supreme act of divine love, the sacrifice of the Son by the Father, which is made manifest on the altar.

Though the Last Supper and the Death of Jesus on Good Friday occurred two millennia ago, they are made present at this time at the Holy Mass on the altar. The one and same sacrifice of Calvary is reenacted in an unbloody manner. The consecration of the bread into the Body of Christ and the separate consecration of the wine into the Blood of Christ represent the separation of body and blood, which causes death.

Yet, it is not dead flesh and blood the believer receives in Holy Communion, but rather the risen Body and Blood, Soul and Divinity of Christ. Death is reenacted, and so is Resurrection. The priest uses the first person singular "this is *my* body . . . this is *my* blood" because through the sacrament of Holy Orders he is made an *alter Christus* (another Christ) who acts *in persona Christi* (in the person of Christ) whenever the sacraments are celebrated.

The priest then begins the offering prayer *(Hanc Igitur)* of the Mass while holding his hands over the chalice with his thumbs overlapped in a cross, representing the sins of the world that Christ took upon himself.

Te Igitur

Te igitur are the first two Latin words of the Roman Canon (Eucharistic Prayer). Often the first or first two words of a Latin document or section of it are used to identify it. The opening phrase is *Te igitur clementissime Pater,* which translates to "to you therefore most merciful Father." It signifies that the Holy Sacrifice of the Mass is offered to God the Father, from God the Son, with God the Holy Spirit.

The priest prays silently:

P. Te igitur clementissime Pater, per Jesum Christum Filium tuum Dominum nostrum, supplices rogamus ac petimus, uti accepta habeas, et benedicas haec dona, haec munera, haec sancta sacrificia illibata, in primis quae tibi offerimus pro Ecclesia tua sancta Catholica; quam pacificare, custodire, adunare, et regere digneris toto orbe terrarum: una cum famulo tuo Papa nostro [N.] et Antistite nostro [N.] et omnibus orthodoxis, atque Catholicae et Apostolicae fidei cultoribus.	P. Therefore, we humbly pray and beseech thee, most merciful Father, through Jesus Christ thy Son, our Lord, to receive and to bless these gifts, these presents, these holy unspotted sacrifices, which we offer up to thee, in the first place, for thy holy Catholic Church, that it may please thee to grant her peace, to guard, unite, and guide her, throughout the world: as also for thy servant [name], our pope, and [name], our bishop, and for all who are orthodox in belief and who profess the Catholic and apostolic faith.

Commemoration of the Living

The Mass is for both the living and the dead, hence the church on earth (Church Militant) is specifically identified just as later in the Canon are the dead (Church Suffering, souls in Purgatory, and Church Triumphant, saints in heaven). Before praying to the saints and asking their intercession, the church prays for the living, particularly the poor, homeless, sick, and dying.

P. Memento Domine famulorum, famularumque tuarum [N.] et [N.] et omnium circumstantium, quorum tibi fides cognita est, et nota devotio, pro quibus tibi offerimus: vel qui tibi offerunt hoc sacrificium laudis pro se, suisque omnibus: pro redemptione animarum suarum, pro spe salutis et incolumitatis suae: tibique reddunt vota sua aeterno Deo vivo et vero.	P. Be mindful, O Lord, of thy servants, [names of special persons for whom the Mass may be offered], and of all here present, whose faith and devotion are known to thee, for whom we offer, or who offer up to thee, this sacrifice of praise, for themselves, their families, and their friends, for the salvation of their souls and the health and welfare they hope for, and who now pay their vows to thee, God eternal, living, and true.

Book III

Catholic Mass

Communicantes

Communicantes means *communion*, and in Catholic theology it is not limited to Holy Communion. The root of the word comes from two separate words: *co* (meaning *with*) and *unio* (meaning *union*) combine to form communio (which means *being united with*). The Communion of Saints are all the living on earth, the souls in Purgatory, and the saints in heaven.

P. Communicantes, et memoriam venerantes, in primis gloriosae semper virginis Mariae genitricis Dei et Domini nostri Jesu Christi: sed {et beati Joseph, ejusdem virginis sponsi} et beatorum Apostolorum ac martyrum tuorum, Petri et Pauli, Andreae, Jacobi, Joannis, Thomae, Jacobi, Philippi, Bartholomaei, Matthaei, Simonis et Thaddaei: Lini, Cleti, Clementis, Xysti, Cornelii, Cypriani, Laurentii, Chrysogoni, Joannis et Pauli, Cosmae et Damiani, et omnium sanctorum tuorum: quorum meritis precibusque concedas, ut in omnibus protectionis tuae muniamur auxilio. Per eumdem Christum Dominum nostrum. Amen.	P. Having communion with and venerating the memory, first, of the glorious Mary, ever a virgin, mother of Jesus Christ, our God and our Lord: likewise of Blessed Joseph, spouse of the same virgin, of thy blessed apostles and martyrs, Peter and Paul, Andrew, James, John, Thomas, James, Phillip, Bartholomew, Matthew, Simon and Thaddeus; of Linus, Cletus, Clement, Sixtus, Cornelius, Cyprian, Lawrence, Chrysogonus, John and Paul, Cosmas and Damian, and of all thy saints: for the sake of whose merits and prayers do thou grant that in all things we may be defended by the help of thy protection. Through the same Christ, our Lord. Amen.

Hanc Igitur

The priest extends his hands over the oblation and prays:

P. Hanc igitur oblationem servitutis nostrae, sed et cunctae familiae tuae, quaesumus, Domine, ut placatus accipias: diesque nostros in tua pace disponas, atque ab aeterna damnatione nos eripi, et in electorum tuorum jubeas grege numerari. Per Christum Dominum nostrum. Amen.	P. Wherefore, we beseech thee, O Lord, graciously to receive this oblation which we thy servants, and with us thy whole family, offer up to thee: dispose our days in thy peace; command that we be saved from eternal damnation and numbered among the flock of thine elect. Through Christ our Lord. Amen.

Quam Oblationem

The bell is rung once before this invocative prayer leading up to the consecration, asking him once more to bless what the Church offers here.

P. Quam oblationem tu, Deus, in omnibus, quaesumus benedictam, adscriptam, ratam, rationabilem, acceptabilemque facere digneris: ut nobis Corpus, et Sanguis fiat dilectissimi Filii tui Domini nostri Jesu Christi.	P. And do thou, O God, vouchsafe in all respects to bless, consecrate, and approve this our oblation, to perfect it and render it well-pleasing to thyself, so that it may become for us the body and blood of thy most beloved Son, Jesus Christ our Lord.

Consecration

The priest repeats the exact words spoken by Christ at the Last Supper over the bread and wine:

P. Qui pridie quam pateretur, accepit panem in sanctas ac venerabiles manus suas: et elevatis oculis in coelum ad te Deum Patrem suum omnipotentem, tibi gratias agens, benedixit, fregit, deditque discipulis suis, dicens: Accipite et manducate ex hoc omnes:	P. Who, the day before he suffered, took bread into his holy and venerable hands, and having lifted up his eyes to heaven, to thee, God, his Almighty Father, giving thanks to thee, blessed it, broke it, and gave it to his disciples, saying: Take ye and eat ye all of this:

The priest then bends over the host and says:

P. Hoc est enim corpus meum.	**P. For this is my body.**

Then the priest adores the host by genuflecting and elevates the now sacred host high enough for everyone to see. The bell is rung. The priest then uncovers the chalice and says:

P. Simili modo postquam coenatum est, accipiens et hunc praeclarum Calicem in sanctas ac venerabiles manus suas: item tibi gratias agens, benedixit, deditque discipulis suis, dicens: Accipite et bibite ex eo omnes:	P. In like manner, after he had supped, taking also into his holy and venerable hands this goodly chalice, again giving thanks to thee, he blessed it, and gave it to his disciples, saying: Take ye, and drink ye all of this:

The priest then bends over the chalice and says:

P. Hic est enim calix sanguinis mei, novi et aeterni testamenti: mysterium fidei, qui pro vobis et pro multis effendetur in remissionem peccatorum. Haec quotiescumque feceritis in mei memoriam facietis.	**P. For this is the chalice of my blood, of the new and everlasting testament, the mystery of faith, which for you and for many shall be shed unto the remission of sins. As often as ye shall do these things, ye shall do them in memory of me.**

The priest then adores by genuflecting and elevates the chalice high enough for everyone to see, and the bell is rung again.

Salvation history

Previous sacrifices by Abel, Abraham, and Melchizadech in the Old Testament are remembered. Their sacrifices were symbols or types of the full and efficacious sacrifice Jesus Christ made on the cross when he died on Good Friday, mystically represented at every Mass.

Book III

Catholic
Mass

Oblation

The priest continues:

P. Unde et memores Domine, nos servi tui, sed et plebs tua sancta, ejusdem Christi Filii tui Domini nostri tam beatae passionis, nec non et ab inferis resurrectionis, sed et in coelos gloriosae ascensionis: offerimus praeclarae majestati tuae de uis donis ac datis, hostiam puram, hostiam sanctam, hostiam immaculatam, Panem sanctum vitae aeternae, et Calicem salutis perpetuae.	P. Wherefore, O Lord, we, thy servants, as also thy holy people, calling to mind the blessed passion of the same Christ, thy Son, our Lord, his Resurrection from the grave, and his glorious Ascension into heaven, offer up to thy most excellent majesty of thine own gifts bestowed upon us, a victim which is pure, a victim which is stainless, the holy bread of life everlasting, and the chalice of eternal salvation.
Supra quae propitio ac sereno vultu respicere digneris: et accepta habere, sicuti accepta habere dignatus es munera pueri tui justi Abel, et sacrificium patriarchae nostri Abraham: et quod tibi obtulit summus sacerdos tuus Melchisedech, sanctum sacrificium, immaculatam hostiam.	Vouchsafe to look upon them with a gracious and tranquil countenance, and to accept them, even as thou wast pleased to accept the offerings of thy just servant Abel, and the sacrifice of Abraham, our patriarch, and that which Melchisedech, thy high priest, offered up to thee, a holy sacrifice, a victim without blemish.
Supplices te rogamus, omnipotens Deus; jube haec perferri per manus sancti Angeli tui in sublime altare tuum, in conspectu divinae majestatis tuae: ut quotquot ex hac altaris participatione, sacrosanctum Filii tui Corpus et Sanquinem sumpserimus omni benedictione coelesti et gratia repleamur. Per eumdem Christum Dominum nostrum. Amen.	We humbly beseech thee, Almighty God, to command that these our offerings be borne by the hands of thy holy angel to thine altar on high in the presence of thy divine Majesty; that as many of us as shall receive the most sacred Body and Blood of thy Son by partaking thereof from this altar may be filled with every heavenly blessing and grace: Through the same Christ our Lord. Amen.

Commemorantes

Commemorantes means to remember or commemorate, and the Church recalls the faithful departed at this part of the Mass. Most Masses are offered specifically for the soul of a deceased person and their names can be mentioned in the space indicated [name].

P. Memento etiam, Domine, famulorum famularumque tuarum [N.] et [N.] qui nos praecesserunt cum signo fidei, et dormiunt in somno pacis. Ipsis Domine, et omnibus in Christo quiescentibus, locum refrigerii, lucis et pacis, ut indulgeas, deprecamur, per eumdem Christum Dominum nostrum. Amen.	P. Be mindful, also, O Lord, of thy servants [name] and [name], who have gone before us with the sign of faith and who sleep the sleep of peace. To these, O Lord, and to all who rest in Christ, grant, we beseech Thee, a place of refreshment, light, and peace. Through the same Christ our Lord. Amen.

The priest strikes his breast, saying:

P. Nobis quoque peccatoribus famulis tuis, de multitudine miserationum tuarum sperantibus, partem aliquam et societatem donare digneris, cum tuis sanctis Apostolis et Martyribus: cum Joanne, Stephano, Matthia, Barnaba, Ignatio, Alexandro, Marcellino, Petro, Felicitate, Perpetua, Agatha, Lucia, Agnete, Caecilia, Anastasia, et omnibus sanctis tuis: intra quorum nos consortium, non aestimator meriti, sed veniae, quaesumus, largitor admitte. Per Christum Dominum nostrum, per quem haec omnia, Domine, semper bona creas, sanctificas, vivificas, benedicis et praestas nobis. Per ipsum, et cum ipso, et in ipso, est tibi Deo Patri omnipotenti, in unitate tus Sancti, omnis honor et gloria.	P. To us sinners, also, thy servants, who put our trust in the multitude of thy mercies, vouchsafe to grant some part and fellowship with thy holy apostles and martyrs; with John, Stephen, Matthias, Barnabas, Ignatius, Alexander, Marcellinus, Peter, Felicitas, Perpetua, Agatha, Lucy, Agnes, Cecilia, Anastasia, and with all thy saints. Into their company do thou, we beseech thee, admit us, not weighing our merits, but freely pardoning our offenses: through Christ our Lord, by whom, O Lord, thou dost always create, sanctify, quicken, bless, and bestow upon us all these good things. Through him, and with him, and in him, is to thee, God the Father Almighty, in the unity of the Holy Ghost, all honor and glory.

The priest ends the Roman Canon (Eucharistic Prayer), and then raises his voice and says:

P. Per omnia saecula saeculorum. Amen.	P. World without end. Amen.

Pater Noster

The Lord's Prayer, or Our Father, was taught to the Apostles by Christ himself. It is now said in preparation for the reception of Holy Communion, which is the true "daily bread." All stand.

P. Oremus. Praeceptis salutaribus moniti, et divina institutione formati, audemus dicere:	P. Let us pray. Admonished by salutary precepts, and following divine directions, we presume to say:
Pater noster, qui es in coelis: sanctificetur nomen tuum: adveniat regnum tuum: fiat voluntas tua sicut in coelo et in terra. Panem nostrum quotidianum da nobis hodie: et dimitte nobis debita nostra, sicut et nos dimittimus debitoribus nostris. Et ne nos inducas in tentationem. Sed libera nos a malo. Amen.	Our Father, who art in heaven, hallowed be thy name; thy kingdom come; thy will be done on earth as it is in heaven; give us this day our daily bread; and forgive us our trespasses, as we forgive those who trespass against us, and lead us not into temptation. But deliver us from evil. Amen.

Book III

Catholic Mass

Libera nos, quaesumus Domine, ab omnibus malis praeteritis, praesentibus, et futuris: et intercedente beata et gloriosa semper Virgine Dei Genitrice Maria, cum beatis Apostolis tuis Petro at Paulo, atque Andrea, et omnibus sanctis, da propitius pacem in diebus nostris: ut ope misericordiae tuae adjuti, et a peccato simus semper liberi, et ab omni perturbatione securi.	Deliver us, we beseech thee, O Lord, from all evils, past, present, and to come: and by the intercession of the blessed and glorious Mary, ever a virgin, Mother of God, and of thy holy apostles Peter and Paul, of Andrew, and of all the saints, graciously grant peace in our days, that through the help of thy bountiful mercy we may always be free from sin and secure from all disturbance.

Fractio Panis

The priest breaks a small piece of the consecrated Sacred Host and places it inside the chalice containing the Precious Blood.

P. Per eumdem Dominum nostrum Jesum Christum Filium tuum. Qui tecum vivit et regnat in unitate Spiritus Sancti Deus. Per omnia saecula saeculorum.	P. Through the same Jesus Christ, thy Son, our Lord, who liveth and reigneth with thee in the unity of the Holy Ghost, God, world without end.
S. Amen.	S. Amen.
P. Pax Domini sit semper vobiscum.	P. May the peace of the Lord be always with you.
S. Et cum spiritu tuo.	S. And with thy spirit.
P. Haec commixtio et consecratio Corporis at Sanguinis Domini nostri Jesu Christi fiat accipientibus nobis in vitam aeternam. Amen.	P. May this commingling and consecrating of the Body and Blood of our Lord Jesus Christ avail us who receive it unto life everlasting. Amen.

Agnus Dei

Agnus dei, Latin for *lamb of God,* is the title St. John the Baptist affirmed Jesus when he baptized Christ at the River Jordan. Jesus is the Lamb slain for the sins of the world. His blood saved souls just as the blood of the lamb on the doorposts spared lives of the Hebrews the night of Passover before the Exodus, when the angel of death passed over the homes of the people. Jesus is called the Lamb of God because he sheds his blood on the doorpost of the cross and thus frees humanity from the slavery of sin.

Three prayers follow the Agnus Dei, preceding the Communion prayer, which comes from the Roman centurion's plea for Christ to heal his sick servant boy.

Bowing down, the priest says:

P. Agnus Dei, qui tollis peccata mundi, miserere nobis. Agnus Dei, qui tollis peccata mundi, miserere nobis. Agnus Dei, qui tollis peccata mundi, dona nobis pacem.	P. Lamb of God, who takest away the sins of the world: have mercy on us. Lamb of God, who takest away the sins of the world: have mercy on us. Lamb of God, who takest away the sins of the world: grant us peace.
Domine Jesu Christe, qui dixisti Apostolis tuis: pacem relinquo vobis, pacem meam do vobis: ne respicias peccata mea, sed fidem Ecclesiae tuae; eamque secundum voluntatem tuam pacificare et coadunare digneris. Qui vivis et regnas Deus, per omnia saecula saeculorum. Amen.	[Prayer 1:] O Lord Jesus Christ who didst say to thine apostles: Peace I leave you, my peace I give you: look not upon my sins, but upon the faith of thy Church, and vouchsafe to grant her peace and unity according to thy will: Who livest and reignest God, world without end. Amen.
Domine Jesu Christe, Fili Dei vivi, qui ex voluntate Patris cooperante Spritu Sancto, per mortem tuam mundum vivificasti: libera me per hoc sacrosanctum Corpus et Sanguinem tuum ab omnibus iniquitatibus meis et universis malis: et fac me tuis semper inhaerere mandatis: et a te nunquam separari permittas: qui cum eodem Deo Patre et Spiritu Sancto vivis et regnas Deus in saecula saeculorum. Amen.	[Prayer 2:] O Lord Jesus Christ, Son of the living God, who, according to the will of the Father, through the cooperation of the Holy Ghost, hast by thy Death given life to the world: deliver me by this thy most Sacred Body and Blood from all my iniquities, and from every evil; make me always cleave to thy commandments, and never suffer me to be separated from thee, who with the same God, the Father and the Holy Ghost, livest and reignest God, world without end. Amen.
Perceptio Corporis tui, Domine Jesu Christe, quod ego indignus sumere praesumo, non mihi proveniat in judicium et condemnationem: sed pro tua pietate prosit mihi ad tutamentum mentis et corporis, et ad medelam percipiendam. Qui vivis et regnas cum Deo Patre in unitate Spiritus Sancti Deus, per omnia saecula saeculorum. Amen.	[Prayer 3:] Let not the partaking of thy Body, O Lord Jesus Christ, which I, all unworthy, presume to receive, turn to my judgment and condemnation; but through thy loving kindness may it be to me a safeguard and remedy for soul and body; who, with God the Father, in the unity of the Holy Ghost, livest and reignest, God, world without end. Amen.

Book III

Catholic Mass

Reception of Holy Communion

The priest genuflects, rises, and says:

P. Panem coelestem accipiam et nomen Domini invocabo.	P. I will take the bread of heaven, and will call upon the name of the Lord.

Taking the Sacred Host with his left hand, the priest repeats the following prayer three times while striking his breast each time, and the bell is rung each of the three times.

P. Domine, non sum dignus ut intres sub tectum meum: sed tantum dic verbo, et sanabitur anima mea.	P. Lord, I am not worthy that thou shouldst enter under my roof; but only say the word, and my soul shall be healed.

Communion of the Faithful

After the priest receives Holy Communion, he gives it to the clergy in the sanctuary next and then goes to the altar or communion rail to give Holy Communion to the faithful (people in the congregation who are baptized Catholics and in the state of grace — not conscious of any mortal sins).

Holding the Sacred Host in his right hand, the priest makes the sign of the cross with it and says:

P. Corpus Domini nostri Jesu Christi custodiat animam meam in vitam aeternam. Amen.	P. May the Body of our Lord Jesus Christ keep my soul unto life everlasting. Amen.

The priest himself then receives Holy Communion and after a brief meditation continues:

P. Quid retribuam Domino pro omnibus quae retribuit mihi? Calicem salutaris accipiam, et nomen Domini invocabo Dominum, et ab inimicis meis salvus ero.	P. What shall I render unto the Lord for all the things that he hath rendered unto me? I will take the chalice of salvation and will call upon the name of the Lord. With high praises will I call upon the Lord, and I shall be saved from all mine enemies.

The priest takes the chalice in his right hand and makes the sign of the cross with it, saying:

P. Sanguis Domini nostri Jesu Christi custodiat animam meam in vitam aeternam. Amen.	P. May the Blood of our Lord Jesus Christ keep my soul unto life everlasting. Amen.

The priest himself then drinks of the chalice.

Here the server recites the *Confiteor* in the name of the communicants, and the priest responds with the *Misereatur* and the *Indulgentiam*.

The priest, holding the ciborium, faces the people and holds up a broken segment from his original host. Before all the communicants, he says:

P. Ecce Agnus Dei, ecce Qui tollit peccata mundi.	P. Behold the Lamb of God, behold him who taketh away the sins of the world.
R: Domine, non sum dignus, ut intres sub tectum meum: sed tantum dic verbo, et sanabitur anima mea. (Repeated three times.)	R: Lord, I am not worthy that thou shouldst enter under my roof; but only say the word, and my soul shall be healed. [Repeated three times.]

Here the lay faithful come forward to the Communion rail to receive our Lord in the Sacrament of Holy Communion. The priest places a host directly on the tongue of each communicant as he kneels. Communicants say nothing and don't take Communion in the hand in the Extraordinary form. While he administers Holy Communion to each person, the priest says:

P. Corpus Domini nostri Jesu Christi custodiat animam tuam in vitam aeternam.	P. May the Body of our Lord Jesus Christ keep your soul unto life everlasting.
R: Amen.	R: Amen.

The Council of Trent (in the 16th century) solemnly defined the dogma that the faithful do not have to receive both the consecrated wine (Precious Blood) and the consecrated host in order to receive Holy Communion because in either the host or in the chalice are *both* the Body and Blood, Soul and Divinity of Christ. In other words, when Catholics receive the host they de facto receive both the Body and the Blood of Christ. Only the priest must consume both elements.

When all have received Communion, the priest returns to the altar and replaces the ciborium in the tabernacle. He then purifies with wine in the chalice, saying:

P. Quod ore sumpsimus Domine, pura mente capiamus: et de munere temporali fiat nobis remedium sempiternum.	P. Into a pure heart, O Lord, may we receive the heavenly food which has passed our lips; bestowed upon us in time, may it be the healing of our souls for eternity.

The priest then goes to the Epistle (right) side of the altar and, while the server pours wine and water over his fingers, says:

P. Corpus tuum, Domine, quod sumpsi, et Sanguis, quem potavi, adhaereat visceribus meis: et praesta, ut in me non remaneat scelerum macula, quem pura et sancta refecerunt sacramenta. Qui vivis et regnas in saecula saeculorum. Amen.	P. May thy Body, O Lord, which I have received, and thy Blood, which I have drunk, cleave to mine inmost parts: and do thou grant that no stain of sin remain in me, whom pure and holy mysteries have refreshed: Who livest and reignest world without end. Amen.

Book III

Catholic Mass

Post Communion Prayer

Before the Communion Prayer, the priest and congregation have the following exchange:

P. Dominus vobiscum.	P. May the Lord be with you.
S. Et cum spiritu tuo.	S. And with thy spirit.

At the Epistle side, the priest recites the Communion Prayer appropriate for the Mass being celebrated.

The priest then returns to the center, kisses the altar, turns toward the people, and says:

P. Dominus vobiscum.	P. The Lord be with you.
S. Et cum spiritu tuo.	S. And with thy spirit.
P. Ite, missa est.	P. Go, the Mass is ended.
S. Deo gratias.	S. Thanks be to God.

The priest bows over the altar and recites the following prayer, known as the *Placeat*, which summarizes the intention of the entire mass:

P. Placeat tibi sancta Trinitas, obsequium servitutis meae; et praesta, ut sacrificium, quod oculis tuae majestatis indignus obtuli, tibi sit acceptabile, mihique et omnibus, pro quibus illud obtuli, sit, te miserante, propitiabile. Per Christum Dominum nostrum. Amen.	P. May the lowly homage of my service be pleasing to thee, O most Holy Trinity: and do thou grant that the sacrifice which I, all unworthy, have offered up in the sight of thy majesty, may be acceptable to thee, and, because of thy loving kindness, may avail to atone to thee for myself and for all those for whom I have offered it up. Through Christ our Lord. Amen.

Blessing

The priest kisses the altar, and at the word *Pater*, turns toward the people, blesses them, saying:

P. Benedicat vos omnipotens Deus, Pater, et Filius, et Spiritus Sanctus.	P. May almighty God, the Father, and the Son, and the Holy Ghost, bless you.
S. Amen.	S. Amen.

Last Gospel

The priest now goes to the Gospel (left) side of the altar; he makes the sign of the cross, first upon the altar, and then upon his forehead, lips, and heart, and then he reads the Last Gospel:

P. Dominus vobiscum.	P. The Lord be with you.
S. Et cum spiritu tue.	S. And with thy spirit.
P. Initium sancti Evangelii secundum Ioannem:	P. The beginning of the Holy Gospel, according to St. John:
In prinicipio erat Verbum, et Verbum erat apud Deum, et Deus erat Verbum. Hoc erat in principio apud Deum. Omnia per ipsum facta sunt, et sine ipso factum est nihil quod factum est. In ipso vita erat, et vita erat lux hominum: et lux in tenebris lucet, et tenebrae eam non comprehenderunt. Fuit homo missus a Deo, cui nomen erat Joannes. Hic venit in testimonium, ut testimonium perhiberet de lumine, ut omnes crederent per illum. Non erat ille lux, sed ut testimonium perhiberet de lumine. Erat lux vera quae illuminat omnem hominem venientem in hunc mundum. In mundo erat, et mundus per ipsum factus est, et mundus eum non cognovit. In propria venit, et sui eum non receperunt. Quotquot autem receperunt eum, dedit eis potestatem filios Dei fieri, his qui credunt in nomine ejus. Qui non ex sanguinibus, neque ex voluntate carnis, neque ex voluntate viri, sed ex Deo nati sunt. (Here all genuflect) *et verbum caro factum est,* et habitavit in nobis et vidimus gloriam ejus, gloriam quasi unigeniti a Patre, plenum gratiae et veritatis.	In the beginning was the Word, and the Word was with God, and the Word was God. The same was in the beginning with God. All things were made by him, and without him was made nothing that was made. In him was life, and the life was the light of men: and the light shineth in darkness, and the darkness did not comprehend it. There was a man sent from God, whose name was John. This man came for a witness to give testimony of the light, that all men might believe through him. He was not the light, but was to give testimony of the light. That was the true light which enlighteneth every man that cometh into this world. He was in the world, and the world was made by him, and the world knew him not. He came unto his own, and his own received him not. But as many as received him, to them he gave great power to become the sons of God: to them that believe in his name: who are born, not of blood, nor of the will of the flesh, nor of the will of man, but of God. And [here all genuflect] *the word was made flesh, and dwelt among us,* and we saw his glory, the glory as of the only begotten of the Father, full of grace and truth.
S. Deo gratias.	S. Thanks be to God.

Book III

Catholic Mass

Prayers after Low Mass

Pope Leo XIII in 1884 asked that the Ave Maria, Salve Regina, and prayer to St. Michael the Archangel be prayed at the end of every Low Mass for the safety of the Church. During that time, the territory of the former Papal States, which had been ruled by the popes since the eighth century, were experiencing great unrest due to the unification of Italy in the late 19th century. The Papal States became part of the new kingdom of Italy, and Vatican City emerged in 1929 as an independent country through a concordat (treaty) signed with Prime Minister Mussolini.

The Leonine Prayers continued even after the Concordat recognized the pope as indepenedent sovereign and Vatican City as a separate nation. The prayers are continued because wars and attacks on the Church still happen around the world from time to time, and prayers for peace should continue.

After Low Mass, the priest kneels at the altar steps and says the following prayers with the people:

Ave Maria

Ave Maria is Latin for *Hail Mary,* which is the prayer taken verbatim from Luke's Gospel when the Archangel Gabriel announces to the Virgin Mary that she is to be the mother of the Savior and she in turn is greeted by her cousin Elizabeth, then pregnant with John the Baptist.

P. Ave Maria, gratia plena, Dominus tecum. Benedicta tu in mulieribus, et benedictus fructus ventris tui, Jesus. Sancta Maria, Mater Dei, ora pro nobis peccatoribus, nunc, et in hora mortis nostrae. Amen. (Repeat three times.)	P. Hail Mary, full of grace, the Lord is with thee. Blessed art thou amongst women, and blessed is the fruit of thy womb, Jesus. Holy Mary, Mother of God, pray for us sinners, now, and at the hour of our death. Amen. [Repeat three times.]

Salve Regina

Hail Holy Queen is the translation of the Latin phrase *salve regina.* This is a hymn to the Virgin Mary that comes from the Middle Ages, when the monks and nuns would chant this before they prayed night prayer.

P. Salve Regina, Mater misericordiae. Vita, dulcedo, et spes nostra, salve. Ad te clamamus exsules filii Hevae. Ad te Suspiramus, gementes et flentes in hac lacrimarum valle. Eja ergo, Advocata nostra, illos tuos misericordes oculos ad nos converte. Et Jesum, benedictum a fructum ventris tui, nobis post hoc exsilium ostende. O clemens, o pia, o dulcis Virgo Maria. Ora pro nobis, sancta Dei Genitrix.	P. Hail, Holy Queen, Mother of mercy, our life, our sweetness, and our hope! To thee do we cry, poor banished children of Eve, to thee do we send up our sighs, mourning and weeping in this valley of tears. Turn then, most gracious Advocate, thine eyes of mercy towards us, and after this our exile show unto us the blessed fruit of thy womb, Jesus. O clement, O loving, O sweet Virgin Mary. Pray for us, O Holy Mother of God.
S. Ut digni efficiamur promissionibus Christi.	S. That we be made worthy of the promises of Christ.
P. Oremus. Deus refugium nostrum et virtus, populum ad te clamantem propitius respice; et intercedente gloriosa et immaculata Virgine Dei Genitrice Maria, cum beato Josepho ejus Sponso, ac beatis Apostolis tuis Petro et Paulo, et omnibus Sanctis, quas pro conversione peccatorum, pro libertate et exaltatione sanctae Matris Ecclesiae, preces effundimus, misericors et benignus exaudi. Per eumdem Christum Dominum nostrum. Amen.	P. Let us pray. O God, our refuge and our strength, look down with favor upon thy people who cry to thee; and through the intercession of the glorious and immaculate Virgin Mary, Mother of God, of her spouse, Blessed Joseph, of thy holy apostles, Peter and Paul, and all the saints, mercifully and graciously hear the prayers which we pour forth to thee for the conversion of sinners and for the liberty and exaltation of holy mother Church. Through the same Christ our Lord. Amen.

Book III

Catholic Mass

St. Michael

The priest prays to St. Michael the Archangel:

P. Sancte Michael Archangele, defende nos in praelio. Contra nequitiam et insidias diaboli esto praesidium. Imperet illi Deus, supplices deprecamur. Tuque princeps militiae caelestis, Satanam aliosque spiritus malignos, qui ad perditionem animarum pervagantur in mundo divina virtute in infernum detrude. Amen.	P. St. Michael, the archangel, defend us in battle. Be our protection against the malice and snares of the devil. We humbly beseech God to command him. And do thou, O prince of the heavenly host, by the divine power thrust into hell Satan and the other evil spirits who roam through the world seeking the ruin of souls. Amen.

Chapter 4

The Tools of the Catholic Mass

A lot goes into a Catholic Mass, and every element of it has a history and significance, from the volumes that inform the readings to the color of the cloth draped over the altar. Those details can vary by rite and by day. In this chapter, you find out about the many physical components of the Catholic Mass, how they differ, and what they mean.

Liturgical Books

Here you get to know the different manuals and textbooks used in Catholic worship. The books that document official rituals have been painstakingly researched and translated so that they conform to Catholic doctrine and are faithful to Catholic liturgy. The Holy Mass is the most central act of Catholic prayer, and the books used at Mass are most important.

Lectionary

The lectionary is a collection of selected passages from the Bible used as Scripture readings for the Mass. The current Catholic lectionary is contained in two books. Volume I is readings for Sundays, solemnities, and feasts of the Lord and the saints, and Volumes II–IV are readings for weekdays and other Masses.

The scriptural readings and responsorial chants used in the Liturgy of the Word during Mass are all contained in the lectionary. The readings from the Bible and chants between the readings are the main part of the Liturgy of the Word. Both the selection and the arrangement of texts follow the Roman *Ordo Lectionem Missae* that was authorized in the apostolic constitution *Missale Romanum* of April 3, 1969, and published by decree of the Congregation for Divine Worship on May 29, 1969. The National Conference of Catholic Bishops later authorized it for use in the diocese of the United States.

The Scripture during the Mass

The practice of reading passages from the Bible in liturgical settings dates back to the Jewish tradition in Old Testament times. In those days, and today, the reading from the Torah, the sacred scroll containing the word of God, was and is the central feature in the liturgy of the synagogue. In the Temple of Jerusalem, the people of Israel had a tradition of reading excerpts from the Bible and singing the psalms. The fourth chapter of Luke's Gospel indicates that Jesus went into the local synagogue in Nazareth and, during the Sabbath service, stood up and read to the people a messianic passage from the Book of the Prophet Isaiah which Jesus dramatically applied to himself when he said "today this Scripture has been fulfilled in your hearing."

The early Christians quickly adapted the Jewish custom of reading passages from the Old Testament in their liturgical assemblies. The New Testament book the Acts of the Apostles refers to the use of readings from Scripture by early Christians when they gathered for the liturgy.

The readings cycles

Until the Second Vatican Council (1962–1965), Western (Latin Rite) Catholic Christians used a single-volume Missal that had all the Scripture readings assigned in a one-year format. The same readings were repeated every year for every weekend and weekday. After the Council, the Missal was divided into two separate books, the lectionary (which contains only Bible readings) and the sacramentary (which contains only Mass prayers). Furthermore, the lectionary was subdivided:

- ✔ The readings in weekdays Masses are more or less chronological and follow an alternating two year cycle (odd years being Year I and even years being Year II).

- ✔ The readings in Sunday Masses follow an independent three-year cycle (A, B, C). The Gospel of Matthew is read in Year A; Mark in Year B; and Luke in Year C. The Gospel of John is read periodically throughout all three years from time to time.

In response to the directives of the Second Vatican Council, the Concillium for the Implementation of the Constitution on the Sacred Liturgy allowed the various Catholic dioceses around the world to develop their own lectionaries. The United States Conference of Catholic Bishops (USCCB) developed the *Lectionary for Mass* using passages from the *New American Bible.* They selected and assigned the readings for Sundays, feasts, weekdays, Masses of the saints, and other special occasions.

Book of the Gospels

The Book of the Gospels contains all four of the Gospels and is used by the celebrant when he reads or chants the Gospel during Mass. The use of the Book of the Gospels is optional because the readings are included in the lectionary for everyday use. However, the Book of the Gospels is the only other item carried in the opening processional at Mass along with the processional cross and candles.

When the deacon or lector reaches the altar, he bows in veneration and places the Gospel Book upon the altar, where it remains until the Alleluia, at which time the priest or deacon retrieves the book and walks with it to the ambo. The book is incensed before it is read and remains at the ambo through the duration of Mass.

When the bishop is celebrating Mass, the Book of the Gospels is brought to him after the reading is proclaimed, and he reverences (kisses) it. After that gesture, everyone may sit. If the celebrant is a priest, the deacon reverences the book (or the priest alone in the absence of a deacon).

Book III

Catholic Mass

Roman pontifical

The Roman pontifical contains the text for special services, such as ordinations, confirmations, rites for dedicating churches, initiation rites, Episcopal services, and more. It is used by the bishop when he is celebrant for any of these services. In Latin, this text is referred to as the *Pontificale* or the *Pontificale Romanum.*

In addition to detailing the bishop's rites, the pontifical contains various historical pontifical manuscripts developed gradually throughout the Middle Ages. They became standardized in the Western Church as various popes issued normative versions that became known as *Roman pontificals.*

The pontifical includes both the texts that are used and the directions for performing each particular ritual, which are known as the rubrics for the liturgical celebration. But the pontifical does not include the rules or directions for the celebration of Mass or praying the Breviary.

Roman Ritual

Although texts for bishops were in common use by the early Middle Ages, priests didn't have a widely accepted text until the 17th century. Priests in the Middle Ages used many different local handbooks to guide their administration of various blessings and ceremonies until the publication of the Roman Ritual by Pope Paul V in 1614.

The *Rituale Romanum* (Roman Ritual) is now one of the official books of the Roman Rite. It contains all the blessings and services performed by the priest that are not contained in the Missal or Breviary. However, it remains the least uniform of all the liturgical books in the Western Church.

In keeping with a desire for uniformity that was growing in the Western Church after the Council of Trent, many books were issued by the Church. In 1586, Cardinal Santorio printed a handbook of different rites to be used by priests, and this book became the foundation of the Roman Ritual that was published by Pope Paul V in 1614.

Pope Paul V didn't abolish all other collections of blessings and sacred rituals, so the Roman Ritual was never meant to be the only text used by the Church on these occasions. As a result, many of the old local rituals from long ago have been preserved in churches around the world. Many countries have retained their own proper and legitimate traditions for marriages, visitations of the sick, and numerous special processions, blessings, and blessings that are not in the Roman Ritual.

The Roman Ritual itself is divided into ten sections, all but the first of which are then subdivided into chapters. Many of these blessings and practices remain in daily use in the Church. But many religious practices that are considered by some Catholics as *old fashioned* or *old-time* are also preserved in the Church through the Roman Ritual.

Today, the one volume Roman Ritual of the pre–Vatican II days has been replaced by separate books of the Roman Ritual for each sacrament, blessings, and exorcism.

Sacramentary (Missal)

The sacramentary, sometimes called the *Mass book,* is the collection of prayers that the celebrant uses for the celebration of the Liturgy of the Eucharist. Before the Second Vatican Council, a single book, the Roman Missal, had all the Bible readings and all the Mass prayers. After the Council, Pope Paul VI authorized the separation of the two into a lectionary of

Scripture readings (used during the Liturgy of the Word) and a sacramentary for altar prayers (used in the Liturgy of the Eucharist).

With the revised English translation of November 27, 2011, the word *Missal* will again be used for the Mass prayers said by the priest and deacon at Mass, replacing the word *sacramentary*. The new Missal issued then will be for use by all English-speaking nations; however, each Episcopal Conference of Bishops will authorize a tailored edition that includes particular feasts for that country and incorporates specific dispensations and regulations unique to that locality.

Unlike the original pre–Vatican II Missal, the new Missal will not contain the Bible passages; they will continue to be in the lectionary, a separate book. Keeping the readings, responsorial psalms, and verses for the Gospel acclamation in the lectionary preserves the important distinction between the parts of Mass.

The Eucharistic prayer, contained in the sacramentary, is an expression of gratitude and a means of growth in holiness. It is the center and summit of the Mass. Following are the main aspects of the Eucharistic prayer:

- **Thanksgiving:** The priest praises and thanks the Father in the name of the entire people of God.

- **Acclamation:** The entire liturgical assembly sings or recites the *Sanctus,* or *Holy, holy,* which acclaims the greatness of God.

- **Epiclesis:** The Church (through the priest) calls on the power of God to ask that the gifts of bread and wine be changed into the Body and Blood of Jesus.

- **Institutional narrative and consecration:** Jesus's sacrifice is celebrated with the words that he used when taking the bread and wine at the Last Supper.

- **Anamnesis:** The Church keeps the memorial requested by Jesus by recalling his Passion, Death, and Resurrection.

- **Offering:** The Church offers the spotless victim to the Father in the Holy Spirit as the assembled faithful offer themselves through Christ the Mediator to an ever more complete union with the Father. The wheat bread and grape wine are offered as Jesus did at the Last Supper. Christ himself is also offered to the Father as a sacrifice to save the souls of the human race.

- **Intercessions:** Prayers are offered by the Church for all its members, both the living and the deceased, who are called to share in the salvation purchased by Christ's sacrifice.

- **Final doxology:** The assembly of the faithful says *amen* to the praise and gratitude offered by the Church to God.

Book III

Catholic Mass

Eastern Catholic books

The Eastern Catholic Church has several liturgical families that are further delineated as separate autonomous Churches in union with Rome. Many of the words used to describe their books, vessels, and vestments have Greek names because the Eastern Church traces itself to the patriarchates of Antioch, Alexandria, and Constantinople that were located in the Eastern part of the Roman Empire.

Following are the Eastern books:

- **Apostolos (Epistle Book):** This book contains Bible readings from the Acts of the Apostles and the New Testament Epistles, arranged according to the liturgical calendar.

- **Archieratikon:** This is the bishop's liturgical service book, which is used when celebrating a Hierarchical Divine Liturgy (formal Divine Liturgy where several prelates and dignitaries are present as opposed to the typical parish liturgy with just the pastor and a deacon). The book contains pontifical editions of the Divine Liturgies of St. John Chrysostom and St. Basil the Great, as well as the Liturgy of the Presanctified Gifts and other Episcopal services, such as ordinations.

- **Euchologion:** Taken from the Greek word for *book of prayers,* the Euchologion is similar to the Roman sacramentary containing the Mass prayers of the priest, deacon, and bishop. The Great (Mega) Euchologion contains all the prayers for the priest to celebrate Divine Liturgy and the sacraments. The Small (Mikron) Euchologion has the blessings and other minor ceremonies.

- **Evangelion (Gospel Book):** Sometimes called the *Tetraevangelion* (Four Gospels), the Evangelion is the Book of the Gospels. It is arranged according to the liturgical calendar. Normally it's kept on the altar in a metal case decorated with icons of the evangelists.

- **Hieratikon:** The Hieratikon, or *Liturgikon,* is the book of the priest. It contains parts of the Mega Euchologion like prayers for Divine Liturgy and for Vespers and Orthros (also called *Matins* or the *Office of Readings*).

- **Octoechos:** Octoechos is the book of the eight tones, an eight-week cycle of liturgical chants used in sacred worship.

Liturgical Vestments

The idea of wearing distinctive clothing for public ceremonies is not unique to Christianity and, in fact, can't even be attributed to Christianity. Most of the priests or officiates of ancient religions wore distinguishing robes, and

Jewish priests wore special vestments when sacrificing bulls or other animals at the Temple in Jerusalem. Rabbis in synagogues wear special ceremonial dress when reading the Torah and proclaiming its contents.

This section describes the attire worn by Catholic priests and explains its meaning. Trust us, style and fashion sense have little to do with the robes and vestments that priests wear when presiding over a Mass.

The origins of liturgical vestments

Catholic Christianity, with its roots in Judaism, borrowed some elements of *vesture,* or apparel, from Temple worship in Jerusalem. Other elements came from more pedestrian origins, such as Roman or Greek daily wear. Tunics and togas worn by average citizens became a pattern for Catholic ceremonial vestments worn by the clergy.

Most vestments worn in the Roman (Western) Church borrow their styles from the unique pattern of public dress characteristic of officials in the ancient Mediterranean world, especially those in imperial Rome. Likewise, the attire worn in the Byzantine Empire greatly influenced the vestments of Eastern Catholic clergy.

Fashions have changed much in the last 21 centuries, but Roman Catholic vestments have largely remained the same. There have been adaptations and even some innovations, but the style is generally the same as it was in the early Church.

The chasuble, the sleeveless outer garment worn by priests, is a prime example of how vestments have changed and yet remained the same. In Roman times the chasuble was long, flowing, and conical in shape, but by the Gothic area it had been shortened, showing more of the sleeve of the underlying vestment. It changed again in the Baroque era, this time taking the shape of two flaps worn over the shoulder and tied at the waist.

What's worn today

The General Instruction of the Roman Missal 2011 explains the essential uses and requirements of Roman vestments: They are used to identify the sign of a particular office of the celebrant, such as bishop, priest, or deacon; they are to contribute to the dignity of the Mass; colors are to be employed throughout the liturgical year and for each Sacrament; and they are to be made of dignified materials and fabrics.

Book III

Catholic Mass

Why is so much emphasis and care placed on these items? Quite simply, they are symbols of the sacredness of the Holy Mass, which is instituted by the Lord Jesus Christ on the eve of his crucifixion at the Last Supper.

Shared vestments in both the East and the West

Pope John Paul the Great once described the Catholic Church as having two lungs, the East and West (also called Latin). Each has its own liturgical style, dress, and regulations. What binds the two is that they celebrate the same Mass in which Christ's sacrifice is made present.

A few vestments are shared by both traditions: the cassock, the biretta, and the zucchetto. The styles of each are different for each tradition, but the purpose and symbolism remain the same.

Cassock

The *cassock* is a floor-length black robe that is considered the ordinary street attire of clerics. In the West, two styles are acceptable: Roman, with 33 fastening buttons and a sash; and a semi-Jesuit model with fasteners and snaps in place of buttons. Latin Rite priests wear a black cassock with black buttons. Monsignors (Chaplains of His Holiness) wear a black cassock with purple trim and a purple sash or (for Prelates of Honor) a purple cassock. Bishops wear a black cassock with red trim and a purple sash, and cardinals wear a red cassock with red sash. The pope is the only person allowed to wear an all-white cassock, but in tropical climates, priests and bishops can wear white with black or purple buttons and trim, respectively.

Because of a strong anti-Catholic climate in the 19th century, priests in the United States wear a black clerical suit rather than the cassock when outside the church or rectory.

In the Eastern Church the inner cassock, *anteri,* is also black, but it has only a few buttons on the shoulder for fastening. Byzantine Catholics also have a secondary cassock, called a *ryasa* or *exorason,* worn over the inner one.

Biretta

The *biretta* is a square cap, usually with three peaks (ridges) on the top, that's worn by all clerics. A four-cornered biretta is worn by someone who has a doctoral degree, with green pom and trim for canon law; red for theology; and blue for philosophy. The biretta is worn in the Extraordinary form of Mass (sometimes called the Traditional Latin Mass, Pre-Vatican II Mass, or Tridentine Mass) by the clergy and removed at different times of the Mass. Celebrants and concelebrants in the Ordinary form (also called the Vatican II, Paul VI, or New Mass; the common Mass used in most parishes) normally do not wear the biretta during Mass, but visiting prelates (high-ranking clergy) and other clergy who are merely attending wear theirs. It can also be worn with a cassock as street attire, but that's usually only done in predominantly Catholic countries.

A celebrating bishop (or archbishop) or cardinal wears a *miter* (a different headdress) instead at Mass, both Ordinary and Extraordinary. The color depends on rank: A priest wears black, a bishop wears purple, and a cardinal wears red. *Kalymavchion* is the stovepipe Eastern Catholic version of the biretta, and its color denotes rank and office.

Zucchetto

A *zucchetto* is a small, round skullcap that is reserved normally for prelates. Because of its shape, the name is derived from the Italian word for gourd. Zucchettos are marked by color: Bishops wear purple, cardinals wear red, and the pope wears white. Bishops and cardinals wear them at Mass, except from the Sanctus until after Communion. Bishops, cardinals, and the pope wear them at Mass with a miter. Clerics (priests and deacons) can also wear a black biretta at Mass (especially in the Extraordinary form), and certain religious orders have retained the custom of donning them in corresponding color of their habits. Only prelates may wear the zucchetto under the biretta; lower clerics (priests and deacons) can wear birettas only at Mass. Eastern Catholic Clergy wear a *skoufos,* which is a soft cap worn much like the zucchetto is by the Latin Rite clergy.

Western Rite vestments

The vestments described in this section are worn by priests in the Western Roman Catholic Church.

Surplice

The *surplice* is a white garment with loose, wide sleeves that is worn over a cassock and typically made from lace, linen, wool, or cotton. It is used by the clergy in services or celebrations of sacraments outside of Mass, with a stole for the ordained. Clerics also wear a surplice with a stole at Holy Communion when attending Mass in choir dress (liturgical attire for clerics who are not concelebrating). Spiritually the surplice represents the white garment that the baptized receives at Baptism.

Mozzetta and rochet

The surplice can be worn by those who are not ordained, such as acolytes and choristers, but it is not worn by prelates, such as bishops, cardinals, and popes. Prelates wear *rochets,* knee-length garments with narrow sleeves, for non-Eucharistic functions. A rochet is worn with a *mozzetta,* a short cape, draped over it. Like a surplice, a rochet is worn in conjunction with a stole. In recent times, the pope has reverted to an earlier custom of wearing a mozzetta of white ermine during Christmas and Eastertide and a velvet one with white ermine trim the rest of the time, with the stole draped over it.

Book III

Catholic Mass

Amice

The *amice* is a rectangular piece of white cloth that has two long ribbons attached from the upper corners of the material, usually with an embroidered cross positioned in the middle. It is always worn under the alb (see the next section) and over the street clothes of the priest (either a cassock or clerical shirt) and is tucked in under the neck. The ribbons are fastened around the waist. Its uses are both practical and spiritual. For practical purposes, the amice protects the vestments that are worn. Spiritually, it is called the *helmet of salvation,* which expresses the idea of putting aside street clothes and enveloping oneself in Christ. If the style of alb worn for Mass covers the Roman Collar, the amice isn't necessary, but some clergy wear it anyway for the symbolic value.

Alb

An *alb* takes its name from the Latin word for white, and it symbolizes purity. This long, flowing gown is worn over the cassock and amice. Albs are normally made from a combination of linen, wool, and now polyester, and sometimes have lace bottoms and cuffs. An alb can be worn loose over a cassock, or it can be tied at the top or made in square yoke shape, in which case an amice has to be worn underneath. The more contemporary style has a high collar and is fashioned for ease. An alb must always be worn underneath vestments (chasuble or dalmatic) for celebrants and concelebrants of Holy Mass. If a cleric is in choir, he then only wears the cassock and surplice.

The alb was an everyday garment for the Roman citizens, but for a priest it is a daily reminder that cleric is ordained to the priesthood of Jesus Christ.

Cincture

The *cincture* is a cord that girds the waist of the alb and is worn by priests and bishops to remind them of their commitment to chastity and purity. It often has tassels at the end and can be made in the liturgical color of the vestment worn. Priests and bishops tie the cincture into two loops in the front so that the stole may go through the loops to fasten it. Deacons and acolytes often wear cinctures, but theirs are fastened on the side. While some albs do not need cinctures, many clergy wear them anyway for the symbolic value.

Stole

The *stole* is a scarf-life garment that marks the ordination of the man wearing it. Whenever a cleric wears an alb, a stole must also be worn to distinguish rank and office. When it's worn over the left shoulder, drawn across the chest and back toward the lower right, it signifies the office of a deacon. In the Extraordinary form of the Roman Rite, priests wear the stole crisscrossed, and bishops wear stoles straight up and down over the neck. In the Ordinary form of the Roman Rite, both priests and bishops wear the stole in the same fashion, hanging straight down around the neck.

During the celebration of the Holy Mass, a stole is worn by deacons under a vestment called a dalmatic and by priests and bishops under a chasuble. It also can be worn over a cassock and surplice for devotions and administrations of some sacraments outside of Mass. Usually stoles are made to match the outer vestment of the clergy, but for non-Eucharistic celebrations they can also be worn in the same liturgical colors as chasubles and dalmatics. Stoles are also worn over choir dress, especially before receiving Holy Communion.

Dalmatic

Deacons sport an outer vestment at Mass known as a *dalmatic,* a long-sleeved tunic. It usually has a two bandings on either side of the panel front and back with two matching cross bandings. The name's origin is Dalmatia, a region of Croatia that lies opposite Italy on the Adriatic Sea. Secularly, it was a garb of rank and privilege. In AD 332, Pope St. Sylvester extended this garment to the order of deacons. It is made in the liturgical colors used at Mass and normally matches the main celebrant's chasuble. In the present Ordinary rite, a lighter version of the dalmatic is worn under a chasuble of a bishop. This signifies that the bishop has fullness of holy orders — deacon, priesthood, and episcopacy.

Tunic

A *tunic* is similar to a dalmatic and is worn in the Extraordinary form of the Mass by subdeacons. This vestment came in popular usage under Pope Gregory I in the seventh century. In the Ordinary form, this level was suppressed since 1972 when Pope Paul VI reformed the rites centering on the priesthood. When the Extraordinary form of the Mass is celebrated, priests often serve in the role of deacons and subdeacons and wear these vestments.

Maniple

No longer required in the Ordinary form of the Mass, the *maniple* is obligatory in the Extraordinary form. It's a band of cloth that is draped over the left arm of the celebrant and is often made of the same material and liturgical colors as the vestment being worn for Mass. It is only worn with either a chasuble, dalmatic, or tunic in a Solemn Mass.

Cope

A *cope* is a long cape fastened in front with clasps. Its origins are quite humble: Because churches were cold and unheated prior to the 20th century, copes provided warmth, and in processions that were led outside, copes provided a layer of protection from the elements. Made from beautiful and ornamental material, this vestment certainly adds solemnity to the celebration.

As a liturgical vestment it comes in the colors associated with the Mass. In the Extraordinary form of the Roman Rite, an archpriest wears a cope in Solemn High Masses. Also, the celebrant uses a cope in the Asperges Rite at

Book III

Catholic Mass

the beginning of Mass. In the Ordinary form, the cope is used only in ceremonies or Eucharistic celebrations outside of Mass. In addition to bishops and priests, deacons may also wear this vestment.

A cope may be worn on the rare occasions when a Rite of Funerals is celebrated in place of a Mass of Christian Burial. During Solemn celebrations of the Liturgy of the Hours, especially evening prayer, the celebrant (either priest or deacon) normally wears a cope. It can either be worn over an alb or cassock and surplice and always with a corresponding matching stole.

Humeral veil

The *humeral veil* is a rectangular vestment that is fastened in the center with clasps, allowing the end to be draped. It's often made of the same material as the cope it's worn with, but the color is generally either white or gold, although in the Extraordinary form of the Mass the humeral veil can be the color of the liturgical season.

In Benediction of the Blessed Sacrament, the officiating clergy covers his hands with the humeral veil and lifts the monstrance containing the Real Presence of the Lord in the Host for blessing of the congregants, and in the Extraordinary form of a Solemn Mass a subdeacon uses a humeral veil in order to hold the paten. The inside of the veil is often made with pockets, making it easier for the celebrant to hold the object. This vestment came into wide use in the Medieval period, and after the Council of Trent in the 16th century it became a normative vestment.

Miter

A *miter* is a type of ceremonial headgear worn by abbots, bishops, cardinals, and popes during Mass and other vested religious functions. It is used in both Western and Eastern Churches, though the style and shape are quite different.

In the Roman Rite (the Western Church), the miter is a tall folding triangular cap consisting of two parts, front and back, forming a peak, with two pieces of matching material suspended from it in the back. Normally, it is made of either white or gold material; however, it can be also of the liturgical color of the day. Byzantine and other Eastern Catholic bishops wear miters that resemble crowns.

Papal tiara

In previous years, popes typically wore a three-tier crown, known as the papal tiara, instead of a miter. The three tiers corresponded with the pope's responsibilities: teach (prophetic), sanctify (priestly), and shepherd (kingly). Paul VI (1963–1978) was the last one to wear the crown, as John Paul I (1978) declined it and John Paul II (1978–2005) followed the example of his immediate predecessor. The papal tiara was never formally suppressed, and any pope is free to use this ancient symbol, though the pallium (see the following section) seems to be the current favorite symbol of papal authority.

Pallium

A narrow band made out of wool worn over the chasuble during Mass by archbishops, the *pallium* is common to both the East and West. In the East it is named *omophor* and is a much wider band than in the West. In the West a pallium takes the shape of a *Y* and contains three golden spikes and six black crosses. They are made of wool from sheep raised by sisters of the Convent of St. Agnes. On the feast of this saint, the lambs are blessed because their wool will be made into these special articles and presented by the pope. The palliums are given to the new archbishops each year and usually are bestowed on the Feast of SS. Peter and Paul, June 29. Since the pope is the Bishop of Rome, in addition to being supreme head of the Universal Church and patriarch of the West, he, too, wears a pallium.

Buskins

Ceremonial liturgical stockings, *buskins,* are worn by bishops in the Extraordinary Rite of the Mass by a prelate. They are worn over the pant leg and come in the liturgical colors of the season. Originally used to protect the cleric from drafts in the days of no central heating in churches, they now have a more ceremonial and festive meaning (in other words, they're used for only the most formal of occasions). They are worn only with special ecclesiastical slippers instead of the common shoe. Often the coat of arms of the prelate is embossed on both the buskin and slipper.

Book III

Catholic Mass

Episcopal gloves

In Solemn Mass of the Extraordinary Rite, prelates also wear the *Episcopal gloves.* Although they can be made in the liturgical colors, most often the gloves are white. They are worn from the start of Mass until the offertory with the Episcopal ring worn on the outside. The gloves are seen as a symbol of purity. The coat of arms of the prelate is often embossed on the glove.

Pectoral crosses

Pectoral crosses are worn by prelates of both rites. When the prelate is wearing a suit, the cross is extended on a gold or silver chain and tucked into a side shirt pocket. With a cassock, it usually hangs on the chain in the center of the chest, and with the rochet and mozzetta, choir dress, it is often worn on a special ornate rope. This same rope is worn under the chasuble and over the alb when the prelate is celebrating Mass. The pectoral cross reflects the dignity of the office of bishop or abbot.

Crozier

A pastoral staff known as a *crozier* is used by a prelate during liturgical ceremonies and at Mass. It is the symbol of the governing office of the bishop. The shape is likened to a shepherd's staff; just as a shepherd watches over his flock, so does the bishop, the chief shepherd of the diocese, watch over his people. In the East the crosier is made in a *T* shape and is called *paterissa,* but it keeps the same meaning as in the Western Church.

The crozier is made of many different materials, ranging from rarer woods to fine metals. Some are ornately decorated with jewels and statuary or even the bishop's coat of arms on the crook or curved part of the staff.

Vimp

A veil or shawl worn over the shoulders of a server is known as a *vimp*. Like a humeral veil, a vimp is a rectangular piece of material fastened in the center. They often have pockets on the inside, allowing the servants to hold onto the bishop's miter and crozier. Practically, a vimp preserves the integrity of the item being held so that it doesn't get worn or dirty.

If a server wears a vimp and holds the crozier for the bishop, the crook should be faced in. Holding it facing out is reserved only for the bishop, as a sign of his openness to guide his flock.

Gremial

The *gremial* is a square piece of cloth with two ribbons at the top that tied around the waist of a celebrant for Mass. In both the Ordinary and Extraordinary Rites of the Mass, this vestment is used by the celebrant of Confirmation and Holy Orders. The bishop is seated during the anointing, and the gremial is placed over his lap to protect his other vestments from being stained by any chrism oil that may leak onto him. It is also used by the celebrant on Holy Thursday at the washing of feet.

In the Extraordinary form of the Mass, prelates use the gremial when seated at the singing of the Kyrie, Gloria, and creed by the choir. This type of gremial is more ornate and usually made to match the vestment. In days of old before central heating in churches, it served to keep the bishop warm during the liturgical ceremony.

Liturgical colors in the West

The General Instruction of the Roman Missal 2011 delineates the use of colors in the Ordinary Rite of the Mass in the West. The diverse colors in the liturgy demonstrate different religious meanings and mysteries of faith being celebrated. Vestments that are worn by the different ordained ministers and the accoutrement for the liturgy in the sanctuary correspond to the prescriptions of the day that can be found in a book known as the Ordo.

Many liturgical pieces change color for particular days. In addition to the vestments of the celebrant and deacons, the antependium of the altar — cloth draped over the altar, chalice veil, burse, and tabernacle veil — are usually coordinated to match the celebrant.

In the Ordinary form the chalice veil, burse, tabernacle veil, and antependium are optional. In the Extraordinary form they are mandatory, and the maniple, cope, humeral veil, and tunics are also used and should match the seasonal or festive color. On solemnities, the highest rank of feast in the church, and Sundays in which Vespers (evening prayer) is celebrated, the color of the anticipated day is normally changed, because liturgically the new day occurs after sundown (even though chronologically it doesn't happen until midnight).

Colors for the Ordinary form of the Roman Rite

For the Ordinary form, the Roman Rite uses the following colors:

- **White:** Used for festive seasons of Christmas and Easter; Holy Thursday; Our Lord's feast day; days of saints; and Feasts of the Blessed Virgin Mary, Angels, Conversion of St. Paul, Nativity of John the Baptist, John the Beloved Disciple, and the beatified. Exclusions include the Lord's Passion and days of martyrs. In addition, it is used for the Sacraments of Marriage, Baptism, First Holy Communion, Holy Orders, and Mass of Christian Burial in the United States of America. White is a symbol of joy, purity, and glory.

- **Red:** Used for Pentecost; Palm Sunday; Passion of the Lord; feasts of the holy cross, martyrs, Apostles, and evangelists (except for John the Beloved Disciple); and Confirmation. Red is a symbol of the burning charity of the martyrs and their generous sacrifice, tongues of fire of the Holy Spirit, and the blood shed by our Divine Lord.

- **Green:** Used in Ordinary Time. It is a symbol of hope in eternal life.

- **Violet or purple:** Used for seasons of Advent and Lent, Sacrament of Reconciliation, and Mass of Christian Burial. Purple is a symbol of penance and mortification.

- **Rose:** Used for Gaudete Sunday (the third Sunday in Advent) and Laetare Sunday (the fourth Sunday of Lent). It is a symbol that the Advent or Lent is half over and soon the Church will be celebrating the joyful season of Christmas or Easter.

- **Black:** Used for All Souls' Day, Masses for the Dead, and Mass of Christian Burial. Black is a symbol of mourning and signifies the sorrow of death.

- **Gold:** Can be used in place of white but is traditionally reserved for solemnities and very important feasts of saints. Often used in the season of Christmas. It is a symbol of richness and festivity.

Book III

Catholic Mass

Colors for the Extraordinary form of the Roman Rite

In the Extraordinary form, white, green, gold, and rose are used in the same ways as in the Ordinary form (see the preceding section). The following colors have different or additional uses:

- ✔ **Red:** Used for the blessing of palms and the procession on Palm Sunday (but not for Mass), Mass of the Holy Spirit, Pentecost, Confirmation, and feasts of the martyrs, Apostles, holy cross, and evangelists (except for John).

- ✔ **Purple:** Used for Ember days, Rogations days, three Sundays before Lent (Septuagesima, Sexagesima, and Quinquagesima), vigils of the Immaculate Conception, Epiphany, Assumption, and Pentecost. In addition, it is used for the seasons of Advent and Lent.

- ✔ **Black:** Used at all requiem Masses, All Souls' Day, and Good Friday (but not including Communion).

Eastern Rite vestments

Many of the vestments in the Eastern Catholic Church are similar to that of the West but with different names. However, distinct vesture peculiar to the Eastern Rite are also used. As with the Roman Rite, Eastern liturgical wear developed out of wear among members of Roman society, but over the years it was used less by ordinary people. Since the items fell out of use by society, the Church could preserve them with sacredness and special character.

- ✔ **Sticharion:** This floor-length, long-sleeved patterned garment is worn by all members of the clergy. Laity can also be dressed in it when they are performing liturgical functions, such as serving the Divine Liturgy. It is compared to the Western alb and is worn over the cassock. It is the oldest liturgical vestment. According to rank of the clergy, the sticharion may vary in weight and color.

- ✔ **Alb:** Like the Western Church's long flowing gown, the Eastern alb is usually white. However, priests and bishops can also wear red and light blue albs for feasts of Easter and the Blessed Mother. For a reader it's made of silk or similar fabric in the appropriate liturgical colors. Albs traditionally have inserts of darker fabric on the shoulders, sleeves, and bottom and are decorated with embroidery. The dark inserts symbolize the Blood shed by Christ during his Sacred Passion.

- ✔ **Orarion:** Deacons wear this long narrow strip of cloth over their left shoulder, extending to the ankle. It can also be worn by subdeacons. It's very similar to a deacon stole of the Western Rite, which is also worn across the shoulder.

✔ **Epitrachelion:** Priests and deacons use this stole, draped around the neck with two adjacent sides buttoned together, as a symbol of their priesthood.

✔ **Epimanikia:** These ornate cuffs are worn on the sleeves and tied. The deacon wears them beneath the alb, and priests and bishops wear them above.

✔ **Zone:** This cloth belt is worn by priests and bishops with a stole and a phelonion (see the following).

✔ **Phelonion:** This vestment for priests is a large, conical, sleeveless garment worn over all the other vestments. The front is cut away so it exposes the ornate matching stole and alb.

✔ **Sakkos:** Instead of wearing a phelonion, bishops wear this tunic. It reaches below the knees with wide sleeves and ornate trim and is buttoned at the sides.

✔ **Epigonation or palitsa:** This vestment is a stiff diamond-shaped cloth draped on the right side and suspended by one corner with strap over the left shoulder. It is reserved for bishops or priests who have been given a special recognition, much like scarlet color denotes monsignors in the West.

✔ **Omophorion:** A wide cloth band draped around the shoulders, this distinctive vestment is worn by bishops.

Liturgical colors in the East

The Eastern Church, which is made up of more than 13 rites, does not have a universal codified system for colors used in vestments. Generally, though, it keeps to the following liturgical norms:

✔ **Gold:** Like the color green in the Roman Rite, used in Ordinary Time

✔ **Light blue:** Feasts of the Blessed Virgin Mary

✔ **Purple or red:** Saturdays and Sundays during Lent

✔ **Red:** Holy Thursday; feasts of the cross, John the Baptist, and martyrs; Nativity Fasts; and Apostles' Fasts

✔ **Green:** Palm Sunday, Pentecost, and feasts of monastic saints

✔ **Black:** Weekdays during Lent and Holy Week, except Holy Thursday

✔ **White:** Easter, Christmas, feasts of the Lord, and funerals

Book III

Catholic Mass

Liturgical Vessels, Altar Linens, and Artifacts

In order for the Sacred Liturgy to operate effectively, it needs certain vessels, furnishings, and equipment in addition to vestments. The Church has always taught that we worship God not only with our minds but with also all our senses. Both the Eastern and Western Rites arrange a feast for the senses: music for the ears; vestments, architecture, vessels, furnishings, and art for the eyes; the reception of the Holy Eucharist for taste; incense and candles for smell; and holy water for the touch.

While the celebration of Mass can take place virtually anywhere — in homes, hospital rooms, or military camps, for instance — for the purposes of our discussion here, we refer to Masses that take place in a building consecrated to the Lord, a church.

In this section, you discover the significance of the various items you typically see in a Catholic Church. The Western or Latin Rite churches and Eastern Rite churches have some minor differences, but the two rites share quite a bit in common.

Common items for both East and West

Although the Eastern and Westerns Rites have many differences, the churches have some consistent features.

Altar

The *altar* is the primary piece of furniture in the church. It is a table that represents Christ, and at the beginning and end of Mass the priest kisses the altar as a sign of reverence for the Lord.

The altar is the furniture at which the Holy Sacrifice of the Mass is offered. Although the Bloody Sacrifice of Christ on the altar of the cross took place once and on Good Friday, it's renewed on the altars of the churches. Therefore, the Mass is not a new or different sacrifice, but rather the same sacrifice of Christ, just in an unbloody manner. Just as the cross was the pulpit for Christ in his office as Prophet (teacher), and throne for Christ in his office as King (leader), the cross was finally the altar for Christ in his office as priest (sanctifier).

The same Jesus who willingly gave up his life on the cross at Calvary on Good Friday is the same Jesus who renews that same sacrifice on the altar at every Holy Mass and Divine Liturgy.

The altar has taken many shapes through the years. In the Extraordinary form of the Roman Rite, the altar often contains a high back drop, *reredos,* made of either wood or marble, which holds the tabernacle and sometimes intricately carved statues of saints or angels. The altar should contain six candles and an altar cross on a ledge just above the mensa (flat, horizontal surface of the altar) where the Holy Mass takes place. The altar has to contain an altar stone that holds the relics of saints and martyrs. The shape of the altar is long and rectangular but not very deep. The relics and shape of the altar harkened back to the days in which Mass was celebrated on martyrs' tombs.

In some churches, especially in the Eastern Rite, a *baldachin* is built over the altar. Baldachins are canopies made of brocade fabric or solid materials, and historically they were used over royal thrones and beds to denote a special place. That meaning transferred to the Catholic Church, as well, and a four-post baldachin over the altar represents the specialness of the altar as the place of the Eucharistic Sacrifice. The most notable example of a baldachin was designed by Bernini and is over the pontifical altar at St. Peter's Basilica.

Tabernacle

The word *tabernacle* has Latin roots and means *a dwelling place.* In the Old Testament Moses was instructed by God to build a tabernacle to house the Ark of the Covenant.

In the Catholic Church, the tabernacle is where priests keep the Blessed Sacrament. After the consecration of the Mass, the consecrated hosts — the Holy Eucharist — that are left are placed in the tabernacle for safekeeping to be later removed and brought as Holy Communion to sick members of the congregation. The leftover consecrated hosts are not only for Holy Communion to the sick, but also just to be there in the tabernacle for adoration of God by the faithful. Often, Catholics spend time in quiet prayer outside of Mass but physically near the tabernacle knowing that it contains the Body and Blood, Soul and Divinity of Christ.

Tabernacles can take many shapes and can be placed on the old high altars with veils or be an *ambry* (a chest or cupboard) built into the wall. Near the tabernacle is a lamp, which is constantly lit to symbolize that the Real Presence of Jesus abides in the Sacrament and is reserved in the tabernacle.

Normally, the Holy Eucharist remains in the tabernacle in the sanctuary. On Holy Thursday it is removed and placed on an altar of Reservation and is not returned to the sanctuary until Easter.

Candles

Candles are used at Mass to signify Christ as the Light of the World. Candles were used to light the church in the days before electric lighting, but today they are used to spiritually note the Light of Christ. In the Ordinary Rite of the Mass, at least two candles are used. In the Extraordinary Rite, two candles are used for Low Mass without a bishop, four are used for Missa Cantata and Low Mass with a bishop, and six candles are used for High Mass. A seventh candle is used in the presence of a bishop.

Candles in the Extraordinary Rite are made of at least 51 percent or more beeswax to symbolize the pure flesh of Jesus. In the Ordinary Rite, candles can be made from oil, usually burning with a wick in a white canister made to look like a beeswax candle.

In the Ordinary Rite of the Mass, servers often carry processional candles and flank the crucifer (the server who carries the cross mounted on a pole, carried in procession at the beginning and end of Mass).

Vessels, artifacts, and linens in the Latin Rite

Some artifacts and vessels are common in each church, but a number of items are specific to the church of either rite.

Chalice

The *chalice* is the sacred vessel containing the wine and drop of water used at Mass. Catholics believe that after the consecration in which the sacred words of Institution are said, the wine turns into the substance of the Precious Blood of Christ. It is the noblest of church vessels, and many legends center on the chalice our Divine Lord used at the Last Supper, also called the Holy Grail.

As with many other vessels of the church, the chalice has taken many styles and shapes over the 21 centuries. The General Instruction of the Roman Missal 2011 reiterates a centuries-old custom on what elements can be used to make a chalice: The chalice should be made from precious metal with the inside gilded in gold or silver, and it should be made of a nonabsorbent material so the Precious Blood doesn't leak through. Some modern liturgists have been tempted to employ nonprecious material in the cup, such as cut crystal, hand-blown glass, alabaster, or rare woods. While incorporating these materials is acceptable, the inside of the cup must be gilded with either silver or gold to secure the Precious Blood from leaking through.

Ciborium

One of the earliest styles of the tabernacle, one that is often still used in Eastern Catholic churches, is type of vessel that looks like a dove. In the

Western Church the dove took the form of a *ciborium* — a covered chalice-like vessel that contains the Blessed Sacrament for distribution. At Mass the unconsecrated hosts that will be distributed to the congregants are placed in the ciborium. After Holy Communion is distributed, the remains are gathered into one ciborium and placed in the tabernacle.

Paten

The *paten* is the second-most illustrious vessel used in Mass (after the chalice). Patens made before the Second Vatican Council, and some still made today, are small disks designed to contain the main celebrant's host. Most patens used in the Ordinary form of the Roman Rite are dish-like and can contain not only the main celebrant's host, but also enough for the congregation.

Monstrance

The *monstrance* or *ostensorium* is a sacred vessel used in exposition, procession, and Benediction of the Most Blessed Sacrament. It stands on a base and rises to height of 2 feet, fanning out in a magnificent sunburst of rays made out of precious metal. The sole purpose is to show the *monstrare,* the Latin word for *consecrated host.* Smaller monstrances that contain relics are called *reliquaries.* The consecrated host is only in the monstrance when it is placed on the altar for public adoration and subsequent Benediction. Otherwise, the monstrance stays in a closet or cabinet or safe and the hosts remain in the tabernacle.

Candlesticks

Candlesticks simply hold the candles that are used for Mass. In the Ordinary form of the Roman Rite, at least two candles must be used, usually placed on either side of the altar. The candlesticks can be either floor-length and free-standing or placed atop the mensa (top, flat part) of the altar. They are usually made of brass and hold either beeswax candles or oil canisters.

Normally in Requiem Masses, the paschal candle and candlestick are used, but in Requiem Masses in the Extraordinary Rite of the Roman liturgy, six candlesticks are place around the bier of the coffin, known as the *catafalque,* instead of the paschal candlestick.

Thurible

Incense is burned at different points of the Mass, exposition and Benediction, Solemn celebration of the Liturgy of the Hours, or at Mass of Christian burial. The item used for burning is known as a *thurible,* or *censer.* Accompanying the censer is the incense boat that contains the aromatic resins to be burned. Thuribles were originally used in Jewish Temple services at the altar of incense. Spiritually, the burning of incense symbolizes prayers going to heaven, reflective of Psalm 140. It symbolizes adoration and worship of God. Practically, burning incense can help purify the air.

Thuribles can either be freestanding or carried at the end of chain by a person called a *thurifer* during the liturgy. In the Byzantine Rite the thurible often has little bells on the chains of the censer. During the celebration of Mass in the Roman Rite and exposition and Benediction of the Blessed Sacrament, the thurifer carries the thurible, which contains burning charcoal. Incense is placed on the burning charcoal and then taken by the celebrant to be used for the incensation. In the Solemn celebration of the Liturgy of the Hours, the handheld thurible is still used; however, recently the stationary style of thurible that's located near the altar has also been permitted. When singing the Benedictus (at Morning Prayer) or the Magnificat (at Evening Prayer), incense is placed in the urn containing burning charcoals.

Bells

Bells are used in the liturgy along with chanting, singing, and the use of other musical instruments. The *Sanctus bells* are held by the servers and used specifically at the Consecration of the Mass. In the Ordinary form of the Roman Rite, they're used four times at the Mass: at the epiclesis, or when the priest invokes the Holy Spirit to bless the Eucharistic bread and wine; at the elevation of the host after the consecration; at the elevation of the Precious Blood after the consecration; and at the reception of Holy Communion by the priest. In the Extraordinary form of the Roman Rite, the Sanctus bells are also rung at the "Holy, Holy . . . ," or Sanctus, which is where they derived their name.

Other bells are also used to prepare the people for the celebration of Mass. The sacristy bell is sometimes rung before Mass to signal people to stand and greet the main celebrant. Bells in the church's tower are used to call people to Mass and are sometimes used in place of the altar bell at the consecration of Mass. They are also used at the Mass of Christian Burial after the closing prayer, and they're used more plentifully at the end of a wedding ceremony. Bells can be rung at end of the angelus or at the recitation of the Regina Caeli during the Easter Season.

Bells are not used in the liturgy between the singing of the Gloria on Holy Thursday and the singing of the Gloria at the Easter Vigil Mass.

Missal stand

A *missal stand* is, quite simply, a stand to hold the missal. It's not always used in Mass in the Ordinary Rite but is a requirement in the Extraordinary form of the Roman Rite. The Roman Missal is placed on the stand so the celebrant of the liturgy can better see it. In the past, the stand has taken the form of a pillow made from beautiful brocades, but it also can be composed of wood, brass, or silver.

Lavabo bowl

The *lavabo bowl* takes its name from the section of the liturgy in which the celebrant washes his hands before the consecration at the offertory. *Lavabo* is a Latin word denoting *washing*. It is also used in the Divine Liturgy of the Eastern Rite after the vesting of the priest before he approaches the altar. In addition to the ordinary use at the Mass, the lavabo bowl is used by the bishop after administering the Sacrament of Confirmation or Holy Orders when using chrism oil. A type of lavabo bowl is used on Holy Thursday when the celebrant in honor of our Divine Lord's initiation at the Last Supper washes the feet of 12 men from the parish who represent the 12 apostles.

The lavabo bowl developed out of a device usually found in the sacristy (the room where sacred items are kept) also known as the lavabo. Before vesting, the celebrant customarily washes his hands and prays a special prayer. The washing of the hands at the offertory is known as the *lavabo proper*.

Cruets

Cruets are small vessels that contain wine and water required for Mass. They may come in all types of materials, such as crystal, silver, blown glass, and other metals. The styles range from the most simple glass to the most ornate Baroque with filigree. In normal parish situations, cruets are typically glass or crystal so they can be easily stored in a refrigerator. The custom of using a large flagon (giant cruet) to consecrate wine and then dispersing it in a chalice is no longer allowed, so either chalices are already filled with wine or it is done at the altar. The water cruet is then used to put a drop of water into each chalice. (The water symbolizes the sharing of divinity the human race enjoys because Christ has a full human nature and a full divine nature in his one divine personhood. As true God and true Man, Christ unites humanity and divinity and thus the one drop of water represents humanity uniting with divinity.) The water cruet is used again at the end of Mass to purify the chalices.

Special cruets without handles are also used in storing the sacred oils blessed at the Chrism Mass. They are often placed in an *ambry,* a cabinet that is placed in a wall near the sanctuary. Newer ambries often have glass fronts and are lit within so the oils are exposed to the congregation.

Book III

Catholic Mass

Crosier

A staff used by bishops and cardinals is called a *crosier.* It is the symbol of the pastoral office of the bishop and is used when the bishop is vested for Mass or celebration of other sacraments, such as Confirmation outside of Mass. The pope does not use a crosier, because his jurisdiction is universal.

During the liturgy, the crosier is held during procession and recession, when listening to the Gospel, during a homily, when accepting vows, during professions of faith, and when blessing someone. The celebrant carries the crosier in his right hand with the crook facing open. It is styled in many different ways from ornate and gothic to contemporary or wooden, and may have the coat of arms of the bishop painted in the crook. Along with the pectoral cross and ring, the crosier designates the office of bishop.

Processional cross

The *processional cross* is generally a crucifix carried in processions by a server known as the *crucifer*. In the order of procession at a Solemn Mass, the crucifer comes between the thurifer and the acolytes holding lit processional candles. In the Ordinary Rite of the Roman Mass, the candles and processional cross often remain in the sanctuary and even serve as the candle for Mass and the cross for the people to reflect upon.

Crosses can be made from a wide variety of materials, from wood to brass, and be gilded in silver or gold. Some have painted representations of the crucifix on them, such as the famous crucifix of San Damiano. Others are made like traditional crucifixes. High Liturgy Protestant churches often incorporate such crosses in their processions along with a crucifix-type processional cross.

Latin Rite altar linens

The following linens are used on the altar during the Latin Mass.

- The **pall** is a stiff square of material that can be made in the liturgical colors of the season: white, red, green, and purple. It's optional in the Ordinary Rite and yet has the practical function of keeping foreign material or insects from flying into the Precious Blood. Some palls are ornately embroidered or have hand-painted images of the Lord, the Blessed Virgin, saints, or other appropriate Christian symbols. They are placed on top of the chalice and underneath the chalice veil and burse.

- A **purificator** is a piece of absorbent fabric draped from the chalice to wipe the cup after someone receives the Precious Blood and used for cleaning the chalice after Communion. The cloth is rectangular, folded twice the long way and, creased in the middle into the shape of an *M* so that it drapes nicely over the chalice. Second, over the purificator and chalice is the paten with celebrant host, and third, the pall over the paten.

- The **chalice veil** usually is made of the same material and color of the vestments worn for Mass and normally has an embroidered cross on the front. It is draped over the chalice after the purificator has been draped over the cup, followed by the paten with unconsecrated host and then with a pall placed on top of all that.

- The **burse,** a sort of envelope that houses the corporal, is placed on top of the chalice veil. The burse is made of the same material as the pall.

✔ The **corporal** is a white, square piece of linen that is folded twice horizontally and twice vertically with an embroidered cross in the middle. It's always made of linen because this is the material believed to be used in the burial of Christ. In the Extraordinary form of the Mass, the host of the priest is taken off the paten and placed directly on the corporal along with the chalice and ciboria. In the Ordinary form of the Mass the host rests on the paten and the chalice and ciboria are next to it. In Masses in which several vessels are used at the consecration, more than one corporal is used. The corporal never remains on the altar after Communion; rather it's placed in the burse and later stored in the sacristy, or if dirty, washed in the sacrarium and then laundered with the other liturgical linens.

Eastern Rite vessels, artifacts, and linens

The following items are used in the Byzantine Rite exclusively.

✔ In the center of Byzantine churches is the **tetrapod,** a table on which an icon of the Christ, Blessed Virgin, or saint being celebrated is placed. It may have candles and be richly adorned with a beautiful cloth. When worshippers come into the church, they go to the tetrapod and make the sign of the cross three times and then kiss the icon.

✔ The **iconostasis** (icon screen) is located between the nave and the sanctuary, because in Eastern Catholic thought, the sanctuary represents the holy place, heaven, and the nave represents the created world. It is a symbol of joining the created with the Creator. The *Royal Doors* located on the iconostasis are opened and closed during the Divine Liturgy to represent the relationship of God with his people. The *Deacon door* is located on the side and suggests the constant communication of God with his people.

✔ The **aspersorium,** or holy water bucket, is the vessel used to contain water that will be blessed for the Asperges rite of the Mass. During this rite, which takes the place of the Penitential Rite in the Ordinary form of the Mass, the people are blessed with holy water to remind them of their Baptism. The holy water bucket is also used at other times, such as at the grave for burial or for the blessing of sacramental or secular items. In the Extraordinary form of the Mass, the Asperges rite takes place before Mass commences. The **aspergillum** is the metal cylindrical device with small holes in the end that the priest uses to dip into the holy water in the aspersorium and sprinkle the people.

✔ The **diskos** is much like the paten in the Roman Rite in that it contains the sacramental bread that will become the Body of Christ. Unlike the paten, however, the diskos sits on a pedestal, and after the Communion it can only be touched by an ordained clergyman.

Book III

Catholic Mass

- The **zeon cup** contains boiling water used in the Divine Liturgy and represents the water that flowed from Christ's side on the cross on Good Friday.

- The **exapteriga** is a fan made with a representation of a six-winged seraphim, the highest rank of angels, mounted on a pole for hand carrying.

- The altar is covered with an arrangement of altar linens. A white linen called the **katasarkion** is placed first. An embroidered cloth called the **endyton** is placed on top of that. Finally, the **eileton** (silk cloth) is placed on top of those two. Inside the eileton is the **antimension,** which is similar to the Roman corporal and altar stone combined. Whereas in the Latin Rite relics of the martyrs are embedded in stone and inserted inside the altar on top of which Mass is celebrated, in the Eastern Rite, relics are sewed inside the antimension cloth.

- **Dikirion** and **trikirion** are liturgical candlesticks used by a bishop when he celebrates the Divine Liturgy. The former has two candles to symbolize the two natures of Christ (human and divine) while the latter has three candles representing the three Persons of the Divine and Holy Trinity (God the Father, God the Son, and God the Holy Spirit).

- An **analogion** is a lectern where the Book of Gospels or an icon is placed for public veneration.

- The **asterisk** is a cross-shaped object which is placed on the *diskos* during the *Proskomedia* (Office of Oblation performed by priest before Divine Liturgy).

- **Prosphora** is leavened bread used in the Divine Liturgy. One part of it, called the *amnon,* is cut during the proskomedia to be consecrated during the Divine Liturgy. The rest is cut up for the *antidoron* (blessed but not consecrated bread) given after the Divine Liturgy.

Chapter 5

The Look and Sound of Mass: Architecture, Art, and Music

. . . .

In This Chapter

▶ Looking at churches, cathedrals, and other buildings of worship

▶ Seeing how architectural styles have evolved

▶ Performing music in services

▶ Displaying art to enhance worship

. . . .

Many aspects of the Catholic Church have remained the same over its 21-century history, but much has changed, as well. The type and architecture of church buildings have been adapted through the years to accommodate changes in liturgy or to avoid expensive construction, and the art and music have changed according to the type of worship experience used in the Church at different times.

Some building styles, such as the ostentatious Baroque style, are just too expensive to try to reproduce nowadays. Other styles, such as neoclassical and neo-Gothic, have been reinvented as new, *(neo)* versions of their early ancestors to better accommodate the changes in worship, because the architecture of churches is more than just a matter of style or taste. In the Catholic Church, worship environment sets an important tone for the worship itself, and therefore the building styles must be right. Here's what Pope Benedict XVI had to say about the Gothic style:

> A merit of the Gothic cathedrals was the fact that, in their construction and decoration, the Christian and civil community participated in a different but coordinated way; the poor and the powerful, the illiterate and the learned participated, because in this common house all believers were instructed in the faith. Gothic sculpture made of cathedrals a "Bible of stone," representing the episodes of the Gospel and illustrating the contents of the Liturgical Year, from Christmas to the Lord's glorification.

This chapter helps you understand how churches and other buildings of worship are designed and laid out. It shows you how architectural styles, art, and music play a part in the buildings and in the Catholic Church itself.

Meeting in Sacred Spaces: Church Buildings

People need a quiet, reserved space for worship. That's not to say the world outside worship is bad or sinful; in fact, Genesis tells us that that the world is good. But as people who are made up of both the material and the spiritual, we need worldly or secular space and a sacred space.

The church building is so important because it's the sacred space dedicated to the worship of God. It is where his written word (the Bible or Sacred Scripture) is read aloud, where hymns are sung, and where ritual worship of God is given with reverence and devotion.

Regardless of its shape, style, or size, the following fundamental elements are needed in each Catholic church:

- ✔ **Sanctuary:** Area in front of church where the altar and Tabernacle reside and where the clergy perform their liturgical ministry
- ✔ **Nave:** Main body of church where congregation stands up or sits on pews (benches to sit on with built in kneelers)
- ✔ **Narthex:** Outer vestibule of church where the casket is brought for funerals and where people get their weekly bulletin as they leave Mass
- ✔ **Baptistery:** Can be a separate room or an area in church reserved for the celebration of Baptism
- ✔ **Sacristy:** Room off of sacristy where clergy vest and where the items needed for Mass are kept (wine, hosts, candles, linens, etc)
- ✔ **Confessional:** Booth or room where faithful go to confess their sins to a priest and receive absolution
- ✔ **Choir:** Area in balcony at rear of church near organ or some other location where members of the choir can sing during the Mass and also where they can rehearse beforehand

As the Church as a body was developing, so was the church as a building. Some elements have been expanded, moved, or even abolished through the years. The location of the choir changed several times throughout the history of the Church; at one time the choir was actually located between the sanctuary and the rest of the congregation. Here are some other examples of design changes through the centuries:

- Side aisles have come and gone through the years. In some early churches the aisles had heavy columns that would obstruct the view for many parishioners, which led to a more open nave in churches built in the 20th century.

- Some older churches were built with several side chapels with altars for private Mass celebrations. It wasn't uncommon for more than one priest to be celebrating Mass at the same time at different altars in the church. Many of the older churches still have these side altars, but they are use mostly as shrines for saints.

- In the early church, many large churches such as cathedrals and basilicas located the baptistery in a separate building. By the mid-20th century, parish churches had separate areas within the building set aside for Baptisms. Before the Second Vatican Council in the 1960s, Baptisms were for the baby and godparents only, so they didn't need much room. After the Council, however, Baptisms could be celebrated at Mass and more people attended the actual sacrament, and holding Baptisms in the small area became increasingly difficult. The baptismal font was relocated to different areas within the church.

The sections that follow describe the form and function of many different types of church buildings.

Parish churches

The *parish church* is the most common and most frequent church building in the *diocese,* the territorial division headed by a bishop appointed by the pope. A diocese contains a cathedral (mother church) and several parishes. A parish church is headed by a priest who is appointed by the bishop and serves as the bishop's representative. The parish church exists on the local level in communities.

The church is the religious center of the parish; it is where the sacraments are celebrated in the lives of ordinary parishioners on a daily basis. In addition to a church building, a parish may have included a rectory, or priest's residence, as well as the offices of the parish, a parochial school to educate the parish children, and a convent to house the religious teachers who teach in the school. However, in the 21st century, many parishes do not have either convents of sisters or parish schools.

Chapels, shrines, and oratories

Chapels, shrines, and oratories are special places of worship and adoration that may be a part of a parish but also can exist independently from a parish. For example, a parochial convent for sisters may have a chapel located within where the sisters pray the Liturgy of the Hours and private devotions. It is not a public place of worship but rather a private place designed for the sisters. A chapel can also be independent and more of a public place for worship. For example, most Catholic hospitals, colleges, and universities have chapels in which Mass is celebrated. Usually these chapels are for people connected to the institutions, but they can be open the general public.

Chapels can also subsist within a larger church structure. For example, in St. Peter's Basilica in Rome, a special chapel exists for the Reservation of the Blessed Sacrament. In this chapel the faithful can come and worship the Lord in the Holy Eucharist in a quiet area of the basilica without the distractions of visitors and tourists who wander around. Many large cathedrals or historical churches have these types of chapels. In addition, a chapel can exist for the housing of relics of a particular saint or martyr. They often become pilgrim destinations in which Catholics visit with the intention of intercession of the saint.

Oratories are similar to chapels. They're designated by ecclesiastical authority for Mass and devotions and are for public, semi-public or private use.

A *shrine* is a designated devotional place, usually for reasons of historical event or specific association. For example, the apparitions of Our Lady in Lourdes, France; Fatima, Portugal; and Guadalupe, Mexico are designated shrines to which the faithful make pilgrimages. Shrines that are dedicated to apparitions, like that of the Blessed Virgin Mary, are often duplicated around the world. For instance, the oldest Shrine of Our Lady of Lourdes, France, was duplicated in Emmitsburg, Maryland, in 1858.

A shrine can also be a burial place of a saint or where a saint lived or died, or it can be dedicated to a particular saint even if the location has no historical importance. For example, the Shrine of St. Anne in Quebec, Canada, was built out of pure devotion to that particular saint.

Cathedrals

A cathedral is the chief church of a diocese, home to the bishop's throne, the *cathedra* (hence the name *cathedral*). Despite their significance within the diocese, cathedrals also serve as parish churches in which parish families worship.

Some cathedrals have or had monasteries attached to them, particularly in Europe. In England, cathedrals that were part of monasteries are called *minster* churches; in Germany, they're called *munster* churches. Cathedrals and monasteries are not connected in the United States.

Like many parish churches, cathedrals come in various sizes and styles but all have the same basic elements inside: choir, sanctuary, and nave. The bishop's throne is located in the sanctuary along with the altar and pulpit, but is a fixed item that can't be moved.

Basilicas

A *basilica* is another distinctive church within a diocese. The canonical status of basilicas has two major divisions: major and minor. Only four basilicas are major, and they all stand within a few miles of each other.

St. Peter's Basilica

The most significant and widely known basilica is the *Basilica of St. Peter* in Vatican City State. The cathedral is the mother church of the diocese, but St. Peter's Basilica is the mother church of the Universal Church. This basilica is on the site of the first-century Christian cemetery where it is believed that St. Peter, the first Bishop of Rome and the first pope, was martyred and buried. This area is known as Vatican Hill, and St. Peter's Basilica is often simply called the Vatican.

The first basilica built over the tomb of St. Peter was built by Emperor Constantine in the traditional Roman basilica style. A palace to serve as the pope's quarters was built near the church. A wall was later built around this area to block barbarian pillagers and invaders. A long wall that houses a causeway to the Tiber River and terminates in a structure known as Castle of St. Angelo served as an escape route for the pope when the area fell under attack.

Basilica of St. John Lateran

St. John Lateran, the oldest of the four major basilicas, is considered the Cathedral of the Archdiocese of Rome. The pope is the Bishop of Rome, and St. John Lateran is where his cathedra (throne) is located. It has been considered the headquarters of the Roman Catholic Church for centuries, and the papal palace and private chapel were originally part of its compounds.

The palace has since been demolished, but the c hapel survives and exists across the street from the basilica. The holy stairs that led to the Praetorium (palace of the Roman governor) of Pontius Pilate in Jerusalem are housed in the chapel, giving the chapel its name, *Scala Sancta.*

The land where the basilica stands originally belonged to the Lateran family. Constantine became the owner of this property and donated it to the church in AD 313. The basilica was dedicated to its patrons, St. John the Baptist and St. John the Evangelist, in the tenth century and was formally named the Basilica of St. John the Baptist and St. John the Evangelist in the Lateran.

Basilica of St. Mary Major

St. Mary Major, the third major basilica, is believed to be the first dedicated to the Virgin Mary after the Ecumenical Council of Ephesus, which defined Mary as the Mother of God. It is built on Esquiline Hill, one of the Seven Hills of Rome. Construction of the basilica began under the reign of Pope Liberius in the fourth century.

According to legend, a wealthy Roman family wanted to honor the Blessed Virgin and prayed to her for help in accomplishing this dream. The city of Rome is typically very hot in the summer, so when it snowed on Esquiline Hill on August 5, the family took that as the sign they needed and built the basilica there. The full title of the basilica is St. Mary Major of the Snow.

One of the most striking relics in the basilica, the holy relic of the crib of Our Lord, resides beneath the baldachin of the main altar. The church also bears a ceiling made with the first gold brought back from the New World and donated to the pope by the king and queen of Spain.

Basilica of St. Paul, Outside the Walls

The fourth and final major basilica is *St. Paul, Outside the Walls,* so named because it was built outside the ancient Roman city walls. The basilica was founded by Constantine in the fourth century and, because it did not have the benefit of city walls to protect it, was pillaged in the ninth century. After the pillaging the pope fortified the basilica with walled courtyards.

Some of the most magnificent mosaics in the world are located inside the apse of the sanctuary, and in one of the side chapels is a miraculous crucifix, in which our Lord came to life in a vision from the cross to St. Bridget. Along the top of the colonnades are medallions of all the popes. Local legend has it that when the last medallion is painted, it will be the end of the world.

Minor basilicas

The next group of basilicas is the canonical minor basilica, those that are smaller and far more numerous. The pope holds the sole authority of naming a church a minor basilica, and certain items must be present in a qualifying church:

- ✔ A papal umbrella that acts as a baldachin, usually decorated with the keys of St. Peter

- ✔ A bell, which is carried in procession on state occasions

- ✔ The cappa magna (exceptionally long and elaborate cape of silk), worn by the canon (priests attached to a cathedral or basilica for honorary purposes and duties) of the basilica when assisting at the Liturgy of the Hours

Over 1,500 minor basilicas exist in the world. In Baltimore, Maryland, the first cathedral built in the United States was designated by Pope John Paul II as the Basilica and National Shrine of the Blessed Virgin Mary.

Four minor basilicas in the world are considered *pontifical minor basilicas,* the highest rank:

- ✔ The Pontifical Basilica of Our Lady of the Rosary, in Pompeii, Italy

- ✔ The Pontifical Basilica of St. Nicholas, in Bari, Italy

- ✔ The Pontifical Basilica of St. Anthony, in Padua, Italy

- ✔ The Pontifical Basilica of the Holy House, in Loreto, Italy

Second division in the minor basilicas are the *papal basilicas,* including the Papal Basilica of St. Francis, Assisi, Italy, and the Papal Basilica of St. Lawrence outside of the Walls, Rome, Italy. The third class is *patriarchal,* denoting that it's attached to an archbishop who has the title of patriarch. The final class is *general,* and countless cathedrals, shrines, and oratories throughout the world have this distinction.

Book III

Catholic Mass

Architectural Styles

Just as buildings changed to meet liturgical needs, so did the styles of architecture. The Church is over 21 centuries old, and much development and variation in design and styles of the buildings have taken place. Sometimes these changing styles worked well with the liturgy, and sometimes they didn't.

Whatever the style may be, churches are places where the faithful meet God: in the Mass, the Sacraments, prayer life, and devotions of the liturgical calendar. The buildings need to be dignified and edifying places that promote worship and prayer instead of inhibiting it. When a design is good it becomes a timeless classic, and with a few modifications it can easily be used in any century.

Roman basilica

One of the earliest styles of churches is based on the *Roman basilica,* which was a public building often found in the forum in Roman cities. Many people turned to Christianity after the Edict of Milan made it became a "respectable" religion, and many wealthy patrons (including Emperor Constantine) donated property and buildings to the Church. These early buildings were oblong and quite large.

Early Roman basilicas contained many features still used today:

- **Sanctuary:** Area in the front of the church where the altar and tabernacle reside and where the clergy perform their liturgical duties
- **Ambo:** The pulpit for the proclamation of the word
- **Apse:** The semicircular roof located in the sanctuary where the altar, bishop's throne, and seats of the clergy are located
- **Side apse:** Where the side altars are located
- **Nave:** The body of the church extending from the sanctuary to the main entrance
- **Aisles:** Interior divisions of the church running parallel with the nave and separated by rows of pillars
- **Choir:** The area for the singers usually located in the front of the nave
- **Court:** The enclosed space wholly or partly surrounded by walls of a building
- **Cloisters:** Covered arcades along the walls of the church or its courts designed for meditation by the monks or nuns
- **Narthex:** The long narrow portico or porch that is in the front of the church

Byzantine

The Roman Empire was not just in Rome, but also in the East, centered in Constantinople (now Istanbul, Turkey). The style of architecture used in that part of the world was *Byzantine.* Although the style originated in the East, it's reflected in church structures that were still under the Byzantine Empire in the West, such as in Venice, Ravenna, and parts of Sicily in Italy. The style is a mixture of classical Greek and Roman coupled with a distinctive Eastern or Middle Eastern Oriental features.

The Byzantine churches differed from Roman basilicas in their vaulted ceilings, domes, and half domes richly adorned in mosaics depicting Christian art. Roman Basilicas also had art, but it was typically *frescoes,* paintings in wet plaster. Some churches in the West mixed styles and had elements of Byzantium and Roman architecture.

Romanesque

Changes and adaptations made within the Byzantine churches gradually developed in the West into the *Romanesque* style of architecture.

This style came in vogue in the early 10th century and lasted until the 12th century when it was supplanted by the Gothic style. Some of the finest examples of Romanesque style can be founded in Italy, France, England, and Spain. It maintained rounded Roman arches, massive, thick walls, and heavy decorations.

Romanesque ornamentation is not subtle, and includes geometric patterns and grotesques of animals or humans. It also incorporated *blind arcading,* brick or stone walls outlined with arches. The doors of Romanesque churches were heavily decorated and emphasized the transition from the secular world on the outside to the spiritual world within.

The footprint of the medieval, Romanesque cathedral is cruciform — that is, it looks like a cross from above. Usually, a Romanesque church has a central nave and two side apses on either side of it. The central nave is separated by a series of columns, and the roof of the aisle and the outer walls help support the upper walls of the vault of the nave, which have an area of windows known as the clerestory. The narthex is the entrance of the church, and the choir is usually located near the sanctuary, sometimes at the transept (the short horizontal bar of the cruciform).

Book III

Catholic Mass

Gothic

By the beginning of the 13th century, the *Gothic* style replaced Romanesque. Its chief difference was the development of the pointed arch that allowed a vast range of new architectural possibilities.

Gothic buildings are taller and have larger windows than preceding structures. French and English Gothic are two great examples of the architectural style, although variations are found in Spain, Portugal, and Italy.

- ✔ French Gothic is typified by great west doors with three pointed rows surrounding each door and topped off by a magnificent rose window. It is normally flanked by two soaring towers with spires. The rib vaults inside are revealed on the outside by flying buttresses.

- ✔ English style is more perpendicular and horizontal than vertical. The ceilings are usually ribbed quite ornately with intersecting arches. The tower is usually located in the center of the transept, but sometimes two towers were built at the west end. On smaller churches, a single tower may be used through which people enter the church. Where two towers are used, the central window is not a circular rose but a very large arched window.

Elaborate stone carvings on Gothic churches create a sense of lightness and delicateness as opposed to the massive feeling of the Romanesque church. Columns and capitals (the structural elements at the tops of columns) often have foliage predominantly carved into them, usually in clusters. Capitals are small, emphasizing the vertical aspect of the Gothic style.

The pointed arch is the quintessential element of Gothic architecture. They're visually lighter, though structurally stronger because the blocks at the top of the arch press inward rather than downward. Fancy lattice and decorative carvings are incorporated into the arches. Moldings of windows and doors also employed the high and pointed arch.

Gothic door sashes and arches above them use the pointed arches, richly decorated by fine moldings and reliefs. The doors themselves may even be elaborately carved. The windows of the Gothic church — plentiful and large, containing stained-glass depictions of Christ, Mary, the saints, and scenes from the Bible — are another hallmark of the style.

The plan of the Gothic church followed the Latin cross, like the earlier Romanesque style. The nave was intersected by the transept to form the cross. Beyond the transept lies the choir and sanctuary. The nave is taller than the side aisle, allowing a series of windows on the top known as the clerestory windows. Directly behind the main altar of the sanctuary, a special chapel was dedicated to the Blessed Virgin Mary.

Renaissance

By the end of the 15th century a new mode came into fashion, the *Renaissance*. This style affected not only architecture but also art, food, poetry, politics, economics, and the sciences. One of the chief characteristics of the Renaissance was a rediscovery of the classics of ancient Greece and Rome.

Classically inspired Renaissance churches incorporate strong horizontal lines, pointed front pediments, flat ceilings, and symmetrically positioned windows. Columns of arcades with their simple curve and Corinthian columns add to the balance of the building. Nothing is out of proportion or overly ostentatious, but rather a unique architectural harmony exists.

The designs were based on designs of buildings from ancient Rome and evoked the glory of the Empire. However, innovations and adaptations were made in this period to the basic classical style. For instance, Renaissance columns are based on a classical style but decorated with roses, leaves, and other naturalistic concepts.

The construction of domes, which had fallen out of style, experienced a rebirth in the Renaissance churches. St. Peter's Basilica, in Vatican City, and the Duomo in Florence are among the two most famous examples. Windows in this period took their basic form from ancient Rome and were usually rectangular with pediments, cornices, classical columns, and pilasters.

The inside plan of a Renaissance church also followed ancient Roman architecture, with long naves columned on the side to allow aisles, and a sanctuary at the top with a rounded apse. A dome was at the transept, instead of an imposing tower as in English Gothic style. The ceiling of the Sistine Chapel at St. Peter's Basilica is an example of the frescoes that adorned these churches. Other ceilings were made of wood and gilded in gold, with fruit or leaves as decoration.

One of the most important architects of this period whose influence has far reaching effects is Andrea Palladio, founder of the Palladian motif, which was the inspiration for Georgian style in England and the Colonial style in America. Christopher Wren's St. Paul's Cathedral of London, England, is a perfect example of Palladian Renaissance architecture in England.

Book III

Catholic
Mass

Baroque

By the 17th century the Renaissance style was being replaced or adapted into the more flamboyant *Baroque*. This style was characterized by grand elaboration of detail and space. Architects took the classical motifs and kicked it up a notch in order to create a sense of drama. In the Church's history, this was the Counter-Reformation Period. Protestant revolt in Northern Europe resulted in a type of iconoclasm or stripping of the churches of any ornamentation. Counter-Reformation preached reform but also the glories of Catholicism, and therefore the churches became even more adorned and splendid.

Some of the chief characteristics of this period included monumental pilasters, curved pediments, and curved floor plans. With the use of rounded shapes, Baroque churches exploited the form with intersecting ovals and circles. The Church of St. Agnes in the Piazza Navona, Rome, is a chief example.

The roofs of Baroque churches carried a style similar to the Renaissance but with more ornamentation. Windows and doors received the decoration of rounded or pointed pediments and sculpture. The famous Church of the Gesu, Rome, is a style that has been copied in many Baroque churches.

The Baroque fashion spread throughout Europe, even in the Protestant countries in the north. However, the style in these areas was limited to palaces and other public places. In Catholic southern and central Europe, particularly Italy, Bavaria, and Austria, many churches being built in this era were constructed in the Baroque design. The Kingdom of the Two Sicilies centered in Naples developed its own distinctive Baroque style.

Some of the greatest architects of the period are Bernini, who designed the colonnade at St. Peter Square, Vatican City, and Borromini, who designed the quintessential oval Baroque Church, San Carlo alle Quatro Fontana, Rome. Many examples of Baroque architecture can be found in the countries that were part of the Spanish Empire in the New World. The Cathedral in Mexico City is the prime example.

Neoclassical

The 18th and 19th centuries gave rise to many revivals. One of the most splendid examples was *neoclassical* architecture, which started as a reaction to the heavily ornate Baroque style. Its style is very similar to Renaissance and classical Greek and Roman.

Andrea Palladio and the Palladian manner heavily influenced this period, often referred to as *romantic classicism*. The trend displayed in architecture in this time was the desire to return to the purity of clean lines of Ancient Grecian buildings, which is why neoclassical architecture is also often called *Greek revival*.

In the United States, many white clapboard churches were built in the Greek revival style. It gave rise to the Federalist style in the United States. Many of our national buildings, such as the Capitol in Washington, D.C., are built in the neoclassical style and architectural motif. Benjamin Latrobe, who designed the United States' Capitol, also designed the United States' first Catholic cathedral, the Basilica of the Blessed Virgin Mary in Baltimore, Maryland, in this neoclassical style.

19th- and 20th-century revivals

In addition to the revival of neoclassicism, both Romanesque and Gothic styles had a resurgence in the 19th century. The Romanesque revival began in the 1830s and lasted into the 20th century, and it was used for secular buildings, from universities to warehouses in the city, as well as for churches. With the use of steel, windows became larger, and so many of the famous department stores of the late 19th century and early 20th centuries were built in the Romanesque style, but with windows. In church architecture, the Shrine Basilica of St. Anne in Quebec is a perfect example of Romanesque revival.

Gothic revival, also referred to as Victorian Gothic or neo-Gothic, became very prevalent in church architecture of the 19th and early 20th centuries. The major difference between the original style and the revival was construction. The latter centuries employed steel for building frames, which made flying buttresses obsolete, and therefore neo-Gothic churches were constructed without them. In the United States, Gothic revival was a favorite style among many immigrants, who wanted to establish churches like the ones in their native lands.

Modern

The 20th century saw the rise to modern art and architecture. Art deco, which took its design from machines, came into vogue in the 1920s. The Chrysler building with its automobile ornamentation of the era is a prime example in secular buildings. However, some suburban Catholic churches also incorporated art deco with traditional architecture and so you have a variation of the design. The Cathedral of Mary Our Queen in Baltimore, Maryland, was built in the 1950s, and its style can be described as art deco meets Gothic revival.

Architecture in the second half of the 20th century was dominated by modernism, with its chief characteristic being a minimalist approach to art and design. Some important monastic chapels, such as Delbarton in Morristown, New Jersey, and St. John Abbey in Collegeville, Minnesota, have incorporated modern design with the simplicity of life. The Cathedral of Archdiocese of Los Angeles is also an example of modernism.

Postmodern

The late 20th and early 21st centuries comprise the period known as postmodernism. In this period many of the designs take inspiration from the styles of the past but reconfigure them for the present. One of the most famous examples of postmodern ecclesiastical architecture, the new chapel at Ave Maria University, Florida, combines modern, art deco, and neo-Gothic.

Many new churches are also being built in the traditional styles of Romanesque, Gothic, Renaissance, and neoclassical. Architects continue to reinvent creatively without being reduced to simply copying existing buildings. One of the most beautiful examples of postmodern classical style is the chapel at St. Thomas Aquinas College in California.

Music in Worship

Music is essential in liturgical art and worship. Christian music can be divided into Gregorian (plain chant), polyphonic (multiple voice levels), English chant (Anglicanism), Baroque concerto Masses, folk music, and hymnal music. In the Church, the king of instruments for over five 500 years has been the pipe organ. However, and especially in Baroque Masses, orchestral ensembles (strings, winds, and brass) have also been employed. Music, like art and architecture, should always complement the Liturgy and not detract from it.

Looking at the early use of music

Christian music has its roots in Judaism. Before it was destroyed in the first century, the Temple of Jerusalem was the center of Jewish worship. Along with Temple ceremonies, music, choir, and instruments accompanied the worship. After the destruction of the Temple, the tradition of music in the synagogues continued. Today, Jewish synagogue cantors continue to bring the Psalms of King David and other literary poems and prayers to life through chant.

Church music is one of the most revered and major components of the Church's heritage. The singing of hymns is in fact a prayer of the Church that cannot be separated from the liturgical celebration. In past centuries, the Church has taught that singing, especially at Mass and the Liturgy of the Hours, should be performed to the best of the choir or congregation's ability. When performed or prayed in this fashioned it expresses a deep meaning of faith that is beautiful and expresses the singers' thoughts and feelings being raised to God.

Christianity was banned for most of the first four centuries AD. Overt displays of music in the "small house" churches and chapels was likely very limited. Even in times of relative peace, music was still restrained, but it did exist. In Ephesians 5:19, St. Paul reminds the early Christians about songs of praise with these words: " . . . addressing one another in psalms and hymns and spiritual songs, singing and making melody to the Lord with all your heart."

Chanting: Pope Gregory's legacy

A significant development in liturgical music can be attributed to Pope Gregory the Great, who was a great liturgical reformer who reigned from 590 to 604. This pope sat on the Throne of St. Peter many centuries after the Edict of Milan, which allowed Christians to worship in public.

After the Edict, larger churches had to be built in the fourth century to accommodate the many converts to Catholicism. The liturgies became more elaborate right along with the grander buildings, and more music was used. In the sixth and seventh centuries, more hymns were written to reflect theological truths of Christ, Mary, and the Church.

By this time, the threat of martyrdom was decreasing, and many people wanted to witness to the Faith in a radical way. This desire lead to the birth of monastic life, which requires many hours to be spent in communal prayer, not only the Holy Sacrifice of the Mass, but also recitation of the Liturgy of the Hours.

These services established a need for music, and Pope Gregory the Great, who started his religious career as a monk, championed a new style of singing known as *Gregorian chant,* which was a perfect fit.

Gregorian chant is a form of plainchant or monophonic chant that almost anyone can learn and do. It has simple melodies and rhythm that are easily learned and when done in choir have a soothing and comforting melody.

In addition, parts of the Mass are still sung in Gregorian chant. They include Kyrie (Lord have mercy), Gloria (Glory to God in the Highest), Credo (Creed), Sanctus and Sanctus (Holy, Holy), and the Agnus Dei (Lamb of God).

Reforming music in the Counter-Reformation

Many political and religious changes occurred at the end of the 15th century, most notably the deep schism in the church that gave rise to the Protestant Revolt. Also at this time the Church convened the Council of Trent to address

Book III

Catholic Mass

some of the abuses in the Church, reiterate Catholic doctrine, and reform the liturgy and Sacraments. This meeting gave rise to the Counter-Reformation period in which many new religious communities were established to disseminate Catholic information.

According to the liturgical reforms, sacred music could not resemble secular music and it could not obscure liturgical texts. But within these restrictions, many new innovations were being added, including *polyphonic chant*. Giovanni Pierluigi da Palestrina was one of the greatest composers of this style of chant.

Polyphony is a more elaborate and sophisticated evolution of plain chant (alias Gregorian chant). Polyphonic chant employs two or more voices whereas plain chant uses only one. Besides the monks and nuns who would chant their Office (Breviary or Liturgy of the Hours), many churches and cathedrals formed choirs to chant parts of the Mass, especially for feasts and holy days.

The Church of England was being established at this time, and so was a variation of polyphonic chant known simply as *Anglican chant*. Today if you attend Evensong, or the Eucharistic Liturgy, the choir traditionally sings in this chant mode. Although it resembles its Roman Catholic counterpart, it is a distinctive style. With the Anglo form of the Roman Rite, this chant is used in liturgies.

As Counter-Reformation church architecture changed in the 17th and 18th century, so did liturgical music, giving rise to the Baroque Masses. Hayden, Scarlatti, Vivaldi, Bach, and Mozart all wrote magnificent Mass settings that at first seem to be more for concerts than a Mass. The Baroque Masses included orchestras and usually were performed for special occasions, such as Christmas, Easter, or for special events such as Coronation Mass.

Using music in the modern Church

By the 20th century excessiveness of the Baroque Masses prompted reform. Pope Pius X wrote in his directive of 1903 that Church music should be of the highest excellence, preserve purity of form, exclude any profane influence, and because the Church is universal, possess collective qualities. By the Second Vatican Council of the 1960s, many reforms were established.

Hymns sung in church originated from the Psalms and developed into the music that's common today. Many were composed to convey a theological teaching of Christ or the Virgin Mary. Since the time of the Protestant Reformation, hymns have been translated and sung in the local language (the vernacular). In the early 20th century, hymns in the vernacular were sung at

Low Masses of the Extraordinary Rite, but today, Latin or the vernacular are common in hymns in the Ordinary Rite. The proper places for hymns are the procession, offertory, Communion, and recession.

When the Second Vatican Council (1962–1965) decided to reform the liturgy, it took place during the time of cultural revolution when popular music took a dramatic turn toward innovative, unconventional, nontraditional, and sometimes bizarre lyrics and melodies. Simultaneously, fold songs (by artists such as Peter, Paul, and Mary) became popular, and tunes like "Kumbaya" as well as music by Simon and Garfunkel and the Beatles crept into Catholic liturgies.

Despite changes in Church music in the 20th century, Gregorian and polyphonic chant are still preferable options and can easily be adapted to the Ordinary form of the Roman Rite.

Art in Churches

Church art is considered the most uplifting effort of humanity. It aims at communicating the divine beauty and directing the faithful to praise and thank God.

Pagans like the ancient Greeks and Romans worshiped statues, images, and amulets. They made gods out of material things and worshiped these idols, which was repugnant to the Hebrew monotheistic religion (the belief that there is but one God). Ancient Jewish tradition does not employ the use of images, lest they be misused as idols, which is firmly forbidden by the First Commandment: "Thou shall not have not strange gods and thou shall not adore them."

Catholic Christianity, on the other hand, has no problems using religious symbols and even depictions of the Almighty, because the Church firmly believes in the Incarnation, which is to say that God the Son had a human nature and was both human and divine. Therefore worship should also include the material and the divine. The images, statues, paintings, mosaics, icons, frescoes, and so on were never objects of worship (as in paganism) but merely tools to remind believers that God created the physical as well as the spiritual world. Jesus is considered both God and Man, and therefore, representing the Divine in art is merely a way to enhance the faith.

The earliest examples of Christian art can be found in catacombs, where Christians drew or painted Christian symbols. One of the finest and oldest examples of this art can be found in the Catacomb of Priscilla on the Via Salaris, Rome, Italy.

Book III

Catholic Mass

Frescoes

Frescoes date from the second century AD in catacombs. The historic image of Christ, the Good Shepherd, is painted in one of the catacomb chapels' apse. Frescoes are painted on specially applied wet plaster. It is a technique found in many churches, basilicas, and cathedrals from throughout the centuries. In the 15th century, Leonardo da Vinci and Michelangelo both used fresco technique when the former painted *The Last Supper* in Milan and the latter painted the Sistine Chapel in St. Peter's Basilica.

Iconography

Also around the second century, *iconography* was growing in popularity in Rome and in the East. This art form is most commonly associated with the East. Icons are flat paintings of God, saints, angels, or scenes from the Bible. They are painted on wood, and the background is usually in gold leaf. St. Luke the Evangelist is believed to have painted the first image of the Blessed Virgin Mary, and he did so in an icon form.

The eighth and ninth centuries saw a great controversy called *iconoclasm*. It was a heresy that harkened a horribly literal interpretation of the First Commandment (forbidding idolatry or the worship of idols). As a result of the movement, many precious icons were lost and destroyed in Eastern Christian Churches. Eventually the pope condemned iconoclasm as a heresy in AD 731, but it wasn't until years later at the Second Council of Nicea that an official articulation guided the veneration of sacred images such as icons. In AD 842 the empress of the Byzantine Empire restored venerations of icons, which lead to the Feast of Triumph over Iconoclasm.

Paintings

In addition to frescoes and iconography, other paintings play an important role in church art. The Florentine school of painters in the 14th and 15th centuries took the first major step forward from the flat artwork of iconography. Depth and drama were added to the figures in order to convey motion and emotion, though like iconography, the paintings were done on wood instead of canvas or plaster. Giotto of the 14th century and Fra Angelico of the 15th century typify the style of the Florentine school.

Painting took a dramatic turn in the 16th century at the dawn of the Renaissance. Artists such as Raphael, Michelangelo, and Leonardo da Vinci used different kinds of color and shading to create almost lifelike sacred images. Cardinals, popes, and bishops were generous patrons, and their support made it possible for such works of art to adorn many of the churches throughout Europe.

In the Romantic period of the 19th and early 20th centuries, artists often made works that were heavily ornate and at times went overboard. Ornamentation was reproduced and copied by artists into apses, walls, and narthexes of churches. These ostentatious displays really didn't reflect the proper dignity that should be used in church art, and it led to an overreaction called *modernism*. A form of minimalism, modernism treats less as better and divests a church of any art.

This antiseptic and sterile response denied the elegant beauty of art and environment. Catholicism firmly teaches the doctrine of the *Incarnation,* that God became Man in Jesus Christ. The Savior is both human and divine. Hence, the material world and the spiritual world need to be used in worship. Today, in the postmodern era, art is used well once again. Thanks to modern technology, many great pieces of art by the old masters can be reproduced on canvas to be displayed in churches.

Mosaics

Art employs many different mediums to achieve its effectiveness. *Mosaics* are small pieces of glass or marble that when put together, like a puzzle, create a scene. Ancient Greeks and Romans used mosaics to adorn their villas, important buildings, and marketplaces. Christian basilicas built in the fourth century often used frescoes and mosaics to decorate the spaces. Ravenna, Italy, is an important town on the Adriatic coast that has a large collection of mosaics throughout the town.

Byzantine churches are often adorned with golden mosaics. This type of art was used all the way through the late Gothic period in the West. Prime examples are the Cathedral of St. Mark in Venice and St. Paul outside the Wall in Rome. The 20th century had a revival of the use of mosaics. The Cathedral Basilica of St. Louis of Archdiocese of St. Louis; St. John on the Mountain, Jersey City, New Jersey; and the Basilica of the Immaculate Conception, Washington, D.C., have some of the largest collections of mosaics in the world.

Statues

What icons are to the Eastern Catholic Church, statues are to the Roman Catholic Church. Statuary in churches was never a problem in Rome as they were in the Eastern Empire. The Iconoclasm heresy never took root in the

West as it did in the East. Additionally, marble quarries, stone masons, and sculptors punctuated the Italian Peninsula for centuries, and they remain viable trades to this day. In fact, statuary from antiquity was the inspiration of the Renaissance artists such as Michelangelo. Who is not inspired by the magnificent David in Florence, Pieta at St. Peter's Basilica, or Moses in Rome?

The practice of carving statues in wood dates from the Romanesque period and reached its pinnacle in the Baroque period. To this day, in northeastern Italy, southwestern Austria, and parts of Bavaria, Germany, are some of the finest wood carvers of statuary on earth. This skill has been handed down from generation to generation. Many postmodern churches that are rediscovering classical architecture are once again adorning them with these beautiful wood carvings.

Stained glass

Stained-glass windows are another means of not only adorning churches but also telling a message. Glass blowing has been around for many centuries, but it really took off in the medieval era. Due to new technology in construction of churches, vast wall space could be converted to windows. Stained-glass windows usually depict God, Jesus, Mary, the saints, scenes from the Bible, or Christian life. The glass is held together by lead ribbing that forms the image. The largest stained-glass window is in the Cathedral of Milan, Italy.

During the Renaissance, Baroque, and neoclassical periods, stained-glass windows fell out of favor. However, with the Romanesque and Gothic revivals, this craft had a resurgence. Many of the beautiful immigrant churches built in the United States in the late 19th and early 20th centuries contain fine examples of stained glass.

Stained glass became the peasant's catechism. As only the nobility and clergy were literate, the poor had to rely on the pictures depicted in the stained glass windows to learn the Christian religion from Bible stories to dogmatic truths.

Book IV

Saints and Other Important Figures

Contents at a Glance

Chapter 1

Understanding Sainthood, Angels, and the Blessed Virgin

In This Chapter

▶ Defining what it means to be a saint

▶ Looking at the canonization process and how it has changed

▶ Honoring and celebrating the saints

▶ Glimpsing angelic beings

▶ Getting to know the Virgin Mary

*I*n this chapter, you find out about sainthood in general — especially how the Catholic Church understands the notion of holiness in its members. You discover the canonization process and how it has evolved over the centuries, how saints are venerated, and the unique role patron saints can play in your spiritual life.

Of all the saints in heaven, the highest honor is given to the Virgin Mary, the Mother of Jesus Christ. She's not only the biological Mother of the Savior but also his most faithful disciple. Mary always put the will of God before her own, and she even says in the Gospel of John, "Do whatever [my son] tells you."

As saints warrant honor and veneration (but never adoration or worship), Catholics and the Eastern Orthodox Church give the Blessed Mother the highest type of honor, though they stop short of crossing the line into adoration (because worshiping Mary would be idolatry). She is given the utmost respect because of her special relationship with Jesus.

The angels are second only to Mary in terms of their dignity. Both are creatures made by God. Though angels are far superior to human beings in terms of intelligence and power, the Virgin Mary outranks them because of her unique position as the Mother of Christ.

Three angelic beings are named in the Bible and a few more in the apocryphal Scriptures. In this chapter, you find out about them and the special woman chosen to be the Mother of the Messiah, the Virgin Mary.

Ordinary Saints versus Official Saints

In the Catholic Church, anyone who goes to heaven is considered a *saint*. Those who make it to heaven but are never canonized are still as saintly as those named so by the pope; in fact, the unnamed and unnumbered saints in heaven are in the majority, and God alone knows who they are and how numerous. These ordinary saints lived normal lives but did so with faith in and love for the Lord. Official *saints,* on the other hand, are men and women who lived lives worthy of recognition, honor, and imitation.

The Catholic Church has never taught that a person has to be perfect or sinless to get to heaven. In fact, it teaches that every man and woman who has been born since Adam and Eve (except for the Virgin Mary, by a special divine grace from God) suffers from the effects of original sin. This means that all of us are sinners and need forgiveness. The saints were all human, with their own vulnerabilities, but by the grace of God they were able to overcome their shortcomings. They lived holy lives, even with their quirks and weaknesses, proving that others can do it, too. To be named a saint (a decision reserved for the pope), candidates are *canonized,* or formally authenticated through an intense study of the person's life. Everything that's known about a candidate — his words, deeds, and writings — comes under close scrutiny. If the details of the candidate's life are determined worthy of formal sainthood, the facts and evidence are presented to the pope for approval. No one becomes a saint until the pope says it's so.

Official sainthood isn't merely an honor for the saints themselves. The saints serve as examples for the faithful who struggle to reconcile their human natures with their spiritual aspirations.

The following sections explore the making of a saint, from the initial nomination process and early examinations, to everything the Church must consider and the events that must take place after the candidate's death.

The Canonization Process Then and Now

As you find in the previous section, any declaration of sainthood must come from the pope. That's true now, but it wasn't always so. Before the 12th century, the local bishop was the one who canonized saints — either on his own or in a council or synod of bishops. In very early and ancient times, saints were declared by *acclamation,* or unanimous consent of the people. If a popular holy person died, usually a martyr, the diocese where he or she lived and died eagerly pushed for sainthood.

But dying for the faith wasn't the only way of sanctity and holiness. Living a good and holy life — even if it didn't end in martyrdom — meant something, too.

The question arose, then: Who gets to be declared a saint? In this section, you look at the development of the formal process by which someone is declared (canonized) a saint.

Centralizing the process with Pope Alexander III

Pope Alexander III was the first to rein in the canonization process. In the late 12th century, he made canonization the exclusive province of the papacy, and he and his successors established elaborate processes and regulations to make sure that every candidate met uniform eligibility guidelines. The result was something very much like a trial. Each investigation involved a promoter for the saint-to-be (sort of a defense attorney) and an opposing side (the equivalent of a prosecuting attorney), called the *devil's advocate,* whose job was to expose any heresies in the candidate's writings or sermons, and/or any immoral behavior in the candidate's life.

For the next 800 years, those who wanted to advocate a particular person for sainthood had to follow a time-consuming path. First was *beatification,* a formal decision that a person can be called "Blessed." Beatification involved a canonical trial with advocates and judges. Those who knew the candidate or witnessed postmortem miracles testified, and the candidate's writings and teachings were examined and entered into evidence. All this took place in Rome, because one of the regulations that came from Alexander's centralization policies was that all such trials be held at the Vatican.

Oh, yes, there was also a 50-year waiting period between a person's death and the earliest date he or she could be considered for sainthood. The purpose of the waiting period was to allow time for emotions to settle, thus reducing the number of grief-induced petitions for sainthood. Fifty years was considered the length of time for one generation to disappear.

Book IV

Saints and Other Important Figures

Revamping the process with Pope John Paul II

In 1983, Pope John Paul II made major changes to the canonization process. For one thing, he reduced the waiting period from 50 years to 5 years, in large part because, after 50 years, finding witnesses who knew the candidate personally can be difficult.

The pope has the authority to reduce or waive this waiting period; in fact, John Paul waived it himself in the case of Mother Teresa.

John Paul II also replaced the trial process with a more scholarly, document-oriented approach. Officials still gather the candidate's writings and facts about the candidate's life, but the contentious roles of the devil's advocate and the trial setting are gone (see the upcoming section "Examining lives and allowing for human nature"). And he returned much of the process to the authority of the local diocese; local bishops and dioceses now do much of the preparatory work and the first phase of research, as they're the ones on location where the proposed saint lived and worked.

When a bishop accepts a case for review, the candidate is called a "Servant of God," until a decision is made to send the case on. When that occurs, the proposed saint is considered Venerable, and research focuses on proof of a miracle connected with the candidate (see the "Confirming miracles" section later in this chapter). After a bona fide miracle is established, Rome decides whether the person can be called "Blessed" and formally beatified.

The next phase is one of waiting for another miracle and the documentation on it. Not all beatifications continue to canonization, but as long as a verifiable second miracle exists, there is hope.

Pope John Paul II reserved all beatification ceremonies to himself, but Pope Benedict XVI has restored the ancient practice of allowing other bishops to beatify their local candidates for sainthood. Benedict still has final say on elevating a "Blessed" to "Saint."

If sufficient evidence exists, and if the pope decides to canonize someone, the feast day is typically the day he or she died. This is considered the saint's "heavenly birthday." Some saints die on a day already taken in the universal calendar, so their feast day is designated on the closest open day to their actual date of death.

Examining lives and allowing for human nature

When people are proposed as possible saints, their lives — their actions and words — are closely examined. No one looks for perfection — just for reassurance that the person in question didn't lead a notorious or scandalous life. Catholic authorities scrutinize the candidate's speeches, sermons, books, and other writings to make sure that they contain nothing contradicting defined doctrines or dogmas.

If the candidate's words and deeds pass muster, examiners then search for *heroic virtue* — the desire and effort to seriously pursue a life of holiness.

Saints are human, and as such, they make mistakes. They're not angels, they don't have wings or halos, and they don't glow in the dark. Saints are simply sinners who never gave up trying to do and to be better.

Confirming miracles

The definition of an *accepted miracle* varies almost as widely as those proposed for sainthood. Traditional miracles involve unexpected healing that's immediate and complete, as well as inexplicable to modern science.

Other miracles can be used as corroborative evidence, such as

- **Incorruptibility:** A phenomenon in which the dead person's body doesn't decay, no matter how many years have elapsed since death. Only non-embalmed bodies are considered for evidence of incorruptibility.

- **The odor of sanctity:** A sweet smell of roses exuding from the dead body, despite rigor mortis and the number of years since death. Again, only non-embalmed bodies are considered for this miracle.

- **Signs of stigmata:** Marks resembling one or more of the five wounds Christ suffered upon crucifixion, present only while the person was alive.

- **Bilocation:** Being in two places at the same time. Because this only happens before death, while the saint candidate is still alive, only the most reliable testimony from unimpeachable witnesses can be used. *Levitation* also can be used as evidence.

Intercession (Patron Saints)

You have mediators and intercessors in your lives every day; you just don't call them "mediator" and "intercessor." Sometimes you call them "doctor" and "nurse," or "store manager" and "clerk." The intercessor is the person you turn to in order to seek help from someone higher up: The nurse relays your information to the doctor; the clerk relays requests or concerns to the store manager.

Book IV

Saints and Other Important Figures

That's how it is with God and saints. Jesus is the mediator in our lives, the one who can speak on behalf of an entire group and who has the authority to negotiate, make agreements or treaties, and represent both parties. The saints are those who make requests to the one and only mediator on behalf of someone else. Their role is optional — not everyone turns to an intercessor, or saint, to address God.

Patron saints serve as intercessors for particular areas. For example, St. Lucy was a martyr in the ancient Church who died a horrible death when her Roman persecutors gouged out her eyeballs. She is invoked as the patron saint for ailments of the eye.

Just as the living on earth can and do pray for others (intercession), the saints in heaven can and do pray for the living here on earth. In both cases, the intercessor prays to the one mediator on behalf of someone else. The Catholic Church sees the intercession of the saints as one big prayer chain in the sky.

Venerating the Saints

Just because saints have their own days on the Church calendar doesn't mean they're to be worshipped — that's held for God alone. Rather, saints are worthy of public honor or veneration, called *dulia* in Latin. Holy men and women in heaven deserve honor just as our nation honors those who died defending our country.

Statues, icons, and images of the saints are not to be considered idols (a claim some have used to criticize Catholicism, citing one of the Ten Commandments warning against worshipping false idols). Again, the proper analogy is not worship but honor. Memorials such as statues of George Washington, Thomas Jefferson, and Abraham Lincoln are public and government-supported ways to honor brave heroes who either died in service of their nation or who spent a good portion of their lives in service to it. The same type of honor exists within the Church. Statues, icons, and images of the saints are memorials meant to remind us of the courage and piety of these holy men and women.

Do you have a picture of a deceased loved one in your wallet or hanging on the wall at home? Those images aren't idols. The pictures of saints displayed in church or in homes are the same thing: a visible reminder of someone you honor and appreciate.

Canonized saints not only have a feast day but also can have churches named after them, such as St. Bernadette's Church or the Church of St. Ann. The building is still a house of God and place of divine worship, yet the place is dedicated to the intercession (see the next section) of this particular saint.

Schools (elementary, high school, college, and university), too, can be named after canonized saints to honor their legacy of faith.

Following the Saints' Examples

By canonizing many new saints, Pope John Paul showed the world that sanctity and holiness don't belong to a clerical minority. Heaven is open to anyone who wants it and is willing to live a good and holy life.

Sainthood is a multi-step process, both in life and after death. In life, achieving holiness may involve a one-time decision to accept God, but that decision must be followed by a lifetime of living according to that decision. Martyrdom — dying in the name of faith — is a one-time act, but making such a strong commitment requires a lifetime of working toward being a true and faithful servant of God.

Sainthood is a reminder that perseverance and dedication to one's faith can bring us to our goals. As Blessed Mother Teresa of Calcutta often said, "God does not call us to be successful; he calls us to be faithful." People aren't perfect and, save for the grace of God, won't be; as such, we should stop trying to reach for that which is out of our grasp. Instead of trying to be perfect, we are called to be faithful in our efforts to do and be better.

Sainthood is also a reminder that even the most hardened sinner isn't without help or hope. Through God's grace, anyone can turn his life around and return to the faithful.

This section looks at the moral, everyday life of the hopeful saint-to-be. Because the saints are normal human beings, they have the same wounded human nature all men and women are born with, thanks to original sin. And because they have the same moral weaknesses every human does, their ability to overcome them by God's grace is also available to everyone else.

Book IV

Saints and Other Important Figures

Setting a moral and ethical foundation with the four cardinal virtues

St. Thomas Aquinas, a brilliant theologian of the 13th century, taught that "grace builds upon nature." This means that before anyone can hope to live a holy life worthy of sainthood (being in heaven), he or she must have a solid moral and ethical foundation upon which the life of grace is built. Being a holy or saintly person is no accident. You must intend and want to be holy. One must first pursue goodness before holiness. The former lays the groundwork for the latter.

The moral or cardinal virtues have been known and discussed since antiquity. Socrates, Plato, Aristotle, Cicero, and the Stoics, just to name a few, were philosophers who lived centuries before Christ and who were Greek or Roman pagans. They had no revealed religion like the Jews and Christians. But they had the use of human reason and saw that there were four cardinal (from the Latin word *cardo,* meaning "hinge" — that is, the hinges to a good moral life) virtues. The ancient philosophers realized that prudence, justice, fortitude, and temperance were the underpinnings of an ethical life and would bring peace and happiness to the individual person and to the community and society at large. Faith complements reason, so religion continues the process by adding to the cardinal or moral virtues the three theological virtues of faith, hope, and love.

The moral (cardinal) virtues can and ought to be practiced by anyone and everyone. They're good for you and help you to be and to do good, as each one is considered a habit you must acquire through effort and practice. The theological virtues come via divine grace through the sacraments, especially Baptism, which is the gateway to the other sacraments (Penance, Eucharist, Confirmation, Matrimony, Holy Orders, and Anointing of the Sick).

To be considered holy, one must first seek a life of virtue — a life guided by the four cardinal virtues of prudence, justice, fortitude, and temperance. As with any life change, each of these virtues must be practiced often before it becomes an ingrained habit.

The following sections give a closer look at each of the cardinal virtues.

Prudence

The premiere of all virtues, prudence is the ability to make good decisions and to have the ability to practice tact — knowing when, where, and how something is appropriate. You wouldn't ask a friend to repay a debt at the friend's mother's funeral. In the same vein, prudence is knowing how to approach a delicate situation with sensitivity and charity.

St. Thomas More (16th century) was a most prudent man. As Lord Chancellor of England and a wealthy nobleman, Thomas always weighed his words and deeds before he said or did them. Some may have called him cautious, but prudent best summarizes his life as a Catholic layman. During his conflict with King Henry VIII, Thomas prudently kept quiet when needed and spoke eloquently and boldly when needed as well. Never rash or impetuous, Thomas prayed and gave deliberation to every aspect of his political, social, and private life. Being wise in knowing the right time and place and the right word and action is what prudence is about. St. Thomas More is also a holy martyr — see his discussion in Book IV, Chapter 4.

Justice

Justice is doing the right thing for the right reason; *quid pro quo* (this for that), the Romans used to say. There are three kinds of justice: commutative, distributive, and social, each defined by the people involved.

- Commutative justice involves just two parties: the buyer and seller, teacher and student, neighbor and neighbor. It involves equity and fairness between the two parties.

- Distributive justice is the balance between the individual and the group, such as between a resident and a government, or a union member and the union. A resident pays taxes and votes in elections; in return, the government provides for safety and well-being.

- Social justice is the responsibility everyone has to preserve natural resources for future generations and look out for one another. When one government oppresses its people, for example, social justice drives other governments and citizens to stand up in defense of the oppressed.

St. Joseph (first century) is literally called a "just" man in the Gospel, and he epitomizes the virtue of justice. He knew what was the right thing to do, and he sought to be fair at all times. His protection of his wife Mary and her son Jesus was motivated out of love, to be sure, but it was his practice of justice that enabled him to be the husband and foster father he needed to be for his family. Being fair to everyone and doing the right thing — and not for reward or recognition — is what justice is all about.

Fortitude

Everyone has been in the position of wanting or needing to do or say something that's necessary, although not easy. Fortitude is having the courage to do or say it anyway.

Blessed Teresa of Calcutta (20th century) is certainly the poster child for fortitude and courage. She was unflinching in her determination to do what had to be done and to say what had to be said, no matter how powerful her opponents. Whether it was helping the poorest of the poor or defending the lives of the unborn in the womb, this little Albanian nun became very familiar with the virtue of fortitude, and hence, she never gave up and never quit. She spoke with charity and kindness but also with firmness of conviction — to leaders of the First, Second, and Third Worlds; the UN; Congress and the White House. Having the guts to do the job (God's will, that is) and not be influenced by ambition or fear is what fortitude is about.

Temperance

Temperance is knowing when enough is enough. Temperate people set limits on their own legitimate pleasures and activities. You may allow yourself a glass of wine, for example, but temperance keeps you from overindulging.

Book IV

Saints and Other Important Figures

St. Josemaria Escriva (20th century) was a very temperate man. He practiced moderation in his work and in his play (leisure and recreation). No party pooper, Josemaria would enjoy parties and responsibly partake of alcoholic beverages, such as wine. But he knew there had to be limits, and he didn't overindulge. He balanced work with rest. Temperance taught him the value of moderation in pleasures so as not to abuse himself or others. Josemaria also practiced some self-denial called mortification, but again in moderate ways so as not to incur injury or harm. A healthy balance is what temperance is about. St. Josemaria Escriva was also a saintly pastor — see his discussion in Book IV, Chapter 6.

Building on moral virtues with the theological virtues

The road to sainthood involves not only the moral virtues but also the *theological* virtues. These virtues are bestowed at Baptism but can be enhanced throughout one's lifetime. Baptism remits original sin and makes a person an adopted "child of God." Sanctifying grace is given at Baptism, which makes a person holy and thus able to enter the holiness of heaven. Along with sanctifying grace, Baptism also makes the soul pliable and ready for actual grace, which is the supernatural gift from God that enables you to do holy things (like pray, forgive your enemies, endure hardships, make sacrifices for others, have courage in the midst of difficulties, and so on).

Following are the theological virtues:

- ✔ **Faith** is believing what God says simply because it comes from God.

- ✔ **Hope** is trusting in promises that God has yet to fulfill, knowing that those promises one day will come to fruition, at a time and place that is right for God.

- ✔ **Love**, theologically, is a spiritual love, wanting what is best for someone else, putting others above one's self. It's not a sexual love or a biological love; it's seeking to love God and to love your neighbor.

The theological virtues build on what the moral, cardinal virtues hopefully establish as a foundation. Faith, hope, and love empower you to believe what God has revealed, to trust in his mercy and providence, to love God with your whole heart and soul, and to love your neighbor as yourself. The daily struggle to live a holy life is made possible by the theological virtues. Hence, people want and need more faith, more hope, and more love every day of their lives until they finally get to heaven, where there is the fullness of grace and the total joy without end.

Sainthood begins with virtue and ends in holiness. It's a lifelong process — there's never a time when a person can stop being prudent, just, temperate, or courageous. In the same way, faith, hope, and love are never fully realized until you get to heaven, but God gives us little morsels to savor along the way.

Understanding Angels (and Why Some Angels Are Considered Saints)

Contrary to popular belief, angels aren't people who've died and gone to heaven and then earned their wings. *Angels* are spirits that God created before he made human beings; they were the first creatures ever created and were the most powerful, most intelligent, and most beautiful. Angels are pure spirits in that they have no bodies — only intellect and will. Men and women — from Adam and Eve to today — are body *and* soul, both material and spiritual.

People who die and go to heaven don't become angels — they become saints. Angels and saints are two separate beings, separate species. Confusion arises when, on occasion, some angels are given the title *saint,* which is typically reserved for humans. The overlap is merely a matter of semantics: The Latin word for saint is *sancta,* which means holy. Once in heaven — saint or angel — one is automatically holy.

It can be confusing, but look at it this way: Angels are spirits in heaven, and saints are human beings in heaven. Angels can be called "saint" (as in the case of St. Michael the Archangel) as a sign of respect and honor. A human being is called "saint" only after death and once in heaven.

Christianity believes that angels and demons (fallen angels) are separated according to their loyalty and obedience to God. The first angels were tested on their loyalty and obedience, and those who failed, like Lucifer, were cast into hell. In hell, the angels became demons with Lucifer (whose name means *bearer of light*), who later became known as the devil (also called the *prince of darkness*).

The Bible names only three specific angels — Michael, Gabriel, and Raphael. *Apocryphal* books (texts that aren't considered authoritative on Sacred Scripture) mention others, such as Uriel and Ramiel. Because these others aren't named in the canonical books of the Bible, their identities aren't considered reliable or above reproach. The three biblical archangels are treated as true angelic beings.

Book IV

Saints and Other Important Figures

Scholars have speculated for centuries on the number of angels. St. Thomas Aquinas — often called the *angelic doctor* — believed that the precise number of angels was beyond human comprehension. Some things, however, are known, such as the fact that angels are separated into nine subdivisions, or choirs.

The nine subdivisions, from greatest to least, are

- Seraphim
- Cherubim
- Thrones
- Dominions
- Virtues
- Powers
- Principalities
- Archangels
- Angels

St. Michael the Archangel

Patron: police officers, the military

Feast day: September 29

Michael means "who is like God?" — a fitting name for one whose mission is to battle the egos of others and remind them that no one is like God. St. Michael is the only angel mentioned in both the Old Testament (Hebrew Scriptures) and New Testament. Daniel 10:13, 21 describes him as the prince of the angels and a protector of Israel. The Epistle of Jude and the Book of Revelation also mention Michael as the one who victoriously battles the devil. He is invoked anytime there is suspicion of demonic or diabolical activity. The prayer to St. Michael is used on such occasions and also was prayed after every Mass in the Catholic rite from 1886 (by Pope Leo XIII) to 1964, when Pope Paul VI dropped it. The prayer to St. Michael is:

> *St. Michael, Archangel, defend us in battle. Be our protection against the wickedness and snares of the devil. May God rebuke him, we humbly pray. And do thou, prince of the heavenly host, by the power of God, thrust into hell Satan and all the other evil spirits who prowl about the world for the ruin of souls. Amen.*

St. Michael is typically depicted in military armor (see Figure 1-1), thrusting a sword or spear into a dragon. The Sanctuary of Monte Sant'Angelo sul Gargano in Apulia, Italy, is the oldest shrine in Western Europe dedicated to St. Michael. Pious tradition holds that the archangel appeared there four times in a 1,000-year period. Pilgrims of St. Padre Pio of Pietrelcina often visit, as St. Pio had a strong devotion to the place and to St. Michael. Also, St. Joan of Arc had visions of St. Michael (accompanied by St. Catherine of Alexandria and St. Margaret) in the 15th century.

Figure 1-1:
St. Michael
the
Archangel.

© National Gallery,
London/Art Resource, NY

Although he's called *archangel,* St. Michael is most likely a member of the seraphim, the highest rank of angels, whose mission is to praise God day and night. Any angel above the rank angel can be called archangel out of respect.

St. Gabriel the Archangel

Patron: messengers, journalists, and communications

Feast day: September 29

St. Gabriel is probably most widely recognized as the angel who comes to Mary and tells her she's carrying the Christ child. He also appears to Zachariah to inform him that his wife Elizabeth — the Virgin Mary's cousin — will give birth to a son, John (the Baptist).

The name *Gabriel* means *strength of God.* Images of St. Gabriel often depict him with a herald's trumpet, as he was the divine messenger to the Virgin Mary.

St. Raphael the Archangel

Patron: travelers

Feast day: September 29

Raphael means *healing of God.* This angel appears in the Book of Tobit, where he is sent by God to help three people: Tobit, his son Tobiah, and his future daughter-in-law Sarah. Sarah had been cursed by the demon Asmodeus so that her husband died on their wedding night before they consummated the marriage, leaving her without offspring.

Widows without children were considered the most desperate and pathetic of society, because in ancient times, women literally depended on their husbands and sons to care for and protect them. Without either husband or children, a widow was as vulnerable as an orphan. For Sarah, the situation was even more tragic: Before she married Tobiah, she had had seven previous husbands, and all of them died on their wedding night.

Tobit, a wealthy and devout Jew, lived among the captives being deported to Nineveh from the northern kingdom of Israel in 721 B.C. According to Jewish tradition, Jews are required to bury their dead, especially the Hebrew victims of King Sennacherib of Assyria. The burial rite was against the law, however, as Hebrew captives had no civil rights whatsoever.

One night, after burying a fellow Israelite, Tobit slept outside his bedroom and was blinded by droppings left by birds. In those times, blindness was as much a tragedy as being a widow or orphan. Raphael was sent to help restore sight to Tobit, to end the curse of Sarah, and to unite Sarah and Tobiah as husband and wife. During his visit, he appeared in human form, and only when he was about to return to heaven did Raphael reveal his true identity. Because of his time accompanying young Tobiah on a journey, St. Raphael is invoked as the patron of travelers, especially those on a pilgrimage.

Tobit is one of the seven books of the Old Testament that are in the Catholic and Eastern Orthodox Bibles but are missing from the Protestant Bibles, or sometimes placed at the back of the book in a section called *Apocrypha* (other writings). Catholicism calls these books *deuterocanonical,* which means from a second (*deutero* in Greek) *canon* (authorized list). The first 39 books are from the first canon and were written originally in Hebrew before the Babylonian Captivity (586 B.C.), when two-thirds of the Jews were exiled from the southern kingdom of Judah. (The northern kingdom of Israel had been conquered by Assyria in 720 B.C.) The seven books of the Deuterocanon (or Apocrypha in Protestant theology) are Baruch, Maccabees I and II, Tobit, Judith, Ecclesiasticus (Sirach), and Wisdom. They were written in Greek during the captivity and were included in the Septuagint (the first Greek translation of the entire Hebrew Bible/Christian Old Testament), written in 250–150 B.C.

The Blessed Virgin Mary

As the Mother of the Son of God, the Virgin Mary is the highest of all saints and deserving of the highest praise possible.

None of the saints can be *worshiped* — that's an honor reserved for God alone. Theologians call the honor given to saints *dulia* to distinguish it from *latria,* the worship of God. The honor given to Mary is called *hyperdulia* because it's the highest form allowed and required.

Mary, Joseph, and baby Jesus

The story of Mary is one of the most repeated stories of the Bible. She had been engaged to be married to Joseph of Nazareth for some time as a young girl. Before the wedding, however, the angel Gabriel appeared to her and announced that she was to give birth to the *Messiah* (Hebrew word for anointed one), also called the *Christ* (from the Greek word for anointed one, *Kristos*).

Mary, a virgin and engaged to be married, was confused — how could she become the Mother of the Savior? Gabriel tells her that through the power of the Holy Spirit, she'll become pregnant with Jesus without the biological cooperation of any human male. It will literally be a virgin birth. This miraculous beginning of Jesus is foretold in the Old Testament prophecy of Isaiah 7:14 that a virgin shall conceive and bear a son.

Joseph, knowing he isn't the biological father but initially ignorant of the divine origin of Mary's pregnancy, plans to divorce her quietly. Gabriel then appears to him in a dream and tells him that Mary has indeed been faithful but is with child by the power of the Holy Spirit. Joseph awakes and takes Mary into his home. When she is about to give birth, the Roman Emperor Caesar Augustus issues a decree for a universal census, making Mary and Joseph travel to their ancestral hometown of Bethlehem, where her baby, Jesus, is born.

Book IV

Saints and Other Important Figures

The family is forced to flee to Egypt after Jesus's birth, when King Herod tries to kill the baby Jesus in an attempt to thwart the prophecy. Herod orders all firstborn males age 2 and under to be slaughtered; Jesus only escaped because his mother and her husband hid in Egypt until the death of their enemy.

Back in Nazareth, Mary and Joseph raised Jesus in a normal home setting, and Jesus became known as a carpenter's son. (See Figure 1-2 for a depiction of the Holy Family.) Jesus lived with Mary and Joseph for 30 years before he began his public ministry. That ministry continued for three years until his Crucifixion, death, and Resurrection in A.D. 33.

Figure 1-2:
The Holy Family of Mary, Joseph, and Jesus.

Réunion des Musées Nationaux/Art Resource, NY

Other key references to Mary in the Bible

Mary is mentioned in the Gospel in the beginning of Jesus's life, from his conception at the Annunciation (when Gabriel tells Mary she's to become the mother of the Messiah) to the Nativity (Christmas Day, when Jesus is born) of Christ, and also at other key moments.

Meeting the Magi

Shortly after Jesus's birth and before the family flees into Egypt, Mary encounters the Magi, or three wise men, who bring gifts to the Christ child (this event is called the Epiphany). One brings a gift of gold, to represent the kingship of Christ; one brings frankincense, to represent the divinity of Christ; and the third brings myrrh, to represent the human mortality of Christ (Matthew 2:1–11).

Seeing the future

On the eighth day after his birth, Jesus was to be circumcised according to Mosaic law, and Mary and Joseph take the child to the Temple in Jerusalem, where he is also presented for a blessing. While there, the family meets Simeon, an old holy man who has been promised by God that he won't die until his eyes see the Messiah. Simeon prophesies that Mary will be pierced by a sword of sorrow as her son will be the rise and fall of many in Israel (Luke 2:22–35). After Jesus's death on the cross on Good Friday, a Roman soldier thrusts a spear into his heart, whereupon blood and water flow out. Mary's maternal heart also must have been wounded, emotionally speaking, as she helplessly watches the horrible ordeal her only son endures for our salvation (John 19:34).

Fearing for a lost child

When Jesus was 12 years old he was thought to be missing for three days (Luke 2:41–52) during the Feast of Passover. It's a mother's nightmare: Your only child is gone, and you have no idea where he is. Mary and Joseph look frantically for three days after leaving Jerusalem, only to find Jesus among the religious teachers, not only listening to them but teaching them, as well. Confronting the adolescent Savior, Mary asks Jesus why he put his parents through all this anxiety and worry. Jesus replies, "Why were you looking for me? Did you not know that I must be in my Father's house?" Like the prophecy of Simeon and the gifts of the Magi, Christ's response to his mother stays with Mary, as Scripture says she "pondered these things in her heart" (Luke 2:51).

After the incident in the Temple, the Bible says nothing more of Jesus until he turned 30 and began his public ministry. Most likely, Jesus lived with his mom and worked in the carpenter's shop with Joseph, because in several places in the Bible, he's called not only the carpenter's son but also a carpenter himself.

Jesus's first miracle

Jesus's first miracle came at the request of his mother. Jesus was in the early days of his ministry after 40 days of fasting and praying in the desert. Mary comes to him as an intercessor for the Church, seeking his mediation. Jesus is the one and only mediator between God and man because he is both human and divine.

Mary and Jesus attend a wedding reception, and Mary notices that the wine has run out. Weddings then were much like weddings today: As long as the food and wine kept coming, the guests were happy. When either ran out, the guests left. So Mary tells Jesus the situation ("they have no more wine") in John 2:3, and he replies mysteriously: "Woman, what does this have to do with me?" (John 2:4).

Book IV

Saints and Other Important Figures

If the story ended there, it would be logical to conclude that Jesus rebuked his mother. When looked at more closely and in context, it's a totally different matter. The original Greek text of John's Gospel says: *gynai, ti emoi kai soi,* which literally translates to "woman, what [is] to me [is] to you," and the Latin of St. Jerome's Vulgate is the same *(quid mihi et tibi est mulier).* Immediately after he responds to his mother, she tells the waiters, "Do whatever he tells you." Then Jesus orders them to take six stone water jars (each holding 20 to 30 gallons), fill them to the brim with water, and then pour some to the wine steward. What he tastes is not water, but the best wine he's ever had.

Standing at the foot of the cross

After all his disciples abandon him during his Crucifixion and death at Calvary, save for St. John the Evangelist, Jesus's mother, the Virgin Mary, stands at the foot of the cross. Her presence gives him comfort, but at the same time, it's a cause of great suffering. It's a comfort because, in his sacred humanity, Jesus has the same human love any son would have for his mother. He also sees that his pain and suffering cause her emotional pain and suffering. What son wants to see his own mother in such agony? Yet it's his physical agony that causes her emotional agony. Knowing that his death is weighing heavily on his mother, Jesus gives his only possession not stolen from him by his persecutors: his mother. He gives her to St. John when he says, "behold, your mother" (John 19:27).

Silent according to Scripture, Mary says nothing — just remains a disciple with Jesus to the very end. After his death, she takes his lifeless body when it comes off the cross and holds it lovingly in her arms (as depicted in Michelangelo's *Pieta*).

Mary's final appearance in the Bible takes place at Pentecost, 50 days after Jesus's Resurrection on Easter Sunday. The Acts of the Apostles tells us that Mary was present in the same Upper Room that Christ had used before on Holy Thursday, when he celebrated the Last Supper with his 12 Apostles. Now, each of those same men, along with the Mother of Jesus, will experience the coming of the Holy Spirit upon them. Her presence at what is considered the birthday of the Church convinced the bishops at Vatican II to call Mary the Mother of the Church.

Mary's perpetual virginity (before, during, and after the birth of Christ her son) is a doctrine of the Catholic faith, as are her Immaculate Conception and her Assumption. These dogmas flow from the same central dogma that any and all privileges and honors given to Mary are based solely on her unique relationship to Christ, her son.

Celebrating Mary's feast days

Mary has several feast days. Being the human Mother of Jesus, her maternal relationship is real and permanent. Therefore, just as any son or daughter would honor special occasions in the life of his or her mother, so, too, the Church observes the unique events in the life of the Mother of the Savior. Following is a quick rundown:

✔ Her birth is celebrated on September 8 in the Latin Church. The Church only celebrates three earthly birthdays: Jesus Christ on December 25; St. John the Baptist on June 24; and the Virgin Mary's. The feast days for the other saints usually mark their heavenly birthdays — that is, the day they died. Mary's earthly birthday is important because Jesus would have honored his mother's birthday.

✔ The Church celebrates Mary's conception just as it celebrates Jesus's. December 8 is the Solemnity of the Immaculate Conception, flowing from the dogma of the Immaculate Conception defined by Pope Pius IX in 1854. This dogma teaches that by a special grace from God, the Virgin Mary was preserved from all sin, even original sin, from the moment of her conception so that when she grew up, she could become the Mother of the Messiah. As such, she would need to be free from sin so she could give Jesus an untainted human nature.

✔ Mary's *Assumption* into heaven is celebrated on August 15. This day marks the taking up of Mary's body and soul by Jesus. (The *Ascension* is when Jesus himself took his body and soul into heaven 40 days after Easter. The Assumption is when he took his mother's body and soul to the same place.)

✔ The *Motherhood* of Jesus is celebrated on January 1. It was formerly the Feast of the Circumcision, but the Second Vatican Council wanted to begin the civil new year by honoring Mary, the Mother of God.

✔ Mary's *Queenship* is celebrated August 22. This feast is relatively new on the calendar, but the title is ancient. It's an extension of the honor due to Christ the King and by extension to Mary, who is the Mother of the King. As Queen Mother, she is honored, venerated, and highly respected above all other humans and angels.

✔ Numerous other Marian feasts honor various *apparitions* (appearances of Mary) such as Lourdes, Fatima, Guadalupe, Knock Ireland, and so on. Other feasts associated with Mary, such as Our Lady of Mount Carmel (July 16) and Our Lady of Seven Sorrows (September 15), are secondary to the major ones listed here.

Book IV

Saints and Other Important Figures

For a fuller description of the role of the Blessed Virgin Mary, see Book IV, Chapter 7.

Chapter 2

Starting at the Beginning: Apostles and Evangelists

In This Chapter

▶ Jesus's followers as the first saints

▶ Early saints who spread the Gospel

The early saints are those who witnessed firsthand (or who personally knew actual eyewitnesses of) the teachings and miracles of Jesus Christ and who helped spread the word of God. This chapter introduces you to the Apostles and Evangelists who walked alongside Christ and documented the journey. It discusses the struggles they faced, the battles they fought, and the way each one met his demise.

An *Apostle* is one of the original 12 men chosen by Jesus to be his follower. *Evangelists* are the four men inspired by the Holy Spirit to write a Gospel account of Jesus.

St. Peter

Galilee (first century B.C.–A.D. 64)

Patron: diocese of Rome, fishermen

Feast day: June 29

Peter, a fisherman, was given the honor of leading the disciples after Jesus ascended into heaven 40 days after his Resurrection from the dead. Born Simon bar Jona (*son of John* in Hebrew), Jesus later called him Peter (from the Greek word *petra,* meaning "rock") to designate that he would be the "rock" on which Christ would establish the Church (Matthew 16:18).

The Gospel mentions Peter's mother-in-law, so he must have had a wife at some time. However, her name is never revealed, and she isn't even mentioned in the telling of Jesus's miraculous cure of her mother (Mark 1:29–31). This anonymity, combined with Peter's travels spreading the Good News, indicates that his wife may have passed away before Jesus called him to be an Apostle.

Of the 12 Apostles handpicked by Jesus, Peter was chosen to be in charge after Christ's Ascension to heaven. The other Apostles recognized Peter's authority and didn't challenge him as the head of the Church on earth. This is evidenced when John ran to the tomb ahead of Peter on Easter Sunday. He was younger and faster, but, although he got there first, he didn't go in; rather, he waited for Peter out of respect for his position as chief Apostle (John 20:4–5).

The Acts of the Apostles (the book following the Gospel of John) discusses several examples of Peter's leadership of the early Church, especially after Pentecost, when the Holy Spirit came upon the Apostles and the Virgin Mary, 50 days after Easter and 10 days after Jesus ascended to heaven.

Peter's authority also is shown when he presides over the election of Matthias to replace Judas (Acts 1:26) and when he leads the Council of Jerusalem (Acts 15). Even St. Paul (after his conversion and change of name from Saul) "goes to see Peter" out of respect for his position (Galatians 1:18).

Peter was martyred in Rome during the reign of Emperor Nero, who ruled from A.D. 54 to A.D. 68. It's believed that Peter was arrested and imprisoned not far from where the Roman Coliseum now stands. Today, the St. Peter in Chains Church marks the spot of Peter's arrest. It's a minor basilica with a great treasure: a statue of Moses that Michelangelo carved out of Carrara marble.

According to pious tradition, Peter didn't consider himself worthy of Christ-like crucifixion because he had denied his association with Jesus three times on Good Friday. Roman soldiers instead crucified him upside down (see the nearby sidebar on "St. Peter's Cross").

Peter is buried on Vatican Hill, the present-day site of the Basilica of St. Peter, where the pope most often celebrates Mass.

Three churches have been built over this site through the centuries. The first was built in the fourth century by Constantine, who first proclaimed the joint feast of Peter and Paul. The second was built in the ninth century directly on top of the earlier edifice. Pope Julius II laid the cornerstone in 1506 and Pope St. Pius V finished the present-day basilica in 1615, again directly over the ninth-century church.

In 1938, Pope Pius XII permitted archaeologists to excavate under the basilicas, all the way to the first-century cemetery, which led to the discovery of the famous "Red Wall." The wall of one of the tombs is marked in red graffiti, noting the final resting spot of Peter and Paul. The first-century tomb lies directly under Bernini's magnificent 16th-century canopy over the high altar.

SS. Peter and Paul are shown together in Figure 2-1. Paul is depicted on the left holding a sword, the means of his martyrdom, while Peter is on the right holding keys, referencing the authority Jesus gave him as head of the Church in the Gospel of Matthew (16:19).

Figure 2-1:
SS. Paul
(left) and
Peter.

© National Gallery, London/
Art Resource, NY

St. Andrew

Bethsaida (first century A.D.–A.D. 69)

Patron: fishermen, Scotland, Greece, Constantinople

Feast day: November 30

Brother to the man who would become their leader, Andrew was the first of Jesus's Apostles.

Andrew was born in Bethsaida in Galilee, the same area in which St. John the Baptist, a cousin to Jesus, first preached that Jesus was the Messiah. Andrew was so impressed that he sought out Jesus for further instruction. Inspired, uplifted, and overjoyed, Andrew recruited his brother (Simon, whom Jesus renamed Peter — see the preceding section), who also became a disciple.

The Sea of Galilee and fishing played an important role in the brothers' lives. Fishing was their livelihood, and the Lord used the sea and fishing many times as points of reference. The Lord used their fishing boat as a pulpit to preach to those gathered along the shore, right before the miracle of the loaves. Andrew and Peter witnessed Jesus walking on the water from their boat. Finally, after a bad night of fishing, Jesus encouraged them to go out once again in their fishing boat, and the brothers came back with their boat overflowing with fish. When they returned, the Lord bid them to become "fishers of men" and to follow him (Matthew 4:18–19).

St. Andrew is believed to have taken the message of the Gospel to Greece and even as far as Constantinople. He was martyred by crucifixion, tied to the cross in the form of an X. To this day, the 24th letter of the alphabet is a symbol of St. Andrew. The Scottish flag is blue with a white X representing its patron.

During the Middle Ages, the relics of St. Andrew were transferred to the Republic of Amalfi on the southwest coast of Italy, where the Basilica of St. Andrew still houses some of his remains; other relics are in Rome. In a gesture of ecumenism, Pope John Paul II returned the relic of St. Andrew's head to the patriarch of the Greek Orthodox Church. Customarily, a 30-day Christmas novena commences on his feast day and continues to the feast of Christmas.

St. James the Greater

Galilee (first century A.D.–A.D. 44)

Patron: Spain, arthritis, hat makers

Feast day: July 25

James is one of a three-man privileged inner circle of Jesus's Apostles, joining St. Peter and St. John the Evangelist. These three were allowed to witness miracles that the other Apostles only heard about. James witnessed the cure of Peter's mother-in-law and the raising of Jarius's daughter from the dead, among other miracles.

James the Greater was the brother of St. John the Evangelist and one of Zebedee's sons. (Two Apostles are named James; this one is known as "the Greater" because he was the older of the two.) Like Peter and Andrew, James earned his living as a fisherman. He and his brother, John, were called by the Lord at the same time he called Peter and Andrew.

Peter, John, and James were the fortunate witnesses to Jesus's Transfiguration on Mount Tabor. This event was most important, for the Lord dazzled the Apostles with his divinity right before his pending passion. As members of the inner circle, their testimony and faithfulness would be needed after the Lord's crucifixion.

Pious tradition holds that, after the Ascension of the Lord, James brought the message of Jesus to Spain and evangelized that country. In fact, there's a magnificent basilica of Santiago (Spanish and Portuguese for *St. James*) in Compostela, in Spain's northwest corner. Compostela lies at the center of the most famous pilgrimage trails throughout all of Europe; since the early Middle Ages, pilgrims have traveled roads from Rome, France, and Spain to this shrine, where relics of St. James are believed to lie in repose. (Other relics of the saint are housed in Rome.)

As he was led outside Jerusalem for martyrdom, James walked by a man crippled with arthritis, who begged James for a cure. James prayed over him and commanded him to stand up, and the man was miraculously cured. Today, despite all the advances in medicine, arthritis has no cure. Those suffering from it may seek relief through prayers to James the Greater.

St. John the Evangelist

Galilee (first century A.D.–A.D. 100)

Patron: editors, writers, burn victims, poison victims

Feast day: December 27

St. John the Evangelist, the Beloved Disciple, was the youngest of the Apostles and the third to be admitted to Jesus's privileged inner circle, alongside St. James the Greater and St. Peter. He wrote the fourth Gospel and is also known as John the Divine for his lofty theology.

John was one of the three Apostles (along with his brother, James the Greater, and Peter) privileged to witness Jesus's Transfiguration on Mt. Tabor (Matthew 17:1–6). On Easter Sunday, John raced to the tomb after hearing that Mary Magdalene discovered it empty. Out of respect for Peter's position as the leader of the Apostles, John waited outside the tomb until Peter entered (John 20:1–9).

Before the Savior died, he entrusted his mother, the Virgin Mary, to the care of John, the Beloved Disciple (John 19:27). Pious tradition holds that she lived with John in Ephesus until her Assumption in Jerusalem.

Book IV

Saints and Other Important Figures

Pious tradition also asserts that after Mary's Assumption, John began his missionary expeditions throughout Asia Minor. He was arrested under the reign of the Emperor Domitian, who tried to boil him in oil. John was miraculously preserved, not only from death but also from any harm.

He was then banished to the island of Patmos in the Aegean Sea. On this island, John received personal revelations that formed the Book of Revelation or the Apocalypse, the last book of the New Testament and of the Christian Bible. He received these revelations in a cave located under the present-day monastery dedicated to his honor. John later traveled to Ephesus, where, inspired by the Holy Spirit and aided by his devoted friends, he wrote the Gospel According to St. John and the three Letters of St. John. In his letters, he addresses the Christian community as *catholic,* meaning "for all."

Figure 2-2 shows an artist's rendering of John on the island of Patmos. The eagle (sitting on the book to the right) is the most ancient symbol for John the Evangelist, just as the lion is for Mark, the ox is for Luke, and the man is for Matthew.

Figure 2-2:
A depiction
of St. John
on the
island of
Patmos.

© National Gallery, London/Art Resource, NY

Compared to the Gospels of Matthew, Mark, and Luke, John's is much more theological and philosophical. He writes for a Christian audience and gives more substance in some areas, such as the Holy Eucharist (John 6). His symbol as Evangelist is the eagle, because he opens his Gospel with lofty ideas of preexistence: "In the beginning was the Word, and the Word was with God and the Word was God." His symbol as Apostle is a cup, with a serpent representing a failed attempt to poison him.

Because John was the youngest of the 12 Apostles, he's often depicted in sacred art as beardless, unlike the other 11. This is why, in Leonardo da Vinci's painting of the Last Supper, John, seated to Jesus's right, looks very young. John is also the only Apostle who wasn't martyred. He lived into his 90s and died of natural causes, probably in Ephesus in present-day Turkey.

St. James the Less

(first century A.D.–A.D. 62)

Patron: fullers, pharmacists

Feast day: May 3

St. James was named the first Bishop of Jerusalem, and because of his location, he became a champion for Jewish converts to Christianity.

James is the author of the New Testament epistle in his name. He is called "the Less" to distinguish him from the older James (see the section on St. James the Greater, earlier in this chapter).

St. James the Less was the son of Alpheus, brother to Joseph (often written as "Joses") and cousin to Simon and Jude. Although he was sometimes referred to as the "brother of the Lord" or the "brother of Jesus," in reality he was a cousin, although no one knows whether the relationship was through the Virgin Mary or her husband Joseph. (Ancient Greeks used the word *adelphos* to refer to any male relative, be it brother, cousin, uncle, or nephew, so precise relationships are often difficult to determine.)

Unlike Paul, St. James the Less favored following the Mosaic laws of circumcision and diet. This debate led to the First Ecumenical Council of Jerusalem. Historic in nature, the council showed the workings of the Church after the Ascension of the Lord. James had been a strong proponent of requiring Gentiles to first convert to Judaism before converting to Christianity. After listening to Peter say in Jerusalem that there was a direct, fast-track conversion from paganism to Christianity, James deferred to that decision.

There are many stories concerning the death of James the Less, but the most credible one comes from the Jewish historian Josephus. He wrote that James was martyred in A.D. 62 by being thrown from a pinnacle off the Temple and then stoned and beaten with clubs.

Book IV

Saints and Other Important Figures

St. Bartholomew

Palestine (first century A.D.)

Patron: shoemakers, cobblers, butchers, tanners

Feast day: August 24

St. Bartholomew is believed to have carried the Gospel to several countries, resulting in a martyrdom of being flayed, or skinned, alive.

Nathaniel Bar-Tholmai is known just by his first name or by the common rendering of his surname, which literally means *son of Tolomai.*

Philip introduced Bartholomew to the Lord. When told that the Messiah had arrived and that he was Jesus of Nazareth, Bartholomew's response was, "Can anything good come from Nazareth?" which prompted Jesus to say, "This man has no guile" (John 1:47); in other words, he speaks his mind.

John's Gospel mentions Bartholomew as one of the Apostles to whom the risen Christ appeared at the Sea of Galilee after his Resurrection. Bartholomew is believed to have carried the Gospel to India, Mesopotamia, Persia, Egypt, and Armenia.

The remains of St. Bartholomew were transferred to two churches in Italy: Benevento and the Church of St. Bartholomew-in-the-Tiber in Rome. This saint's main symbol consists of three knives representing his gruesome death.

Because of the manner in which he died, St. Bartholomew became the patron saint of butchers, tanners, and leather workers, who peel the hide off animals before the carcasses are sent to the butcher.

St. Thomas

Galilee (first century A.D.–A.D. 72)

Patron: India, Pakistan, doubters

Feast day: December 21

St. Thomas is perhaps best known for his post-Resurrection confession to the risen Savior.

After the Crucifixion, most of the Apostles were devastated; they didn't quite grasp the fact that Jesus was the Messiah. When the Lord appeared to them on that first Easter Sunday, Thomas was missing. When the other Apostles told Thomas about seeing the risen Lord, Thomas said he wouldn't believe it was Jesus until he had seen and felt the Lord's wounds for himself — thereby becoming known as Doubting Thomas (and thus the namesake of skeptics who demand proof before being convinced).

A week later, the risen Lord once again appeared to the Apostles, and this time Thomas was present. He had Thomas probe his wounds, and Thomas made his solemn confession of faith in the risen Savior. Thomas's doubt has become the certitude of faith for all those who weren't eyewitnesses to the Resurrection. His famous confession is a classic for all those preparing to receive Holy Communion at Holy Mass: "My Lord and my God!"

There are many folkloric tales concerning Thomas, but most historians agree that he evangelized India, where he was martyred. Christians belonging to the Syro-Malabar Rite attribute their group's foundation to Thomas.

Legend has it that King Gundafor commissioned Thomas to build a palace. He gave Thomas the money and then left on a long journey. When he returned, the monarch asked to see his new home. Thomas had spent all the money to help the poor and told the king that he had built him a heavenly home instead. Gundafor ordered Thomas's death, but the night before the execution, the king dreamt of his dead brother, who told him of the gorgeous home Thomas had built for him in heaven. The next day, the king released Thomas, and his whole family converted to Christianity. King Mazdai, however, didn't convert and was enraged when his wife did. He had Thomas speared to death in A.D. 72.

The apocryphal Gospel ascribed to Thomas was probably written by Gnostics who sought to vindicate their heretical ideas, and thus it isn't part of the *Canon* (approved lists of inspired books) of the Bible.

St. Jude Thaddeus

Galilee (first century A.D.)

Patron: lost causes, hopeless cases, impossible burdens

Feast day: October 28

Jude is Aramaic for *support of God.* Jude Thaddeus was the brother of James the Less and author of the New Testament epistle named after him. The epistle isn't addressed to any particular Christian community; rather, it's a general exhortation concerning the scandalous behavior of some converts who have no intention of following the Lord.

After the commissioning of the 12 Apostles, Jude aligned with Simon and went to preach the Gospel in Persia. There he was martyred by being clubbed to death. He's often pictured holding or resting on this instrument of torture.

St. Jude became the patron saint of lost causes partially because he was often mistaken for Christ's betrayer, Judas (Jude) Iscariot, as they had the same first name.

This devotion as patron of desperate cases has two celebrated shrines in the United States. The first, in Chicago, was built as a place of hope for people hit hard by the Great Depression. The other is in Baltimore, the famous St. Jude Shrine on Paca Street, founded by Italians in 1873. The devotion to St. Jude at this church expanded during World War II, and many prayed for the safe return of the nation's armed service men and women. Today, St. Jude's Shrine in Baltimore is still a popular pilgrim destination for East Coast Catholics.

Another famous place is St. Jude Children's Hospital in Memphis, Tennessee. Actor Danny Thomas prayed to St. Jude Thaddeus in the early 1950s when he was a young, unknown, and struggling entertainer with a baby on the way. Penniless, he promised St. Jude he would build a shrine if the saint would intercede on his behalf before the Lord. Soon his career in television took off, but he never forgot his promise and helped build the now-famous children's hospital in honor of St. Jude, who had helped him many years before.

St. Matthew

Galilee (first century A.D.)

Patron: tax collectors, accountants, bookkeepers

Feast day: September 21

Matthew, originally known as Levi, may have been the last person Jesus's followers would have chosen as an Apostle. He was a tax collector, a profession loathed as being traitorous and collaborating with the occupying Romans. So despised were these "civil servants" of the Roman Empire that Jews were forbidden to marry or even associate with them.

Because of Matthew's profession, there was something of a scandal when Jesus approached him. Yet, as Jesus himself often said, he came not for the healthy but for the sick, to seek the lost that they may be found. While not physically ill, Matthew was spiritually in need of healing. The invitation to become a follower of Christ was too great to resist, so he became a disciple when asked.

Author of the first Gospel in the New Testament, Matthew wrote for a predominantly Hebrew audience — that is, to Jews who were curious about or interested in Jesus but didn't know the story. This is seen in his meticulous attention to biblical references in the Old Testament prophesying the Messiah. His genealogy of Christ in the first chapter begins with Abraham and ends with Joseph, the husband of Mary. (Although Jesus wasn't the biological son of Joseph, he was the adopted and legal heir in Mosaic law, so Jesus was properly known as the "son" of Joseph.)

Matthew also accentuates the connection between Jesus and Moses, the hero of the Old Testament, particularly through his comparison of Jesus's Sermon on the Mount (Matthew 5:1) to Moses receiving the Ten Commandments from God (Exodus 19).

How St. Matthew was martyred isn't known. His symbol is the figure of a man with wings, because he begins his Gospel with the genealogy of Jesus that shows the humanity of the Lord united to his divinity in one divine person.

St. Matthias

Judaea (first century A.D.–A.D. 80)

Patron: reformed alcoholics, tailors

Feast day: May 14

St. Matthias, whose name in Hebrew means *gift of the Lord,* was appointed an Apostle following the betrayal and suicide of Judas Iscariot, one of the original 12 Apostles. Matthias was one of the original 72 disciples of the Lord from the time of Jesus's baptism in the Jordan River.

After the Ascension of Jesus to heaven and the descent of the Holy Spirit at Pentecost, Peter and the other Apostles met to decide what to do about the vacancy left by Judas. The choice was between Matthias and Barsabas, and the Apostles chose Matthias by casting lots (Acts 1:26).

St. Clement of Alexandria explains how Matthias preached throughout Judea, Greece, and Cappadocia (in present-day Turkey), as well as the great discipline Matthias practiced. Based on his experiences with the Lord, he was able to abstain from legitimate pleasures in order to control the lower passions. Subsequently, he became one of the patron saints for alcoholics.

He was martyred in Jerusalem, stoned to death. In the fourth century, St. Helena transferred his relics to Rome.

Book IV

Saints and Other Important Figures

St. Philip

Galilee (first century A.D.–A.D. 80)

Patron: pastry chefs, jockeys and horsemen, Uruguay, Luxembourg

Feast day: May 3

Little is known about St. Philip, other than he was with the other 11 Apostles for the Last Supper, for the Ascension, and for Pentecost.

A Galilean from Bethsaida, Philip was probably a disciple of John the Baptist before being called to follow Jesus. He introduced Nathaniel (also known as Bartholomew) to Jesus and is the one who said to Christ, "Show us the Father," to which he responded, "Philip, whoever has seen me has seen the Father" (John 14:8–9).

He was present at the miracle of the loaves and fishes as Jesus directly asks him, "Where are we to buy bread so as to feed them [the five thousand]?" Philip replies, "Two hundred denarii would not buy enough" (John 6:5,7).

Philip is believed to have traveled to Ephesus in present-day Turkey and to Phrygia and Hierapolis in present-day Greece, where he was martyred and buried. He was crucified upside down under the reign of Emperor Domitian. In the seventh century, his relics were transferred to the Basilica of the Apostles in Rome, where they are venerated today. His name means *lover of horses,* and so he is the patron saint of jockeys, horse breeders, and horse-back riders.

St. Simon the Zealot

Cana (first century A.D.)

Patron: lumberjacks, woodcutters

Feast day: October 28

In Hebrew, Simon's name means *God has answered.* He is also known as the zealot because of his religious zeal for the Hebrew religion. Not much more is known about Simon except the fact that he is listed as one of the 12 Apostles in the Gospels.

Pious tradition maintains that he preached in Egypt and Mesopotamia and was martyred in Persia in the first century by being sawed in half. He's often pictured holding a lumberjack's saw as his symbol.

St. Mark

Palestine or Libya (first century A.D.–A.D. 68)

Patron: Venice, lion trainers

Feast day: April 25

St. Mark, one of the original 72 disciples, was never appointed an Apostle. He was the youngest follower of Christ; when Jesus was arrested prior to his Crucifixion, Mark fled from the Temple guards so quickly that he left his tunic behind.

Author of the second Gospel, Mark wrote for a Roman audience. His Greek (the language used by all four Evangelists to write the Gospels) was so good that scholars believe he was a Greek convert to Judaism before becoming a follower of Jesus. His mother was the sister of St. Barnabas, companion to St. Paul.

Mark used the same kind of literary tools as Matthew in that he reported what he knew a Roman would want to hear — no more and no less. Mark is the shortest of the four Gospels and is very active with short sentences.

Mark eventually preached the Gospel all the way to Alexandria, Egypt, where he was martyred. Arrested for his faith, Mark was bound and gagged and then dragged by horses through the streets of the city.

His symbol is the lion with wings, as his Gospel opens describing John the Baptist as a "voice crying in the wilderness," much like a lion would do (Mark 1:3). The relics of St. Mark were transferred to Venice more than a thousand years ago, and even today, there are lions all over the city. Even the great basilica, originally the Doge's Chapel, was renamed St. Mark.

St. Luke

Antioch, Syria (first century A.D.–A.D. 84)

Patron: physicians, healthcare workers, painters

Feast day: October 18

St. Luke, a Greek physician and convert to Christianity, wrote the third Gospel and the Acts of the Apostles in his native language. After his conversion, he belonged to the Christian community in Antioch and met St. Paul. Eventually, Luke accompanied Paul on some of his missionary journeys. St. Paul was physically not very healthy, and it's widely believed that Luke took care of him.

Besides being a physician, Luke was also a historian and documented happenings of the day. His attention to detail is reflected in his writing. Only in St. Luke's Gospel are there such details as the Annunciation of Mary, the Visitation, 6 miracles, and 18 parables. The miracles are especially poignant, because Luke was a doctor and naturally concerned with physical illness. In Acts, Luke shares wonderful insights into the workings of the first-century Church.

Luke's Gospel accentuates Jesus in his universal call to holiness to save all men and women, not just the chosen people of Abraham. He mentions the conspicuous times Jesus speaks and interacts with non-Jewish persons, like Samaritans, Greeks, and Romans. The Gospel of Luke has been called the "gospel of mercy" for all the miraculous healings it describes, and the "gospel of women" for the prominent role women play, in contrast to the other Gospels.

Legend relays that Luke was also an artist. The first icon of Mary and the baby Jesus is attributed to him.

Luke eventually met up with the Virgin Mary in Ephesus. This is where he learned about the infancy of Christ and everything that surrounds the Lord's birth.

Not much is known about Luke's death. Some early Church Fathers declare he died at the age of 84; others say he was martyred. In any event, his relics were transferred to Constantinople, the new capital of the empire in the fourth century. Before the fall of the Byzantine Empire, his relics were moved to Rome.

St. Paul

Tarsus (first century A.D.–A.D. 65)

Patron: preachers, writers, tent makers

Feast day: January 25 (Conversion of St. Paul)

Known before his conversion to Christianity as Saul of Tarsus, Paul is probably the most mentioned in all of the New Testament Scriptures — 14 of the 27 books of the New Testament are ascribed to his name. While he wrote no Gospel, he did write pastoral letters to early Christian communities with a message that transcends time and space and which the Church considers divinely inspired.

He was born in Tarsus and was thus a Roman citizen. A member of the Pharisees, Saul was a militant persecutor of the new-found sect of Christianity. He saw Christians as disloyal to their Hebrew religion and considered Christianity a perversion, not a valid expression of Judaism. He was present at the stoning of St. Stephen, the first Christian martyr and deacon of the Church (Acts 7:58).

Saul's outlook irrevocably changed while he was on the way to Damascus to round up Christians (men, women, and children). He was knocked to the ground and heard the voice of Jesus say, "Saul, Saul, why do you persecute me?" (Acts 9:4). He realized that he was persecuting Jesus by persecuting his followers. Christ had already died, risen, and ascended when Saul had this encounter. From that moment onward, he was known as Paul. Temporarily blinded after hearing the voice, Paul fully recovered his sight when Ananais laid hands on him and baptized him (Acts 9:18).

After his conversion, Paul went on three missionary journeys. On the first journey, he wrote his Epistle to the Galatians. On his second journey, he wrote his Epistles 1 and 2 Thessalonians. On his third journey, he wrote his Epistles 1 and 2 Corinthians and Romans.

Paul had to use his Roman citizenship to escape the death penalty in Jerusalem by his former colleagues, the Pharisees and Sadducees. During his imprisonment he wrote letters (epistles) to Christian communities, encouraging whenever possible but also chastising when necessary. These epistles include Colossians, Ephesians, Philemon, Philippians, 1 Timothy, Titus, and 2 Timothy. His whole journey on foot and at sea is seen as a living symbol of the spiritual journey every Christian must make to get from this world to the next.

Because of his Roman citizenship, he couldn't be crucified and could only be executed by the sword (beheading); he also appealed his case to Emperor Nero. This assured him safe passage to Rome, and at imperial expense. He was shipwrecked for a while in Malta, but eventually was sent on to Rome, where he was martyred in the same place as St. Peter before him.

Today, a magnificent basilica marks the spot of Paul's martyrdom, known as St. Paul Outside the Walls because it's literally located outside the Aurelian Walls of the city of Rome.

Book IV

Saints and Other Important Figures

Chapter 3

Looking at Undecayed Saints (Incorruptibles)

In This Chapter

▶ Looking good after death

▶ Showing God's favor

A small handful of saints have the extraordinary holiness of having been *incorruptible,* meaning that their bodies didn't decay or decompose the way a body normally does after death. Their bodies weren't embalmed or otherwise preserved, yet they remained intact long after decomposition normally would set in. In this chapter, you get the lowdown on some of these saints, finding details of their lives and experiences as well as the circumstances in which their bodies were unearthed and examined.

St. Bernadette Soubirous

Lourdes, France (1844–1879)

Beatified: 1925

Canonized: 1933

Patron: those suffering from poverty

Feast day: April 16

The Virgin Mary made 18 visits to a poor, uneducated girl in France at a time when Catholicism was still viewed with suspicion. Although she was born into a prosperous wheat-milling family, Bernadette Soubirous's fate changed at an early age. Her parents fell on hard times when she was 13 and eventually made their home in a one-room building that was once the town jail but had been deemed unfit for housing prisoners.

Because of her impoverished upbringing as a teen, Bernadette didn't receive Holy Communion at the appropriate age and was quite a bit older than those with whom she served in preparation. She was often ridiculed for her lack of knowledge and understanding in both the spiritual and secular disciplines.

Bernadette's first apparition came on a trip to the town dump with her sisters to collect firewood. She didn't know the woman who came to her until after her first few apparitions, when she came to know the woman dressed in white with a blue sash as "The Immaculate Conception," a term that meant little to a girl of low intellect living in a remote Pyrenees village.

At this time in France there remained a residue of anti-Catholicism from the French Revolution. Processions, religious devotions, and especially shrines marking apparitions weren't approved by the extremely secular government. For years, Bernadette underwent examinations, tests, and observations from both government leaders and the Church. Eventually, authorities determined that her apparitions were authentic.

Bernadette entered the Sisters of Notre Dame of Nevers, the same order that staffed her parish. She died from complications due to chronic asthma and tuberculosis of the bone, a horribly painful disease.

Bernadette was buried at the motherhouse chapel in Nevers on April 16, 1879. Her body was first exhumed in 1909 in front of doctors, representatives for the cause of her canonization, and the sisters of the order. Upon exhumation, they found no decay on Bernadette's body; only the clothing, the wood around the casket, and the rosary she held had perished. The casket was opened again in 1919, and the body of the future saint was found in the same condition as it was in 1909. Today, you can visit the motherhouse of the Sisters of Notre Dame of Nevers and venerate the saint in a beautiful glass retainer located in the chapel.

St. Catherine Laboure

Fain-les-Moutiers, France (1806–1876)

Beatified: 1933

Canonized: 1947

Feast day: November 25

Zoe Laboure was a French farmer's daughter whose mother died when she was 8. Zoe entered the Sisters of Charity on the Rue du Bac in Paris on the same day a celebration was being held as the relics of St. Vincent de Paul were transferred to the convent chapel. (As you can read in his section later in this chapter, St. Vincent de Paul had influenced Sister Louise de Marillac to establish the Sisters of Charity.) Upon entrance to the Sisters of Charity, Zoe took the name of Catherine.

The same evening that she entered the order, Sister Catherine began receiving apparitions. The first was the Lord bidding her to chapel; then came the Blessed Virgin Mary. Mary gave Catherine a task that was quite challenging for a young postulant, particularly at a time when France and the French Catholic Church were recovering from the devastating effects of the French Revolution and weren't inclined to be impressed with a nun receiving miraculous visits from heaven.

The Blessed Virgin instructed Catherine to create a medal with the image of Our Lady of Grace stomping on a serpent and the words, "O Mary, conceived without sin, pray for us who have recourse to thee." On the back of the medal, two hearts were to represent the Sacred Heart of Jesus and the Immaculate Heart of Mary. Those who wore the medal with devotion would receive great graces from God.

Fifteen hundred medals were made in 1832; by 1834, more than 130,000 had been made. Out of humility, Sister Catherine didn't want her name to be attached to the medal or the miraculous information. After the first medals were cast, Sister Catherine returned to normal convent life in obscurity; only her confessor and the Mother Superior knew of Catherine's apparitions. It was only eight months before Catherine's death, under specific instructions from the Mother Superior, that the facts regarding the medal and the miraculous information were revealed for posterity.

Sister Catherine died in 1876 and was buried in the crypt of the chapel. In 1933, Rome announced her beatification and, following routine, the casket was excavated. The outer wooden casket had deteriorated while the inner casket, made of lead, remained intact. The third, wooden casket began to crumble upon opening, but the future saint's body was in good condition and intact. The body of St. Catherine was transferred to the motherhouse chapel on the Rue du Bac, where her religious life had begun.

In this chapel, pilgrims can see St. Catherine Laboure in her blue habit with white coronet at the side altar. To the side of the high altar is the blue chair that the Blessed Virgin sat in when she appeared to St. Catherine.

St. Charbel Makhlouf

Bika'Kafra, Lebanon (1828–1898)

Beatified: 1965

Canonized: 1977

Patron: Lebanese Catholics

Feast day: September 5

Following his ordination into the priesthood at age 31, Father Charbel joined a monastery of strict observances and lived his life in solitude as a hermit.

Hermits generally take a vow of silence and live alone in small buildings known as *hermitages*. They generally come together for work, meals, and prayer, but live alone in an effort to solidify their relationship with God. During Father Charbel's solitude, he practiced extreme penances of fasting and wearing a hair shirt to further discipline his body and make him even freer to love and worship God. His reputation for holiness increased, and people began to seek him out for prayers and blessings.

In 1898, Father Charbel suffered a fatal stroke. His tremendous love of the Holy Eucharist was apparent in that the host had to be physically removed from his hands after the stroke. He was buried in the monastery cemetery without being embalmed. Indeed, he wasn't even placed in a casket because it was customary for the poor order to place their deceased members directly into the earth. When Father Charbel was buried, a bright light shone from his grave for more than 45 days. This marvel necessitated that his body be unearthed and examined. Despite abundant rain and no embalming or hermetically sealed casket, the body was in excellent condition. In addition, oil resembling blood dripped from his pores in such abundance that the monks had to change Father Charbel's habit twice a week.

In 1927, the body was examined again and was still in excellent condition. Father Charbel's body was then laid to rest undisturbed until 1950, when oil exuded from the crack of the tomb. Again, the body was examined, and again it was in perfect condition, pliable and oozing this oil. Father Charbel was beatified in 1965 and canonized in 1977. At the time of his beatification, the Blessed Charbel's body began to deteriorate. Today, only the bones of the saint remain, clothed in the vestiture of a priest with wax hands and face. His body is displayed in the St. Maron Monastery in Ananaya, Lebanon.

St. Francis de Sales

France (1567–1622)

Beatified: 1662

Canonized: 1665

Patron: journalists and writers

Feast day: January 24

Despite his father's discouragement, Francis de Sales pursued the virtuous order of religious life early on. After ordination, he served as a missionary to the Lake Geneva region, an area that had fallen to the radical Calvinist Protestants. With the help of pamphlets explaining the Catholic faith, Father Francis recatechized the region of Chablis.

Upon the death of the Bishop of Geneva, Father Francis was named his successor. He continued to work to reeducate people about the Catholic faith and authored *The Introduction to the Devout Life,* a practical guide for Catholics to give up old sinful habits and bring them in closer union with God. The guide is still used in spiritual direction and read by those who want to advance in the spiritual life.

Along with then-Sister Jane Frances de Chantal (see the next section), Francis founded the Visitation Sisters of Holy Mary. He also established a congregation of men known as the Oblates of St. Francis de Sales, who were devoted to preaching parish missions-retreats, staffing colleges, and working in parishes. His legacy had a powerful influence on other men and women in the centuries that followed, including St. John Bosco, founder of a congregation dedicated to the education of poor boys. This community, the Salesians, follows the spirituality of St. Francis de Sales.

Francis de Sales was canonized in 1665 and was declared a Doctor of the Church in 1877. His body was laid at rest in the Visitation Convent in Annecy next to St. Jane Frances de Chantal. When his body was exhumed in 1632, it was in perfect condition, but in subsequent years only the bones were found. Today, St. Francis de Sales can be venerated at the Basilica of the Visitation in Annecy, where his bones are placed under bishop's clothing and a wax mask covers his face.

St. Jane Frances de Chantal

Dijon and Moulins, France (1572–1641)

Beatified: 1751

Canonized: 1767

Patron: people who feel abandoned and people with in-law problems

Feast day: August 12

Book IV

Saints and Other Important Figures

Unlike many saints, Jane Frances didn't immediately turn to a life of religious service. Her mother died when she was quite young, leaving her upbringing to her father. Jane married the Baron de Chantal, and for nine years she lived a peaceful and religious life as a good wife and mother of four children. A hunting accident claimed the life of her husband, leaving Jane Frances to sink into a deep depression.

Upon the urgings of her father, Jane devoted her life to her children as well as to the poor and sick in her area. She also ministered to the dying, to whom she offered much comfort, and continued to practice works of charity, mortifications, and prayer. Following a Lenten retreat and hearing the great Francis de Sales (see the preceding section), Jane wanted to enter the cloistered Carmelite Nuns. Francis became Jane's spiritual director, regulating her penances and devotional practices and sharing with her his vision of a new community of sisters, the Visitation Sisters of Holy Mary. Jane expressed great interest in helping Francis to establish this new community.

Jane overcame many obstacles in seeing the dream become a reality. She left her son with her father and took her three daughters to the convent. Within a year, one daughter passed away; the other two eventually married. The deaths of her father, son, son-in-law, and many sisters from the plague added to Jane's suffering. In 1641, Jane died at the age of 69 in the state of grace and was buried near St. Francis de Sales in Annecy, France.

In 1722, her tomb was unearthed, and with the exception of some mold on her habit, Jane's body was perfectly intact. During the French Revolution in 1793, the relics of St. Francis de Sales and St. Jane Francis de Chantal were carried by boat and hidden during the night for protection until the restoration of the church in 1806. In the restoration, the relics suffered much, and only the bones remained of the two saints. St. Jane was canonized in 1767 and her relics are on display for veneration at the Basilica of the Visitation. The bones are dressed in the habit of the order and a wax mask covers her face.

St. John Marie Vianney

Dardilly and Ars, France (1786–1859)

Beatified: 1905

Canonized: 1925

Patron: parish priests

Feast day: August 4

John Marie Vianney was born in the South of France just before the French Revolution. A national church was created after the Revolution, and priests or religious persons loyal to the Roman Catholic Church were banned from serving and were often martyred as a result.

By the time John Vianney wanted to enter the priesthood, seminaries and most Catholic institutions were closed. After the restoration of the hierarchy of the Church, instruction of candidates for the priesthood was left to parish priests and later to the bishops of the dioceses. Education of candidates was sporadic and fell short of typical preparation in the great seminaries and institutions of higher education.

John received his religious education under these circumstances. That, and the fact that he was a poor learner, created doubt that he would ever be ordained. Churches and entire parishes were without priests, however, and bishops felt the urgency to ordain men, even if the new priests weren't intellectually equipped. John Vianney was ordained in 1818. He began his ministry under tutelage of a very holy pastor, and upon the death of his pastor, Father Vianney became pastor of a small, abandoned parish in Ars, France.

The town was remote and Catholic only in name and revealed the full effect of the French Revolution. The church building and priest house were in great disrepair, people didn't attend church services, men frequented the bars and brothels to the abandonment of their families, and children weren't properly educated in the Catholic faith. Father Vianney took the challenge and, little by little, began to turn things around in Ars. He repaired, cleaned, and restored the church building. He began catechism classes for the children and wrote a catechetical book easy enough for the children to grasp. Along with a wealthy patron of the village, Father Vianney even founded a school for girls. He went to village bars and dragged husbands back to their families, preached magnificent but down-to-earth homilies, and conducted parish missions — a type of retreat that resulted in a boom of confessions.

All his efforts to restore the Church community came at quite a cost for John Vianney. Clergy in surrounding towns soon became jealous and maliciously maligned him. He was personally attacked by the devil when he tried to sleep. His health deteriorated due to extreme penances and denial of nourishing food. Yet, people from Ars and around the region came to the village to seek the Cure of Ars for confession and spiritual direction. Habitually, Father Vianney would stay in the confessional for eight to ten hours a day.

John Vianney died after receiving the Sacrament of the Sick, commonly known as the last rites, on August 4, 1859. In 1904, his body was unearthed. Though a bit dried and darkened, his body was entirely intact. After his beatification, St. John Vianney was placed in a gold reliquary in a newly constructed shrine. Today, his body lies in a glass casket above the high altar in a newly constructed basilica near the old parish church in Ars.

St. Josaphat

Volodymyr, Poland (Lithuania) (1580–1623)

Beatified: 1643

Canonized: 1867

Patron: Ukraine

Feast day: November 12

Josaphat entered religious life at a time of strife within the Church. He had been baptized in the Ruthenian Orthodox Church, but that branch of the Orthodox Church later reunited with Rome. The reunification was a source of hostility and derision among the Orthodox, who still call the groups that have reunited with Rome the *Uniates.*

It was in this environment that young Josaphat entered the Basilian Order of Religious Men. He was soon ordained a bishop and later an archbishop. Despite the dangers, he labored and preached for the reunification of the Orthodox Church to Rome, which caused him political and personal strife.

Josaphat was killed and thrown into a river, and when his body was retrieved a week later by faithful followers, it was in good condition. It didn't show the normal signs of deterioration that would be evident after a week in water. Twenty-seven years after his death, while the body was being prepared for a new elaborate reliquary, fresh blood flowed from the saint's mortal wound. Because of the many wars in the region, the body was moved to St. Peter's in Rome and can be seen today in this basilica. With the passage of time and many moves, Josaphat's body has seen some deterioration in the face but otherwise remains in good condition. Pope Leo XIII canonized Josaphat in 1867 and, because of his successful proselytizing among the Orthodox Church, he was given the title "the Apostle of Union."

St. Lucy Filippini

Corneto-Tarquinia, Italy (1672–1732)

Beatified: 1926

Canonized: 1930

Patron: schoolteachers

Feast day: March 25

Lucy Filippini dedicated her life to the education of poor girls, establishing a community of sisters further dedicated to that pursuit in the 17th century.

Cardinal Barbarigo, aware of the piety of the young Lucy, was instrumental in bringing her to an institute for teachers, where she excelled in study, devotion, and service. She later founded the Maestre Pie Filippini, or the Religious Teachers Filippini, an organization that helped expand the pontifical community and establishment of schools for girls.

Pope Clement XI summoned Sister Lucy Filippini and her sisters to launch a school in Rome. The number of students far surpassed the available space, and the community soon expanded throughout Italy, offering education to young, poor girls at a time when education wasn't mandatory.

Sister Lucy Filippini died in 1732. Her body was uncovered in 1926 and found to be nearly undamaged, save for minute deterioration on her face. Her body is located under the Baroque Domo of St. Margaret in Montefiascone, in a chapel carved out of an earlier church. Opposite St. Lucy Filippini are the remains of Cardinal Barbarigo.

In 1910, Pope Pius X responded to the needs of Italian immigrants to the U.S. by sending five sisters to America to staff parochial schools with the Maestre Pie Filippini. In 2010, the community will celebrate 100 years in America. The provincialate of the Religious Teachers Filippini is located in Morristown, New Jersey, and they retain the same charisma of St. Lucy. The sisters are now located in Italy, the U.S., Ireland, England, Brazil, and India.

St. Mary Magdalene de Pazzi

Florence, Italy (1566–1607)

Beatified: 1626

Canonized: 1669

Patron: Naples, Italy

Feast day: May 25

Sister Mary practiced an ascetic way of life, often denying herself food other than bread and water. She suffered numerous attacks from the devil in the areas of chastity and gluttony. He would tempt her with impure thoughts, which she immediately rejected, and he would also tempt her to overeat, even when she wasn't hungry. At other times, she experienced extreme dryness in her prayer life that left her with no compensation at all. It wasn't until later in life that Mary Magdalene began to experience the spiritual phenomenon of ecstasy and on several occasions was found to be in an almost comatose state.

As novice mistress and director of the young nuns at the monastery in Florence, Sister Mary Magdalene encouraged the sisters to exercise the penances that she imposed upon herself, but she also cautioned that they strive for a balance in prayer, work, and relaxation. She acknowledged that not everyone was called to the extremes, as she was.

Sister Mary Magdalene died in 1607 and was entombed underneath the high altar in the monastery's chapel. A year after her death, she was exhumed, and her remains were still intact. Her body soon began to emit a fragrant oil, a phenomenon that continued for 12 years. Three additional unearthings took place, the final one in 1663; Sister Mary Magdalene's body remained flexible.

Book IV

Saints and Other Important Figures

Today, the relic of the saint lies in the chapel of the monastery in a glass casket for all to view. She's clothed in the Carmelite habit *discalced* (without shoes). Although her face is now colored, the flesh, muscle, and bones of her head, feet, and hands (that which is exposed to the public) remain intact.

St. Philip Neri

Florence, Italy (1515–1595)

Beatified: 1615

Canonized: 1622

Patron: Rome

Feast day: May 26

A young man born and raised into wealth, Philip Neri gave it all up at the age of 17 when he left home and chose to serve the Lord rather than pursue a career in business.

Philip went to Rome and found the city in great physical and spiritual deterioration. There were many slums, and children of the city often ran amok. Suffering from the ill effects of the Renaissance, the city of Rome saw a decline in papal authority and in the education and sense of loyalty of the clergy. Philip committed himself to the re-evangelization of the city.

He began with the youth. Philip established pilgrimages for the children during the middle of the day, when they were most likely to get into mischief. He took the children to the seven churches of the city, talking to them all the way. Eventually, the children began to confide in Philip.

The practice of the pilgrimages to the seven churches is still followed today, especially on Holy Thursday, with the visits to seven repositories. (*Repositories* are temporary mini-chapels where a smaller tabernacle is used to keep the Blessed Sacrament after the Mass of the Lord's Supper on Holy Thursday evening until the Easter vigil on Holy Saturday evening, thus leaving the main tabernacle in the church empty.)

Philip also reached out to young businessmen, offering weekly informal talks on theology and religion, which eventually led to the men staying for prayers. The gatherings were moved to a larger facility to accommodate the growing number of attendees.

After his ordination into the priesthood, Philip remained a champion of the Catholic faith, becoming an instrument for many to return to the sacraments and the Church. He instituted the devotion known as *Forty Hours,* in which the Blessed Sacrament is exposed on the altar of a church for 40 hours while continuous prayer is made. This devotion to the Holy Eucharist is based on the 40 hours Jesus spent in the tomb from his death on Good Friday until his Resurrection on Easter Sunday. Some parishes in the diocese are assigned a 3-day (40-hour) time slot on the calendar every year where the Blessed Sacrament is exposed on the altar for public adoration. He also established a group of priests, known as the Oratorians, for which liturgy and youth conferences were a hallmark.

Philip died in 1595. Four years later, his body was exposed and was found to be in good condition despite damp conditions. His body was embalmed in 1602, when it was moved to the new Oratorian Church, or *Chiesa Nuova,* where it still rests today. In 1622, Pope Gregory XV canonized St. Philip Neri and gave him the title "The Apostle of Rome."

St. Rose of Lima

Lima, Peru (1586–1617)

Beatified: 1667

Canonized: 1671

Patron: Latin America and the Philippines; gardeners

Feast day: August 23

After ten years of disagreements with her parents regarding her desire to live as a cloistered nun — and her parents wishing to see her married — Rose of Lima was finally allowed to join the Third Order of Dominicans.

The order was a pious organization designed for laypeople, and it allowed Rose to continue to live at home while following the Rule of St. Dominic and wearing a habit. She eventually moved to an outer house on the property where she could practice her religious virtues.

As their fortunes began to wane, Rose helped support her family. She continued to practice her charity to those less fortunate by opening a small clinic in her family home to provide essential medical treatment to the poor.

From the days when she would disfigure herself by rubbing pepper on her skin, hoping to keep potential suitors at bay, Rose always practiced mortifications on herself. She continued to do so while in the order, but with the

Book IV

Saints and Other Important Figures

permission of her priest-confessor. In addition to the many penances, self-denials, and prayers, she wore a crown of thorns over her veil. Eventually worn out by her penances, charitable work, and long hours of meditation, Rose died in 1617 at the age of 31. She was canonized in 1671 by Pope Clement X as the first saint of the New World.

Eighteen months after her death, her body was unearthed and found to be in excellent condition. Signs of deterioration were present, however, when her body was exhumed again a few decades later. Today, her relics are on display in the Dominican Church of Santo Domingo and in a small shrine church built on the spot where she lived.

St. Veronica Giuliani

Mercatello, Duchy of Urbino, and Citt'di Castello, Italy (1660–1727)

Beatified: 1804

Canonized: 1839

Feast day: July 9

Sister Veronica developed a somewhat mystical devotion to the Passion of Christ in the early years of her religious life. After some disagreement with her father regarding her desire to become a cloister nun rather than marry, she was finally allowed to enter the Capuchin Order of Nuns based on the reform rule of the Poor Clares.

Sister Veronica experienced many mystical phenomena as a cloister nun, most notably the vision of the Lord offering the chalice of suffering to her. The apparitions and the impression of the stigmata of Christ led to a formal investigation by the bishop of the diocese who observed her wounds.

For a time, Sister Veronica was isolated from any outside influences and couldn't even receive Holy Communion. The isolation was a heavy cross for her to bear, yet the young nun endured the trial with patience and obedience, eventually being allowed to return to convent living.

Sister Veronica served for 34 years as a novice-mistress and forbade her young charges from dwelling on or reading any forms of extreme, mystical, theological works. Eventually, she was elected abbess of the order; she took care of the mundane problems of the convent with the same fervor she gave her spiritual life, thus living a well-balanced religious life while keeping her sufferings and stigmata private.

Following her death, Sister Veronica's body remained incorrupt until the Tiber River overflowed its banks in a terrible flood. Now the bones of the saint are preserved with a wax facial mask and the habit of her order. Her heart is kept separately and miraculously remains in very good condition. Her remains are at the Monastery of St. Giuliani (Monastero Santa Veronica Giuliani) in Città di Castello, Italy.

St. Vincent de Paul

Gascony, France (1580–1660)

Beatified: 1729

Canonized: 1737

Patron: charitable societies

Feast day: September 27

Immediately upon ordination, Vincent's life was dedicated to the corporal and spiritual works of mercy, notably among the sick, the poor, and the galley prisoners in France. To better meet those needs, he founded the Congregation of Missions, more commonly known as the Vincentians. The priests worked among the poor in missions and helped establish seminaries to provide proper education for future clergy.

Vincent's work inspired St. Louise de Marillac, who cofounded the Daughters of Charity (also known as the Sisters of Charity). These sisters worked in hospitals and among the destitute. In the United States, the Sisters of Charity are known through St. Elizabeth Ann Seton, who established an American branch of that community. The Daughters of Charity is what the worldwide religious community of women is known by today. It includes both the American and French sisters as well as those all over the world.

Vincent died at the age of 80 and was buried in the St. Lazare Church in Paris. In 1712, his body was exposed and found to be in good condition except for some decay in the face. However, when the body was exhumed again, there was additional damage because of a flood. His bones are now encased in wax in the provincial headquarters of the Congregation of the Missions in Paris. His perfectly preserved heart is at the motherhouse of the Sisters of Charity on the Rue du Bac in Paris.

Frederic Ozanam was inspired by Vincent's work and in 1832 created the St. Vincent de Paul Society. This society, made up of laymen and women, quietly performs the corporal works of mercy among the destitute in local parishes.

Book IV

Saints and Other Important Figures

St. Zita

Monte Sagrati and Lucca, Italy (1218–1271)

Canonized: 1696

Patron: servants

Feast day: April 27

Born to devout Catholic parents, Zita was a pious girl at a very young age. When she was 12, she moved into the home of a wealthy wool merchant in Lucca, Italy, as part of the cleaning staff. She considered her work part of her prayer life. She attended daily Mass, recited morning and evening prayers, and slept on the bare floor for penance.

Zita's colleagues didn't initially understand her devotions; some were jealous, and others felt guilty for not practicing their own faith. She was persecuted for her piety, to the point that a male colleague made advances toward her and she was forced to physically defend herself. Her employers at first refused to believe her side of the story that she was an innocent victim and object of lustful and indecent intentions. They and many of her fellow servants preferred to believe the worst and presumed she had led the man on or had wanted to seduce him. She was totally chaste and pure but refused to answer their lewd interrogations because they had already decided she was guilty. Her innocence was later established and she was vindicated.

Zita's reputation for charity soon spread throughout Lucca. During a famine, people lined up for food, and Zita gave away almost all of the family's dry beans. She'd intended to restock the pantry but didn't get the chance before the master of the house decided to take stock of the beans and sell them at market. Fearful that she would be fired or thrown into jail because of the missing food, Zita prayed, and, miraculously, the dry beans were restored.

Zita died at age 60 and lies in state at the local parish of San Frediano in Lucca. Her casket was opened three times, the last time being in 1652. Each time, the body remained perfectly incorrupt. Today, the saint's body remains the same except for a bit of dryness and darkness to the skin.

Chapter 4

Holy Martyrs

. . . .

In This Chapter

▶ John the Baptist and other famous martyrs

▶ Lesser-known martyrs

. . . .

*M*artyrs are people who believe in their faith so strongly that they're willing to die for it. The original Greek word means "witness," and these people are witness to their love of Jesus Christ and the Church in that they'd rather die than betray their God. Martyrs don't murder anyone — suicide bombers aren't martyrs, they're homicide bombers. Martyrs don't cause the death of innocent victims — martyrs are victims themselves. The martyrs in this chapter were in love with the Lord and heaven more than with this world.

St. Agatha

Sicily (birthdate unknown–AD 251)

Patron: Sicily and Malta, women at risk of sexual assault, bell makers, and against breast cancer

Feast day: February 5

Agatha lived during the persecution of Emperor Decius. She decided very early to dedicate her life to Christ and to live in a pure and chaste manner. She forsook all advances from men, even Roman dignitaries.

One dignitary Agatha spurned was Quintian, a Roman official. Angered by her rejection and knowing she was a Christian, he reported her to the emperor. She was arrested and brought before a judge, but even threats of torture and death didn't influence Agatha's loyalty to God.

Quintian subjected Agatha to many forms of torture and abuse. He placed her in a house of ill repute and ordered her stretched on the rack and burned with iron hooks. Her breasts were tortured and then cut off, and she was then returned to prison without medication. Through it all, Agatha became more cheerful in her love for Christ.

St. Peter came to Agatha in prison and healed her wounds. Quintian was a witness to the miracle, but instead of converting to a life of faith, he increased his torturous efforts, ordering that Agatha be rolled naked over hot coals. It was after this last event, when she was returned to prison, that Agatha died.

The early Christians so revered Agatha that her name is in the Roman Canon of the Mass, also known as Eucharistic Prayer I. Devotion to St. Agatha soon spread throughout the empire and especially in Rome, where Pope Symmachus built a church in her honor in AD 500 on the Aurelian Way.

St. Agnes

Rome, Italy (AD 291–AD 304)

Patron: chastity, gardeners, girls, engaged couples, rape victims, and virgins

Feast day: January 21

Agnes consecrated her life to Christ at a young age and considered herself his spiritual bride. Like Agatha, Agnes came from a noble family and was much sought after by Rome's noblemen. She thwarted their affections, however, and stood by her vows of purity and chastity. Her determination didn't sit well with her prospective suitors, and they accused her of being a Christian, which was outlawed by Emperor Diocletian.

The Roman governor first tried simple things to influence Agnes and move her away from her consecration to the Lord. Seeing he was having no effect, he turned to threats. Agnes remained courageous, even while being dragged before Roman pagan idols and ordered to make an offering and worship. She refused, vowing to worship only the one true God. She was sent to a house of prostitution with orders that her virginity be violated.

A series of miracles kept Agnes pure. She was ordered to participate naked in a processional through the streets, but once outside, her hair grew from her head to cover her. At the house of ill repute, the governor allowed everyone to have his way with Agnes, yet when people approached her, they were instantly blinded. One of the attackers was carried back to her room; Agnes prayed over him, and his sight was restored.

This final act so infuriated the governor that he ordered that Agnes be beheaded, and she went to the gallows cheerfully.

Agnes was buried in a cemetery on the Via Nomentana, and Emperor Constantine built a basilica in her honor over the cemetery. Pope Innocent X built a second church in Rome on the site where her chastity was threatened.

On her feast day, it's customary to bring lambs into St. Agnes Basilica in Rome for a special blessing; afterward, the lambs are raised in a local monastery until shearing. The wool is spun into strips of cloth, known as *pallia.* The pallia are blessed by the pope and given out to all the new archbishops on the feast of St. Peter and Paul.

St. Agnes is commemorated in the Roman Canon of the Mass. She is always pictured with a fern and a lamb. John Keats wrote the poem "The Eve of St. Agnes" in 1819, which is based on folkloric romanticism of a girl and a dream on the day before the saint's feast day.

St. Blasé (Blaise)

Armenia (third century AD–AD 316)

Patron: the city of Dubrovnik, the wool industry, wild animals; and against ailments, diseases, and throat cancer

Feast day: February 3

Blasé was born in Armenia at the end of the third century. He was a pious young man who had a Christian education and became both a physician and an ordained bishop of the diocese of Sebaste in Armenia. He suffered persecution under the reign of Emperor Diocletian. When harassment reached his see, Blasé retreated to the forests and lived in a cave, where many wild animals would gather around him peacefully.

While Blasé was in the cave, the Roman governor of Cappadocia, Agricola, came to Sebaste to continue mistreating the Christians. He sent men into the nearby forests to capture animals for their games in the amphitheater. The men found Blasé, deep in prayer and surrounded by wild animals. Agricola had him arrested and tried him for being a Christian, but Blasé wouldn't give up his faith. Exasperated, the governor sent him to prison.

While on his way to prison, Blasé was approached by a mother whose son was choking on a fish bone. Blasé prayed over the child, and the bone was dislodged.

It's customary on his feast day to receive the traditional blessing of the throats in honor of St. Blasé. Two candles placed in the shape of a cross are used in the blessing. The prayer that's invoked for the special blessing reads: "Through the intercession of St. Blasé, bishop and martyred, may the Lord deliver you from all sicknesses of the throat and every other evil."

Book IV

Saints and Other Important Figures

One of the most beautiful shrines in his honor is in the port city of Dubrovnik, part of old Yugoslavia. In the 11th century, he became its special patron, and through his intercessions, he warned the people of the city about an imminent attack of the Venetian Republic, which ruled the Adriatic.

St. Boniface

Crediton (Devon, England) (AD 673–AD 754)

Patron: Germany, brewers, file cutters, and tailors

Feast day: June 5

Boniface was educated in a Benedictine monastery in Exeter, England, and was instrumental in reorganizing the Church in France. King Charles, the last Merovingian (the French dynasty that preceded the Carolingian, made famous by Charlemagne) king, was a tyrant and left the Church in decay. Although it was customary for the kings to appoint bishops, Charles often left positions empty or sold them to the highest bidder. And many of the bishops of the time were uneducated and lived lives of decadence.

After Charles's death, his sons Pepin and Carloman ascended to the throne, and Boniface had much greater influence with these men. He was able to convene a synod, or church council, that approved decrees calling for improved education and discipline among the clergy.

The relationship between the papacy and the Frankish king, Pepin, improved greatly. The Carolingian dynasty became a great supporter of the Holy See, and the seeds that Boniface sowed helped make the Church in France the Holy See's eldest daughter.

Boniface was sent to Germany to establish the first diocese there in Fulda in AD 722. The Lord granted him great gifts of preaching and teaching as well as strong discipline to learn the many dialects of language in the region.

Boniface is often depicted with an axe, an image that dates back to a legend in which he is thought to have chopped an oak tree that was a sacred part of pagan ceremonies in Germany. After chopping the tree, he is said to have built a chapel in honor of St. Peter the Apostle on that very site.

The new chapel marked a turning point for Christianity in Germany. Boniface then established abbeys — schools staffed by Anglo-Saxon nuns. The monasteries served as a basis for the beginning of missionary work, while the schools helped to further Christianity.

When he returned to Germany after visiting the pope in Rome, Boniface encountered a common problem: The newly converted Christian Germanic people, left without a strong structure, reverted to the old pagan religion. This occurred in the area where Boniface first established the Church. In AD 754, he returned to celebrate the Sacrament of Confirmation, but he and his companions were attacked and martyred.

St. Cecilia

Rome, Italy (second century AD)

Patron: musicians

Feast day: November 22

Much of the information available about Cecilia is *pious tradition* (possible legend, or oral history without any other evidence); little about her life has actually been recorded as fact. The dates of her birth and death are unknown. Originally thought to have lived in the third century, later scholarship now dates her 100 years earlier to the second century AD.

Common belief is that Cecilia was given in marriage to a pagan nobleman, Valerian, after she had already vowed to live a life of chastity. On the night of the wedding, Cecilia was able to not only convince her new husband to let her remain a virgin but also to convert him to Christianity. The two also converted Valerian's brother, Tiburtius, and the two men were baptized.

Valerian and Tiburtius were such staunch defenders of the faith that they sought the bodies of martyred Christians and buried them, an act that wasn't looked upon with favor in those times. They were arrested and refused to recant their faith; both were put to death.

Cecilia found their bodies and buried both men. She, too, was captured. When she wouldn't offer sacrifice to pagan idols, she was sentenced to death by suffocation in the bathroom of her home. She survived the suffocation and was ordered beheaded, but somehow remained alive for three days.

When Cecilia died, her hands were beside her confessing in the Trinity — three fingers extended for the three persons in one God, and two clutched to denote the second person's incarnation.

She was originally buried in the Catacombs of St. Callixtus, where a statue of her was erected that depicted her real martyrdom of beheading. In the ninth century, Pope St. Paschal I transferred her body to a basilica in her honor.

Cecilia's body is recorded as incorrupt, or non-decaying (see Book IV, Chapter 3 for more on incorruptibles). Since the third century, without embalming and after laying at rest at first in the humid, subterranean conditions of the catacombs, her body miraculously remains intact. The last time it was exhumed, in the 17th century, her body remained the same.

St. Denis

Italy (third century AD–AD 258)

Patron: Paris, and against diabolical possession and headaches

Feast day: October 9

Denis was one of seven bishops sent on a missionary expedition to present-day France. He was the first Bishop of Paris and is considered the city's patron. He and the other bishops were quite successful in gathering several conversions on their mission trip, a feat that angered the pagan religious leader. Denis was beheaded on Montmartre — mount of martyrs — and his body was dumped into the Seine River. Some of his faithful followers went to retrieve his body and his head.

According to witnesses, Denis picked up his head and walked two miles, delivering a sermon the entire way, stopping only when it was time to die. A basilica was built in his honor at this site, and today, statues and images of St. Denis portray him holding his head in his hands. A monastery, St. Denis, was built on the site of his martyrdom and today houses his relics.

SS. Felicity and Perpetua

Birthplace unknown (AD 181–AD 203)

Patron: Carthage, mothers, expectant mothers, ranchers, and butchers

Feast day: March 7

Felicity and Perpetua were arrested during the Christian persecutions ordered by Emperor Septimius Severus. Felicity was Perpetua's maid and companion; Perpetua was a married noblewoman who'd just given birth. Perpetua's mother and two of her brothers were Christians; her father was a pagan. Her brothers and her mother were arrested alongside Perpetua and Felicity.

Felicity was eight months pregnant and Perpetua was nursing her newborn when they were arrested and martyred. At the time, many Christians and *catechumens* (pagans who were studying to convert to Christianity) were tortured by being fed to hungry animals. The Romans did this to appease the crowds and to dissuade others from following the new religion of Christianity. The emperor ordered that all citizens and inhabitants worship him and the Roman gods. When Christians like Perpetua and Felicity refused to commit idolatry, they were brutally martyred. Instead of discouraging others, the murder of these holy women actually encouraged more people to sacrifice — even sacrifice their lives — in order to gain heaven.

Perpetua wrote a detailed account of her imprisonment and the murders of her companion Christians. It was known as the *Acta* (account) and was very popular soon after their deaths.

St. Fidelis of Sigmaringen

Sigmaringen, Prussia (1577–1622)

Beatified: 1729

Canonized: 1746

Feast day: April 24

Fidelis was acutely aware of and in service to the poor and the sick, often giving up his own meals and tending to the ill — administering the sacrament as well as praying over them — at various infirmaries. He was recognized very early in life for his piety, wearing hair shirts under his clothes for a penance he knew no one else would see.

He was very successful in bringing people back to the Church during the Counter-Reformation. Because of his knowledge of philosophy and theology and his skill as a preacher, he was sent with a group to Switzerland with hopes to reconvert those who left the Catholic Church to follow Zwibgili and the new Protestant religion.

His success in bringing people back to the Church angered the Calvinist Protestants, and they threatened his life. They made an unsuccessful attempt to kill him on April 24, 1622. A pious Protestant offered to house Fidelis for protection, but Fidelis refused. On his way home to his base at Grusch, Switzerland, he was murdered by 20 Calvinist soldiers.

Fidelis is depicted with a sword to denote his fidelity as a soldier of Christ and a palm branch to denote martyrdom.

Book IV

Saints and Other Important Figures

St. George

Nicomedia, Mesopotamia (AD 275–AD 303)

Patron: England, Catalonia, The Netherlands, Georgia (the former Soviet country), Bavaria, Aragon, agricultural workers, equestrians, soldiers, and knights

Feast day: April 23

George was a Roman soldier for Emperor Diocletian at a time when being a Christian was a dangerous endeavor — never mind being a Christian in the emperor's army.

Emperor Diocletian issued an edict in AD 302 calling for Christian soldiers to be arrested if they didn't offer sacrifice to the pagan gods. George refused, but, remembering the bravery of George's father as a soldier, Diocletian wasn't prepared to lose him. He tried to bribe George with money, property, and titles if he would renounce Christianity, but George remained steadfast.

The emperor ordered that George be beheaded on April 23, AD 303.

The popularity of St. George soon spread through the East, and during medieval times, a story called the "Golden Legend" brought his popularity to the West as well. It tells of a dragon living in a lake near Silena, Libya. Entire armies tried to defeat the creature and lost their lives. The beast ate two sheep a day, but when they were gone, the local villagers sacrificed their own maiden daughters to spare the entire town. St. George arrived and, hearing the dire fate of a young princess about to be eaten by the fiery dragon, he blessed himself with the sign of the cross and charged off to battle the serpent, killing it with a single blow of his lance. He then preached a moving sermon and converted the local pagans to the Christian faith. He was rewarded with a generous gift from the king whose daughter he rescued. St. George immediately distributed it to the poor and rode off to his next adventure.

St. Hippolytus of Rome

Rome, Italy (AD 170–AD 235)

Patron: Bibbiena (town in Italy), prison guards, and horses

Feast day: August 13

It may seem a bit odd that a man who once established himself as the first rival pope, or anti-pope, would reunite with the Church and become a saint, but that is the life of Hippolytus. He was born in the second half of the second century AD and was ordained a priest of Rome. An astute man and a great preacher and teacher, he was considered a rising star in the ecclesiastical chain. Yet his pride and knowledge got the best of him.

Hippolytus tangled with Pope Zephyrinus and Pope St. Callixtus and was eventually elected as a rival bishop in Rome. Pope St. Pontian had Hippolytus banished to the island of Sardinia under the new Christian persecution initiated by Emperor Maximinus. Life on the island was abysmal and provided

Hippolytus ample time to think. He reconciled himself with the Church, made amends for his pride, and confessed his loyalty to the true successor of St. Peter and authentic Bishop of Rome.

He was martyred in a most gruesome manner: Hippolytus was strapped to two wild horses who were then turned loose to drag him to death.

St. Ignatius of Antioch

Antioch (AD 50–AD 107)

Patron: the Church in the eastern Mediterranean and North Africa; throat disease

Feast day: October 17

Ignatius was a convert to Christianity under St. John the Evangelist and was named third Bishop of Antioch, the same diocese that once had St. Peter the Apostle as its bishop. Ignatius remained the bishop until his death.

Emperor Trajan started a fresh wave of persecutions against Christians who wouldn't offer worship to the pagan gods. Although considered a good emperor, Trajan nevertheless was thankful to the gods for his victories, and he persecuted those who didn't worship these gods.

Ignatius was arrested and brought to Rome for trial. On his journey, he stopped at Smyrna and wrote four important letters: one each to the churches in Ephesus, Magnesia, Tralles, and Rome. In the town of Troas, he wrote three more letters, these to the churches in ancient Philadelphia (also called Alaşehir, located in modern-day Turkey), Asia Minor, and Smyrna, as well as a letter to St. Polycarp. In Rome, he was fed to the lions.

His relics are housed at St. Peter's Basilica in Rome, and he is represented as a bishop surrounded by lions.

St. Irenaeus

Smyrna, Asia Minor (AD 125–AD 202)

Patron: archdiocese of Mobile, Alabama

Feast day: June 28

Many of Irenaeus's early writings attacked the Gnostic heresy, holding that only Catholic bishops, those in communion with the pope, could provide correct interpretation of the Sacred Scriptures. He hoped to counter the ill effects of Gnosticism and stress Christianity.

His writings include a famous five-volume series, *On the Detection and Overthrow of the So-Called Gnosis.* He wrote quite extensively about the heresy of Gnosticism, pointing to the fact that it was a sect with very limited reaches in the Church. In other words, these so-called Gnostic Gospels were not universal in nature, like the four authentic Gospels, and were tied to a particular people, message, and time. At the same time, he emphasized the four authentic Gospels of Matthew, Mark, Luke, and John.

He was likely martyred in Lyon, France, in AD 202. Unfortunately, his relics were destroyed as a result of the Protestant revolt in the 16th century.

St. Januarius

Benevento, Italy (AD 275–AD 304)

Patron: Naples, blood banks, and against volcanic eruptions

Feast day: September 19

Januarius was a fourth-century bishop of Benevento, Italy, who lived and died during the reign of Emperor Diocletian. He was among a group of Christians arrested and taken to Pozzouli, a section of modern-day Naples, to be food for wild bears. The beasts wouldn't touch the Christians, so the Christians were all beheaded by Roman authorities.

More interesting than Januarius's life is what happened to him in death. At first, the relic of his head was left in Naples and the rest of his body was taken to Benevento, where he had served as bishop. Eleven hundred years later, in the 15th century, his head and body were reunited and placed in the Cathedral of Naples, and he was made patron of the city.

A phenomenon involving the saint's blood has occurred since the 14th century: When the relics of the saint and vials of his blood are brought in procession and unite, the blood liquefies. The liquefaction of the blood can take many forms: boiling, turning a bright crimson color, or turning sluggish and dull in color.

St. Januarius has specific days set aside in the Church year on which he is celebrated. September 19 is the day of his martyrdom, and the Saturday before the first Sunday of May memorializes the reunification of his relics.

December 16 commemorates the aversion of the eruption of the Mt. Vesuvius volcano (he's the patron saint against volcanic eruptions, because Naples exists in the shadow of Mt. Vesuvius, still a very active volcano).

St. John the Baptist

Palestine (5 BC–AD 30)

Patron: Baptism, converts, the Knights of Malta, lambs, and tailors; the dioceses of Charleston (South Carolina), Dodge City (Kansas), Paterson (New Jersey), Portland (Maine), and Savannah (Georgia); invoked against convulsions, epilepsy, spasms, and hail

Feast days: birth, June 24; beheading, August 29

John the Baptist is the cousin of the Lord Jesus and son of Zachary and Elizabeth, who was the cousin of the Blessed Virgin Mary. According to Jewish genealogy, he is from the line of Aaron. Zachary, a Jewish priest, was struck mute when he doubted the veracity of an angel's news that his wife was pregnant. When the infant was born and Zachary was asked the infant's name, his voice returned and he proclaimed the baby "John."

When both Elizabeth and Mary were pregnant, Mary came to visit her cousin (see Figure 4-1 for an artist's rendering of this event). John is said to have leapt inside his mother's womb when he encountered Jesus in Mary's womb. Those in the pro-life movement in the Catholic Church today look to the visitation of Elizabeth and the meeting of John and Jesus in the wombs as an inspiration for the sanctity of life beginning in the womb.

Figure 4-1: The Virgin Mary visiting her cousin Elizabeth, with Zachary (far left) and Joseph, husband of Mary (far right).

© Réunion des Musées Nationaux/Art Resource, NY

John started his ministry at the age of 27, living a penitential life in the desert. He preached of repentance and baptized many people in the River Jordan — a baptism that was different from that Sacrament of Baptism instituted by the Lord. The Lord's Baptism is a purification of the body; the baptism performed by John was a means of interior repentance.

John's staunch preaching against vices and evil caught the ear of King Herod, who was living in sin with his brother's wife, Herodias, who also happened to be his niece. John preached rather severely against this particular sin and was arrested. The king both feared and revered John but was not in favor of his preaching. Herod threw a party attended by many guests, and the king got drunk. Herodias's daughter, Salome, performed an exotic dance that pleased the king so much he granted her anything she wanted. Salome conspired with her mother to silence John the Baptist, and so he was beheaded.

Today, the relics of St. John the Baptist are in Rome and Amiens, France. He's often depicted in art clothed in a hair shirt ready to baptize, or with his severed head on a platter.

St. John Fisher

Beverley (Yorkshire, England) (1469–1535)

Beatified: 1886

Canonized: 1935

Patron: diocese of Rochester, New York

Feast day: June 22

John Fisher's defense of the bonds of marriage and his refusal to dissolve that of King Henry VIII to Catherine of Aragon were the ultimate reason he was put to death.

Henry wanted to divorce Catherine because she couldn't produce a male heir, but that wasn't a valid reason for annulment in the Catholic Church. Bishop John Fisher defended the marriage bond, and the case was eventually upheld by the Roman Rota, the highest court in the Church. Henry broke with the Catholic Church and named himself head of a new church. The bishops who were in their positions as a result of nepotism or other royal favors soon swore allegiance to the new church, but not to John Fisher. He swore allegiance to Henry as the king of England but not head of the church.

Bishop John Fisher was arrested and sent to the Tower of London, despite having once been chaplain to the king's mother. He languished in prison for 18 months until Pope Paul III appointed him a cardinal. That was the last straw for King Henry, who ordered Fisher to be beheaded for treason.

His body was buried unceremoniously in a churchyard not far from the tower, but his head was placed on a stake on Tower Bridge to be viewed by the populace. It was only removed two weeks later to make room for Thomas More's head (see the Thomas More entry later in this chapter).

St. Lucy

Siracusa, Sicily (AD 283–AD 304)

Patron: Sicily and Syracuse (Siracusa), ailments, injuries, and eye cancer

Feast day: December 13

Lucy had devoted her life to Christ, but after her father's death, her mother betrothed the girl to a rich pagan. She wanted to retain her consecration, but it took three years and an intercession from another Sicilian martyr, Agatha, to convince her mother to let her remain chaste.

Her fiancé was not pleased and accused her of being a Christian, and then turned her over to the Roman governor. The governor sentenced Lucy to a house of prostitution, but the Lord came to protect her. She was then tortured by having her eyes plucked out. She eventually succumbed to the torturous orders from the governor, but not before her eyesight was restored. Lucy's name was added to the Roman Canon of the Mass.

St. Lucy, pictured in Figure 4-2, is often shown with two eyeballs on a plate, or, as in this rendering, two eyeballs on a spike, to indicate the horrible method of her martyrdom.

Figure 4-2: St. Lucy.

© DeA Picture Library/Art Resource, NY

Lucy's name means "way of light." On the Julian calendar, which predates the Gregorian calendar, Lucy's day of martyrdom, December 13, is the darkest day in the Northern Hemisphere.

St. Maximilian Kolbe

Poland (1894–1941)

Beatified: 1971

Canonized: 1982

Patron: prisoners, drug addicts, journalists

Feast day: August 14

Maximilian's life was filled with strife. He was born in the section of Poland that was under enemy control of the Russians, and he died during the Nazi regime. His parents were industrious workers who faced many hardships: Many of Maximilian's siblings died, and his father was hanged for working for independence. His mother eventually entered a Benedictine convent, and his surviving brother became a priest.

In 1907, Maximilian entered the Conventuals, a reform branch of the Franciscan Order, and he later went to the Pontifical Gregorian College in Rome. In Rome, he founded an organization to promote the Catholic Church, the Army of Mary.

Maximilian received another doctorate, this one in theology, from the Pontifical University of St. Bonaventure, and then returned to Poland to teach in a seminary. He later joined four other men on a missionary trip to Japan, where they founded a monastery and established a Catholic newspaper.

The Nazis were in power when he returned to Poland. Many congregations were shut down, Catholic presses came to a halt, and the infamous prison camps were filling up. Maximilian entered the Auschwitz death camp on May 28, 1941, and ministered as a priest calmly and quietly to other inmates. He was beaten, starved, dehydrated, and eventually given a lethal drug.

St. Polycarp

Birthplace unknown (AD 69–AD 155)

Patron: people who suffer from earaches or dysentery

Feast day: February 23

Polycarp was a disciple of St. John, the Beloved Disciple, and was part of the apostolic fathers, those who were instructed firsthand by the Apostles. Soon after his conversion in AD 80, he became a priest and then Bishop of Smyrna, which is located in present-day Turkey.

Polycarp traveled to Rome to meet with the pope. There, he also met the great *heretic* — a teacher of false doctrines — Marcion, who was quite indignant that Polycarp said anything to him. A new wave of Christian persecution welcomed Polycarp when he returned to Smyrna. He refused to worship the pagan Roman gods, partake in emperor worship, or offer incense to the pagan deities. He was arrested at the age of 86 and was burned to death.

St. Sebastian

Milan, Italy (AD 257–AD 288)

Patron: archers, athletes, bookbinders, gunsmiths, lace makers, police officers, soldiers, stonecutters, victims of arrow wounds, and victims of the plague

Feast day: January 20

Sebastian is commonly known by his means of death. According to pious tradition, he volunteered to become a soldier in Caesar's army, specifically becoming a Praetorian Guard (the elite personal protectors of the emperor). He wanted to be close to the Christians awaiting martyrdom. It's said that he would comfort them, give them courage, and properly bury them after death — an act punishable by his own death under orders of Emperor Diocletian.

Sebastian was brought to his execution site, tied to a stump, and shot with arrows. The soldiers left, believing him dead, but Irene, a pious woman, went to retrieve his body and found he was still alive. She nursed him back to health, and rather than flee, Sebastian returned to his post as a Praetorian Guard, which startled Caesar. Sebastian reproached Diocletian for persecuting Christians and was sentenced to death by beating.

Sebastian was buried in a common catacomb that would later take his name. A magnificent basilica stands over the cemetery in his honor.

Book IV

Saints and Other Important Figures

St. Thomas Becket

London, England (1118–1170)

Beatified: 1173

Canonized: 1174

Patron: secular (diocesan) clergy, Exeter College, and Portsmouth, England

Feast day: December 29

Thomas Becket was a loyal friend and supporter to King Henry II. As a supporter, he worked tirelessly for the monarch; as a friend, he accompanied the king on hunting expeditions.

At the death of the Archbishop of Canterbury, Henry wanted Thomas to take over. Thomas warned the king that their relationship would change, but Henry was too intent on controlling the Church with his friend to listen.

Conflicts arose, and Thomas sought to halt the king's interference in Church matters, which didn't sit well with Henry. On December 29, 1170, four knights set out for Canterbury seemingly under direction of the king. They tried to bring Thomas back to Winchester but killed him upon his refusal.

St. Thomas More

London, England (1478–1535)

Beatified: 1886

Canonized: 1935

Patron: lawyers and attorneys

Feast day: June 22

Thomas More was a lawyer and writer who became a friend and personal adviser to King Henry VIII. Thomas was elected Speaker of the House of Commons in 1523 and, when the king was still Catholic, assisted him in writing the *Defense of the Seven Sacraments*. Henry made him the Chancellor of England from 1529 to 1532, a position that he ultimately resigned.

The men retained their friendship until Henry challenged the validity of his marriage to Catherine of Aragon. Thomas agreed with the presiding bishop that the bond was valid. When the Church in Rome also ruled that the marriage was valid, Henry left the Church and set himself up as the Supreme Head of the Church of England, which denied the pope's authority. To recognize Henry as head of the church was against Thomas's faith.

Thomas resigned his position and was imprisoned in the Tower of London and martyred for his refusal to take the Oath of Supremacy. On July 6, 1535, he was beheaded and buried at the Tower of London. His head was placed on a lance to be viewed from the Tower Bridge.

Other Notable Martyrs

Not all martyrs' stories are complete; in some cases, very little is known about them other than that they lived — and ultimately died — for their love of neighbor and love of God.

- ✔ **St. Charles Lwanga and companions (1865–1886):** Charles was from Uganda and was abused as a page as a young man. He became head of pages and wanted to protect other young pages, converting them to Catholicism. King Mwanga separated the Christians from the pagans and ordered them killed when they refused to renounce their faith.

- ✔ **St. Cyprian (died AD 258):** Cyprian was an excellent rhetorician before his conversion to Christianity. A highly educated man, he wrote many theological treatises. Christian persecutions were commonplace, and the Emperor Valerian started a new wave in AD 256, making martyrs of Pope Stephen I, Pope Sixtus II, and Pope St. Cornelius. Cyprian prepared the people of his diocese in Carthage, and he was arrested and put to death by the sword for refusing to offer sacrifice to pagan gods.

- ✔ **First martyrs of the Church of Rome (died AD 64):** The city of Rome was a blaze of fire in AD 64. Emperor Nero, seeing the charred remains, needed someone to blame. The emerging Christians, to Nero, were the perfect scapegoat. They were rounded up and put to death.

- ✔ **Holy Innocents:** The Holy Innocents are commemorated in Matthew 2:16–18, in which the Evangelist recounts the anger of King Herod over the Magi not returning to reveal where the baby Jesus, the Messiah, was located. Herod ordered all boys 2 years old and younger to be massacred in Bethlehem and its environs (see the entry on the Blessed Virgin Mary in Book IV, Chapter 1). The victims of this act of barbarism are considered to be the first martyrs for Christ. In the later part of the 20th century, the Holy Innocents came to be the patron saints of all the aborted babies in the world.

- ✔ **St. Josaphat (1580–1623):** Josaphat joined the Basilian Fathers (in Lithuania) and was ordained a priest in 1609. In 1617, he was ordained a bishop and was later made archbishop. He worked tirelessly to restore the Byzantine Catholic Church in areas that had gone over to the Orthodox Church, and in doing so, he created enemies. Animosity and jealousy eventually led to his martyrdom in 1623. St. Josaphat is also one of the incorruptible saints — see his discussion in Book IV, Chapter 3.

- ✔ **St. Lawrence of Rome (died AD 258):** Lawrence was one of seven deacons to serve the Church in the third century, protecting the goods and property. When a prefect from Rome came looking for the Church's riches, Lawrence presented him with the elderly, needy, and sick, indicating that they were the true riches. The prefect wasn't amused, and Lawrence was sentenced to death by being grilled over a gridiron.

Book IV

Saints and Other Important Figures

✔ **SS. Marcellinus and Peter the Exorcist (died AD 304):** Marcellinus and Peter were jailed for their positions in the Church — notably, Peter's position as an *exorcist* (one who recites the exorcism prayer at Baptism). They are said to have converted the head jailer and his family, an act that so angered Emperor Diocletian that he ordered them beheaded.

✔ **SS. Nereus and Achilleus (died AD 98):** Nereus and Achilleus were brothers. They served as guards to the noblewoman, Domitilla, a niece to Emperor Domitian. Domitilla converted to Christianity and consecrated herself as a virgin to the Lord, and the brothers were baptized by St. Peter the Apostle. All three were arrested and sent to the island of Ponza in the Mediterranean Sea, near the island of Capri. Nereus and Achilleus were beheaded, and Domitilla was burned for her refusal to offer sacrifice to the pagan idols.

✔ **St. Pancras (AD 290–AD 304):** Pancras and his uncle, Dionysius, were beheaded for not offering worship to the pagan Roman gods and were buried in the catacombs, which later took Pancras's name. In the sixth century, a basilica was built over the site, and the head of St. Pancras was placed in a splendid reliquary in the new basilica.

✔ **SS. Paul Chong Hasang and Andrew Kim Taegon and companions (1793–1839):** Paul and his friends were martyrs from Korea. Paul was a layperson who was very instrumental in getting more clergy into Korea. Andrew Kim was the first Korean-born Catholic priest. Catholics in Korea had to practice their faith secretly because the ruling dynasty persecuted Christians. Andrew was beheaded in 1846, along with hundreds of other Catholics.

✔ **St. Paul Miki and companions (1562–1597):** Paul was born to rich parents in Japan, entered the Jesuit community, and was ordained a priest. Paul and other Catholics marched 600 miles to Nagasaki, where he was crucified.

✔ **St. Peter Chanel (1803–1841):** Peter, a Frenchman, was ordained in 1827 and sent to a parish that fell into decline following the French Revolution. With papal approval, Peter and his companions were sent to the South Pacific. They were the first Catholic missionaries, specifically to the Futuna Islands. To the native king's dismay, most of the island converted to Catholicism. The king ordered Peter to be killed.

✔ **St. Stanislaus (1030–1079):** Stanislaus was ordained a priest and later became Bishop of Krakow, Poland. He was well known for his eloquent preaching, generosity, and penitential living. Because of his strict discipline and defense of morality, he came into conflict with King Boleslaus of Poland. The confrontation eventually led to Stanislaus being hacked to death while celebrating Mass.

Chapter 5

Founding Fathers and Mothers

· ·

In This Chapter

▶ Looking at the founders of the Franciscans and Dominicans

▶ Checking out some other Church Fathers and Mothers

· ·

*J*ust as a country honors its founding fathers and mothers, the Church honors the holy men and women who helped establish religious communities that have served the needs of many throughout the centuries. In this chapter, you discover the men and women who are considered the founders of various religious orders.

These founding fathers and mothers determined the name of the society they established as well as the *charism,* or spirit of the group. Even though a more formal name may have been used when these religious communities were created by their founders, many times the nickname of the organization comes from the personal name of the founding mother or father (Dominicans for the Order of Preachers; Franciscans for the Order of Friars Minor; Vincentians for the Congregation of the Mission; and so on).

St. Alphonsus Ligouri

Campania, Kingdom of Naples (current Italy) (1696–1787)

Beatified: 1816

Canonized: 1839

Patron: moral theologians, ethicists, arthritis sufferers

Feast day: August 1

Alphonsus was something of a child prodigy, earning his doctorate in law by the age of 16 and having his own legal practice at age 21. Despite his legal prowess, however, just one significant loss forced Alphonsus to reassess his life choices and realize his true calling was the priesthood.

With his legal background and thinking style, Alphonsus was able to teach moral theology in a manner that was neither too lax nor too rigorous. His manuals in ethics have been considered classics for centuries, although he was met with some early opposition from those who considered him either too progressive or too reactionary.

Alphonsus was ordained in 1726, and in less than six years, he inaugurated a new religious community for men known as the Redemptorists after Our Lord and Savior, Jesus Christ the Redeemer. The Congregation of the Most Holy Redeemer (CSsR from the Latin initials) was established as an order of missionary preachers who, to this day, are renowned for their eloquent homilies and sermons.

St. Augustine of Hippo

Algeria (AD 354–AD 430)

Patron: theology and philosophy professors, former playboys

Feast day: August 28

Augustine — the same man who would go on to establish a religious order of monks called the Augustinians — spent his early adult years in a life of debauchery and moral decadence. He immersed himself in a lifestyle filled with overindulgence and illicit pleasure, mimicking what was happening in the Roman Empire at the time. Once a stoic and respected empire, it had degenerated into rampant drunkenness, promiscuity, and hedonism.

As the empire crumbled and barbarians raided and invaded the frontier and the capital, Augustine's desire for ultimate pleasure at all costs began to wane. At the age of 18, he had already fathered a son out of wedlock, Adeodatus (meaning "gift from God"), but "the good life" took its toll, and Augustine began to yearn for something more substantial. He realized that a spiritual realm coexisted with the material world.

Unfortunately, Augustine turned from his hedonistic lifestyle to dualism, or Manichaeism — the belief that anything physical is intrinsically evil, and only the purely immaterial is good. Instead of turning to religion as his mother, St. Monica, had prayed he would, Augustine adopted a Persian philosophy that viewed the battle of good and evil as being fought between the spiritual and material.

The book of Genesis tells us that God created both the spiritual and the material and that it was "good." Christianity takes this concept a step further: The doctrine of the Incarnation teaches that God took on a human nature in Jesus Christ. In other words, the pure spirit (God) took a physical body. How could this happen if the body were evil?

St. Ambrose of Milan first broke through to Augustine, explaining that, while the world contains both good and evil, they are not equal forces. Evil is the absence of a good that ought to be present. A physical evil, for example, would be a violent hurricane that destroys a peaceful village. A moral evil is when a human being does something wrong instead of doing the right thing (like telling a lie rather than telling the truth).

Augustine pondered Ambrose's words, and after much thought and prayer — and with the help of divine grace — he accepted the faith and became a believer. He and his son were baptized in AD 384 and became ardent Christians. Augustine became a staunch defender of the faith and used the philosophy of Plato to explain and defend Catholic doctrine. After the death of his beloved mother, he sold his possessions and founded the first monastery in the West.

Augustine also fought the Pelagian heresy, a belief that any man or woman could get into heaven on his or her own merit, without the assistance of God. Augustine staunchly opposed Pelagianism and taught that any and all supernatural good works are the result of divine grace.

Augustine's religious order was named after him, the Order of St. Augustine. The abbreviation OSA comes at the end of the name of an Augustinian monk — for example, Rev. Dudley Day, OSA. Augustine initially intended to live the life of a hermit — one of solitude and little or no influence from the outside world — in an effort to escape the brutality of the Barbarians.

Augustine wrote *Confessions,* an autobiography in which he admits his wild, decadent youth and his imprudent overreaction in embracing dualism. He then explains that the Judeo-Christian religion is true because it's rooted in reality; namely, that God created both the material and the immaterial, the physical and the spiritual. Either one can be abused and misused for nefarious purposes, but good ultimately triumphs because it's inherently superior to evil.

St. Benedict of Nursia

Cassino, Italy (AD 480–AD 543)

Canonized: 1220

Patron: Europe, poison victims

Feast day: July 11

In sharp contrast to St. Augustine's early years, Benedict was turned off by the wild and rampant living taking place in Rome and fled to Subiaco, Italy, where he lived in a cave for three years. He later moved to the mountains of Monte Cassino, where he established a monastic way of life. He and his monks lived by the creed *ora et labora,* or "prayer and work," which left him to divide his days equally between spiritual reflection and manual labor. At his monastery, the chapel bells rang every three hours to call the monks to prayer.

Benedict offered stablility and guidance in the darkness of invasions and the collapse of Western civilization. His monasteries grew and spread quickly. Benedictine monasteries proliferated in Western Europe during the Middle Ages. The monks initially left the dangerous cities to live a life of simplicity, but after the Roman Empire fell (AD 476) and the barbarians became civilized, the monks' mission evolved into preserving the culture, art, literature, and education from antiquity. The monks not only preserved the Latin and Greek languages but also taught the former barbarians how to read and write. Eventually, people moved out of the old cities, and, over time, they built new ones surrounding the monks.

Benedict's twin sister, Scholastica, established the female counterpart to her brother's monastic order. Benedictine nuns operate much like their male contemporaries, also following the "*ora et labora*" way of life. Both men and women of the Benedictine order have the letters OSB after their proper names to designate that they're members of the Order of St. Benedict.

St. Clare of Assisi

Assisi, Italy (1194–1253)

Canonized: 1255

Patron: television, goldsmiths

Feast day: August 11

When she was 18 years old, Clare heard a popular preacher, St. Francis of Assisi (see his entry later in this chapter), for the first time and was so moved that she immediately decided to found her own branch of religious women to be of spiritual support to the Franciscans.

Clare established the community of the Poor Ladies (now known as the Poor Clares) to meditate day and night and offer prayers for the Church. She was joined by her sister, Agnes, as well as many other women who lived in religious poverty, much like their Franciscan counterparts. With no money or land, they begged for their daily sustenance.

The Poor Clares are still active today, with likely the most active group in Alabama at Eternal Word Television Network (EWTN) — the international Catholic media network that includes radio, Internet, shortwave radio, and satellite and cable television.

St. Dominic de Guzman

Calaruega, Province of Burgos, Kingdom of Castile (current Spain) (1170–1221)

Canonized: 1234

Patron: preachers, astonomers, the Dominican Republic

Feast day: August 8

The first vision to affect Dominic's life happened before he was even born; while she was pregnant, Dominic's mother had a vision of a dog with a torch in its mouth. The religious order Dominic would one day establish is called the Dominicans (Order of Friars Preachers) — *domini cani,* the Italian equivalent, means "hounds of the Lord," a phrase used to describe steadfast preaching.

Dominic was ordained a priest in 1194. By 1215, he formed his own religious community as a *mendicant,* or beggar, much like St. Francis of Assisi. The Dominicans, like the Franciscans, are technically not monks but friars, and they live in friaries, not monasteries.

Dominic's greatest challenge was the Albigensian heresy. Similar to the Manichaeism and dualism that St. Augustine battled centuries before, Albigensianism held that Christ didn't have a true human nature. These heretics believed that anything material or physical was intrinsically evil and that Jesus only pretended to have a real humanity along with his divinity. Creation was not good, according to the Albigensians, and Jesus was only divine and not human.

Despite his eloquent preaching talent, Dominic was unable to dissuade the lay faithful in Spain and France from this growing heresy. Discouraged, he prayed for assistance, and the Virgin Mary gave him an answer. In a vision, he saw the Blessed Mother with the child Jesus, and she gave Dominic a Rosary (prayer beads). Since Hebrew times of the Old Testament, believers have used prayer beads to keep count when they pray the 150 Psalms as found in the Bible. Those same 150 beads could also be used to help defeat Albigensians, according to Dominic's vision.

Book IV

Saints and Other Important Figures

Common folk used prayer beads to pray the Psalms. St. Dominic asked them to use those same beads to think about the mysteries of Christ (see the nearby sidebar, "Contemplating the mysteries of Jesus"), which reveal both His humanity and His divinity. Only a man can suffer pain and death, yet only a god can rise from the dead and ascend into heaven. The spiritual "tool" of the Rosary worked, and the Albigensian heresy was defeated. The people embraced the orthodox teaching that Christ is true God and true Man, one divine person with two complete natures, human and divine.

St. Francis de Sales

Château de Thorens, Savoy, France (1567–1622)

Beatified: 1662

Canonized: 1665

Patron: journalists

Feast day: January 24

Francis was destined by his father to study law and enter into politics, but it was his Holy Father who calmed him during a stressful and overwhelming time, causing Francis to resign himself completely to the Divine Providence. He decided to become a priest and was ordained in Geneva in 1593. He was later named Bishop of Geneva and consecrated in 1602.

Francis established the Oblates of St. Francis de Sales (*Oblati Sancti Francisci Salesii*, O.S.F.S) to help promote the faith beyond the confines of the parish and diocese. The spirituality is based on *Introduction to a Devout Life,* a book Francis wrote for those struggling to become better Christians.

St. Francis also is one of the incorruptible saints; see his entry in Book IV, Chapter 3.

St. Francis of Assisi

Assisi, Italy (1181–1226)

Canonized: 1228

Patron: animals, pet owners, veterinarians; San Francisco

Feast day: October 4

Francis — known now for his life of poverty and his work with the poor and needy — was once a spoiled young man who lived a life of ease, partying through the day and night and spending time with his friends.

Italy didn't become a unified kingdom until the 19th century, so in Francis's time, frequent battles took place between the cities and states. The people of Assisi and Perugia often were at battle; in one fight, Francis and his friends went to defend Assisi. The Perugians defeated Assisi, however, and Francis was jailed for a year.

Francis became ill with fever while in jail and spent time in the infirmary, providing him with plenty of time to think of how he had wasted his life thus far. He decided to join the military and serve with honor when he was released and went to join Count Walter of Brienne. While traveling, he had a vision of the Lord saying to him, "Go, Francis, and repair my house, which as you see is falling into ruin."

Francis misunderstood the Lord's request. He ran to his father's cloth shop and took the most expensive materials he could find. He sold the materials and his horse and took the money to the priest of a church in San Damiano that was in disrepair. Knowing that Francis had stolen the materials from his father, the priest refused the money.

Francis's father, Bernadone, was incensed when he learned what his son had done. His temper was so intense that Francis fled and hid in a cave in San Damiano for a month. He emerged dirty, unshaven, undernourished, and a general mess, making himself the subject of ridicule. His father dragged him home, beat him, and locked him in a closet. His mother helped him escape one day when his father was away on business.

Francis returned to the church in San Damiano and helped the priest there. When his father came looking for him, he told him: "Up to now I have called you my father on earth; henceforth I desire to say only 'Our Father who art in Heaven.'" He then stripped himself of his clothes and handed them to his father, donning instead the clothing of a beggar. Over time, Francis acquired some companions who sought to rebuild the Church, and he realized what the Lord had meant: The Church he wanted Francis to rebuild was not the buildings but rather the people who came to worship in them. Francis realized his mission was to preach spiritual renewal to the people of God. Pope Innocent III gave permission for him to establish a new religious community, the Order of Friars Minor (OFM), which would later be known as the Franciscans.

Book IV

Saints and Other Important Figures

Francis and the others took vows of poverty, chastity, and obedience. However, unlike the monks in the monasteries who also took a vow of stability to live and die at that monastery, the Franciscans and their colleagues, the Dominicans, were mendicants; they begged for their sustenance, as they had no land and no money of their own. They literally had to live on the generosity of others.

St. Francis is known as the patron saint of animals and animal lovers because he spent time in meditation outside and was sometimes found conversing with these creatures. He even befriended a wolf in Gubbio that had been bullying the local villagers. He admonished the beast to behave, which the wolf did from then on.

Francis also traveled to the Holy Land in an attempt to convert the Muslim Saracens and thus end the Crusades peacefully. He was unsuccessful in that specific goal, but he did secure the admiration of the Caliph, who ordered that certain Christian shrines in Jerusalem be placed in the care of the Franciscans — a role the Franciscans have carried out for centuries.

Well before his life ended, Francis was blessed with the gift of the *stigmata,* the manifestation of the five wounds of Jesus on the person without any physical harm (stigmata disappears immediately at death, however). Figure 5-1 shows St. Francis with the stigmata on his hands, meditating on the Gospel while praying over a skull (a symbol of the dying self, or replacing the ego with the will of God).

Figure 5-1:
St. Francis.

St. Ignatius of Loyola

Loyola, Spain (1491–1556)

Beatified: 1609

Canonized: 1622

Patron: military personnel

Feast day: July 31

Ignatius had long sought a soldier's life, and in 1517, he entered the army and served in numerous campaigns with bravery and distinction. His life took a turn, however, when his leg was shattered by a cannonball in 1521.

Recuperation was long and painful, and Ignatius had little to do but read the Bible and the *Lives of the Saints.* Ignatius plowed through both, eventually determining that he shouldn't be risking his life for an earthly king when the King of Kings promised him eternal life. Ignatius laid down his secular sword and became a "soldier for Christ," allying himself with Jesus. He established a community of men he called the Society of Jesus, later to be known as the Jesuits (see Figure 5-2).

Figure 5-2: St. Ignatius contemplating the Holy Name of Jesus (*IHS*, the first three letters of Jesus's name in Greek).

© *Réunion des Musées Nationaux/ Art Resource, NY*

Ignatius saw the advantage of training men in all the classics of theology and philosophy, as well as geography, science, math, languages, and other humanities. He planned to conquer error and heresy with truth and knowledge, which is why the Jesuits to this day are one of the most educated of religious communities. In addition to taking solemn vows of poverty, chastity, and obedience, Ignatius added a fourth vow, of complete service to the pope.

Popes in different times used the Jesuits and their growing influence to promote and defend the faith. Secular kings and princes, however, resented and envied the Jesuits' success and finally pressured Rome to suppress the Order in 1767. Not until the Council of Vienna in 1814 after the Napoleonic Wars was the Society of Jesus (Jesuits) restored.

Book IV

Saints and Other Important Figures

St. Lucy Filippini

Corneto, Tuscany, Italy (1672–1732)

Beatified: 1926

Canonized: 1930

Patron: Catholic grammar schools

Feast day: March 25

After being orphaned as a young child, Lucy was taken under the wing of Cardinal Marc'Antonio Barbarigo, who inspired and protected her and encouraged her to work among the younger girls of the diocese. The Cardinal wanted Lucy to help make sure that the girls received a Christian education and upbringing.

Lucy established the Religious Teachers Filippini in 1692 to educate and train religious women, who in turn taught the young, especially young women, to prepare them for life, whether they married or entered the convent. Boys commonly received instruction to prepare them to become priests or lay Christian gentlemen, but young women seldom received such spiritual and academic guidance. The Religious Teachers Filippini was established to give these young women the tools they needed to spiritually succeed. St. Lucy Filippini also is one of the incorruptible saints — see her discussion in Book IV, Chapter 3.

St. Philip Neri

Florence, Italy (1515–1595)

Beatified: 1615

Canonized: 1622

Patron: U.S. Special Forces

Feast day: May 26

Philip spent most of his life as a devout layman, only becoming ordained to the priesthood in 1551, when he was in his mid '30s. Until then, he studied and prayed and worked in the hospitals helping the sick.

He had a strong devotion to the Holy Eucharist and encouraged others to spend time in prayer before the Blessed Sacrament. After he was ordained,

Philip established the Congregation of the Oratory (CO) to help priests become holier and thus help their parishioners as well.

St. Philip Neri's oratories were and remain today an innovative creation: priests living together in a quasi-community but still working as typical parish priests. The fraternity and camaraderie, as well as spiritual support, is an attempt to compensate for what's missing in most rectories (where most parish priests live). One of the most famous oratories is in London, England, where Cardinal Newman, the Anglican convert, spent his final years. St. Philip Neri also is one of the incorruptible saints; see his entry in Book IV, Chapter 3.

St. Vincent de Paul

France (1581–1660)

Beatified: 1729

Canonized: 1737

Patron: social workers, seminary professors

Feast day: September 27

Vincent de Paul's priesthood got off to a somewhat turbulent start. Five years after being ordained, he was captured by Turkish pirates and held hostage for two years. He eventually converted his "owner" to Christianity and was granted freedom. He returned to Rome to expand his studies and eventually ended up in a wealthy parish in Paris.

In Paris, he befriended some affluent parishioners and convinced them to use their wealth to help the poor, one of two great needs he recognized in the early 17th century. The other great need he saw was the education of the clergy; poorly educated priests helped sow the seeds of the Reformation, and ignoring the plight of the poor was equally devastating to the church and society at large.

The Black Death (bubonic plague in 1348–1350) decimated a third of the population of Western Europe and killed two-thirds of the clergy. So desperate were people for priests to administer the sacraments that sometimes uneducated and incompetent men were ordained, and their misbehavior and/or unorthodox ideas made fertile ground for religious revolution.

Book IV

Saints and Other Important Figures

Vincent established the Congregation of the Mission (CM) to work on those two priorities: service to the poor and education of the clergy (seminary formation). The Council of Trent had met from 1545–1563 in response to Martin Luther and the Protestant Reformation. One of the council's decrees was the establishment of adequate seminaries to educate and supervise the formation of clergy to better serve the spiritual needs of the people in the parish. St. Vincent de Paul also is one of the incorruptible saints — see his discussion in Book IV, Chapter 3.

Chapter 6

Saintly Pastors

Some saints spent their lives serving the Church as pastors — priests or bishops who cared for people's spiritual lives. *Pastor* means "shepherd," and just as the good shepherd tends to the needs and safety of his flock, so too did these men. They were exemplary in their spiritual care of those entrusted to them. This chapter discusses just some of these important men.

St. Aloysius Gonzaga

Lombardy, Italy (1568–1591)

Beatified: 1605

Canonized: 1726

Patron: young students (because of his early catechetical work with them), Jesuit novices, and people with AIDS and their caregivers

Feast day: June 21

Aloysius was the eldest son of the Marquis of Castiglione, and, as such, he was born into certain expectations and demands. His father had hopes that he would enter the military and be a strong commander, but Aloysius wanted to live a religious life.

He and his brother were sent to various royal courts, most notably to Spain as part of the child prince's retinue. That life grew tiresome for young Aloysius, and instead of taking part in the available pleasures, he continued to practice his devotions and disciplines. He fasted, rose early to pray and make a holy hour, and performed severe penances.

The death of the Spanish prince freed Aloysius from all royal duties, and he then worked toward entering a religious life. He had read journals and other material on saints and religious men and was interested in the Jesuits' account of their missionary work in India. He wanted to join the Counter-Reformation congregation.

Aloysius joined the Jesuit novitiate in Rome in 1585 as a frail young man afflicted with kidney disease and prone to chronic headaches. Schooling was in Milan, but Aloysius's health prevented him from continuing. He returned to Rome as a plague epidemic hit the city. He volunteered in the Jesuit hospital and helped care for the sick.

Aloysius contracted the plague and died in 1591. He is enshrined in Rome at the Church of St. Ignatius.

St. Ansgar

France (A.D. 801–A.D. 865)

Feast day: February 3

Ansgar was a child of nobility raised in the Abbey of Corbie near Amiens, France. He grew up in piety and devotion to the Blessed Virgin Mary and entered monastic life at the same abbey. He later transferred to Westphalia (a region in Germany), where he continued his preaching and teaching.

New opportunities for Catholicism and Christianity began to open in the northern European regions, and Ansgar stood at the forefront of those who sought to introduce Christianity to Denmark and Sweden. He was quite successful in establishing churches in these areas.

Upon being summoned by Holy Roman Emperor Louis the Pious, he returned to France and was made Archbishop of Hamburg in A.D. 831. He continued to promote the Church through education and the building of churches and monasteries.

When Emperor Louis died in A.D. 840, the empire was divided among his three sons, and new churches came under attack, including the archdiocese in Hamburg. Eventually, the new emperor, Louis II, was able to bring peace, and Ansgar rebuilt his see.

Ansgar didn't pastor to only the Church as a whole; he was also very much a pastor to the individual. Throughout his career as archbishop, he personally fed and tended to the sick and the poor, and his works of charity were known throughout the diocese. He dismissed any praise for his role of Christian service.

He is considered an apostle of northern Europe and patron saint of Denmark. He is also venerated in the Eastern Orthodox Church, as well as the Lutheran and Anglican religions.

St. Anthony, the Abbot

Egypt (A.D. 251–A.D. 356)

Patron: basket makers, butchers, victims of eczema, and hermits (a type of monk); invoked against pestilence

Feast day: January 17

Although monasticism had been in existence for some time, Anthony is considered the father of Eastern monasticism for making it known and popular in a way no other monk was able to do. As a child, he led a life of extraordinary solitude and didn't attend school outside the home. When his parents died, he inherited vast amounts of money and property and became his unmarried sister's caretaker.

While attending church services, Anthony heard a gospel passage about a wealthy young man selling all he had and giving it to the poor. He took this message as a sign that God wanted him to do the same thing, so he placed his sister in the care of consecrated virgin women — which would later become the beginning of convent life — and sold all his property.

Anthony sequestered himself in solitude and entered a period of deep prayer, fasting, reading, and manual labor, thus beginning to perfect the virtues of humility, charity, and chastity.

In A.D. 305, Anthony founded the first of what would be several monasteries. He is believed to have died at the age of 105 after living a life of austerity and discipline.

The city of Vienna, in Austria, has a major shrine of St. Anthony, and a monastery also exists in his honor.

St. Anthony Claret

Spain (1807–1870)

Beatified: 1934

Canonized: 1950

Patron: textile merchants, weavers, Catholic press, Claretian missionaries, and the diocese of the Canary Islands

Feast day: October 24

Anthony was born in Spain to a family involved in wool manufacturing. The family lived comfortably and stressed the importance of education. As a young adult, Anthony moved to Barcelona to continue the woolen trade but discovered he was more interested in religious life.

Anthony had hoped to enter the monastery of the strictest observance, the Carthusians, but his health wasn't strong enough to allow him to follow that austere lifestyle. Instead, he was ordained a priest for his home diocese of Vic in Catalonia, Spain. He tried missionary work by joining the Jesuits in Rome, but again, his health began to deteriorate.

Returning to Spain, he preached missions in his native diocese and the Canary Islands. He established a religious community, the Congregation of Missionary Sons of the Immaculate Heart of Mary, known as the Claretians.

Anthony's holiness, organizational skills, and missionary zeal soon caught the eye of Queen Isabella II of Spain. At her request, Pope Pius IX appointed Anthony Archbishop of Santiago in Cuba. The diocese was a physical and spiritual mess, having suffered the effects of a revolution. Archbishop Claret reorganized the diocese, established schools, emphasized clerical discipline, and restructured the seminary.

Anthony was called back to Spain to be the queen's confessor, and he worked at the military palace, Escorial, where he established a science laboratory in the monastery. In Barcelona, he established a library.

The political situation deteriorated in Italy and Spain, and Anthony went to Rome to prepare for the First Vatican Council, which would define papal infallibility. At the time, Italy was undergoing unification, the Papal States were threatened, and Anthony Claret proved to be a good support for Pope Pius IX.

St. Anthony Zaccaria

Italy (1502–1539)

Beatified: 1890

Canonized: 1897

Patron: the Barnabite community

Feast day: July 5

Anthony Zaccaria was educated in medicine and returned to his hometown to serve as a physician. It wasn't long before he felt a deep attraction to religious life, and he was ordained into the priesthood in 1527. Anthony practiced works of charity among the poor and in hospitals.

He organized three religious institutions for priests, sisters, and laypeople. The Clerks Regular of St. Paul took vows of chastity, poverty, and obedience without being monastic or mendicants. The Angelic Sisters of St. Paul was founded to help young women avoid falling into the evil ways of the world. Finally, the Laity of St. Paul was established for married couples as support in their vocation.

The Clerks Regular chose the Church of St. Barnabas in Rome as their home and thus became known as the Barnabites. Their main apostolate was to promote the sacred liturgy and the sacraments, and to that end, Anthony started a devotion of exposing the Blessed Sacrament on the altars of churches for three days, known today as the Forty Hours' Devotion. This custom was inaugurated in the United States by St. John Neumann.

Anthony practiced severe *asceticism* — rigorous self-denial and self-mortification — and it took a toll on his health. He caught a fever while preaching a mission in 1539 and died a short time later.

Pope Leo XIII canonized him, and a shrine in his honor is in the Convent of St. Paul's in Milan, Italy.

St. Augustine of Canterbury

Canterbury, England (unknown–A.D. 605)

Patron: Canterbury; England; Great Britain

Feast day: May 27

Augustine was a Benedictine monk and prior of a monastery near Rome. Pope Gregory the Great became aware of Augustine's gifts and talents and appointed him to missionary work in England. Because of several wars and pagan invasions, England was, at the time, divided into factions of small Christian religious communities.

Christians in England asked the pope to send more missionaries, and Augustine was chosen to lead them. The pope sent many things with Augustine to use in reestablishing the Church, including relics, sacred vessels, altar furnishings, vestments, and books. After Augustine baptized the English king, he returned to France to be ordained a bishop.

Augustine then founded a new see and built a monastery and church at the site where the Canterbury Cathedral now stands. He also established the diocese of London and Rochester and had to deal with the remnant Catholic Church that had been exiled to Cornwall and Wales by pagan invasions. Augustine's hope of reuniting this group with his reinvigorated church ultimately failed, but through his work and the missionaries that were sent by Rome, the Catholic Church now had a strong foundation in England.

St. Bernadine of Siena

Italy (1380–1444)

Canonized: 1450

Patron: advertisers, people with chest problems, gambling addicts, public relations personnel, and the diocese of San Bernardino, California

Feast day: May 20

St. Bernadine was born on September 8, the same date as the Virgin Mary, so his birth date held a special significance to him. That date served as his baptismal date, the day he was invested with the Franciscan habit, and the day of his ordination.

Information about the first 12 years of Bernadine's religious life is scarce, except that he lived the strict observance of the Franciscans, a movement within the broader order. Apparently, one of his religious brothers had a vision that Father Bernadine was to go and preach to the region of Lombardy.

Wherever he went, Bernadine preached of repentance and turning away from vices. He spread the devotion to Jesus's holy name and used the term IHS to denote his name — IHS being the first letters of Jesus's name in Greek, which was later translated to Latin. Drawn rays of sunshine emanate from the initials of this beautiful logo.

Bernadine preached throughout Italy. When he took the habit of the strict observance of St. Francis, the order had only 300 men; his preaching was so powerful and successful that at the time of his death, the order had grown to 4,000 men.

St. Bernadine was canonized by Pope Nicholas V and is buried in Aquila, Italy, the last place he preached.

St. Bruno

Germany (1030–1101)

Canonized: 1623

Patron: Ruthenia, victims of demonic possession

Feast day: October 6

As chancellor of the church in Rheims, France, Bruno witnessed many abuses and worldliness in the clergy, including those involving Archbishop Manasses of Rheims, who appointed him to his post. He reported what he saw and an investigation ensued; Archbishop Manasses was quite clever, however, and was returned to his see. Bruno and his clerical companions who challenged the archbishop were persecuted.

Bruno wanted to retire and devote himself entirely to religious life, and he went on to found the Carthusian Order in Chartreuse, France. Pope Urban II heard of Bruno's piety and called him to Rome to help him in Church government. Bruno recognized obedience to one's legitimate superior as a virtue and set out for Rome. He created a hermitage and worked on reforms in clerical life for the pope.

When Bruno was ready for a more secluded religious life, the pope granted him permission to go to Calabria, Italy. He developed two monasteries in the area and continued communication with his monastery in Chartreuse.

St. Cajetan

Italy (1480–1547)

Beatified: 1629

Canonized: 1671

Patron: the unemployed and job seekers

Feast day: August 7

Book IV

Saints and Other Important Figures

Cajetan was born with the name "Gaetano" in Vicenza, Italy, and lived during a time of great political and religious upheaval. He was sent to Padua, where he received a doctorate in law and worked under Pope Julius II in the protonotary office (the church equivalent of a notary public). When Julius died, Gaetano resigned his office and studied for the priesthood. He was ordained in 1516 and took the name Cajetan.

He worked for the restoration of clergy by reviving an association of priests called Divine Love. This group worked among the poor and in hospitals.

Cajetan returned to Vicenza and, recognizing the need for reform in the Church, worked with other priests to establish the Congregation of Clerks Regular, known as the Theatines. The Theatines' mission was to revive spirit and zeal in the clergy, as Cajetan believed that no true reform could take place in the Church until the priests reformed themselves.

He died on August 7, 1547, in Naples, Italy, and was canonized in 1671 by Pope Clement X.

St. Casimir

Poland (1458–1484)

Canonized: 1522

Patron: Poland and Lithuania

Feast day: March 4

Casimir was the third eldest child of King Casimir IV and Elizabeth of Austria — daughter of Emperor Albert II — and was the grand duke of Lithuania. Very early in his life, he committed himself to chastity and celibacy and worked tirelessly for the poor. He influenced his father and older brother to distribute alms.

Casimir reluctantly obeyed his father and accepted the throne in Hungary. He was forced into politics at a time when the people of Hungary were tired of their lax king, and the Muslim Ottoman Empire was threatening to enter Christendom through Hungary. But Casimir's army was outnumbered, and he returned to Poland. His father wasn't pleased and imprisoned his son in a castle outside Kraków.

During his imprisonment, Casimir's faith, asceticism, and devotion to God blossomed. He was eventually trained in political affairs and, during his father's travels, ruled Poland in a prudent and judicious manner. He died of tuberculosis on March 4, 1484, and is buried in the cathedral Vilna in Lithuania.

St. Charles Borromeo

Italy (1538–1584)

Beatified: 1602

Canonized: 1610

Patron: catechists, catechumens, seminarians, and the diocese of Monterey, California; invoked against abdominal pain, intestinal disorders, stomach diseases, and ulcers

Feast day: November 4

Charles was named cardinal-deacon by his uncle, Pope Pius IV. Upon the death of his father, Count Gilberto Borromeo, he inherited money, land, and the title of count, all of which he renounced so he could be ordained a priest. He was soon ordained Archbishop of Milan.

Charles worked tirelessly with his uncle at the Council of Trent. When Pius IV died, the new pope, Pius V, retained Charles Borromeo. He worked on many of the deliberations of the council during the Church's Reformation, while personally working on the reformation of liturgy and sacrament as well as the establishment of the catechism of the Council of Trent.

Along with Pope St. Pius V, St. Philip Neri, and Ignatius of Loyola, the Church was armed with the renewed spirit of reform, known as the *Counter-Reformation.* Still, Charles wanted to work in his diocese; years of neglect had taken a toll on the archdiocese of Milan. He started his reforms in 1566 by implementing the deliberations of the Council of Trent, and then he regulated clerical life by establishing rectories — residences for priests. He founded seminaries for the training of priests and spent his life and fortune on the people of Milan.

St. Columban

Italy (A.D. 540–A.D. 615)

Patron: bookbinders, poets, and against floods

Feast day: November 23

Columban was born to Irish nobility in the sixth century and traveled with a small band to Iona, Scotland, and then on to France. He was ordained and founded monasteries throughout Ireland, Scotland, Italy, and France, and he adopted the rule of St. Benedict in all of them.

The rule — or *regula* in Latin — refers to the disciplines used to keep order in a religious community. The rule delineates who's in charge and of what, and it defines what the members can and can't do in everyday life. St. Benedict's rule is one of the oldest and simplest in that it centers on two aspects — prayer and work *(ora et labora).*

Book IV

Saints and Other Important Figures

In addition to St. Columban's rule for monastic living, he wrote a number of letters and poetry. He died on November 23, A.D. 615, in Bobbio, Italy, where his monastery became a bastion of faith and learning. His body is preserved in the abbey church at Bobbio.

St. Eusebius of Vercelli

Sardinia (A.D. 283–A.D. 371)

Patron: the diocese of Vercelli, Italy

Feast day: August 2

Eusebius was instituted as a lector in Rome before eventually going to Vercelli in northern Italy to become the region's first bishop. While he was Bishop of Vercelli, the Arian heresy was infiltrating the Church. In response, Pope Liberius sent Bishop Eusebius to ask the emperor to convene a council to return the heretics to Catholicism.

The synod was held in Milan in A.D. 355, but Eusebius saw that the tide had turned and that reconciliation wasn't imminent. The emperor refused to accept the decrees of the Council of Nicea and condemned St. Athanasius. The emperor expected all bishops to sign this condemnation, but Eusebius refused, believing in the innocence of Athanasius and the validity of the Council of Nicea.

(Athanasius was the opponent of Arius, who denied the divinity of Christ. Nicea vindicated Athanasius and condemned Arius.)

Eusebius was then exiled to Palestine. After the ascension of the new emperor, exiled bishops were allowed to return to their sees. Eusebius met with Athanasius in Alexandria to work on clarifying other Christological doctrine.

Eusebius eventually returned to Vercelli and died there on August 1, A.D. 371.

St. Francis of Paola

Calabria, Italy (1416–1502)

Canonized: 1519

Patron: Calabria (a region in Italy), boatmen, mariners, and naval officers

Feast day: April 2

Francis was educated by Franciscan priests and established the Franciscan Order of Minim Friars, a type of hermit, in 1492. The strict observance of the rule of St. Francis attracted many to his new monastery in Cosenza.

Francis was known for his holiness and as a miracle worker. When King Louis XI of France became gravely ill, he summoned Francis, who initially refused. The king beseeched the pope to intercede, and Francis felt compelled to obey. He traveled to France and prepared the king for death.

Upon the king's death, Francis wanted to return to Italy, but the new king wouldn't allow him to leave, wanting Francis to stay in France because of his holiness.

Francis died at the age of 91 in France. French Protestants broke into Francis's tomb in 1562 and found his body incorrupt, or non-decayed. They burned his body, and devout Catholics retrieved fragments of his bones for veneration.

St. Jerome Emiliani

Italy (1481–1537)

Beatified: 1747

Canonized: 1767

Patron: orphans, abandoned people, and Taos Indians

Feast day: February 8

Like most men of his social status at the time, Jerome started his career in the military in the Republic of Venice. Venice's power was then being challenged, and there was a call to arms.

Jerome was captured in the northern Italian town of Treviso and jailed. While in prison, he had time to reflect on his worldly life, which was fairly devoid of God. At a church in Treviso, at the altar of Our Lady, Jerome laid down his arms and consecrated his life to the Mother of God.

Jerome was ordained a priest in 1518 and devoted himself to the sick, the poor, orphans, and victims of the plague. His apostolate attracted other men to join in his works, and he founded a new congregation of men, the Clerks Regular of Somascha, known as the Somaschi Fathers. They were dedicated to the poor and often preached in the fields where the peasants worked.

Book IV

Saints and Other Important Figures

He caught a fever on one of his preaching expeditions to the fields and died in Somascha in 1537.

St. John Baptist de la Salle

France (1651–1719)

Beatified: 1888

Canonized: 1900

Patron: educators, teachers of youth, and school principals

Feast day: April 7

John was born to parents of noble origins, and upon their death, he donated his inheritance to the poor. He studied for the priesthood and was ordained in 1678. John became interested in the education of poor children early on in his priestly life and established a new religious community, the Brothers of Christian Schools, which was devoted to teaching.

John's new community soon became the largest teaching order in the post-Reformation Church. Schools sprouted up throughout France, all dedicated to the education of poor boys. The brothers used the native language of the countries they were living in rather than teach the courses in Latin.

Secular schools felt threatened, and John Baptist and his community faced great opposition. The perseverance of the community grew, and so did the construction of its schools.

One major change to the apostolate happened when King James II of England, exiled in France, wanted a school built for his sons and gentry alike. John drew up a manual for his school that set the standard for all Christian Brothers schools in terms of following a certain curriculum and code of conduct.

John's principal shrine is located in Rome at the de la Salle Generalate.

St. John Cantius (Kanty)

Poland (1390–1473)

Beatified: 1676

Canonized: 1767

Patron: Lithuania and Poland

Feast day: December 23

John taught Scripture at the University of Kraków and was a noted professor, which caused jealousy among the other professors. Already an ordained priest, he was reassigned to a parish. He was nervous about the administrative tasks of the pastor, and at first, the people in his parish didn't like him. John persevered, however, and his solemn celebration of the Mass and excellent preaching and teaching changed the parishioners' attitudes. When he was sent back to the university to teach Scripture, his parishioners didn't want him to go.

John was a great friend of the poor, often distributing his own food, materials, and money to them. So humble was he that, when traveling on pilgrimage to Rome, he walked all the way, carrying his few possessions on his back.

He died at the age of 83. A religious community founded in Chicago, the St. John Cantius Society, is named after him. This society is devoted to the restoration of the Latin liturgy, and its members celebrate the extraordinary form of the Mass — the Mass that was used before the Second Vatican Council.

St. John of Capistrano

Italy (1386–1456)

Beatified: 1650

Canonized: 1690

Patron: judges, jurists, military chaplains, and the Spanish-American Catholic Mission in San Juan Capistrano, California

Feast day: October 23

As a young man, John studied law at the University of Perugia and was eventually elected governor of the region. All of Italy was undergoing political and economic change and hardship; one city-state was at war with another.

John was captured and imprisoned, giving him time to reflect on his life. His marriage was dissolved because it had never been consummated, and he decided to enter the Franciscan Order.

John was ordained into the priesthood in 1420 and became known as a powerful orator. Emperor Frederick III called upon his talents to preach against a heretic religious group, the Hussites, that was flourishing in central Europe. The group originated in Prague and was led by reformer John Huss. Although

Huss was condemned and put to death as a heretic, his movement lived on, but John of Capistrano's powerful preaching brought people back to the Church.

Catholic Europe was under great threat with the fall of Constantinople at the hands of the Muslim Turks. Pope Nicholas V called upon John to lead a crusade against the Turks, and he preached to the people of Austria and Hungary, exhorting them to come to arms. The Turks were deterred, at least for a time.

John became ill on the battlefields where he was administering the sacraments, celebrating Holy Mass, and preaching. He died on October 23, 1456.

St. Josemaria Escriva

Rome, Italy (1902–1975)

Beatified: 1992

Canonized: 2002

Patron: lay workers

Feast day: June 26

By the time he was 15, Josemaria had seen three of his sisters die as children and his father go through bankruptcy. Feeling called to the priesthood, he went to the seminary, earned degrees in theology and civil law, and was ordained in 1925.

While a parish priest, Josemaria discerned the Lord calling him further, and he founded Opus Dei, Latin for *work of God*. Nearly 35 years before the Second Vatican Council would even use the phrase "universal call to holiness," Josemaria conceptualized it and founded Opus Dei as a means by which ordinary Catholic Christians could sanctify their entire lives by sanctifying their daily work.

During the Middle Ages, the peasants thought that only the monks and nuns were capable of holiness, whereas the common folk (non-nobility) had to settle for a watered-down version of monastic spirituality. Monastic life centered on work and prayer, while secular life had lots of work but little time for prayer.

Instead of going to the chapel whenever the bell rang (as the monks and nuns had to do each day), Josemaria meditated on the lives of St. Joseph and the Virgin Mary, the two holiest people next to Jesus Christ himself. Joseph and his wife were humble, simple folk. They spent most of their day doing manual labor. As faithful Jews, Joseph and Mary did go to synagogue or temple, but not daily. It just wasn't practical to do so.

Likewise, Josemaria thought, one's personal holiness isn't solely contingent on how much time one spends in holy places, but rather on how much of the daily work is consecrated to God. While daily prayer is absolutely essential, so is making your daily work a "prayer." Josemaria discovered that if you do your best at whatever your regular job entails and dedicate your best effort to God, then that work is made holy.

St. Martin of Tours

Upper Pannonia, Hungary (A.D. 316–A.D. 397)

Patron: beggars, equestrians, and the Pontifical Swiss Guard; invoked against alcoholism, impoverishment, and poverty

Feast day: November 11

Born to pagan parents in what is now Hungary, Martin studied and converted to Christianity at the age of 10. He became a soldier and served in the emperor's army.

When Martin was a soldier, he visited Amiens in present-day France. It was a cold morning, and at the city gate stood a beggar — cold, hungry, and with very few clothes. Martin didn't have much to offer, because soldiers were poorly paid. He got off his horse and offered what he had: half his cape.

Observing the tearing of his cloak in half, some made fun of him, while others felt guilty that they didn't do their part in helping a poor old man. As the story continued that night, Martin had a dream in which Christ the Lord came to him dressed in the remnants of his cloak. The story reflects the ways in which Christians are known for their good actions.

Martin continued as a soldier, and after a successful campaign, the emperor was ready to pay him fairly well, but Martin refused and wanted to be released from the army. This angered the emperor, because Martin was a good soldier, and he imprisoned Martin on charges of treason with hopes that he would change his mind. He was eventually released to St. Hilary of Poitiers, France.

Martin wanted to live a quiet life as a hermit and began the first monastery in this area. Upon the death of the Bishop of Tours, the people wanted him to become their new bishop. He preferred to remain a quiet monk, but he accepted the call to become their bishop. Through his preaching, teaching, and fine holy example, he won over many from paganism. Idols and temples were soon destroyed, and Catholic churches were built.

At the same time, many heretical groups began to form over confusion in doctrine. One such group was the Priscillianists — a Gnostic, Manichean

Book IV

Saints and Other Important Figures

religious sect. Martin successfully preached against this heresy, but when the emperor condemned members to death, Martin pleaded for leniency.

St. Nicholas of Bari

Turkey (A.D. 270–A.D. 346)

Patron: sailors, children in the West, fishermen, merchants, the falsely accused, prostitutes, repentant thieves, and pawnbrokers

Feast day: December 6

Nicholas was Bishop of Myra in Asia Minor. In his time, girls couldn't marry unless they had a proper endowment. One man, the father of three girls, lost all his money and was going to sell his daughters into prostitution. Nicholas heard this, and in the middle of the night, he took a sack of gold, enough for the eldest daughter to marry, and threw it through the open window of the man's house. He also did this for the other two daughters, and the father made it a point to see who this generous benefactor was.

As the legend grew, St. Nicholas became Sinter Klaas in Dutch and Santa Claus in English. The jolly old St. Nicholas mentioned in many Christmas carols is actually St. Nicholas of Bari. However, the present-day secular representation has little to do with the real St. Nicholas. He didn't wear a red-and-white suit, nor did he have a sleigh and eight reindeer. These were elements of the mythical "Father Christmas" that became identified with St. Nicholas after European immigrants came to the New World. The real St. Nick did dress as a bishop of his time, did many good deeds, and performed many miracles for children, whom he loved and cherished dearly.

He is revered among the Orthodox and Byzantine Catholic churches for his defense of the Christian faith against the many heresies plaguing the Church in the third and fourth centuries, especially Arianism. He is patron of sailors because, according to legend, sailors in the Mediterranean Sea invoked his name during storms, and the saint guided them safely to port. His feast is kept with great solemnity and festivity in Nordic countries.

During the Muslim takeover of many Christian cities and sites in the eastern Mediterranean, the relics of St. Nicholas were successfully moved in the 11th century to Bari, Italy, where they are today. A magnificent basilica was built in his honor in this port city. He was greatly revered among the Russians as the defender of orthodoxy, so much so that, until the Communist Revolution, Russians would travel to Bari on pilgrimage.

St. Patrick

Britain (A.D. 387–A.D. 461)

Patron: Ireland, many dioceses throughout the English-speaking world, and engineers; invoked against the fear of snakes and snakebites

Feast day: March 17

Patrick was born just south of Hadrian's Wall in Britain, which was part of the Roman Empire. He was captured by Irish pagans in his early teens and taken to Ireland, where he was enslaved for six years. During that time, he grew to like the spirit of the Irish. When he escaped and returned to his family, he vowed to one day return to Ireland.

He studied at monasteries on the continent and was eventually ordained a priest and then a bishop. Pope Celestine I commissioned Patrick to be an apostle to Ireland.

Patrick initially encountered many hardships among the pagans, particularly the druids. They weren't willing to give up their power over the old religion and feared Patrick and Christianity. Although the ruling monarch, King Laoghaire, didn't convert to Christianity, many of his family members did, and little by little, the old religion began to fade. Patrick traveled from town to town, tearing down idols and temples and establishing the Catholic Church. By A.D. 444, the primatial see and first cathedral of Ireland were built in Armagh.

He baptized, confirmed, and ordained priests, and he erected schools and monasteries. Thousands came into the Church under his direction. He accomplished all these activities in less than 30 years, during which time the whole island nation of Ireland was converted. Toward the end of his life, he wrote *Confessions,* in which he gives a record of his life and mission. He died on March 17, A.D. 461, of natural causes. He is buried in Downpatrick in present-day Northern Ireland.

Many stories are told in connection with St. Patrick. The three-leaf clover was said to be used by the saintly bishop to explain the Blessed Trinity to the pagans. Another legend has Patrick driving all the snakes out of Ireland; snakes were a popular symbol among the Irish pagans. He is certainly one of the most revered saints in the Catholic Church. The famous prayer, "St. Patrick's Breastplate," is attributed to him.

Book IV

Saints and Other Important Figures

St. Paul of the Cross

Italy (1694–1775)

Beatified: 1853

Canonized: 1867

Patron: Ovada, Italy

Feast day: October 19

Paul developed a devotion to the sacred passion of Christ very early on in his life, instilled first by his mother, who taught him to spiritualize pain and inconveniences he encountered.

Paul received a vision when he was a young man that inspired him to establish a new congregation of priests, the Congregation of the Passion of Jesus Christ, commonly known as the Passionists, in 1720. The new community devoted itself to preaching missions in parishes and giving retreats in seminaries, houses of formation, and monasteries. Toward the end of his life, Paul also founded a cloistered, contemplative community of religious women, known as the Passionist Nuns.

Today, many shrines throughout Europe and in America are staffed by Passionists, including the famous shrine of St. Gabriel of the Passion in the Abruzzi Mountains in Italy and, in the U.S., the Shrine of St. Ann in Scranton, Pennsylvania. In addition, these priests work in various monasteries and retreat centers.

Paul's major shrine, which contains his relics, is the Church of St. John and Paul in Rome.

St. Vincent Ferrer

Spain (1350–1419)

Canonized: 1455

Patron: builders, construction workers, plumbers, brick makers, and tile makers

Feast day: April 5

Vincent had a great love for the poor and often shared what little he had with them. He entered the Order of Preachers, also known as the Dominicans, and was ordained a priest. Soon he became a scholarly man and received a doctorate. He was well versed in philosophy, theology, and Sacred Scripture. It is said that he had a vision of St. Dominic and St. Francis early in his priesthood and from that time on had many mystical experiences.

His great knowledge would soon be put to good use. During the Western (Papal) Schism of 1378–1417, three men claimed at the same time to be pope. Vincent began to preach the unity of the Church throughout Europe. He begged the anti-popes to resign in order to preserve this unity. This was no easy task. Anti-Pope Benedict XIII, who held court in Avignon, France, was counseled by Vincent to end the schism.

Vincent advised King Castile of Spain to withdraw his support of the Avignon anti-pope, which ended the usurped reign of Benedict. The resignation of the authentic pope and the deposing of the two anti-popes paved the way for the election of the true successor to St. Peter, which would be Vincent's greatest legacy.

Several miracles were attributed to the saint before and after his death. The major shrine is in the city of Vannes (in France) in the Vannes Cathedral, where his remains are buried.

Chapter 7

Women in the Bible: Six Impactful Ladies

The Bible contains many more stories of men than of women . . . and in much greater detail. Although many people know the stories of biblical men, many biblical women remain mysteries. Yet women play critical roles in the Bible and in salvation history. Some are famous, and others are unknown; some are powerful, and others are powerless. Like their biblical male counterparts, some women used their gifts and abilities for good, and some for evil. But no matter what their individual personalities and contributions, their stories are often crucial to understanding salvation history. Their examples provide a perspective on another time, as well as enlightenment on the modern-day world. Here, you find details about six of those ladies who made quite a mark.

And Then There Was Woman: Eve

Eve is sometimes given a bad rap as a temptress to Adam. She is, according to the Bible, the first woman, the first wife, and the first mother of the human race. Eve isn't the first to sin, however. She shares that dishonor equally with her husband, Adam. That's why the act of disobedience these two commit is called *the sin of Adam and Eve* (what Christians call *original sin*). She was tempted by the serpent and then, in turn, she tempted Adam. Eve could have said *no,* and Adam could have, too.

Before you look at Eve's mistake, you need to see her place in creation, not just chronologically but, more important, her spiritual place in salvation history. Eve is created by God and in the image and likeness of God. She has the same free will and rational intellect as her mate, Adam, the first man. They are united into one flesh before they break God's law. Her importance to the human race is partially her sin but also the good she still possesses even after the fall.

Paul claims in one of his New Testament epistles that death entered the human race through one man, Adam, but that eternal life also came through one man, Jesus Christ (1 Corinthians 15:22). Eve is therefore not blamed with bringing death to the human race — Adam gets that dishonor.

Oops, I probably shouldn't have done that

Soon after God creates Eve and she and her husband Adam begin their domestic life, they get into some trouble, which is documented in Genesis 3. Their first act of disobedience to God was the first sin committed by the human race, and it is therefore known as *original sin* or *the sin of Adam and Eve.* According to the Bible, because they were the original parents of humanity, their sin is handed on or transmitted to each and every subsequent descendant — in their case, the rest of humankind.

"The devil made me do it!"

Eve is alone until the serpent enters the picture. The Bible describes the serpent as the most crafty or cunning of all the animals. (The Hebrew word *nachash* can be translated as "serpent" or "snake." Some Bibles and Bible commentaries use the word "snake" rather than "serpent" but the two mean the same thing.)

A dialogue develops between Eve and the serpent. Although it may be tempting to pick apart the story of a talking serpent — stupid pet tricks are perhaps better left to late-night talk shows — neither the author nor Eve concerns themselves with this detail. The point of the Bible story is that someone or something other than Eve and Adam — a nonhuman — is the catalyst for the original sin.

Biblical scholars point out that the Hebrews were very familiar with the pagan fertility idolatry practiced by the Canaanites — their nemesis — much of which involved worship of a serpent or snake god. Hearing that a serpent was a part of the Fall would make perfect sense to a Hebrew. In addition, some theologians speculate that the devil, a fallen angel, took the form of a serpent or used a snake as a puppet tool to communicate his insidious temptation.

The serpent asks Eve if God said that she and her husband could eat of any tree in the garden. She replies that God said they could eat the fruit of any tree — except the one in the middle. If they touch it or eat from it, they'll die.

The serpent then tells Eve that she won't die if she eats from the tree, but that her eyes will be opened and she and Adam will become Godlike, knowing good and evil. Eve sees that the tree does indeed have food on it that is pleasing to the eye, and the potential to have divine wisdom and knowledge entices her to eat from it.

Although most people think that the forbidden fruit was an apple, the Bible never once uses the word *apple.* The tree of knowledge is not described as an apple tree, nor is the fruit ever referred to as an apple. Christian artists depicted Eve biting into an apple or Eve handing a half-eaten apple to her husband, Adam. All it took was one artist to choose a fruit, and from then on, subsequent artists followed suit.

Share and share alike

Eve eats the forbidden fruit and gives some to Adam. He also eats the fruit, thereby disobeying the command of God himself. Sure enough, after they consume the food from the tree of knowledge, "the eyes of both were opened, and they knew they were naked" (Genesis 3:7), so they sewed fig leaves together and made loincloths for themselves.

Didn't Adam and Eve know they were naked before they ate the forbidden fruit? No. How would they know they were naked unless they saw another human being with clothes?

Genesis says that God couldn't find Adam and Eve at first because they were hiding. The Lord calls out to Adam, "Where are you?" Adam steps forward and admits that he and his wife hid because they were naked. The Hebrew word used is *eyrom,* which can mean unclothed (naked) or also unprotected. Adam and Eve are both unclothed and unprotected (not counting the loincloths) because, before this time, God had protected them, but now they're on their own.

The blame game and passing the buck then ensues, as told in Genesis 3:8–13. God asks, "Who told you that you were naked?" It's obvious that Adam and Eve have eaten of the forbidden fruit and thus disobeyed God. The man points the finger at his wife. "The woman gave it to me." When God then questions Eve, she blames the snake: "The serpent tricked me into doing it."

Time out for both of you!

When Adam and Eve admit what they did, God punishes them, along with the serpent who tempted Eve in the first place, and the day of reckoning thus begins:

- ✔ God punishes Eve by telling her that she'll bear children in pain (no one had invented the labor epidural yet). Giving birth and raising children won't be easy, and her relationship with her husband will be disrupted at times. The point? Sin causes division, not just between God and the sinner but also between human beings.

- ✔ God punishes Adam by making him toil and labor for his food. He also tells Adam that he will die and his body will decay and decompose and turn back into dust (Genesis 3:19). "You are dust, and to dust you shall return" are the ominous words.

- ✔ God also punishes the serpent (who is Satan, or the devil) with a promise: He says that one day an offspring of the woman will conquer the serpent once and for all:

> The LORD God said to the serpent: "Because you have done this, cursed are you among all animals and among all wild creatures; upon your belly you shall go, and dust you shall eat all the days of your life. I will put enmity between you and the woman, and between your offspring and hers; he will strike your head, and you will strike his heel."
>
> —Genesis 3:14–15

Eve's offspring who will crush the head of the serpent is considered by Christians to be Jesus. Catholic religious art (especially statues) often depicts the Virgin Mary standing on the head of a serpent. This image represents that Mary is the new Eve, whose offspring, Jesus, is the new Adam. Mel Gibson's film *The Passion of the Christ* also alludes to this promise when he has Jesus, during his agony before the crucifixion, stomp on a snake — the devil — that slithers toward him (an event that is not found in the Bible). The idea here is that the promise that was made involving the first Eve took form in the offspring of the second Eve — Mary, whose offspring, Jesus, would destroy the power of evil when he died on the cross to save humankind.

Understanding original sin

Just as genetics pass on physical traits like eye and hair color from parent to child, original sin is the spiritual inheritance passed on to children from their parents, and ultimately from Adam and Eve themselves. According to Christian and Jewish theology, *original sin* is a spiritual disease of the human soul, a disease that is passed on to future generations as much as physical characteristics or physiological defects.

The phrase *the Fall* is used by Jewish and Christian theologians to describe the consequence of original sin. Prior to their disobedience, Adam and Eve were created and endowed by God with spiritual integrity and sanctifying grace. After they sinned, they lost that integrity and grace, hence the idea of fallen human nature or wounded nature. In other words, they fell from the spiritual level of being in communion with God to the level of being in sin. In turn, sin divides and causes further division.

The point of the story of original sin is not to pick apart the details, but to understand the message. Had Adam and Eve remained obedient, God would have revealed to them what was good and what was evil. But they wanted to know for themselves. Because of their transgression, human beings would have to learn the hard way, discovering good and evil for themselves, instead of being told and believing in what God says. Men and women would have to struggle to discern morally correct behavior.

Bible scholars use this analogy to clarify the lesson: Think of a curvy roadway. Without a speed limit sign to tell you how fast you should go, you have no way of knowing how fast you can drive before your speed becomes dangerous. Without a road sign, you must determine the correct speed on your own and, as a result, you're at greater risk of getting into a nasty accident. Before Adam and Eve sinned, God would have functioned as that road sign. Instead, pride caused the first man and woman to drive recklessly, ignoring every traffic code in the book. So they, and in turn humankind, now have to figure things out by using their conscience and their reason, which are not perfect and certainly not infallible.

Mother of all

Despite original sin, which causes the fall of humankind and allows death to enter the human equation, life nevertheless continues in the form of future generations, and Eve is the matriarch of all humankind.

In Genesis 3:20, Eve is first called Eve: "The man named his wife Eve, because she was the mother of all living." The Hebrew word *Chavvah,* which is the proper name for Eve, comes from the word *chay,* which means "the living."

Experiencing tragedy

The beginning of Genesis 4 reveals that Eve gives birth to two children — Cain and Abel. Nothing is said of their childhood, and the boys eventually grow up and get jobs: Abel as a shepherd and Cain as a farmer. Unfortunately, sibling rivalry raises its ugly head and leads to a heinous tragedy.

Book IV

Saints and Other Important Figures

One day, each man offers a sacrifice to God. Abel contributes the best of his herd, but Cain offers only the rotten produce he himself wouldn't eat. Abel gave the best he had; Cain gave the worst. When the smoke from their respective sacrifices emanates from the fire, Abel's goes straight up to heaven (a sign of God's approval), and the smoke from Cain's offering blows into his face (guess what that means).

Envy fills Cain's heart. He becomes so angry and hateful he actually kills his brother Abel. God punishes Cain by making him an outcast. He places a mark on Cain so that no one will take revenge by killing him, and he can never again see his mom and dad. (Genesis 4:1–16 details the events leading up to and including the murder of Cain.)

Thus, the first act of murder takes place very early in human history. And Eve becomes the first mother to grieve the death of a child; even worse, she must live with the knowledge that her other son is a murderer. She must not only bury Abel but also must say goodbye forever to her only other son, Cain. Eve endures this nightmare the best she can.

Giving birth again

Though she loses two sons, Eve is at least comforted in her third child, Seth. Fittingly, his name translates from the Hebrew word meaning "compensation."

The Bible says that when Adam was 130 years old, he became the father of Seth, and that he and Eve also had other sons and daughters until his death at the age of 930 (now that's an old man). The Bible doesn't say anything, however, about Eve's age when she died, or whether she lived as long as her husband.

Appearing in the New Testament

Only two more references to Eve are made in the Bible. Those references appear in the New Testament: 2 Corinthians 11:3 ("But I am afraid that as the serpent deceived Eve by its cunning, your thoughts will be led astray from a sincere and pure devotion to Christ") and 1 Timothy 2:13–14 ("For Adam was formed first, then Eve; and Adam was not deceived, but the woman was deceived and became a transgressor"). The first one uses Eve as an example of being duped by false teaching, and the second is using her submission to Adam's authority as a reason why the apostle Paul says the husband is head of the family.

In the nonbiblical (and mostly Gnostic) books the *Apocalypse of Adam,* the *Life of Adam and Eve,* and the *Testament of Adam,* you can find stories about the missing years between the birth of Seth and the death of Eve. However, no Jewish or Christian community considers these books to be inspired or factual.

The three Faces of eve

So what does Eve represent to humankind in general, and what does she represent to women in particular? The following sections take a look at these questions. Eve was made in the image and likeness of God just as much as her husband, Adam. She committed sin but apparently learned from her mistake because the Bible doesn't mention any further sins or punishments. Finally, Eve was created to be a partner for man and vice versa.

Woman as likeness of God

Because the Bible says that God created humankind "male and female" (Genesis 1:26) and that both were made "in the image of God" (Genesis 1:27), woman is as much an integral expression and reflection of God as is man. God, being a pure spirit, is neither male nor female, but human nature is both. Divinity has no gender, but humanity does. Only when male and female are together is the full expression of God reflected here on earth.

In addition, humankind and God are represented within the larger symbolic sense of marriage. The entire human race — both male and female — represents the bride, and God is the ever faithful and loving groom. The metaphoric use of marriage is intended to make all human beings feel they are in an intimate and personal relationship with God. Humans are not simply creatures and God the creator.

Eve as believer

After her decision to eat the forbidden fruit, Eve learns her lesson, and she emerges from the Garden of Eden a little bit wiser, along with her husband, Adam. She experiences the pain of giving birth to her children, the joys of raising those children, and the sorrows of burying one of them killed by his own brother. Eve is an example to believers in that she is truly a repentant sinner. After the Garden incident, the Bible doesn't mention any other incident where she disobeyed the Lord. Like someone recovering from alcohol or drug abuse, Eve is a recovering sinner striving to stay on the straight and narrow.

A message for women

Eve isn't only the first woman on earth; she's also the only one of God's creations who can be a suitable partner for Adam. Genesis 2:20 uses the Hebrew word *ezer,* which can be translated as "partner" or "companion." The Greek word *Boethos* is used in the Septuagint version of the Old Testament, and one of its meanings is "helper." Nowhere is Eve described as being a servant or slave to Adam. She is his partner, and because she is made in the image and likeness and God, just like her husband, Eve deserves the same respect

Book IV

Saints and Other Important Figures

and honor. Her value as a woman is that, with man, they together reflect the image and likeness of God. Neither gender alone can do that.

As wife, Eve epitomizes the biblical teaching that in marriage, two become one flesh. Not someone who merely agrees to a contract, Eve is a person who enters a *covenant* (sacred oath) with her husband, Adam, and their covenant symbolizes the covenant between God and all humankind. (For more on the complementary roles of Adam and Eve, see Book I, Chapter 3.)

A Famous Mom: Mary, the Mother of Jesus

According to Christian belief, God became man and lived among humans for 33 years. Now, God didn't just pretend to be human, nor did he merely use a human body (like some sci-fi movie where aliens take on human form). Christians believe that divinity and humanity were united in one person known as Jesus of Nazareth. As God, he existed from all eternity, but as man, he was born in time and space like you. The God-Man Jesus Christ had a real, flesh-and-blood human mother who conceived him in her womb and nine months later gave birth to him. That woman was Mary.

Other than Jesus himself, Mary is one of the most important persons in the New Testament. The number of references to her in the Gospels alone merits attention, as well as her dynamic interaction with her son, Jesus.

Motherhood is but one dimension of Mary's role in the Bible. She is also a *disciple* (a student and follower of Christ) and powerful symbol of the new Christian church. This section examines the various roles that Mary plays in Christian theology. It also looks at the parallels that some Christian religions draw between Mary and Eve.

The life and times of Mary

No other woman of the Bible has captured imaginations or captivated millions as much as Mary of Nazareth, the mother of Jesus. And neither has a biblical woman been the center of as much controversy as Mary. Her name in Hebrew is Miriam, but because the Gospels were written in Greek, she is known by her Hellenized name, Mary. Loved by many, she is also confusing to some and even problematic to others.

The earliest references to Mary are made in Luke's Gospel. Luke wasn't one of the original 12 apostles. He was a Gentile (that is, a non-Jew) before he accepted Christ, and he didn't witness many of the events of Christ's life as had the other Gospel writers who were apostles (like Matthew and John). Yet Luke's book contains more details than any other Gospel regarding the miraculous Virgin Birth. Many scholars suspect Luke interviewed an excellent source — the mother of Jesus herself — to get his information. After all, who else would know and remember with such vivid details about the events leading up to and including the birth of the Savior?

Her early life

The Bible is silent about the birth and background of Mary. She first appears in scripture (Matthew 1 and Luke 1) as a young maiden engaged to a man named Joseph, who was from the tribe of Judah and of the lineage of King David (back when there *was* a Kingdom of Israel). Nonbiblical sources like the Apocryphal Protoevangelium of James give the names Joachim and Anne for Mary's parents (who would be Jesus' maternal grandparents, of course). This text was written around A.D. 120 and attributed to James the Less or the Just, but most likely written by one of his pupils — this short document offers some peripheral information on the infancy of Jesus and on his mother as well. However, nothing is said in the officially accepted texts (those books that all Christian religions consider to be inspired) of sacred scripture about Mary's past before the *Annunciation* — the day when the Angel Gabriel announced that she would become the mother of the Messiah.

Receiving the good news: You're gonna have a baby!

According to the Gospel of Luke, when Mary is a young woman, the Angel Gabriel visits Mary in Nazareth, a city of Galilee. Luke describes Mary as a virgin (*parthenos* in Greek), and Gabriel greets her with these words: "Hail, full of grace, the Lord is with you!" (Douay-Rheims Bible).

The angel's phrase "full of grace" is *kecharitomene* in Greek from the root word *charis* (grace). Mary is full of grace because, as Gabriel says, "the Lord is with [her]" *(kyrios meta sou)*. No one has ever said this to Mary before, nor has anyone in the entire Bible been addressed in such a fashion. Because of this special greeting, you already know that something's up.

The Latin Vulgate Bible reads *"Ave Maria, gratia plena, Dominus tecum,"* which is the first phrase of the prayer known as the Hail Mary or Ave Maria. Much of the text of this oft-spoken prayer is taken right from the Gospel. The phrase of the Angel Gabriel (Luke 1:28) is joined with one from Elizabeth (Luke 1:42) to form: "Hail, Mary, full of grace, the Lord is with you. Blessed are you among women, and blessed is the fruit of your womb, Jesus."

Book IV

Saints and Other Important Figures

The words startle Mary, so the angel tells her not to be afraid, for she has found favor with God. Gabriel goes on to say:

> *And now, you will conceive in your womb and bear a son, and you will name him Jesus. He will be great, and will be called the Son of the Most High, and the Lord God will give to him the throne of his ancestor David. He will reign over the house of Jacob forever, and of his kingdom there will be no end.*
>
> —Luke 1:31–33

Stop the presses: Mary wonders if she heard correctly. Conceive and bear a child? She asks Gabriel how this can happen. Although she's officially engaged to Joseph the Carpenter, they don't live together yet as husband and wife. Some translations, such as the Douay-Rheims Bible, say that Mary said, "How can this be since I know not man?" while others, such as the New Oxford Annotated Bible, render it "since I am a virgin?"

No problem, implies the angel. He tells Mary that the Holy Spirit (God) will come upon her and the power of the Most High (God again) will "overshadow" her. (Although the meaning of the word "overshadow" remains mysterious, Christian theologians explain it in terms of Mary becoming pregnant solely by divine intervention and without any human father.)

Gabriel then reveals that Elizabeth, Mary's 80-year-old cousin whom everyone thought was barren, is six months pregnant, "for nothing will be impossible with God" (Luke 1:37). Despite what was probably wonder, confusion, and awe about all this news, Mary nevertheless gives her consent: "Here am I, the servant of the Lord; let it be with me according to your word" (Luke 1: 38).

Visiting Elizabeth

As soon as Gabriel goes back to heaven, Mary goes "with haste" to the hill country to see her pregnant cousin, Elizabeth. In the first chapter of his Gospel, Luke tells of Elizabeth's conception. Her husband, Zechariah, it seems, had been visited by the Angel Gabriel, who told him that she would give birth to a son, John the Baptist.

The meeting of these two expectant mothers, also cousins, is called the Visitation. In Luke 1:42, Elizabeth greets Mary with these words: "Blessed are you among women, and blessed is the fruit of your womb!" She continues her greeting with "And why has this happened to me, that the mother of my Lord comes to me?" (Luke 1:43). Elizabeth makes this bold proclamation of faith because the very moment she heard Mary enter the house, the unborn baby in her womb leapt for joy. John the Baptist, only six months in the womb, already assumes the role of prophet and heralds the arrival of Christ — only a few days conceived in his mother's womb. The meeting of these four — Mary with Jesus and Elizabeth with John — is what makes this a "pregnant" moment.

When Elizabeth gives birth to John three months later, Mary, now in her third month of pregnancy, goes back home. Her state of impending motherhood will soon be evident to anyone who sees her.

Reacting to the news: Joseph

In Matthew's Gospel, Joseph is the last one to find out about Mary's pregnancy. At the time, he and Mary were engaged, probably by arrangement through their parents, as was the custom back then. Even though the wedding contract had been signed, they weren't yet fully husband and wife because Joseph hadn't taken Mary into his home and they hadn't consummated the marriage. So when he learns his fiancée is with child, he knows he isn't the father.

Joseph is a just man. Without recriminations and accusations, he decides to divorce Mary quietly and get on with his life. Matthew 1:19 says that Joseph could have exposed Mary (but was unwilling to do so) to public shame as an unwed mother of sorts, because even though they were legally united on paper, they were not yet united spiritually. He and Mary were *betrothed* (engaged) but not married by the rabbi. If he drew attention to her situation, someone might erroneously conclude that Mary had cheated on Joseph. So Joseph plans a discreet and gentlemanly way out — until, that is, he goes to sleep and has a dream. In his dream, an angel tells Joseph not be afraid to take Mary into his home as his wife, because she has conceived by the power of the Holy Spirit (Matthew 1:20–23). Joseph complies.

Giving birth to Jesus

Every Christmas Eve around the world, children re-enact Luke 2:1–7 just before Christian worship services or Mass. In this passage, the Roman Emperor, Caesar Augustus, orders a census that requires all the people to register in their native hometowns. For this reason, Joseph has to take his very pregnant wife all the way from Nazareth to Bethlehem (about 90 miles) to comply with the order. Late in her pregnancy, Mary can't travel easily, but when Caesar commands, people listen.

When Joseph and Mary arrive in Bethlehem, the city of King David of old, there is literally no room at the inn; the town is packed with people who have also returned because of the census. So there they are: Mary is about to give birth, and Joseph can't find them a decent place to stay the night. Finally, someone offers the use of a stable where the animals were protected from the elements. While the stable is certainly no four-star hotel (not even a one-star), it nevertheless provides much-needed shelter and privacy. There, Mary gives birth to a son, whom they name Jesus (Luke 2:7, 21).

Book IV

Saints and Other Important Figures

Receiving visitors — kings and shepherds

After the birth of Jesus, Mary has some visitors. First to come are the shepherds, who were told by angels "to you is born this day in the city of David a Savior, who is the Messiah, the Lord" (Luke 2:11). The next guests are the Magi (also known as the three Wise Men or the Three Kings), who came from the East after having been guided by a star (Matthew 2:1–12). These visitors arrived to give homage to the child. Luke 2:19 says that Mary pondered (*symballousa* in Greek) all these things in her heart, meaning that she meditated and thought about the visitors and what they told her and often wondered what they meant.

Escaping King Herod

After the Magi come to pay their respects to Jesus, King Herod gets wind of it and feels threatened. He seeks to destroy the child, whom he sees as a potential rival. Like Pharaoh centuries before, Herod orders the massacre of all male infants 2 years of age and under. Jesus, Mary, and Joseph flee into Egypt to escape the bloodbath of King Herod (Matthew 2:16–18).

When Herod is dead, Mary, Joseph, and baby Jesus can return. They don't go back to Bethlehem, however, because Herod's son Archelaus now rules Judea. Instead, they settle in Nazareth, where Jesus grows up. He is hence sometimes called "the Nazarene" or "Jesus of Nazareth." (See Matthew 2:19–23 for the account of these events in Mary's life.)

Hearing a prophecy

Mary and Joseph were devout Jews and followed the laws and customs of the Hebrew religion. So eight days after his birth, Jesus was circumcised according to the Law of Moses, and 40 days after giving birth, Mary went to the Temple of Jerusalem to present her firstborn son and to receive the ritual purification required of all mothers (Luke 2:21–24). While in the Temple, two elderly people who had been patiently waiting for the arrival of this child greet Joseph and Mary.

Simeon is one of them. He says to Mary, "This child is destined for the falling and the rising of many in Israel, and to be a sign that will be opposed so that the inner thoughts of many will be revealed — and a sword will pierce your own soul too" (Luke 2:34–35). Bible scholars consider the last phrase, about a sword piercing her soul, to be a prophecy of the pain Mary will experience when she witnesses Jesus' death, some 33 years later.

Trying times with a preteen

The period in Jesus' life between birth and the age of 30, when he begins his public ministry, is often called the "hidden years." Luke does record one story that occurs when Jesus is around 12 years old. The Bible jumps from

Jesus' presentation in the Temple as an infant to a dozen years later when he and Mary and Joseph are in Jerusalem for Passover.

As told in Luke 2:41–52, after the Passover religious festival, Jesus stays behind in the Temple while Mary and Joseph head back to Nazareth. Each one thinks that Jesus is with the other — an assumption that is easy to understand if you consider that the men and women were separated in the Temple and often traveled in segregated groups. Until Jesus is bar mitzvahed, he spent most of his time with his mother; after that rite of passage, he spent more time with Joseph and the other adult men. So because they didn't travel as a family unit and because each thought Jesus was with the other, neither Mary nor Joseph initially panicked when he wasn't with them when they left.

But then, of course, the mistake is realized, and Mary experiences a mother's worst nightmare. She and Joseph search for their missing son for three days. Just as it would be today, a missing adolescent is no light matter. She must have worried herself sick wondering if he were alive or dead, hurt or injured, or even sold into slavery. Mary and Joseph finally find Jesus in the Temple, conversing with the scholars and teachers. When asked the typical questions that mothers pose to their children in situations like these — "Where in the world have you been?!" and "Don't you know your father and I have been looking all over for you?!" — Jesus merely replies "Did you not know I must be in my Father's house?" (Luke 2:49).

Supporting Jesus' mission

The next time Mary appears, she is at a wedding feast (John 2:1–11). Because Joseph is no longer mentioned, it's presumed that he died sometime during those so-called hidden years, when Jesus was between the ages of 12 and 30. John says that Mary had been invited to a wedding in Cana, a little village in Galilee near Capernaum. Jesus and his disciples were also invited.

At one point, the wedding reception runs out of wine. Mary notices the fact and informs Jesus that they have no more wine. His response to her is very interesting and has been interpreted in different ways, depending on what translation and version of the Bible are being examined.

The original Greek text of Jesus' response to his mother reads "*gynai, ti emoi kai soi,*" which literally means "woman, what to me and to you." (Greek often implies a verb instead of stating it explicitly.) Here is how some different Bibles translate this phrase (John 2:4):

- ✔ "Woman, what does this have to do with me" (English Standard Version).
- ✔ "You must not tell me what to do" (Good News Translation).
- ✔ "How does that concern us, woman" (International Standard Version).

✔ "Dear woman, why do you involve me" (New International Version).

✔ "Woman, what do you want from me" (New Jerusalem Bible).

✔ "Woman, what have I to do with thee" (King James Version).

✔ "What to thee and to me, woman" (Young's Literal Translation).

Some of these translations sound like a sharp rebuke from Jesus. Yet the literal translation is much more benign, especially when taken in context of the very next verse in which Mary says to the servants "Do whatever he tells you" (John 2:5). Following this response, Jesus performs his first public miracle, changing water into wine.

This context — that Jesus actually responds to Mary's request rather than ignoring it — tends to encourage a softer interpretation of John 2:4. It's more likely that Jesus said to his mother something like, "What affects me, affects you, and vice versa." If the fact that the groom was going to be embarrassed when they ran out of wine bothered Mary; then it would bother Jesus as well. Others speculate that Jesus may have meant that after he performs this miracle, the quiet life he and his mother have enjoyed up to now will be over. Word about the miracle does, in fact, spread, and Jesus is asked to do more miracles, mostly healings and exorcisms. His quiet life ceases, and so does hers, because he won't be staying home anymore.

Mary's biological connection to Jesus is no small matter, but her emotional bond is no less real, because Christians firmly believe he had a true human nature as well as a divine one. Because Christians hold that Jesus is both God and man, human and divine, his human emotions (like when he wept at the grave of his friend Lazarus, John 11:35) must be equally real and authentic. So Mary and Jesus did love each other, as mothers and sons do.

Witnessing Jesus' death

Mary is conspicuously present at the Crucifixion of her son, Jesus. The "brothers" or "brethren" of the Lord, whether you believe them to be siblings or other relatives, are noticeably absent. The Bible says in John 19:25 that the following people are with Jesus as he dies: his mother, Mary; his mother's sister (Mary, the wife of Clopas); and Mary Magdalene. Verse 26 mentions the presence of only one of the 12 apostles, "the disciple whom Jesus loved." This was an affectionate term for John, the Gospel writer and the brother of James.

Alongside the one apostle (John) who attended Jesus' crucifixion, Mary says nothing while she helplessly watches her son suffer for three hours before he finally dies. Just before his last breath, however, Jesus speaks to Mary: "Woman," he says, "Here is your son" (John 19:26). Then he speaks to John: "Here is your mother" (John 19:27).

The act of entrusting Mary to John the Beloved is both practical (if there are no siblings to care for her) and spiritual. Because they are present at the crucifixion while the rest fled, these two will have to continue their discipleship and thus preserve the infant church until the coming of the Holy Spirit at Pentecost (Acts 2:1–4).

Jesus uses the same word for "woman" as he did at the wedding feast of Cana: *gyne* in Greek or *ishshah* in Hebrew. Many scholars believe the use of "woman" was intended as a compliment, rather than an insult, to his mother, affirming Mary's role as disciple as well as mother. Genesis 3:15 — when God curses the serpent and says that he will put enmity "between you [the serpent] and the woman" — uses that same word. This language affirms that Mary is the true human mother of Jesus, a faithful daughter of God the Father, and, because of the Virgin Birth, a spouse of the Holy Spirit. Despite her elevated status, she is still a human being, so she has no divine prerogatives or attributes.

When Jesus finally dies and is taken down from the cross, his body is placed in Mary's arms. This heart-wrenching scene is poignantly portrayed in the *Pietà* (from the Italian word for *pity* or *sorrow*), a marble sculpture by Michelangelo (A.D. 1499). Whether you believe Mary had other children or that Jesus was her only son, no doubt she felt the pain that only a mother can know at the death of a child.

Despite Jesus' divine nature, he was also her son, her flesh and blood. She bore him in her womb for nine months, gave birth to him, nursed him, and fed, clothed, and educated him. Mary loved and cared for Jesus like any normal mom. Perhaps, while she mournfully held his body in her arms, she remembered Simeon's prophecy spoken to her 33 years earlier: "A sword will pierce your own soul too" (Luke 2:35).

Serving the early Church

The last explicit reference to Mary, the mother of Jesus, is in the Acts of the Apostles. She is in the upper room with the apostles on the day of Pentecost (50 days after Jesus' resurrection on Easter Sunday). "All these were constantly devoting themselves to prayer, together with certain women, including Mary the mother of Jesus, as well as his brothers" (Acts 1:14). This same upper room is where Jesus had his Last Supper with the 12 apostles on what some refer to as Holy Thursday, the day before his death (the day called Good Friday).

Book IV

Saints and Other Important Figures

The importance of Mary

Mary's role in the Christian faith is both instrumental (she was the real and true human mother of Jesus the Savior) and educational (she shows how to be a disciple of the Lord). She is a woman, a wife, a mother, and a disciple. As a woman, she shares in being made in the image and likeness of God, and she possesses the strength, courage, and faithfulness of the woman in the Bible who preceded her.

As the mother of Jesus, Mary embodies these traditional characteristics:

- ✔ **Humility:** Mary's humility is exemplified when she accepts the will of God after the Angel Gabriel tells her she is to be the mother of the Messiah. Her submission is not a surrender of her personal dignity, however. She freely allows God's will to replace her own will and thus becomes a humble servant of the Lord.

- ✔ **Obedience:** Mary obeys the Word of God, but her submission isn't a surrender of her personal dignity. She isn't an unwilling slave but a willing and faithful servant of the Lord who does what she is asked to do.

- ✔ **Service:** Mary serves the Word made Flesh by caring for and loving Jesus, from the time he was a baby who nursed at her breasts to the time his lifeless adult body lay in her sorrowful arms the day he died. She is a servant in good times and in bad, in joy and in sorrow.

Mary's role isn't incidental or peripheral; it's always contingent and secondary to the unique and singular work of her son, the Redeemer and Savior, Jesus Christ. She shows that a woman can play an important part in salvation history as did Sarah, Rebekah, Rachel, Deborah, Miriam, Esther, Judith, Ruth, and so on.

As a pillar of faith

Most of all, Mary demonstrates the ability to trust the Lord even when she didn't understand what was going on or how things were going to happen later on. Reverend Benedict Groeschel, CFR (a spiritual writer), has often said that Mary had a lot of unanswered questions like any human being. Why did she have to give birth in a stable rather than a clean hotel? Why did she have to take the baby and flee into Egypt? Why couldn't something happen to Herod to prevent such a journey? Why would an old man tell her that a sword will pierce her heart, or why did Jesus go missing for three days when he was only 12 years old? Mary "pondered in her heart" all these unanswered questions but never found the answers.

Mary's claim to fame wasn't that she had insider information, as if God had whispered the secrets of the universe into her ears; rather, it was that she had the courage and strength to trust enough to live with those unanswered questions.

As a disciple of Christ

Mary relates to Jesus in both his human and divine natures. She is his mother in terms of his humanity, and she is his obedient servant and discile in terms of his divinity. She loves him as her son, and she loves him as God. Her love for him, in fact, is just as powerful as his love for her. The best description of Mary is that she was faithful to the Word, especially the Word made Flesh (Jesus).

Trusting completely and totally in God and especially in Jesus Christ, Mary epitomizes what it means to be a disciple. Her words to the servants at the wedding feast in Cana are succinct and profound: "Do whatever he tells you" (John 2:5). Her existence isn't limited nor is it totally defined by her role as wife to Joseph, as daughter to Joachim and Anne, or even as mother to Jesus. She is first and foremost a child of God — like the rest of us. She is human with a heart and soul made of flesh and blood. She is no goddess or superhero from another planet.

As a symbol of the church

The early Church always saw itself not as a neutral, abstract institution or organization, but as a living and mystical body of believers. The assembly, or *ekklesia* as it was called in Greek, cannot exist separate from its founder, Jesus Christ. Like Mary, the church is always in a relationship with Jesus. Mary is his mother in terms of his humanity, and she is a disciple in terms of his divinity. The church, too, is both disciple (one who studies and learns from the teacher) and simultaneously is also the bride of Christ (the beloved spouse whom he is willing to die for). Mary symbolizes the church in that both hear the Word (Mary hears it from Gabriel; the church hears it from the lips of Jesus himself) and both obey the Word. Mary's response to Gabriel's message is "Let it be with me according to your word." The church likewise is expected to do what Jesus commands: "Go therefore and make disciples of all nations, baptizing them in the name of the Father and of the Son and of the Holy Spirit" (Matthew 28:19), "proclaim the good news" (Mark 16:15), and "love one another as I have loved you" (John 15:12).

As the new Eve

In Romans 5:14, Paul says that Adam is a "type," meaning that he *typologically references* or symbolically predicts Christ, the one who was to come. *Typology* is a literary device in which something from the past, such a person or an event, predicts something in the future. This typology is so strong that Christian scholars often say Jesus is the new or last Adam (1 Corinthians 15:45). If there is a new Adam, it makes sense that there would be a new Eve. This new Eve, according to Eastern Orthodox and Catholic Christians, is Mary, the mother of Jesus.

Book IV

Saints and Other Important Figures

The reason Mary is called the new Eve is because of the comparisons that can be drawn between the women's stories:

✔ Each woman launches a different Testament (Old and New).

✔ Each had a choice to make: submit to God's will or not. Although Eve, in Genesis, disobeyed God's request to avoid eating from the tree of knowledge, Mary embraced God's word when told she would be the mother of the savior: "Let it be with me according to your word" (Luke 1:38).

✔ According to some Christians, the connection between Eve and Mary is most evident in Genesis 3. The passage tells the story of God cursing the serpent for tempting Eve, when he makes this prophecy, "I will put enmity between you and the woman, and between your offspring and hers; he will strike your head, and you will strike his heel" (Genesis 3:15).

The point of the story is this: Although the serpent was successful in tempting Adam and Eve, humankind's first parents, he will ultimately lose and be conquered. And the offspring who will conquer the serpent is Christ. Although the devil will try to strike at Christ's heel in myriad ways — Judas's betrayal, the disciples' abandonment of Jesus at the Crucifixion, and so on — Jesus, who is Mary's offspring in his human nature, will nevertheless vanquish Satan.

Other Christians do not readily accept nor embrace the connection between Mary and Eve. The connection is subtle to be sure. Depending on your faith tradition, you may appreciate or disregard the typological aspect of Mary as the new Eve, but at least you now know where it came from.

Befriending Jesus: Mary Magdalene

Mary Magdalene is one of the most famous — yet most mysterious — women of the Bible, a woman who lived and served in close proximity to Jesus. A contemporary of Christ, Mary Magdalene lived in the early first century A.D. and was probably around the same age as Jesus.

Some of what we know about Mary Magdalene is stated explicitly in the Bible. Other info is speculation, based on biblical text. This section pieces together a picture of Mary Magdalene that relies on biblical accounts and traditional Christian belief. We examine what the Bible says about her enigmatic past, her conversion of faith, her fraternal love of and devotion to Christ, and her impact on Christianity and the Christian church.

Her role in Jesus' life has inspired a great deal of speculation, particularly in the pop culture of recent years. For that reason, this section examines the nonbiblical speculation — like the suggestions that perhaps she was more to Jesus than a faithful follower and that she is the matriarch of a line of European royalty.

What the Bible says about her

Chronologically, Mary Magdalene first appears in the Gospel of Luke:

> *The twelve were with him, as well as some women who had been cured of evil spirits and infirmities: Mary, called Magdalene, from whom seven demons had gone out, and Joanna, the wife of Herod's steward Chuza, and Susanna, and many others, who provided for them out of their resources.*

> —Luke 8:1–3

Supporting Jesus and the apostles

Luke 8:1–3 show that Mary Magdalene generously supported the material needs of Jesus and the apostles. This role was an important one, particularly during that time period in history. Jesus and his apostles spread their message by traveling from town to town, and they didn't have the luxury of inexpensive motels or cheap fast food. Nor did the carpenter's son or the former fishermen who followed him get a weekly salary for their preaching and teaching. They depended on the kindness of followers and on the hospitality of new believers to stay alive. Mary Magdalene, along with Joanna, Chuza, and Susanna, took care of the guys from their own means.

Where Mary Magdalene got her modest wealth no one can say with certainty. She may have inherited it from her father (if he had no sons), or she may have been the widow of a man who was well-off. Some speculate that she may have had a lucrative nest egg from a former life as a high-class call girl — a supposition that is hotly contested and considered in greater detail in the section "What Folks Speculate about Her," later in this chapter. The Bible never explicitly explains how she provided or what she provided, just that she helped Jesus.

Being possessed by demons

Luke's initial passage also says that Mary Magdalene was possessed by demons — seven devils, to be exact, haunted her. Though the Bible never describes when she was delivered from her spiritual bondage, Mark 16:9 specifies that Jesus was the one who exorcised her demons. Why and how she became possessed is never said, but certainly being cured of such a malady would make most people extremely grateful to the person who healed them. This gratitude may be part of the reason why Mary Magdalene became such a devout follower and supporter to Jesus.

Book IV

Saints and Other Important Figures

Staying with Jesus as he died

Biblical accounts also affirm that Mary Magdalene was one of the women who stayed with Jesus at the foot of the cross the day he was crucified and died (the anniversary of that day is honored as Good Friday by many Christians). Matthew 27:56, Mark 15:40, and John 19:25 explicitly mention Mary Magdalene as being at Calvary, the place where Jesus was crucified, with the Virgin Mary and a few other ladies. John the Apostle is the only man recorded as being there (John 19:26).

Tradition has it that the other men and apostles abandoned Jesus and left him, while the women, like his mother and Mary Magdalene, remained faithful and stayed with him. Magdalene's act of solidarity — while others chose to run and hide to protect themselves — illustrates her fraternal love for Jesus.

Witnessing the Resurrection

Mary Magdalene is present not only at the cross when Jesus dies but also at his burial (Matthew 27:61 and Mark 15:47). Most significant, however, is her role as the first one to discover his empty tomb on Easter morning.

Jesus had just risen from the dead when Mary Magdalene dutifully went to the tomb on Sunday to complete the Jewish burial rituals. (According to Christian tradition, Jesus died on Friday and rose on Sunday. Saturday was the Jewish Sabbath, and no work was allowed on that day, not even burial rituals.)

Matthew 28:1, Mark 16:1, Luke 24:10, and John 20:1 all tell essentially the same story:

Mary Magdalene goes to the tomb where Jesus was buried. When she arrives, she finds the *sepulcher* (a tomb or crypt) empty and fears that someone has stolen the body. She sees two angels in the tomb dressed but no Jesus. Usually the sight of angels invokes either fear or joy, but Mary Magdalene is so overwhelmed with grief about Jesus' death and now suspected desecration, that their presence has no effect on her. She cries intensely, and when the angels ask her why, she replies, "They have taken away my Lord, and I do not know where they have laid him" (John 20:13).

Turning around, Mary Magdalene sees Jesus standing there, but she doesn't recognize him because he has just risen from the dead. (Christian theologians claim that his glorified, resurrected body was the same body crucified on the cross, but it was also changed in some way.) Thinking that the man before her is the gardener, she asks him where he put Jesus' body so she can retrieve it; she doesn't realize she's talking to Jesus in his resurrected body. Jesus then calls her name, and she finally recognizes who he is. (You can read this account in John 20:14–16.)

Reporting to the apostles

After this awesome and emotional reunion, Jesus sends Mary Magdalene to the apostles to bring the good news. She tells them, "I have seen the Lord" (John 20:18). Because Mary Magdalene was sent by Jesus to bring the message that Christ is risen, she is often metaphorically called the "apostle to the Apostles." Peter, James, John, and the rest first learn of the Resurrection from Mary Magdalene. Although they don't initially believe her, almost dismissing her claim as hysterical grief, Peter and John still go to the empty tomb to see for themselves.

Mark 16:9 emphasizes that the resurrected Jesus appeared to Mary Magdalene first before anyone else, even before Peter or John — let alone the rest of the 11 apostles (Judas hanged himself, so their number went down from 12). She is also the bearer of the greatest message in Christian theology: that Christ has risen from the dead. She is the one sent by God to deliver that news to the apostles.

This is where the Bible ends its mention of Mary Magdalene. Her name doesn't appear in the rest of the New Testament, either in the Acts of the Apostles or in any of the epistles. She seems to almost disappear, while the apostles begin to build the early church. Where her story in the Bible ends, however, some of the writings that haven't earned a seal of approval attempt to fill in the blanks.

What folks speculate about her

This section looks at the various opinions, theories, and hypotheses about this very mysterious woman of the New Testament. The Bible offers few details about Mary Magdalene's history, her occupation, her activities, and even her actual involvement with the early church. The ambiguity of scripture has encouraged speculation for the past 2,000 years. Some speculation is based on reasonable and logical arguments from what the Bible and history tell us; some is conjecture that has no proof or evidence but that makes interesting reading nonetheless.

One question that has been hotly debated and argued by biblical scripture scholars for centuries is what Mary Magdalene did for a living. Some scholars maintain she was a *harlot* (the biblical name for a prostitute). Others say she was a notorious adulteress. Still others claim that she was merely one of several middle-class women of modest wealth who provided for the material needs of Jesus and his apostles — in other words, a benefactor — and nothing else.

The public sinner

Through the ages many people have speculated that Mary Magdalene is the woman featured in the story that begins in Luke 7:37. Because this woman is never named — either as "Mary" or as "Mary Magdalene" — the speculation continues to this day.

Luke's story describes a notorious public sinner — a woman — who comes to Jesus while he is visiting a Pharisee. This unnamed woman washes his feet with her tears, dries them with her hair, and anoints them with costly perfumed oil. The host, who knows of this woman's past, wonders why, if Jesus is really a prophet, he doesn't reject her for what she is — a public sinner. Jesus recognizes this man's thoughts and asks him who is more grateful — a man who owes 500 days' wages and whose debt is dissolved, or the man who owes 50 days' wages and has his debt erased? The Pharisee believes it is the man who owes more money, and he tells Jesus so.

Jesus then turns toward the woman and says that her many sins are forgiven and that she has shown great love.

Though the name of this "public sinner" is never mentioned, tradition says this woman was Mary Magdalene.

The adulteress

Mary Magdalene is also frequently given credit as a woman in another well-known story of the New Testament. Again, the woman in the passage is never called by name, and so her identity is cause for speculation.

John 8:3–11 tells of an unnamed woman caught in adultery who is about to be stoned to death. Jesus confronts her potential executioners, saying, "Let anyone among you who is without sin be the first to throw a stone at her." Jesus then begins writing in the dirt in such a way that the men can see what he writes. One by one the potential executioners leave the scene, dropping their rocks and going away.

What Jesus wrote is unknown, but his actions somehow convince the men to give up, even after they'd been so sure of this woman's fate. After they leave, Jesus and the woman are alone. He says to her "Woman, where are they? Has no one condemned you?" She replies, "No one, sir." So Jesus says, "Neither do I condemn you. Go your way, and from now on do not sin again" (John 8:10–11).

Biblical scholars debate both the identity of the woman and the content of Jesus' writings in the dirt. Some experts hypothesize that he wrote the names of other women on the ground, the adulteresses and prostitutes whom some of these very righteous men may have been secretly intimate with. Others think that Jesus may have written other sins in the dirt, like lying, cheating, stealing, and so on, whereby each man saw his own sin identified.

Whatever he doodled in the sand, the result was that the woman's life was spared. More important to Christians, Jesus saved her soul. So the next conclusion that many scholars draw is that this adulteress is the very same woman depicted as Luke's public sinner, the one who would later anoint Jesus' feet and dry them with her hair and who would be very grateful to Jesus. For this reason, these scholars believe that the women in each story are one and the same. Their next conclusion, of course, is that this woman in both cases was Mary Magdalene.

Weighing the interpretations

The problem is that all the evidence pointing to the fact that these stories are about Mary Magdalene is very circumstantial and not incontrovertible. Making the leap that the public sinner, the woman caught in adultery, and the woman who wiped the feet of Jesus are Mary Magdalene is a difficult theory to prove beyond a reasonable doubt. However, disproving it just on grounds that such a notorious sinner couldn't possibly repent and rise to the level of friend and disciple denies the message of the Gospel completely.

Mary Magdalene may not have been the woman featured in any of these stories. But if the woman was Mary, it certainly portrays, in Christian minds, God's great mercy as well as any sinner's potential to repent, be forgiven, and become close to God. The scriptural evidence that the woman who washed the feet of Jesus and identified as Mary in John 12:3 is the same nameless woman who washed the feet of Jesus in Matthew 26:6 and Mark 14:3 and is the same woman as the public sinner in Luke 7:37–38 who washed Jesus' feet is persuasive. Matthew, Mark, and Luke all mention the detail that the ointment was contained in an alabaster jar. The very uncommon, possibly unheard of, practice of a Hebrew woman washing a Hebrew rabbi's feet also lends to the conclusion that this incident happened only once.

Although the circumstantial evidence is good that one woman washed Jesus' feet, anointed them, and dried them with her hair and that the woman's name was Mary, the evidence to support that Mary, the sister of Martha and Lazarus, is also Mary Magdalene is much less solid and self-evident. The implication that Mary the sister of Martha was a repentant, forgiven public sinner doesn't seem unlikely or incredible. The suggestion that she was also the Magdalene is somewhat more tenuous.

Some people believe that it's a violation of Mary's dignity to claim she is the one portrayed as a former prostitute or adulteress. They point out that it is a subtle attempt to denigrate, demean, and diminish the importance of Mary Magdalene by insinuating she was at one time a harlot. But some other Christians insist those folks are missing the point of what Christianity believes Jesus came to do — forgive sins. Luke 15:7 states that there is more joy in heaven over 1 repentant sinner than in 99 righteous who have no need of repentance. Scripture never explicitly identifies Mary Magdalene as the woman caught in adultery (John 8:3), but Christian tradition from ancient to medieval times has associated the public sinner of Luke, the woman caught in adultery of John, and the woman who washed the feet of Jesus in Matthew and Mark as being one and the same woman. This idea was never a doctrine of faith, however, and recent historians and biblical scholars agree that the evidence for Mary Magdalene being all these women is a little unconvincing — but it was believed for some time to be true.

Even the identification of Mary Magdalene as a reformed prostitute is hotly debated today. Remember that the Bible often poses more questions than it provides answers to, in terms of details and the like. During the early days of the church and especially during the Middle Ages, western Christians took for granted that Mary Magdalene was a repentant sinner, and they named many charitable homes for unwed mothers and for recovering prostitutes after her to encourage women who had fallen into sin to believe that anyone was capable of being forgiven and of being given a second chance. Even if Mary Magdalene wasn't the woman caught in adultery or the public sinner who washed Jesus' feet, she is still a woman who was healed of seven demons and who conspicuously was present at the foot of the cross the day Jesus died.

If conclusive evidence is ever discovered disproving Mary Magdalene's lurid past, it won't change the fact that, according to the New Testament, Jesus forgave a woman known as a public sinner and a woman caught in adultery. Even if one of the women or both women turn out not to have been Mary Magdalene, the story's message remains the same, no matter her identity.

Controversial references to Mary

Some controversial references and theories about Mary Magdalene go beyond the theological and scriptural ones of her past and whether or not she was the woman who washed the feet of Jesus. The speculation on her relationship to Jesus is the epicenter of current discussion. Another hot topic is her role in the early Christian Church. We examine both subjects in this section.

Despite recent theories brought on by fictional books such as *The Da Vinci Code* by Dan Brown (Doubleday) and subsequent media speculation, the Bible and Christian tradition do not indicate any kind of a romantic relationship between Jesus and Mary Magdalene. Many Christian believers find this type of speculation offensive, and in the professional opinion of these authors and many other biblical scholars and historians, there is no credible evidence to support it. Each of the many varieties and denominations of Christianity, whether Protestant, Catholic, or Orthodox, officially denounce the idea of any romantic involvement between Jesus and Mary Magdalene, although some Christians may believe in such a theory.

So where does this theory come from? And from where do other theories about Mary Magdalene's actions stem? In the following sections, we examine references to Mary Magdalene from beyond the Bible and sacred tradition.

Apocryphal accounts

Apocryphal writings of the New Testament (ones you won't find in any Bible of any religion or denomination) mention Mary Magdalene. The Apocryphal Gospel of Peter and Apocryphal Epistle of the Apostles say that she went to the burial place of Jesus on the third day to fulfill the Jewish funeral rituals that were not completed because of the Sabbath. But no mention is made here about any deeper relationship between Mary Magdalene and Jesus.

Gnostic accounts

The most controversial accounts of Mary Magdalene's life come from Gnostic writings, like the apocryphal Gospel of Philip and the Pistis Sophia (Greek for "faith wisdom"). These manuscripts depict Mary as a *companion* of Jesus, a term that some folks today interpret in romantic terms. The Gnostic accounts of Mary Magdalene purport her to be the real "Beloved Disciple" and author of the Fourth Gospel (rather than John, the brother of James and the son of Zebedee) and a competitor with Peter for leadership in the early church, among other claims. Still, none of these Gnostic gospels ever refer to Jesus and Mary Magdalene as being husband and wife.

The Gnostic Gospel of Mary Magdalene is the epicenter of controversial theories about her and Jesus. This nonbiblical manuscript was discovered in the late nineteenth century and features Mary Magdalene and Peter fighting with each other over an alleged revelation she had from Jesus after his resurrection and ascension. The Gospel of Mary Magdalene has Mary revealing secrets from Jesus, now in heaven, telling the select few that the body is evil while only the soul is good — the essence of Gnostic belief. Christians would say the idea that the body is inherently evil contradicts what the biblical New Testament says — specifically, that because Christians believe Jesus is both divine and human, their doctrine of the union of God and man in a human body shows the intrinsic good of the material as well as the spiritual worlds, rather than a battle between the good spirit and evil body. Even Genesis 1 speaks of the creation of the material world, from the planets to the human body, and says that God saw that it was good.

Later theories

Unproven theories also exist about Mary Magdalene and Jesus producing offspring, either inside or outside wedlock, and these children allegedly became the ancestors of some of the Western European monarchies.

Dan Brown's wildly popular work of fiction, *The Da Vinci Code,* capitalized and expanded on some of these notions. Interesting though they may be, no scholarly evidence supports these theories.

Book IV

Saints and Other Important Figures

Claims that Leonardo da Vinci actually painted Mary Magdalene into the Last Supper as one of the apostles are implausible. Using feminine qualities to symbolize the innocence and softness of youth was a common technique of Renaissance artists. Museum and art curators agree that medieval and Renaissance artists such as da Vinci used this style to distinguish young men from old ones. So depicting John the Beloved Disciple with feminine qualities was just to draw a contrast between him (youthful) and the older, rougher, and more mature (manly) apostles.

Meeting Ruth

The Book of Ruth is a story about family loyalty. A mother-in-law and her daughter-in-law share joys and sorrows in this brief biblical saga. Ruth, a foreigner, shows as much love and devotion to her mother-in-law, Naomi, as would a full-blooded offspring. Trial and tribulation are on the menu for these two women, but they endure together, and sharing their suffering makes them closer.

The Book of Ruth is unlike many books of the Bible in that most of the text is dialogue. It's divided into four chapters but seven sections:

- In the first section (1:1–6), we read about Naomi's husband's family line dying out.

- The widows return to Naomi's homeland in the second section (1:7–22).

- In the third section (2:1–23), Ruth encounters her father-in-law's kinsman.

- The fourth section (3:1–18) recounts a widow's demand and the kinsman's dilemma.

- A solution to the dilemma is found in the fifth section (4:1–12).

- The family line is restored in the sixth section (4:13–17).

- The seventh section is an appendix (4:18–22), which briefly gives the lineage from Perez, the son of Tamar and Judah, down to Boaz and Ruth, who were the great-grandparents of King David.

The Book of Ruth was written during the reign of King David, but the main characters lived about 200 years earlier, during the turbulent era of tribal conflict in which a group of leaders known as the Judges ruled Israel. This was after the Exodus from Egypt. The 12 tribes of Israel fought with each other under the king's rule (successively, these kings were Saul, David, and Solomon). Family squabbles among clans were the first phase when the originators of the tribes (the sons of Jacob, otherwise known as Israel) were still alive. (*Clans* are merely subdivisions among the tribes representing closer familial relations, whereas the *tribes* were larger and more encompassing classifications.) As each clan grew and expanded, they became less connected and interwoven and almost existed as separate nations even though all were considered Hebrew. When a king was anointed to rule over all the tribes and a monarchy established, a short-lived but unified nation of Israel existed (under three kings: Saul, David, and Solomon). After the death of Solomon, the unified kingdom is divided into two parts, northern kingdom of Israel (capital = Samaria) and southern kingdom of Judah (capital = Jerusalem).

Introducing the main character

Ruth, wife of Mahlon, was the daughter-in-law of Naomi, and her relationship with Naomi is the best-known relationship in the Bible. We know nothing of Ruth's background, origin, or family, except that she is a *Moabite,* meaning she's from the country of Moab. Despite that she was looked down on by some Hebrews at the time as a foreigner, the Bible describes her through her character, her loyalty, her strength, and her resolve. Ruth stands out as the epitome of a good daughter-in-law to Naomi. She is completely devoted and loyal to her husband's family, which she makes her own. After Ruth's husband (Mahlon) dies, she stays with her mother-in-law, while Orpah (Naomi's other daughter-in-law, whose husband, Chilion, also dies) leaves. Ruth takes care of her mother-in-law, who, in return, helps her daughter-in-law find a good husband.

Leaving Moab

Ruth is living in Moab when Naomi moves to that country with her husband, Elimelech, and her two sons, Mahlon and Chilion, because of a famine in their homeland of Judah. Elimelech soon dies. Mahlon, Naomi's son, takes Ruth as a wife, and his brother, Chilion, marries a woman named Orpah. But tragedy soon strikes again, and both sons die. Ruth, like her mother-in-law, Naomi, and her sister-in-law, Orpah, is left to fend for herself as a widow. The three decide to head toward Bethlehem for better pastures. (See Ruth 1:1–7 for specifics.)

On the way to the land of Judah, however, Naomi realizes that her two daughters-in-law won't find life easy in Bethlehem because they're foreigners. Even though they married Hebrew men, as foreign widows they won't fare as well as a Hebrew widow. In those days, the only hope for these widows would be to marry other sons of Naomi, which she expects she is too old to have — and even if she could, Ruth and Orpah would have to wait an awfully long time. So, with great kindness, Naomi, weeping, advises them to turn back. You can find this story in Ruth 1:8–14.

Book IV

Saints and Other Important Figures

Orpah decides to leave, but Ruth won't abandon Naomi, in spite of the circumstances. Ruth decides that she will tough it out with Naomi no matter what. She believes they will be stronger together than apart. Although Ruth must have been tempted to return to Moab, her own homeland, her love and loyalty to Naomi are stronger. Ruth utters her now famous quote often repeated at weddings and religious ceremonies: "Where you go, I will go . . . your God [is] my God" (Ruth 1:16). When they return to Bethlehem, they are warmly greeted. But they are still husbandless, childless, and poor.

Trying to escape poverty

To deal with their poverty, Ruth goes to work in the only way she can — collecting the *gleanings* from the fields, the leftover grain that remains after reapers have harvested their crop. Although this work is demeaning and difficult, it enables Ruth to provide for herself and Naomi, who is too old to work herself.

Providentially, Ruth ends up gleaning in a field owned by a relative of Elimelech, Naomi's dead husband. This man's name is Boaz, the son of Rahab of Jericho. (Head to Ruth 2:1–18, where this story is described.) Naomi realizes that Ruth's job situation presents an opportunity. A custom of the day dictated that a relative could marry a childless widow. Their firstborn son would be considered the continuation of the deceased father's line.

Naomi sees this ancient practice as a way to help her daughter-in-law, Ruth. She suggests that Ruth doll herself up in her best outfit and visit Boaz. Ruth does as she's told, and Boaz is impressed by this Moabite woman who shows so much love and loyalty to her mother-in-law — word of the plan had already gone around Judah and ultimately to Boaz himself (Ruth 3:1-3:15). Apparently news traveled fast even before cellphones and e-mail.

Happy endings

Boaz falls in love with Ruth's character. She is an honorable and virtuous woman, and Boaz finds these characteristics most attractive. He proposes marriage to Ruth. Scholars speculate that perhaps Boaz was more likely to marry and help Ruth, a foreigner, because his own mother had been a foreigner — his mother, Rahab, had been instrumental in helping Moses, Joshua, and the Hebrews overtake Jericho to secure Israel.

There is one fly in the ointment, however. Although Boaz is a relative to Naomi and Ruth, there is another, unnamed relative who is more closely related to them. Boaz wants to marry Ruth and purchase the property Naomi wants to sell (her dead husband's land before they left for Moab during the famine), but the closer relative has first dibs on buying the place and on any marriage proposals.

Boaz is a shrewd negotiator. He approaches the other kinsman of Naomi and Ruth and asks him in front of witnesses if he intends to buy Naomi's property from her. The mystery man (we never find out who he is) says he does want to exercise his prerogative and purchase the land. Presumably, this relative knew Naomi was a widow whose sons also passed away and that she is well beyond childbearing years. What he probably didn't know, however, was that Naomi had a daughter-in-law, Ruth, who was also a widow and childless. Under levirate custom, a relative was to marry her and if a son were born, he would be the heir to the deceased father's legacy.

Ruth is something the kinsman didn't anticipate. Boaz is counting on him seeing only one way out of his dilemma. On the one hand, if the relative marries Ruth and she has a son, junior inherits the land his stepfather would have purchased from grandma Naomi. On the other hand, if he doesn't marry Ruth and buy the land, he will be violating the law that required the nearest relative to help the widow. When he thought there was just an elderly widow in the bargain (Naomi), he did not mind the thought of marrying her because she would not pose any threat by having an offspring who could claim the property for himself. Now that he knows there is a younger widowed daughter-in-law who is also part of the mix, his appetite disappears.

Boaz hoped this would happen: that the kinsman wouldn't want to buy the land from Naomi and marry Ruth because the firstborn son she would have would be the heir of the deceased first husband under levirate law. So Boaz offers to buy the land and marry Ruth as if offering a gentleman's way out of a difficult duty.

The relative doesn't know that Boaz loves Ruth and wants to marry her, purchase the property from Naomi, and raise their first son as the heir of Mahlon. All he knows is that custom required him to have preference in being the first to consider buying the land and in taking a widow as his own wife. Playing his cards well, Boaz has convinced the man to relinquish his claims to buying the property and to asking Ruth to marry him and instead allow Boaz to take on the "burden" (not knowing that Boaz is in love with Ruth).

After Ruth and Boaz marry, she gives birth to a son, Obed. Obed later becomes the father of Jesse, who in turn has a son named David. This David is the man who slays the giant Goliath and one day becomes King David of Israel, the father of King Solomon and an ancestor of Jesus. You can read this account in Ruth 4:13–17. Ruth isn't mentioned again until her name appears in the lineage of Jesus in the Gospel of Matthew (1:5). Her fame, though, is remembered in sacred art, often depicting Ruth with her mother-in-law, Naomi, to whom she was a most devoted daughter-in-law.

Book IV

Saints and Other Important Figures

Ruth's example

Naomi and Ruth didn't act like victims of circumstance. They didn't blame or curse God for their misfortune. Neither of them allowed tragedy to make them hard of heart, nor did it turn them into cranky old widows. The dynamic duo goes through major hardships — death, famine, and ostracism, to name a few — but their loyalty to one another and, ultimately, to God, ensures that their difficulties are transformed to joy over the course of their lifetimes. Ruth's fidelity to her mother-in-law, and her embracing of her mother-in-law's religion as well, makes Ruth, although born a foreigner, a shining example to converts as well as those born into the faith. Ruth and Naomi's names are still held in high respect to this very day by the faithful who read the Bible.

But Naomi was indeed discouraged at one point (heck, her husband and two sons died suddenly). She was so discouraged that she says, "Call me no longer Naomi [which means "pleasant"], call me Mara [which means "bitter"]" (Ruth 1:20). She was merely speaking about her unpleasant run of bad luck, however. Naomi never allowed the tough times to make her nasty or indifferent; it was just that she simply didn't enjoy the pains and suffering she had to endure. She shows that a person can be faithful and still not enjoy the misfortunes life may bring from time to time. Faithfulness, as Naomi and Ruth demonstrate, is not in taking pleasure in adversity but in bravely persevering.

Getting to Know Judith

Judith is one of the most unique and independent women in the Bible. Her incredible faith in God leads her to save the Hebrew nation. Her bravery is equal to that of any Biblical man. And her lifestyle is more akin to today's norms than those of the patriarchal society in which she lived. She is remembered for bravery, courage, and ingenuity in defeating the enemy, accomplishing what none of her male counterparts had the nerve to attempt.

The book of Judith can be broken into two parts. The first seven chapters of Judith detail the political and military doings of sixth century B.C.. These chapters supply a backdrop to the climate in which Judith lived. The remaining chapters discuss the role Judith played in saving her people and her nation from a powerful and dangerous enemy.

Judith enters the picture

Chapter 8 in the book of Judith introduces her as the daughter of Merari and the widow of Manasseh. Scripture says she was gorgeous, wealthy, and well-respected. A long genealogy is given, showing her prestigious Hebrew pedigree. Judith is a Jew living in Judea when Nebuchadnezzar ruled the Assyrians. He had asked the neighboring nations to help him in his war with the Medes, but many turned him down, including the Jews of Judea. Nebuchadnezzar wants to teach these nonconsenting Jews a lesson, so he sends his military chief of staff, Holofernes, to take care of them. Holofernes is warned, however, that the Hebrews have a powerful God and the only way to defeat them is to lure them into losing faith.

When the Hebrew people of the nation break God's laws and thus show religious infidelity, punishment results.

Holofernes comes up with a plan to cut off the water supply to the Hebrews. He hopes that after days of thirst and no relief, his adversaries will lose hope and trust in God and surrender (Judith 7:8–14).

Uzziah, the local Jewish religious leader, pleads with the people to wait five days before they abandon all hope and surrender to the Assyrians (Judith 7:30–32). But this offends Judith, who addresses the town elders and rebukes them for giving God a five-day ultimatum. She questions their judgment: How dare they give the Lord five days to rescue them or else threaten him with idolatry (Judith 8:9–17)? Judith reminds them of the many times that God has saved his people, despite their infidelity to him.

Some may question why Judith was the one to speak to the elders in this way, but the Bible doesn't comment on any reasons behind her bold actions. It does indicate that this woman is wealthy, and she probably comes from the upper class, but nothing more is explained about why she possesses some divine insight or intuition that enables her to see clearly what has to be done. No one but Judith saw any alternative to surrendering.

Saving her people

Judith decides to take action in the face of the elders' inaction. She fasts, prays, and wears sackcloth and ashes to do penance for the nation. Then she decides to use her beauty to her advantage. While the Israelites sit back and wait for the fifth day to arrive and then surrender, Judith hatches a brilliant plan to outwit Holofernes and defeat the Assyrian enemy before the Jews are wiped out according to Nebuchadnezzar's vendetta.

Before the fifth day comes, she gussies herself up in her finest linens and silks. Her beautiful body and face and stunning attire are breathtaking. If she can somehow lure Holofernes into a trap before the Israelites lose faith on the fifth day, all is not lost.

Book IV

Saints and Other Important Figures

Judith leaves town to seek out Holofernes, going under the pretext that she wishes to defect before he attacks and destroys Bethulia. Dazzled by her beauty, he agrees to see her. She explains once again that the only way he'll succeed in his quest is if the Israelites sin against God. She assures Holofernes that, after a few more days with no food or water, the inhabitants will lose faith and slay animals to eat forbidden foods (non-kosher fare), and thus incur the wrath of God. She explains that only then can the commander march in and capture the city. (See Chapter 11 of the Book of Judith for more info.)

Meanwhile, her story is a ruse to spend time with him. Judith gets Holofernes to drink copious amounts of strong wine so that he passes out in his tent. The true reason for her meeting then becomes clear. She takes his own sword, decapitates the feared general, and hands the severed head to her maid who shoves it into her food bag! (Read this account in Judith 13:1–10.) This story gives a whole new meaning to "brown-bagging it."

Judith then slips out of the camp as if to go and pray, and none of the soldiers are the wiser. She returns to Bethulia with the severed head of Holofernes and instructs the town leaders to hoist the head of their enemy on the city wall. Then she tells them to fake an attack against Holofernes' army, knowing that the chain of command will require the officers to inform the supreme commander himself. (Judith 13:10–14:5 describes this story.)

When they discover their leader decapitated, the soldiers realize it was by a woman's hand and that she had escaped under their noses. The rank and file are completely demoralized, and mutiny and defections run rampant. The great army of the king of the earth is in utter disarray and shambles. Bethulia is saved thanks to Judith's wits, beauty, and bravery. Instead of surrendering in despair, she single-handedly saved her country from destruction and ruin.

Not only does Judith save her own people, but she also inspires others to follow the Hebrew way. Achior the Ammonite, the man who had originally warned Holofernes against attacking the Hebrews, is summoned to verify the identity of Judith's prized head. When he sees Holofernes' head, he passes out. He is so amazed and moved by Judith's accomplishment and God's will that he professes the faith and is circumcised a Jew. (You can read this account in Judith 14:6–10.)

Remaining independent

Judith is indeed an independent woman for her time. After her heroic acts, she receives many offers but never remarries, despite the fact that she is child-less. It is believed that she remains unmarried to honor her dead husband. She is also the only woman of the Bible who has another woman (her maid) in charge of her estate. In fact, before her death, she disposes of her property and releases her servant from her obligations to make her a free woman.

Even though she displays much independent thinking and chutzpah — first for chastising the men who were willing to surrender and then by bravely killing the enemy — she also respects convention and tradition by observing the custom of praying, fasting, and wearing sackcloth before she embarks on her secret mission. She is bold and daring, yet still seeks to serve the Lord. Despite the fact that she flouts patriarchal society, her leadership is accepted and her ruse works because of her obvious faith in God.

Judith lives a long life (105 years), which is seen as a reward for her goodness. (For the particulars of her later years, see Judith 16:21–25.) She is remembered by Jews and Christians alike as a woman of bold and decisive action.

Esther: Becoming a Queen

Esther was a Persian Jew who lived in the fifth century B.C. during the *Diaspora*, which was the massive exile of three-quarters of the Jews from the Holy Land. During this time, being discreet (if not secretive) about your religion was very prudent, especially if you were Jewish. Anti-Semitism was prevalent wherever significant populations of Jews were present. Esther was born with the Hebrew name Hadassah, but her parents later gave her the name Esther. Despite her Persian name, Esther was a very devout Hebrew woman.

No other woman is mentioned as often in the Bible as Esther. Her name appears 56 times while the name of Sarah, herself a pivotal figure, appears only 54 times. Esther, who becomes queen, has a life filled with risk, bravery, and faith in God. Twice she risks death for her people. Esther could have kept quiet to save her own hide, but her faith doesn't allow her to remain safe while her people are threatened.

Esther's courage enables her to save her people from genocide during a time in which they had little or no power. Over the ages, her story has given hope to exiled Jews, encouraging them to practice their faith, even outside their homeland. The book of Esther also gives an explanation for the Jewish spring festival of Purim, which commemorates Esther's brave actions that saved the Jews.

The Book of Esther has eight main sections:

- ✔ The first section contains a prologue and Mordecai's dream.
- ✔ In the second section, Esther replaces Queen Vashti.

Book IV

Saints and Other Important Figures

✔ Haman plots to destroy all the Jews in the third section.

✔ Esther and Mordecai pray to God for divine assistance in the fourth section.

✔ In the fifth section, God answers Esther and Mordecai's prayers.

✔ The tables are turned in the sixth section.

✔ In the last section, you find the epilogue.

✔ Last is the interpretation of Mordecai's dream.

Vying for the king's hand

During Esther's day, the Persian King Ahasuerus (Xerxes in Greek) ruled the kingdom. During the third year of his reign, the king has a 187-day feast to celebrate his victory over his enemies (those folks knew how to party). He has reason to celebrate: His Persian empire is extremely powerful and wealthy, and his palace is adorned with gold and silver and exquisite marble, not to mention fine Persian rugs.

After much wine, the king summons Queen Vashti, his wife, so that he can show off her beauty, but she refuses to come. To refuse a royal summons was a big no-no indeed, and King Ahasuerus wasn't used to rejection. He immediately orders Vashti's removal from the palace and divorces her on the spot. (See Esther 1:10–22 for the story.) King Ahasuerus then seeks to replace her with a new wife. All the eligible virgin maidens of the realm enter a beauty contest, and Esther's Uncle Mordecai encourages her to vie for the king's hand. Esther enters the royal harem for consideration.

While in the harem, Hegai, the *eunuch* in charge (a castrated male; a eunuch was in charge of the harem because his physical condition made him no threat), gives Esther beauty treatments and a special diet so she'll over-shadow the other women. After 12 months in the harem, Esther wins the king over. And so the beautiful, intelligent, and engaging Esther is chosen over all the other concubines to be the new queen. However, the king doesn't realize that Esther is Jewish, and she heeds her Uncle Mordecai's advice to hide her Jewish identity because anti-Semitism is still very prevalent (Esther 2:1–20).

Foiling an evil plot

In the meantime, a powerful and influential man in the king's court named Haman, the grand vizier, starts to cause problems. His status in the kingdom requires that ordinary citizens bow before him. One day he encounters Mordecai, Esther's uncle, and Mordecai refuses to bow. Mordecai explains that, as a Jew, he bows to no one but God. Ego bruised, Haman is outraged, and he seeks death not only for Mordecai but also for all Jews in the kingdom.

The evil vizier goes before King Ahasuerus and convinces him that the Jews in his kingdom are traitors and that they need to be eliminated as soon as possible. Haman is given the imperial seal to issue a death warrant for all the Jews. Mordecai is on the top of his list, and Haman has a huge gallows constructed to execute him, as well as the rest of his people. (See Chapter 3 of the Book of Esther, where this plot is detailed.)

Mordecai sends word of the death decree to Queen Esther, who fasts and prays for three days to discern what she should do next. She then uses her sharp intelligence to formulate a plan.

With her Jewish identity still a secret, Esther knows that if she reveals it carelessly, she will also become a victim of the death penalty. She understands that she must approach the king — and soon. Unfortunately, in those days, talking to your husband the king was more complicated than just calling his office. She had to approach him at court, which was fraught with risk — law dictated that only the king could issue a summons, and the queen had no right to appear at court on her own. By doing so, she risks death. Nonetheless, she is so moved by the potential plight of her people that she forges ahead with her plan. (See Chapter 4 of the Book of Esther, where more of this story is told.)

Esther knows that two things can happen when she appears at court. If the king extends his scepter to her upon her arrival, this gesture signifies that he welcomes her presence. If he withholds the scepter, he doesn't want to see the queen, and she faces execution for her show of disrespect.

Fortunately, Esther's gamble pays off. When he sees her, Ahasuerus extends his scepter in welcome. He not only tolerates her presence but also offers her the ultimate public display of affection, saying, "What is your request? It shall be given you, even to the half my kingdom" (Esther 5:3). Esther tells the king that she would like to host a banquet for his majesty and the grand vizier Haman. The king approves of her idea, and the dinner goes forward as planned. At its conclusion, Esther invites Haman over for a second dinner the following night. Haman is gleeful about his repeat invitation, believing he's getting in the good graces of the royal family. On his way home, Haman revels at the sight of the gallows, where his nemesis Mordecai is to be executed. Everything seems to be going his way, or so he thinks.

Book IV

Saints and Other Important Figures

Exposing the rat

Later that night, the king can't sleep, so he requests that the royal chronicles be read aloud to him. His courtiers recount how a certain Mordecai had actually once saved King Ahasuerus's life by exposing a plot to assassinate him, but Mordecai was never rewarded for his act of loyalty. In fact, it was Haman who had reaped the rewards for saving the king's life, even though Mordecai had exposed the plot. (See Chapter 6 of the Book of Esther.)

The king summons Haman and asks him what kind of reward should be given to someone to whom the king wants to show gratitude for faithful service and loyalty. Thinking to himself, "Whom would the king wish to honor more than me?" (Esther 6:6). Haman gives a most elaborate reply:

> *For the man whom the king wishes to honor, let royal robes be brought, which the king has worn, and a horse that the king has ridden, with a royal crown on its head. Let the robes and the horse be handed over to one of the king's most noble officials; let him robe the man whom the king wishes to honor, and let him conduct the man on horseback through the open square of the city, proclaiming before him: "Thus shall it be done for the man whom the king wishes to honor."*
>
> —Esther 6:7–9

The King then throws Haman a curve ball. He commands that all the rewards Haman just suggested should be given to Mordecai the Jew for his former act of patriotism and loyalty. You can imagine the jaw of the vizier dropping to the floor. His worst enemy, the man he has planned to execute, is now to be given the royal treatment (literally). (Esther 6:6–13 describes these events.)

Because this command comes from the king, Haman must endure the ignoble shame of honoring his enemy. He must lead the horse upon which Mordecai rides. When it's over, Haman returns home with his head held low, and the soldiers whisk him away to the palace for his second dinner with the king and queen.

Confessing and protecting her people

It's time for Esther to spring her trap. While at dinner, King Ahasuerus again asks the queen what he can do for her. She decides to expose her secret, an act that once again puts her at great risk. Esther asks the king to spare the lives of all her people — and her own life, because she too is a Jew. She begs the king's mercy, explaining that neither she nor any of her fellow Jews has ever done anything close to treason against the throne. Her Jewish identity is now out in the open. (See Chapter 7 of the Book of Esther for this part of the story.)

The king responds by asking Esther who it is that's responsible for threatening her life — and the lives of all her people. She replies, "the wicked Haman" (Esther 7:6). The vizier's day then goes from bad to worse. When one of the eunuchs shows the king from his window the gallows where Haman intended to hang Mordecai, the king wreaks justice against Haman. "Hang him on that!" (Esther 7:9) Ahasuerus orders. Haman is then killed by the very instrument he intended to use against Mordecai. (You can find these incidents in Esther 7:1–10.)

But Esther isn't yet content, because the death decree is still in effect. She approaches the king and asks for his intervention. Unfortunately, the custom of the day prevents the king from rescinding an order previously given, but Ahasuerus does what he can. He issues another order allowing every Jew to defend himself, even with force of arms. When the order is implemented, the Jews fight back because they are allowed to keep swords as protection, and they defeat any attempt to exterminate them.

The festival of Purim commemorates when the Jews were allowed to defend themselves thanks to Esther's intervention. She is remembered every year around March 14 and 15, when Jews continue to celebrate Purim.

As further reward for his loyalty, Mordecai replaces Haman as vizier. Queen Esther continues as the beloved wife of King Ahasuerus. Esther could have laid low and kept her Hebrew origins secret to save her own skin, but she intervenes for her people and uses her political position as queen and the romantic connection with her husband, the king, to right an injustice. Queen Esther leaves the Bible stage at this point after the book of Esther ends, but her bravery and her invaluable assistance in saving her people are remembered not only by Jewish ritual but also in Christian art, which often depicts heroes of the Old and New Testaments.

Book IV

Saints and Other Important Figures

Book V
All About the Pope

Five Popes Who Became Saints

- **Pope St. Peter:** The first pope
- **Pope St. Sixtus II:** Began his career as a Greek philosopher
- **Pope St. Marcellinus:** Like St. Peter, was beheaded by Emperor Diocletian
- **Pope St. Julius I:** Built two churches in Rome that are still standing
- **Pope St. Gregory I:** Both his mother and grandfather are also saints

Ever wonder where hell is? Read about it online at www.dummies.com/extras/catholicismaio.

Contents at a Glance

Chapter 1

How the Pope Becomes Pope, and What Happens Next

*B*est known throughout the world and among more than 1 billion Catholics as *the pope,* the bishop of Rome is the supreme and visible head of the Catholic Church. The word *pope* is actually an English translation of the Italian *il Papa,* meaning *father,* which leads you to another title for the pope — *Holy Father.* Just as a Catholic priest is called "Father" in a spiritual sense, the pope is called "Holy Father" by Catholics all over the world.

He has a slew of other titles, too: Successor of St. Peter, Vicar of Christ, Primate of Italy, Supreme Pontiff, Roman Pontiff, Sovereign of the Vatican City State, and Head of the College of Bishops. The most common and best-known titles, however, are pope, Holy Father, and Roman Pontiff.

Think you're under pressure at work? The pope has *two* big jobs: He's the bishop of Rome *and* the head of the entire Catholic Church.

Getting the Job

The *College of Cardinals* elects the pope. Nope, that's not a university where priests and bishops learn how to become cardinals. Unlike Notre Dame and The Catholic University of America, the *College of Cardinals* merely refers to all the cardinals around the world, just as the *College of Bishops* is a way of describing all the world's Catholic bishops.

The pope handpicks bishops to become *cardinals,* and their primary function in life is to elect a new pope when the old pope dies or resigns. Because most modern popes live at least ten years in office (except Pope John Paul I, who lived only one month), cardinals do have other work to do instead of just waiting around for the boss to pass on. (For details about cardinals and their jobs, see the section Book I, Chapter 5.) Cardinals under the age of 80 are eligible to vote for the next pope.

The limit of electors is set at 120, but at one point Pope John Paul II (who was pope from 1978 to 2005) had appointed so many that the number of eligible voters reached 137. With retirements and deaths, only 117 eligible voting cardinals remained when Pope John Paul II died in 2005. His successor, Pope Benedict XVI, created 90 new cardinals in five consistories. Pope Francis has, as of this writing, created 39 cardinals in two consistories, yet with retirements and deaths through are currently 122 electors.

The electors can vote for any other cardinal or any Catholic bishop, priest, deacon, or layman, anywhere in the world and of any liturgical rite, such as Latin, Byzantine, and so on. Normally, the cardinals select another cardinal, both because they know each other better and because the number of cardinals to choose from is small compared to the 5,000 bishops around the world and more than 410,000 priests. Although extremely rare, if a layman is elected pope (as in the case of Benedict IX), he first has to be ordained a deacon, then a priest, and then a bishop before he can function as pope, because the authority resides in his office as bishop of Rome. If a priest is chosen, he needs to be ordained a bishop prior to being installed as pope.

Are there pope primaries?

The government of the Catholic Church, called the *hierarchy,* is more like a monarchy than a democracy. Catholicism is hierarchical in that one person, the pope, is supreme head over the universal Church. Yet bishops govern the local churches in a geographical district called the *diocese,* and pastors (or priests) represent the bishop in each local parish. Individual Catholics don't vote for the next pope or for their bishop or pastor. The Catholic hierarchy operates like a military chain of command as opposed to an elected, representative government. So, nope — no local primaries, no election campaigns, no debates, no political ads, and no popular vote.

Other religions and Christian churches allow for lay participation in positions of authority from a little to a lot, but Catholicism has been predominantly monarchical since the appointment of St. Peter. Laypersons are encouraged to participate in other ways. While they aren't allowed to have jurisdictional power, laity serve as consulters and advisors to pastors and bishops. Parish councils and finance committees are composed of lay parishioners who advise the pastor before he makes important decisions. Laity also even serve in the Vatican to advise, counsel, and represent the Holy See to organizations like the United Nations.

You may have heard the saying: He who enters the conclave a pope leaves a cardinal. The meaning? When a pope becomes sick or elderly or dies, rumors run rampant as to who will take the Chair of St. Peter. Often, the press names certain cardinals as the most likely candidates; they're called *papabile* (meaning *pope-able*) in Italian. But the *papabile* are usually the ones that the other cardinals *never* elect. So if a man enters the *conclave* — the private meeting of all the cardinals for the specific purpose of electing the pope — as a favorite (or worse yet, if he comes off as wanting the job), chances are he will leave a cardinal because his fellow cardinals will choose someone more humble.

Dimpled, pimpled, or hanging chads?

No sooner than 15 days and no later than 20 days after the death or resignation of the pope, all the cardinals are summoned to Rome for the secret conclave. *Conclave* comes from the Latin *cum clave,* meaning *with key,* because the cardinals are literally locked into the Sistine Chapel, the pope's private chapel at the Vatican, until they elect a new pope.

After the cardinals from around the world assemble inside the conclave, they begin discussions and deliberations. Almost like a sequestered jury, the cardinals are permitted no contact with the outside world during the conclave. Under pain of excommunication, no cardinal is ever allowed to discuss what transpires at these elections — to keep the element of politics and outside influence to a bare minimum.

Historically, the election of a new pope could take place in one of three different forms:

- ✔ **Acclamation:** A name is presented, and everyone unanimously consents without the need of a secret ballot.

- ✔ **Compromise:** Each cardinal casts a secret ballot. If no one achieves a two-thirds majority after several rounds of voting, then the entire College of Cardinals may choose one or several electors to select a candidate, and the entire body is bound to accept that choice. A unanimous vote to employ compromise is necessary for it to be valid.

- ✔ **Scrutiny:** Each cardinal proposes a candidate and gives reasons for his qualifications before the individual cardinals cast their secret ballot. A two-thirds majority decision is needed to elect a new pope.

  This is the only valid method currently permitted in papal conclaves.

Want a peek at what's going on behind those closed doors? When voting for a new pope, each cardinal writes a name on a piece of paper, which is placed on a gold *paten* (plate). The paten is then turned upside down, so the ballot can fall into a *chalice* (cup) underneath. This symbolism is deep, because the paten and chalice are primarily used at the Catholic Mass to hold the wafer of bread and cup of wine that, when consecrated, become the body and blood of Christ during the Eucharistic Prayer.

If no one receives two-thirds of the votes or if the nominee declines the nomination, then wet straw is mixed with the paper ballots and burned in the chimney. The wet straw makes black smoke, which alerts the crowds gathered outside that a two-thirds majority decision hasn't yet been made. One vote occurs in the morning and one in the evening. The election continues twice a day, every day. In 1996, Pope John Paul II introduced a variation in which if no one was elected by a two-thirds majority after 21 votes, then on the 22nd ballot, the man who received a simple majority (50 percent plus one) was elected pope. Pope Benedict XVI subsequently rescinded that change in 2007 and returned the requirement of two-thirds no matter how long the conclave takes. If someone receives two-thirds of the votes and he accepts, the ballots are burned without the straw, which blows white smoke to alert the crowds.

After a cardinal has received a two-thirds majority vote, he's asked whether he accepts the nomination. If he accepts, he's then asked, "By what name are you to be addressed?"

Pope John II (A.D. 533) was the first to change his name when he was elected pope because he was born with the name Mercury after the pagan god. So he chose the Christian name John instead. But it was not until Sergius IV (1009) that all subsequent popes continued the tradition of changing their name at the time of election. So, for example, Pope Pius XII (1939) was originally Eugenio Pacelli, John XXIII (1958) was Angelo Roncalli, Paul VI (1963) was Giovanni Montini, John Paul I (1978) was Albino Luciani, John Paul II (1978) was Karol Wojtyla, and Benedict XVI (2005) was Josef Ratzinger.

Is He Really Infallible?

Catholicism maintains that the pope is *infallible,* incapable of error, when he teaches a doctrine on faith or morals to the universal Church in his unique office as supreme head. When the pope asserts his official authority in matters of faith and morals to the whole church, the Holy Spirit guards him from error. Papal infallibility doesn't mean that the pope can't make *any* mistakes. He's not infallible in scientific, historical, political, philosophical, geographic, or any other matters — just faith and morals.

It boils down to trust. Catholics trust that the Holy Spirit protects *them* from being taught or forced to believe erroneous doctrines by preventing a pope from issuing them. Whether the Holy Spirit's intervention is as subtle as getting the pope to change his mind or as drastic as striking him dead, in any event, Catholics firmly believe that God loves them and loves the truth so much that he would intervene and prevent a pope from imposing a false teaching upon the whole Church. This belief doesn't mean that personally and individually the pope is free from all error. He could privately be wrong as long as he doesn't attempt to impose or teach that error to the universal Church, because at that point the Holy Spirit would somehow stop him from doing so.

So what does infallibility mean?

Infallibility is widely misunderstood. It's *not* the same as the Catholic beliefs of *inspiration* or *impeccability:*

✔ **Inspiration** is a special gift of the Holy Spirit, which He gave to the *sacred authors,* those who wrote the Sacred Scripture (the Bible), so that only the things God wanted written down *were* written down — no more, no less. So the pope isn't inspired, but Matthew, Mark, Luke, and John were when they wrote their Gospels.

✔ **Impeccability** is the absence and inability to commit sin. Only Jesus Christ, being the Son of God, and His Blessed Mother had impeccability — via a special grace from God. Popes aren't impeccable, so they're capable of sin — which, by the way, was visible in the case of the first pope, St. Peter, when he denied Christ three times just before the Crucifixion (Matthew 26:69–75).

Everything the sacred authors wrote in the Bible is inspired, but not everything every pope says or writes is infallible. *Infallibility* means that if the pope attempts to teach a false doctrine on faith or morals, the Holy Spirit prevents him (even by death) from imposing such an error on the faithful. So, for example, no pope can declare, "As of today, the number of commandments is nine instead of ten." Nor can he declare, "Jesus was not a man" or "Jesus was not the Son of God."

Infallibility also doesn't mean perfection. Infallible statements aren't perfect statements, so they can be improved so that subsequent popes can use better or more accurate language. Yet infallible statements can never be contradicted, rejected, or refuted.

So according to Catholicism, an immoral pope (you'll find several in Church history) can sin like any man and will answer to God for his evil deeds. However, as supreme head of the Church, the pope retains his infallibility on matters of faith and morals as long as he remains pope.

No pope in 2,000 years has formally and officially taught an error of faith or morals to the universal Church. Individually, some may have been poor or inadequate theologians or philosophers, and some may have had erroneous ideas about science. That has nothing to do with papal infallibility, however, because the main objective is to preserve the integrity of Catholic faith for all the members at all times and in all places.

The pope can exercise his papal infallibility in two ways. One is called the *Extraordinary Magisterium,* and the other is called *Ordinary Magisterium.* The word *magisterium* is from the Latin word *magister* meaning *teacher,* so the *Magisterium* is the teaching authority of the Church, which is manifested by the pope alone and or the pope along with the bishops all over the world.

The Extraordinary Magisterium

Extraordinary means just that, out of the ordinary. When an Ecumenical (General) Council is convened, presided over, and approved by the pope, and he issues definitive decrees, they're considered infallible because they come from the Extraordinary Magisterium. The Church has held an all-time total of only 21 councils. These are gatherings of the world's bishops and cardinals. Sometimes priests, deacons, and laity are invited to observe, but only bishops and the pope can discuss and vote. The culmination of these councils is a written letter that explains the faith, interprets Scripture, or settles disputed topics of faith and morals. They never contradict the Bible but apply biblical truths to contemporary concerns and problems, as well as giving more understanding to essential core beliefs. The names and years of the councils throughout Church history are as follows:

1. Nicea (325)
2. First Constantinople (381)
3. Ephesus (431)
4. Chalcedon (451)
5. Second Constantinople (553)
6. Third Constantinople (680–81)
7. Second Nicea (787)
8. Fourth Constantinople (869–70)
9. First Lateran (1123)
10. Second Lateran (1139)
11. Third Lateran (1179)
12. Fourth Lateran (1215)
13. First Lyons (1245)
14. Second Lyons (1274)
15. Vienne (1311–12)
16. Constance (1414–18)
17. Basel-Ferrara-Florence (1431–45)
18. Fifth Lateran (1512–17)
19. Trent (1545–63)
20. First Vatican (1869–70)
21. Second Vatican (1962–65)

The Ecumenical Councils have defined doctrines such as the divinity of Christ (Nicea); the title of Mary as the Mother of God (Ephesus); the two natures of Christ, human and divine, being united in the one divine person (Chalcedon); *transubstantiation* to describe how the bread and wine are changed at Mass into the Body and Blood of Christ (Lateran IV); the seven sacraments, Sacred Scripture and Sacred Tradition (see Book I, Chapter 2), and other responses to the Reformation (Trent); and papal infallibility (Vatican I). These conciliar decrees and *ex cathedra* papal pronouncements form the Extraordinary Magisterium.

Ex cathedra (Latin for *from the chair*) pronouncements from the pope are considered infallible teachings. The only two *ex cathedra* pronouncements in 2,000 years have been the dogmas of the Immaculate Conception (1854) and the Assumption (1950). When the pope teaches *ex cathedra,* he's exercising his universal authority as Supreme Teacher of a doctrine on faith or morals, and he's incapable of error. Catholics consider the Assumption of Mary and the Immaculate Conception infallible teachings because they involve the solemn, full, and universal papal authority. (See Book IV, Chapter 7 for more information on Mary, the Immaculate Conception, and the Assumption.)

The word *cathedral* comes from the Latin *cathedra* because it's the church where the bishop's chair *(cathedra)* resides. The chair is symbolic of authority going back to Roman days when Caesar or his governors sat on a chair and made public decisions, pronouncements, or judgments. When the pope teaches *ex cathedra,* he's not physically sitting on a particular chair but exercising his universal authority as Supreme Teacher.

Unlike governments that separate their executive, legislative, and judicial branches, in the Catholic Church, the pope is all three rolled into one. He's the chief judge, the chief lawmaker, and the commander in chief all at the same time. That's why the triple crown (also known as a *tiara* or *triregnum*) was used in papal coronations — to symbolize his three-fold authority and that he's higher in dignity and authority than a king (one crown) or even an emperor (double crown). (Pope Paul VI was the last pope to wear the tiara. It's a matter of personal choice and preference now.)

The Ordinary Magisterium

The second way that an infallible teaching is taught to Catholics is through the *Ordinary Magisterium,* which is the more common and typical manner, hence the reason why it's called *ordinary.* This teaching of the popes is consistent, constant, and universal through their various documents, letters, papal encyclicals, decrees, and so on. It's never a new doctrine but rather one that has been taught *ubique, semper et ab omnibus* (Latin for *everywhere, always and by all*). In other words, when the pope reinforces, reiterates, or restates the consistent teaching of his predecessors and of the bishops united with him around the world, that's considered the Ordinary Magisterium and should be treated as infallible doctrine.

When popes write papal documents (anything authored by a pope), the title they use to refer to themselves the most is *Servant of the Servants of God* (*Servus Servorum Dei* in Latin). St. Gregory the Great (590–604) was the first pope to use this title. Check out the different types of papal documents from the most solemn on down:

- Papal Bulls
- Papal Encyclicals
- Papal Briefs
- Apostolic Exhortations
- Apostolic Constitutions
- Apostolic Letters
- Motu Proprios

Prior to the Second Vatican Council (1962–65), more commonly known as Vatican II, the type of papal document the pope chose determined how much authority he intended to exercise. The preceding list indicates the order of authority that various papal documents traditionally had. For example, the lowest level was the *Motu Proprio,* which is a Latin phrase meaning *of his own initiative.* Somewhat like an international memo, it's a short papal letter granting a dispensation or making a modification applying to the whole world but on a disciplinary matter only, such as an issue that has nothing to do with doctrine. An example of Motu Proprio was when John Paul II granted permission to celebrate the Tridentine Mass (the order and structure of the Mass as it was celebrated between the Council of Trent and Vatican II). On the other hand, *Papal Bulls* were considered the highest authority.

Since Vatican II, however, the *content* and *context* of the document determine the degree of authority and not just the type of papal document. If the pope intends to definitively teach the universal Church on a matter of faith or morals, then he is expressing his supreme authority as head of the Church. When John Paul II issued his Apostolic Letter *Ordinatio Sacerdotalis* in 1994, he officially declared that the Catholic Church has no power to ordain women. (See Chapter 14 for more on the role of women in the Church.) *Ordinatio Sacerdotalis* was *not* an ex cathedra papal statement, but it's part of the Ordinary Magisterium, and thus, according to the Prefect for the Sacred Congregation for the Doctrine of the Faith, the teaching is infallible. The Cardinal Prefect is the pope's watchdog to investigate all suspected cases of *heresy* (false teaching) and to explain official church dogma.

Papal encyclicals are letters addressed to the world on contemporary issues and concerns. *Encyclical* comes from the Latin word for *circular*, because these documents are meant to circulate around the world. The name of each letter consists of the first two words of the letter in Latin, because every official document coming from the Vatican is still written in Latin. Encyclicals aren't *ex cathedra* pronouncements. Some examples of popes who put encyclicals to good use include:

- **Leo XIII** wrote *Rerum Novarum* in 1891, which discusses capital and labor. It defends private property and business, as well as the right of workers to form trade unions and guilds.

- **Paul VI** presented the Church's teaching on abortion and artificial contraception in *Humanae Vitae* in 1968. It's not an *ex cathedra* statement, but *Humanae Vitae* is a part of the constant, consistent, and universal teachings of the popes and bishops over the ages. (For more about the church's stand on artificial contraception, as well as other sticky issues, turn to Book II, Chapter 6.)

- **John Paul II** wrote *Laborem Exercens* in 1981 on human work; *Veritatis Splendor* in 1993 on the natural moral law; *Evangelium Vitae* in 1995 on the dignity, sanctity, and inviolability of human life and the things that threaten it, such as abortion, euthanasia, and the death penalty; and *Fides et Ratio* in 1998 on the compatibility of faith and reason.

- **Benedict XVI**'s first encyclical was *Deus Caritas Est* (2005) on the biblical passage that "God is Love." It explains that divine love and human love are based on the same premise: All love must be both "give and take," sacrificial and possessive.

Encyclicals are the routine, day-to-day, consistent teaching of the Ordinary Magisterium, which is equally infallible when it concerns faith and morals and reiterates the constant, consistent, and universal teaching of the popes and bishops. Their content requires religious submission of mind and will of faithful Catholics around the world. So-called dissent from papal teaching in encyclicals isn't part of Catholic belief. The Catholic faithful willfully conform to papal teaching and don't dispute it.

Now That's Job Security!

Popes are elected for life unless they voluntarily — without pressure or coercion — resign from office. (Pope Pontian was the first one to abdicate from the office in A.D. 235. Pope St. Peter Celestine V was the most famous one to resign, going back to monastic life in 1294. Pope Gregory XII quit in 1415, and for nearly 600 years no one else did so until Pope Benedict XVI resigned in 2013. No one can depose a pope even if he becomes insane, sick, or corrupt. No ecumenical council has the authority to remove him from office. So when a bad pope gets in (and from time to time, a bad pope has been elected), the only course of action is to pray to St. Joseph for a happy death of the pope in question. (St. Joseph is the patron of a happy death, because he probably died of natural causes in the arms of Mary and Jesus.)

Although even one bad pope is one too many, Jesus himself picked 12 imperfect sinners to be his apostles. The first pope, St. Peter, weakened and denied Christ three times, and Judas, one of the first bishops, betrayed him for 30 pieces of silver. One repented; the other hanged himself instead of seeking mercy.

This is our two cents' worth: Of the 266 popes in history, only a dozen were real scoundrels and caused great scandal. Eighty popes are recognized as holy saints, leaving 174 pretty good, all-right guys. Better stats than for presidents, prime ministers, or monarchs around the world.

Where the Pope Hangs His Hat

The pope's home is *Vatican City,* an independent nation since the Lateran Agreement of 1929, when Italy recognized its sovereignty. Vatican City covers only 0.2 square miles (108.7 acres), has fewer than a thousand inhabitants, and rests in the middle of Rome.

After 300 years of Roman persecution, the Emperor Constantine legalized Christianity in A.D. 313 with the Edict of Milan and thus formally ended the state-sponsored persecutions of the Christians. In A.D. 321, he donated the imperial property of the Lateran Palace to the bishop of Rome, which began a trend of donating property in recompense for all the land and possessions that the Romans took from the early Christians during the pagan era.

The donation of large estates stopped around A.D. 600, but 154 years later, King Pepin (the Short) of the Franks (who was also the father of Charlemagne) issued the Donation of A.D. 754: The pope would govern the territory of central Italy (16,000 square miles). From 754 to 1870, Vatican City was part of the Papal States, also known as *Patrimonium Sancti Petri* (the Patrimony of St. Peter). During the unification of Italy, Giuseppe Garibaldi and Count Camillo Benso di Cavour, the two men most responsible for creating the Kingdom and modern nation of Italy in 1870, seized the Papal States and, for all practical purposes, ended the secular rule of the popes. Today, Vatican City is the smallest independent nation in the world. Ironically, it also has the largest number of embassies and ambassadors around the globe. Guglielmo Marconi, the inventor of radio, built a radio for Pope Pius XI; thus Vatican Radio began in 1931. Now, in addition to a radio and short-wave antennae, the Vatican also has television and Internet programming.

The only real citizens of Vatican City, aside from the pope, are the cardinals who live in Rome, directors of other Vatican offices, and full-time diplomats who work for the *Holy See* (the pope and the various offices of Church government in the Vatican). These diplomats, clergy and laity alike, come from countries all over the world. They still retain their own nationality and citizenship but are given a Vatican passport while employed to represent the Vatican. Originally sent to Rome in 1506, about 107 Swiss guards protect the pope, decorating the *Piazza* (outdoor square where people gather) with their colorful costumes. In addition, plain-clothes Swiss guards, with electronic surveillance and sophisticated weapons, also keep a close eye on the Holy Father, especially since the attempted assassination of John Paul II in 1981.

Chapter 2

John Paul II: A Man for All Seasons

● ●

In This Chapter

▶ Seeing how he plotted his own course

▶ Reading his writings

▶ Understanding his philosophy and theology

▶ Knowing where he stood

▶ Taking a look at everything he accomplished

● ●

*R*obert Bolt's play titled *A Man for All Seasons* (1960) was about the life of Sir Thomas More, Lord Chancellor of England, who remained completely faithful to his God, his church, and his conscience even to the point of death. Although fidelity is easy when things are going well, maintaining and persevering in one's faith in times of trial and tribulation is not an easy task. Thomas More was called a "man for all seasons" because he didn't allow public opinion or political pressure to infect his soul.

Karol Wojtyła, who became Pope John Paul II, can also be called a "man for all seasons," because he did not allow anything to weaken his faith. Neither the German Nazis who invaded his homeland during World War II nor the Soviet Russians who occupied Poland throughout the Cold War could discourage this man's convictions and commitment to his religion. Despite a would-be assassin's bullets and Parkinson's disease, JP2 never succumbed to discouragement.

Both Thomas More (1478–1535) and John Paul II were poets, philosophers, and men of many talents. They were truly spiritual men who loved their countries but loved their God even more than their own lives. Like More, JP2 was a man of conscience and a *Renaissance man* (someone who has a broad education and has some proficiency in the arts, humanities, and sciences).

In this chapter, you discover how Pope John Paul II was a true pioneer in the sense that he went into uncharted waters and territory. We show you how he made an impact on the world itself, how he left an indelible mark on the Catholic Church, how he injected his own style and flavor into the papacy, and how he brought his Polish culture and personal faith into his public role as leader of the world's largest religion. Groundbreaker, innovator, defender, protector, shepherd, and pastor — these are but a few of the hats Pope John Paul II wore.

Being a Groundbreaker, Shepherd, and Reformer

John Paul II came from an ancient land steeped in tradition, was raised in a 2,000-year-old religion, and would become the visible defender of traditional morality and orthodox doctrine. At the same time, JP2 was innovative, not in content but in presentation. He showed his followers how the Church and especially the papacy could — and should — adapt to the modern world.

JP2 broke the stereotype of popes being elderly Italian church bureaucrats. Unlike some of his predecessors, he was elected at the young age of 58; was the first non-Italian pope since the 16th century; and traveled more than any other pope in history. He had the third longest reigning papacy (after St. Peter and Blessed Pius IX). The non-Catholic world, however, will remember John Paul II for his groundbreaking efforts to open dialogue with members and leaders of other faiths and religions. His gestures to heal wounds between Christians and Jews and between Catholics and Protestants were sincere and profound — if not totally successful.

The first Polish pope — and the first non-Italian in 455 years

The first mold John Paul II broke was the origin of the popes. JP2 was the first non-Italian pope in 455 years. The last non-Italian was Cardinal Adrian Florensz Boeyens, a Dutchman, elected Pope Adrian VI in 1522. From the time of St. Peter (the Jewish fisherman Jesus chose to head his church, whom Catholics consider the first pope) to Benedict XVI (the current pope, as of this writing), we've had 217 popes from Italy, 17 from France, 8 from Germany, 3 from Spain, and 1 each from Africa, Argentina, England, Portugal, the Netherlands, Poland, and Palestine (present-day Israel).

Why the Italian monopoly? Believe it or not, no strong-arm tactics were involved here. The practical reason was that, until the era of John Paul II, the papacy was very much involved in local concerns involving the diocese of Rome, of which the pope is the bishop, and surrounding Italian dioceses of Italy. It made sense to elect a local, an Italian, who not only spoke the language but who knew the culture and the problems the local and national churches were experiencing.

These days, the popes no longer need to worry about national defense and other domestic issues that other world leaders have to contend with every day. The small 109 acres of land that make up the Vatican are merely a home, a place of pilgrimage, and a center of ecclesiastical administration.

Since the time of Pope Paul VI (1963–1978), who was the first pontiff to visit five continents (and was called the "pilgrim pope" until the arrival of John Paul II), the universal ministry of the office became more relevant. Instead of just handling the affairs of the diocese of Rome or the Catholic Church in Italy, the papacy in the latter half of the 20th century became much more global in its perspective.

With the College of Cardinals comprising representatives from almost every nation on Earth, the unofficial Italian "monopoly" over the papacy ceased to exist. The year Pope John Paul II was elected (1978) was as good a time as any to elect a non-Italian, even if it hadn't been done for 455 years.

The last pope of the 20th century — and the first pope of the 21st

John Paul II has the unique claim of being the last pope of the 20th century and the first pope of the 21st century; he reigned from 1978 to 2005. Because of the unique time in which he was pope, a time of numerous technological advances, Pope John Paul II was able to bring the Church and the papacy into the 21st century, embracing technology instead of shunning it.

The *message* would be the same: perennial teaching of Christ as found both in Sacred Scripture (the Bible) and Sacred Tradition and as taught for two millennia by the Catholic Church. The *medium* by which the message was delivered would utilize the best the contemporary world had to offer. Pope John Paul II used modern tools to bring time-honored values and principles to a new generation.

JP2 inaugurated the Vatican Web site on Easter (March 30) 1997, and was considered the first "high-tech pope." Unlike previous popes who occasionally used modern media like radio and television, John Paul II was the first to capitalize on and utilize the full potential of high-tech communications. His weekly Wednesday audiences were broadcast by radio, television, satellite, short-wave radio, and Internet to all corners of the Earth.

Reaching out: Around the world, across religions, and to young people everywhere

John Paul II certainly broke the mold when he took the papacy on the road. Other popes had traveled, but none of his successors would cover as many miles, visit as many nations, and be seen and heard by as many people of every age, race, and background. Some old-time Vatican bureaucrats thought he traveled too much and should have stayed home more to "mind the store." But in practice, Vatican City (as an independent country) and the Holy See (as the administrative center of the one-billion-member organization) virtually run by themselves in terms of the day-to-day business and work that has to be done. The pope does not micromanage every diocese or nation. For the most part, he lets the local bishop shepherd his own flock.

Pope John Paul II's 104 pastoral trips to 129 countries around the globe were always media events, attracting reporters and journalists from every nation. He used the press to help communicate his message to the universal flock he was shepherding, even if those who covered him did not completely agree with him. He was the first pope to actually hold press conferences on airplanes during his worldwide travels.

JP2 was a true groundbreaker not only because he used modern media, but also because he was the first to make monumental advances in *ecumenism* (efforts to bring more unity and cooperation among all religions). As the first pope to visit a Jewish synagogue (in 1986) since St. Peter, he referred to all Jews as "our elder brothers." John Paul II was also the first pope ever to visit an Islamic mosque (in Damascus in 2001) and was the first pope ever to preach in a Lutheran church (in 1983).

Besides his efforts to communicate with the spiritual leaders of other religions and with the political leaders of other nations — whether capitalist, socialist, or communist — JP2 was also a groundbreaker in reaching out to the youth. He was the first pope to have World Youth Day, an annual event in which young people across the globe get together with the head of the Catholic Church. Since 1986, these events have brought together anywhere from 300,000 to more than 4 million young men and women at one place and time.

Author, Author

Most people know of John Paul II's papal encyclicals and letters. What a lot of people don't know is that he authored many books:

✔ *Sign of Contradiction* (1979)

✔ *Love and Responsibility* (1960, Polish; 1980, English translation)

✔ *The Way to Christ: Spiritual Exercises* (1982)

✔ *Crossing the Threshold of Hope* (1994)

✔ *Gift and Mystery: On the Fiftieth Anniversary of My Priestly Ordination* (1996)

✔ *The Theology of the Body: Human Love in the Divine Plan* (1997)

✔ *Pope John Paul II: In My Own Words* (1998)

✔ *Forgiveness: Thoughts for the New Millennium* (1999)

✔ *Get Up, Let Us Go* (2004)

✔ *Lessons for Living* (2004)

✔ *Memory and Identity: Conversations at the Dawn of a Millennium* (2005)

JP2 is best known for being the first Polish pope, and then as a theologian and philosopher in his own right, before and during his papacy. He was also a poet and playwright. Like the several languages he spoke fluently, this man was also of several talents, interests, and abilities. During Nazi occupation and then under Communist control, freedom of thought was not encouraged and freedom of speech not tolerated. Plays and poetry were two ways that patriotic citizens maintained their heritage.

Playwright

Not only did John Paul II write books, he also wrote plays. Besides plays based on biblical characters like *David, Job,* and *Jeremiah,* he also wrote plays like *Our God's Brother, The Jeweler's Shop,* and *The Radiation of Fatherhood: A Mystery,* dealing with the universal themes of faith and practicing it in day-to-day life. The last two he wrote under the pseudonym of Andrzej Jawien to avoid being caught by KGB agents in Soviet-controlled Poland.

Since the time of the Nazi occupation during World War II and throughout the Soviet control of Poland during the Cold War, resistance to Fascism and Communism took expression in the arts, especially in plays, prose, and poetry. Authors tried to keep the flames of freedom burning in the hearts of their countrymen despite the occupation and oppression. A common safeguard to avoid arrest and possible torture was to use a pseudonym whenever writing such material.

The Jeweler's Shop is a three-act play still available in English today. The setting is, as the title suggests, a jewelry shop, and the main characters are three couples who enter the store. Each couple has a different struggle, as well as a different understanding and experience of love, doubt, fear, disappointment, disillusion, and hope. The moral of the story is to not give up, which applies not just to married life, but also to religious and spiritual life and to an oppressed people whose country has been occupied or controlled by another nation.

Poet

John Paul II also wrote poetry. Through his poems, you get a glimpse into his heart and soul as a man and a human being. He wrote some poems during and after World War II, during his priesthood, during his *episcopacy* (the time spent in the government of the church as a bishop, archbishop, and a cardinal), and even during his pontificate. The poems show a tender, vulnerable, yet still very confident nature of the man who became the Bishop of Rome and head of the Catholic Church.

Here is a sample of his poetry from a poem he wrote in 1939 about his mother, Emilia, who had died tragically when Karol (John Paul's name at birth and his baptismal name) was only 9 years old.

> "Over This, Your White Grave"
>
> Over this, your white grave
> the flowers of life in white —
> so many years without you —
> how many have passed out of sight?
> Over this your white grave
> covered for years, there is a stir
> in the air, something uplifting
> and, like death, beyond comprehension.
> Over this your white grave
> oh, mother, can such loving cease?
> for all his filial adoration
> a prayer:
> Give her eternal peace —

John Paul II had a very strong devotion to the Virgin Mary, which was probably based not only on his staunch Catholic upbringing, but also on his Polish heritage and his need to be a son and have a mother he could turn to for comfort. Mary was not a substitute for his mother, Emilia, but the mother of Christ was still his spiritual mother, because Jesus, her biological son, was also his spiritual brother.

Becoming a Philosopher-Theologian

When John Paul II was still Karol Wojtyła, a teenager in high school, he was so good at public speaking that he was chosen to give the welcome address to a very special dignitary visiting the school one day. Prince Adam Stefan Stanisław Bonfatiusz Józef Sapieha (that's a mouthful), the Archbishop of Krakow and one of the most dignified members of Polish aristocracy, came for a visit. When he heard the eloquent speech given by Wojtyła, he asked one of his teachers if the lad was headed for the seminary. His professor replied that Karol had designs on going to Jagiellonian University to study philology (linguistics). Momentarily disappointed, thinking the church was losing a potential intellectual jewel for the priesthood, the archbishop merely replied, "Too bad." Little did he know then that divine providence had another plan for Karol Wojtyła.

Loving linguistics

As an incoming freshman, Karol Wojtyła had a heavy load. He studied not only Polish grammar, phonetics, and etymology but also the Old Slavonic and Russian languages. He loved language because it conveyed to others what was in the mind and heart of the writer or speaker of that tongue.

Language is the cornerstone of civilization, because it unites individuals and ideas. Without language, or without a means of communication, no society, no community can exist. Many occupying powers impose a foreign language on a conquered nation and often outlaw the native dialect to prevent a national identity. Yet, a common language, even if foreign, would sometimes have the opposite effect and unite people of the same nation who initially spoke completely different dialects and who, beforehand, could not easily communicate with those outside their own region. John Paul II not only had a talent for learning languages, he truly loved being able to communicate with others in their native tongue. He understood the philosophy of language and showed how to communicate verbally and nonverbally throughout his pontificate. A multilingual pope who traveled the world made the *catholic* (universal) part of his job and of his church have more meaning than ever before.

Showing a keen mind for linguistics, the young Karol developed a love of theater and poetry. In both of these, language was at its best. Polish plays and poems not only showed pride in the motherland but also instilled appreciation of the culture, art, and history of the people who lived in that country. He even helped form a student theater group known as Studio 39, and it was there that he felt an attraction to the stage. Even though he was not known as a "ham" actor seeking attention and applause at every opportunity, Wojtyła nevertheless recognized the power of presence. As a linguist, he knew the importance and effect of words. As an actor, he knew the importance of how those words were spoken and even the impact of saying nothing at all, just allowing the symbols and gestures to speak for themselves.

Secretly studying philosophy

In 1942, seminaries were officially closed like the colleges and universities, so Wojtyła pursued a covert underground education. Hidden in the residence of Archbishop Sapieha of Krakow, he discovered the sublime beauty of philosophy. He learned about the great philosophers such as Plato, Aristotle, Augustine, and Aquinas.

He was ordained a priest on November 1, 1946; two weeks later, he was sent to Rome to continue his studies and earn his first doctorate. His bishop sent him to the Angelicum, a seminary run by the Dominicans (brothers and priests of a religious community who follow the spirituality of St. Dominic from the 13th century, a contemporary of St. Francis of Assisi). St. Thomas Aquinas was not only the preeminent theologian of the Catholic Church, but also one of its finest philosophers and he happened to be a Dominican. No mystery then that Father Wojtyła would be immersed in scholastic philosophy, sometimes called *Thomism,* after Thomas Aquinas.

He threw himself into understanding such complex topics as objective realism, Natural Moral Law, and the three levels of truth (scientific, philosophical, and theological). So, to Karol Wojtyła, science and faith were not at odds with each other. Instead, they were two ways of examining the same reality.

Wojtyła defended his dissertation and passed his examinations with flying colors in 1948 but could not get the degree from his alma mater, the Angelicum. He was too poor to have his doctoral dissertation printed, and the seminary required that the dissertation be printed prior to conferring the degree. When he returned to Poland, Father Wojtyła resubmitted his paper to Jagiellonian University, and it awarded him a doctorate in theology. He earned a second doctorate in theology in 1954.

Thomistic philosophy and theology and other philosophies shaped the mind of Karol Wojtyła. Whether it was abortion, euthanasia, contraception, or the death penalty; economic, political, and social justice; he was always on the same page: promoting and defending what is good for humans, individually and communally. John Paul II believed that the ultimate good was the happiness found in knowing and doing the Will of God.

Becoming a Philosopher-Theologian

After his ordination, the Cardinal Archbishop of Krakow recognized the intellectual character of the young priest Father Wojtyła. The archbishop assigned Karol further studies in Rome and concentrated his academics in the philosophy of St. Thomas Aquinas and the Spanish mystics like St. John of the Cross and St. Theresa of Avila. In the summer of 1948, Father Wojtyła returned to Poland.

Karol's academic career in Rome was much more than the classroom and library. He had the chance to see historic churches, catacombs, and shrines, and meet hosts of other students from all over the world. Rome, with its Catholic universities, was a center of international activity. It was here that the future pope received a valuable education in the fine art of Roman diplomacy. With clergy, bishops, ambassadors, professors, students, and cardinals from all over the world, Father Wojtyła was able to practice the many languages he knew from his younger days. These interactions served as a basis for the future pope, who, some would argue, was the most diplomatic pontiff the Holy See ever had.

During this period, Father Wojtyła still wrote poetry, prose, and plays. His most famous drama was *Brother of Our God.* This play, in a theatrical way, outlined his beliefs in the social doctrines of the Church. Later these theological ideas would become more concise and articulate in the various encyclicals that he wrote and addressed to the Universal Church.

Receiving doctoral degrees

At the conclusion of his postgraduate studies, Father Wojtyła had defended his thesis on "evaluation of the possibility of founding a Christian ethic on the ethical system of Max Scheler." This he did at his alma mater, Jagiellonian University. His was the last doctoral defense before the Communists closed the institution. All the while, Father Karol continued his work with young students, choirs, study groups, and retreats. He earned a doctorate in philosophy in 1948 from the Roman University of the Angelicum and a doctorate in sacred theology in 1953 from the Jagiellonian University in Krakow, Poland.

In 1951, Father Wojtyła took another sabbatical in which he continued to study philosophy and theology. At this time, he began to develop his philosophy of man. Along with help from such greats as Dietrich von Hildebrand and Edith Stein (20th-century philosophers who taught in Germany and Austria before World War II — Stein was born a Jew, converted to Catholicism, and became a Carmelite nun before being sent to a Nazi death camp, and von

Hildebrand escaped to New York City in 1940), Father Wojtyła started a new school of thought that became known as Christian *phenomenology* (a method of inquiry based on the premise that reality consists of objects and events as they are perceived or understood in human consciousness and not anything independent of human consciousness).

Becoming a professor and faculty member

Later, Father Wojtyła became professor of moral philosophy and social ethics at a seminary in Krakow and a professor of philosophy at the Catholic University of Lublin. He assumed the Chair of Ethics and lectured for 25 years before his election as pope in 1978. He became a commuter, shuttling between Lublin and Krakow on the overnight train to teach and counsel in one city and study in the other.

In Lublin, Father Wojtyła endured the harshness of the Communist regime. The government had already arrested the university's *rector* (equivalent to chancellor or president) and nine priests on the faculty. As during World War II and the Nazi occupation, which lead to underground movements, Father Wojtyła joined professors who met secretly and became a nucleus of academics who sought ways to undermine Communism peacefully and philosophically.

During this period, Father Wojtyła continued his work on marriage preparation. He composed his thoughts into a book titled *Love and Responsibility*. This book was not merely a set of instructions for marriage, but a study on the vocation of marriage and sexual love that marriage entails. By explaining marital love and chastity, it also proved to be a valuable tool to counter the sexual revolution that plagued the West after World War II. In his book, Father Wojtyła explained that human sexuality was good because sexual desire leads men and women into marriage. Chastity was explained as a virtue to love others as persons, not objects. These personal concepts helped to pave the way for his general teachings on man and woman as persons and not as impersonal objects, a view that was adopted by secular society as a whole in the 20th century.

Being a Shepherd (Bishop)

On July 4, 1958, Father Wojtyła became Bishop Wojtyła. Pope Pius XII named him auxiliary bishop of Krakow. The circumstances surrounding the announcement of Father Wojtyła becoming bishop is classic Karol. He was an ardent sportsman and worker with the young. Naturally, the two converged in the summer with outings in the country. One such outing took place in July 1958. Father Wojtyła and friends went on a kayak and camping trip. It was in the midst of this camping trip that he received word to return to the cathedral in Krakow. Karol docked his boat, changed his clothes, went to the bishop's residence, and was informed of his elevation to the *episcopacy* (the office of bishop). Later, he returned to his boat, changed his clothes, and went back to camping, boating, and soccer, saying nothing to his companions, because he did not want to overshadow their planned holiday. Such humility had been a hallmark of Karol ever since he was a young boy.

Book V

All About the Pope

Karol Wojtyła was consecrated 11 days before Pope Pius XII died. This pope was the one he had met years before in Rome while doing his graduate work, and he was the same Holy Father who wrote extensively on Mary and the liturgy, two loves of Pope John Paul II. The next pope, John XXIII, would prove to be very important in the life of the young bishop when he convened the Second Vatican Council in Rome.

During these early years as auxiliary bishop of Krakow, Karol preached on a host of different occasions such as retreats, recollections, and symposia. He developed a theme of renewal, a theme that Pope John XXIII would also reiterate to the Universal Church at the new council he would convene.

Besides writing his theological treatise on marriage, chastity, and marital sexual love, called *Love and Responsibility,* Karol also wrote a play titled *In Front of the Jeweler's Shop.* The overall theme of the play is moral and inspirational. The play is about wedding rings, a symbol of the sanctity of marriage, the central theme of the play. The play highlights Bishop Karol's views on the equality of partners in marriage. The second act deals with a troubled marriage, and the third act deals with a couple who gets engaged after the war. The son is the product of the couple from the first act, and the daughter is the product of the couple from the second act. The play is a modern commentary on the challenges, responsibilities, and benefits of modern Catholic marriage.

Participating in the Second Vatican Council

The Second Vatican Council convened in 1962, and Bishop Wojtyła took part. The Council was monumental. It was an *ecumenical council,* which means it was a meeting of bishops of the whole Church to discuss and settle matters of Church doctrine and practice. Pope John XXIII invited other Christian churches to send observers to the Council. There was a great, historic meeting between Catholics, Orthodox, and major Protestant denominations.

The First Vatican Council was held only a century before and came to an end with the unification of Italy and the dissolution of the Papal States. As a result, the First Council was truncated, only dealing with the papacy. Another council would have to be convened in order to finish what the first could not, especially in areas of pastoral and dogmatic issues concerning the whole Church.

A typical day for Bishop Karol at the Council began with Mass at 6:45 a.m. at the Polish Institute, where he was staying. Then he made the short, ten-minute walk to St. Peter's. He attended another Mass at St Peter's Basilica at 9 a.m., with all the bishops in attendance. All the sessions of the Council took place here. Imagine the magnitude of the event, with the attendance of 108 cardinals, 9 primates, 5 patriarchs, 543 archbishops, 2,171 bishops, 128 major superiors of men's religious orders, and 93 abbots. Sessions included deliberations and speeches by the various clergy in attendance. (Indeed, Bishop Karol addressed the Council for the first time in November 1962.) In the afternoon, Bishop Karol returned to his residency. He would then go over the documents discussed during the day. In the evening, he would attend meetings of Council commissions and subcommittees to which he belonged.

A brief history of the Second Vatican Council

Pope Pius XII laid the groundwork for change in the 1950s, a whole decade before the Second Vatican Council. His encyclical Mediator Dei (1947) paved the way for the first document of Vatican II, Sacrosanctum Concilium (Constitution on the Sacred Liturgy), in 1963. In *Mediator Dei,* Pius XII encouraged and exhorted Catholics not to be mere bystanders and not to just sit as a passive audience when at Mass or any sacred celebration of the sacraments. Even when the liturgy was exclusively in Latin, the goal was to foster participation by having the congregation verbally respond to prayers from the priest, join together in singing hymns, and make the same external gestures (like kneeling, standing, and sitting) with one another. These external signs of participation were to be combined with an interior, internal, and spiritual participation of uniting heart, mind, and soul to what was happening in the sanctuary and on the altar.

Vatican II took place in the 20th century, almost a hundred years after its predecessor, Vatican I, which defined the dogma of *papal infallibility* (the Catholic teaching that the pope is prevented by the Holy Spirit from teaching an erroneous doctrine on faith and morals when speaking to the Universal Church). The Franco-German war abruptly ended the First Vatican Council (1869–1870), which was supposed to discuss other issues besides papal infallibility, such as Church law and discipline, missionary work, the sociopolitical world, and the issue of the Oriental (Eastern) Christian churches.

Unlike the previous 20 councils, Vatican II was not a *doctrinal council* (a council convened to resolve theological controversy); instead, it was called to be a *pastoral council* (one that did not define any new doctrines and instead focused on the pastoral and spiritual welfare of the Church).

When Angelo Roncalli was elected Pope John XXIII in 1958, he wanted to revise the then archaic 1917 *Code of Canon Law.* This body of ecclesiastical laws governed the Universal Church, from the Vatican all the way down to the local bishop and diocese to the local pastor and parish. Pope John XXIII and his immediate successor, Pope Paul VI, wanted to update the Catholic Church. They weren't interested in changing the content of teaching or the substance and essence of worship — they wanted to change the way and manner in which the doctrine was explained and the liturgy was celebrated.

It was clear from day one that the pope did not intend in any way, shape, or form to alter, revise, change, remove, or add to the ancient deposit of faith. The content of faith (in other words, doctrine) and the celebration of faith (sacraments) would remain intact, while the mode and manner in which they are explained and conducted would adapt to modern expressions and experiences. The *what* would remain the same, but the *how* would be another matter.

Pope John XXIII died in 1963, soon after he convened Vatican II in 1962. The Council was suspended until the College of Cardinals elected a successor, Giovanni Montini, who took the name Paul VI. Pope Paul VI reconvened the Council and later implemented many of its recommendations and resolutions. Some of those proposals included

- ✔ Allowing greater use of the vernacular (until then religious ceremonies were celebrated in the Latin language)

- ✔ Restoring the order of permanent deacon

- ✔ Promoting Christian unity (ecumenism) among the various denominations and religions (Protestant, Roman Catholic, and Eastern Orthodox)

- ✔ Respecting Christianity's Jewish origins and roots

- ✔ Using modern technology and contemporary perspectives to explain the faith

The Sacred Liturgy was the first area of discussion and dealt with the public worship of the Church. The entire Mass (or Eucharistic liturgy) was revamped, not in substance but in appearance. The common language of the local people replaced the universal ecclesiastical tongue of Latin. The priest was allowed to face the people as he celebrated from the altar. Larger selections from the Bible were incorporated so that, in a three-year period, nearly all of the scripture would be read and heard in church by the faithful.

Byzantine (Eastern) Catholics had already been accustomed to vernacular as well as liturgical Greek, Old Slavonic, Aramaic, Arabic, and Syriac in their Divine Liturgies, and they always had a permanent diaconate and married clergy. Latin (Western) Catholics, however, thanks to Vatican II, experienced some of these modernizations for the first time. The purpose of the changes was to foster and promote full, active, and conscious participation of the faithful in sacred worship and public liturgy.

According to Vatican II, worship shouldn't be seen as the exclusive work of the clergy. Vatican II allowed for lay involvement, such as reading the scriptures, serving at the altar, and, when necessary, assisting with distribution of Holy Communion as extraordinary ministers. The hierarchy was still very much alive and maintained teaching authority and governance over Church matters. But the wisdom, experience, and counsel of the laity were to be solicited and valued. Parishioners would be invited to join pastoral councils and finance committees, which have consultative though not deliberative authority to guide the pastor with his pastoral leadership.

Marriage and the single life were respected and honored as equal vocations from God along with Holy Orders (deacon, priest, and bishop) and religious life (nuns, monks, brothers, and sisters). Laity were encouraged to use their role in the world to enter political, economic, and social life and make it better by using the values and principles of their religious convictions.

Vatican II was not only pastoral and practical but truly *catholic* (universal) in the sense that 489 bishops from South America, 404 from North America, 374 from Asia, 84 from Central America, and 75 from Oceania participated and many non-Catholics (Eastern Orthodox, Protestants, and Muslims, for example) were also invited as guests. Nearly 3,000 people attended the Council in some fashion in the years it was convened, from 1963 to 1965.

Identifying the effects of the Council

Two main effects came from the Second Vatican Council. The first effect was the true intent of the Council, which sought neither to remake the Church nor to redefine the Church's teachings, but to speak and use the language of the time to communicate, explain, and defend what had been believed and taught for 2,000 years. This segment (the hierarchy) of the Church included the pope and most of the bishops who attended Vatican II. Their goal was not to "modernize" Catholicism as much as it was to use modern expressions and perspectives to present the ancient religion to a modern world.

The other effect was the elite group of "professional" theologians, journalists, liturgists, and ecclesiastical bureaucrats who attempted to hijack the Council in the claim of defending the "spirit of Vatican II." Although the bishops still met in Rome during the sessions of discussions, the spin-masters of their day distorted principles and propositions of the Council Fathers and proliferated them around the world. Liturgical experimentation, innovation, and alteration without any papal or Episcopal sanction rampaged Europe and the United States while Vatican II was being held. Aberrations and violations of liturgical regulations and *rubrics* (rules that govern how sacraments are celebrated) before, during, and after the sessions of the Second Vatican Council confused many of the laity and discouraged many of the older clergy who had only known one way of doing things. *Dissident theology,* which contradicted the official dogmas and doctrines of the *Magisterium* (the official teaching author-ity of the Church), were spread in numerous Catholic classrooms, colleges, universities, and seminaries.

At the same time that this distorted version of Vatican II was being followed, the bishops, priests, deacons, religious, and lay faithful loyal to the authentic "spirit of Vatican II" found their guidance in the "letter of Vatican II," or in the actual documents of the Council. Greater exposure to, reflection on, medita-tion on, and interpretation of the Bible by Catholic teachers and students did not conflict with official and ancient teachings and disciplines; instead, it gave them new meaning and enthusiasm. One of the greatest consequences of the authentic interpretation of Vatican II had nothing to do with power and authority in the Church, which remained hierarchical with the pope and bishops in control, but focused on the "universal call to holiness."

Almost 20 centuries had passed since Jesus walked the Earth and founded his church on the rock of Peter (Matthew 16:18). During that time, an unofficial notion crept into the common mind, not intended by the Church but never aggressively addressed, either. The idea arose among the regular laity that *sanctity* (holiness or saintliness) was only possible for professional religious people (like priests, monks, and nuns) — someone in Holy Orders or religious vows who wore a *habit* (religious garb), took vows (of poverty, chastity, and obedience), and lived in community (a monastery, friary, convent, abbey, or rectory). The clergy and religious only composed at most 5 to 10 percent of the Church at any one time in Church history, yet many people erroneously thought only the religious or clerical life could make a person holy. And with-out holiness, you can't go to heaven. Yet, it is erroneous to think that only clergy and religious have access to holiness. All the baptized are offered the same grace and same opportunity to live holy lives.

This false idea came about because, years ago, the clergy and religious spent a good quarter to a third of their day in formal prayer, while most if not all the lay faithful spent 99 percent of their time laboring and working for lords and ladies who owned the property and allowed the peasants to work them for survival. The amount of time spent in prayer at a chapel, oratory, church, or cathedral in many people's minds meant everything. A common person didn't have the time or the opportunity to spend quality time praying in sacred space.

Vatican II reminded the faithful that everyone who is baptized is called to live a life of holiness. The common priesthood of the laity was not an attempt to clericalize the laity or to laicize the clergy. The idea was simply that Baptism enables anyone and everyone to worship God and to practice the *corporal* (of the body) and spiritual works of mercy regardless of their state in life (vocation, career, or job). (For more on the corporal and spiritual works of mercy, see the nearby sidebar.)

Reading the Bible, doing mental prayer, saying the Rosary, and other devotions are not the exclusive activity of the clergy. Any baptized person since Vatican II is encouraged to pray, study, and get involved with teaching the faith (or *catechesis*) and living the faith (like the *apostolate* — a ministry suited to the individual believer — and practicing works of mercy). The brainstorm of Vatican II was that any vocation could help achieve holiness and sanctity and, thus, help someone get to heaven, because all vocations are considered ultimately from God. So, a single man or woman working in the office, store, factory, or classroom, the average husband and wife, mother and father, all had the same chance and opportunity of growing and receiving *divine grace* (the supernatural gift from God that makes you holy) as the priests, nuns, and monks had.

Religion, faith, piety, devotion — these were no longer considered the restricted tools of the ordained and consecrated religious. Being a good, devout, and practicing Catholic Christian as a husband or wife, mother or father, single man or woman was not only a possibility, but also a necessity. Doing a good job at work, home, or school; obeying the Ten Commandments and Natural Moral Law; reading the Bible, the Lives of the Saints, papal encyclicals, and other religious works; and cultivating a daily prayer life, a regular sacramental life (weekly Mass and frequent confession), and an active *apostolate* (works of mercy) were seen as duties and obligations of everyone by virtue of their Baptism. Church authority was not what conferred sanctity — divine grace did that. And grace is made available to everyone — clergy and laity alike.

The proper implementation of Vatican II made official Church worship more participatory, not in terms of geographic location (sanctuary or pews), but in terms of external and internal involvement of body (gestures and verbal responses) and soul (intellect and will). Listening to the revealed Word of God (as proclaimed at Sunday Mass) and feeding on the word (made flesh in Holy Communion) empowers the lay and ordained faithful to seek lives of holiness (in other words, doing the Will of God in everything that is said or done — words and deeds).

Although some people improperly used Vatican II to promote their own agendas or portray it as some wild revolution against ancient doctrine and traditional discipline, the sons of Vatican II (the bishops like JP2 who actually attended and participated in it) understood the real spirit of the Council, namely to *renew* instead of *reform* the Church.

Implementing reforms in the diocese

One of the first things Bishop Wojtyła did when he returned to Poland after attending the Second Vatican Council was to mobilize the *laity* (everyone in the Church except the clergy). Because they shared in the common priesthood by virtue of Baptism, the lay faithful, as well as the clergy and religious, were all called to a life of holiness. Teaching the faith, called *catechesis,* was the duty of all the baptized.

Because the Communists outlawed teaching religion in schools, Bishop Wojtyła got nuns and laity to teach in private homes, church social halls, and other places not under control of the civil authorities. He also formed a diocesan synod and Priests' Council to get input from his clergy and to give them direction and guidance as they sought to serve the spiritual needs of their parishioners. He challenged all the faithful to get involved in their religion, from the personal level (daily prayer, weekly Mass, and monthly confession) to the communal level (study groups to learn more about the faith, Bible study, and social action, like feeding the hungry, sheltering the homeless, visiting the sick, and so on).

An educated Catholic is one who is more active in his Church, so the message of Christ truly becomes liberating, not only from oppressive political regimes, but also from sin and ignorance itself.

Moving Up the Ranks

Karol Wojtyła was a remarkable man, with his athletic bearing, flare for public speaking, command of languages, and sincere faithfulness. He impressed his parishioners, superiors, and fellow clergy. He was afforded opportunities to speak the faith on the world stage and made the most of them. He rose through the ranks of the Catholic Church with uncommon speed, which culminated in an uncommon papacy.

Becoming the archbishop of Krakow

Pope Paul VI appointed Wojtyła archbishop of Krakow in 1964, during the Second Vatican Council. This important and prestigious promotion was not automatic, even though Wojtyła had been an auxiliary bishop of the same archdiocese. In giving Wojtyła this assignment, the pope showed his confidence in Wojtyła's abilities to be a spiritual leader and shepherd of souls.

Receiving the red hat: Cardinal Wojtyła

Historically, the archbishop of Krakow would also be elevated to the rank of *cardinal* (a senior ecclesiastical official of the Catholic Church, ranking just below the pope), and Archbishop Wojtyła was no different in this regard: He was made a cardinal in 1967.

Cardinals wear a red hat known as a *biretta*. The color of this ecclesiastical headgear, a precursor to the academic mortarboard, indicates the hierarchal rank of the cleric: Priests wear a black biretta; monsignors wear a black one with a purple pom-pom on top; bishops wear a violet biretta. So when a cardinal is elected, we say he received the red hat.

Over the next 11 years — before the College of Cardinals elected him pope — Cardinal Wojtyła had to deal with the Communists and his poor people who were persecuted by them. Religious education at all levels was a primary focus in his administration. (This theme was one he would pick up again when he issued a new *Catechism of the Catholic Church* in 1994.) Banned from public schools, Cardinal Wojtyła standardized alternative programs to continue to educate his flock, including the following:

- ✔ **Youth ministry:** Wojtyła used outdoor activities with young people — such as hiking, skiing, and camping — to share and teach the faith while having wholesome fun.

- ✔ **Works of charity:** Wojtyła got volunteers to help the poor in soup kitchens, homeless shelters, health clinics, orphanages, and other outreach programs. Part of their training and work was to be exposed to the teachings of the Church, because he was thoroughly convinced that good works only have value when motivated out of love of God and love of neighbor.

Electing a new pope: John Paul I

In August 1978, following Pope Paul VI's death, Cardinal Wojtyła voted in his first papal conclave since being made a cardinal. There were many possible contenders to the Throne of St. Peter. Yet the conclave elected an Italian from Venice, Albino Luciani, who was 65 years old. He broke with tradition and was the first pope to take two names, John Paul I to honor his two immediate predecessors, John XXIII and Paul VI. Luciani reigned as pope and as sovereign of Vatican City State from August 26, 1978, to September 28 of the same year. His one-month papacy is one of the shortest in history.

Being elected pope

The Second Vatican Council had only been over for 13 years when John Paul I was elected, and many of its implications were still being worked out. He took the name to alert the Universal Church that he would continue the reforms of the two previous pontiffs. Sadly, Pope John Paul I lived only 33 days. This plunged the Church into another conclave. This period of the Church would be referred to by historians as the "Year of the Three Popes" (Paul VI, John Paul I, and John Paul II).

Upon the death of the pope, the period is known as the *sede vacante* (meaning empty chair, the symbol of authority since the time of the Roman Empire) or as the *interregnum* period. This period lasts between the pope's death and the election of his successor. Cardinal Wojtyła, who had returned to Poland after the election of Pope John Paul I, once again boarded a plane back to Rome to vote for the next pope. Little did he know that he would be elected the 264th pope of the Roman Catholic Church and the first non-Italian pope in over 400 years.

At the second papal conclave, two strong candidates allegedly emerged, Cardinal Siri of Genoa and the Archbishop of Florence, Cardinal Benelli. (No one knows for sure, because the cardinals take a solemn oath to keep the deliberations of a conclave absolutely confidential before they even enter the Sistine Chapel.) Cardinal Wojtyła was supposedly considered the compromise candidate because Siri was thought too conservative or traditional while Benelli was considered too liberal or progressive by many of their brother cardinals.

Cardinal Wojtyła, on the other hand, was seen as a centrist in that he was a true son of the Second Vatican Council (meaning, he participated in the Second Vatican Council and vigorously worked to properly implement the reforms). At the same time, as a bishop behind the Iron Curtain, he was a staunch defender of *orthodoxy* (the official teachings of the Church on faith and morals) against the old enemy of atheistic Communism. Yet, this so-called compromise candidate was who the College of Cardinals wanted to lead the Church in the 20th century — a church that was fighting Communism on all levels. Who better a candidate to fight against atheism and Marxism than a cardinal who had suffered under its evil regime?

At the age of 58, Cardinal Wojtyła was one of the youngest popes. He chose the name Pope John Paul II in order to continue the reforms of the Second Vatican Council. As part of his reforms, he got rid of the traditional *papal coronation* (a long ceremony in which a new pope was crowned head of the Roman Catholic Church and sovereign of the Vatican City State) and instead was installed pope at a pontifical Mass.

During the traditional papal coronations, the pope was crowned with the three-tiered papal tiara to show that he was the chief priest, prophet, and king of the Church. The last coronation was that of Paul VI. His tiara, which was a gift from the Archdiocese of Milan, is now on display at the National Shrine in Washington, D.C.

Instead of the traditional papal coronation, Pope John Paul II chose a simple papal inauguration. At the new ceremony, the pope received a *pallium,* which is a narrow band of wool. It's worn over the *chasuble* (which is the long sleeveless vestment worn by a priest over other garments) at Mass. The pallium symbolizes the early image of Christ, who is the Good Shepherd and carries the lamb on his shoulders. The pallium is decorated with three jeweled lances to symbolize the nails driven into Christ at his crucifixion. Next, the pope received the ring of the fisherman, which is decorated with a relief of St. Peter fishing and is worn by the Sovereign Pontiff until his death, when it is ceremoniously crushed.

Upon his election as the 264th pope, the theme of his pontificate was "Be Not Afraid." These words ring true in many areas, from religious to political, economic, and even social freedom. "Be not afraid," for the Holy Spirit will guide you to the truth and to witness to it, he would tell young people at World Youth Day, so that they could recognize that old people were being killed by euthanasia.

The new pope was a beacon of light who would clarify the teachings of the Second Vatican Council in a church that was suffering from internal dissent and abusive experimentation. Everything from the Sacred Liturgy to the *Code of Canon Law* would see an imprint from the third longest reigning pope in the history of the Catholic Church. He would earn, we believe, the title of "the Great."

At the same time he was also a world leader. Pope John Paul II became a loud voice for social justice in rich and poor nations. He touched the hearts of many in his numerous trips to various countries. He was known as the most traveled pope in the history of the Church. And he used the media and technology to benefit the Church in spreading the message of the gospel.

Revisiting His Legacy

The legacy of John Paul II is still materializing and developing. The quarter-century he led the Church encouraged many vocations to the priesthood and religious life. After the confusion that followed after Vatican II — not from the documents themselves but from what many claimed to be the "spirit of Vatican II" rather than the actual and literal message of Vatican II — some priests and nuns abandoned their vows, there was a rise in the divorce rate, fewer people attended Mass, there was more dissent among theologians, and more Catholics ignored Church teaching and discipline altogether.

Paul VI had closed Vatican II in 1965, but it was under his pontificate that much of the spiritual decay had begun to infect the mystical body of Christ. Paul VI tried to preserve, protect, and repair the damage, but the sexual and cultural revolutions were simultaneously transforming the world into a place of greater instability and uncertainty. John Paul II came in 1978 and did not repeal or repudiate the Second Vatican Council; rather, he sought to fully, properly, thoroughly, and correctly implement what the Council Fathers had intended but that time and circumstance had previously prevented from happening.

JP2 did not come to set back the clock to before 1963. He came to prepare the Church and the world for the third millennium, which would come as soon as the 20th century ended and the 21st began. He sought reconciliation where possible. He defended the consistent, perennial teachings of the 2,000-year-old religion. He used modern tools — like the jet plane, the Internet, television, and radio — to spread his message. He preserved the rich heritage and patrimony of Catholicism, while at the same time he shook some of the dust off the places that had become complacent and lethargic.

John Paul II did not define any new dogmas, nor did he deny, dilute, or tamper with the revealed truths he was entrusted with as Supreme Pastor of the Universal Church. He did explain the age-old doctrines in a brighter light and with full enthusiasm and gusto. Prolific in his writings and speeches, Pope John Paul II had an important message — but as a former actor and poet, he also knew the importance of how the message was delivered.

The pope is considered by Catholics to be the head of the entire Universal Catholic Church while a local bishop is head of the diocese and the local pastor is the head of the parish church. *Universal Church* is used to refer to the Catholic Church as a whole.

JP2 could defend the tradition of priestly celibacy while extolling the virtues of married love between one man and one woman for the rest of their lives. He could defend the doctrine of a male priesthood while denouncing the exploitation of women through pornography and abortion. He spoke of the sacredness of each human person and the beauty of conjugal love open to the possibility of new life. He associated with all who suffer, because of the sufferings of his own past — losing his mother, brother, and father at an early age; living under Nazi and Communist oppression; surviving a would-be assassin's bullet; and his long battle with Parkinson's disease.

He was not able to convince all Catholics to embrace completely and totally all that the Church teaches, all the doctrines, disciplines, and sacred rituals. He could not get the Eastern Orthodox, for example, to come any closer to ecclesiastical unity, and the Protestant churches did not pack up and move to Rome.

Since 1054, the Roman Catholic and Eastern Orthodox churches have been divided. Prior to that, there was one Christian Church with several patriarchs (bishops from historical places of antiquity — for example, Jerusalem, Antioch, Alexandria, Rome, and Constantinople). The division was called the *Eastern Schism,* and the churches that separated and sought to be autonomous from Rome and the pope are called Eastern Orthodox. The patriarch of Moscow became independent in 1589. Although the Orthodox churches do not accept the primacy of jurisdiction of the pope as Supreme Pastor of the Universal Church, they do share the same theology, have the same seven sacraments, and have a strong devotion to the Virgin Mary as the Mother of God. Though very similar in substantial areas, the political and jurisdictional differences have historically prevented a formal reunion of the Eastern Orthodox and Western (Roman) Catholic churches.

The Protestant Reformation, which began in 1517 with Martin Luther then with John Calvin, John Knox, Thomas Cranmer, John Wesley, and others, broke from Rome and created the Lutheran, Calvinist, Presbyterian, Anglican, and Methodist churches. Unlike the Eastern Schism in the 11 century, the 16th-century Protestant Reformation divided Western Christendom along doctrinal and liturgical lines as well as jurisdiction.

Does the fact that JP2 wasn't able to achieve all of his goals mean he failed? Should he have even tried? Well, look at it this way: For a long time, nothing was said about the dangers of cigarette smoking. Then doctors and the surgeon general began telling everyone that smoking can cause cancer. Despite the amount of information and the scope to which it has been disseminated, there are still those who choose not to believe or to just ignore the warnings. Likewise, despite the global access John Paul II had, the 26 years he had it, and the wonderful manner he had in spreading it, not everyone paid attention. Those who did will never forget. Those who actually embraced it will never regret it. Not a waste then, after all.

A People's Pope: John Paul the Great?

Even before his death, some were calling him John Paul the Great. At his funeral and after his burial, the usage has become prolific. Only three other popes in history have had the honor of the title "the Great." Whereas only a pope can canonize a saint, it has been the prerogative of the people and posterity to bestow the title "the Great." It's an informal but rare moniker saved for those very few who surpassed their contemporaries and many of their predecessors in achievements, accomplishments, impact, and overall influence.

Many contemporary scholars believe that Karol Wojtyła will eventually inherit the title "John Paul the Great" for several reasons:

- ✔ **On the global level, he was instrumental in the dissolution of the Soviet Empire with the breakup of the Soviet Union, the unraveling of the Warsaw Pact, and the tearing down of the Berlin Wall.** Although he did not personally coordinate or participate in any of those incidents, he did make it easier for them to occur, and many people consider him the catalyst history needed at the time. He preached a nonviolent resistance to those who are denied human rights and dignity, like the freedom to worship.

- ✔ **He made the papacy truly international by taking it on the road.** By visiting millions of people in hundreds of nations, he showed how universal the Catholic Church was. Speaking several languages fluently, he visited foreign lands, made many *cardinals* (the guys who advise the pope and who elect the new one when the old one dies) from almost every nation, and invited the youth of the planet to gather every year at World Youth Day. He made the papacy and the Catholic Church extremely visible during his pontificate.

- ✔ **He was the first pope in a century to revise the Code of Canon Law (which had not been done since 1917) and the first pope to revise the Catechism in 450 years.** He canonized more saints than any of his predecessors and did so from all four corners of the Earth, from every race and nation.

Being "great" does not mean John Paul II was perfect or sinless. Even the Catholic doctrine of papal infallibility does not cross that line. Designating John Paul as "the Great" is not a dogmatic or spiritual judgment on the man. It is merely a title of convention given by history to those few who influenced so many people for the good. Mistakes? Sure, he made some — and he would've been the first to admit it. He acknowledged that he was like the rest of us sinners, in need of mercy and forgiveness. And he confidently — and regularly — went to confession.

Chapter 3

Pope Francis

* *

* *

*N*amed *Time* magazine's Person of the Year just months after he was elected to the position, Pope Francis has been lauded as a progressive, liberal leader in the church. His stands on controversial issues have drawn worldwide attention and have kept him in the public eye as a surprising and powerful leader.

Born Jorge Mario Bergoglio, Pope Francis was elected Bishop of Rome and Supreme Head of the Catholic Church on March 13, 2013. He is the 266th pope and 265th successor to Saint Peter the Apostle (whom the Catholic Church considers to be the first pope). He was preceded by Pope Benedict XVI, who resigned from office on February 28 that same year for health reasons.

In the Days before the Election: The Early Years of Pope Francis

Before he was Pope Francis, he was a Jesuit in Argentina. This section gives you a glimpse into the personal history, running through the "pre-pope" days of this unique person from South America.

Italian roots, Argentinian upbringing

Jorge Mario Bergoglio was born on December 17, 1936, in Buenos Aires, Argentina, to Mario Giuseppe Bergoglio Vasallo (an accountant for the railway) and his wife, Regina María Sivori Gogna (a housewife). Jorge's dad was born in Piedmonte, Italy, and emigrated to Argentina in the 1920s. His mom was born in Buenos Aires, Argentina but the daughter of Italian immigrants from Piedmonte.

Fluent in both Italian and Spanish, the Bergoglio family, like most families who immigrated to Argentina from Italy, was most likely fleeing the totalitarian regime of the dictator, Benito Mussolini.

Although his blood and DNA are Italian, Bergoglio also grew up and spent most of his life in Argentina, South America. He is one of five children, having two brothers (Oscar and Alberto) and two sisters (Maria and Marta). Maria is the only surviving sibling.

Pursuing religious vocation

Jorge was a natural scholar and loved to study. He had a keen intellect and yet enjoyed a normal life growing up with siblings and even having a girlfriend early in his young adulthood. His last surviving sister says he always had an infectious smile and a great sense of humor. He enjoyed life, yet he never over-indulged nor crossed the moral line. Moderation best described his lifestyle: not too much and not too little.

After his high school graduation, Jorge studied at the University of Buenos Aires, where he earned a master's degree in chemistry. He soon felt a calling to the Catholic priesthood, broke up with his girlfriend, and enrolled in the local diocesan seminary, but later entered the novitiate for the Society of Jesus (also known as the Jesuits) in 1958.

He continued his studies of the humanities in Chile and then returned to Argentina in 1963 where he graduated with a degree in philosophy from the Colegio de San José in San Miguel.

Bergoglio taught literature and psychology from 1964 to 1966. Then from 1967 to 1970, he studied theology.

On December 13, 1969, he was ordained a priest and continued studies and spiritual training from 1970 to 1971 in Spain. Bergoglio made his final profession with the Jesuits on April 22, 1973.

Developing a promising career

Almost immediately, Jorge Bergoglio became *Provincial*, which is almost the equivalent of being a bishop in that he has jurisdiction over a territory (province) and is the religious superior for Jesuits in that region. Members of the Province (other Jesuits) elect the Provincial for a term of office. He would assign and transfer his confreres (fellow Jesuits) as a diocesan bishop would the priests of his diocese.

After six years, he went from being Provincial to being rector of a Jesuit college from 1980 to 1986. His superiors then sent him to Germany to complete his doctoral thesis, after which he was reassigned to Buenos Aires and finally to Cordoba, Argentina, as confessor and spiritual director.

Pope St. John Paul II appointed him Auxiliary Bishop of Buenos Aires on May 20th, 1992 and was ordained and consecrated on May 27th in the cathedral.

Bishop Bergoglio was quickly appointed Episcopal Vicar of the Flores district and on December 21st, 1993, was made Vicar General of the Archdiocese. In less than four years he was then named Coadjutor Archbishop of Buenos Aires. A coadjutor bishop is usually made when the Pope wants an auxiliary bishop to immediately succeed the current local bishop of a diocese.

Cardinal Quarracino, Archbishop of Buenos Aires, died in 1998, and Bergoglio then became his successor as Archbishop and Primate of Argentina. Three years later he was made a cardinal by Pope St. John Paul II in 2001.

Living like Saint Francis of Assisi

As a bishop then archbishop and as a Cardinal, Jorge Bergoglio was a man of humility who constantly championed the causes of justice and service to the poor. Much like Saint Francis of Assisi who lived in the 12th century and worked among the poor, Bergoglio, too, lived a life of simplicity.

Despite his office as bishop, he took public transportation rather than being chauffeured in an expensive car as had been tradition. Riding the bus and subway with the poor in Buenos Aires, Bergoglio chose to renounce any external signs of prestige or privilege.

Considered by some to be an *ascetic* (someone who voluntary gives up most comforts in life for the sake of holiness), Cardinal Bergoglio became one of the more popular prelates in Latin America. His solidarity with the poor and his simple lifestyle enamored him to the disenfranchised, the marginalized, and the poor.

Following tradition, unconventionally

Though he was somewhat unconventional in his stark simplicity, Bergoglio was no radical or dissident when it came to Church doctrine or discipline. A humble man of the cloth, he often referred to himself as a "faithful son of the Church."

He openly opposed efforts by the Argentine government and judiciary to recognize same-sex marriages and allow gay couples to adopt children on the grounds that it would threaten and "seriously damage the family." Bergoglio wrote a letter to all the Carmelite nuns in Argentina asking them to fast and pray that the nation would not forsake traditional marriage (one man and one woman).

At the same time, he consistently reiterated the Church teaching in the Catechism (#2358) "[homosexuals] must be accepted with respect, compassion, and sensitivity. Every sign of unjust discrimination in their regard should be avoided."

He also publicly opposed government efforts to promote free contraception and artificial insemination. His stance against abortion, euthanasia, and attempts to redefine traditional marriage were well known in Argentina and all of South America.

The Unexpected Papacy

Pope Benedict XVI shocked the world as well as the entire Catholic Church when he announced on February 11, 2013 that he was going to resign as Supreme Head of the Church. Effective February 28 that same year, less than a month later, the announcement meant that Benedict XVI would become Pope Emeritus, and the See of Saint Peter would then become vacant. A new pope would have to be elected by the College of Cardinals. The last Bishop of Rome to resign as pope had taken place 600 years before (Pope Gregory XII in 1415).

The Conclave assembled on March 12, 2013, and the next day on the fifth ballot, Cardinal Jorge Bergoglio was elected successor to Pope Benedict XVI and the 265th successor of Saint Peter. He was the first Latin American pope, the first pope from the "New World," and the first Jesuit pope as well. Lastly, Francis is the first non-European pope since the Syrian Pope Gregory III in 741 AD.

Francis took his name after Saint Francis of Assisi who lived in the 12th century and is the co-patron of Italy (along with St. Catherine of Siena). St. Francis is one of the most famous and most popular of saints among Catholics and non-Catholics alike. St. Francis lived a life of poverty and worked among the poor. Jorge Bergoglio practiced a similar lifestyle as priest, bishop and cardinal before being elected Pope, so his choice seemed quite natural.

Like his moniker saint, Pope Francis embodies humility and simplicity. Unlike Pope Benedict XVI, who was a scholar and professor par excellence, Pope Francis, although no intellectual slouch, often speaks off the cuff. Pope St. John Paul was a philosopher, and Pope Benedict a theologian. Pope Francis is seen as a pastor more than anything else.

Living with less pomp: The Francis effect

Uncomfortable with formality, Pope Francis has shunned some of the minor traditions associated with the papacy. He chose to ride on the same bus with the cardinals after his election just as he had done before he was chosen pontiff. He has preferred to ride in more economical and modest automobiles than his predecessors, even though their cars were all gifts and no Vatican money was spent to purchase them.

Popes have traditionally lived in the Apostolic Palace (or Papal Palace) at Saint Peter's in Rome. It is called a palace not because it is a lavish residence, rather, because the pope is the ruler of Vatican City, an independent sovereign nation. Just as Queen Elizabeth II of England lives in Buckingham Palace in London, Popes have lived in the Apostolic Palace at the Vatican for centuries.

Francis, however, has chosen to live in the same hotel where all the Cardinals stayed during the papal conclave. The Domus Santa Marta (House of St. Martha) was built by Pope JP2 in 1996 to replace the ancient custom of having the cardinals sleep on cots in rooms located in the Apostolic Palace. The actual voting for a pope still takes place, though, in the Sistine Chapel.

John Paul II had the hotel built to accommodate the elderly and infirm cardinals who attended the conclave and who found the living arrangements at the Papal Apartments too spartan and inconvenient for those with disabilities and other age-related issues. The Domus is not a five-star hotel but is spacious and friendly for those who have difficulty getting around on their own.

The hotel rooms have no television or radio and are simply adorned. Because of the secrecy of the papal conclave, cell phone coverage inside is nil. The pope (or anyone for that matter) who lives at Domus Santa Marta must go outside if not further to make a cell call.

This change of residence was neither meant nor intended to be a slight on the humility of his immediate predecessors. Popes Benedict and John Paul and others lived in modestly furnished apartments. What Francis wanted, however, was to live and dine with others. As a Jesuit, he was accustomed to eating and living in a community. Rather than live alone (albeit with his personal secretary nearby), Pope Francis never left the Domus Santa Marta. He currently uses suite 201.

His simple and down-to-earth style has trickled down to cardinals, archbishops, bishops, priests, and deacons around the globe. Sometimes called the Francis Effect, it refers more to a style of governance that is seen as very pastoral, much like how a pastor shepherds his parish as opposed to a monarch ruling his kingdom.

Avoiding opulence and trappings of vainglory, Pope Francis has initiated a renaissance of simpler times and procedures. Old habits are hard to break, however, and Rome (especially the Vatican) moves slowly. The Church has been around 2,000 years, and the city has existed since 753 BC. Historically, there were a few decadent popes during the Renaissance (coming from the Medici and Borgia families, for example) who lived lives of comfort and refinement that had no rival among the kings and queens and emperors of Europe.

Recent pontiffs, especially in the 20th and 21st centuries, were men of learning, holiness, and saintly humility. Francis, however, through symbols and gestures, is bringing attention and focus to living a simple life. The first week of his papacy was filled with unsubstantiated stories in the press about rumors going about Rome, such as the one where he allegedly made a sandwich lunch for a Swiss Guard to the one of him sneaking out of the Vatican at night to give food to the poor.

Speaking his mind

Pope Francis is famous for saying precisely what he is thinking without any political or diplomatic filter. As some would say, Pope Francis likes to be frank. He is akin to Saint Nathaniel's description by Jesus in John 1:47 "behold, . . . [someone] who has no guile." In other words, here is someone who speaks plainly.

Unlike Pope B16 and JP2, F1 (Pope Francis I) prefers to speak more colloquially, that is, in common conversational style rather than in formal, theological and philosophical vocabulary. Sometimes called "tweet theology" (after the social media Twitter), Pope Francis likes to use short sentences and brief phrases instead of delivering fancy lectures. It helps to have a Francis lexicon of sorts — something to help understand the context of what the Pope says to more accurately get the proper meaning. When taken out of context, his words can disturb some conservatives while giving some liberals false hopes that he is changing doctrine or discipline.

Following are some examples of his comments:

✔ **"This is what I ask of you. Be shepherds with the 'smell of the sheep'."**

This comment was not meant to be derogatory but a vivid reminder to parish priests, pastors, and bishops that they are first and foremost shepherds and as such should be accessible to their flock. So much so, that they have the odor of the sheep — that is, they are identifiable as one of them. Another fellow pilgrim on the road to heaven.

✔ **"I see the church as a field hospital after battle. It is useless to ask a seriously injured person if he has high cholesterol and about the level of his blood sugars. You have to heal his wounds. Then we can talk about everything else."**

In a hospital emergency room, someone needs to triage and ascertain who is in trauma and therefore in most urgent need of treatment. Likewise, Pope Francis is saying that the church, be it the parish or the diocese, needs to prioritize people's spiritual needs and address the urgent ones first.

✔ **"We cannot insist only on issues related to abortion, gay marriage, and the use of contraceptive methods. The teaching of the church is clear, and I am a son of the church, but it is not necessary to talk about these issues all the time."**

Pope Francis is *not* saying the church and her leaders should avoid reiterating the consistent teachings of the church on the sanctity of human life from conception to natural death, but he is reminding everyone that there are other issues of social justice and moral theology which cannot be ignored or overlooked. Like his predecessors, JP2 and B16, Francis sees a hierarchy of moral values, and they also recognize that there are several if not many dimensions to the moral and spiritual life besides the controversial issues.

✔ **"The confessional is not a torture chamber, but the place in which the Lord's mercy motivates us to do better."**

The Sacrament of Penance or Confession is never meant to be an Inquisition nor is it a trial, but Pope Francis reminds Catholics that God's forgiveness of sins is an act of Divine Mercy and meant to encourage us to improve.

✔ **"It makes me sad when I find sisters who aren't joyful. They might smile, but with just a smile they could be flight attendants!"**

Religious sisters and nuns are not being dissed here. Francis is using a little satire to remind those in consecrated vows (poverty, chastity, and obedience) that discipleship is not a chore or drudgery, rather it is a joy and pleasure to serve the Lord and our fellow human beings.

✔ **"Gossip can also kill, because it kills the reputation of the person! It is so terrible to gossip! At first it may seem like a nice thing, even amusing, like enjoying a candy. But in the end, it fills the heart with bitterness, and even poisons us."**

Verbal character assassination is the byproduct of gossip. Rumor-mongering and backstabbing injure others' reputations but also eat away at the integrity of the one spreading the gossip.

✔ **"If a person is gay, who am I to judge them if they're seeking the Lord in good faith?"**

This is the most controversial quote and most taken out of context. Yes, Pope Francis was asked about someone at the Vatican who was gay but not actively practicing. There was an official who was accused of financial misdeeds and in the subsequent investigation it was disclosed that he had been involved in homosexual activity when he was a young man.

The Pope's point was that any sin, once confessed, absolved, and forgiven, cannot be held liable against that person. "Who am I to judge" someone who has repented and made amends for his/her mistakes? He was not saying that sexual misconduct is permissible nor is it acceptable. Any and all sexual activity is reserved for marriage, which is between one man and one woman.

✔ **"If my [someone] says a curse word against my mother, he can expect a punch in the nose . . . It's normal. You cannot provoke. You cannot insult the faith of others. You cannot make fun of the faith of others."**

Pope Francis was not condoning the violence committed by Islamist extremists, particularly the heinous massacre committed against *Charlie Hebdo* journalists in France. Violence is never the proper nor acceptable response. He was, however, reminding the world that free speech is not absolute. Freedom of speech does not trump freedom of religion. Respecting other faiths and religions does not compromise freedom of the press.

Just as the law puts limits on free speech so that perjury, slander, and libel are crimes punishable by the court, and just as one cannot shout "fire" in a crowded auditorium when there is none, so, too, one's freedom of speech has reasonable limits. Nonviolent and peaceful response is always the route to follow. His "punch in the nose" was intended as a metaphor and not meant to be taken literally.

Drawing historic crowds

Over six million people attended a papal mass celebrated in Manila by Pope Francis when he visited the Philippines. Papal audiences in Rome have drawn enormous size crowds in all kinds of weather. The numbers of pilgrims and visitors to the Vatican have reached an all-time high since Bergoglio's election as Pope.

Pope St. John Paul II and Pope Emeritus Benedict XVI attracted impressive crowds, but Pope Francis has by far hit a grand slam, as they say in baseball. Young and old alike, Italians, Latinos, rich and poor, and people from various nations, languages, and ethnic traditions flock to any gathering where they might grab a glance or hear a word from Pope Francis. That popularity is rooted in his down-to-earth and pastoral approach which reminds folks more of their own.

The Vatican reported that during the year 2014, more than 5,900,000 faithful participated in the various encounters with Pope Francis. General audiences (1,199,000) and special audiences (567,100) along with liturgical celebrations in the Vatican Basilica and St. Peter's Square (1,110,700) and the Angelus (3,040,000) hit historic highs.

Initially thought just a curiosity with a new Pope and the first from Latin America, Pope Francis has continued to attract large numbers of crowds. Whether or not that translates into more Catholics returning to the church or more converts coming in is still to be seen.

Popularity can be fleeting, however. Crowds that cheered Pius IX (1846–1878) would later threaten to throw his body into the Tiber River when he died. Francis is not seeking to appease everyone but he does want to reach out to as many as possible.

Making His Positions Official in Papal Encyclicals

Papal Encyclicals are official documents written by the pope to address a particular moral or doctrinal concern. Their name is determined by the first two words of the Latin text, because Latin is the official language of the Catholic Church. So, *Humanae Vitae* is the encyclical written by Pope Paul VI in 1968 on Human Life, and *Veritatis Splendor* (Splendor of Truth) was from Pope John Paul II (1993).

Lumen Fidei

Pope Francis' first official letter was entitled *Lumen Fidei* (Light of Faith). It was released on June 29, 2013. His predecessor Pope B16 did a lot of the preliminary drafts, and his other two encyclicals centered on Love (*Deus est Caritas*, 2005) and on Hope (*Spe Salvi*, 2007). *Lumen Fidei* this would have been his third had he not resigned from the papacy in 2013.

Lumen Fidei is still an encyclical of Pope Francis, for he edited and added to it as well as promulgated it as his first papal document. It centers on the supernatural virtue of faith and how it enlightens the mind of the believer.

Faith is believing what God has divinely revealed. It is an assent of the intellect (mind) to accept a concept as being true even though one is unable to completely understand it. It is a mystery one embraces because of Who it is that reveals this truth.

Pope Francis uses familiar Catholic notions such as truth being the object of the mind. Theological truth is revealed directly by God and contains information necessary for salvation but is beyond the capacity of human reason (via philosophical truth or scientific truth) to know on its own.

Pope Benedict wrote two papal letters on love and on hope. These are two of the three theological virtues. The last one is faith and so it made sense that this would be the next document, even if by the new pope. Pope Francis speaks of faith as both an intellectual activity (enlightenment) and a personal activity (having a loving relationship with Jesus Christ).

Evangelii Gaudium

Written in 2013, this letter addresses the issues of spreading the Gospel (called evangelization) and includes some reflections on a fair and just economic system. Some in the secular media falsely interpreted it to mean that Pope Francis was condemning capitalism. In fact, the word never appears in the document. *Consumerism* is what is rebuked as an overemphasis of acquiring material goods to the exclusion and neglect of the moral and spiritual needs of human beings.

Pope Francis also spoke of concern for the poor and for the promotion of justice at home and abroad. He explained the centrality of the Gospel and its message of hope and the joy, which the Word of God brings to the hearts of men and women — hence the name, *Evangelii Gaudium* (Joy of the Gospel).

The letter includes a section on promoting global peace through social dialogue and ecumenical engagement. He underscores the pursuit of the common good as the principal goal of society and culture.

Pope Francis is not a controversial pope in that he seeks to undo or unravel what was said and done by his predecessors. His aims and goals are not to reinvent the Catholic Church or to redesign it. He does intend to reform the papacy and the church, but from within. Unlike the Protestant Reformation of the 16th century, which resulted in formal separation of denominations that differ theologically, liturgically, and in governance, Francis seeks an internal reformation in that he brings the efforts of Pope John Paul II and Pope Benedict XVI to their logical conclusion.

Pope John XXIII convened the Second Vatican Council. Pope Paul VI implemented the liturgical and structural reforms. JP2 and B16 brought the papacy to the modern world with their international visits and by their international expansion of the college of cardinals, as well as by the number of saints canonized during their reigns.

Some in the secular press and media misinterpret Pope Francis and see him as a loaded gun or as an unpredictable innovator. Spontaneity is not the same as rashness, nor is informality the same as irreverence. Francis' persona is such that he wants to be and to look accessible. He uses a more casual style than his predecessors, but he has no desire to abandon ritual and tradition just for the sake of doing so.

He still wears the traditional white cassock popes have worn since Pope St. Pius V began the custom in the 16th century. Although he lives in the Doma Sanctae Martae hotel rather than in the papal palace, his residence is still within the Vatican, whereas some early popes lived at Saint John Lateran in Rome, and for 70 years popes lived in Avignon, France. Francis chose an unconventional name when he was elected, but John Paul I was the first one to choose two names in 1978. Francis kept the custom of changing his name, that is, of not using his baptismal name (a custom first begun in 533 and done consistently since 1555). Hence, it cannot be said Pope Francis has turned his back on all custom and tradition, but he does make minor changes now and then.

Pope Francis, like all popes, will defend the 2000-year history of doctrine and dogma, but he will do so in his own style. He chooses to be more of a pastor, whereas some of his predecessors were more like teachers. All popes take on both hats, so to speak. In fact, the ancient *tiara* (three-level crown) that was used in papal coronations represented the three-fold powers of every pope: priest (sanctifying office), prophet (teaching office), and king (governing office). It also symbolizes the legislative, judicial, and executive powers of the bishop of Rome.

No one should pigeonhole Pope Francis or box him into one category or classification. He is neither liberal nor conservative. He is different, as are all popes, but no one can deny he has been one of the most popular among Catholics and non-Catholics alike, rivaling only John XXIII and John Paul II.

The term "Francis effect" has been used to describe the more informal style and the overt attention to the poor and needy. Cardinals, bishops, and priests around the world are emulating his kind and gentle manner to remind their flocks that their shepherds are human just like them and that they are approachable and available for their main mission, which is to serve and not be served. It is not about being soft on morality or doctrine, rather, it is about being patient and compassionate and just being there, as well as teaching and leading the fold.

Chapter 4

One Last Promotion: Popes Who Became Saints

· ·

In This Chapter

▶ Getting to know the popes great enough to be deemed saints

▶ Finding out about saintly popes of the early Catholic Church

· ·

*T*he supreme head of the Catholic Church is the pope, from the Italian "papa," or "father." Every Bishop of Rome has been the pope, and every pope has been the Bishop of Rome. Most popes lived in Rome; those who didn't physically live there still served as Bishop of Rome, even if by long distance.

In this chapter, you find out about those popes who've been canonized as saints and briefly describe what's known of their earthly service. The popes appear in chronological order for easier reference and provided the dates of their pontificate (papacy) but not their birth, because ancient records didn't keep birth information as accurately as ordination information. You don't find patronage information either, as none of these popes are listed as patron saints. (FYI, the two most recent popes to become saints were Pope St. John XXIII and Pope St. John Paul II, both canonized by Pope Francis on April 27, 2014.)

Pope St. Peter

Pontificate: A.D. 33–A.D. 64

Feast days: SS. Peter & Paul, June 29; Chair of St. Peter, February 22

Peter became head of the Church and leader of the Christians following Christ's Resurrection and Ascension. As the premier pope of the Catholic Church, St. Peter set the stage for those to follow; every pope to serve after his reign is considered a successor to St. Peter and the Bishop of Rome (see the nearby sidebar, "Early Church hierarchy"). He established the first Christian community in the empire's capital just before being martyred in A.D. 64.

Pope St. Linus

Pontificate: A.D. 64–A.D. 76

Feast day: September 23

Not much is known about Linus, but he is mentioned in the New Testament in St. Paul's Epistle, 2 Timothy 4:21. He was likely made a bishop by Paul.

Linus, who was probably from Tuscany, was the second pope of the Church and the first successor to St. Peter. His name appears in the Roman Canon, the part of the Catholic Mass where the Last Supper is reenacted and the priest speaks the words of Christ over the bread and wine, changing them into the body and blood of Jesus. One authoritative source *(Liber Pontificalis)* states that Linus was buried next to his predecessor, St. Peter, the first pope, on Vatican Hill. Recent archeological research has cast some doubts on the remains currently identified as Linus, but his existence is not disputed.

Pope St. Clement I

Pontificate: A.D. 88–A.D. 97

Feast day: November 23

Clement, the fourth pope, is believed to have known Peter and Paul; his writings are a great resource for their preaching and teaching. Scholars also believe that Paul refers to Clement in Philippians 4:3. Clement was an educated man who wrote numerous letters that still survive today — many of which were responses to requests to settle disputes. His decisions were sought because he was the successor to St. Peter, and as the Bishop of Rome, he was considered to have universal primacy.

Clement is venerated as a martyr, though no historical data can back this view. Like St. Linus, Clement's name appears in the Canon of the Mass. He died in Crimea, but his remains were brought back to Rome and are enshrined at the minor basilica of St. Clement *(Basilica di San Clemente al Laterano)*.

Pope St. Alexander I

Pontificate: A.D. 105–A.D. 115

Feast day: May 3

As with many of the early popes, not much is known about Alexander except for some minor liturgical additions he made, such as the blessing of holy water mixed with salt. He also encouraged the use of holy water in private homes.

Some historians believe that Alexander was a martyr and died under Emperor Hadrian or even Trajan, but no documented record indicates this. He was martyred by decapitation and is buried on the Via Nomentana in Rome.

Pope St. Telesphorus

Pontificate: A.D. 125–A.D. 136

Feast day: January 5

St. Telesphorus instituted a 7-week fast to prepare for the solemnity of Easter, thereby laying the foundation for the modern-day season of Lent (although Lent today lasts only 40 days). He also established the practice of celebrating Easter only on a Sunday so as to commemorate the actual day of the week that Jesus rose from the dead. Previously, people had celebrated Easter three days after Passover, and so it didn't always fall on a Sunday. Telesphorus was also the first pope to establish the Christmas midnight Mass. He was martyred for his faith and is buried near St. Peter in the Vatican.

Pope St. Hyginus

Pontificate: A.D. 136–A.D. 140

Feast day: January 11

St. Hyginus had talents in theology that were put to use against the heresy of Gnosticism during his reign. *Gnosticism* was the idea that salvation could be achieved only through secret knowledge. Followers also believed that human souls are prisoners in physical bodies. Only the invisible, spiritual realities are considered good, while anything visible and material is evil.

Book V

All About the Pope

Gnosticism originated in Egypt, and some of its proponents came to Rome in the hopes of winning over converts. Hyginus successfully eliminated the threat from Rome, but Gnosticism wasn't completely eradicated until the fifth century. Hyginus is buried near the tomb of St. Peter at the Vatican.

Pope St. Zephyrinus

Pontificate: A.D. 199–A.D. 217

Feast day: August 26

Zephyrinus, a Roman of modest means and humble beginnings, faced several heresies during his reign, including two that created a heavy burden for this pope: adoptionism (the idea that Christ only became divine upon his baptism) and modalism (the idea that the Holy Father, the Resurrected Son, and the Holy Spirit are one entity rather than the Holy Trinity).

Zephyrinus is considered a *dry martyr* because, though he certainly suffered persecution, he may not have died a martyr's death. He's buried in a cemetery near the Catacombs of St. Callixtus in Rome.

Pope St. Callixtus I

Pontificate: A.D. 217–A.D. 222

Feast day: October 14

Callixtus I reigned much the same way he lived — surrounded by struggles and misfortune. He was a Roman from Trastevere, the son of Domitius. While a slave of Carpophorus, Callixtus was given care of a bank, but he lost the money and ran away. Historians believe that customers took advantage of his inexperience and good nature.

Callixtus was caught and sentenced to hard labor. He was released early for good behavior, only to be jailed again for fighting in a synagogue (most likely trying to recover the money he lost). He was sent to work in the mines of Sardinia but was again released at the request of the emperor's mistress.

Knowledge of his papacy comes from his most vocal opponents and enemies. Tertullian and Hippolytus vigorously disagreed with Callixtus's decision to allow former adulterers, and even murderers, to receive Holy Communion after performing some tough penance and showing full contrition. They preferred the more strict response of total and perpetual excommunication for very grave sins. Callixtus's view on the mercy of God and the use of the Sacrament of Penance (confession) prevailed, and his enemies are now remembered as heretics.

His relics are buried in the Church of Santa Maria in Trastevere.

Pope St. Pontian

Pontificate: A.D. 230–A.D. 235

Feast day: August 13

Pontian, a Roman by birth, held a *synod* (a meeting of clergy) in Rome in A.D. 230 to condemn the heresy of *origenism* — the loose interpretation of scripture and subordination of the doctrine of the Trinity. He was exiled to Sardinia during the reign of Emperor Maximinus Thrax, who eagerly persecuted the Church. In most cases, being exiled was considered a death sentence.

Popular belief holds that Pontian abdicated his office so his nephew could be chosen as his successor. Buried in Sardinia, Pontian's remains were later moved to a papal cemetery on the Appian Way known as the Catacombs of St. Callixtus. Later, his bones were moved again to the Vatican, with other popes.

Pope St. Fabian

Pontificate: A.D. 236–250

Feast day: January 20

Fabian was one of the few laymen to be elected pope. After his selection, he was ordained a deacon, and then a priest, and finally, Bishop of Rome. When Pope Anterus died, many notable candidates were considered to succeed him. The crowd saw a white dove alight upon Fabian's head, almost like the scene from the Gospel when the Holy Spirit descends in the form of a dove. The crowd interpreted this as a sign from heaven and unanimously chose Fabian as the next Bishop of Rome and Pope of the Church.

Fabian ruled during the reign of Emperor Gordian III, a time of peace in which the Church was able to expand. He divided the diocese of Rome into seven sections, built churches, and expanded cemeteries. He was responsible for the return of the remains of both Pope Pontian and the reconciled anti-pope Hippolytus.

After Emperor Gordian's rule, persecution once again threatened the Christian Church in Rome. Emperor Decius had Fabian imprisoned, and he died there in A.D. 250. Originally buried in the Catacombs of St. Callixtus, he was later moved to the Basilica of St. Sebastian.

Pope St. Cornelius

Pontificate: A.D. 251–A.D. 253

Feast day: September 16

Cornelius was a Roman priest when he was chosen to succeed Pope Fabian. He was displeased with *confessors* (priests and bishops who absolved the sins of contrite sinners via the sacrament of *penance,* also known as *confession*), whom he considered lax with allegedly repentant Christians — those who sought reconciliation with the Church after having denounced their faith during the Roman persecutions. At the same time, he rebuked the harshness of those who maintained that the *lapsi* (lapsed Christians) were unforgivable.

Cornelius believed that the mercy of God allowed the Church to forgive repentant sinners but that divine justice demanded a proper penance.

The persecution of Christians was renewed and Cornelius was exiled; he died pending his trial and is therefore considered a martyr. He's buried in the Catacombs of St. Callixtus.

Pope St. Lucius I

Pontificate: A.D. 253–A.D. 254

Feast day: March 4

Lucius was born in Rome and served just 18 months as pope. Like Cornelius, he condemned those who refused reconciliation with repentant lapsi, because he believed any sin was forgivable as long as the person had true contrition and a sincere desire to avoid sin in the future.

Lucius and other Christians were exiled by Emperor Gallus, but after Gallus's death, his successor, Valerian, allowed Pope Lucius and other Christians to return to Rome after previously being exiled. Lucius died a natural death in A.D. 254 and is buried in the papal chambers of the Catacombs of St. Callixtus.

Pope St. Stephen I

Pontificate: A.D. 254–A.D. 257

Feast day: August 2

Stephen was a priest in Rome when he was elected pope and faced the issue of heretics conducting baptisms. Some claimed that heretics' baptisms were invalid, while others maintained that the grace of the sacrament worked regardless of the spiritual state of the minister. Pope Stephen agreed with the latter position, and thus it became doctrine for the entire Church, angering some of his opponents.

St. Stephen is buried in the papal chapel of the Catacombs of St. Callixtus.

Pope St. Sixtus II

Pontificate: A.D. 257–A.D. 258

Feast day: August 6

Sixtus (also Xystus) was a Greek philosopher before he became pope in Rome. At the time, Emperor Valerian was vehemently anti-Christian and prohibited worship, instead requiring Christians to participate in state religious ceremonies. In defiance, Sixtus II gathered the faithful in a cemetery for a mass of commemoration, for which he was arrested and beheaded.

Sixtus is buried in the papal section of the Catacombs of St. Callixtus, and his name appears in the Canon of the Mass.

Pope St. Dionysius

Pontificate: A.D. 259–A.D. 268

Feast day: December 26

Dionysius was elected Pope at a time when many priests were martyred and church property was confiscated. Dionysius exercised his papal authority in many different ways, first by settling disputes in theology over the Blessed Trinity, and then by reaffirming the Church's teaching that the Sacrament of Baptism is received only once.

In areas of government, Dionysius was left with the restructuring of the Church in Rome after Emperor Valerian's campaign of persecution. After the emperor's son ascended the throne, church land and property were returned. Dionysius reorganized the property and revitalized the decimated clergy. He's buried in the papal section of the Catacombs of St. Callixtus.

Pope St. Caius

Pontificate: A.D. 283–A.D. 296

Feast day: April 22

Caius insisted on maintaining the mandate that bishops first be ordained priests before being consecrated to the episcopacy, which some had tried to make optional. Although he was likely a relative of the Emperor Diocletian, Caius had to escape to caves and catacombs when the Diocletian persecution of Christians went into full swing. He's buried in the new part of the papal cemetery in the Catacombs of St. Callixtus.

Pope St. Marcellinus

Pontificate: A.D. 296–A.D. 304

Feast day: June 2

Marcellinus is remembered along with St. Peter as an exorcist of Rome. Both men were beheaded under the particularly vicious reign of Emperor Diocletian and are remembered in the Roman Canon of the Mass. Marcellinus guided the church for eight years, between A.D. 296 and A.D. 304.

Marcellinus was originally buried in a private cemetery, but the Christian Emperor Constantine later translated his relics, built a church over them, and buried his own mother, St. Helena, in it as well. In the ninth century, portions of the relics of both saints were gifted by the Holy See to monasteries in Germany. Miracles were attributed to the intercession of these saints during this last transfer.

Pope St. Melchiades

Pontificate: A.D. 311–A.D. 314

Feast day: December 10

Melchiades was the first pope to see the end of Roman persecution of Christians. Constantine defeated Maxentius in A.D. 312, and the new emperor issued his famous Edict of Milan the following year, legalizing Christianity.

At the urging of his mother, St. Helena (a devout Christian), Constantine gave Melchiades and the Church many imperial estates, like the Lateran Palace (which became the Basilica of St. John Lateran, the pope's actual cathedral) and Vatican Hill (where St. Peter's Basilica is located and where the pope now lives and works every day).

Melchiades is buried in the papal chapel of the Catacombs of St. Callixtus.

Pope St. Sylvester I

Pontificate: A.D. 314–A.D. 355

Feast day: December 31

According to pious tradition, Emperor Constantine was miraculously cured of leprosy when he was baptized by Pope Sylvester after he had issued the Edict of Milan.

Two significant meetings took place during Sylvester's reign: the Synod of Arles, which condemned the heresy of Donatism, and the Ecumenical Council of Nicea, which condemned the heresy of Arianism. The latter council also developed the formula creed recited in the Catholic Church, based on an earlier creed of the Apostles.

On the Via Salaria he built a cemeterial church over the Catacomb of Priscilla. He is buried in this church.

Pope St. Julius I

Pontificate: A.D. 337–A.D. 352

Feast day: April 12

Julius had to deal with the problem of the Arian heresy (Arianism denies the divinity of Christ). So much of the Christian world came under the influence of this heresy that Catholic bishops were deposed from their dioceses. Julius convened a synod, which resulted in reaffirming the pope's authority over questions of theology or governance in the Church.

Julius also built two churches in Rome that still stand today: St. Mary Trastevere and The Church of the Holy Apostles.

Pope St. Damasus

Pontificate: A.D. 366–A.D. 384

Feast day: December 11

Damasus's papacy was filled with heresies and political strife. He worked with St. Basil in the Eastern Church to enforce the documents of the Council of Nicea in Antioch, which at the time was divided between two bishops. He was also a productive laborer, working alongside St. Jerome in the Latin Vulgate translation of the Gospels, building a number of churches in Rome, restoring the catacombs, and refurbishing older places of worship. He wrote a treatise on virginity and poems on the Roman martyrs and popes. He's buried in one of the churches he built in Rome, St. Lorenzo in Damaso.

Pope St. Siricius

Pontificate: A.D. 384–A.D. 399

Feast day: November 26

Siricius was the first pope to mandate celibacy in the Latin Church. (Eastern Catholic clergy were always given the option of marriage or celibacy before ordination). Even where married clergy were permitted, only celibates could be promoted. Siricius also condemned a heresy that attacked the veracity and necessity of the perpetual virginity of Mary. He's buried in the Catacomb of Priscilla.

Pope St. Innocent I

Pontificate: A.D. 401–A.D. 417

Feast day: July 28

Innocent stressed that dioceses should refer all major problems to the Bishop of Rome, as the pope is the supreme pastor of the universal church. A common expression was coined in this era: *Roma locuta est, causa finita est* (Rome has spoken, and the case is closed).

Innocent is buried next to his father, Pope Anastasius I, whose papacy ended prior to the celibacy mandate.

Pope St. Boniface I

Pontificate: A.D. 418–A.D. 422

Feast day: September 4

Boniface has earned much recognition for his efforts to strengthen the papacy. He was an old man when elected pope, and some of his dissidents seized the Lateran Palace and elected their own anti-pope, Eulalius. Emperor Honorius initially tried to sort out the situation, and for a while, he asked both men to suspend their rule. Boniface complied; Eulalius did not. The emperor and those in government were angered by Eulalius's disobedience and unanimously recognized Boniface I as the authentic pope.

Boniface I also battled heresy and, along with St. Augustine of North Africa, was a champion supporter of orthodoxy. He is buried in the cemetery of Maximus on the Via Salaria, Rome.

Pope St. Celestine I

Pontificate: A.D. 422–A.D. 432

Feast day: April 6

Much controversy existed in the Church at the time Celestine reigned, especially from North Africa. Two heresies, Pelagianism and Nestorianism, plagued orthodox theology. Pelagius denied the necessity of grace and held that human works alone could earn your way into heaven; Nestorius denied the divinity of Christ and the title of Mary the Mother of God.

With St. Augustine, Bishop of Hippo in North Africa, Celestine dealt with the heresies by convening a council in Rome that laid the groundwork for the great Ecumenical Council in Ephesus, which dealt with these heresies on an authoritative basis. At this council in Rome, Celestine asserted the primacy of Peter and his successors in the Church and in matters of faith and morals. He is buried in the Catacombs of Priscilla.

Pope St. Sixtus III

Pontificate: A.D. 432–A.D. 440

Feast day: March 28

Sixtus continued the condemnation of the heresies of Pelagianism and Nestorianism during his papacy, although his pastoral demeanor and patience led some to conclude erroneously that he had heretical sympathies with these two. In reality, he was just a kinder, gentler pope than his predecessors.

He enlarged the Basilica of St. Mary Major on Esquiline Hill in Rome, dedicated St. Peter in Chains, and built a beautiful baptistery at the Basilica of St. John Lateran.

Pope St. Leo I

Pontificate: A.D. 440–A.D. 461

Feast day: April 11

Leo was a deacon under Pope Celestine I and Pope Sixtus III. Along with Pope Gregory and Pope Nicholas, he's one of only three popes to be given the title "the Great."

A learned, erudite, and accomplished orator, Leo dealt with heresies head-on. Ninety-six of his sermons and 143 letters survive today that concern the major theological errors of Leo's time.

Although he couldn't attend the Ecumenical Council of Chalcedon (A.D. 451), he wrote a letter known as the "Tome of Pope St. Leo" that was so clear and well received that the council fathers said, "God has spoken to us through Peter and in the person of Leo, his successor."

Historically, Leo is remembered as the one man in all of human history who was able to dissuade Attila the Hun from sacking Rome. As Attila prepared for war in his camp outside of Rome, Leo rode up on his horse, not in armor but wearing the ecclesiastical vestments of a bishop. Attila had great awe and respect for Leo after seeing such faith and courage in an old man.

Leo is buried in St. Peter's Basilica.

Pope St. Hilarius

Pontificate: A.D. 461–A.D. 468

Feast day: February 28

Hilarius narrowly escaped death at the "Robber Council" of Ephesus (A.D. 449), and, when he was elected pope, he showed his gratitude by building a chapel of St. John the Apostle in the baptistery of the Basilica of St. John Lateran. Centralizing the papacy's authority in France and Spain proved to be a hallmark in his reign. He is buried at St. Lorenzo Fuori le Mura.

Pope St. Gelasius I

Pontificate: A.D. 492–A.D. 496

Feast day: November 21

Gelasius was the first pope to use the title "Vicar of Christ." He also created a fourfold division of church donations and offerings. One part went to the poor, another to upkeep of the local parish, one portion to the bishop, and the fourth to the minor clergy.

Gelasius was an educated man and left a great depository of writings, ranging from theological letters and treatises to additions to the Roman Missal. He is buried in St. Peter's Basilica.

Pope St. John I

Pontificate: A.D. 523–A.D. 526

Feast day: May 27

John was used as a pawn of sorts by Theodoric, the king of Italy, in an effort to mitigate the persecution and exile of Arian heretics. Emperor Justin I, a champion of orthodoxy, sought to root out the last vestiges of Arianism, but Theodoric, an Arian sympathizer, wanted John to intervene. One thing the pope didn't agree to was a concession to allow once-converted Arian heretics to return to their old ways.

That concession aside, the pope did go to Constantinople to temper the passion of the emperor. This was the first trip that any pope commenced to the capital of Byzantium. The results were bittersweet — the trip was quite successful in that the emperor received the pope with great joy and enthusiasm; on the other hand, when Pope John returned to Italy he was imprisoned by the mad king. He died in prison in A.D. 526.

Pope St. Felix III (IV)

Pontificate: A.D. 526–A.D. 530

Feast day: September 22

This Felix was concerned with heresies, particularly in France, where practitioners were following teachings that denied the workings of grace and free will. The pope reaffirmed the teachings of St. Augustine, who had dealt with this issue in North Africa a century earlier.

Felix was a good steward of the Church: He increased its funds and church property, converted pagan temples back into churches (including pagan temples in the Roman Forum, two of which he converted into Christian basilicas of SS. Cosmas and Damian), presided over numerous ordinations to the priesthood, and performed many charitable works. Known as a man of simplicity, humility, and charity, he was also a staunch defender of the faith.

He decreed that clerics were under ecclesiastical jurisdiction, not civil, and that only Church courts could try accused clergy and impose sentencing.

Pope St. Agapetus I

Pontificate: A.D. 535–A.D. 536

Feast day: April 22

Agapetus was an archdeacon and somewhat elderly when chosen to be pope. He was a cultured and well-learned man who owned a vast library and who hoped to establish a university in Rome with the books he collected.

Although unsuccessful, the pope traveled from Rome to Constantinople to meet with Emperor Justinian in an effort to dissuade him from invading Italy. He died in Constantinople.

Pope St. Gregory I

Pontificate: A.D. 590–A.D. 604

Feast day: September 3

Gregory was quite literally born into a saintly heritage. He was the grandson of Pope St. Felix III and the son of Gordianus, a wealthy patrician, and Silvia, who was also a saint. Gregory started his religious life as a monk and converted the family villa in Rome to a monastery. His piety and monastic discipline marked his spiritual life as pope.

When he assumed the papacy, Rome was in shambles from wars, invasions, earthquakes, fires, and abandonment by the empire. Rome went into a steady decline as power shifted to Constantinople. Pope Gregory served to help the material needs of the people he also led spiritually in the Eternal City.

He reorganized all the patrimony due to the Holy See from estates throughout Italy; created the Gregory Missal, a compilation of changes in the traditional liturgy; and established the Gregorian chant musical style. He was a great supporter of missionary activity to England, where he sent St. Augustine of Canterbury and 49 missionaries. He is buried in St. Peter's.

Pope St. Boniface IV

Pontificate: A.D. 608–A.D. 615

Feast day: May 8

Historians believe Pope Boniface worked closely with the great reforming pope Gregory I and was a champion of monasticism in the West. He was a member of the Benedictine Order.

He appointed the first Bishop of London and assembled a synod concerning monasticism, reforms that the bishop took back to England. The saintly pope was buried in the portico of St. Peter's, and his relics were later translated into the interior of the church.

Pope St. Martin I

Pontificate: A.D. 649–A.D. 655

Feast day: November 12

Martin was a nuncio (papal ambassador) to Constantinople for Pope Theodore I before succeeding him in the papacy.

During his reign, Martin dealt with the heresy of *Monothelitism* — which denied that Christ had both a divine and a human will — and in so doing found himself in conflict with Emperor Constans II, who favored the Monothelists and silenced any opposition. Martin convened a council at the Lateran Palace, the official residence of the pope, in which Monothelitism was condemned, and appointed a vicar in the East to carry out his dictates, infuriating the emperor.

In retribution, the emperor sent a special dignitary to arrest the pope for high treason, but the representative converted upon seeing the pope's popularity and the doctrine's reasonableness. The emperor had to send another representative to arrest Martin and bring him to Constantinople. The arduous journey to the seat of the Byzantine Empire was difficult for Martin, who was already in failing health. He was found guilty in a mock trial and sentenced to death, but later his sentence was commuted to banishment.

It wasn't the humiliation or the terrible conditions of ill health that created Pope Martin I's suffering; rather, it was that the people of Rome had forgotten him. Nobody attempted to help or rescue him, and the Romans had in fact elected another pope.

Martin died in exile in A.D. 655. In A.D. 680, the sixth general council ratified his teachings, and Martin was venerated as the last papal martyr. He is buried at St. Martin di Monti.

Pope St. Vitalian

Pontificate: A.D. 657–A.D. 672

Feast day: January 27

Like many of his predecessors, Vitalian was forced to confront Monothelitism, the denial of the two wills of Christ. Both the emperor and the Constantinople patriarch supported this denial.

The pope maintained the Roman position but let the argument remain idle for a time. The emperor bestowed gifts upon him, and the patriarch included his name in the Constantinople diptych. When the emperor visited Rome, Vitalian received him warmly and, in another diplomatic decision, passed over the emperor's terrible treatment of his predecessor, Pope St. Martin I.

When the emperor was murdered in Sicily, Pope Vitalian backed the emperor's son, the logical successor to the empire. The son wasn't interested in doctrine, providing Vitalian an opportunity to come out with strong teachings against Monothelitism. The Constantinople patriarch wasn't amused and tried to remove his name diptych, but the new emperor, remembering Vitalian's support, wouldn't allow it.

Vitalian is buried in St. Peter's Basilica.

Pope St. Agatho

Pontificate: A.D. 678–A.D. 681

Feast day: January 10

A Sicilian monk from Palermo, Agatho was married for 24 years before going into the monastery. He was instrumental in developing a friendly relationship between the Catholic Church and the Byzantine Empire. He convened a council in Rome, attended by more than 150 bishops, that not only condemned the Monothelitism heresy but also reaffirmed the pope's role as the custodian of the true faith.

Another great filial concern was the church in England. He sent a special envoy from Rome to look after the emerging church in this area and to teach Roman liturgical norms and chants, at the same time keeping a closer eye on the emerging church. Agatho was a well-loved pope; he gave what little money he had to his clergy in Rome and endowed St. Mary Major, one of the four major basilicas.

Pope St. Sergius I

Pontificate: A.D. 687–A.D. 701

Feast day: September 8

Sergius, the son of a Syrian merchant, became pope under enormous controversy as anti-pope Paschal attempted to buy his way to the papacy through bribes. The influence of Constantinople and the Byzantine Empire were on the decline during Sergius's papacy. The emperor called a council, to which the pope wasn't invited, yet the emperor required him to sign the rules from the proceedings. Sergius refused, so the emperor sent troops to force the pope's signature; the troops, however, supported the pope. The emperor was eventually deposed in Constantinople and sent into exile.

Sergius turned his attention toward the new church in England and tried to reinforce Roman Christianity's foothold. He baptized the king of the Saxons, granting a *pallium* — sign of an archbishop — and thereby creating Canterbury and an archdiocese. In Rome, he restored, rebuilt, and enriched the basilicas of St. Peter, St. Paul, and St. Susana. He also established four feasts for the Blessed Virgin Mary: Annunciation, Assumption, Nativity, and Presentation. He is buried in St. Peter's.

Pope St. Gregory II

Pontificate: A.D. 715–A.D. 731

Feast day: February 11

Gregory was born in Rome. He was a librarian for four popes and was known as a brilliant scholar, but he was perhaps best known for his defense of doctrine. Emperor Leo wanted church icons destroyed, making the Church appear more accessible to Jews and Muslims, who banned such images. When the decree reached Italy, Gregory immediately rejected it, reaffirming Catholic teaching that only idols (objects or images for worship of false gods) were prohibited. Sacred art depicting Jesus and the saints was a good thing. Most illiterate people learned the faith by looking at icons and stained glass windows, often called the poor man's catechism.

Gregory also repaired the city walls and churches and opened institutions for the care of the elderly. He was a great supporter of monasticism: He turned his family estate into a monastery, restored the famous monastery of Monte Casino, and encouraged monastic vocations.

Pope St. Zacharias

Pontificate: A.D. 741–A.D. 752

Feast day: March 15

Zacharias, an Italian, was a learned man who knew how to read and write in Greek, skills that proved useful in dealing with the Byzantine emperor. At the time of his reign, the dispute over uses of sacred art and images still plagued the Church in the East; Zacharias, wise and diplomatic, cast the issue aside in favor of a better relationship with Constantinople.

Emperor Constantine V also put aside his religious differences and didn't persecute the pope and the West for retaining sacred images in worship. The emperor needed the support of the pope in dealing with the Lombards, who wanted to invade Ravenna, the last Byzantine stronghold in Italy.

Zacharias visited the king of the Lombards in a gesture of peace, forming a truce that resulted in the papal estates and political prisoners being returned to Rome. To the north, in the area of the Holy Roman Empire, the pope had excellent relations with the emperor and supported Boniface in his reign.

Pope St. Paul I

Pontificate: A.D. 757–A.D. 767

Feast day: June 28

Paul was the brother of Pope Stephen III and became his immediate successor in A.D. 757. He met the challenges of his time with diplomacy, fortitude, and at times clemency, granting his allegiance to the Holy Roman emperor upon coronation. King Pepin and the pope shared a favorable relationship in which recognition of the newly formed Papal States was solidified.

Unfortunately, his relationships with the Lombard king and the emperor of Constantinople were clouded by controversy over sacred images in churches and their use in worship. Paul I died at St. Paul's Outside the Walls Basilica.

Pope St. Leo III

Pontificate: A.D. 795–A.D. 816

Feast day: June 12

Leo's papacy was one of intrigue and slander, as a splinter group begrudged his election and sought to overturn it. First, they kidnapped and beat the pope to near death. When he recovered, the group brought false charges against him — charges serious enough that Charlemagne, king of the Franks, came to Rome to help defend Leo. The pope was cleared of all charges, and, on Christmas Day, Pope Leo III crowned Charlemagne as the peace-loving emperor of the Romans, commencing the Holy Roman Empire of the West.

Pope St. Paschal I

Pontificate: A.D. 817–A.D. 824

Feast day: February 12

Paschal's papacy was plagued by intrigue, calumny, and disobedience. He was elected and consecrated pope immediately, not waiting for the approval of the Holy Roman emperor. The emperor was such a good friend of Paschal's that he enacted a series of laws protecting the rights of the pope, the Papal States, and elections of future popes. The emperor's son visited Rome after being granted co-rule of the empire and was crowned co-emperor by the pope. From that time on, Holy Roman emperors traveled to Rome for their coronation by the pope.

Calumny inundated the pope when his papal household was involved in foul play and the pope was accused of being involved in the plot. He took a pledge of innocence before bishops to prove his innocence; however, upon his death the old lies resurfaced, and the Romans barred his burial at St. Peter's. Instead, he's buried in one of the churches he built, St. Praxedis.

Pope St. Leo IV

Pontificate: A.D. 847–A.D. 855

Feast day: July 17

The major threat during Leo's reign came from the Muslims, known as the Saracens, who attacked and destroyed cities up and down Italy's coast. Pope Leo IV rebuilt the walls of Rome and added new walls around the Vatican. He aided the reconstruction of many destroyed churches and took care of those displaced by the Saracen invasions. Internally, he worked to improve his clergy's moral status by adding several canons to Church law, reforming their education and discipline.

Pope St. Nicholas I

Pontificate: A.D. 858–A.D. 867

Feast day: November 13

When Nicholas assumed the papacy, the church was faced with many challenges, not the least of which was the fall of Charlemagne and the resulting division of the Holy Roman Empire. No central political power existed — bishops were appointed and deposed at the whim of local nobility.

Nicholas was a champion for the sacrament of marriage, making many decisions regarding royal weddings that were being called into question. He also favored the freedom to marry over the veto powers of kings and fathers.

He ensured that food was prepared and delivered to poor invalids every day, setting aside substantial funds for their care and working to end their personal suffering. All these qualities made him one of the finest popes of his age and a true leader in the temporal and spiritual aspects of the Church — which the Church has recognized by designating him "Nicholas the Great," one of only three popes to earn the title.

Pope St. Gregory VII

Pontificate: 1073–1085

Feast day: May 25

Gregory VII was one of the most powerful popes in history, remembered for vigorously defending the independence and autonomy of the Church from the secular authority of the kings and the Holy Roman emperor.

This period was a truly trying time for the Church. Of the secular rulers — William the Conqueror of England, Philip I of France, and Henry IV of Germany — Henry IV was the most tiresome. Gregory excommunicated him twice for his infidelity; Henry IV is believed to have supported an anti-pope, or illegal rival pope.

Things inside the Church weren't much better. Gregory VII was confronted with a range of problems, including clerical laxity and a decline of moral leadership. He ordered archbishops throughout the empire to come to Rome to receive the sign of their office, the pallium, in an effort to consolidate the authority of the Holy See. He died at the monastery in Monte Casino.

Pope St. Celestine V

Pontificate: 1294

Feast day: May 19

Born Pietro di Murrone, Celestine was a hermit, from the Abruzzi section of Italy. He was not well-schooled in theology, Latin, or diplomacy; and was an unlikely choice to become a successor of St. Peter. The fact that he was made pope is testament to the terrible state of the Church in the 13th century. The throne of St. Peter had been vacant for more than two years when Pietro di Morone exhorted the cardinals to put their differences aside and elect a pope.

The five months of his papacy proved difficult for the 85-year-old Celestine. The king of the Two Sicilies, Charles II, saw an opportunity to make poor Celestine a puppet to his wishes. Charles had the pope create 13 cardinals, many of whom were French, in a bid to secure the next election of the pope.

Devastated by these machinations, Celestine wanted to abdicate the throne of Peter, which was unprecedented. With the help of Cardinal Gaetani, who eventually succeeded him as Boniface VIII, Celestine laid aside his papal robes, begged the cardinals' forgiveness, and returned to life as a hermit. Boniface VIII, worried that Celestine might be kidnapped and used to create a schism, kept Celestine a benign prisoner until the elderly hermit's death. Boniface canonized him a saint in 1313.

Pope St. Pius V

Pontificate: 1566–1572

Feast day: April 30

Michele Ghisleri, who became Pius when elected pope, was a great reformer. He accepted the "shoes of the fisherman" at a time when the Church was suffering from the Protestant revolt in most of Northern Europe. The Council of Trent had been convened before his papacy, and he implemented many of its reforms. He issued a new Roman Missal for Mass, the Roman Breviary — a scriptural prayer book for priests, and catechism — as the basis for other catechisms from children to adults, and a vernacular translation of the Bible. In addition, he enforced reform among bishops and priests, demanding that they live in the diocese and parish to which they were assigned; and he fought against *simony* (the buying and selling of ecclesiastical favors) and nepotism. These moves ushered in the age of the Counter-Reformation. Many new religious communities were formed, which helped create the armies of reform and bring back those souls lost to Catholicism.

As a politician, however, Pius V received mixed reviews. When monarchs, such as Queen Elizabeth I, left the Church and followed a new brand of religion, Pius excommunicated them. But the monarchs themselves were hardly affected. To the Catholics who remained in England, however, the excommunication proved disastrous. Those who remained in the faith were persecuted; many were sentenced to death for "high treason."

When it came to dealing with the Turks and the Muslim Ottoman Empire, however, the pope was more successful. The West united in the famous Battle of Lepanto, in which Christianity was victorious. Pius V saw the victory on October 7, 1571, as a gift from God through the intercession of the Blessed Virgin. He proclaimed a celebration known to this day as the Feast of Our Lady of the Most Holy Rosary. Originally, Pius V's feast was observed on May 5. In the new Roman calendar of 1969, it was moved to April 30.

Pope St. Pius X

Pontificate: 1903–1914

Feast day: August 21

Another great reformer of the Church, Giuseppe Melchiorre Sarto, also took the name Pius at the start of his papacy.

Among his many reforms were his attempts to address the heresy of modernism. In an encyclical 1907 letter, "Lamentabili," he condemned 65 modernist propositions. He sought to renew Bible study and liturgical music, reform the Roman Missal, and renew the Code of Canon Law — the laws that govern Church practice. He renewed and revised seminary life and training, encouraged children to receive Holy Communion at the age of reason, and championed daily Communion for all.

St. Pius X condemned the secular French states for breaking with an earlier agreement in matters of property. He defended the rights of the downtrodden in Peru, Ireland, Poland, and Portugal. He sent many missionaries to the United States to help the newly established immigrant church. Some received miracles from God through the prayers of this kind, religiously devout, and charitable pope while he was alive.

Pope Pius XII canonized him a saint in 1954.

Other Saintly Popes of the Early Catholic Church

Details about many popes who served in the earliest days of the Catholic Church have been lost to the mists of time, yet they're still considered saints. Here's a brief recap of what is known about these holy men.

Pope St. Cletus (A.D. 76–A.D. 88): Born a Roman as Cletus, he was also known by his name in Greek, Anacletus. He's listed in the Roman Canon of the Mass. His feast day is April 26.

Pope St. Evaristus (A.D. 97–A.D. 105): Evaristus, of Greek origin, was the fifth pope. He's buried next to St. Peter in the Christian cemetery on Vatican Hill, the site of the 16th-century basilica. His feast day is October 26.

Pope St. Sixtus I (A.D. 115–A.D. 125): St. Sixtus reigned for ten years before meeting a martyr's death. He's believed to be buried near the site of the first-century cemetery on Vatican Hill. He is remembered on April 3.

Pope St. Pius I (A.D. 140–A.D. 155): St. Pius I battled heretics that threatened the faith. So clear were Pope Pius I's teaching and preaching that he won over converts, including St. Justin Martyr. His feast is celebrated on July 11.

Pope St. Anicetus (A.D. 155–A.D. 166): St. Anicetus hung out with some notable theologians, such as St. Polycarp of Smyrna and St. Justin Martyr. He's most likely a martyr as well, even though no official details are known. His feast is on April 16.

Pope St. Soter (A.D. 166–A.D. 175): St. Soter introduced the solemnity of Easter as an annual celebration. Though no conclusive proof is available, he is traditionally considered a martyr and is remembered on April 22, along with another pope, St. Caius.

Pope St. Eleutherius (A.D. 175–A.D. 189): Eleutherius was a deacon in Rome before becoming a priest and then a bishop. He's remembered for his declaration that anything suitable for human consumption is suitable for Christians to eat. His feast is on May 26.

Pope St. Victor (A.D. 189–A.D. 199): Victor so strongly believed that the Church should observe a uniform date for the solemnity of Easter that he excommunicated certain churches in the East who preferred their own calendar and calculations. His feast is celebrated on July 28.

Pope St. Urban I (A.D. 222–A.D. 230): Urban reigned during the rule of Emperor Alexander Severus. Not much is known about him, other than the fact that he was a charitable and kind leader. He's buried in the papal chapel of the Catacombs of St. Callixtus, and his feast is noted on May 25.

Pope St. Anterus (A.D. 235–A.D. 236): Anterus, a Greek, was responsible for creating the Acts of the Martyrs, a collection of biographies on the early Christian martyrs documenting when, where, and how they died. He was only pope for 43 days before being martyred himself by order of Emperor Maximinus Thrax; he was buried in the newly built papal chamber of the Catacombs of St. Callixtus. His feast is celebrated on January 3.

Pope St. Felix I (A.D. 268–A.D. 274): Felix ordered the celebration of Mass over the tombs of martyred Christians in the catacombs. His feast is May 30.

Pope St. Eutychian (A.D. 275–A.D. 283): Eutychian wasn't martyred but has been considered a saint since antiquity. He reigned during a very peaceful respite between persecutions. He was the last pope to be buried in the papal chamber of the Catacombs of St. Callixtus. His feast day is December 7.

Pope St. Marcellus I (A.D. 308–A.D. 309): Marcellus wanted repentant *lapsi* to perform appropriate penances, an unpopular position that led to riots. Emperor Maxentius exiled Marcellus in an effort to calm down the populace. He died in A.D. 309 and is buried in the church named after him in Rome. His feast is memorialized on January 16.

Pope St. Eusebius (A.D. 309): Eusebius sought substantial penances from repentant *lapsi,* leading Emperor Maxentius to exile him to Sicily, where he died. Eusebius's body was transferred to Rome and buried in the Catacombs of St. Callixtus. His feast is celebrated on August 17.

Pope St. Mark (A.D. 336): Mark's pontificate only lasted eight months, but he established two churches in Rome: one named after the evangelist Mark, currently incorporated in Palazzo di Venezia, and the second in the cemetery of St. Balbina, which has since been destroyed. Two important documents also came out of his pontificate: the Episcopal and Martyr Deposits, both of great historical value for the Church. His feast is recalled on October 7.

Pope St. Anastasius I (A.D. 399–A.D. 401): Anastasius settled theological controversies concerning an early Church father of theology, Origen. Origen had many good theological points but had confusing ones as well. Anastasius had to clarify matters and condemn those parts that were heretical, which earned him praise from St. Jerome. Anastasius's feast day is celebrated on December 19.

Pope St. Zosimus (A.D. 417–A.D. 418): In his short time as pope, Zosimus dealt with heresy and battled against episcopal intrigue and skulduggery surrounding imperial politics. Though not the most astute in areas of Church politics, he was a holy, kind, and charitable man. His feast is December 26.

Pope St. Simplicius (A.D. 468–A.D. 483): Simplicius saw the western Roman Emperor, Romulus Augustus, defeated by barbarian invaders, thus causing the city and empire to fall once and for all in A.D. 476. Pope Simplicius also had to deal with the usual heresies of the times. His feast is March 10.

Pope St. Felix II (III) (A.D. 483–A.D. 492): Some historians, to separate him from the anti-pope Felix II, list this pope as Felix III. He worked with the emperor to fight heresy throughout the empire. He's buried at the Basilica of St. Paul Outside the Walls; his feast is March 1.

Pope St. Symmachus (A.D. 498–A.D. 514): Symmachus was archdeacon of the Eternal City (another name for Rome); his election to the papacy, however, was fraught with controversy as he faced struggles with the anti-pope Laurence. Symmachus embellished many churches throughout Rome and helped refugees in exile from heretical tyrants. He died on July 19 and is buried at St. Peter's Basilica.

Pope St. Hormisdas (A.D. 514–A.D. 523): Not much is known about Hormisdas, who, like the first pope, St. Peter, had a wife. She died and left him a son, who later became Pope Silverius. Hormisdas compiled a confession of faith, *Hormisdas Formula* allowing heretics to reenter the Church. His feast day is August 6.

Pope St. Silverius (A.D. 536–A.D. 537): Silverius was a subdeacon in Rome when elected pope. He was forced to abdicate his papacy in A.D. 537, falling victim to scheming by Empress Theodora, who wanted the pope to restore heretical leaders to their respective dioceses. When Silverius refused, the enraged empress plotted his downfall. He was reinstated to the throne of St. Peter by the emperor, who wasn't aware of his wife's skullduggery. Pope St. Silverius's feast day is June 20.

Pope St. Adeodatus I (A.D. 615–A.D. 618): After more than 40 years as a priest, Adeodatus was elected to the papacy at a late age. He was the first pope to use lead seals on papal decrees (called *bulls*). In his will, he left a year's salary to local clergy. His feast is November 8.

Pope St. Eugene I (A.D. 654–A.D. 657): Eugene was a priest in Rome when chosen pope and struggled with the emperor over Monothelitism. Unlike his predecessor, Pope Martin I, who openly condemned the Patriarch of Constantinople for his Monothelite opinions, Eugene chose to be more diplomatic and tone down the rhetoric without denying the faith. He did refuse to sign a document that the patriarch sent to the pope, further confusing the issue of how many wills Christ had. The advancing Muslim troops against the Eastern Empire preoccupied the emperor and the patriarch, and Eugene was spared the humiliation and imprisonment suffered by his predecessor, Martin. He died in A.D. 657; his feast is June 2.

Pope St. Leo II (A.D. 682–A.D. 683): Leo II was an outstanding preacher who loved music but cared for the poor even more. The emperor often interfered with Church policies, and this was the case in Leo's election. It took 18 months before the emperor gave his approval and Leo could go through the coronation ceremonies. The controversy centered on the sixth ecumenical council of Constantinople III (A.D. 680), which condemned both the heresy of Monothelitism and Pope Honorius I (accusing him of having heretical opinions). Leo confirmed the condemnation of the heresy itself and of his predecessor's (Honorius) private opinions while making it clear that these theories never enjoyed formal approval. His feast is celebrated on July 3.

Pope St. Benedict II (A.D. 684–A.D. 685): When it came time for Benedict, proficient in both sacred music and Scripture, to be considered for the papacy, the Church of Rome still elected the popes, and they had to wait for imperial recognition before they could actually ascend the throne. Benedict got the emperor to agree to cede his approval authority to the local ruler in Italy, thus saving time between election and papal coronation. His feast is May 8.

Index

About the Authors

Rev. Kenneth Brighenti, PhD: A native of New Britain, Connecticut, Father Brighenti is the Director of Pastoral Field Education and an assistant professor at Mount Saint Mary University and Seminary (Emmitsburg, Maryland). He is the managing editor of *Sapientia* magazine and a member of the Board of Directors for the Con-fraternity of Catholic Clergy, and he cohosted three weekly TV series on Eternal Word Television Network (EWTN). Father Brighenti also served as a U.S. Naval Reserve Chaplain for ten years and was ordained a priest for the Diocese of Metuchen (New Jersey) in 1988. He and Father Trigilio coauthored *Catholicism For Dummies* (2003), *The Everything Bible Book* (2004), *Women in the Bible For Dummies* (2005), *John Paul II For Dummies* (2006), and *Saints For Dummies* (2010), and he authored *Marriage as Covenant* (2009). Fathers Brighenti and Trigilio are also Knights of Columbus and members of the Order Sons of Italy of America (OSIA) and the National Italian American Foundation (NIAF).

Rev. Msgr. James Cafone, STD: A native of Belleville, New Jersey, Msgr. Cafone serves as tenured assistant professor in the Religion Department of Seton Hall University, South Orange, New Jersey. He is the vice-chair of its Board of Trustees and a member of the Board of Regents and the Committee on Mission and Identity. He teaches full-time at the university and serves as minister to the 47 members of the Priest Community at Seton Hall. He also serves as chaplain to the Alumni Board of the university. Monsignor wrote the foreword to *John Paul II For Dummies* (2006), written by Frs. Brighenti, Toborowsky, and Trigilio.

Rev. Jonathan Toborowsky, MA: A native of Port Reading, New Jersey, Father Toborowsky serves as Pastor of St. Lawrence Roman Catholic Church (Lawrence Harbor, NJ). He is the host and moderator of Proclaim the Good News, a weekly radio show, and an online theological advisor for Ave Maria Single Catholics Online. He was ordained a priest for the Diocese of Metuchen (New Jersey) in 1998.

Rev. John Trigilio, Jr., PhD, ThD: A native of Erie, Pennsylvania, Father Trigilio serves as the pastor of Our Lady of Good Counsel (Marysville, Pennsylvania) and St. Bernadette Catholic Churches (Duncannon, Pennsylvania). He is the president of the Confraternity of Catholic Clergy and executive editor of its quarterly journal, *Sapientia* magazine. Father Trigilio cohosted several weekly TV series on the Eternal Word Television Network (EWTN): *Web of Faith, Council of Faith, Crash Course in Catholicism,* and *Crash Course in Pope John Paul II.* He also serves as a theological consultant and online spiritual advisor for EWTN. He is a Cooperator in Opus Dei, was listed in *Who's Who in America* and *Who's Who in Religion,* and is a member of the Fellowship of Catholic Scholars. He was ordained a priest for the Diocese of Harrisburg (Pennsylvania) in 1988.

Publisher's Acknowledgments

Acquisitions Editor: Tracy Boggier

Editor: Corbin Collins

Technical Editor: Rev. Patrick J. Beidelman, STL

Art Coordinator: Alicia B. South

Production Editor: Suresh Srinivasan

Cover Image: ©iStock.com/onepony